JOURNAL

OF THE

CONSTITUTIONAL CONVENTION

OF THE

STATE OF MICHIGAN.

1850.

Printed by order of the Convention, under the supervision of

JOHN SWEGLES, JR.,

PRINCIPAL SECRETARY OF THE CONVENTION.

LANSING:

R. W. INGALS, STATE PRINTER.

1850.

JOURNAL OF THE CONVENTION.

Lansing, Monday, June 3, 1850.

Pursuant to the provisions of law, the delegates elected by the people to revise the Constitution of the State, met in convention at the Capitol, at Lansing, at 2 o'clock P. M., and were called to order by the Hon. Charles H. Taylor, Secretary of State, who called the roll of delegates by counties, and the following answered to their names:

Allegan—Oka Town.

Barry—Joseph W. T. Orr.

Berrien—Calvin Britain, Jacob Beeson, Charles W. Whipple.

Branch—Wales Adam, Alvarado Brown, Asahel Brown.

Calhoun—Isaac E. Crary, Milo Soule, William V. Morrison, John D. Pierce, Nathan Pierce.

Cass—George Redfield, Mitchel Robinson, James Sullivan.

Chippewa—Elijah J. Roberts.

Clinton—David Sturgis.

Eaton—Charles E. Beardsley, John D. Burns.

Genesee—John Bartow, Elbridge G. Gale, Dewitt C. Leach.

Hillsdale—John P. Cook, Daniel Kinne, John Mosher.

Ingham—Charles P. Bush, Ephraim B. Danforth.

Ionia—Henry Bartow.

Jackson—Robert H. Anderson, John L. Butterfield, Jerry G. Cornell, Elisha S. Robinson, Wilbur F. Storey.

Kalamazoo—Hezekiah G. Wells, Samuel Clark, Volney Hascall.

Kent and Ottawa—Rix Robinson, Thomas B. Church, Timothy Eastman.

Lapeer—Noah H. Hart, Jonathan R. White.

Lenawee—Addison J. Comstock, Alexander R. Tiffany, Peter R. Adams, Charles Chandler, George C. Harvey, Nelson Green.

Livingston—Daniel S. Lee, Robert Crouse, Robert Warden, Jr., Ely Barnard.

Michilimackinac—Wm. Norman McLeod.

Macomb—Dewitt C. Walker, Charles W. Chapel, Andrew S. Robertson.

Monroe—Robert McClelland, Alexander M. Arzeno, Emerson Choate, Henry B. Marvin.

Oakland—James Webster, Alfred H. Hanscom, Seneca Newberry, Jacob Van Valkenburgh, Ebenezer Raynale, Gideon O. Whittemore, William Axford, Zebina M. Mowry, Elias S. Woodman.

Saginaw—Jabez G. Sutherland.

St. Clair—John Clark.

St. Joseph—William Connor, Joseph R. Williams, Edward S. Moore.

Van Buren—Isaac W. Willard.

Washtenaw—James Kingsley, Elias M. Skinner, Earls P. Gardiner, Daniel Hixon, Morgan O'Brien, William S. Carr, Benjamin W. Wait.

Wayne—Daniel Goodwin, Benjamin F. H. Witherell, John Gibson, Ammon Brown, Henry J. Alvord, Henry Fralick, Peter Desnoyers, Henry T. Backus, Joseph H. Bagg, Ebenezer C. Eaton.

On motion of Mr. Kingsley, of Washtenaw,

Isaac E. Crary, of Calhoun county, was appointed President *pro tempore*.

On motion of Mr. Hanscom, of Oakland county,

D. P. Bushnell, of Wayne county, was appointed Secretary *pro tempore*.

On motion of Mr. Raynale, of Oakland county,

Diodate Hubbard, of Oakland county, was appointed Sergeant-at-Arms *pro tempore*.

Mr. Kingsley moved that the Convention proceed to ballot for a President.

Mr. Hanscom moved that the Convention elect a President *viva voce*.

Mr. McLeod moved to lay the motion of Mr. Hanscom on the table. Lost.

The question was then taken on said motion, and the same was not agreed to.

Mr. Flavius J. Provost, delegate elect from the county of Shiawasse, presented his credentials and took his seat.

The Convention then proceeded to appoint a President by ballot, as provided by law.

Messrs. Storey, of Jackson county, and Hanscom, of Oakland, having been appointed tellers,

The ballots being counted, the following was the result:

For Daniel Goodwin, 75.
" H. T. Backus, 3.
" C. W. Whipple, 2.
" J. R. Williams, 3.
" D. C. Walker, 1.
" I. E. Crary, 2.
" B. F. H. Witherell, 1.
" H. G. Wells, 1.
" N. Pierce, 1.
" W. F. Storey, 1.

The president *pro tem.* announced that Daniel Goodwin of Wayne county, having received the highest number of votes, was duly appointed President of the Convention.

On motion of Mr. Whipple, of Berrien County,

A committee of two was ordered to be appointed to wait upon the President elect to the chair.

The President *pro tempore* appointed Messrs. Whipple, of Berrien, and McClelland, of Monroe, such committee.

The President having been conducted to the chair, addressed the Convention as follows:

Gentlemen of the Convention:

I tender to you my sincere thanks for the flattering expression of your confidence in selecting me to preside over your deliberations upon this interesting occasion. When I look around this Hall, and behold congregated here so much of ability, of intelligence, and of experience in public affairs—so many who have occupied various stations in different departments of public service, with honor to themselves and usefulness to their fellow citizens; and when I consider further the importance of the objects for which we are convened, I cannot but be impressed with deep sensibility for the distinguished honor conferred. The best requital which I can make will be in the devotion of my best powers to the faithful and impartial performance of the highly responsible duties of the station. This I shall endeavor to do in all sincerity. And though I do not bring to the task great familiarity with parliamentary proceedings, yet with the aid (which I doubt not will be kindly and generously accorded) of the knowledge and experience that pervade this assembly of representatives of enlightened and free citizens, it is my hope that I shall be enabled so to fulfill it as to meet your approbation.

In conclusion, allow me to express the fervent desire, that our deliberations may be so guided by that All-Wise Being, in whose hands are the destinies of States and Nations, that their results may tend to establish the more firmly and permanently those benign principles of civil freedom and popular sovereignty upon which our institutions are based, and promote in the highest degree the prosperity of our State and happiness of our people.

On motion of Mr. Cook, of Hillsdale county, it was

Resolved, That John Swegles, jr., be and he is hereby appointed Secretary of this Convention.

Resolved, further, That Horace S. Roberts and Charles Hascall be and they hereby are appointed Assistant Secretaries of this Convention.

Mr. Hanscom offered the following resolution:

Resolved, That the rules of the last House of Representatives of this State be adopted, so far as the same are applicable, for the government of the proceedings of this Convention, until otherwise ordered.

Agreed to.

Mr. Roberts, of Chippewa county, offered the following:

Resolved, That David Hubbard, jr., be and he is hereby appointed Sergeant-at-Arms of this Convention. Agreed to.

Mr. Kingsley offered the following:

Resolved, That a committee of seven be appointed to prepare rules for the government of this convention in its proceedings.

Agreed to.

The President announced that Messrs. Kingsley, Britain. McClelland, Tiffany, Backus, Walker and Hanscom would constitute such committee.

Mr. Crary offered the following:

Resolved, That the President of this Convention appoint a door-keeper and four messengers.

Mr. Fralick, of Wayne county, moved to strike out the words "door-keeper and." Lost.

The question was then taken on the resolution of Mr. Crary, and the same agreed to.

Mr. McClelland offered the following resolution:

Resolved, That a committee of nine be appointed by the President of the Convention to report as to the best mode of proceeding to the revision of the Constitution of the State.

Adopted.

Mr. Cook offered the following:

Resolved, That there be printed for the use of the Convention 500 copies of the daily journal.

Mr. Redfield, of Cass county, moved to strike out 500 and insert 1000.

Agreed to, and the resolution as amended was adopted.

Mr. Cook also offered the following:

Resolved, That the daily sessions of the Convention shall commence at 9 o'clock, A. M., until otherwise ordered.

Adopted.

Mr. Hascall, of Kalamazoo county, offered the following resolution:

Resolved, That the members of the Convention now go into a draft for their respective seats.

Which, the yeas and nays being ordered thereon, was lost as follows:

YEAS.

Mr. Axford,	Mr. Dimond,	Mr. Newberry,
Backus,	Gale,	O'Brien,

Bagg,
H. Bartow,
Britain,
Ammon Brown,
Burns,
Bush,
Carr,
J. Clark,
S. Clark,
Conner,
Cornell,
Crary,
Gardiner,
Green,
Hascall,
Hixon,
Kingsley,
Kinne,
Leach,
Lovell,
Mason,
McLeod,
Moore,
Mowry,
Orr,
N. Pierce,
Prevost,
Roberts,
E. S. Robinson,
Town,
Wait,
Wells,
Whipple,
Williams,
Willard,
President, 42

NAYS.

Mr. W. Adams,
Alvord,
Anderson,
Arzeno,
Barnard,
J. Bartow,
Beeson,
Alvardo Brown,
Asahel Brown,
Butterfield,
Chapel,
Choate,
Church,
Comstock,
Cook,
Crouse,
Mr. Danforth,
Desnoyers,
Eastman,
Eaton,
Fralick,
Gibson,
Hanscom
Hart,
Harvey,
Lee,
Marvin,
McClelland,
Morrison,
Mosher,
Raynale,
Mr. Redfield,
M. Robinson,
Rix Robinson,
Robertson,
Skinner,
Storey,
Sullivan,
Sutherland,
Tiffany,
Van Valkenbur g,
Walker,
White,
Whittemore,
Witherell,
Warden, 45

Mr. Britain, of Berrien county, offered the following:

Resolved, That the State Printer be instructed to forward by mail, one copy of the daily journal to the publishers of each newspaper in this State, during the session of this Convention.

Adopted.

Mr. Storey, of Jackson, offered the following, which was adopted;

Resolved. That a committtee of three be appointed by the President, to inquire into the propriety of securing the services of three reporters, to report the proceedings and debates of this Convention.

Mr. Butterfield, of Jackson county, offered the following:

Resolved, That the Secretary of the convention be instructed to procure papers equal to one daily for each delegate, of such papers as each delegate shall direct. Lost.

Mr. Hanscom, of Oakland county, offered the following:

Resolved, That a committee of three be appointed to ascertain and report to this convention what arrangement, if any, can be made in reference to newspapers and postage.

Which resolution was adopted, and Messrs. Hanscom, Danforth and Britain were appointed such committee.

Mr. Crouse, of Livingston county, offered the following:

Resolved, That the commitee on rules be required to cause the rules which this convention shall adopt to be printed in the form of a manual, embracing the present constitution of this State, together with other like information which appears in the manual of the legislature of A. D. 1849.

Which, on motion of Mr. Witherell,

Was laid on the table.

Mr. White, of Lapeer county, offered the following:

Resolved, That there be a committee of five appointed by the chair to furnish the members of this convention with stationery.

Mr. Cook moved to amend the resolution so that the amount to be furnished each member should not exceed five dollars.

On motion of Mr. Hanscom,

The resolution and amendment were ordered laid on the table.

Mr. Whittemore, of Oakland county, offered the following:

Resolved, That a committee of three be appointed to furnish for the use of this Convention such stationery as is allowed by law.

Which was ordered laid on the table.

When, on motion of Mr. J. D. Pierce,

The Convention adjourned.

Lansing, Tuesday, June 4, 1850.

The Convention met pursuant to adjournment and was called to order by the President.

The roll was called by the Secretary, and a quorum found to be present.

The journal of yesterday was read and approved.

The President announced the following committees appointed under resolutions of yesterday:

Committee on resolution as to reporters—Messrs. Story, Church and Wells.

Committee on resolution as to the mode of proceeding, &c.—Messrs. McClelland, Crary, S. Clark, Tiffany, Williams, R. Robinson, Whittemore, Walker and Witherell.

Mr. Van Valkenburg offered the following resolution:

Resolved, That a committee of two be appointed to invite the resident clergymen of this place to meet with us alternately and open our daily sessions with devotional exercises.

Mr. Roberts moved to lay the resolution on the table.

Which motion was lost.

The resolution was then adopted by yeas and nays, as follows:

YEAS:

Mr. P. R. Adams,	Mr. Cornell,	Mr. J. D. Pierce,
W. Adams,	Crouse,	N. Pierce,
Alvord,	Danforth,	Prevost,
Anderson,	Desnoyers,	E. S. Robinson,
Backus,	Eastman,	M. Robinson,
Bagg,	Fralick,	Rix Robinson,
Barnard,	Gardiner,	Skinner,
J. Bartow,	Gibson,	Soule,
Beardsley,	Green,	Storey,
Beeson,	Hart,	Sturgis,
Britain,	Harvey,	Sullivan,
Alvarado Brown,	Hascall,	Sutherland,
Asahel Brown,	Hixon,	Tiffany,
Burns,	Kingsley,	Town,
Bush,	Kinne,	Van Valkenburg,
Butterfield,	Leach,	Walker,
Carr,	Lee,	Webster,
Chandler,	Lovell,	Wells,
Choate,	Marvin,	White,
Church,	Mason,	Whipple,
J. Clark,	McClelland,	Whittemore,
S. Clark,	Mowry,	Witherell,
Comstock,	O'Brien,	Warden,
Conner,	Orr,	President,
Cook,		73

NAYS:

Mr. Arzeno,	Mr. Gale,	Mr. Roberts,
Axford,	Hanscom,	Robertson,
Ammon Brown,	McLeod,	Williams,
Chapel,	Newberry,	Willard,
Crary,	Raynale,	Woodman,
Eaton,		16

The President announced as such committee, Messrs. Van Valkenburg and J. D. Pierce.

Mr. Roberts offered the following resolution, which was unanimously adopted:

Resolved, That the thanks of this Convention be tendered D. P. Bushnell, Esq., for the able and courteous manner in which he has performed the duties of Secretary *pro tempore.*

On motion of Mr. Roberts,

Resolved, That a committee of three be appointed to make arrangements for the raising of the national flag at the hour of the opening of the daily sessions of this Convention.

And the President appointed Messrs. Roberts, Bush, and Willard, such committee.

On motion of Mr. Witherell,

Resolved, That his Excellency, the Governor, be invited by the President to take a seat within the bar of the Convention during its session.

Mr. McClelland offered the following, which was adopted:

Resolved, That the committee relative to reporters, &c., inquire into the propriety of having the proceedings of this convention published in the German, Dutch and French languages.

Mr. J. D. Pierce called up the following resolution, laid on the table yesterday:

Resolved, That a committee of three be appointed to furnish for the use of this Convention such stationery as is allowed by law, and the officers such stationery as they may require.

Mr. Crary moved to amend the resolution by adding: "*Provided* the allowance to each member do not exceed the sum of five dollars."

Mr. Fralick moved to amend by striking out "five," and inserting "three."

And the question being taken first upon striking out, the same was not agreed to.

Mr. Hanscom moved to lay the resolution on the table.

Which motion did not prevail.

The question being taken upon Mr. Crary's amendment, it was agreed to.

On motion of Mr. Story,

The resolution was further amended by striking out "committee of three," and inserting "committee on supplies, when appointed."

And the resolution as amended was then adopted.

Mr. Story offered the following resolution:

Resolved, That the Secretary be instructed to procure —— copies of a work containing the Constitutions of all the different States, for the use of this Convention.

Mr. Witherell moved to fill the blank with "20."

Mr. Bagg moved to fill the same with "100."

Mr. Story offered the following substitute:

Resolved, That the Secretary procure a sufficient number of copies of a work containing the Constitutions of all the States, for the use of each of the standing committees, and that at the end of the session they be deposited in the State Library.

When, on motion of Mr. Fralick,

The resolution and substitute were laid on the table.

The President announced the following communication from the Secretary of State:

OFFICE OF THE SECRETARY OF STATE,
Lansing, June 4, 1850.

Hon. DANIEL GOODWIN,

President of the Convention to revise the Constitution:

In compliance with the requirements of Joint Resolution No. 19 of the session laws of 1850, I have the honor to transmit herewith an abstract of the reports of the county clerks of the several counties relative to the expenses of the circuit and county courts of this State, so far as the same have been received at this office.

The Joint Resolution above referred to also required of me a further report "of the whole expenses of courts and officers in the year 1846." I have made thorough search and have been unable to find any reports or documents in this office giving the information desired.

Very respectfully, yours,

C. H. TAYLOR,

Secretary of State.

On motion of Mr. Cook,

The accompanying papers were laid on the table, and 500 copies ordered printed for the use of the Convention.

Mr. Kingsley, from the committee on rules, reported the following, which,

On motion of Mr. Cook,

Was laid on the table and ordered entered on the journal:

RULES OF THE CONVENTION.

RULE 1. The President shall take the chair at the time to which the Convention stands adjourned, and the Convention shall then be called to order and the roll of the members called.

RULE 2. Upon the appearance of a quorum, the journals of the preceding day shall be read by the Secretary, and any mistake therein may be corrected.

RULE 3. The President shall preserve order and decorum, and shall decide questions of order, subject to an appeal to the Convention.

RULE 4. The President shall vote on all questions taken by yeas and nays, (except on appeals from his own decisions.)

RULE 5. When the Convention adjourns, the members shall keep their seats until the President announces the adjournment.

RULE 6. Every member, previous to his speaking, shall rise from his seat, and address himself to the President.

RULE 7. When two or more members rise at once, the President shall designate the member who is first to speak.

RULE 8. No member shall speak more than twice on the same question, without leave of the Convention, nor more than once until every member who chooses to speak, shall have spoken.

RULE 9. No motion shall be debated or put, unless the same be seconded; it shall be stated by the President before debate, and any such motion shall be reduced to writing.

RULE 10. After a motion shall be stated by the President, it shall be deemed to be in possession of the Convention; but may be withdrawn at any time before decision or amendment; but another member may renew the same.

RULE 11. When a question is under debate, no motion shall be received but to adjourn; for the previous question; to lay on the table; to postpone indefinitely; to postpone to a day certain; to commit or to amend; which several motions shall have precedence in the order in which they stand arranged.

RULE 12. A motion to adjourn shall always be in order; that and the motion to lay on the table shall be decided without debate.

RULE 13. The previous question shall be in this form: "Shall the main question be now put?" And if demanded by a majority of the members present, its effect shall be to put an end to all debate, and bring the Convention to a direct vote upon amendments, if any are pending, and then upon the main question.

RULE 14. All incidental questions of order, arising after a motion is made for the previous question, during the pendency of such motion, or after the Convention shall have determined that the main question shall be now put, shall be decided, whether on appeal or otherwise, without debate.

RULE 15. Petitions, memorials and other papers, addressed to the Convention, shall be presented by the President, or a member in his place.

RULE 16. Every member who shall be present when a question is last stated from the Chair, and no other, shall vote for or against the same, unless the Convention shall excuse him, in which case he shall not vote.

RULE 17. When the President is putting the question, no member shall walk out or across the House; nor when a member is speaking, shall any person entertain any private discourse, or pass between him and the Chair.

RULE 18. If the question in debate contains several points, any member may have the same divided.

RULE 19. A member called to order, shall immediately sit down, unless permitted to explain, and the Convention, if appealed to, shall decide the case; if there be no appeal, the decision of the Chair shall be submitted to; on an appeal, no member shall speak more than once, without leave of the Convention, except when a member is called to order for offensive language, in which case there shall be no debate.

RULE 20. In forming a committee of the whole, the President shall appoint a chairman to preside.

RULE 21. Propositions committed to a committee of the whole, shall first be read through by the Secretary, and then read and debated by clauses. All amendments shall be entered on a separate piece of paper, and so reported to the Convention by the chairman, standing in his place.

RULE 22. All questions, whether in committee or in the Convention, shall be put in the order they were moved, except in the case of privileged questions; and in filling up blanks, the largest sum and the longest time shall be first put.

RULE 23. No motion for reconsideration shall be in order, unless within three drys after the decision proposed to be reconsidered took place. A motion for reconsideration being put and lost, (except in case of privileged motions,) shall not be renewed on the same day, nor shall any subject be a second time reconsidered on the same day without unanimous consent.

RULE 24. Any member may be at liberty to move for a reconsideration; and a motion for reconsideration shall be decided by a majority of votes.

RULE 25. The rules of the Convention shall be observed in committee of the whole, so far as they may be applicable, except that the yeas and nays shall not be called, the previous question enforced, nor the time of speaking limited.

RULE 26. A motion that the committee rise shall always be in order, and shall be decided without debate.

RULE 27. In all cases where an order, resolution or motion, shall be entered on the journals of the Convention, the name of the member moving the same shall be entered on the journals.

RULE 28. No person, unless introduced by a member, shall be admitted within the bar, but the Executive, the heads of departments of the State Government, Judges of the Supreme Court, members of Congress, those who have been members of Congress, of the State Convention forming the Constitution, of the State Legislature, or of the Legislative Council when Michigan was a Territory, and such other persons as the President shall, on application, assign places as stenographers.

RULE 29. On the meeting of the Convention, after reading the journal of the preceeding day, the order of business shall be as follows: 1st, presentation of petitions; 2d, reports of standing committees—reports of select commiitees; 3d, motions, resolutions and notices; 4th, reading resolutions; 5th, unfinished business of the preceding day; 6th, special orders of the day; 7th, general orders of the day.

Rule 30. When the Convention have arrived at the general orders of the day, they shall go into committee of the whole upon such orders, or a particular order designated by a vote of the Convention, and no other business shall be in order until the whole are considered or passed, or the committee rise; and unless a particular subject is ordered up, the committee of the whole shall consider, act upon, or pass the general orders, according to the order of their reference.

Rule 31. No rule of the Convention shall be suspended, altered or amended, without the concurrence of two-thirds of the members present.

Rule 32. Upon the call of the Convention, the names of the members shall be called by the Secretary, and the absentees noted; but no excuse shall be made until the Convention shall be fully called over; then, the absentees shall be called over the second time, and if still absent, excuses are to be heard; and if no excuse, or insufficient excuse be made, the absentees may, by order of those present, if there are fifteen members present, be taken into custody, where-ever to be found, by the Sergeant-at-Arms.

Rule 33. The President may leave the chair and appoint a member to preside, but not for a longer time than one day, except by leave of the Convention.

Rule 34. The rules of parliamentary practice comprised in Jefferson's Manual, shall govern the Convention in all cases to which they are applicable, and in which they are not inconsistent with the standing rules and orders of the Convention.

Rule 35. The ayes and noes may be called for by ten members.

Rule 36. A majority of the members elected shall constitute a quorum for the transaction of business; but a less number may adjourn.

Rule 37. A journal of the proceedings in committee of the whole shall be kept.

The President announced to the Convention the following appointments under the resolution of yesterday:

For Door-keeper—Edwin C. Merrifield.

For Messengers—Moses Goodridge, Daniel Bloss, William C. Stockton, Charles E. Toan.

On motion of Mr. Cook, the Convention adjourned.

Lansing, Wednesday, June 5, 1850.

The Convention met pursuant to adjournment and was called to order by the President.

Prayer by the Rev. W. W. Atterbury.

Hon. Ebenezer Daniels, of Lenawee county, appeared and took his seat.

The roll being called, there was found absent Messrs. Graham, Edmunds and Hathaway.

Mr. Leach moved to dispense with the reading of the journal.

Which motion was lost.

The journal was partly read by the Secretary, when,

On motion of Mr. J. Bartow,

The further reading of the same was dispensed with, and the journal corrected and approved.

The President announced to the Convention, that, in pursuance of a resolution of yesterday, his Excellency, the Governor, had been invited to take a seat within the bar, and had accepted the same.

REPORTS.

Mr. McClelland, from the committee on resolution as to mode of proceedings, &c., submitted the following:

1. A committee of seven on the bill of rights.
2. do do five on the elective franchise.
3. do do five on the division of the power of the government.
4. do do nine on the Legislative department.
5. do do nine on the Executive department.
6. do do nine on the Judiciary department.
7. do do five on State officers, except the Executive.
8. do do seven on county officers and county government.
9. do do seven on township officers and township government.
10. do do five on the organization and government of cities and villages.
11. do do five on impeachments and removals from office.
12. do do seven on the militia.
13. do do nine on education.
14. do do nine on finance and taxation.

15. A committee of nine on banking and corporations other than municipal.
16. do do seven on salaries.
17. do do five on the seat of government.
18. do do seven on exemptions, real and personal, and the rights of married women.
19. do do seven on the punishment of crimes.
20. do do seven on miscellaneous provisions.
21. do do five on the mode of amending and revising the constitution.
22. do do seven on the schedule.
23. do do eleven on arrangement and phraseology of the constitution.

By consent of the Convention, the report was laid on the table.

Mr. Story, from the committee appointed to inquire into the propriety of employing competent persons to report the proceedings of this Convention, submitted a report and resolutions, and

On motion of Mr. Crary,

The same were accepted and the committee discharged.

On motion of Mr. Danforth,

The report was laid on the table and the accompanying resolutions ordered placed upon the journals, as follows:

Resolved, That C. J. Fox, Joseph Coates and William Coates, be and they are hereby appointed Reporters to this Convention, with a per diem allowance of three dollars each. It shall be their duty to make full and minute reports of the proceedings and debates of this Convention, and to furnish such reports, legibly wrltten, to the State Printer, from day to day, as soon as possible after such proceedings and debates transpire.

Resolved, That there be printed in octavo form, in bourgeois type, for the use of the members of this Convention, one thousand copies of the proceedings and debates, as furnished by the Reporters; such proceedings and debates to be delivered to the members in sheets as fast as printed.

Resolved, That there be printed in book form, upon the same type used in printing the sheets provided for in the foregoing resolution, (without any extra pay for composition,) one thousand copies of the proceedings and debates of this Convention; and that such books be bound in leather, and distributed as follows, to-wit: One copy to be transmitted to the Secretary of State of the United States; one copy to the Library of Congress; one copy to the Secretaries of State of each of the States and Territories in the Union; one copy to each of the State Institutions in this State; one copy to each of the Judges of a court of record in this State; one copy to each of the members and officers of this Convention; one copy to each of the town clerks in this State, to be deposited in the town Libraries; ten copies to be deposited in the State Library, and one copy in each of the State offices; and the remainder to be deposited in the office of the Secretary of State for transmission to the town clerks of such new towns as may be hereafter organized.

Resolved, That the printing provided for in the forgoing resolutions shall be done under the supervision of the committee on printing.

On motion of Mr. Cook,

The report of the committee on rules was taken from the table, and the Convention resolved itself into committee of the whole on the same,

Mr. Hanscom in the chair.

And after some time spent thereon, rose and reported the same back to the Convention with amendments, and asked the concurrence of the Convention therein.

On motion of Mr. Cook,

The amendments were concurred in in gross, with the exception of that to the 23d rule.

The 23d rule being under consideration,

Mr. Walker offered the following substitute for the same:

"Motions for reconsideration shall be in order at any time within three days after the decision proposed to be considered took place. But a motion for reconsideration being put and lost, (except in case of privileged motions,) shall not be renewed on the same day, nor shall any subject be a second time reconsidered on the same day without a vote of two-thirds."

On which the yeas and nays were ordered, when

3

On motion of Mr. McClelland,

The original and substitute were laid on the table.

Mr. J. Clark called up the report of the committee on resolution as to mode of proceedings, &c.

Mr. J. D. Pierce moved to amend by combining the committees numbered 8 and 9, and that the committee consist of nine delegates.

Which motion was lost.

The report of the committee was then adopted.

Mr. Hanscom, from the committee appointed pursuant to the resolution relative to postage and newspapers, asked and obtained leave to report:

That upon conferring with his Excellency, the Governor, they learned that there was, by an act of the last legislature, placed in his hands, as part of the contingent fund, the sum of five hundred dollars, for the purpose of employing or retaining a private secretary until after the close of this Convention. That he had dispensed with the services of a private secretary, and consequently the sum of $500, designed for payment for the services of such officer, was now in the contingent fund, and that he would use such sum for the payment of such postage as might be directed by the Convention.

The committee would further beg leave to state, that under the construction given to the law under which the Convention is organized, by the Auditor General, that officer would not feel himself authorized to draw a warrant upon the Treasurer upon the certificate of the Secretary and President of the Convention, for postage or other contingent expenses, other than those specially contemplated by the terms of the act.

Upon the subject of newspapers, the committee have been informed by the proprietors of the Detroit Free Press and the Advertiser, that they will furnish such papers as the Convention may direct, under the recommendation of the Convention to the next Legislature to make an appropriation to pay for the same.

It is perhaps proper in conclusion to state that at the time of the appropriation to the contingent fund above referred to, the Governor had in his employ as private secretary, Mr. Horace S. Roberts, a gentleman eminently qualified for the performance of the duties, and whose services were only dispensed with from considerations of economy; the Governor preferring to perform his own appropriate duties, and also those devolving upon that officer, rather than impose additional burthens upon the treasury.

All of which is respectfully submitted.

The report was accepted, the committee discharged and the report laid on the table.

On motion of Mr. Storey,

The first resolution relative to Reporters of the Convention, was taken from the table, and the same was adopted.

Mr. Hanscom offered the following resolution, and the same was agreed to:

Resolved, That there be added to the standing committees of the Convention, one on supplies and expenditures, to consist of five members.

On motion of Mr. Hanscom,

The subject of postage and newspapers was referred to the committee on supplies and expenditures.

On motion of Mr. Roberts,

The Convention then adjourned.

Lansing, Thursday, June, 6, 1850.

The Convention met pursuant to adjournment and was called to order by the President.

Prayer by the Rev. Mr. Sapp.

Hon. J. M. Edmunds, of Washtenaw county, appeared and took his seat.

The roll being called, the delegates answered to their names with the exception of Messrs. Graham and Hathaway, absent.

On motion of Mr. Leach,

The reading of the journal was dispensed with, and the same was corrected and approved.

The President announced the following committee on supplies and expenditures: Messrs. Hanscom, Danforth, Beeson, Chapel and Eaton.

REPORTS.

Mr. Hanscom presented the following:

The committee on supplies and expenditures, recommend to the Convention the adoption of the following resolutions:

Resolved, That the committee on supplies and expenditures be and they are hereby authorized and required to procure for the use of the Convention an amount of such stationery as will be required, not exceeding in value three hundred dollars, and that the same be delivered to the respective members and officers, under the direction and supervision of the Secretary of the Convention, and an account kept of the amount delivered to each member and officer of the Convention, and that if, after the adjournment of the Convention, any portion of the same should be unappropriated, the same shall be delivered by the Secretary of the Convention to the Secretary of State for the use of the state.

Resolved, That the Secretary of the Convention be required to order for the members of this Convention such newspapers as they may direct, not exceeding two dailies for each, during the setting of the Convention, and that this Convention recommend that the next Legislature make an appropriation to pay therefor.

Resolved, That all postage on mailable matter (not exceeding the sum of five hundred dollars) received or sent, except letters sent by members of the Convention, be by the Post Master of this village charged to the Convention, and that his Excellency, the Governor, be and is hereby requested to pay such sum to said Post Master, upon the certificate of the Secretary of the Convention countersigned by the President, as may be due for postage, not exceeding said sum of $500; and that the Post Master be required to keep an account with each member of the Convention.

The report was accepted, the committee discharged and the resolutions laid on the table.

Mr. Van Valkenburg, from the committee appointed to invite resident clergymen to officiate at the opening of the daily session of the Convention, reported that they had performed that duty, and the committee was discharged.

RESOLUTIONS.

Mr. Gardiner offered the following, which was adopted:

Resolved, That a standing Committee of five be appointed to superintend the printing to be done for this Convention, to be called the committee on printing.

The President appointed Messrs. Gardiner, Hascall, Church, Roberts and Bush such committee.

Mr. Storey offered the following:

Resolved, That the State Printer be instructed to print an edition of 250 copies of the daily official journal of this Convention, in book form, for binding; and that he be instructed to print a like number of all reports of committees for binding.

Resolved, That the contractor for doing the binding for the State, be instructed to bind in the same manner the journals of the Legislature are now bound, the journals and such documents as may be printed by order of this Convention, in one volume—the reports to be inserted as an appendix to the journals.

On motion of Mr. Britain,

The resolutions were referred to the committee on printing.

Mr. Arzeno offered the following resolution:

Resolved, That a certificate for five dollars be drawn and presented to each member of this Convention, to be used by such member in the purchase of stationery; which

On motion of Mr. Crary,

Was laid on the table.

Mr. Roberts offered the following which was adopted:

Resolved, That a Committee on Governmental and Judicial policy of the Upper Peninsula, be added to the standing committe, to consist of nine members.

Mr. N. Pierce moved that the vote by which the 34th rule was stricken from the report of the committee on rules to govern this Convention, be reconsidered.

Which, on motion of Mr. Cornell,

Was laid on the table.

Mr. Bush called from the table the report of the committee on supplies and expenditures, and moved the adoption of the report.

The first resolution being under consideration, Mr. Van Valkenburg offered the following substitute for the same:

Resolved, That a certificate for five dollars be drawn and presented to each member of this Convention, to be used by such member in the purchase of stationery.

Mr. Morrison moved to amend by striking out "five" and inserting "three;" and a division of the question being called, the question was first taken upon striking out, and the same prevailed.

The blank was then filled with "three."

On motion of Mr. Morrison,

The substitute was so amended as to appropriate two dollars in addition to the chairman of each standing committee, for the use of the committee.

And the question recurring upon the adoption of the substitute as amended, the same was not adopted.

Mr. Butterfield offered the following as a substitute for the first resolution:

Resolved, That the Secretary of the Convention be instructed to purchase five hundred dollars worth of stationery for the use of the Convention, and that the Secretary distribute to the members, not exceeding three dollars worth each, and such stationery as their official duties may require, to the chairmen of standing committees.

Mr. Morrison moved to strike out "three," and insert "two," in the substitute. And a division of the question being ordered,

The motion to strike out, was lost.

The question being taken on the adoption of the substitute, as offered by Mr. Butterfield,

The same was not adopted.

The question then recurring on the adoption of the first resolution reported by the committee,

On motion of Mr. Mason,

All after the word "*Resolved,*" was stricken out; when

On motion of Mr. Whipple,

The remainder of the resolution was laid on the table.

The second resolution being under consideration,

Mr. Hascall moved to strike out the word "two," and insert "one." And a division of the question being called,

The motion to strike out did not prevail.

Mr. Leach moved to strike out all after the word "*Resolved,*" which motion was lost; and

The second resolution, as reported by the committee, was then adopted.

The third resolution being under consideration,

On motion of Mr. Hanscom,

The last clause of the resolution, relative to the Post Master keeping an account with delegates, &c., was stricken out.

Mr. Mason moved to lay the resolution on the table.

But the motion did not prevail.

Mr. Britain offered the following as a substitute, which was lost:

Resolved, That the Post Master at Lansing be and he is hereby authorized to charge to the State the postage on all mail matter received by members and officers of said Convention, and all journals and documents of said Convention sent from this post office by said members and officers, *Provided,* Said amount do not exceed five hundred dollars.

Whereupon, the third resolution was adopted.

On motion of Mr. Cook,

The report of the committee on rules was taken from the table.

The question being upon the adoption of the substitute to the 23d rule, proposed by Mr. Walker,

By general consent the words "without a vote of two-thirds," were stricken therefrom.

Mr. Britain moved to amend the substitute by striking out the two first lines, as printed, and inserting:

A motion for reconsideration shall be in order at any time, and may be made by any member of the Convention; but if the motion to reconsider shall not be made on the same day or the day after that on which the decision proposed to be reconsidered was made, three days notice of the intention to make the motion shall be given.

Which motion to amend did not prevail.

The question then recurring upon the adoption of the substitute, as offered by Mr. Walker,

The same was lost by yeas and nays, as follows:

YEAS.

Mr. P. R. Adams, W. Adams, Anderson, Arzeno, Axford, Barnard, Britain, Alvarado Brown, Asahel Brown, Burns, Chapel, Mr. Conner, Cook, Crouse, Daniels, Desnoyers, Edmunds, Gale, Gardiner, Kinne, Marvin, Moore, Mr. Mosher, Raynale, Redfield, Roberts, Robertson, Sullivan, Town, VanValkenburg, Walker, Webster, Woodman, 33

NAYS.

Mr. Alvord, Backus, Bagg, H. Bartow, J. Bartow, Beardsley, Beeson, Ammon Brown, Bush, Butterfield, Carr, Chandler, Choate, Church, S. Clark, Comstock, Cornell, Eastman, Mr. Fralick, Gibson, Green, Hart, Harvey, Hascall, Hixon, Kingsley, Leach, Lovell, McClelland, Morrison, Mowry, Newberry, Orr, J. D. Pierce, N. Pierce, Prevost, Mr. E. S. Robinson, M. Robinson, Rix Robinson, Skinner, Soule, Sturgis, Sutherland, Tiffany, Wait, Wells, White, Whittemore, Williams, Willard, Witherell, Warden, President, 53

Mr. Morrison offered the following as a substitute, which was not adopted:

"When a motion has been once put, and carried in the affirmative or negative, it shall be in order for any member who voted in the majority, to move for a reconsideration thereof, on the same or the succeeding day. And it shall be in order for any member thereafter to make such motion, by giving at least two days notice of his intention to do so. But a motion for reconsideration being put and lost, shall not be a second time renewed, without a vote of a majority of the members elect.

Mr. J. D. Pierce offered the following as a substitute:

No motion for reconsideration shall be in order unless on the same day or day following that on which the decision proposed to be reconsidered took place, nor unless one of the majority shall move such reconsideration. A motion for reconsideration being put and lost, shall not be resumed, nor shall any subject be a second time reconsidered, without the consent of the Convention.

Which did not prevail.

The Convention then concurred in the report of the committee of the whole, regarding the 23d rule.

The question being upon the adoption of the rules, as concurred in,

Mr. J. Bartow moved to amend the 8th rule by adding after the word "question," the words "nor more than one hour at any one time."

Mr. Morrison moved to amend the amendment by striking out "one hour" and inserting in lieu thereof "fifteen minutes."

Which motion was lost.

Mr. Desnoyers moved to strike out the same and insert "thirty minutes."

A division of the question being called for, the Convention refused to strike out.

The amendment offered by Mr. J. Bartow was then adopted.

Mr. J. D. Pierce moved to amend the 33d rule by striking out "ten" and inserting "twenty" in lieu thereof.

But the motion did not prevail.

On motion of Mr. Roberts,

The 28th rule was amended as follows:

After the words "ministers of the gospel," insert "ladies, farmers, mechanics, laborers, and other citizens and strangers."

When, on motion of Mr. Hanscom,

The 28th rule was stricken out.

On motion of Mr. N. Pierce,

The vote by which the Convention concurred in the report of the committee of the whole, striking out the 34th rule, was reconsidered.

And the question again arising on concurring in the same,

The Convention refused to concur.

Mr. Bush offered the following as a substitute for the 2d rule.

Upon the appearance of a quorum, the journal of the preceding day shall he corrected, and, when demanded by a majority, shall be read by the Secretary.

Mr. Van Valkenburg moved to amend the substitute by striking out "majority," and inserting the word "member" in lieu thereof.

Which motion did not prevail, and the substitute was adopted.

The rules as amended were then adopted in gross.

On motion of Mr. Cook,

The rules were ordered placed upon the journal.

Mr. Hascall moved a reconsideration of the resolution appointing a committee to invite the Clergymen of Lansing to open the morning sessions of the Convention with prayer, passed yesterday.

Pending which, on motion of Mr. Cook,

The Convention adjourned.

Rules of the Convention.

Rule 1. The President shall take the chair at the time to which the Convention stands adjourned, and the Convention shall then be called to order and the roll of the members called.

Rule 2. Upon the appearance of a quorum, the journal of the preceeding day shall be corrected, and when demanded by a majority, shall be read by the Secretary.

Rule 3. The President shall preserve order and decorum, and shall decide questions of order, subject to an appeal to the Convention.

Rule 4. The President shall vote on all questions taken by yeas and nays, (except on appeals from his own decisions.)

Rule 5. When the Convention adjourns, the members shall keep their seats until the President announces the adjournment.

Rule 6. Every member, previous to his speaking, shall rise from his seat, and address himself to the President.

Rule 7. When two or more members rise at once, the President shall designate the member who is first to speak.

Rule 8. No member shall speak more than twice on the same question, nor more than one hour at any one time without leave of the Convention, nor more than once until every member who chooses to speak, shall have spoken.

Rule 9. Every motion shall be reduced to writing, if required by the President or any member, and shall be stated by the President, before debate.

RULE 10. After a motion shall be stated by the President, it shall be deemed to be in possession of the Convention; but may be withdrawn at any time before decision or amendment; but another member may renew the same.

RULE 11. When a question is under debate, no motion shall be received but to adjourn; for the previous question; to lay on the table; to postpone indefinitely; to postpone to a day certain; to commit or to amend; which several motions shall have precedence in the order in which they stand arranged.

RULE 12. A motion to adjourn shall always be in order; that and the motion to lay on the table shall be decided without debate.

RULE 13. The previous question shall be in this form: "Shall the main question be now put?" And if demanded by a majority of the members present, its effect shall be to put an end to all debate, and bring the Convention to a direct vote upon amendments, if any are pending, and then upon the main question.

RULE 14. All incidental questions of order, arising after a motion is made for the previous question, during the pendency of such motion, or after the Convention shall have determined that the main question shall be now put, shall be decided, whether on appeal or otherwise, without debate.

RULE 15. Petitions, memorials and other papers, addressed to the Convention, shall be presented by the President, or a member in his place.

RULE 16. Every member who shall be present when a question is last stated from the Chair, and no other, shall vote for or against the same, unless the Convention shall excuse him, in which case he shall not vote.

RULE 17. When the President is putting the question, no member shall walk out or across the House; nor when a member is speaking shall any person entertain any private discourse, or pass between him and the Chair.

RULE 18. If the question in debate contains several points, any member may have the same divided.

RULE 19. A member called to order shall immediately set down, unless permitted to explain, and the Convention, if appealed to, shall decide the case; if there be no appeal the decision of the Chair shall be submitted to; on an appeal, no member shall speak more than once, without leave of the Convention, and when a member is called to order for offensive language, there shall be no debate.

RULE 20. In forming a committee of the whole, the President shall appoint a chairman to preside.

RULE 21. Propositions committed to a committee of the whole shall first be read through by the Secretary, and then read and debated by clauses. All amendments shall be entered on a separate piece of paper, and so reported to the Convention by the chairman, standing in his place.

RULE 22. All questions, whether in committee or in the Convention, shall be put in the order they were moved, except in the case of privileged questions; and in filling up blanks, the largest sum and the longest time shall be first put.

RULE 23. No motion for reconsideration shall be in order, unless within three days after the decision proposed to be reconsidered took place. A motion for reconsideration being put and lost, (except in case of privileged motions,) shall not be renewed on the same day.

RULE 24. Any member, having voted with the majority, may be at liberty to move for a reconsideration; and a motion for reconsideration shall be decided by a majority of votes.

RULE 25. The rules of the Convention shall be observed in committee of the whole, so far as they may be applicable, except that the yeas and nays shall not be called, the previous question enforced, nor the time of speaking limited.

RULE 26. A motion that the committee rise shall always be in order, and shall be decided without debate.

RULE 27, In all cases where an order, resolution or motion, shall be entered on the journals of the Convention, the name of the member moving the same shall be entered on the journals.

RULE 28. On the meeting of the Convention, after correcting the journal of the preceding day, the order of business shall be as follows: 1st, presentation of petitions; 2d, reports of standing committees—reports of select committees; 3d, motions, resolutions and notices; 4th, reading resolutions; 5th, unfinished business of the preceding day; 6th, special orders of the day; 7th, general orders of the day.

RULE 29. When the Convention have arrived at the general orders of the day, they shall go into committee of the whole upon such orders, or a particular order designated by a vote of the Convention; and no other business shall be in order until the whole are considered or passed, or the committee rise; and unless a particular subject is ordered up, the committee of the whole shall consider, act upon, or pass the general orders, according to the order of their reference.

RULE 30. No rule of the Convention shall be suspended, altered or amended, without the concurrence of two-thirds of the members present.

RULE 31. Upon the call of the Convention, the names of the members shall be called by the Secretary, and the absentees noted; but no excuse shall be made until the Convention shall be fully called over; then the absentees shall be called over the second time, and if still absent, excuses are to be heard; and if no excuse, or insufficient excuse be made, the abseentees may, by order of those present, if there are fifteen members present, be taken into custody, wherever to be found, by the Sergeant-at-Arms.

RULE 32. The President may leave the chair and appoint a member to preside, but not for a longer time than one day, except by leave of the Convention.

RULE 33. The rules of parliamentary practice comprised in Jefferson's Manual, shall govern the Convention in all cases to which they are applicable, and in which they are not inconsistent with the standing rules and orders of the Convention.

RULE 34. The ayes and noes may be called for by ten members.

RULE 35. A majority of the members elected shall constitute a quorum for the transaction of business; but a less number may adjourn.

RULE 36. A journal of the proceedings in committee of the whole shall be kept.

Lansing, Friday, June 7, 1850.

The Convention met pursuant to adjournment and was called to order by the President.

Prayer by the Rev. Mr. Atterbury.

The roll being called, Messrs. Graham, Hanscom and Hathaway were found to be absent.

Mr. Storey asked and obtained leave of absence for Mr. Hanscom till Monday next.

The journal, as printed, was approved.

The President announced the following

STANDING COMMITTEES:

1. *On the Bill of Rights*—Messrs. S. Clark, Rix Robinson, Gardiner, Gibson, Webster, P. R. Adams, Prévost.

2. *On the Elective Franchise*—Messrs. Whittemore, Alvord, Hascall, Lovel, Wait.

3. *On the Division of the Powers of Government*—Messrs. J. Clark, Newberry, Hart, Barnard, Asahel Brown.

4. *On the Legislative Department*—Messrs. McClelland, Bagg, Crouse, E. S. Robinson, Soule, Alverado Brown, Beeson, Gale, Chandler.

5. *On the Executive Department*—Messrs. Whipple, Skinner, Mowry, Eaton, Anderson, Sutherland, M. Robinson, N. Pierce, Daniels.

6. *On the Judicial Department*—Messrs. Crary, S. Clark, Church, Hanscom, Sullivan, Walker, Kingsley, Tiffany, Backus.

7. *On State Officers, except the Executive*—Messrs. Redfield, Roberts, Mosher, Orr, Carr.

8. *On County Officers and County Government*—Messrs. Rix Robinson, Cornell, Ammon Brown, Conner, Hixon, Green, Wait.

9. *On Township Officers and Township Government*—Messrs. Bush, Eaton, Chapel, Town, Beeson, Harvey, Leach.

10. *On the Organization of the Government of Cities and Villages*—Messrs. J. Bartow, Skinner, Marvin, Witherell, Raynale.

11. *On Impeachments and Removals from office*—Messrs. Sullivan, J. Clark, W. Adams, Beardsley, P. R. Adams.

12. *On the Milita*—Messrs. Hanscom, Arzeno, Dimond, O'Brien, White, Anderson, Daniels.

13. *On Education*—Messrs. Walker, Van Valkenburg, Butterfield, Eastman, Desnoyers, J. D. Pierce, Barnard, Williams, Edmunds.

14. *On Finance and Taxation*—Messrs. Britain, Bush, Fralick, Axford, Morrison, Burns, Choate, Wells, Chandler.

15. *On Banking and other Corporations, except Municipal*—Messrs. Cook, Raynale, Hascall, Danforth, Gardiner, Crouse, Moore, White, Comstock.

16. *On Salaries*—Messrs. Storey, Van Valkenburg, Mason, Desnoyers, Eastman, Morrison, Williams.

17. *On the Seat of Government*—Messrs. Kingsley, Axford, Danforth, Storey, Willard.

18. *On Exemptions and the Rights of Married Women*—Messrs. J. D. Pierce, Newberry, Lee, Chapel, Fralick, H. Bartow, Tiffany.

19. *On the Punishment of Crimes*—Messrs. Witherell, Sturges, M. Robinson, Woodman, Warden, Kinne, Prevost.

20. *On Miscellaneous Provisions*—Messrs. Church, Whittemore, Sutherland, Alvarado Brown, Marvin, Dimond, Carr.

21. *On the Mode of Amending and Revising the Constitution*—Messrs. McLeod, Mosher, Webster, Gibson, Harvey.

22. *On the Schedule*—Messrs. Mason, Hart, Robertson, Moore, Alvord, Wells, Backus.

23. *On Arrangement and Phraseology of the Constitution*—Messrs. Crary, McClelland, Whipple, S. Clark, Gardiner, Walker, Redfield, Britain, Wells, Tiffany, Williams.

24. *On the Government and Judicial Policy of the Upper Peninsula*—Messrs. Roberts, McLeod, Cornell, Willard, Hanscom, Edmunds, Gale.

RESOLUTIONS.

Mr. Kingsley submitted the following:

Resolved, That the committee on printing procure, in convenient form, for the use of each member of this Convention, a copy of the present Constitution of the State.

The resolution was adopted.

Mr. N. Pierce offered the following:

Resolved, That the committee on supplies and expenditures be instructed to employ some suitable person to repair the locks that are upon the tables of the members of this Convention, or so many of them as are not in repair.

And the same was agreed to.

On motion of Mr. McClelland,

Resolved, That the present constitution be referred to the appropriate committees, and that said committees be requested, when they report, to embody their suggestions for a constitution in articles and sections: that they copy into such articles, the sections of the present constitution applicable thereto, to which they propose no amendments or alterations, and in such sections as they propose to amend and alter, they shall incorporate such amendments and alterations.

Mr. N. Pierce offered the following, which was not adopted.

Resolved, That this Convention will on Monday next proceed to revise and amend the Constitution of this State; that this Convention will resolve itself into the committee of the whole Convention, and take the present constitution up by articles and by sections and in such other subdivisions as will best suit the convenience of the committee, and proceed from day to day to revise and amend said Constitution in committee and in Convention, until the labors of this Convention shall be finished.

On motion of Mr. Storey,

Resolved, That the resolutions reported by the committee appointed to inquire into the expediency of employing Reporters, be taken from the table and referred to the committee on printing.

Mr. Raynale offered the following resolution:

Resolved, That a committee of three members of this Convention be appointed to invite the resident clergy of this village to attend alternately, and open the sessions by prayer; and that no other compensation be allowed for the services of clergymen than the members of the Convention may deem proper to pay from their own private funds; and that said committee be required to inform the clergymen already invited of the action of the Convention on this subject.

Mr. Danforth moved to lay the same upon the table. Which motion was lost.

Mr. Roberts submitted the following substitute:

Resolved, That the services of the resident clergymen be dispensed with, and that the Rev. J. D. Pierce and Rev. Mr. Webster, members of this body, be requested to officiate alternately.

Mr. Witherell moved to indefinitely postpone the resolution and substitute. Mr. Axford called for the yeas and nays, and being sustained, the motion was lost, as follows:

YEAS.

Mr. Anderson,
Backus,
J. Bartow,
Bush,
Carr,
Chandler,
S. Clark,
Comstock,
Danforth,
Daniels,
Edmunds,
Gardiner,
Mr. Green,
Hart,
Harvey,
Kingsley,
Leach,
Lee,
Lovell,
Orr,
J. D. Pierce,
N. Pierce,
Prevost,
Mr. E. S. Robinson,
Sutherland,
Tiffany,
VanValkenburg,
Wait,
Webster,
White,
Whipple,
Whittemore,
Witherell,
President,
34

NAYS.

Mr. P. R. Adams,
W. Adams,
Alvord,
Arzeno,
Axford,
Bagg,
Barnard,
H. Bartow,
Beardsley,
Beeson,
Britain,
Alvarado Brown,
Ammon Brown,
Asahel Brown,
Burns,
Butterfield,
Chapel,
Choate,
Church,
J. Clark,
Conner,
Mr. Cook,
Cornell,
Crouse,
Desnoyers,
Dimond,
Eastman,
Eaton,
Fralick,
Gale,
Gibson,
Hascall,
Hixon,
Kinne,
Marvin,
McLeod,
McClelland,
Moore,
Morrison,
Mosher,
Mowry,
Mr. Newberry,
O'Brien,
Raynale,
Redfield,
Roberts,
Robertson,
M. Robinson,
Rix Robinson,
Skinner,
Soule,
Storey,
Sturgis,
Sullivan,
Town,
Walker,
Warden,
Wells,
Williams,
Willard,
Woodman,
61

And the substitute proposed by Mr. Roberts was not adopted.

Mr. J. Clark moved to strike from the resolution the last clause, providing for the payment of Chaplains.

Which motion was lost.

Mr. White moved to lay the resolution on the table.

But the motion did not prevail.

Mr. McLeod offered the following as a substitute for the resolution:

Resolved, That the Convention proceed on Monday next to the election of a Chaplain.

To which Mr. Britain offered the following amendment, which was accepted by the mover:

"Who shall receive for his services such compensation as shall be subscribed by the members of this Convention for that purpose."

And the yeas and nays being taken thereon, the same was lost, as follows:

YEAS:

Mr. Anderson,	Mr. Hascall,	Mr. Robertson,
Axford,	Kinne,	E. S. Robinson,
Beardsley,	Leach,	Soule,
Beeson,	Lee,	Storey,
Alvarado Brown,	McClelland,	Town,
Bush,	McLeod,	Van Valkenburg,
Choate,	Morrison,	Wait,
S. Clark,	Mowry,	Webster,
Cook,	O'Brien,	Wells,
Danforth,	J. D. Pierce,	Whittemore,
Edmunds,	N. Pierce,	Willard,
Gale,	Prevost,	Witherell,
Gibson,	Roberts,	38

NAYS:

Mr. P. R. Adams,	Mr. Comstock,	Mr. Mosher,
W. Adams,	Conner,	Newberry,
Alvord,	Cornell,	Orr,
Arzeno,	Crouse,	Raynale,
Backus,	Daniels,	Redfield,
Bagg,	Desnoyers,	M. Robinson,
Barnard,	Dimond,	Rix Robinson,
H. Bartow,	Eastman,	Skinner,
J. Bartow,	Eaton,	Sturgis,
Britain,	Fralick,	Sullivan,
Ammon Brown,	Gardiner,	Sutherland,
Asahel Brown,	Green,	Tiffany,
Burns,	Hart,	Walker,
Butterfield,	Harvey,	Warden,
Carr,	Hixon,	White,
Chandler,	Lovell,	Williams,
Chapel,	Marvin,	Woodman,
Church,	Moore,	President,
J. Clark,		55

And the question being on the resolution offered by Mr. Raynale

Mr. Alvord called for the yeas and nays, and the same being ordered, the resolution was adopted by the following vote:

YEAS.

Mr. P. R. Adams,	Mr. Conner,	Mr. Newberry,
W. Adams,	Cook,	Raynale,
Alvord,	Cornell,	Redfield,
Arzeno,	Crouse,	Roberts,
Axford,	Desnoyers,	Robertson,
Barnard,	Dimond,	E. S. Robinson,
H. Bartow,	Eastman,	M. Robinson,
J. Bartow,	Eaton,	Rix Robinson,
Beardsley,	Fralick,	Storey,
Beeson,	Gale,	Sturgis,
Britain,	Gibson,	Sullivan,
Alvarado Brown,	Hascall,	Town,
Ammon Brown,	Kinne,	Walker,
Asahel Brown,	Leach,	Warden,
Burns,	Marvin,	Webster,
Butterfield,	McClelland,	Williams,
Chapel,	Morrison,	Willard,
Choate,	Mosher,	Woodman,
Church,	Mowry,	56

NAYS.

Mr. Backus,	Mr. Green,	Mr. Skinner,
Bagg,	Hart,	Soule,
Bush,	Harvey,	Sutherland,
Carr,	Hixon,	Tiffany,
Chandler,	Lovell,	VanValkenburg,
J. Clark,	McLeod,	Wait,
S. Clark,	Moore,	Wells,
Comstock,	O'Brien,	White,
Danforth,	Orr,	Whittemore,
Daniels,	J. D. Pierce,	Witherell,
Edmunds,	N. Pierce,	President,
Gardiner,	Prevost,	35

On motion of Mr. Backus,

Resolved, That the committee on the legislative department be instructed to inquire into the expediency of reporting a provision in the Constitution that no act of the Legislature shall embrace more than one subject, which shall be clearly expressed by its title.

Mr. Church asked to be and was excused from serving upon the committee on printing.

Whereupon, Mr. Britain was appointed in his stead.

Mr. Witherell moved that when the Convention adjourn, it stand adjourned till Monday next.

But the motion was lost; and

On motion of Mr. McLeod,

The Convention then adjourned.

Lansing, Saturday, June 8, 1850.

The Convention met pursuant to adjournment and was called to order by the President.

Mr. Cook announced the presence of his colleague, Hon. Jonathan B. Graham, who appeared and took his seat.

Mr. Walker announced that Hon. Hiram Hathaway of Macomb county, was in attendance; and Mr. Hathaway took his seat.

The roll being called, Mr. Hanscom was absent on leave.

The journal was corrected and approved.

PETITIONS.

By Mr. Cook: of H. Waldron, E. H. C. Wilson and others, of Hillsdale county, asking that the word "white," may be stricken out of the revised Constitution;

Referred to committee on elective franchise.

By Mr. Crary: of Lewis Wilmarth and 241 citizens of Calhoun county, praying the Convention to abolish the institution of the Grand Jury;

Referred to committee on bill of rights.

REPORTS.

Mr. McLeod, from the committee on the mode of amending and revising the Constitution, submitted a report, which was read, accepted, and

On motion of Mr. Mason,

Laid upon the table and ordered printed.

Mr. S. Clark, from the committee on the bill of rights, submitted a report; which,

On motion of Mr. Crary,

Was referred to the committee of the whole and ordered printed.

Mr. Gardiner, from the committee on printing, to whom was referred the resolutions relative to printing journals, &c., reported the following resolutions, and recommended their adoption:

Resolved, That the State Printer be instructed to print an edition of 480 copies of the daily official journal of this Convention, including the Constitution adopted by this Convention, in book form, for binding; and that he be instructed to print a like number of all reports of committees for binding.

Resolved, That the contractor for doing the binding for the State, be instructed to bind, in the same manner the journals of the Legislature are now bound, the journals and such documents as may be printed by order of this Convention, in one volume—the reports to be inserted as an appendix to the journals.

On motion of Mr. Crary,

The report was accepted and the committee discharged from the further consideration of the subject.

On motion of Mr. J. D. Pierce,

The amendments proposed by the committee were severally concurred in and the resolutions as amended were adopted.

RESOLUTIONS.

Mr. Butterfield offered the following:

Resolved, That there be added to the committee on the judiciary department six members from other occupations and professions than that of the law.

Mr. Robertson moved to amend by striking out "six," and inserting "ten."

And the resolution was so amended.

Mr. Butterfield demanded the yeas and nays on the passage of the resolution, and the same being ordered, the resolution was adopted, as follows:

YEAS:

Mr. P. R. Adams,	Mr. Cornell,	Mr. Newberry,
W. Adams,	Crary,	O'Brien,
Alvord,	Crouse,	Orr,
Anderson,	Danforth,	J. D. Pierce,
Arzeno,	Daniels,	N. Pierce,
Axford,	Eastman,	Prevost,
Backus,	Eaton,	Raynale,
Bagg,	Edmunds,	Robertson,
Barnard,	Fralick,	E. S. Robinson,
H. Bartow,	Gale,	M. Robinson,
J. Bartow,	Gardiner,	Rix Robinson,

Beardsley,
Beeson,
Britain,
Alvarado Brown,
Ammon Brown,
Asahel Brown,
Burns,
Bush,
Butterfield,
Carr,
Chandler,
Chapel,
Choate,
Church,
J. Clark,
Comstock,
Conner,
Cook,
Gibson,
Graham,
Green,
Hart,
Harvey,
Hascall,
Hathaway,
Hixon,
Kingsley,
Kinne,
Leach,
Lee,
Lovell,
Marvin,
McClelland,
Moore,
Morrison,
Mosher,
Skinner,
Storey,
Sturgis,
Sullivan,
Sutherland,
Tiffany,
Town,
Wait,
Warden,
Webster,
Wells,
Whittemore,
Williams,
Willard,
Witherell,
Woodman,
President, 85

NAYS:

Mr. S. Clark,
Desnoyers,
Dimond,
Mason,
Mr. McLeod,
Mowry,
Redfield,
Roberts,
Mr. Soule,
Van Valkenburg,
White, 11

Mr. Witherell offered the following, which was referred to the committee on the judiciary:

Resolved, That the committee on the judiciary be instructed to inquire into the expediency of establishing a supieme court to consist of three judges; and to provide for a division of the State into judicial circuits, and for the election of a circuit judge in each circuit. And that the Legislature be empowered to increase the number of circuits and circuit judges at the expiration of every five years, and not oftener.

Mr. Alvord offered the following:

Resolved, That the committee on education be instructed to inquire into the expediency of establishing a system of free schools to be supported by general taxation.

Mr. Crary moved to refer to the committee on education.

Which motion did not prevail.

The resolution was then adopted.

On motion of Mr. Bagg,

Resolved, That the committee on banks and incorporations be and hereby are directed to inquire into and report upon the expediency of incorporating into the Constitution of this State, as a distinct section thereof, the following, to wit: The Legislature shall have no power to pass any act granting any charter for banking purposes,

On motion of Mr. Wells,

Resolved, That the committee on the judiciary be instructed to inquire into the expediency of requiring the judges of the Supreme Court to report to the Legislature at the commencement of each session, what defects they have observed in existing laws, and propositions for amendment.

On motion of Mr. Eaton,

Resolved, That the committee on the elective franchise, &c., inquire into the expediency of so amending the constitution of this state as to secure to the people of this state an annual registry of the names of all legal voters previous to the election.

On motion of Mr. Eaton,

Resolved, That the committee on education inquire into the expediency of making constitutional provision for the establishment of such a system of common schools as will, by taxation, bestow the facility of acquiring a good education on every child in this State.

On motion of Mr. Warden,

Resolved, That the committee on the elective franchise be instructed to inquire into the expediency of allowing the right of suffrage to aliens, who shall have declared their intention to become citizens of the United States, in accordance with the naturalization laws thereof, and who shall have resided in this State for one year next preceding any election.

On motion of Mr. Roberts,

Resolved, That the State Printer be instructed to print 480 copies of all articles, and 480 copies of all reports ordered printed for the use of this Convention.

On motion of Mr. J. D. Pierce,

Resolved, That the committee on the judiciary be instructed to inquire into the expediency of providing that all acts of the Legislature be submitted to the justices of the supreme court, to decide upon their constitutionality before they take effect, and that subsequently they have no power to declare any act so passed upon to be unconstitutional.

And also, that said committee inquire into the expediency of so simplifying judicial proceedings, as to have but one form of action. And also to provide that the Legislature at its first session after the adoption of the Constitution, shall appoint three commissioners, whose duty it shall be to reduce to a written code, the whole body of the law of this State, or so much thereof, as to them shall seem expedient.

On motion of J. D. Pierce,

Resolved, That the committee on incorporations be instructed to inquire into the expediency of providing as follows:

1. That the credit of the state shall not be loaned to any person or persons, nor to any company or association, nor shall the state ever be liable for the stock of any corporation whatever.

2. The legislature shall have no power to pass acts of incorporation, except for municipal purpose.

3. In all cases where damage is done by any corporation to private property, the corporation shall pay to the full amount of such damage.

4. The legislature may pass general laws, under which associations may be formed for all purposes of business, and for religious and charitable objects; but no rights, exemptions, privileges or immunities shall be granted to any association or corporate body which are not secured to every person in the state.

5. No special charters shall be granted for banking purposes, and no association or corporation now existing, or hereafter to exist by virtue of general laws, shall issue any bills under a less denomination that five dollars after the first of January, 185–.

6. The legislature shall have no power to pass any act sanctioning the refusal of any person or persons, association or corporate body, issuing bills, to pay the same on demand.

7. Whenever any banking association shall become insolvent, the bill-holders shall be entitled to preference in payment over all other creditors, and the stockholders shall be responsible in their individual capacity for all the debts and liabilities of the same.

8. No act under which banking associations may be formed shall go into operation until the same shall have been approved by a direct vote of the people at some general election subsequent to its passage.

Mr. Tiffany moved that the committee on the judiciary be instructed to report a judiciary system which shall not include the present system of county courts.

Mr. Bagg moved to amend by adding "with the exception of the county of Wayne."

When the resolution was laid upon the table.

On motion of Mr. Storey,

Resolved, That the committee on the legislative department be instructed to inquire into the expediency of a constitutional provision which shall require the legislature, in making an amendment to an existing law, to re-enact and publish the entire act.

On motion of Mr. Fralick,

Resolved, That the committee on the legislative department be instructed to inquire into the expediency of providing for single Representative and Senatorial districts, and for bienniel sessions of the Legislature, in the new Constitution.

Mr. Crouse offered the following; which,

On motion of Mr. J. D. Pierce,

Was referred to the committee on printing.

Resolved, That the committee on printing be required to cause —— copies of the rules of this Convention to be printed in the form of a manual, together with such other information as they shall deem useful and appropriate.

On motion of Mr. Bagg,

Resolved, That the committee on the legislative department be instructed to inquire into the propriety and expediency of incorporating a provision in the Constitution, for any person to sell or vend ardent spirits, or other intoxicating liquors, wholesale or retail, in this State, without license: *Provided*, That such person or persons shall be liable for all the pernicious consequences arising from such sale, to be collected in a court of law; and that the only proof necessary for conviction and judgment, shall be that the defendant or defendants had sold or given to such person or persons ardent spirits, or other intoxicating drinks, twenty-four hours prior to the commission of such offence or offences; and all persons who shall have sold to such defendant or defendants, shall be joined in defence, and pay after judgment, in proportion to the quantity sold or given to the offender by each, respectively.

On motion of Mr. Warden,

Resolved, That the committee on the punishment of crimes be instructed to inquire into the expediency of providing for the abolition of capital punishment.

On motion of Mr. Van Valkenburg:

Resolved, That the committee on township officers and township government be instructed to inquire into the propriety of reducing the number of town officers and town expenses.

On motion of Mr. Orr,

Resolved, That the judiciary committee be instructed to inquire into the expediency of dispensing with our present grand jury system.

On motion of Mr. McClelland,

Resolved, That the committee on banking and corporations inquire into the expediency of engrafting upon the constitution a provision requiring all banking institutions to be established by general laws, and to be based on State stock securities so as to make the bill-holder perfectly secure, and that such general laws, before they take effect, be submitted to a vote of the people.

On motion of Mr. McClelland,

Resolved, That the committee on county officers and county government be instructed to inquire into the propriety of adopting the commissioner system in the counties or of reducing the number of supervisors to three or five in each county, either electing them by districts or by the whole county.

On motion of Mr. McClelland,

Resolved, That the committee on the judiciary be instructed to inquire into the propriety of abolishing the county court system, and of organizing a supreme court system, and requiring the judges thereof to discharge circuit duties.

Mr. Britain offered the following:

Resolved, That the committee on state officers be instructed to inquire into the expediency of providing for the election of the Speaker of the House of Representatives by the people.

Which, on motion of Mr. Redfield,

Was amended by adding "whose per diem shall be the same as other members of that body."

And the resolution as amended was adopted.

Mr. Beardsley offered the following:

Resolved, That the committee on the elective franchise be instructed to inquire into the expediency of granting to aliens now residents, and who shall hereafter become residents of this state, all the privileges of United States citizens within this state.

Mr. Bagg moved to amend by inserting the word "white" before "aliens," which was accepted by the mover, and the resolution was adopted.

On motion of Mr. Sutherland,

Resolved, That the committee on finance and taxation be instructed to inquire into the expediency of abolishing the office of Auditor General, and requiring the legislature to provide for the transaction of the business of that officer at the county seat of the several counties, so far as such business concerns taxation.

On motion of Mr. Bush,

Resolved, That the committee on the legislative department be instructed to inquire into the expediency of entitling each county at present organized to at least one Representative.

On motion of Mr. H. Bartow,

Resolved, That the committee on education be instructed to inquire into the expediency of requiring the free schools to be English schools.

On motion of Mr. Soule,

Resolved, That the committee on the judiciary be instructed to inquire into the expediency of abolishing the distinction between law and equity proceedings; that all causes may be tried upon their merits, and allowing all persons to act as attorneys, in any court.

Also, provide that all appeals shall be submitted to a jury, if either party in the suit shall require it.

On motion of Mr. Walker,

Resolved, That the committee on the legislative department be instructed to inquire into the expediency of providing that the regular sessions of the Legislature shall not be held oftener than once in two years; and that after the first 60 days of any session, the members shall receive no compensation. Also, so that it shall require a vote of two-thirds of all the members elected to each House, to create, alter or amend any law, except at such sessions as an entire revision of the laws shall have been ordered to be made in pursuance of a constitutional provision.

On motion of Mr. Fralick,

Resolved, That the committee on township officers and township government be instructed to inquire into the expediency of providing that the public business of townships and township offices be performed by 3 persons, instead of a larger or the present number.

On motion of Mr. Hascall,

Resolved, That the committee on State officers be instructed to inquire into the expediency of diminishing the number of State officers, and embracing the duties of two or more into one.

On motion of Mr. Butterfield,

Resolved, That the committee on finance and taxation be instructed to inquire into the expediency of so forming the organic law as to require the Legislature to pass such laws as shall provide for the final collection of all taxes within the townships.

On motion of Mr. Beeson,

Resolved, That the committee on exemptions and the rights of married women be instructed to inquire into the expediency of securing to married women all property owned by them at the time of their marriage, or that they may at any time acquire by inheritance.

On motion of Mr. Sturgis,

Resolved, That the committee on the legislative department be instructed to inquire into the expediency of reducing the per diem of representatives of the Legislature to two dollars.

On motion of Mr. Fralick,

Resolved, That the committee on the judicial department be instructed to inquire into the expediency of the organization of police courts in cities and villages with a limited criminal jurisdiction.

On motion of Mr. Alvord,

Resolved, That the committee on the Legislative department be instructed to inquire into the expediency of employing the services of chaplains in legislative and conventional bodies, and allowing the same pay as members of those bodies.

On motion of Mr. Robertson,

Resolved, That the committee on the legislative department be instructed to inquire into the expediency of vesting all legislative powers in one House—the Lieutenant Governor to be President of the House.

Mr. Witherell offered the following:

Resolved, That the committee on the judiciary be instructed to inquire into the expediency of a constitutional provision rendering the Governor of the State ineligible to the office of United States Senator during the term for which he may be elected.

Mr. Hascall moved to amend by inserting after "United States Senator" the words "or any other office;" which was adopted.

Mr. Backus moved to amend by inserting after the word "State," "and Judges of the Supreme Court."

Mr. Witherell moved to amend the amendment by inserting after "Supreme," the words "and Circuit;" which motion prevailed, and the amendment was adopted.

On motion of Mr. Cornell,

The resolution was amended by adding thereto the words "and for one year thereafter."

The resolution as amended was adopted.

On motion of Mr. Hart,

Resolved, That the committee on the judiciary be required to inquire into the expedieney of abolishing the Probate Court and creating some kind of County Court with Surrogate and Probate jurisdiction.

Mr. Leach offered the following, which by his request, was laid upon the table:

Resolved, That this Convention is in favor of biennial sessions of the Legislature.

Mr. Willard offered the following:

Resolved That when this Convention adjourn it adjourn to meet at Detroit, on ———

Mr. Leach moved to indefinitely postpone the same. Upon which motion,

Mr. Bush demanded the yeas and nays. And the call being sustained,

The resolution was indefinitely postponed, as follows:

YEAS.

Mr. W. Adams,	Mr. Danforth,	Mr. O'Brien,
Axford,	Dimond,	Orr,
Barnard,	Eastman,	J. D. Pierce,
H. Bartow,	Edmunds,	N. Pierce,
J. Bartow,	Gale,	Prevost,
Beardsly,	Gardiner,	Redfield,
Britain,	Graham,	Robertson,
Alvarado Brown,	Green,	E. S. Robinson,
Ammon Brown,	Harvey,	Rix Robinson,
Burns,	Hascall,	Soule,
Bush,	Hathaway,	Storey,
Carr,	Hixon,	Sturgis,
Church,	Kingsley,	Sullivan,
S. Clark,	Kinne,	Town,
Comstock,	Leach,	Wait,
Conner,	Lee,	Walker,
Cook,	Lovell,	Warden,
Cornell,	McClelland,	White,
Crary,	Mosher,	Williams,
Crouse,	Mowry,	59

NAYS.

Mr. P. R. Adams,	Mr. Daniels,	Mr. M. Robinson,
Alvord,	Desnoyers,	Skinner,
Anderson,	Eaton,	Sutherland,
Arzeno,	Fralick,	Tiffany,
Backus,	Gibson,	VanValkenburg,
Bagg,	Hart,	Webster,
Beeson,	Marvin,	Wells,
Asahel Brown,	McLeod,	Whittemore,
Butterfield,	Moore,	Willard,
Chandler,	Morrison,	Witherell,
Chapel,	Newberry,	Woodman,
Choate,	Raynale,	President,
J. Clark,	Roberts,	38

On motion of Mr. Britain,

Resolved, That the committee on printing, who were on the 7th inst. ordered to procure in convenient form for the use of each member of this Convention, a copy of the present Constitution of this State, be instructed to procure the printing, in the form of a manual, of the rules adopted by this Convention, with said Constitution, with lists of members and officers, showing their place of nativity, occupation, post office and present boarding house. Also, a calendar and statement of all standing committees of this Convention; and that 240 copies of the same be published for the use of this Convention.

On motion of Mr. Beardsley,

Resolved, That the committee on exemptions and the rights of married women be instructed to inquire into the expediency of allowing married women to dispose of any property, real or personal, by will, without the consent of their husbands.

On motion of Mr. Beardsley,

Resolved, That the committee on the judiciary be instructed to inquire into the expediency of establishing one or more judges, to be elected in each organized county, to hold township courts within such county, for the trial of all causes in which the amount of damages claimed shall not exceed two hundred dollars; and of such criminal jurisdiction as shall be provided by law; and of prohibiting justices' courts for the trial of civil and criminal causes.

On motion of Mr. Orr,

Resolved, That the committee on banking and other corporations, (except municipal,) be instructed to inquire into the expediency of reporting a constitutional provision making the stockholders in such corporations individually liable for the term of one year after they cease to become such stockholders.

On motion of Mr. Moore,

Resolved, That the committee on the legislative department be instructed to inquire into the propriety of settling contested elections in their respective counties and districts. and save the expense of coming before the Legislature with such disputed claims.

Mr. Van Valkenburg offered the following:

Resolved, That one hundred and twenty copies of the manual of this Convention be bound in the same form and of the some material as the manual of the Legislature of this State at its session of 1850.

Mr. J. Clark moved to lay the resolution on the table, which was not agreed to.

Mr. Bush moved to adjourn, but the Convention refused to adjourn.

The resolution, as offered by Mr. Van Valkenburg, was then adopted by yeas and nays, as follows:

YEAS:

Mr. W. Adams,	Mr. Cook,	Mr. N. Pierce,
Alvord,	Cornell,	Prevost,
Arzeno,	Crouse,	Raynale,
Axford,	Danforth,	Roberts,
Bagg,	Desnoyers,	M. Robinson,
Beeson,	Eastman,	Skinner,
Britain,	Fralick,	Soule,
Alvarado Brown,	Gardiner,	Storey,
Ammon Brown,	Gibson,	Van Valkenburg,
Asahel Brown,	Graham,	Wait,
Burns,	Kingley,	Walker,
Bush,	Kinne,	Webster,
Butterfield,	Marvin,	Whittemore,
Choate,	McLeod,	Willard,
Church,	Moore,	Woodman,
Conner,	Mosher,	47

NAYS.

Mr. P. R. Adams,	Mr. Eaton,	Mr. O'Brien,
Backus,	Edmunds,	Redfield,
Barnard,	Gale,	Robertson,
H. Bartow,	Green,	Sturgis,
J. Bartow,	Harvey,	Sullivan,
Carr,	Hascall,	Tiffany,
Chandler,	Hathaway,	Town,
Chapel,	Hixon,	Warden,
J. Clark,	Leach,	Wells,
S. Clark,	McClelland,	White,
Comstock,	Morrison,	Williams,
Daniels,	Mowry,	Witherell,
Dimond,	Newberry,	President, 39

On motion of Mr. Hascall,

Resolved, That the committee on exemptions and the rights of married women be instructed to inquire into the expediency of abolishing all law for the collection of debts under a limited amount.

Mr. Wells moved that Mr. Witherell be excused from serving upon the committee on the punishment of crimes.

But the motion to excuse was lost.

The President announced the following committee on the invitation of clergymen, &c.:

Messrs. Raynale, J. D. Pierce and Webster.

On motion of Mr. Cook,

The Convention adjourned till Monday morning.

Lansing, Monday, June 10, 1850.

The Convention met pursuant to adjournment and was called to order by the President.

Prayer by the Rev. Mr. Atterbury.

The roll being called, Messrs. Roberts and Whipple were absent without leave.

PETITIONS.

By Mr. Fralick: of E. J. Penniman, D. H. Rowland, Bethuel Noyes, and 409 others, of Wayne county, in favor of biennial sessions of the Legislature of limited duration, and single districts for Senators and Representatives, and county boards of Supervisors, dividing counties when required into Representative districts.

Referred to committee on the legislative department.

By Mr. Van Valkenburg: of Hiram Barrett and 44 others, of Oakland county, asking the adoption of several features in the revised constitution.

Referred to committee on miscellaneous provisions.

Mr. Backus presented the proceedings of the common council of the city of Detroit, tendering the use of the city Hall for the use of the Convention, should it adjourn to that city.

Laid upon the table.

The President announced a communication from Orville B. Dibble upon the same subject.

Read and laid on the table.

REPORTS.

Mr. McClelland, from the committee on rules of proceeding, &c., submitted the following, to be added to the standing rules of the Convention:

RULE 37. Every article shall receive three several readings previous to its being passed; and the second and third readings shall be on different days; and the third reading shall be on a day subsequent to that in which it has passed a committee of the whole, unless the Convention, by a vote of two-thirds of the members present, shall direct otherwise.

RULE 38. No article shall be committed or amended unless it has been twice read.

RULE 39. Every article, when read a third time and passed, shall be referred to the committee on arrangement and phraseology.

The rules were severally adopted by a two-thirds vote.

Mr. J. Clark, from the committee on the division of the powers of government, submitted a report, which was read a 1st and 2d time by its title, and

On motion of Mr. Cook,

Referred to the committee of the whole and ordered printed.

The committee on printing, to whom was referred the resolutions relative to printing the proceedings and debates of this Convention, have had said resolutions under consideration, and report the same back to the Convention and recommend the following amendments, viz: strike out of the first resolution, "one thousand copies," and insert "twelve hundred."

Strike out of second resolution, "one copy to each of the judges of a court of record in this State," and insert "one copy for the use of the office of each county clerk in this State, and one copy for the clerk of the Supreme Court;" to which they ask the concurrence of the Convention.

All which is respectfully submitted.

E. P. GARDINER, Ch'n.

The amendments proposed by the committee were severally concurred in.

When, on motion of Mr. Gardiner,

The second resolution was further amended by striking out the words "one thousand," and inserting "twelve hundred."

On motion of Mr. Storey,

The second resolution was amended by striking out "ten," and inserting "one hundred," so it shall read "one hundred copies to be deposited in the State Library.

And the resolutions as amended were severally adopted.

RESOLUIONS.

On motion of Mr. Britain,

Resolved, That the committee on printing cause the rules this morning adopted to be printed in the manual.

Mr. Witherell offered the following, which was not adopted:

Resolved, That for the purpose of preserving the purity and efficiency of future conventions to revise the Constitution, the committee on the legislative department be instructed to inquire into the expediency of providing for an election by the people of presidents of such conventions, and in case of any doubt existing as to such expediency, said committee be instructed to consult precedents.

Mr. Fralick offered the following:

Resolved, That the committee on the legislative department be instructed to provide for single reepresentative districts in their re-report.

Which, on motion of Mr. Van Valkenburg,

Was laid upon the table.

Mr. Ammon Brown offered the following, which, on motion of Mr. Crary,

Was laid upon the table:

Resolved, That the committee on the legislative department be instructed to report an article or articles providing for single senatorial districts.

Mr. Morrison offered the following:

Resolved, That corporations for banking purposes shall be formed, extended or renewed by special laws, but no such act of incorporation, extension or renewal shall take effect until the same shall have been submitted to the people at the next general election, succeeding the passage of the same, for representatives, and approved by a majority of all the votes cast at such election for and against such law; and that but one act of incorporation, extension or renewal of any corporation with banking powers shall be passed during any one session of the Legislature. No such corporation shall be formed, extended or renewed for a longer period than fifteen years.

Referred to the committee on banking and other incorporations.

Mr. Morrison offered the following, which was referred to the committee on miscellaneous provisions:

Resolved, That when private property is taken for the use or benefit of the public, the necessity of using such property and the just compensation to be made therefor shall be ascertained by a jury of twelve freeholders, residing in the vicinity of such property, or by not less than three commissioners appointed by a court of record, as shall be prescribed by law. That private roads may be opened in the manner to be prescribed by law; but in every case the necessity of the road, and the amount of all damages to be sustained by the opening thereof, shall be first determined by a jury of freeholders, and such amount, together with the expenses of the proceeding, shall be paid by the person to be benefitted.

Also, the following, which was referred to the committee on exemptions and the rights of married women:

Resolved, That any person, in order to avail himself of any provision in this constitution, or of law exempting property from forced sale on executions, shall make and file (at such time as shall be prescribed by law, once in each year, with some officer to be designated by law in the township, village or city in which he resides,) an affidavit, setting forth a description of the property of which he is the owner, and the value thereof. Also a statement of the amount of his indebtedness.

On motion of Mr. Bagg,

Resolved, That the committee on the judiciary department be instructed to inquire into the expediency of establishing in incorporated cities, municipal courts, with civil and criminal jurisdiction.

On motion of Mr. Storey,

Resolved, That the committee on miscellaneous provisions be instructed to inquire into the expediency of a constitutional prohibition against the employment of state prisoners in those branches of mechanical labor which interfere with mechanical trades in this state.

Mr. Van Valkenburg offered the following:

Resolved, That the committee on the legislative department be instructed to insert a provision into the Constitution authorizing each House of the Legislature to employ a Chaplain during their sessions, who shall be entitled to the same per diem allowance as members of their respective bodies.

On motion of Mr. McLeod,

The resolution was referred to the committee on the legislative department.

Mr. Beardsley offered the following:

Resolved, That the committee on the judicial department be instructed to inquire into the expediency of allowing any white male resident of this State, twenty-one years of age, to practice as an attorney and counsellor in any of the courts of law, and as a solicitor in chancery in this State, on filing a written notice of his intention in the office of the clerk of the Supreme Court.

On motion of Mr. McLeod,

The resolution was amended, by striking out the word "white."

Mr. S. Clark moved to lay the resolution upon the table; which motion was lost; when

On motion of Mr. Crouse,

The resolution was indefinitely postponed.

On motion of Mr. Beardsley,

Resolved, That the committee on the judicial department be instructed to inquire into the expediency of including the fees of counsel and attorneys and solicitors in the costs of suits at law and in equity, and enforcing their payment by execution, against the losing party: and also, of restricting counsel to certain fees in all the courts of this State; and attorneys and solicitors to such fees as shall be provided by law.

On motion of Mr. Beardsley,

Resolved, That the committee on the judicial department be instructed to inquire into the expediency of prohibiting special and dillatory pleas and demurrers in all the courts of this State.

Mr. Beardsley offered the following, which did not prevail:

Resolved, That the committee on the elective franchise be instructed to inquire into the expediency of granting the right of suffrage to all white and single females, twenty-one years of age, and who are now or who shall hereafter become residents of this State.

On motion of Mr. Witherell,

Resolved, That the committee on the Legislative department be instructed to inquire into the expediency of providing that no property of individuals shall be taken for the use of the State or of any corporation without payment therefor being first made.

On motion of Mr. Backus,

Resolved, That the committee on the legislative department be instructed to inquire into the expediency of reporting a provision in the constitution, that the Legislature shall pass no retrospective laws.

On motion of Mr. Backus,

Resolved, That the committee on miscellaneous provisions be instructed to inquire into the expediency of reporting a provision in the constitution, that private property shall not be taken for public use, or the use of corporations, municipal or otherwise, without compensation first provided and actually paid or tendered.

On motion of Mr. Backus,

Resolved, That the committee on the legislative department inquire into the expediency of reporting a provision in the Constitution, that every person holding claims against the State may sue for such demand in like manner and with the same facility as suits may be brought against individuals.

On motion of Mr. O'Brien,

Resolved, That the committee on exemptions, &c., are requested to inquire into the expediency of exempting the property of every individual to the amount of five hundred dollars, from sale on execution or other process of law or equity.

On motion of Mr. Alvord,

Resolved, That the committee on judiciary be instructed to inquire into the expediency of abolishing the court of probate.

On motion of Mr. Town,

Resolved, That the committee on connty officers and county government be instructed to inquire into the expediency of uniting the offices of county clerk and register of deeds into one office, and of reducing the fees of both.

On motion of Mr. S. Clark,

Resolved, That the committee on education be instructed to inquire into the expediency of providing for the establishment of an agricultural school and model farm connected therewith.

On motion of Mr. Gibson,

Resolved, That the committee on elective franchise be instructed to inquire into the expediency of prohibiting duelists and persons guilty of betting on elections from exercising the right of suffrage.

On motion of Mr. Skinner,

Resolved, That the committee on the judiciary be and they are hereby instructed to inquire into the expediency of authorizing the supervisors of each county to make as many judicial districts in each county, (not exceeding the number of representative districts,) as, in their opinion, will best suit the convenience and wants of the people thereof; in each of which shall be elected a district justice for the term of four years; with such civil and criminal jurisdiction as shall be conferred by law.

On motion of Mr. Britain,

Resolved, That the State Printer be requested to print twelve hundred copies of the daily jonrnal for the use of this Convention, instead of ten hundred, as heretofore ordered.

On motion of Mr. Storey,

Resolved. That the committee on the legislative department be instructed to inquire into the expediency of a constitutional provision prohibiting the legislature from legislating on any claim against the state.

Resolved, That the committee on state officers (except executive) be instructed to inquire into the expediency of creating a board of state auditors, who shall act upon all claims against the state, and from whose decision there may be an appeal to the supreme court.

On motion of Mr. Daniels,

Resolved, That the committee on punishment of crime be instructed to inquire into the propriety of incorporating into the constitution the establishment of a house of refuge or correction, for the punishment of juvenile and female offenders.

On motion of Mr. Robertson,

Resolved, That the committee on education be instructed to inquire into the expediency of providing for the election of one school superintendent in each county, whose duties shall be prescribed by law, and to be in lieu of the present system of township school inspectors.

Mr. Moore offered an amendment to the bill of rights, as follows:

Any citizen of this State who may hereafter be engaged, either directly or indirectly, in a duel, either as principal or accessory before the fact, shall forever be disqualified from holding any office under the Constitution and laws of this State.

Referred to the committee of the whole.

Mr. Chapel offered the following:

Resolved, That in the opinion of this Convention, no member is entitled to his per diem, unles his name appears daily upon the journal of this Convention. Sickness only, excepted.

On motion of Mr. Mason,

The resolution was laid upon the table.

On motion of Mr. Hart,

Resolved, That the committee on the jndiciary be required to inquire into the expediency of incorporating in the Constitution authority to the Legislature to establish courts of conciliation.

On motion of Mr. Williams,

Resolved, That the committee on the judicial department be instructed to report a provision for the new Constitution, authorizing the Legislature to establish courts of conciliation, with powers and duties prescribed by law, whose jurisdiction shall be co-extensive with organized towns; and after such courts shall have been established for seven years, to create similar courts of a wider jurisdiction.

On motion of Mr. Williams,

Resolved, That the committee on finance and taxation be instructed to inquire into the expediency of so restricting any system of taxation as to prevent one citizen acquiring the right to the property of another by virtue of a tax title; and that they be further instructed to inquire into the expediency of having all lands escheat to the State on which taxes have not been paid for —— years.

On motion of Mr. Williams,

Resolved, That the committee on miscellaneous provisions be instructed to inquire into the expediency of inserting in the Constitution a provision substantially as follows: "Lands now flowed and unimproved lands which may hereafter be flowed by the erection of mill dams, shall be paid for in the manner to be provided by law; and the actual value of the land flowed shall be determined by a jury of freeholders, and such value and the expenses of determining the same, shall be paid by the party erecting the dam."

On motion of Mr. Williams,

Resolved, That the committee on exemptions and the rights of married women be instructed to inquire into the expediency of abolishing all laws for the compulsory collection of debts after the year 1854.

On motion of Mr. Hixon,

Resolved, That the committee on the judicial department be instructed to inquire into the expediency of abolishing all laws for the collection of debts.

On motion of Mr. Witherell,

Resolved, That the committee on the schedule be instrscted to inquire into the expediency of providing in said schedule for the payment of such expenses of this Convention as have not been provided for by the Legislature.

On motion of Mr. Cornell,

Resolved, That the committee on towns be instructed to inquire into the expediency of merging the offices of supervisos, assessor, commissioners of highways and directors of the poor into one office, and the duties to be performed by three persons, denominated "board of supervisors."

On motion of Mr. Raynale,

Resolved, That the committee on miscellaneous provisions be instructed to inquire into the propriety of prohibiting the Legislature from passing any resolution of instructions to our Senators in Congress, unless by a two-thirds vote of the members elected to each House.

On motion of Mr. Chapel,

Resolved, That the committee on the legislative department inquire into the expediency of so altering the present mileage of members of the Legislature to and from the capital of this State as not to exceed eight cents per mile.

The President announced the following additional members of the committee on the judicial department, under the resolution of the 8th inst.:

Messrs. Butterfield, Hixon, Comstock, Cook, Asahel Brown, Hathaway, Mowry, Lee, Town and Bagg.

Additional members of the committee on the governmental and judicial policy of the upper peninsula, under resolution of the 8th inst.:

Messrs. Robertson and Graham.

On motion of Mr. Cook,

The House resolved itself into committee of the whole on the bill of rights,

Mr. Britain in the chair.

PROCEEDINGS IN COMMITTEE.

Mr. Walker offered the following substitute to Sec. 3:

"All men are entitled to equal rights and privileges."

Which substitute was not adopted.

Mr. Redfield moved to strike out of section 3, the words "or separate."

Which motion did not prevail.

On motion of Mr. J. D. Pierce,

Section 6 was amended by striking out of 1st line, the word "religious," and inserting "political."

Mr. J. Bartow moved to amend section 7, by striking out from lines 4 and 5, the words "and was published with good motives and for justifiable ends."

Which motion did not prevail.

Mr. N. Pierce moved to amend section 8, line 1, by inserting after "papers," the word "property."

Which motion was not agreed to.

Mr. Hanscom moved to amend sec. 8, by striking out "unreasonable," in line 1, and inserting after "seizures," in line 2, "except pursuant to authority of law."

But the committee refused to so amend.

On motion of Mr. McLeod,

Sec. 9 was amended by striking out "and," in second line, and inserting "but," and by adding at the end of the section, "not of record."

Mr. Walker moved to further amend said section by striking out "all," in 3d line, and by adding after "record," "and in civil causes in all courts."

Pending which, on motion of Mr. White,

The committee rose, reported progress, and asked leave to sit again.

The committee, through their charman, reported their proceeding to the Convention, (as above,) and asked and obtained leave to sit again.

On motion of Mr. Church,

Resolved, That when the Convention adjourn it adjourns to meet to-morrow morning at 8 o'clock.

On motion of Mr. Gardiner,

The Convention then adjourned.

Lansing, Tuesday, June 11, 1850.

The President called the Convention to order at 8 o'clock.

Prayer by the Rev. Mr. Sanford.

Upon calling the roll, Messrs. Bush, Chapel, Lee, Whipple and Willard appeared to be absent.

The journal was corrected and approved.

REPORTS.

Mr. McClelland, from the committee on the Legislative department, reported "Article 4, Legislative Department."

The Article was read the first and second time by its title, referred to the committee of the whole, and ordered printed.

Mr. Storey moved that double the usual number of copies be ordered printed, but

The motion did not prevail.

Mr. Bagg, from a majority of the same committee, to whom was referred the resolution of the 8th inst., directing an inquiry into the expediency of inserting a clause in the constitution authorizing the sale of ardent spirits without license, &c., reported an additional section to the foregoing article; which was read a first and second time by its title, referred to the committee of the whole, and ordered printed with article 4.

The committee on the legislative department was discharged from the further consideration of all resolutions heretofore referred to it, and

On motion of Mr. Crary,

The same were referred to the committee of the whole.

Mr. Sullivan, from the committee on impeachments and removals from office, submitted "Article —, Impeachments and Removals from Office."

The article was read the first and second time by its title, and referred to the committee of the whole, and ordered printed.

LEAVE OF ABSENCE.

Mr. McLeod asked and obtained leave of absence for Mr. McClelland for an indefinite period.

Mr. J. Bartow asked leave of absence for Mr. Whipple, until Friday next, which was granted.

RESOLUTIONS.

On motion of Mr. Eaton,

Resolved, That the committee on finance and taxation be instructed to inquire into the propriety of engrafting the following provision in the Constitution: that all bonds, mortgages, judgments, and all other evidences of debt which are liens on real estate shall not be taxed as personal property, and that all real estate shall be taxed to the owner or occupant at its fair value, and that any person or persons owning or holding any bond, mortgage, judgment, or any other evidence of indebtedness, which are liens on real estate shall be liable to the person or persons to whom the same shall have been taxed for his, her or their proportion of said tax, in proportion to the interest he, she or they may have held or owned in said real estate.

On motion of Mr. Sutherland,

Resolved, That the Committee on impeachments and removals from office be instructed to inquire into the expediency of providing for the trial and determination of impeachments and charges against officers, involving their removal, in some court of judicature.

On motion of Mr. Comstock,

Resolved, That the committee on the militia be instructed to inquire into the expediency of incorporating into the Constitution of this State, a provision exempting from militia duty any inhabitant of this state, of any religious denomination whatever, who from scruples of conscience is averse to bearing arms, upon such conditions as shall be prescribed by law.

Mr. White offered the following, which, by consent, was laid upon the table:

Resolved, That the Auditor General of this State be, and he is hereby requested to furnish for the use of this Convention, a statement of the annual expenses of the State Government since its organization. That such statement embrace a list of the State officers, the number of clerks and other persons employed by them respectively in each year, and the salary or compensation paid to each; also, the annual expenditure of the several departments of government, Executive, Judicial and Legislative. That the Auditor General be requested to furnish to the Convention, a statement of the annual amount of State tax apportioned to be paid by each county; the yearly amount of delinquent or unpaid taxes returned to the Auditor's office from the several counties, and showing the amount of the original tax levied; the amount of interest which accrued thereon; the amount of office fees and other contingent expenses, if any, charged to said tax; and the amount of taxes rejected with interest, &c., which have been charged back to the respective counties in each year.

On motion of Mr. Backus,

Resolved, That the committee on counties be instructed to inquire into the expediency of reporting a provision in the constitution, that no county or counties, township or city, shall be liable for the expense of laying out or establishing any road or roads, authorized by special act of the Legislature.

On motion of Mr. Fralick,

Resolved, That the committee on militia be instructed to inquire into the expediency of providing for the enrollment of all persons liable to military duty, and the abolition of militia trainings, except those of independent companies.

Mr. Orr offered the following:

Resolved, That the judiciary committee be requested to inquire into the expediency of reporting a constitutional provision dispensing with the present law on evidence which now governs in our courts of justice.

Which was not agreed to.

Mr. McLeod offered the following:

Resolved, That the committee on the seat of government be instructed to report on to-morrow the permanent location of the capital at Lansing.

Mr. Bagg offered the following as a substitute for the foregoing:

Resolved, That the committee on the location of the capital be instructed to report a distinct article in the constitution, to be referred to the people, locating the capitol permanently at the city of Detroit.

On motion of Mr. Alvord,

The resolution was laid upon the table.

On motion of Mr. Burns,

Resolved, That the committee on county offices and county government, be instructed to inquire into the expediency of a constitutional provision, that no county seat shall be removed, until the place to which it is proposed to be removed shall be fixed by law, and a majority of two-thirds of the voters of the county voting on the question, have voted in favor of its removal.

On motion of Mr. Church,

Resolved, That the daily sessions of the Convention shall commence at 8 o'clock A. M., until otherwise ordered.

Mr. Eaton submitted the following resolution:

Resolved, That when this Convention adjourns, it adjourn to meet again at 3 o'clock this afternoon; and that it will hold afternoon sessions, commencing at 3 o'clock each day, until further ordered by the Convention.

Which was laid on the table.

Mr. Woodman offered the following:

Whereas, The chairman of the committee on the punishment of crimes, (Mr. Witherell,) refuses to act as their chairman;

And whereas, No member of said committee feels at liberty to act as chairman; therefore

Resolved, That the committee on the punishment of crimes be discharged.

Which was not adopted.

On motion of Mr. Backus,

Resolved, That the committee on counties be instructed to inquire into the expediency of reporting a provision in the constitution, authorizing the erection of any city into a separate county government, without regard to the territorial extent of such county.

On motion of Mr. Danforth,

The Convention resolved itself into committee of the whole on the Bill of Rights, Mr. Britain in the chair.

PROCEEDINGS IN COMMITTEE.

Mr. Walker's amendment to section 9 being under consideration, it was modified by the mover so as to read as follows, viz:

Amend section 9 by striking out all after the word "law" in 2d line, and inserting "but the Legislature may authorize a trial by jury of a less number than twelve men for the trial of misdemeanors and civil cases."

Mr. Goodwin moved to amend the amendment by adding at the end thereof "in courts held by Justices of the Peace."

On motion of Mr. Hanscom the further consideration of Sec. 9 was dispensed with and said section passed over, when the committee proceeded to consider section 10.

Mr. S. Clark moved to amend sec. 10 by adding:

"Nor shall any person be held to appear for a criminal offence unless on the presentment or indictment of a Grand Jury, except in cases of impeachment, or in cases cognizable by Justices of the Peace, or arising in the army or militia when in actual service in time of war or public danger."

Which motion did not prevail.

Mr. Sutherland moved to amend as follows.

Sec. 10. Line 3. Amend by striking out the words "and in all civil cases in which personal liberty may be involved, the trial by jury shall not be refused."

But the committee refused to so amend.

Mr. Tiffany moved to amend sec. 10, line 2, by striking out "to be confronted with the witnesses against him."

Which motion did not prevail.

Mr. Sullivan moved to amend sec. 10 by adding "the institution of the Grand Jury is hereby abolished."

Pending which Mr. McLeod moved that the committee rise, report progress, and ask leave to sit again.

Which motion was not agreed to.

When, on motion of Mr. Cook, sec. 10 was passed over,

And the committee proceeded to the consideration of Sec. 11.

Mr. Crary moved to amend Sec. 11 by striking out of line 1, all after the word "person," to and including the word "punishment," and inserting "after acquittal, shall be tried for the same offence."

Mr. J. Bartow moved to amend the amendment by inserting after the word "acquittal," the words "upon the merits."

Pending which, on motion of Mr. Daniels, the committee rose, reported progress, and asked leave to sit again.

The Chairman, Mr. Britain, reported the same back to the Convention, and asked and obtained leave to sit again; when,

On motion of Mr. Danforth,

The Convention adjourned.

Lansing, Wednesday, June 12, 1850.

The Convention met at 8 o'clock A. M., and was called to order by the President.

Prayer by the Rev. Mr. Tooker.

Roll called, and members all present except Messrs. McClelland and Whipple, absent on leave.

The journal was approved.

REPORTS.

Mr. Redfield, from the committee on state officers, except the executive, reported

"Article —. Of State Officers."

The article was read a first and second time by its title, and referred to the committee of the whole and ordered printed.

Mr. Kingsley, from the committee on the seat of government, submitted the following:

"*Article —. Of the Seat of Government.*

"The seat of government of the state shall be in the township of Lansing in the county of Ingham, where it is now located."

And the same was read the first and second time by its title and referred to the committee of the whole.

RESOLUTIONS.

On motion of Mr. Beardsley,

Resolved, That the committee on the judiciary department be instructed to inquire into the expediency of prohibiting appeals and certioraris, and of providing for new trials instead thereof; and also as to the propriety of making a second verdict or judgment in favor of a party final and irreversible in all cases.

On motion of Mr. Cornell,

Resolved, That the committee on townships be instructed to inquire into the expediency of abolishing the offices of assessors, commissioners of highways and directors of the poor; and empowering the legislature to provide for the election of a supervisor, township clerk and treasurer, who shall, together with the oldest justice of the peace, constitute the township board and board of elections, and who shall perform such other duties as shall be prescribed by law.

On motion of Mr. Wells,

Resolved, That the committee on education be instructed to inquire into the propriety of reporting a constitutional amendment which shall forever prevent the legislature from enacting any law relating to the university and school lands, unless such law is general in its application and effect.

On motion of Mr. Morrison,

Resolved, That the committee on the elective franchise be instructed to inquire into the expediency of incorporating in the constitution the following provision:

That for the pnrpose of voting, no person shall be deemed to have gained or lost a residence during his attendance as a student of any seminary of learning.

On motion of Mr. Cook,

The Convention then resolved itself into committee of the whole and resumed the consideration of "Article 1. Bill of Rights,"

Mr. Britain in the chair.

PROCEEDINGS IN COMMITTEE.

Mr. J. Bartow's amendment to Mr. Crary's amendment being under consideration, after some debate, the amendment was adopted.

The question recurring on Mr. Crary's amendment, and a division of the question being called for, the words "for the same offence shall be twice put in jeopardy of punishment," were stricken out.

The words "after acquittal upon the merits, shall be tried for the same offence," were then inserted.

On motion of Mr. Lovell,

Section 11, line 2, was amended by striking out "capital offences," and inserting "murder and treason."

Mr. Skinner offered the following:

Resolved, That section 11 be amended by adding after the word "merits," "*Provided*, however, that no acquittal or conviction on his own complaint, or at his instance, shall be a bar to a second trial and conviction for the same offence.

Which was not adopted.

Section 12 being under consideration,

Mr. Bagg moved to amend by inserting between "every" and "person," the word "white."

Which was not agreed to.

Mr. Crouse moved to amend section 12, by striking out "person," and inserting "citizen."

Which motion did not prevail.

Mr. Bagg moved to amend section 12 by striking out the words "and the State."

But the committee refused to strike out.

Section 14 being under consideration,

On motion of Mr. S. Clark,

The same was amended by inserting after "owner," the words "or occupant."

Section 16 was then considered, when

Mr. Butterfield moved to amend by adding after the word "contracts," the words "or their remedies."

Which motion did not prevail.

Mr. Fralick moved that the committee pass over section 16.

Which motion was not agreed to.

Mr. Warden moved to insert after the word "contract," in section 16, "and no law altering or changing any law exempting property from levy or sale on execution, having retrospective action."

Which motion did not prevail.

Mr. Butterfield offered the following substitute for section 16:

No bill of attainder, or ex post facto law either civil or criminal, shall be passed, nor any law impairing the obligation of a contract or the remedy existing at the time such contracts shall be made.

And a division of the question being called for, the committee refused to strike out section 16.

Section 17 being under consideration,

On motion of Mr. Witherell,

It was amended by striking out "and unjust," and inserting "or unusual."

Section 18 was amended,

On motion of Mr. Williams,

By adding at the end thereof:

Private roads may be opened in the manner to be prescribed by law; but in every case the necessities of the road, and the amount of all damage to be sustained by the opening thereof shall be first determined by a jury of free holders, and such amount, together with the expenses of the proceeding, shall be paid by the person or persons to be benefitted.

Mr. Witherell moved to amend section 18 by adding after "for," in the 1st line, "the use of the state or of any corporation," and by adding after "therefor," the words "previously made therefor or tendered."

Which was not adopted.

Mr. Tiffany moved to amend as follows:

Add at the end of section 18, "first paid or tendered, or otherwise disposed of, as shall be prescribed by law, for the benefit of the person whose property shall be intended to be taken, except when to be appropriated for the benefit of municipal corporations or for common roads.

Which motion was lost.

On motion of Mr. Hanscom,

The last vote was reconsidered.

And the question being on the amendment of Mr. Tiffany,

Mr. Witherell moved to amend the amendment, by adding after "therefor," in 1st line, "nor for the use of any corporation without compensation previously made or tendered."

Pending which,

On motion of Mr. Storey,

The committee rose, reported progress, and asked leave to sit again.

The committee, through their chairman, reported the article back to the Convention, and asked and obtained leave to sit again.

On motion of Mr. Storey,

The Convention then adjourned.

Lansing, Thursday, June 13, 1850.

The Convention met pursuant to adjournment and was called to order by the President.

Prayer by the Rev. Mr. Atterbury.

Roll called, and Messrs. Lee and McLeod absent without leave, and Mr. McClelland with leave.

Journal approved.

PETITIONS.

By Mr. P. R. Adams: of John Crawford and 108 others, of Lenawee county, relative to the management of the State Prison.

Referred to committee on miscellaneous provisions.

By Mr. Town: of John Mabbs and 26 others, praying that the word "white" be dispensed with in the revised Constitution.

Referred to the committee on the elective franchise.

REPORTS.

Mr. Raynale, from the select committee to invite the resident clergy of this village to attend alternately and open the sessions by prayer, reported that they had performed that duty in part; and that the Rev. Mr. Atterbury, Mr. Sandford, and Mr. Tooker have been in attendance. And the Rev. Mr. Atterbury has directed the committee to say to the Convention that he declines any remuneration in the manner proposed.

The report was accepted and the committee continued.

On motion of Mr. Cook,

The convention then resolved itself into committee of the whole, and resumed the consideration of Article 1, Bill of Rights, Mr. Britain in the chair.

The question being upon Mr. Witherell's amendment to Mr. Tiffany's amendment,

Mr. Witherell withdrew his amendment.

Mr. J. D. Pierce moved to amend by striking out all after the word "tendered," of Mr. Tiffany's amendment.

Which motion did not prevail.

Mr. Cook offered the following substitute for the amendment:

Section 18, line 1, after "therefor," insert "being first made or tendered in such manner as the legislature may provide."

The substitute was not adopted.

Mr. Tiffany modified his amendment so as to read as follows:

Section 18, line 1, after "therefor," insert "to be first paid or tendered, except when to be appropriated for public highways."

And the question being on the adoption of the amendment the same was not adopted.

Section 19 being under consideration,

On motion of Mr. Bush,

It was amended by striking out "shall," in 1st line.

Section 22 being under consideration,

Mr. Raynale offered the following substitute, which was not adopted:

"Involuntary servitude, unless for the punishment of crime, shall never be tolerated in this state."

On motion of Mr. Witherell,

Section 23 was amended by striking out the words "mesne or final process."

Mr. Sullivan moved to amend as follows:

Section 23, line 2, after "fraud," insert "but the provision shall not extend to actions of debt for fines, penalties or forfeitures, or to actions founded on promises to marry, or for moneys collected by any public officer, or in any professional employment."

Mr. Whipple moved to amend the amendment by striking out the words "or to actions founded on promises to marry."

Which motion did not prevail.

The question recurring on Mr. Sullivan's amendment, the same was not adopted.

On motion of Mr. Crary,

All after "debt," to and including "fraud," was stricken out, and the following words inserted, viz: "arising out of, or founded on a contract expressed or implied."

On motion of Mr. S. Clark,

Section 24 was stricken out.

Mr. Hanscom moved to strike out all after "proceedings," in first line of section 26.

But the Committee refused to strike out.

Mr. Robertson offered the following substitute for sec. 27:

The Legislature shall have no power to appropriate the public moneys or property for local or private purposes."

Pending which,

Mr. Cook moved that the committee rise, report progress, and ask leave to sit again.

Which motion did not prevail.

The question recurring on Mr. Robertson's substitute, the same was not adopted.

On motion of Mr. Whipple,

Section 28 was stricken out.

On motion of Mr. Witherell,

Section 29 was amended by inserting between "estate" and "for," in 1st line, the words "hereafter acquired."

Mr. Skinner moved to strike out "actually," in second line, and insert the word "necessarily."

Which motion was not agreed to.

Mr. Walker moved to amend by inserting after "no," in 1st line, the word "private."

Which was not adopted.

Mr. Van Valkenburg moved that the committee rise, report progress and ask leave to sit again.

But the committee refused to rise.

Mr. Lee moved to strike out section 29.

But the committee refused to strike out.

Mr. Leach moved to strike out section 31.

Which motion was lost.

On motion of Mr. Cook,

The committee rose, reported progress and asked leave to sit again.

The committee, through their chairman, reported the same back to the Convention, and asked and obtained leave to sit again.

On motion of Mr. Eaton,

The Convention then adjourned.

Lansing, Friday, June 14, 1850.

The Convention met pursuant to adjournment and was called to order by the President.

Prayer by the Rev. Mr. Sanford.

Roll called and Mr. Orr absent without and Mr. McClelland with leave.

Journal approved.

ABSENCE.

Mr. Church asked and obtained leave of absence for Mr. Orr until Tuesday next.

MOTIONS.

Mr. Witherall moved that the committee of the whole be discharged from the consideration of "Article —. Of the Seat of Government."

Mr. Britain calling for the yeas and nays thereon, and the same being sustained, the motion was lost, as follows:

YEAS.

Mr. P. R. Adams,	Mr. Desnoyers,	Mr. Prevost,
Alvord,	Eaton,	Roberts,
Arzeno,	Fralick,	M. Robinson,
Backus,	Gibson,	Skinner,
Bagg,	Green,	Storey,
J. Bartow,	Hanscom,	Sullivan,
Beeson,	Harvey,	Sutherland,
Alvarado Brown,	Hathaway,	VanValkenburg,
Ammon Brown,	Hixon,	Wait,
Asahel Brown,	Kingsley,	Wells,
Butterfield,	Marvin,	Whipple,
Carr,	Mason,	Williams,
Chandler,	McLeod,	Willard,
Choate,	Morrison,	Witherell,
J. Clark,	O'Brien,	President,
Daniels,		46

NAYS.

Mr. W. Adams,	Mr. Crary,	Mr. Newberry,
Anderson,	Crouse,	J. D. Pierce,

Axford,	Danforth,	N. Pierce,
Barnard,	Dimond,	Raynale,
H. Bartow,	Eastman,	Redfield,
Beardsley,	Gale,	Robertson,
Britain,	Gardiner,	E. S. Robinson,
Burns,	Hart,	Soule,
Bush,	Hascall,	Sturgis,
Chapel,	Kinne,	Town,
Church,	Leach,	Walker,
S. Clark,	Lee,	Warden,
Comstock,	Lovell,	White,
Conner,	Moore,	Whittemore,
Cook,	Mosher,	Woodman,
Cornell,	Mowry,	47

On motion of Mr. Bush,

The Convention resolved itself into committee of the whole, and resumed the consideration of "Article 1. Bill of Rights,"

Mr. Britain in the chair.

PROCEEDINGS IN COMMITTEE.

Section 9 being under consideration,

Mr. Kingsley offered the following substitute:

The right of trial by jury shall remain inviolate; but to entitle a party to a jury in a civil case, he shall demand it as the law shall direct; and the legislature may provide that a less number than twelve may constitute a jury in the trial of civil causes.

Mr. Witherell moved to amend the substitute by adding at the end thereof the words "in courts not of record."

Which was not adopted.

Mr. Robertson offered the following substitute, which was accepted by Mr. Kingsley:

9. The right of trial by jury shall remain inviolate; but shall be deemed to be waived, in all civil cases, unless demanded by one of the parties, in such manner as shall be directed by law; and the legislature may authorize a trial by a jury of a less number than twelve men.

Mr. Walker moved to amend the substitute by striking out the words "the right of trial by jury shall remain inviolate," and inserting "parties in civil suits shall have a right to a trial by a jury."

Mr. Van Valkenburg moved to amend the substitute by inserting between "by" and "jury," in 1st line, the word "a."

Which motion did not prevail.

The question recurring on Mr. Walker's amendment, and a division of the question being called for,

The committee refused to strike out the words proposed.

The question then recurring on the substitute of Mr. Robertson, and a division of the question being demanded,

Section 9 was stricken out, and the substitute was then adopted.

Section 10 being under consideration, and the question being upon Mr. Sullivan's amendment, (which was in the words following: add at the end of section 10, "the institution of grand jury is hereby abolished,")

Mr. Walker offered the following substitute for the amendment:

All justices of the peace shall be, by virtue of their office, grand jurors, and when complaint shall be made to any one of said grand jurors that a criminal offence has been committed, upon sufficient evidence to induce the belief that the accused is guilty of an offence not cognisable by a justice of the peace, then such juror shall associate with him two other grand jurors within the county, and cause the accused to be brought before them for an examination; and upon such examination the accused shall have a right to make a full defense; and if it shall appear upon such examination, after a full hearing, that there is reasonable cause to believe the accused is guilty of the offence charged against him, then such jurors shall transmit a certified copy of the proceedings and evidence before them to the prosecuting attorney of the county, and he shall draw a bill of indictment against the accused for the offence charged, and cause the accused to be arraigned for trial thereon.

Pending which, on motion of Mr. Skinner,

The committee rose, reported progress and asked leave to sit again.

The committee, through their chairman, reported the same back to the Convention, and asked leave to sit again.

Leave was granted.

Mr. Eaton moved that the Convention adjourn till 3 o'clock this afternoon.

Pending which, on motion of Mr. McLeod,

The Convention adjourned.

Lansing, Saturday June 15, 1850.

The President called the Convention to order at the usual hour.

Prayer by the Rev. Mr. Tooker.

Roll called, and Messrs. P. R. Adams, Backus, Beeson, Edmunds, Marvin, M. Robinson, Tiffany and Witherell, were absent without leave; and Mr. Orr with leave.

Journal approved.

LEAVE OF ABSENCE.

Mr. Comstock asked leave of absence for Messrs. Tiffany and P. R. Adams until Friday next.

Mr. Alvord for Messrs. Bacnus and Witherell until Tuesday next.

Mr. Whipple for Mr. Beeson until Tuesday next; and Mr. Redfield for Mr. M. Robinson for an idefinite period.

Leave was granted.

PETITIONS.

By Mr. Alvord: of George Duffield and 419 others of Wayne county, praying that the right of suffrage may be extended to persons of color.

Referred to committee on the elective franchise.

By Mr. McLeod: of Robert Banks and 134 other citizens of Detroit, praying for certain alterations in the present constitution.

Referred to the committee on the elective franchise.

Also, memorial of Wm. M. Johnston, in behalf of sundry civilized Indians, praying the right of American citizenship.

Referred to committee on the government and judicial policy of the Upper Peninsula.

By Mr. Gardiner: of citizens of Pittsfield, Washtenaw county, for incorporation of an article in the revised constitution, prohibiting the legalization of the traffic in ardent spirits as a beverage.

Referred to select committee of five.

By Mr. Walker: memorial of a public meeting held at Romeo, in Macomb county, relative to various amendments to the constitution.

Referred to committee of the whole.

By Mr. Church: of A. D. Rathbone and 165 others, residents of Kent county, praying that ordained ministers of the gospel may be prohibited holding offices of honor or trust under the constitution.

Referred to committee on miscellaneous provisions.

REPORTS.

Mr. Hanscom, from the committee on the militia, reported "Article —, Militia."

Read first and second time by its title, and referred to committee of the whole and ordered printed.

RESOLUTIONS.

Mr. Cook offered the following:

Resolved, That on and after Monday next, the Convention will hold two daily sessions; morning sessions to commence at eight o'clock, A. M.—the afternoon session to commence at two and one-half o'clock, P. M.

Mr. White moved to strike out "two and one-half" and insert "three."

Which motion did not prevail.

On motion of Mr. Desnoyer,

The resolution was amended by striking out "eight" and inserting "half-past eight."

Mr. Robertson moved to strike out "two and one-half" and insert "two."

Which motion was lost.

Mr. White moved to lay the resolution on the table.

But the Convention refused to lay on the table.

The question recurring upon the adoption of the resolution as amended,

Mr. Cook demanded the yeas and nays upon the same,

And the resolution was passed, as follows:

YEAS:

Mr. W. Adams,
Anderson,
Axford,
Bagg,
Barnard,
H. Bartow,
Alvarado Brown,

Mr. Daniels,
Desnoyers,
Dimond,
Eaton,
Gale,
Gardiner,
Gibson,

Mr. Mowry,
Newberry,
O'Brien,
N. Pierce,
Prevost,
Redfield,
E. S. Robinson,

Ammon Brown,	Graham,	Skinner,
Bush,	Green,	Soule,
Butterfield,	Hanscom,	Sullivan,
Chandler,	Harvey,	Sutherland,
Chapel,	Hascall,	Town,
Choate,	Hathaway,	Van Valkenburg,
J. Clark,	Kinne,	Wait,
S. Clark,	Leach,	Walker,
Comstock,	Mason,	Whipple,
Cook,	McClelland,	Whittemore,
Cornell,	Moore,	Williams,
Crary,	Morrison,	Warden,
Crouse,	Mosher,	59

NAYS:

Mr. Alvord,	Mr. Conner,	Mr. Robertson,
Arzeno,	Danforth,	Storey,
J. Bartow,	Eastman,	Sturgis,
Beardsley,	Hart,	Webster,
Britain,	Kingsley,	Wells,
Asahel Brown,	Lee,	White,
Burns,	Lovell,	Willard,
Carr,	McLeod,	Woodman,
Church,	Roberts,	President, 27

Mr. McLeod offered the following:

That the use of the Hall be allowed to Mr. Bibb, of Detroit, this afternoon, to explain the views of the colored inhabitants of Michigan in reference to the elective franchise.

Mr. Chapel moved to amend the resolution by adding "unless occupied by this Convention."

But the motion was lost.

The resolution was then adopted.

On motion of Mr. Cook,

The Convention went into committee of the whole, and resumed the consideration of Article 1, Bill of Rights,

Mr. Britain in the chair.

PROCEEDINGS IN COMMITTEE.

The question being on Mr. Walker's substitute offered yesterday for Mr. Sullivan's amendment,

The same was not adopted.

Mr. Hascall offered the following as a substitute for Mr. Sullivan's amendment:

"The Legislature may abolish a grand jury, except for crimes where the penalty is death or imprisonment for life."

Which was not adopted.

The question then recurring on Mr. Sullivan's amendment, which was to add at the end of section 10, "the institution of the grand jury is hereby abolished,"

The committee refused to so amend.

Mr. Skinner offered the following amendment, to commence section 10:

"No person shall be holden to answer for any crime, the punishment of which may be death or imprisonment for life, unless on a presentment or indictment of a grand jury, except in the land or naval forces, in the militia when in actual service in time of war or public danger; and grand juries shall have cognizance of no other offences."

On motion of Mr. Robertson,

The words "in the land or naval forces," of the amendment were stricken out.

Mr. Whipple offered the following substitute for the amendment:

1. No person shall be held to answer for an offence punishable by imprisonment in the State prison, unless on presentment of a grand jury.

2. A grand jury shall consist of not less than nine, nor more than thirteen persons.

Which was not adopted.

The question then recurring on Mr. Skinner's amendment, the same was lost.

On motion of Mr. Robertson,

Section 10 was amended by inserting in the second line, after the word "jury," the words, "which may consist of less than twelve men in all courts not of record."

On motion of Mr. McClelland,

Section 10 was amended by inserting after the preceding amendment, the words, "to be informed of the nature and cause of the accusation."

Mr. Beardsley moved to amend section 10, article 1, by inserting after the word "defence," in second line, the following, viz: "Who shall have the right of reply."

Which did not prevail.

On motion of Mr. Leach,

The committee rose, reported the article back to the Convention, and asked to be discharged from its further consideration.

—

The committee rose, and through their chairman, reported the same back to the Convention, with sundry amendments, in which the concurrence of the Convention was asked.

The committee of the whole were discharged from the further consideration of the same, and

On motion of Mr. J. D. Pierce,

The article as amended was laid upon the table and ordered printed.

On motion of Mr. Moore,

The committee of the whole were discharged from the further consideration of an amendment to the bill of rights, offered by him on the 10th inst., relative to persons engaged in duels, &c.

On motion of Mr. White,

The Convention then adjourned.

Lansing, Monday June 17, 1850.

The Convention met pursuant to adjournment, and was called to order by the President.

Prayer by the Rev. Mr. Merrill.

Roll called, and Messrs. Burns, Lee, McLeod, Morrison, Roberts and Soule were absent without leave; and Messrs. P. R. Adams, Backus, Beeson, M. Robinson, Tiffany and Witherell with leave.

Journal approved.

The President announced the following select committee on the petition of citizens of Pittsfield, Washtenaw county, for incorporation of article in revised constitution, prohibiting legalization of the traffic in ardent spirits as a beverage:

Messrs. Gardiner, Leach, Ammon Brown, Hathaway and W. Adams.

ABSENCE.

Mr. Arzeno asked leave of absence for Mr. Marvin, for the day:

Mr. McClelland for Mr. McLeod, for the same period.

Mr. Walker for Mr. Roberts, for like time.

Mr. Britain for Mr. Hascall, for the day.

Mr. Barnard for Mr. Lee, till Wednesday next; and

Mr. Beardsley for Mr. Burns, for the same period.

Leave was granted as asked-

PETITIONS.

By Mr. Kingsley: of 205 citizens of Washtenaw county, praying that the amended constitution may provide for extending the right of suffrage to colored people.

Referred to the committee on the elective franchise.

REPORTS.

Mr. Whipple, from the committee on the Executive department, submitted Article —, Executive Department.

Which was read the first and second time by its title, referred to the committee of the whole, and ordered printed.

Mr. Crary, from the committee on the judicial department, to whom was referred the following resolution:

"*Resolved*, That the committee on the judicial department be instructed to inquire into the expediency of providing that the Legislature, at its first session after the adoption of the constitution, shall appoint three commissioners, whose duty it shall be to reduce to a written code, the whole body of the law of this State, or so much thereof as to them shall seem expedient;"

Reported the same back to the Convention, asking to be discharged from the further consideration of the same, and recommending its reference to the committee on the schedule.

The committee was discharged, and the resolution so referred.

RESOLUTIONS.

Mr. Green offered the following:

Resolved, That the chairman of the committee on education be instructed to address letters of inquiry to the present and late superintendents of public instruction of this State, soliciting their opinions as to the propriety of establishing the free school system, and particularly what in their opinion would be its effects upon general education in the State.

Which, on motion of Mr. Danforth, was laid upon the table.

Mr. White called up his resolution of the 11th inst., asking information of the Auditor General; and

The resolution was then adopted.

Mr. Britain submitted the following preamble and resolutions:

Whereas, It is desirable that the business of this Convention should be completed at the earliest practicable period;

And whereas, the practice of distributing newspapers and other mail matter among members of the Convention, and the practice of reading newspapers and other mail matter by the members and others within the bar, during the hours of business, disturbs the harmony and impairs the efficiency of the Convention, retards the progress of public business, and should be prohibited by this Convention; therefore,

Resolved, That the following be adopted as one of the standing rules of this Convention:

No newspaper or other mail matter shall be distributed among the members of this Convention between the opening and the closing of its sessions. Nor shall any member of this Convention, or other person within the bar, read any newspaper or other matter foreign to the business of the Convention, between the opening and the closing of its sessions.

Mr. Willard moved as an addition to the rule proposed, the words "unless when long and dull speeches are being made."

Pending which,

The proposition of Mr. Britain was laid on the table.

On motion of Mr. Cook,

The Convention resolved itself into committee of the whole on the general order,

Mr. McClelland in the chair.

PROCEEDINGS IN COMMITTEE.

The committee proceeded to the consideration of the general order.

No amendments were made to

Article —. Mode of amending and revising the constitution, and

Article —, Division of the powers of government.

Article —, Impeachments and removals from office, being under consideration,

Mr. Sullivan moved to amend section 2, 1st line, by inserting after "Senate" the words "and judges of the Supreme Court."

Which motion did not prevail.

Mr. Leach moved to amend by striking out all after the word "preside," in the second line, to and includng the word "and," in the fourth line.

But the committee refused to so amend.

On motion of Mr. Lovell,

The word "present," in 5th line, section 2, was stricken out, and "elect" was inserted.

On motion of Mr. Crary,

Section 5, line 1, was amended by striking out "Executive," and inserting "Governor."

Mr. Walker moved to amend section 6, line 2, by striking out "shall" and inserting "may."

Which motion was lost.

On motion of Mr. Williams,

Section 6 was amended by striking out in line 2 the word "of," between "two-thirds" and "each," and inserting "of the members elected to."

On motion of Mr. Hanscom,

Section 6, line 2, was further amended by striking out "an address" and inserting "a concurrent resolution."

Mr. Lovell moved to strike out in first line of section 7 the words "justices of the peace and," and insert "all."

Which motion did not prevail.

On motion of Mr. Cook,

The committee rose and by their chairman reported the articles back with amendments, asked the concurrence of the Convention, and to be discharged from the further consideration of the above named articles.

The committee, through their chairman, reported back articles number 2 and 3 without amendment, and number 4 with amendments, in which they asked the concurrence of the Convention.

The committee were discharged from the consideration of the same, and

Article —. Mode of amending and revising the constitution, being under consideration, the same,

On motion of Mr. Bartow,

Was laid upon the table.

Article —. Division of the powers of government, reported back without amendment,

Was ordered engrossed for a third reading.

The Convention having under consideration

Article —. Impeachments and removals from office,

The amendments made in committee were concurred in in gross.

On motion of Mr. McClelland,

The article was further amended by inserting after the word "shall," in line 1 of section 3, the words "when an impeachment is directed."

Mr. Walker moved to amend seetion 6, line 2, by striking out "shall," and inserting in lieu thereof the word "may,"

Which did not prevail.

The article was then ordered engrossed for a third reading.

On motion of Mr. J. D. Pierce,

Article 1. Bill of Rights, was taken from the table, and the same being under consideration,

The amendments made in committee of the whole were severally concurred in, with the exception of the one striking out section 28, which was non-concurred in by the following vote, the yeas and nays being demanded by Mr. Britain:

YEAS

Mr. W. Adams,
J. Bartow,
Asahel Brown,
Butterfield,
Carr,
Comstock,
Crouse,
Daniels,
Dimond,
Mr. Green,
Hanscom,
Harvey,
Hathaway,
Kingsley,
Mowry,
Robertson,
E. S. Robinson,
Mr. Skinner,
Sutherland,
Wells,
White,
Whipple,
Williams,
Woodman,
President,

25

NAYS.

Mr. Anderson,	Mr. Danforth,	Mr. Orr,
Arzeno,	Eaton,	J. D. Pierce,
Bagg,	Edmunds,	N. Pierce,
Barnard,	Fralick,	Prevost,
Beardsley,	Gale,	Raynale,
Britain,	Gardiner,	Redfield,
Alvarado Brown,	Gibson,	Rix Robinson,
Ammon Brown,	Graham,	Storey,
Bush,	Hart,	Sturgis,
Chandler,	Hascall,	Sullivan,
Chapel,	Hixon,	Town,
Choate,	Kinne,	VanValkenburg,
Church,	Leach,	Wait,
J. Clark,	Lovell,	Walker,
S. Clark,	Mason,	Webster,
Conner,	McClelland,	Whittemore,
Cook,	Moore,	Willard,
Cornell,	Mosher,	Worden,
Crary,		55

On motion of Mr. Crary,

The article was further amended in line 1 of section 21, by striking out the word "foreigner," and inserting in its stead "alien."

Mr. Whipple moved to add after the word "contracts," in section 16, the words "or affecting the vested rights of private persons, or retrospective in its operation." Pending which,

On motion of Mr. Storey,

The article was made the special order for Thursday next.

On motion of Mr. Danforth,

The Convention adjourned.

Afternoon Session.

The Convention met at half-past 2 o'clock; when, on calling the roll, a quorum being present,

On motion of Mr. Crary,

The Convention resolved itself into committee of the whole on Article —, Legislative Department, Mr. Wells in the chair.

PROCEEDINGS IN COMMITTEE.

Mr. Fralick offered the following amendment to section 2:

Strike out all after "districts," in third line, and insert "the Senate shall consist of not less than twenty-four nor more than thirty-two members, and shall be elected for four years and by single districts."

Mr. Raynale moved to amend the amendment by striking out "four" and inserting "two."

Which motion was not agreed to.

Mr. Britain offered the following as a substitute for Mr. Fralick's amendment:

Add to section two as follows: "and by double districts; Senators after the first election under this constitution to be elected from each half of the district alternately."

Which was not adopted.

Mr. Hanscom moved to strike out all after "members," of the amendment.

But the committee refused to strike out.

Mr. Chapel moved to amend the section by inserting between "Senators" and "two," the words "at least."

Which motion did not prevail.

The question then recurring upon Mr. Fralick's amendment,

The same did not prevail.

Mr. Bush moved to amend by striking out in third line the word "two" and inserting "one," and to strike out "four" in fourth line and insert "two."

Mr. Moore moved to amend by striking out "two" in third line and inserting "three."

Which motion did not prevail.

And the question recurring upon Mr. Bush's amendment,

The same was not agreed to.

On motion of Mr. S. Clark,

The word "two" in fourth line was stricken out and "one" inserted.

Mr. Bagg moved to strike out in third line "and by single districts."

But the committee refused to strike out.

Mr. Sutherland moved to amend section 3, by adding at the end as follows: "Each organized county shall be entitled to at least one representative."

Mr. Chapel offered the following as a substitute:

"Every organized county containing 2,000 white inhabitants shall be entitled to one representative."

Pending which,

On motion of Mr. J. D. Pierce,

The committee rose, reported progress and asked leave to sit again.

The chairman reported the same back to the Convention, and asked and obtained leave to sit again.

On motion of Mr. Cook,

The Convention then adjourned.

Lansing, Tuesday, June 18, 1850.

The Convention met pursuant to adjournment and was called to order by the President.

Prayer by the Rev. Mr. Atterbury.

Roll called, and members all present except those absent on leave.

No corrections made to the journal.

PETITIONS.

By Mr. Hanscom: of Randolph Manning and 90 others, citizens of Oakland county, on the subject of the judiciary.

Referred to the committee of the whole.

By Mr. Comstock: of Israel Pennington, John H. Osborn and 233 others, of Lenawee county, praying that the elective franchise may be extended to colored persons of this State; and that the word "white" be rejected wherever it occurs to the prejudice of colored citizens.

Referred to committee on the elective franchise.

By Mr. Kingsley: of 200 citizens of Washtenaw county, praying that the elective franchise may be extended to colored persons in this State.

Referred to committee on the elective franchise.

By the President: of Wm. P. Patrick and 9 others, that provision may be made in the revised Constitution for the location of the office of Adjt. and Qr. Master General and of the State Armory at the seat of government.

Referred to the committee on the militia.

RESOLUTIONS.

On motion of Mr. Leach,

Resolved, That the state printer be instructed to forward by mail one copy of the debates in the Convention to each newspaper in this state.

On motion of Mr. Cook,

Resolved, That there be allowed to the Secretaries of this Convention three dollars per day each, to the Sergeant-at-Arms and Door Keeper three dollars per day each, to the Messengers one dollar per day each.

On motion of Mr. McClelland,

The Convention then resolved itself into committee of the whole and resumed the consideration of "Article 4, Legislative Department,"

Mr. Wells in the Chair.

PROCEEDINGS IN COMMITTEE.

Section 3 of Article –, "Legislative Department," being under consideration, and the question being on Mr. Chapel's substitute for Mr. Sutherland's amendment, the committee,

On motion of Mr. White,

Passed over section 3.

On motion of Mr. Woodman,

Section 4 was amended by striking out the first line, to the word "in," and by inserting "The Boards of Supervisors."

Mr. Van Valkenburg moved to pass over section 4; but the Committee refused to pass over.

On motion of Mr. Williams,

The committee resumed the consideration of section 3, and the question being upon Mr. Chapel's substitute for Mr. Sutherland's amendment, Mr. Sutherland withdrew his amendment and offered the following:

Provided, That until the next apportionment under the census of 1855, the counties of Saginaw, Tuscola, Midland, and Gratiot shall be entitled to one representative each; the county of Mackinaw and the counties thereto attached, to one representative; the counties of Chippewa, Houghton and Marquette to one representative.

Mr. White moved that the committee rise, report progress, and ask leave to sit again.

But the committee refused to rise.

Mr. Chapel then renewed his substitute, and it having been accepted by Mr. Sutherland, the same was adopted.

Mr. Van Valkenburg moved to amend Section 3, line 5, by inserting after "inhabitants," the words "and such colored persons and Indians as are taxed."

Which motion did not prevail.

Mr. Comstock moved to strike out "white," in fifth line, and insert after "inhabitants," the words "excludings Indians not taxed."

And the question being upon striking out,

The committee refused to strike out.

Mr. Gale moved to insert after "inhabitants" the words "excluding all aliens."

But the committee refused to so amend.

Mr. Cook offered the following as a substitute for section 5:

The state shall be divided into thirty-two districts to be called Senate districts, each of which shall choose one Senator. The districts shall be numbered from one to thirty-two inclusive. The Senators chosen by the odd numbered districts shall go out of office at the expiration of two years; the Senators chosen by the even numbered districts shall go out of office at the expiration of four years, and thereafter the Senators shall be chosen for the term of four years. No county shall be divided in the formation of Senate districts except such county shall be equitably entitled to two or more Senators.

On motion of Mr. J. Bartow,

The words "from their respective districts" was stricken out of line two of section five.

The question being upon Mr. Cook's substitute, and a division being called for, section five was stricken out.

On motion of Mr. Hanscom,

That portion of the substitute included between the word "inclusive" and the words "no county," was stricken out.

The substitute as amended was then adopted.

On motion of Mr. Cook,

The following words were added to section seven: "and all votes given for any such person shall be void."

On motion of Mr. Hanscom,

The word "postmaster," was stricken out of first line of section seven.

Mr. Storey moved to strike out "notaries public, and officers of the militia and of townships excepted."

But the committee refused to strike out.

Mr. Bush offered the following substitute for section seven:

No person holding any United States office or State office, (notaries public and officers of the militia excepted,) shall be eligible to a seat in either house of the Legislature; and votes given for such person shall be void.

Mr. J. Clark moved that the committee rise, report progress, and ask leave to sit again.

But the committee refused to rise.

Mr. Morrison moved to amend Mr. Bush's substitute by inserting between "militia" and "excepted" the words "county and township officers."

Pending which, on motion of Mr. Danforth,

The committee rose, reported progress, and asked leave to sit again.

—

The committee, through their charman, reported the same back to the Convention, and asked leave to sit again.

Leave was granted.

On motion of Mr. Woodman,

The Convention then adjourned.

—

Afternoon Session.

Half past two o'clock.

The president called the Convention to order.

Roll called, and a quorum being in attendance,

On motion of Mr. McClelland,

The Convention resolved itself into committee of the whole on Article —, "Legislative Department,"

Mr. Wells in the chair.

PROCEEDINGS IN COMMITTEE.

The question being upon Mr. Morrison's amendment to Mr. Bush's amendment, Mr. Fralick moved to amend sec. 7, so that it would read as follows:

No person holding any office under the United States or this State, or any county office, notaries public, officers of the Militia and officers elected by townships excepted, shall be eligible to, or have a seat in either house of the Legislature.

Mr. Sullivan moved to amend the amendment by striking out the words "be eligible to or."

Which motion did not prevail.

Mr. Fralick's amendment was then adopted.

Mr. Bush then withdrew his substitute.

Mr. Fralick moved to amend Section 9 by striking out in 1st line "members elected to."

Which motion was not agreed to.

Mr. Robertson moved to strike out of 1st and 2d lines of section 11, the words "except such parts as may require secrecy."

But the committee refused to strike out.

On motion of Mr. Hanscom,

Section 11 was amended by inserting after "act," in line 4, the word "proceeding."

Mr. Hanscom moved to amend section 15 by striking out "two-thirds," in lines 4 and 6.

Which motion did not prevail.

On motion of Mr. J. D. Pierce,

The word "present," in 4th line, was stricken out, and "elected" inserted; and "present," in sixth line was stricken out, and "elected to" inserted.

Mr. Willard moved to amend section 17 by striking out "three," where it occurs, and inserting "two."

And a division of the question being called for,

The committee refused to strike out.

Section 17 was amended, on motion of Mr. McClelland, by inserting in 1st line, after the word "services," the word "only;" by striking out "unless" in the second line, and inserting "and when;" by striking out "more" in 3d line and inserting "thereafter," and by striking out "no more," in fourth line, and inserting "nothing thereafter."

On motion of Mr. Walker, section 17 was amended by inserting after "proclamation," in 5th line, "or submitted to them by his special message."

On motion of Mr. Storey, the committee rose, reported progress, and asked leave to sit again.

The committee, through their Chairman, reported the same back to the Convention, and asked and obtained leave to sit again.

On motion of Mr. J. Clark,

The Convention then adjourned.

Lansing, Wednesday, June 19, 1850.

The Convention met at the usual hour and was called to order by the President.

Prayer by the Rev. Mr. Tooker.

Roll called and Messrs. Backus, Beeson, Mason, Prevost, Whipple and Witherell were absent without leave, and Messrs. P. R. Adams, M. Robinson and Tiffany with leave.

The journal was approved.

LEAVE OF ABSENCE.

Mr. Lovell asked leave of absence for Mr. Prevost.

Mr. Dimond for Mr. Mason for an indefinite period.

Leave was granted.

PETITIONS.

By Mr. Hanscom: of Moses S. Collins and 299 others, citizens of the county of Washtenaw, praying that the elective franchise be extended to every male citizen over the age of 21 years.

Referred to the committee on the elective franchise.

By Mr. Bush: of 89 citizens of the town of Lansing, asking that the word "white" may be stricken from the Constitution.

Referred to committee on elective franchise.

REPORTS.

Mr. Walker, from the committee on education submitted a report accompanied by "Article —, Education."

The article was read the first and second time by its title, referred to the committee of the whole and ordered printed; and

On motion of Mr Skinner,

Double the usual number of copies of the accompanying report were ordered printed.

RESOLUTIONS.

On motion of Mr. Roberts,

Resolved, That the committee on printing be instructed to direct the state printer to print the debates of this convention in such form and on such type as they may deem prudent and serviceable.

On motion of Mr. McClelland,

The convention resolved itself into committee of the whole and resumed the consideration of "Article 4, Legislative Department,"

Mr. Wells in the chair.

PROCEEDINGS IN COMMITTEE OF THE WHOLE.

Section 17 being under consideration, it was,

On motion of Mr. Britain,

Amended as follows:

Add to section 17 as follows: "Each member of the legislature shall be entitled to one copy of the laws, journals and documents of the legislature of which he was a member; but the legislature shall not, at the expense of the State, provide for its members books, newspapers and other perquisites of office, not expressly authorized by this Constitution."

Mr. Beardsley moved to amend section 18, by inserting after "matter," in first line, the words "sent and," and by striking out the words in last line, "but not for any sent or mailed by them."

Which motion did not prevail.

Mr. Van Valkenburg moved to add at end of section 18, "except documents of said legislature."

But the committee refused to so amend.

On motion of Mr. Hascall,

Section 19 was amended as follows:

Strike out all after "shall," in the first line, and insert the following: "receive no additional compensation in virtue of their offices."

On motion of Mr. McClelland,

The 7th line of section 20 was stricken out and the following inserted after "elected," in sixth line: "and for one year thereafter."

Mr. Bush moved to amend section 23 by striking out the words "every" and "object," in first line, and inserting "no" and "subject."

Which motion did not prevail.

On motion of Mr. McClelland,

Section 23, line 1, was amended by striking out "every" and inserting "no," and by striking out "but" and inserting "more than."

Mr. Bush moved to amend said section by striking out "object," in first line, and inserting "subject."

But the committee refused to strike out.

On motion of Mr. Raynale,

The words "in case of emergency," in third line of section 23, were stricken out.

On motion of Mr. Morrison,

The words "all the members elected to," were inserted at the end of third line of section 23.

Mr. Hascall offered the following:

Amend section 25, 4th line, after the word security, by inserting as follows: "for the performance thereof, in the manner following; with such other conditions as shall be prescribed by law:

1. All printed matter except bills and resolutions shall be set solid, and as compact as the nature of the case will admit.

2. Bills and resolutions shall be done in the usual manner, and the price of composition shall be one-third that of solid matter.

3. Blank pages or fractions of pages, shall not be computed in the estimate of compositon, and no charge except for reading matter actually set shall be allowed.

4. No division of sheets or multiplication of signatures shall be permitted for the increasing of press-work; and only the smallest amount of press-work of which the nature of the particular kind of work is capable, shall be allowed.

5. All printed matter called for by the legislature shall be ordered by the token."

Pending which, on motion of Mr. Gardiner,

The committee rose, reported progress and asked leave to sit again.

The committee, through their chairman, reported the same back to the Convention and asked leave to sit again, and

Leave was granted.

Mr. Hanscom offered the following resolutions:

Resolved, That from and after this day the post master of this village be not authorized to charge to the Convention or state any postage on any mailable matter, sent or mailed by members or officers of the Convention, and that the Secretary notify the post master accordingly.

Resolved, That from and after this date there be printed for the use of the Convention but 240 copies of the journal.

Mr. Storey offered the following as a substitute:

Whereas, The amount of Buncombe that has been expedned by members of this Convention this morning, on the subject of postage, has cost the state more money than all the postage of members is likely to amount to, therefore

Resolved, That the whole subject be dropt.

Mr. White moved to adjourn, but

The motion did not prevail.

Mr. J. D. Pierce moved to lay the resolution of Mr. Hanscom on the table; which was lost.

The substitute offered by Mr. Storey was not adopted.

The question recurring on the adoption of the first resolution, the same prevailed by the following vote:

YEAS.

Mr. W. Adams,	Mr. Crouse,	Mr. Newberry,
Alvord,	Danforth,	O'Brien,
Anderson,	Daniels,	Orr,
Arzeno,	Dimond,	J. D. Pierce,
Axford,	Eastman,	N. Pierce,
Bagg,	Eaton,	Raynale,
Barnard,	Edmunds,	Redfield,
H. Bartow,	Fralick,	Robertson,
Britain,	Gardiner,	E. S. Robinson,
Alvarado Brown,	Gibson,	Rix Robinson,
Ammon Brown,	Graham,	Skinner,

Asahel Brown,	Green,	Soule,
Burns,	Hanscom,	Sturgis,
Bush,	Hart,	Sullivan,
Butterfield,	Harvey,	Town,
Carr,	Hascall,	VanValkenburg,
Chandler,	Hathaway,	Wait,
Chapel,	Hixon,	Walker,
Choate,	Kingsley,	Webster,
Church,	Kinne,	Wells,
J. Clark,	Leach,	White,
S. Clark,	Lovell,	Whittemore,
Comstock,	McClelland,	Williams,
Conner,	Moore,	Willard,
Cook,	Morrison,	Worden,
Cornell,	Mosher,	Woodman,
Crary,	Mowry,	President, 81

NAYS.

Mr. McLeod, Mr. Storey, 2

The second resolution being under consideration, the same was adopted.

On motion of Mr. Morrison,

The convention then adjourned.

Afternoon Session.

½ past 2 o'clock.

The Convention was called to order by the President.

Roll called and a quorum present.

Mr. Roberts offered the following, which was not adopted:

Resolved, That the committee on supplies be instructed to direct the carpet on the floor of this Hall to be removed, and such arrangements made as they may deem conducive to health.

On motion of Mr. Roberts,

Resolved, That the resolution authorizing subscription for newspapers, equal to two daily papers, be and the same is hereby rescinded, and that the post master be requested to give notice to publishers to that effect.

On motion of Mr. McClelland,

The Convention resolved itself into committee of the whole on "Article 4, Legislative Department,"

Mr. Wells in the chair.

PROCEEDINGS IN COMMITTEE.

The question being on Mr. Hascall's amendment,

Mr. Roberts offered the following substitute for section 25.

A State Printer shall be elected at the same time that state officers are to be chosen, and hold his office for a like period. He shall be a practical printer, and the prices to be paid him shall be fixed at forty cents for the composition of every thousand *ems*, and forty cents *per white token* for press work.

But the substitute was not adopted.

The committee then adopted Mr. Hascall's amendment, with the following addition:

"6. All accounts for public printing shall be certified by the contractor to be in accordance with the conditions of his contract, and the same shall be under oath."

On motion of Mr. Whittemore,

Section 26 was stricken out.

Mr. Britain offered the following:

Add to section 27, as follows: "but the legislature shall provide by law for a simple and cheap method of selling, with the approbation of the judge of probate, the real estate of minors, and of married women whose husbands shall be incapable of selling the same."

Mr. Lovell moved to amend the amendment by striking out the words "with the approbation of the judge of probate."

Which was not agreed to.

On motion of Mr. Hanscom,

The words "a simple and cheap," were stricken from the amendment.

The question then recurring upon Mr. Britain's amendment as amended, the same was not adopted.

Mr. Robertson moved that the committee rise, report progress and ask leave to sit again.

But the committee refused to rise.

On motion of Mr. Kingsley,

The words "or conveyance," was inserted in line one, after the word "sale."

Mr. Raynale moved to strike out the words "individual or individuals," and insert "person," in the 2d line.

On motion of Mr. McClelland,

The amendment was amended by inserting "person or persons."

Mr. Raynale's amendment was then adopted.

On motion of Mr. Newberry,

The following was adopted as a substitute for section 28.

The legislature shall have no power to appropriate money from the treasury to pay chaplains, or for any religious services performed in either house.

On motion of Mr. McClelland,

All after "title," in 1st line of section 29, was stricken out, and the following inserted:

"Only, but the act revised, and section or sections of the act amended, shall be published at length."

On motion of Mr. J. D. Pierce,

The committee rose, reported progress, and asked leave to sit again.

The committee, through their chairman, reported the same back to the convention and asked leave to sit again.

Leave was granted.

Mr. Butterfield offered the following resolution:

Resolved, That hereafter the afternoon sessions of this Convention shall commence at two o'clock, until otherwise ordered.

Mr. White moved to strike out "two" and insert "three" in its stead; pending which,

On motion of Mr. Cook,

The resolution was laid upon the table.

Mr. Church moved to reconsider the resolution passed this morning, relative to the printing of debates, &c., which motion,

On motion of Mr. Hanscom,

Was laid upon the table.

On motion of Mr. Van Valkenburg,

The convention then adjourned.

Lansing, Thursday, June 20, 1850.

The Convention met pursuant to adjournment and was called to order by the President.

Prayer by the Rev. Mr. Sanford.

Roll called, and Messrs. Beeson, Gale, Whipple and Witherell were absent without leave, and Messrs. P. R. Adams, Mason, Prevost, M. Robinson and Tiffany with leave.

Journal approved.

LEAVE OF ABSENCE.

Mr. Leach asked and obtained leave of absence for Mr. Gale for the day.

PETITIONS.

By Mr. Morrison: of James Russell and 71 citizens of Calhoun county, praying that a clause be inserted in the Constitution prohibiting the legislature from enacting any law authorizing the sale of ardent spirits as a beverage. Also, of James Finch and 31 others, of the county of Calhoun, for a like prohibition.

Referred to the committee of the whole.

REPORTS.

Mr. Cook, from the committee on banking and other corporations, except municipal, reported back the following resolution, asking to be discharged from its further consideration and recommending its reference to the committee on finance and taxation:

Resolved, That the committee on incorporations be instructed to inquire into the expediency of providing as follows:

1. That the credit of the state shall not be loaned to any person or persons, nor to any company or association, nor shall the state ever be liable for the stock of any corporation whatever.

The committee was discharged, and the resolution so referred.

Mr. Cook, from the same committee, reported

"Article —. Incorporations."

Which was read a first and second time by its title, referred to the committee of the whole and ordered printed.

Sundry resolutions referred to the same committee were reported back, from the consideration of which they were discharged.

Mr. Crary, from the committee on the judicial department, reported

"Article —. Judicial Department."

Which was read the first and second time by its title, when

Mr. Crary offered the following resolution:

Resolved, That the article on the judicial department be recommitted to the judiciary committee with instructions that such committee so alter and modify their report as to provide that the judges of the circuit courts shall be judges of the supreme court.

And upon his motion,

The report and resolution were ordered printed and made the special order for Tuesday next.

MOTIONS AND RESOLUTIONS.

On motion of Mr. McClelland,

The vote of yesterday by which was adopted the resolution offered by Mr. Roberts, relative to newspapers, &c., was reconsidered.

And the question being again on the adoption of the same,

Mr. Alvord moved to lay the resolution upon the table.

Which motion did not prevail.

Mr. J. Clark moved to strike out "Post Master," in the resolution, and insert in its stead, "Secretary." When

Mr. Hanscom moved the indefinite postponement of the matter.

On which Mr. Britain demanded the ayes and noes, and the result was as follows:

YEAS:

Mr. W. Adams,	Mr. Crary,	Mr. McLeod,
Alvord,	Crouse,	Morrison,
Arzeno,	Danforth,	Mosher,
Anderson,	Desnoyers,	O'Brien,
H. Bartow,	Eastman,	J. D. Pierce,
J. Bartow,	Gardiner,	Raynale,
Beardsley,	Green,	E. S. Robinson,
Alvarado Brown,	Hanscom,	Rix Robinson,
Burns,	Hart,	Soule,
Bush,	Harvey,	Storey,
Butterfield,	Kingsley,	Sullivan,
Carr,	Kinne,	Sutherland,
Chandler,	Lovell,	Webster,
Choate,	Marvin,	White,
Church,	McClelland,	Whittemore,
Conner,		46

NAYS:

Mr. Axford,	Mr. Edmunds,	Mr. Roberts,
Bagg,	Fralick,	Robertson,
Barnard,	Gibson,	Skinner,
Britain,	Graham,	Sturgis,
Ammon Brown,	Hascall,	Town,
Asahel Brown,	Hathaway,	Van Valkenburg,
Chapel,	Hixon,	Wait,
J. Clark,	Leach,	Walker,
S. Clark,	Lee,	Warden,
Comstock,	Moore,	Wells,
Cook,	Mowry,	Williams,
Cornell,	Newberry,	Willard,
Daniels,	Orr,	Woodman,
Dimond,	N. Pierce,	President,
Eaton,	Redfield,	44

So the resolution of Mr. Roberts was indefinitely postponed.

On motion of Mr. Butterfield,

The motion of Mr. Church, offered yesterday, to reconsider the vote on the resolution relative to debates, was taken from the table.

The motion to reconsider was carried.

The resolution being again before the Convention,

Mr. Roberts offered the following as a substitute, which was lost:

Resolved, That the printing of the debates of this Convention be dispensed with, and the Reporters relieved from further attendance.

Mr. Butterfield offered the following substitute:

Resolved, That the State Printer be directed to proceed with the printing of the debates as already begun.

When, on motion of Mr. Crary,

The resolutions were indefinitely postponed.

Mr. Church offered the following:

Resolved, That the committee on printing be instructed to cause the following items to be inserted in the volume of printed debates, in their appropriate place and order,

1st. The law providing for this Convention;

2d. The present Constitution and the new one to be presented to the people;

3d. That part of the Manual comprising the list of members, the rules and standing committees of the Convention;

4th. The articles reported by the several committees;

5th. The debates and an index of subjects.

Mr. Alvord moved to amend by adding, " but no speeches evidently made for Buncomb shall be printed in the debates."

Which was lost.

On motion of Mr. Britain,

The resolution was amended by adding the following: "and that said committee be relieved from procuring the printing said reports in bourgeois type."

The resolution as amended was then adopted.

Mr. Sutherland offered the following, which was lost:

Resolved, That on and after this day the Convention will hold but one session a day—that it will commence at 8 o'clock, A. M.

On motion of Mr. S. Clark,

The special order of the day was postponed until to-morrow.

On motion of Mr. McClelland,

The Convention then resolved itself into committee of the whole, and resumed the consideration of "Article 4. Legislative Department,"

Mr. Wells in the chair.

PROCEEDINGS IN COMMITTEE.

Mr. Hanscom moved to strike out section 32.

Mr. Walker moved to amend by adding at the end thereof, "except in cases in which there shall be reasonable grounds to doubt as to the respective rights of the contestants."

Which motion did not prevail.

On motion of Mr. McClelland,

Section 32 was amended by inserting after "receive," in first line, the words "from the State."

The question then recurring upon Mr. Hanscom's motion to strike out,

The committee refused to strike out.

On motion of Mr. McClelland,

The committee rose, reported progress, and asked leave to sit again.

The committee, through their chairman, reported the same back to the Convention, and asked and obtained leave to sit again.

On motion of Mr. J. D. Pierce,

The Convention then adjourned.

Afternoon Session.

Half-past two o'clock.

The Convention was called to order by the President.

Roll called and a quorum present.

Mr. Graham asked and obtained leave of absence for Mr. Cook until Monday next.

On motion of Mr. McClelland,

The Convention resolved itself into committee of the whole on "Article 4. Legislative Department,"

Mr. Wells in the chair.

PROCEEDINGS IN COMMITTEE.

On motion of Mr. McClelland,

All after the word "account," in section 34, was stricken out.

Mr. McClelland moved to amend section 36 by striking out "January" and inserting "February."

Mr. Witherell moved to amend by inserting "June."

Which motion did not prevail.

The question being on striking out, "January" was stricken out.

On motion of Mr. Raynale,

"Monday" was stricken out and "Wednesday" inserted.

The committee then inserted "February" in lieu of "January."

Mr. Storey offered the following, to stand as section 38:

All general laws shall be published in one newspaper in every county where there is a paper printed, which paper shall be designated by the Secretary of State; and the publisher of every such paper shall receive six cents per folio for such publication.

Mr. Bagg moved to strike out "6 cents per folio."

But the committee refused to strike out.

On motion of Mr. Morrison,

The following was added to the proposed section: "and such papers shall be sent by the publishers to every inhabitant in the county in which the paper is published."

Mr. Hanscom moved to strike out all after "Secretary of State."

But the committee refused to strike out.

The question recurring upon the adoption of the section as amended, the same was not adopted.

On motion of Mr. Britain,

Section 36 was amended so as to read as follows:

"The legislature shall meet on the 1st Wednesday of February next, and on the 1st Wednesday of February in every 2d year thereafter, and at no other period, unless as provided by this Constitution."

On motion of Mr. McClelland,

All after "1851" was stricken out, and the following inserted:

"And on the Tuesday succeeding the 1st Monday of November in every second year thereafter."

Mr. Hanscom moved that the committee rise, report progress, and ask leave to sit again.

But the committee refused to rise.

Mr. Britain offered the following, to stand as section 39:

"The Legislature may authorize a compilation and reprint of the laws actually in force, whenever such reprint shall be necessary; but no revision or alteration of the laws shall at any time be authorized, except so far as shall be necessary to adapt them to amendments of the constitution."

When, on motion of Mr. Woodman,

The committee rose, reported progress and asked leave to sit again.

—

The committee, through their chairman, reported the same back to the Convention, and asked and obtained leave to sit again.

Mr. Hanscom moved that there be added to the standing rules of the Convention, the following, to stand as rule —.

"A motion that the Convention resolve itself into committee of the whole upon the general order, shall always be in order, and shall be decided without debate."

And the same was adopted.

On motion of Mr. Danforth,

The Convention then adjourned.

Lansing, Friday, June 21, 1850.

The Convention met at the usual hour and was called to order by the President.

Prayer by the Rev. Mr. Merrill.

Roll called, and there were absent with leave, Messrs. Cook, Mason, Prevost and M. Robinson, and without leave, Messrs. P. R. Adams, Beeson and Tiffany.

No corrections made to the journal.

PETITIONS.

By Mr. Alvord: of David Thomas and 185 others, inhabitants of the county of Genesee, praying that the right of suffrage may be extended to persons of color.

Also, of J. H. Sanford and 200 others, of Lapeer county; and

Of Wiley Bancroft and 74 others, of the county of Macomb, praying for a like provision.

Referred to the committee on the elective franchise.

RESOLUTIONS.

Mr. Graham offered the following:

Resolved, That when this Convention adjourn on Monday, July 1st, the same shall stand adjourned until Tuesday, July 9th.

Mr. Moore offered the following substitute for the resolution:

Resolved, That this Convention adjourn on Friday, the 28th inst., until Tuesday, 9th July.

Mr. Witherell moved to amend the proposed substitute, by adding the words, "then to meet at Marshall, in the county of Calhoun."

Mr. Hathaway moved to lay the resolution and substitute upon the table.

Which motion was lost by yeas and nays, as follows:

YEAS:

Mr. W. Adams,
Arzeno,
Bagg,
Barnard,
Beardsley,
Britain,
Ammon Brown,
Bush,
Butterfield,
Chapel,
Mr. Crary,
Danforth,
Fralick,
Gardiner,
Green,
Hascall,
Hathaway,
Kingley,
Lee,
Lovell,
Mr. Orr,
J. D. Pierce,
N. Pierce,
Raynale,
Redfield,
Robertson,
E. S. Robinson,
Rix Robinson,
Soule,
Storey,

Church,	McClelland,	Sturgis,
J. Clark,	Mosher,	Town,
S. Clark,	Newberry,	Warden,
Conner,		40

NAYS.

Mr. Alvord,	Mr. Dimond,	Mr. Mowry,
Anderson,	Eastman,	O'Brien,
Axford,	Eaton,	Roberts,
Backus,	Edmunds,	Skinner,
H. Bartow,	Gale,	Sullivan,
J. Bartow,	Gibson,	Sutherland,
Alvarado Brown,	Graham,	Van Valkenburg,
Asahel Brown,	Hanscom,	Walker,
Burns,	Hart,	Webster,
Carr,	Harvey,	Wells,
Chandler,	Hixon,	White,
Choate,	Kinne,	Whittemore,
Comstock,	Leach,	Williams,
Cornell,	Marvin,	Willard,
Crouse,	McLeod,	Witherell,
Daniels,	Moore,	Woodman,
Desnoyers,	Morrison,	President, 51

Mr. Bush moved to indefinitely postpone the same; and the yeas and nays being demanded, the Convention refused to postpone, as follows:

YEAS:

Mr. W. Adams,	Mr. Cornell,	Mr. Newberry,
Arzeno,	Crary,	Orr,
Bagg,	Crouse,	J. D. Pierce,
Barnard,	Danforth,	N. Pierce,
Beardsley,	Eaton,	Raynale,
Britain,	Fralick,	Redfield,
Ammon Brown,	Gardiner,	Robertson,
Burns,	Green,	E. S. Robinson,
Bush,	Hascall,	Rix Robinson,
Butterfield,	Hathaway,	Soule,
Chapel,	Kingsley,	Storey,
Church,	Lee,	Sturgis,
J. Clark,	Lovell,	Town,
S. Clark,	McClelland,	Walker,
Conner,	Mosher,	Warden, 45

NAYS:

Mr. Alvord,	Mr. Edmunds,	Mr. Roberts,
Anderson,	Gale,	Skinner,
Axford,	Gibson,	Sullivan,
Backus,	Graham,	Sutherland,

J. Bartow,
H. Bartow,
Alvarado Brown,
Asahel Brown,
Carr,
Chandler,
Choate,
Comstock,
Daniels,
Desnoyers,
Dimond,
Eastman,
Hanscom,
Hart,
Harvey,
Hixon,
Kinne,
Leach,
Marvin,
McLeod,
Moore,
Morrison,
Mowry,
O'Brien,
Van Valkenburg,
Wait,
Webster,
Wells,
White,
Whittemore,
Williams,
Willard,
Witherell,
Woodman,
President,
47

At this stage of the proceedings, Mr. Witherell withdrew his amendment.

Mr. Walker offered the following amendment to the substitute proposed by Mr. Moore, to come in at the end of the same: "and the members and officers of this Convention shall receive no compensation for the time that shall transpire between such adjournment and the re-assembling of the Convention."

When, after some discussion,

Mr. Axford moved the previous question, which was demanded.

And the main question was ordered to be now put.

The same being first upon the amendment proposed by Mr. Walker, it was agreed to.

And the substitute, as amended, being then under consideration, the same was lost.

The main question now being on the original resolution proposed by Mr. Graham, the yeas and nays were called, with the following result:

YEAS.

Mr. Alvord,
Backus,
J. Bartow,
Graham,
Hanscom,
Hart,
Mr. Kinne,
McLeod,
Roberts,
VanValkenburg,
Webster,
Mr. Wells,
White,
Whipple,
Witherell,
President,
16

NAYS.

Mr. W. Adams,
Anderson,
Arzeno,
Axford,
Bagg,
Mr. Crouse,
Danforth,
Desnoyers,
Dimond,
Eaton,
Mr. Mowry,
Newberry,
O'Brien,
Orr,
J. D. Pierce,

Barnard,	Edmunds,	N. Pierce,
H. Bartow,	Fralick,	Raynale,
Beardsley,	Gale,	Redfield,
Britain,	Gardiner,	Robertson,
Alvarado Brown,	Gibson,	E. S. Robinson,
Ammon Brown,	Green,	Rix Robinson,
Asahel Brown,	Harvey,	Skinner,
Burns,	Hascall,	Soule,
Bush,	Hathaway,	Storey,
Butterfield,	Hixon,	Sturgis,
Carr,	Kingsley,	Sullivan,
Chapel,	Leach,	Town,
Choate,	Lee,	Wait,
Church,	Lovell,	Walker,
J. Clark,	Marvin,	Warden,
S. Clark,	McClelland,	Whittemore,
Comstock,	Moore,	Williams,
Conner,	Morrison,	Willard,
Cornell,	Mosher,	Woodman,
Crary,		73

So the resolution was not adopted.

Mr. Hanscom offered the following:

Resolved, That when this Convention adjourns on Monday, July 1st, the same shall stand adjourned until Wednesday, July 10th, and that the members and officers shall receive no compensation for the time of said adjournment.

Pending which, on motion of Mr. McClelland,

The Convention resolved itself into committee of the whole and resumed the consideration of "Article —, Legislative Department,"

Mr. Wells in the chair.

PROCEEDINGS IN COMMITTEE.

The question being upon Mr. Britain's proposed section, as offered yesterday, Mr. Witherell moved to amend by inserting between "no" and "revision," the word "general."

Pending which Mr. Britain withdrew his proposition.

On motion of Mr. Morrison,

A new section was added, to stand as section 38:

"No appropriation of the public money shall be made for the publication of the laws of this State in any newspaper."

Section 39 being under consideration, Mr. Van Valkenburg offered the following substitute:

"The Legislature shall have no power to pass any act to grant licenses for the sale of ardent spirits or intoxicating drinks, except for mechanical or medicinal purposes."

Mr. Chapel moved to amend as follows, to come in after "Legislature:" "shall have no power to pass any act, or grant any license to members of the Legislature to use intoxicating liquors as a drink or beverage, except for medicinal purposes."

Mr. Hanscom offered the following substitute for the whole matter:

"The Legislature shall never pass any act authorizing or permitting the making or vending of ardent spirits, except for medicinal and mechanical purposes."

Mr. Leach moved that the committee rise, report progress, and ask leave to sit again.

But the committee refused to rise.

Mr. Eaton moved to strike out of the section as reported by the committee, the words "as a drink or beverage."

But the committee refused to strike out.

The question being on Mr. Chapel's amendment to Mr. Van Valkenburg's substitute,

The amendment did not prevail.

Mr. Chapel moved to amend Mr. Hanscom's substitute by striking out "making and vending ardent spirits," and inserting "raising and selling corn."

Which was not adopted.

The question then being upon Mr. Hanscom's substitute, the same was not adopted.

Mr. Danforth moved that the committee rise, report progress and ask leave to sit again.

But the committee refused to rise.

The question then recurring upon Mr. Van Valkenburg's substitute, the same was not adopted.

Mr. Walker offered the following substitute for section 39:

"The Legislature shall have no power to impose any specific tax, fee or compensation, to be paid by any person or persons, except corporations, as a compensation for the privilege of exercising any moral employment or profession, nor to authorize or legalize on any conditions the exercise of any immoral profession or employment."

Which was not adopted.

On motion of Mr. Gardiner,

Section 39 was stricken out.

On motion of Mr. J. Clark,

The committee rose, reported progress, and asked leave to sit again.

The committee, through their chairman, reported the same back to the Convention, and asked leave to sit again.

Leave was granted.

On motion of Mr. Pierce,

Resolved, That the use of this hall be granted for the purpose of a temperance lecture, on Saturday evening of this week.

On motion of Mr. Eaton,

The Convention then adjourned.

Afternoon Session.

Half-past two o'clock.

The Convention was called to order by the President.

Roll called, and a quorum present.

On motion of Mr. McClelland,

The Convention then resolved itself into committee of the whole on Article 4, "Legislative Department,"

Mr. Wells in the chair.

PROCEEDINGS IN COMMITTEE.

Mr. Raynale moved to strike out the words "or any county thereof," in 5th and 6th lines of section 20.

But the committee refused to strike out.

On motion of Mr. McClelland,

The committee rose, reported the article back with amendments, and asked the concurrence of the Convention therein.

The committee, through their chairman, reported the same back with sundry amendments, in which they asked the concurrence of the Convention.

On motion of Mr. McClelland,

The article was laid upon the table and ordered printed, with the amendments made in committee.

Mr. Axford offered the following, which was laid upon the table:

Resolved, That in the opinion of this Convention, no member should be entitled to his *per diem* unless in actual attendance upon this Convention—sickness only excepted.

Resolved, That no appropriation be made for the purpose of paying any member of this Convention his *per diem,* except for the time he shall be in actual attendance in this Convention, except prevented by sickness.

THIRD READING OF ARTICLES.

The articles entitled "Division of the powers of Government;" and

"Impeachments and removals from Office," were severally read a third time and passed.

The Convention having arrived at the

SPECIAL ORDER,

Being the Bill of Rights, and the same being under consideration, the amendment proposed by Mr. Whipple, on the 17th inst., to section 16 did not prevail.

Mr. Fralick moved to amend section 16 by inserting after the word "obligation," the words "or remedies."

The yeas and nays being called thereon, the amendment was lost, as follows:

YEAS.

Mr.	Axford,	Mr.	Fralick,	Mr.	Newberry,
	Ammon Brown,		Gale,		N. Pierce,
	Asahel Brown,		Gibson,		Raynale,
	Burns,		Graham,		Wait,
	Bush,		Lee,		Webster,
	Chapel,		McLeod,		Whipple,
	Cornell,		Moore,		Williams,
	Desnoyers,		Morrison,		Witherell,
	Eastman,		Mosher,		26

NAYS.

Mr.	W. Adams,	Mr.	Dimond,	Mr.	J. D. Pierce,
	Alvord,		Eaton,		Redfield,
	Anderson,		Edmunds,		Robertson,

Arzeno,	Gardiner,	E. S. Robinson,
Bagg,	Green,	Rix Robinson,
Barnard,	Hanscom,	Skinner,
H. Bartow,	Hart,	Soule,
Beardsley,	Harvey,	Storey,
Britain,	Hascall,	Sturgis,
Alvardo Brown,	Hathaway,	Sullivan,
Carr,	Hixon,	Town,
Choate,	Kingsley,	Van Valkenburg,
Church,	Kinne,	Walker,
J. Clark,	Leach,	Warden,
S. Clark,	Lovell,	Wells,
Comstock,	Marvin,	White,
Conner,	McClelland,	Whittemore,
Crary,	Mowry,	Willard,
Danforth,	O'Brien,	Woodman,
Daniels,	Orr,	President, 60

On motion of Mr. McClelland,

Section 26 was stricken out.

Mr. Moore offered the following, to stand as an additional section to the article:

"Any citizen of this State who may hereafter be engaged, either directly or indirectly, in a duel, either as principal or accessory before the fact, shall forever be disqualified from holding any office under the Constitution and laws of this State."

On motion of Mr. Whittemore,

The proposed section was amended by adding thereto the words, "nor be permitted to vote at any election."

And the section was adopted.

On motion of Mr. Witherell,

Section 30 of the article was amended by adding thereto the words "and shall be appropriated exclusively to the support of primary schools."

Mr. Morrison moved to amend section 29 by inserting after "corporation," the words "except for educational purposes."

Which amendment did not prevail.

Mr. Raynale submitted the following as a substitute for section 22:

"Involuntary servitude, unless for the punishment of crime, shall never be tolerated in this State." Which was lost.

On motion of Mr. Robertson,

Section 10 was amended by striking out all after the word "defense," in the 4th line.

Mr. Walker offered the following as a substitute for sec. 3:

"No man or set of men are entitled to exclusive or separate emoluments or privileges from the community, but in consideration of public services."

But the same did not prevail.

Mr. Hanscom moved to strike out sec. 7, and insert the following:

"Any person may publish his sentiments on any subject, being responsible for the abuse of that liberty; and in all prosecutions for libel, the truth, unless published from malicious motives, shall be sufficient defense to the person charged, and the jury shall be judges of the law and the fact."

A division of the question being had, the motion to strike out the section did not prevail.

Mr. S. Clark moved to amend section 10 by adding thereto the following:

"Nor shall any person be held to answer for a criminal offense unless on the presentment or indictment of a grand jury, except in cases of impeachment, or in cases cognizable by justices of the peace, or arising in the army or militia when in actual service in time of war or public danger."

Pending which, on motion of Mr. J. Bartow,

The Convention adjourned.

Lansing, Saturday, June 22, 1850.

The President called the Convention to order at the usual hour.

Prayer by the Rev. Mr. Atterbury.

The roll being called, there were found absent with leave, Messrs. Cook, Mason, Prevost, and M. Robinson.

Without leave, Messrs. P. R. Adams, Butterfield, Chandler, Crouse, Eaton and Walker.

No corrections made to the journal.

LEAVE OF ABSENCE.

Mr. Storey asked for and obtained leave of absence for Mr. Butterfield until Tuesday next.

Mr. Lee for Mr. Crouse,

Mr. Tiffany for Mr. P. R. Adams until Wednesday,

Mr. Bagg for Mr. Eaton until Thursday, and

Mr. Daniels for Mr. Chandler indefinitely.

REPORTS.

Mr. Whittemore, from the committee on the elective franchise, reported back sundry petitions and resolutions referred to them, from the further consideration of which they asked to be and were discharged.

Mr. Whittemore, from the same committee, reported an article entitled "Elections," accompanied by a resolution, the passage of which was recommended.

The article was read a first and second time by its title, and, with the resolution, referred to the committee of the whole and ordered printed.

RESOLUTIONS.

Mr. Robertson moved to take from the table the resolutions offered by Mr. Axford yesterday relative to the absence and *per diem* of members.

The motion was lost.

The resolution offered yesterday by Mr. Hanscom, relative to an adjournment from the "1st of July," to the "tenth," being under consideration, Mr. Chapel moved to amend the same by striking out "Wednesday, July 10th," and inserting in its stead, "1st day of October next."

When, on motion of Mr. McClelland,

The resolution was laid on the table.

The Convention having reached the order of

UNFINISHED BUSINESS.

The same being the "Bill of Rights,"

The question recurred on the amendment proposed by Mr. S. Clark to section 10, as follows:

Add thereto the words, "Nor shall any person be held to answer for a criminal offense unless on the presentment or indictment of a grand jury, except in cases of impeachment, or in cases cognizable by justices of the peace, or arising in the army or militia when in actual service in time of war or public danger."

Mr. McClelland offered the following as a substitute: "It shall be competent for the Legislature to change, modify or abolish the present grand jury system."

Pending which, on motion of Mr. White,

The Convention adjourned.

Afternoon Session.

½ past 2 o'clock.

The President called the Convention to order.

A quorum of members in attendance.

Mr. Mowry asked and obtained leave of absence for Mr. Woodman until Tuesday next.

Mr. Williams for Mr. Willard; and

Mr. Kingsley for Mr. Edmunds for an indefinite period.

The President announced a communication from the Auditor General, in answer to a resolution of inquiry adopted by the Convention on the 17th inst.

The same was read and laid upon the table.

The Bill of Rights being under consideration,

Mr. McClelland withdrew the substitute he proposed for Mr. Clark's amendment.

Mr. J. D. Pierce offered the following substitute for the same:

"The present grand jury is hereby abolished."

Mr. Storey moved the previous question; when

Mr. Bagg moved to adjourn. Which was lost.

The previous question was then demanded, but the vote seconding it was reconsidered; and

Mr. Storey withdrew his motion.

The question recurring on the substitute offered by Mr. J. D. Pierce, the same was lost by yeas and nays, as follows:

YEAS.

Mr. Anderson,	Mr. Hart,	Mr. Rix Robinson,
H. Bartow,	Hathaway,	Skinner,
Beardsley,	Kinne,	Soule,
Carr,	Lovell,	Storey,
Church,	McLeod,	Sturgis,
Crary,	Mosher,	Sullivan,
Eastman,	O'Brien,	Wait,

Gardiner, Graham, Green, Orr, J. D. Pierce, N. Pierce, Walker, Webster, 29

NAYS.

Mr. W. Adams, Arzeno, Backus, Bagg, Barnard, J. Bartow, Beeson, Britain, Alvarado Brown, Ammon Brown, Asahel Brown, Burns, Bush, Chapel, Choate, J. Clark, S. Clark, Comstock, Mr. Conner, Cornell, Daniels, Desnoyers, Fralick, Gale, Gibson, Hanscom, Harvey, Hascall, Hixon, Kingsley, Leach, Marvin, McClelland, Moore, Mowry, Mr. Newberry, Raynale, Redfield, Roberts, Robertson, E. S. Robinson, Sutherland, Tiffany, Town, VanValkenburg, Warden, Wells, White, Whittemore, Williams, Witherell, President, 52

Mr. Williams proposed the following amendment to the one offered by Mr. S. Clark, and the same was accepted by the mover:

Strike out "a criminal offence," and insert "any criminal offence punishable by imprisonment in the State Prison."

Mr. Williams proposed further to amend, by adding to the amendment proposed by Mr. Clark:

"Grand juries may be so modified as not to consist of more than thirteen men."

Which did not prevail.

The amendment proposed by Mr. Clark was then lost, as follows:

YEAS.

Mr. Backus, Bagg, J. Clark, S. Clark, Desnoyers, Mr. Hanscom, Moore, Raynale, Van Valkenburg, Wells, Mr. White, Williams, Witherell, President, 14

NAYS:

Mr. W. Adams, Alvord, Anderson, Arzeno, Mr. Daniels, Eastman, Fralick, Gale, Mr. Newberry, O'Brien, Orr, J. D. Pierce,

Barnard,	Gardiner,	N. Pierce,
H. Bartow,	Gibson,	Redfield,
J. Bartow,	Graham,	Roberts,
Beardsley,	Green,	Robertson,
Beeson,	Hart,	E. S. Robinson,
Britain,	Harvey,	Rix Robinson,
Alvarado Brown,	Hascall,	Skinner,
Ammon Brown,	Hathaway,	Soule,
Asahel Brown,	Hixon,	Storey,
Burns,	Kingsley,	Sturgis,
Bush,	Kinne,	Sullivan,
Carr,	Leach,	Sutherland,
Chapel,	Lovell,	Tiffany,
Choate,	Marvin,	Town,
Church,	McClelland,	Wait,
Comstock,	McLeod,	Walker,
Conner,	Morrison,	Warden,
Cornell,	Mosher,	Webster,
Crary,	Mowry,	Whittemore, 69

Mr. Roberts moved that the further consideration of the Article entitled "Bill of Rights," be postponed until all other articles to be acted upon by this Convention have been considered and disposed of except the schedule; which

On motion of Mr. Church,

Was laid upon the table.

The Convention then adjourned.

Lansing, Monday, June 24, 1850.

The Convention met pursuant to adjournment, and was called to order by the President.

Prayer by the Rev. Mr. Sanford.

Members all present except Messrs. P. R. Adams, Butterfield, Cook, Crouse, Eaton, Edmunds, Mason, Prevost, M. Robinson, Willard and Woodman, absent on leave.

Journal approved.

PETITIONS.

By Mr. Storey: of Geo. F. Gardner and 150 others, citizens of Jackson county, praying that the elective franchise may be extended to every male citizen above the age of 21 years; and also, that the word "white" may be excluded from the Constitution, whenever and wheresoever the same may occur to the detriment of the colored citizens of the State of Michigan.

REPORTS.

Mr. Comstock, from a minority of the committee on banking and other incorporations, except municipal, submitted a report, accompanied by an Article entitled "Corporations other than municipal."

The article and report were referred to the committee of the whole and ordered printed.

RESOLUTIONS.

On motion of Mr. Williams,

The use of the Hall for to-morrow evening was allowed to Messrs. Clark and Smith for the purpose of delivering a lecture on scientific subjects.

UNFINISHED BUSINESS.

The Bill of Rights being under consideration,

Mr. Bagg offered the following, as an additional section to the article:

"No person shall be held to answer for a capital, or otherwise infamous crime, unless on a presentment or indictment of a grand jury, except in cases arising in the land or naval forces, or in the militia, when in actual service in time of war or public danger.

Mr. Crary raised a point of order, that the amendment proposed embraced matter that had been once disposed of by the Convention.

The President decided the amendment in order.

Mr. Alvord offered the following as a substitute for Mr. Bagg's amendment:

"And the institution of the grand jury is hereby abolished."

When, after some discussion,

Mr. Bagg, by Mr. Alvord's consent, withdrew his proposition.

Mr. Beardsley offered the following amendment to section 10:

Strike out all after the word "favor," in the 4th line of said section, and in lieu thereof insert as follows, viz: "to be aided by counsel in his defence, who shall have the right to close the argument to the jury, when one may be empannelled."

The yeas and nays were demanded by Mr. Hanscom, and the amendment was negatived, as follows:

YEAS.

Mr. W. Adams,
Anderson,
Arzeno,
Axford,
Barnard,
H. Bartow,
Beardsley,
Ammon Brown,
Asahel Brown,
Burns,
Bush,
Church,
Cornell,
Mr. Crary,
Dimond,
Gale,
Gardiner,
Hanscom,
Hart,
Hascall,
Hathaway,
Leach,
Lee,
Mosher,
O'Brien,
Mr. Orr,
J. D. Pierce,
Prevost,
Redfield,
Rix Robinson,
Soule,
Town,
Van Valkenburg,
Webster,
Wells,
Whittemore,
Williams,
37

NAYS.

Mr. Backus,
Bagg,
J. Bartow,
Beeson,
Britain,
Alvarado Brown,
Carr,
Chapel,
Choate,
J. Clark,
S. Clark,
Comstock,
Conner,
Danforth,
Daniels,
Desnoyers,
Mr. Eastman,
Fralick,
Gibson,
Graham,
Green,
Harvey,
Hixon,
Kingsley,
Kinne,
Lovell,
Marvin,
McClelland,
McLeod,
Moore,
Morrison,
Mowry,
Mr. Newberry,
N. Pierce,
Robertson,
E. S. Robinson,
Skinner,
Storey,
Sturgis,
Sullivan,
Tiffany,
Wait,
Walker,
White,
Whipple,
Witherell,
President,
47

On motion of Mr. McClelland,

Section 10 was amended by striking out in the 3d line, the words "and cause."

Mr. Barnard proposed to amend section 16 by inserting after the word "contracts," in the first line, the words "or rendering the remedies thereon less effective."

Pending which,

On motion of Mr. J. D. Pierce,

The Convention adjourned.

Afternoon Session.

Half-past two o'clock.

The President called the Convention to order.

A quorum of members in attendance.

The amendment proposed by Mr. Barnard to section 10, Bill of Bights, being under consideration,

He withdrew the same, and proposed the following as a substitute for the section:

"No ex post facto law, or law impairing the obligation of contracts, or depriving a party of any remedy for enforcing a contract which existed when the contract was made, shall be passed."

Mr. J. D. Pierce raised a question of order, that the subject matter had already been disposed of.

The President decided the amendment in order.

And the yeas and nays being demanded, the substitute was lost, as follows:

YEAS.

Mr. Axford,
Backus,
Barnard,
Beeson,
Ammon Brown,
Asahel Brown,
Burns,
Bush,
Choate,
J. Clark,
Cornell,
Desnoyers,
Mr. Eastman,
Fralick,
Gale,
Gibson,
Graham,
Hanscom,
Hart,
Leach,
Lee,
McLeod,
Moore,
Mr. Morrison,
Mowry,
Newberry,
N. Pierce,
Kaynale,
Robertson,
Tiffany,
Wait,
Whipple,
Williams,
Witherell, 34

NAYS.

Mr. W. Adams,
Alvord,
Anderson,
Arzeno,
Bagg,
J. Bartow,
Beardsley,
Britain,
Alvarado Brown,
Carr,
Chandler,
Chapel,
Church,
S. Clark,
Comstock,
Conner,
Crary,
Mr. Daniels,
Dimond,
Gardiner,
Green,
Harvey,
Hascall,
Hathaway,
Hixon,
Kingsley,
Kinne,
Lovell,
Marvin,
McClelland,
Mosher,
O'Brien,
Orr,
J. D. Pierce,
Mr. Prevost,
Redfield,
E. S. Robinson,
Rix Robinson,
Skinner,
Soule,
Storey,
Sturgis,
Sullivan,
Sutherland,
Town,
Van Valkenburg,
Walker,
Wells,
Whittemore,
President. 50

Mr. Roberts moved to take from the table his motion of Saturday, to postpone the further consideration of Bill of Rights until all other articles were disposed of.

The motion did not prevail.

On motion of Mr. Church,

The vote by which the Convention refused to strike out section 7, on the 21st inst., and insert a substitute offered by Mr. Hanscom, was reconsidered.

And the substitute proposed as follows, was lost:

"Any person may publish his sentiments on any subject, being responsible for the abuse of that liberty; and in all prosecutions for libel, the truth, unless published from malicious motives, shall be sufficient defence to the person charged, and the jury shall be judges of the law and the fact."

Mr. Sullivan offered the following amendment to section 23:

Insert after the word "implied," in first line, the following: "except in cases of fraud or breach of trust, or of moneys collected by a public officer, or in any professional employment."

Mr. Raynale moved to amend the amendment by striking out the words "or in any professional employment;" which was lost.

And the amendment proposed by Mr. Sullivan was adopted.

Mr. McLeod proposed the following, to be incorporated in the Bill of Rights:

"The universal education of the youth of our country is indispensable to the purity and permanency of our democratic institutions and system of government."

Which did not prevail.

The article was ordered to a third reading, and so read, when,

On motion of Mr. Church,

Resolved, That sections 5, 7, 8, 9, 10, 11, 12, 13, 14, 15, 16, 17, 18, 20, 21, 22, 23, 25, 27, 28, 29, 30 and 31, be referred to the committee on the arrangement and phraseology of the Constitution, with instructions to insert the same in the appropriate articles, and to adapt them thereto.

Mr. McLeod moved that the residue of the article be laid on the table; which was lost.

On motion of Mr. S. Clark,

The same was referred to the committee on arrangement and phraseology.

Mr. White moved to adjourn.

But the Convention refused to adjourn; when,

On motion of Mr. Crary,

The Convention resolved itself into committee of the whole, on the Article entitled "State Officers,"

Mr. J. D. Pierce in the chair.

PROCEEDINGS IN COMMITTEE.

On motion of Mr. Crary,

The words "and an attorney general," were stricken out of 2d line of 1st section.

Mr. Hanscom moved to strike out the words "an auditor general."

But the committee refused to strike out.

Mr. Whittemore moved to insert in 1st line, after the word "State," the words, "who shall be ex-officio."

Which motion did not prevail.

Mr. Robertson moved to strike out the words "who shall be ex-officio," in 2d line.

Pending which,

On motion of Mr. Hanscom,

The committee rose, reported progress, and asked leave to sit again.

The committee, through their chairman, reported the same back to the Convention and asked leave to sit again.

Leave was granted.

On motion of Mr. McClelland,

The Convention then adjourned.

Lansing, Tuesday, June 25, 1850.

The Convention met at the usual hour and was called to order by the President.

Prayer by the Rev. Mr. Tooker.

Roll called and Messrs. P. R. Adams, Eaton, Edmunds, M. Robinson and Willard, absent with leave, and Messrs. Warden and Woodman without leave.

Journal corrected and approved.

LEAVE OF ABSENCE.

Mr. Barnard asked and obtained leave of absence for Mr. Warden until Wednesday next.

PETITIONS.

By Mr. Lovell: of D. L. Case and 13 others praying that there may be submitted to the people for their approval or disapproval, a provision prohibiting the sale, manufacture and importation of intoxicating drinks as a beverage, from and after the first day of January, 1854, which provision, if approved by the people, shall become a part of the new Constitution.

Referred to the select committee appointed on the 17th inst.

By Mr. Beeson: of Charles Jewett and 106 others, citizens of Berrien county, requesting such action by this Convention as will check the emigration of slaves into this State from others; and also, a remonstrance against the submitting of any provision granting the right of suffrage to any other than "free white citizens."

Referred to the committee of the whole.

REPORTS.

Mr. J. D. Pierce, from a majority of the committee on exemptions and the rights of married women, submitted an article entitled, "Exemptions and the Rights of Married Women," which was read a first and second time by its title, referred to the committee of the whole and ordered printed.

RESOLUTIONS.

Mr. White offered the following:

Resolved, That when this Convention adjourn at noon, on Monday the 1st day of July next, it stand adjourned until Wednesday morning, July 10th, ensuing.

Upon which, Mr. Hanscom moved the previous question, and the same being seconded by a majority of the members present.

The main question was ordered to be now put, and the resolution was lost by the following vote:

YEAS:

Mr. Alvord,	Mr. Eastman,	Mr. Prevost,
Anderson,	Gibson,	Robertson,
Axford,	Graham,	Sullivan,
Backus,	Hanscom,	Sutherland,
Beeson,	Hart,	VanValkenburg,
Alvarado Brown,	Harvey,	Webster,
Asahel Brown,	Kinne,	Wells,
Burns,	Leach,	White,
Choate,	Marvin,	Whipple,
J. Clark,	McLeod,	Whittemore,
Comstock,	Moore,	Witherell,
Danforth,	Mowry,	President,
Desnoyers,	O'Brien,	38

NAYS:

Mr. W. Adams,	Mr. Cornell,	Mr. J. D. Pierce,
Arzeno,	Crary,	N. Pierce,
Bagg,	Daniels,	Raynale,
H. Bartow,	Dimond,	Redfield,
J. Bartow,	Fralick,	E. S. Robinson,
Beardsley,	Gale,	Rix Robinson,
Britain,	Hascall,	Skinner,
Ammon Brown,	Hathaway,	Sonle,
Carr,	Kingley,	Storey,
Chandler,	Lovell,	Sturgis,
Chapel,	McClelland,	Tiffany,
Church,	Morrison,	Town,
S. Clark,	Mosher,	Wait,
Conner,	Newberry,	Walker,
Cook,	Orr,	Williams, 45

On motion of Mr. Church,

Resolved, That the Commissioner of the Land Office be and he is hereby requested to furnish to this Convention with all convenient dispatch, a statement embracing, as far as practicable, the following particulars:

1st. What quantity of Primary School Lands is still unsold.

2d. " " University " "

3d. " " Salt Spring " "

4th. " " State Building " "

5th. " " Asylum " "

6th. What quantity of Assett lands is still unsold.

7th. " " Normal School " "

8th. " " Internal Improvement "

9th. What number of accounts have been opened in the Land Office, upon sales of these several classes of lands, and what number thereof for each year.

10th. What number of forfeitures have occurred on sales of Primary School Lands and University Lands during the current year, and the amount of penalties on said forfeitures.

On motion of Mr. Backus,

Resolved, That the committee on finance and taxation be instructed to inquire into the expediency of reporting a provision in the Constitution that all assessments and taxes shall be equal.

Mr. Whipple moved that the Convention go into committee of the whole on the article entitled "State Officers."

Which was not agreed to.

On motion of Mr. McClelland,

The special order of the day, being the report of the committee on the judiciary, was postponed until Monday the 8th July next.

On motion of Mr. Britain,

The Convention resolved itself into committee of the whole, on the article entitled "Militia,"

Mr. J. Clark in the chair.

PROCEEDINGS IN COMMITTEE.

On motion of Mr. Comstock,

The following was added to section one:

"But all such inhabitants of this State, of any religious denomination whatever, as, from scruples of conscience, may be averse to bearing arms, shall be excused therefrom, upon such conditions as shall be prescribed by law."

Mr. Leach moved to amend 1st section, 1st line, by striking out the word "white."

But the committee refused to strike out.

Mr. Hixon moved to amend section 2, line 1, by striking out the words "and disciplining."

Which motion was not adopted.

Mr. Leach moved to amend 1st line, section three, by striking out the words, "or appointed."

Which was not agreed to.

Mr. Witherell offered the following, to stand as a new section:

"The Legislature may make such provisions for the support of independent or volunteer companies as they may deem expedient."

Mr. Britain moved to amend by striking out "support," and inserting "organizing."

Mr. Chapel offered the following substitute, which was not adopted:

"The Legislature may provide for the organization of independent companies, provided no tax shall be levied, or appropriation from the treasury for such object shall be made, except in times of public danger."

The question being upon Mr. Britain's amendment, the same was lost.

The question then recurring upon Mr. Witherell's proposition, the same was not agreed to.

On motion of Mr. Cook,

The committee rose, reported the article back with an amendment, asked the concurrence of the Convention therein, and to be discharged from the further consideration of said article.

The committee, through their chairman, reported the same back to the Convention with an amendment, in which the concurrence of the Convention was desired.

And the article being under consideration, the amendment was concurred in.

Mr. Witherell proposed the following, as an additional section:

"The Legislature may provide by law for the organization and support of independent or volunteer companies, as they may deem expedient."

Mr. Witherell asked the yeas and nays, and the same being ordered, the result was as follows:

YEAS.

Mr. Backus,	Mr. Desnoyers,	Mr. McLeod,
Bagg,	Gibson,	Moore,

J. Bartow,	Graham,	Witherell,
Comstock,	Harvey,	President.
Crouse,		13

NAYS.

Mr. W. Adams,	Mr. Danforth,	Mr. N. Pierce,
Alvord,	Dimond,	Prevost,
Anderson,	Eastman,	Raynale,
Arzeno,	Fralick,	Roberts,
Axford,	Gale,	Robertson,
Barnard,	Gardiner,	E. S. Robinson,
H. Bartow,	Green,	Rix Robinson,
Beardsley,	Hanscom,	Skinner,
Beeson,	Hart,	Soule,
Britain,	Hascall,	Storey,
Alvarado Brown,	Hathaway,	Sturgis,
Ammon Brown,	Kingsley.	Sullivan,
Asahel Brown,	Kinne,	Tiffany,
Bush,	Leach,	Town,
Butterfield,	Lovell,	Van Valkenburg,
Carr,	Marvin,	Wait,
Chandler,	McClelland,	Walker,
Chapel,	Morrison,	Webster,
Choate,	Mosher,	Wells,
S. Clark,	Mowry,	White,
Conner,	Newberry,	Whipple,
Cook,	O'Brien,	Whittemore,
Cornell,	Orr,	Williams, 69

So the proposed amendment was disagreed to.

The article entitled "Militia," was then ordered engrossed for a third reading.

On motion of Mr. Crary,

The Convention resolved itself into committee of the whole on the article entitled "Executive Department,"

Mr. Walker in the chair.

PROCEEDINGS IN COMMITTEE.

Mr. Britain offered the following:

Section 1, line 1, after "Lieutenant Governor," insert "Speaker of the House of Representatives, each of whom."

Which was disagreed to.

Mr. Hanscom moved to strike out of section two, all after "election," in third line.

But the committee refused to strike out.

On motion of Mr. Britain,

Section two was amended by inserting after "Lieutenant Governor," the words "or Speaker of the House of Representatives."

Mr. Lovell moved to amend section two, lines one and two, by striking out "have been five years," and inserting the word "be."

Which motion did not prevail.

Mr. Bagg moved to amend section two by adding, "or over 70 years."

Which motion was disagreed to.

On motion of Mr. Britain,

Section 3 was amended by inserting after "Lieutenant Governor," wherever it occurs, the words "Speaker of the House of Representatives."

On motion of Mr. Kingsley,

The following words were added to section 4: "and he shall have power to call forth the militia to execute the laws of the State, to suppress insurrection, and repel invasion."

On motion of Mr. Crary,

The words "or the Senate only," were stricken out of 1st line of section 7.

Mr. Bush moved to insert in line 4 of section 9, after "upon," the word "a."

Which was not agreed to.

On motion of Mr. Britain,

Section 11 was amended by striking out "President of the Senate," and inserting "Speaker of the House of Representatives."

On motion of Mr. Britain,

A new section was added to stand as section 13, as follows:

"The Speaker of the House of Representatives shall, by virtue of his office, be the presiding officer of the House of Representatives. In the committee of the whole, he may debate all questions; and when there is an equal division, he shall give the casting vote."

Mr. Backus moved to add at the end of section 13, "nor shall the Governor be eligible to any office or appointment from the Legislature or either branch thereof, for the term for which he may have been elected."

On motion of Mr. Morrison,

The amendment was amended by inserting after "Governor," the words "Lieutenant Governor and Speaker of the House of Representatives."

On motion of Mr. Witherell,

The amendment was further amended by adding "and all votes given for either of them for any such office shall be void."

Mr. Storey moved that the committee rise, report progress and ask leave to sit again.

But the committee refused to rise.

The amendment of Mr. Backus, as amended, was then adopted.

On motion of Mr. Britain,

Section 14 was amended by inserting after "Lieutenant Governor," in 1st line, "or Speaker of the House of Representatives."

Mr. Hart moved that the committee rise, report progress and ask leave to sit again.

But the committee refused to rise.

On motion of Mr. McClelland,

All after and including "when," in 2d line of section 15, was stricken out.

Mr. Witherell moved to strike out "continue to," and to insert between "the" and "great," the word "present," in 1st line of section 16.

Which was disagreed to.

On motion of Mr. Britain,

The words "President of the Senate, pro tempore," in 1st line of section 15, were stricken out, and "Speaker of the House of Representatives," inserted.

On motion of Mr. J. Clark,

The committee rose, reported the article back with amendments, asked the concurrence of the Convention therein, and to be discharged from the further consideration of the same.

The committee, through their chairman, reported the same back with sundry amendments, in which they asked the concurrence of the Convention; when,

On motion of Mr. McClelland,

The Convention adjourned.

Afternoon Session.

Half-past two o'clock.

The Convention was called to order by the President, and the roll being called, a quorum of members were in attendance.

Mr. Mowry asked and obtained leave of absence for Mr. H. Bartow, for an indefinite period.

Mr. Backus, by consent, offered the following:

Resolved, That a special committee of five be appointed to inquire and report to this Convention the relative quantity of land received from the general government by this state, as compared with the other north-western states, and also to report a memorial to congress on that subject.

And the resolution was adopted.

The article entitled "Executive Department," being under consideration, and the question being on concurring in the amendments made in committee,

The 1st amendment was non-concurred in by the following vote:

YEAS.

Mr. Axford,	Mr. Hart,	Mr. J. D. Pierce,
Bagg,	Hascall,	Prevost,
Beardsley,	Hathaway,	Raynale,
Beeson,	Hixon,	Redfield,
Britain,	Kingsley,	Robertson,
Burns,	Leach,	Skinner,
Chandler,	McLeod,	Storey,
Choate,	Morrison,	Sturgis,
Comstock,	Mosher,	Town,
Conner,	Mowry,	White,
Eastman,	Newberry,	Williams,
Gardiner,	O'Brien,	Witherell,
Green,	Orr,	38

NAYS.

Mr. W. Adams,	Mr. Cook,	Mr. N. Pierce,
Alvord,	Cornell,	Roberts,
Anderson,	Crary,	E. S. Robinson,
Arzeno,	Crouse,	Rix Robinson,
Backus,	Danforth,	Soule,
Barnard,	Daniels,	Sullivan,
J. Bartow,	Desnoyers,	Sutherland,
Alvarado Brown,	Dimond,	Tiffany,
Ammon Brown,	Fralick,	Van Valkenburg,
Asahel Brown,	Gale,	Wait,

Bush,
Butterfield,
Carr,
Chapel,
Church,
J. Clark,
S. Clark,
Gibson,
Graham,
Hanscom,
Harvey,
Lovell,
McClelland,
Moore,
Walker,
Webster,
Wells,
Whipple,
Whittemore,
President, 50

The 2d, 3d and 4th amendments, being to section 3, were also non-concurred in.

The 5th and 6th amendments were concurred in.

In the 7th and 8th amendments the Convention refused to concur.

The 9th amendment to the article being under consideration, the words "Speaker of the House of Representatives" were stricken out.

Mr. Hanscom moved to amend the amendment proposed, by striking out "Lieutenant Governor."

Which did not prevail.

The amendment as amended was then concurred in as follows:

YEAS:

Mr. W. Adams,
Alvord,
Anderson,
Arzeno,
Axford,
Backus,
Bagg,
Barnard,
J. Bartow,
Beardsley,
Britain,
Alvarado Brown,
Ammon Brown,
Asahel Brown,
Burns,
Bush,
Butterfield,
Carr,
Chandler,
Choate,
Church,
J. Clark,
S. Clark,
Comstock,
Conner,
Cornell,
Mr. Crary,
Crouse,
Daniels,
Desnoyers,
Dimond,
Eastman,
Fralick,
Gale,
Gardiner,
Gibson,
Graham,
Green,
Hart,
Harvey,
Hascall,
Hathaway,
Hixon,
Kingsley,
Leach,
Lovell,
Marvin,
McClelland,
Moore,
Morrison,
Mosher,
Mowry,
Mr. Newberry,
O'Brien,
Orr,
J. D. Pierce,
N. Pierce,
Prevost,
Redfield,
Robertson,
E. S. Robinson,
Rix Robinson,
Skinner,
Soule,
Sullivan,
Sutherland,
Town,
Van Valkenburg,
Walker,
Webster,
Wells,
White,
Whipple,
Whittemore,
Williams,
Wtiherell,
President. 77

NAYS:

Mr. Chapel,	Mr. McLeod,	Mr. Storey,
Cook,	Raynale,	Tiffany,
Danforth,	Roberts,	Wait.
Hanscom,		10

In the 10th and 11th amendments the Convention refused to concur, and in the 12th and last amendment made in committee, the Convention concurred.

On motion of Mr. Williams,

Section 7 of the article was further amended by striking out, " to the Legislature at every session," in the secsnd line, and inserting, " at such times as he may deem necessary and proper to the existing Legislature, and at the close of his official term of service to the next Legislature."

Mr. McClelland moved to strike from the 2d section, the last clause, as follows: " nor shall any person be eligible to the office of Governor who shall not have attained the age of thirty years."

And the yeas and nays being demanded, the result was as follows:

YEAS:

Mr. W. Adams,	Mr. Hart,	Mr. Roberts,
Alvord,	Hascall,	Robertson,
Anderson,	Leach,	E. S. Robinson,
Beardsley,	Marvin,	Soule,
Choate,	McClelland,	Storey,
Cook,	McLeod,	Sutherland,
Crary,	Morrison,	Van Valkenburg,
Eastman,	J. D. Pierce,	Walker,
Gibson,	Raynale,	Webster,
Hanscom,		28

NAYS.

Mr. Arzeno,	Mr. Conner,	Mr. Mowry,
Avford,	Cornell,	Newberry,
Backus,	Crouse,	O'Brien,
Bagg,	Danforth,	Orr,
Barnard,	Danieis,	N. Pierce,
J. Bartow,	Desnoyers,	Prevost,
Beeson,	Dimond,	Redfield,
Alvarado Brown,	Fralick,	Rix Robinson,
Ammon Brown,	Gale,	Skinner,
Asahel Brown,	Gardiner,	Sullivan,
Burns,	Graham,	Tiffany,
Bush,	Green,	Town,
Butterfield,	Harvey,	Wait,

Carr,	Hathaway,	Wells,
Chandler,	Hixon,	White,
Chapel,	Kingsley,	Whipple,
Church,	Kinne,	Whittemore,
J. Clark,	Lovell,	Williams,
S. Clark,	Moore,	Witherell,
Comstock,	Mosher,	President, 60

So the proposed amendment was negatived.

Mr. Tiffany moved to amend section 8 by striking out the words "a contagious" before "disease;" and the same prevailed.

On motion of Mr. McLeod,

The words "after its adjournment," were stricken out of the 2d line of section 8.

Mr. Barnard moved to strike out "dangerous," in the same section, and insert "endangered;" which did not prevail.

Mr. J. D. Pierce moved to amend the same section, by inserting after "Legislature," the words, "after their adjournment."

But the motion was lost.

Mr. Van Valkenburg submitted the following as a substitute for section 8:

"He may direct the Legislature to meet at some other place than the seat of government, if it shall become dangerous from a common enemy, or from disease."

Which was not adopted.

Mr. Beeson offered the following as a substitute for the same, which was not adopted;

"He may direct the Legislature to meet at some other place than the seat of government, if that shall become, when the Legislature are not in session, dangerous from a common enemy or disease."

The article entitled "Executive Department" was then ordered engrossed for a third reading.

Mr. White moved that the article be printed as amended; which motion did not prevail.

On motion of Mr. Crary,

The Convention resolved itself into committee of the whole on the article entitled "Education,"

Mr. S. Clark in the chair.

PROCEEDINGS IN COMMITTEE.

On motion of Mr. Walker,

Section 1 was amended by striking out all in first line to the word "Superintendent," and inserting "the." Also striking out in 2d line the words "who shall hold his office for the term of two years;" and also by striking out "whose," in 3d line, and inserting "his."

Mr. Hanscom moved to strike out of last line of section 2, the words "upon such fair and equitable basis," and insert "in such manner."

Which motion did not prevail.

On motion of Mr. Walker,

The words "free and," were stricken out of 2d line of section 3.

On motion of Mr. Williams,

Section 3 was amended by striking out in 1st line, the words "by which;" and by striking out in 3d and 4th lines, the words "and shall provide that."

On motion of Mr. Skinner,

The committee rose, reported progress, and asked leave to sit again.

The committee, through their chairman, reported the same back to the Convention, and asked and obtained leave to sit again.

The President announced the committee under resolution in relation to government land, &c.: Messrs. Backus, Church, Lovell, Bartow, Graham.

On motion of Mr. Lovell,

The Convention then adjourned.

Lansing, Wednesday, June 26, 1850.

The Convention met pursuant to adjournment and was called to order by the President.

Prayer by the Rev. Mr. Merrill.

The roll being called, there were found absent on leave, Messrs. P. R. Adams, H. Bartow, Eaton, Edmunds, Mason and Willard, and Mr. Barnard without leave.

PETITIONS.

By Mr. Storey: of Samuel Higby, Leander Chapman, and 38 others, citizens of Jackson cnunty, praying that the Judges of the circuit courts may be the Judges of the supreme court.

Referred to the committee of the whole.

By Mr. Arzeno: of H. V. Man and 40 others, citizens of Monroe county, praying that the right of suffrage be extended to persons of color.

Referred to the committee of the whole.

RESOLUTIONS.

On motion of Mr. McClelland,

Resolved, That the committee on the mode of revising and amending the Constitution be instructed to report an article designating the time of election for the several officers mentioned in this Constitution.

Mr. Alvord submitted the following:

Resolved, That when this Convention adjourn on Monday next, July 1st, the same stand adjourned until Saturday, July 6th.

Mr. Roberts moved a call of the House, and the call being sustained, the roll was called, and Messrs. Barnard, Ammon Brown, Burns, J. Clark, O'Brien and N. Pierce were found absent without leave.

On motion of Mr. Roberts,

All further proceedings under the call were dispensed with.

Mr. Alvord moved the previous question, which was seconded by a majority of the members present.

And the question being, "Shall the main question be now put?" it was decided in the affirmative.

The yeas and nays being ordered, the resolution was adopted by the following vote:

YEAS:

Mr. Alvord,	Mr. Gale,	Mr. O'Brien,
Anderson,	Gardiner,	J. D. Pierce,
Backus,	Gibson,	Prevost,
J. Bartow,	Graham,	Roberts,
Beeson,	Green,	M. Robinson,
Alvarado Brown,	Hanscom,	Sullivan,
Asahel Brown,	Hart,	Sutherland,
Burns,	Harvey,	Tiffany,

Bush,	Hascall,	VanValkenburg,
Chandler,	Kinne,	Warden,
Chapel,	Leach,	Webster,
Choate,	Lee,	Wells,
S. Clark,	Marvin,	White,
Comstock,	McLeod,	Whipple,
Daniels,	Moore,	Whittemore,
Desnoyers,	Morrison,	Witherell,
Dimond,	Mowry,	President,
Eastman,		52

NAYS:

Mr. P. R. Adams,	Mr. Crouse,	Mr. Redfield,
W. Adams,	Danforth,	Robertson,
Arzeno,	Fralick,	E. S. Robinson,
Axford,	Hathaway,	Rix Robinson,
Bagg,	Hixon,	Skinner,
Beardsley,	Kingsley,	Soule,
Britain,	Lovell,	Storey,
Butterfield,	McClelland,	Town,
Carr,	Mosher,	Wait,
Conner,	Newberry,	Walker,
Cook,	Orr,	Williams,
Cornell,	N. Pierce,	Woodman,
Crary,	Raynale,	38

Before an announcement of the result, Mr. Crary moved that Messrs J. D. Pierce and Soule be excused from voting, but the Convention refused to excuse, and the delegates recorded their votes as above.

Mr. Chapel moved a reconsideration of the vote by which Mr. Alvord's resolution was adopted; upon which Mr. Hanscom moved the previous question, which was demanded, and the main question was ordered to be now put.

The yeas and nays having been ordered, the motion to reconsider was lost, as follows:

YEAS.

Mr. W. Adams,	Mr. Cornell,	Mr. Raynale,
Anderson,	Crary,	Redfield,
Arzeno,	Crouse,	Robertson,
Axford,	Fralick,	E. S. Robinson,
Bagg,	Hathaway,	Rix Robinson,
Beardsley,	Hixon,	Skinner,
Britain,	Kingsley,	Soule,
Ammon Brown,	Lovell,	Storey,
Bush,	McClelland,	Town,
Butterfield,	Mosher,	Wait,

Chapel,	Newberry,	Walker,
Church,	Orr,	Warden,
Conner,	J. D. Pierce,	Williams,
Cook,	N. Pierce,	Woodman, 42

NAYS.

Mr. Alvord,	Mr. Gale,	Mr. O'Brien,
Backus,	Gardiner,	Prevost,
J. Bartow,	Gibson,	Roberts,
Beeson,	Graham,	M. Robinson,
Alvardo Brown,	Green,	Sturgis,
Asahel Brown,	Hanscom,	Sullivan,
Burns,	Hart,	Sutherland,
Carr,	Harvey,	Tiffany,
Chandler,	Kinne,	Van Valkenburg,
Choate,	Leach,	Webster,
S. Clark,	Lee,	Wells,
Comstock,	Marvin,	White,
Danforth,	McLeod,	Whipple,
Daniels,	Moore,	Whittemore,
Desnoyers,	Morrison,	Witherell,
Dimond,	Mowry,	President,
Eastman,		49

Mr. Williams proposed the following resolution:

Resolved, That no pay shall be allowed to the members of this Convention between Monday, July 1st, and Saturday, July 6th, for which period the Convention stands adjourned, except to those members who remain at the Capitol in attendance upon their duties.

Mr. Webster moved to amend by adding: "and that no per diem be paid to those who have been, or may be absent, except such absence was occasioned by sickness of himself or some member of his family."

Mr. Leach moved to indefinitely postpone the motion; when,

Mr. McClelland moved the previous question; and the same being seconded, the main question was ordered to be now put.

The main question being first on the amendment proposed by Mr. Webster, the same was agreed to.

And the question now recurring on the adoption of the resolution as amended, Mr. Axford called the yeas and nays, and the same being ordered, the resolution was lost, by a tie vote, as follows:

YEAS:

Mr. W. Adams,	Mr. Cornell,	Mr. O'Brien,
Anderson,	Danforth,	Orr,

Axford,
Backus,
Bagg,
Beardsley,
Britain,
Burns,
Bush,
Butterfield,
Chapel,
Choate,
Church,
Conner,
Cook,
Fralick,
Gardiner,
Gibson,
Hanscom,
Hathaway,
Hixon,
Lee,
Marvin,
McClelland,
Morrison,
Mosher,
Mowry,
Newberry,
N. Pierce,
Raynale,
Redfield,
Robertson,
E. S. Robinson,
Rix Robinson,
Sturgis,
Town,
Walker,
Warden,
Whipple,
Williams,
Witherell, 45

NAYS.

Mr. Alvord,
Arzeno,
Barnard,
J. Bartow,
Beeson,
Alvarado Brown,
Ammon Brown,
Asahel Brown,
Carr,
Chandler,
S. Clark,
Comstock,
Crary,
Crouse,
Daniels,
Mr. Desnoyers,
Dimond,
Eastman,
Gale,
Graham,
Green,
Hart,
Harvey,
Kinne,
Leach,
Lovell,
McLeod,
Moore,
J. D. Pierce,
Prevost,
Mr. Roberts,
M. Robinson,
Skinner,
Soule,
Storey,
Sullivan,
Sutherland,
Tiffany,
Van Valkenburg,
Wait,
Wells,
White,
Whittemore,
Woodman,
President, 45

Mr. Hascall offered the following:

Resolved, That during the adjournment voted this morning, the per diem allowance of members and officers of this Convention be suspended, and no charge be allowed therefor.

Pending which, Mr. Hanscom moved that the Convention resolve itself into a committee of the whole on the article entitled "Education."

And the yeas and nays being ordered, the result was as follows:

YEAS:

Mr. Alvord,
Anderson,
Arzeno,
Backus,
Bagg,
Barnard,
J. Bartow,
Mr. Daniels,
Desnoyers,
Dimond,
Eastman,
Fralick,
Gale,
Graham,
Mr. Orr,
J. D. Pierce,
Prevost,
Raynale,
Roberts,
E. S. Robinson,
M. Robinson,

Beeson,
Alvarado Brown,
Asahel Brown,
Burns,
Bush,
Butterfield,
Carr,
Chandler,
Choate,
Comstock,
Crary,
Hanscom,
Hart,
Harvey,
Kingsley,
Kinne,
Leach,
Lee,
Lovell,
Marvin,
Moore,
O'Brien,
Skinner,
Sturgis,
Sullivan,
Sutherland,
Van Valkenburg,
Wait,
Webster,
Wells,
White,
Whittemore,
Witherell, 54

NAYS:

Mr. W. Adams,
Axford,
Britain,
Ammon Brown,
Chapel,
Church,
S. Clark,
Conner,
Cook,
Cornell,
Crouse,
Danforth,
Gardiner,
Mr. Gibson,
Green,
Hascall,
Hathaway,
Hixon,
McClelland,
McLeod,
Morrison,
Mosher,
Mowry,
Newberry,
N. Pierce,
Redfield,
Mr. Robertson,
Rix Robinson,
Soule,
Storey,
Tiffany,
Town,
Walker,
Warden,
Whipple,
Williams,
Woodman,
President, 38

So the Convention resolved itself into a committee of the whole on the article entitled "Education,"

Mr. S. Clark in the chair.

PROCEEDINGS IN COMMITTEE.

Mr. Williams moved to strike out "that may exist," and insert "in means."

And a division of the question being demanded,

The committee agreed to strike out.

Pending the question to insert,

On motion of Mr. Hascall,

The committee rose, reported progress, and asked leave to sit again.

The committee, through their chairman, reported the same back to the Convention, and asked leave to sit again.

Leave was granted.

On motion of Mr. Raynale,

The Convention then adjourned.

Afternoon Session.

Half-past two o'clock.

The President called the Convention to order.

The roll being called, and a quorum of members being in attendance,

The President announced a communication from the Commissioner of the Land Office; which,

On motion of Mr. Cook,

Was laid upon the table and ordered printed.

On motion of Mr. Alvord,

The Convention resolved itself into committee of the whole, on the article entitled "Education,"

Mr. S. Clark in the chair.

PROCEEDINGS IN COMMITTEE.

The question being upon Mr. William's motion to insert "in means," the same was agreed to.

Mr. Cornell offered the following substitute for section 3:

"The Legislature shall establish free schools throughout the State, and provide for their support. After applying the Primary School Fund and such other funds as shall be set apart for the support of such schools, the balance shall be raised by a tax upon the taxable property of the State."

Mr. Witherell moved to strike out "shall" and insert "may."

Which was not adopted.

Mr. Crouse moved to strike out "of" and insert "in." Lost.

On motion of Mr. Witherell,

All after "tax" was stricken out, and "State" inserted before "tax."

Mr. Leach offered the following as a substitute for Mr. Cornell's substitute:

"A primary school shall be kept in each school district in this State at least months in each year.

"The right to attend such schools without charge for tuition, is guarantied to all persons between the ages of four and eighteen years.

"For the support of primary schools, there shall be raised annually, a State tax of not less than cents per scholar, for each scholar returned to the office of the Superintendent of Public Instruction; and such tax, and also the interest of the primary school fund, shall be annually distributed among the several school districts in this State, in proportion to the number of scholars in each, as shown by their returns to the office of the Superintendent of Public Instruction; and any deficiency that may exist in the districts, after the distribution of said moneys, shall be raised by tax on all the taxable property in such districts.

"No district failing to comply withthe requirements of the law shall be entitled to any portion of the State tax or interest of the primary school fund.

The English language shall be taught in all the primary schools in this state."

Mr. Raynale moved to amend the above by striking out "and," eighteen," and inserting after "years," the words "and upwards;" and also, strike out "between," and insert "of."

Which motion did not prevail.

Mr. Walker moved to amend Mr. Cornell's substitute by adding at the end as follows: "and the instruction in all such schools shall be conducted in the English language."

Which the committee disagreed to.

Mr. Raynale moved to strike out of Mr. Leach's substitute the word "eighteen" and insert "twenty-one," which was accepted by Mr. Leach.

Mr. J. D. Pierce moved to strike out all after "instruction," to the words "the taxable."

Mr. Sutherland moved that the committee rise, report progress and ask leave to sit again.

But the committee refused to rise.

The question recurring upon Mr. Pierce's motion, the same was agreed to.

The question then recurring upon Mr. Leach's substitute as amended, the same was disagreed to.

Mr. Bush moved to amend Mr. Cornell's substitute by striking out "shall," and inserting "may."

Which was accepted by Mr. Cornell.

Mr. Fralick moved to amend section 3, by striking out all after "shall," in 1st line, and inserting "provide for a system of primary schools, by which a school shall be kept up and supported in each school district, at least three months in every year; and any school district neglecting to keep up and support such a school, may be deprived of its equal proportion of the interest of the public fund. And the legislature may levy a tax on the whole taxable property of the several townships or cities of this state for the support of said schools."

On motion of Mr. Bagg,

The word "up" was stricken out wherever it occurs in the amendment.

On motion of Mr. Axford,

The committee rose, reported progress, and asked leave to sit again.

The committee, through their chairman, reported the same back to the Convention, and asked and obtained leave to sit again.

On motion of Mr. Van Valkenburg,

The Convention then adjourned.

Lansing, Thursday, June 27, 1850.

The Convention met pursuant to adjournment and was called to order by the President.

Prayer by the Rev. Mr. Atterbury.

The roll being called, Messrs. H. Bartow, Eaton, Edmunds and Willard were absent with leave, and Messrs. J. Clark, Cook, Green, Hart, McClelland, McLeod and White, without leave.

Journal approved.

LEAVE OF ABSENCE.

Mr. Dimond asked and obtained leave of absence for Mr. J. Clark for an indefinite period;

Mr. Arzeno for Mr. McClelland,

Mr. Storey for Mr. McLeod,

Mr. Tiffany for Mr. Green,

Mr. Graham for Mr. Cook, and

Mr. Gardiner for Messrs. Hart and White until Saturday.

THIRD READING OF ARTICLES.

"Article —. Militia," was read a third time, passed, and referred to the committee on arrangement and phraseology.

The Article entitled "Executive Department," coming up for a third reading,

On motion of Mr. Hanscom,

It was laid upon the table.

UNFINISHED BUSINESS.

Mr. Hascall's resolution of yesterday being under consideration, he modified the same so as to read as follows:

Resolved, That during the adjournment voted this morning, the per diem of members of the Convention be suspended. Also, the per diem of officers, except such as shall remain at their duties at the capitol.

Mr. Alvord moved to indefinitely postpone the same.

And the yeas and nays being demanded, the result was as follows:

YEAS:

Mr. P. R. Adams,	Mr. Dimond,	Mr. Prevost,
Alvord,	Eastman,	Raynale,
Arzeno,	Gale,	Roberts,
Barnard,	Graham,	M. Robinson,
J. Bartow,	Harvey,	Soule,
Beardsley,	Hathaway,	Storey,
Beeson,	Kinne,	Sullivan,
Alvarado Brown,	Leach,	Sutherland,
Asahel Brown,	Lee,	Tiffany,
Butterfield,	Marvin,	Van Valkenburg,
Chandler,	Mason,	Webster,
Crary,	Moore,	Wells,
Crouse,	Mosher,	Whittemore,
Desnoyers,	Mowry,	41

NAYS:

Mr. W. Adams,	Mr. Danforth,	Mr. Redfield,
Anderson,	Daniels,	Robertson,
Axford,	Fralick,	E. S. Robinson,
Backus,	Gardiner,	Rix Robinson,
Bagg,	Gibson,	Skinner,
Britain,	Hanscom,	Sturgis,
Ammon Brown,	Hascall,	Town,
Burns,	Hixon,	Wait,
Bush,	Kingsley,	Walker,
Carr,	Lovell,	Warden,
Chapel,	Morrison,	Whipple,
Choate,	Newberry,	Witherell,
Church,	Orr,	Woodman,
S. Clark,	J. D. Pierce,	President,
Conner,	N. Pierce,	44

So the motion to indefinitely postpone was lost.

Mr. Alvord moved to amend the resolution by adding thereto the following:

"And all members who have been heretofore, are now, and who may be hereafter absent, and also those who remain at the capitol during the adjournment, shall receive no per diem."

When, on motion of Mr. Hanscom,

The Convention resolved itself into committee of the whole on the general order,

Mr. J. Bartow in the chair.

PROCEEDINGS IN COMMITTEE.

"Article —, Seat of Government," being under consideration, Mr. Alvord moved to strike out all after "the," in 1st line, and insert "City of Detroit in the county of Wayne."

Mr. J. D. Pierce moved to amend by striking out "Detroit in the county of Wayne," and inserting "New Buffalo in the county of Berrien."

Which did not prevail.

Mr. Alvord's amendment did not prevail.

The committee then proceeded to the consideration of "Article —. Elections."

Mr. Morrison moved to strike out the words included between the word "inhabitant," in third line of section one, and the word "shall," in fifth line, and to insert "of the age aforesaid, who may be a resident of the State at the time of the signing of this Constitution."

But the committee refused to so amend.

Mr. Raynale offered the following substitute for section one:

"In all elections, every white male citizen, above the age of 21 years, having resided in this State six months next preceding an election, shall be entitled to vote at such election; and every white male inhabitant of the age aforesaid, having resided in this State two years in all, shall be entitled to vote at all elections: *Provided*, Such inhabitant shall have resided in this State for the six months next preceding such election, but no such citizen or inhabitant shall be entitled to vote, except in the township or ward of which he is an actual resident."

Mr. Sutherland moved to amend as follows:

Add at the end of section 1: "all foreigners who shall have resided in this State one year previous to the adoption of this Constitution, shall be entitled to vote at any election: *Provided*, That they shall not have such right after five years, if, during that period, they do not become naturalized, and be able to read and speak the English language."

Mr. Witherell moved to amend the above by striking out "and be able to read and speak the English language."

Which motion did not prevail.

Mr. Sutherland's amendment was then rejected.

Mr. Hanscom moved to amend section 1, by inserting in 2d line, after "election," where it first occurs, as follows: "and every white male inhabitant above the age aforesaid, who has resided in this State two years next preceding the adoption of this Constitution, and has declared his intention to become a citizen of the United States, pursuant to law."

Mr. Morrison moved to strike out "two" and insert "one."

Which was not agreed to.

Mr. Goodwin moved to strike out "two years next preceding the adoption of this Constitution," and insert "one year prior to the signing of this Constitution."

Which motion did not prevail.

Mr. Walker moved to strike out "has resided," and insert "shall have resided;" also, strike out the words "next preceding the adoption of this Constitution."

Which was disagreed to.

The question then recurring upon the amendment of Mr. Hanscom, the same was not adopted.

Mr. Witherell moved to amend section 1 by inserting after "aforesaid," in 5th line: "but no person, not a citizen of the United States, shall be allowed to vote after he may have resided five years in this State, unless he has or shall become naturalized."

But the committee refused to so amend.

Mr. Beeson moved to insert after the word "election," in 5th line, "if born within the United States."

Mr. Storey moved to strike out all after "resident," in sixth line of section one.

But the committee refused to strike out.

The question then recurring upon Mr. Raynale's substitute, the same was not adopted.

Mr. Orr moved to strike out "white," in 1st line of section 1.

Pending which,

On motion of Mr. S. Clark,

The committee rose, reported back "Article —, Seat of Government," without amendment, and asked to be discharged from its further consideration; also reported progress on "Article —, Elections," and asked leave to sit again.

The committee, through their chairman, reported back to the Convention the Article entitled "Seat of Government," without amendment, from the further consideration of which they asked to be and were discharged.

On motion of Mr. Kingsley,

The Convention then adjourned.

Afternoon Session.

Half-past two o'clock.

The Convention was called to order by the President.

And a quorum of members being in attendance,

The article entitled "Seat of Government," as follows: "The seat of government of the State shall be in the township of Lansing in the county of Ingham, where it is now located," was ordered engrossed for a third reading; when,

On motion of Mr. Crary,

The 37th rule was suspended.

And the question being, "shall the Article pass?" it was decided in the affirmative, as follows:

YEAS.

Mr. P. R. Adams,	Mr. Danforth,	Mr. N. Pierce,
W. Adams,	Daniels,	Raynale,
Alvord,	Desnoyers,	Redfield,
Anderson,	Dimond,	Roberts,
Arzeno,	Eastman,	Robertson,
Axford,	Fralick,	E. S. Robinson,
Backus,	Gale,	M. Robinson,
Bagg,	Gardiner,	Rix Robinson,

Barnard,	Gibson,	Skinner,
J. Bartow,	Hanscom,	Soule,
Beardsley,	Harvey,	Storey,
Beeson,	Hascall,	Sturgis,
Britain,	Hathaway,	Tiffany,
Ammon Brown,	Hixon,	Town,
Asahel Brown,	Kingsley,	VanValkenburg,
Burns,	Leach,	Wait,
Bush,	Lee,	Walker,
Butterfield,	Lovell,	Warden,
Carr,	Marvin,	Webster,
Chandler,	Mason,	Wells,
Chapel,	Moore,	Whipple,
Choate,	Morrison,	Whittemore,
Church,	Mosher,	Williams,
S. Clark,	Newberry,	Witherell,
Cornell,	O'Brien,	Woodman,
Crary,	Orr,	President,
Crouse,	J. D. Pierce,	80

NAYS. 0

Mr. Whittemore, by consent, asked and obtained leave of absence for Mr. Mowry till Monday, 8th July, next.

On motion of Mr. N. Pierce,

Resolved, That the vote of this Convention adjourning from Monday, July 1st, until Saturday, July 6th, be and the same is hereby rescinded.

On motion of Mr. Raynale,

The Convention resolved itself into committee of the whole on the general order,

Mr. J. Bartow in the chair.

PROCEEDINGS IN COMMITTEE.

"Article —, Elections," being under consideration; and

The question being upon Mr. Orr's motion, to strike out "white," of section 1,

The committee refused to strike out.

Mr. Raynale offered the following as a substitute for section one:

"In all elections, every white male citizen above the age of 21 years, having resided in this State six months next preceding an election, shall be entitled to vote at such election: and every white male inhabitant of the age aforesaid, having resided in this

State two years in all, and having filed his intentions to become a citizen of the United States, shall be entitled to vote at all elections: *Provided*, Such inhabitant shall have resided in this State for the six months next preceding such election; but no such citizen or inhabitant shall be entitled to vote, except in the township or ward of which he is an actual resident."

Which was not adopted.

Mr. Williams moved to strike out "or while a student of any seminary of learning," in section 5.

Which motion did not prevail.

On motion of Mr. Crary,

The words "Constitution or," were inserted at the end of 1st line of section 6.

On motion of Mr. Gale,

The words "*non compos mentis*," in 4th line of section 6, were stricken out, and "not of sound mind," inserted.

On motion of Mr. Crary,

Section 8 was stricken out.

On motion of Mr. Leach,

The blanks in the resolution were filled with "1st January, 1851."

Mr. Raynale moved to strike out all after "*Resolved.*"

But the committee refused to strike out.

Mr. Crary moved to strike out of section 6, the words "or who shall make or become directly or indirectly interested in any bet or wager, pending upon the result of any election in this State," and insert "and for depriving any person who shall make or become directly or indirectly interested in any bet or wager depending upon the result of any election, from the right to vote at such election."

Which was agreed to.

Mr. Raynale moved to strike out of section 6, the words "all persons who have been or may be convicted of bribery, or larceny, or any infamous crime."

On motion of Mr. Bush,

Section six was stricken out.

On motion of Mr. Hanscom,

The following was substituted for said section:

"Laws may be passed excluding from the right of suffrage, and from holding any office under the laws of this State, persons who may be convicted of an infamous crime, are *non compos mentis* or insane."

On motion of Mr. Witherell,

The committee rose, reported the article back to the Convention with amendments, asked their concurrence therein, and to be discharged from the further consideration of said article.

The committee, through their chairman, reported back the Article entitled "Elections," with sundry amendments, in which the concurrence of the Convention was asked.

The committee was discharged from the further consideration of the article; and the same was laid upon the table.

On motion of Mr. J. Bartow,

The Convention then adjourned.

Lansing, Friday, June 28, 1850.

The Convention met at the usual hour and was called to order by the President.

Prayer by the Rev. Mr. Sanford.

Roll called, and Messrs. H. Bartow, J. Clark, Cook, Edmunds, Hart, McClelland, McLeod, White and Willard were absent on leave, and Messrs. P. R. Adams, Alvord, Barnard, Beeson, Alvarado Brown, Chandler, Comstock, Connor, Dimond, Graham, Harvey, Kinne, Mowry, J. D. Pierce, Sullivan, Wait and Webster were absent without leave.

Journal approved.

LEAVE OF ABSENCE

Was granted to Messrs. P. R. Adams, Alvord, Alvarado Brown, Beeson, Chandler, Dimond, J. D. Pierce, Sullivan and Webster for an indefinite period.

To Messrs. Barnard, Harvey, Hixon and Waite till Wednesday next, and

To Mr. Whittemore till Monday, July 8th, next.

REPORTS.

Mr. Rix Robinson, from the committee on county officers and county government, submitted an article entitled "County Officers and County Government," which was read a first and second time by its title, referred to the committee of the whole and ordered printed.

RESOLUTIONS.

Mr. Redfield offered the following:

Resolved, That when the Convention adjourn, it shall stand adjourned until Monday, the eighth of July, and that during the said adjournment, the pay of members and officers shall be suspended.

Mr. Bagg offered as a substitute for the same, the following:

Resolved, That the remaining members, and the officers of this Convention have leave of absence till July 6th, to take place from and after the 29th instant.

Mr. Storey moved to lay the resolution on the table; and the motion prevailed by the following vote:

YEAS.

Mr. W. Adams,	Mr. Green,	Mr. Roberts,
Arzeno,	Hanscom,	E. S. Robinson,
Axford,	Leach,	M. Robinson,
J. Bartow,	Lee,	Skinner,
Beardsley,	Lovell,	Soule,
Bush,	Marvin,	Storey,
Carr,	Moore,	Sturgis,
Choate,	Mosher,	Sutherland,
Crary,	Newberry,	Tiffany,
Crouse,	O'Brien,	VanValkenburg,
Daniels,	Orr,	Warden,
Eaton,	N. Pierce,	Woodman,
Gale,	Raynale,	38

NAYS.

Mr. Backus,	Mr. Fralick,	Mr. Rix Robinson,
Britain,	Gardiner,	Town,
Asahel Brown,	Hascall,	Walker,
Burns,	Hathaway,	Wells,
Chapel,	Mason,	Whipple,
Church,	Prevost,	Williams,
S. Clark,	Redfield,	Witherell,
Cornell,	Robertson,	President, 24

Mr. Britain submitted the following:

Resolved, That when this Convention adjourn, it adjourn to meet on Wednesday, the 10th day of July next, and that no compensation be allowed the members and officers of this Convention during said adjournment.

Mr. Woodman moved to indefinitely postpone the same.

Pending which,

Mr. Storey moved to go into committee of the whole on the general order.

Mr. Britain demanded the yeas and nays, and the same were taken with the following result:

YEAS.

Mr. Arzeno,	Mr. Green,	Mr. N. Pierce,
Axford,	Hanscom,	Raynale,
J. Bartow,	Kingsley,	E. S. Robinson,
Beardsley,	Leach,	Skinner,
Bush,	Lovell,	Soule,
Carr,	Marvin,	Storey,
Crary,	Moore,	Sturgis,
Crouse,	Morrison,	Sutherland,
Danforth,	Mosher,	Tiffany,
Daniels,	Newberry,	Van Valkenburg,
Eastman,	O'Brien,	Walker,
Eaton,	Orr,	Woodman,
Gale,		37

NAYS.

Mr. W. Adams,	Mr. Gardiner,	Mr. Rix Robinson,
Backus,	Hascall,	Town,
Britain,	Hathaway,	Warden,
Asahel Brown,	Lee,	Wells,
Chapel,	Mason,	Whipple,
Church,	Prevost,	Williams,
S. Clark,	Redfield,	Witherell,
Cornell,	Robertson,	President,
Fralick,		25

So the Convention resolved itself into committee of the whole on the general order,

Mr. Williams in the chair.

PROCEEDINGS IN COMMITTEE.

Mr. Walker moved that the committee rise.

Which was not agreed to.

The committee took up for consideration, "Article —, State Officers;"

And the question being upon Mr. Robertson's motion to amend by striking out "who shall be ex officio," and inserting "a," of section 1, line 2, made on the 24th inst.,

On motion of Mr. Hathaway,

The committee rose, reported progress, and asked leave to sit again.

—

The committee, through their chairman, reported progress and asked leave to sit again.

Leave was granted.

On motion of Mr. Mason,

The Convention adjourned.

—

Afternoon Session.

Half-past two o'clock.

The Convention was called to order by the President.

A quorum of members in attendance.

Mr. Moore asked leave of absence for Mr. Conner for an indefinite period.

The yeas and nays were ordered on the question, when,

On motion of Mr. Rix Robinson,

The same was laid upon the table.

Mr. Britain asked leave of absence for Mr. Hascall indefinitely.

Upon which the yeas and nays were ordered.

Mr. Crary moved to lay the same upon the table.

Pending which,

On motion of Mr. Crary,

The Convention resolved itself into committee of the whole on the general order, by the following vote:

YEAS:

Mr. W. Adams,	Mr. Eaton,	Mr. N. Pierce,
Anderson,	Fralick,	Prevost,
Arzeno,	Gale,	Raynale,
J. Bartow,	Green,	E. S. Robinson,
Bush,	Hanscom,	Rix Robinson,
Butterfield,	Hathaway,	Skinner,
Carr,	Kingley,	Storey,
Chapel,	Lovell,	Sturgis,
Church,	Mason,	Tiffany,

Cornell,	Morrison,	VanValkenburg,
Crary,	Mosher,	Walker,
Crouse,	Newberry,	Warden,
Danforth,	O'Brien,	Whipple,
Daniels,	Orr,	Woodman,
Eastman,		43

NAYS:

Mr. Axford,	Mr. Asahel Brown,	Mr. Robertson,
Backus,	S. Clark,	Witherell,
Beardsley,	Gardiner,	President,
Britain,	McLeod,	11

Mr. Morrison in the chair.

PROCEEDINGS IN COMMITTEE.

"Article —, State Officers," being under consideration,

And the question being on Mr. Robertson's motion to strike out "who shall be ex officio," and inserting "a," the same prevailed.

Mr. Crouse moved to strike out "Superintendent of Public Instruction," in 1st line, and insert after "years," in 4th line, "and a Superintendent of Public Instruction, who shall hold his office for four years."

And a division of the question being demanded, the committee refused to strike out.

Mr. Fralick offered the following as a substitute for section 1:

"There shall be a Secretary of State, who shall be ex officio Superintendent of Public Instruction, a State Treasurer, who shall be ex officio Commissioner of the Land Office, and an Auditor General elected at each biennial general election, who shall hold their respective offices for the term of two years, and shall perform such duties as may be prescribed by law."

Which was disagreed to.

Mr. Chapel offered the following substitute:

"There shall be a Secretary of State, who shall be ex officio Superintendent of Public Instruction, a Commissioner of the Land Office, who shall be ex officio State Treasurer, an Auditor General and an Attorney General, elected at each biennial general election, who shall hold their respective offices for the term of two years, and shall perform such duties as may be prescribed by law."

Which was not adopted.

On motion of Mr. Britain,

Section 1 was amended by inserting after "years," in line 4 "each of whom shall keep an office at the seat of government."

Mr. McLeod moved to strike out section 2.

But the committee refused to strike out,

On motion of Mr. Hanscom,

The words "a temporary," in 2nd line of section 3, were stricken out.

On motion of Mr. Bush,

All after "shall," in 1st line of section 4, to "constitute," in 2nd line, were stricken out.

Mr. Backus moved to strike out all after "government," in 2nd line as printed to "and," in 4th line.

Which was disagreed to.

Mr. Hanscom moved that the committee rise, report progress and ask leave to sit again.

But the committee refused to rise.

On motion of Mr. Chapel,

"Auditor General" was stricken out, and "Commissioner of the State Land Office" inserted.

On motion of Mr. Crary,

The following was inserted at the end of section 6:

"The inspectors shall have the charge and superintendence of the State Prison, and shall appoint all the officers therein. All vacancies in the office of inspector shall be filled by the Governor, till the next election."

On motion of Mr. Raynale,

The word "two" was stricken out of last line of section 6, and "six" inserted.

On motion of Mr. McLeod,

The committee rose, reported the article back with amendments in which the concurrence of the Convention was asked, and to be discharged from the further consideration of the same.

—

The committee, through their chairman, reported "Article —, State Officers," with certain amendments, in which the concurrence of the Convention was asked.

Mr. McLeod moved a call of the House, which was demanded, and there being a quorum in attendance,

On motion of Mr. Britain,

All further proceedings under the call were dispensed with.

The article entitled "State Officers" being under consideration, Mr. Backus moved that the same be laid upon the table and ordered printed.

A division of the question being had, the article was laid upon the table, but the Convention refused to print.

Mr. Hanscom moved the Convention adjourn.

Which was lost.

The question now recurring on the motion to lay upon the table. the application for leave of absence for Mr. Hascall, made prior to going into committee of the whole,

The motion to lay upon the table was lost as follows:

YEAS.

Mr. Arzeno,	Mr. Lee,	Mr. Raynale,
Asahel Brown,	Mason,	Rix Robinson,
Carr,	McLeod,	President. 9

NAYS.

Mr. W. Adams,	Mr. Daniels,	Mr. Robertson,
Axford,	Eastman,	E. S. Robinson,
Backus,	Eaton,	Skinner,
Beardsley,	Fralick,	Soule,
Britain,	Gale,	Storey,
Burns,	Gardiner,	Sturgis,
Bush,	Hathaway,	Sutherland,
Butterfield,	Kingsley.	Tiffany,
Chapel,	Lovell,	Van Valkenburg,
Church,	Morrison,	Walker,
S. Clark,	Mosher,	Warden,
Cornell,	Newberry,	Whipple,
Crary,	O'Brien,	Witherell,
Crouse,	Orr,	Woodman,
Danforth,	N. Pierce,	44

Upon the question of granting leave, the yeas and nays having been ordered, the result was as follows:

YEAS.

Mr. W. Adams,	Mr. Eastman,	Mr. Orr,
Anderson,	Eaton,	N. Pierce,
Arzeno,	Fralick,	Robertson,
Backus,	Gale,	E. S. Robinson,

Beardsley,	Gardiner,	Skinner,
Asahel Brown,	Hanscom,	Soule,
Burns,	Hathaway,	Storey,
Bush,	Kingsley,	Sturgis,
Chapel,	Lee,	Sutherland,
Church,	Lovell,	Tiffany,
Cornell,	Mason,	Van Valkenburg,
Crary,	McLeod,	Walker,
Crouse,	Morrison,	Whipple,
Danforth,	Mosher,	Woodman,
Daniels,	O'Brien,	President, 45

NAYS.

Mr. Axford,	Mr. Newberry,	Mr. Rix Robinson,
Carr,	Roberts,	Warden,
S. Clark,		7

So leave was granted Mr. Hascall for an indefinite period.

On motion of Mr. Britain,

Resolved, That article 8, entitled "Executive Department," be recommitted to the committee on executive department, with instructions to inquire into the expediency of so amending said article as to provide for the election of Speaker of the House of Representatives by the people.

Mr. Gale asked and obtained leave of absence for Mr. Leach for an indefinite period.

Mr. Hanscom moved that the Convention adjourn.

But the Convention refused to adjourn.

Mr. Hanscom moved that the Convention resolve itself into committee of the whole on the general order.

Upon which, the yeas and nays were demanded.

When, upon calling the roll, a quorum of members not being in attendance,

On motion of Mr. Storey,

A call of the House was ordered.

The roll being called, and a quorum of members answering to their names,

On motion of Mr. Storey,

All further proceedings under the call were dispensed with; when

On motion of Mr. Danforth,

The Convention adjourned.

Lansing, Saturday, June 29, 1850.

The Convention met at the usual hour and was called to order by the President.

Prayer by the Rev. Mr. Tooker.

Roll called, and Messrs. P. R. Adams, Alvord, Barnard, H. Bartow, Beeson, Alvarado Brown, Chandler, J. Clark, Cook, Dimond, Edmunds, Hart, Harvey, Hascall, Hixon, Leach, McClelland, McLeod, J. D. Pierce, M. Robinson, Sullivan, Wait, Webster, White, Whittemore and Willard were absent with leave; and Messrs. Bagg, Ammon Brown, Choate, Comstock, Conner, Desnoyers, Gibson, Graham, Green, Kinne, Lee, Marvin, Moore, Morrison, Mowry, O'Brien, Redfield, Town, Wells and Williams without leave.

The President called Mr. Roberts to the chair.

RESOLUTIONS.

Mr. Hanscom offered the following, which were adopted:

Resolved, That the President of this Convention be paid the same amount of mileage allowed to other members, and that he receive six dollars per day for his per diem, and that the same shall be paid upon the certificate of one of the Secretaries of the Convention.

Resolved, That the same per diem and mileage allowed to the present officers of the Convention, be paid to the Secretary and Sergeant-at-Arms *pro tem*, and that the usual certificate be drawn therefor.

On motion of Mr. S. Clark,

The vote by which the above resolutions were adopted, was reconsidered.

Mr. Butterfield moved the indefinite postponement of the 2d resolution.

Which was lost.

On motion of Mr. Eaton,

So much as related to mileage in the same, was stricken out.

The resolutions were then severally adopted.

Mr. Storey moved the Convention resolve itself into committee of the whole on the general order.

But the motion did not prevail.

On motion of Mr. Witherell,

A call of the House was had, and a quorum being found present,

All further proceedings under the call were dispensed with.

Mr. Storey renewed his motion to go into committee of the whole.

And the same was again lost.

The President took the chair.

Mr. Roberts moved to adjourn till Monday, 8th July next.

Mr. Van Valkenburg moved to amend by inserting "Wednesday, 10th."

Mr. Chapel offered the following as a substitute.

Resolved, That this Convention adjourn till Monday, July 8th, next, and that during the period of adjournment, no member or officer shall be entitled to his per diem.

Mr. Eaton moved to insert in lieu of "July 8," "September 1."

A call of the House being had, and a quorum of members not being in attendance,

All further proceedings under the call were dispensed with.

Mr. Storey offered the following:

Whereas, a majority of the members of this Convention, by obtaining leave of absence, or otherwise, have absented themselves, and the number present is now reduced to less than a quorum, and the only power left those in attendance is to adjourn or send the Sergeant-at-Arms after the absentees; and

Whereas, there is no reasonable prospect of obtaining the attendance of a quornm at an earlier day than Tuesday, July 9th; therefore,

Resolved, That this Convention stand adjourned until the 9th day of July, at half-past 8 o'clock, A. M.

The yeas and nays being asked for, and the President deciding that it was in order to demand the same,

Mr. Mason appealed from the decision of the chair.

And the question being, "shall the decision of the chair stand as the decision of the Convention," it was decided in the affirmative.

A division of the question was ordered, and the resolution was adopted by the following vote:

YEAS.

Mr. Arzeno,	Mr. Hanscom,	Mr. Skinner,
Axford,	Hathaway,	Soule,

J. Bartow,	Kingsley,	Storey,
Beardsley,	Mason,	Sutherland,
Burns,	Mosher,	Tiffany,
Butterfield,	Newberry,	Van Valkenburg,
Carr,	Prevost,	Walker,
Church,	Kaynale,	Whipple,
Crary,	Roberts,	Witherell,
Eastman,	Robertson,	Woodman,
Gardiner,	E. S. Robinson,	32

NAYS.

Mr. W. Adams,	Mr. S. Clark,	Mr. Gale,
Anderson,	Cornell,	Orr,
Backus,	Crouse,	N. Pierce,
Britain,	Danforth,	Rix Robinson,
Asahel Brown,	Daniels,	Sturgis,
Bush,	Eaton,	President.
Chapel,	Fralick,	20

So the President declared the Convention adjourned until Tuesday, the 9th day of July next, at half-past 8 o'clock, A. M.

Lansing, Tuesday, July 9, 1850.

The Convention met pursuant to adjournment and was called to order by the President.

Prayer by the Rev. Mr. Sanford.

The roll being called a quorum of members was in attendance.

The journal of the last days proceedings was approved.

On motion of Mr. Roberts,

The Convention resolved itself into committee of the whole on the general order,

Mr. Eaton in the chair.

PROCEEDINGS IN COMMITTEE.

Mr. Crary moved to take up for consideration the article on corporations.

Which did not prevail.

On motion of Mr. Walker,

The article on education was passed over.

The committee then proceeded to the consideration of

Article —. County Offices and County Government.

Mr. Fralick moved to strike out of line 2, section 2, the word "six," and insert "four."

And a division of the question being had, the committee refused to strike out.

Mr. Fralick moved to add at the end of section 2, "except the county of Wayne."

Which was not agreed to.

Mr. Hanscom moved to strike out section 2.

But the committee refused to strike out.

On motion of Mr. Crary,

The words "and one or more coroners," were stricken out of the 3d line of section 3.

On motion of Mr. Kingsley,

The words "who shall be ex efficio," in 2d line of section 3, were stricken out, and "a" inserted.

Mr. Church moved to amend section 3 by inserting after "county," where it first occurs in line 2, "and register of deeds," and by striking out in lines 2 and 3 the words "register of deeds." Also, by adding at the end of the section, "in counties containing more than 25,000 inhabitants, the offices of county clerk and register of deeds may be separated by the legislature."

Pending which, on motion of Mr. Bagg,

The committee rose, reported progress, and asked leave to sit again.

The committee, through their Chairman, reported the same back to the Convention, and asked and obtained leave to sit again.

On motion of Mr. Cook,

The Convention then adjourned.

Afternoon Session.

½ past 2 o'clock.

The Convention was called to order by the President.

Roll called and a quorum present.

On motion of Mr. McClelland,

The Convention then resolved itself into committee of the whole on the general order.

Mr. Eaton in the chair.

PROCEEDINGS IN COMMITTEE OF THE WHOLE.

The committee resumed the consideration of "Article —. County Officers and County Government."

The question being upon Mr. Church's amendment, and a division of the same being had, the committee refused to strike out.

Mr. Morrison moved to add at the end of section 3, "it shall be competent for the Board of Supervisors in the several counties containing less than 25,000 inhabitants, to combine the offices of County Clerk and Register of Deeds in one office."

Mr. J. D. Pierce moved to strike out "25,000" and insert "20,000," and a division of the question being called for, the committee struck out "25,000."

Mr. Cook moved to fill the blank with "30,000."

Which motion did not prevail.

The question recurring upon filling the blank with "20,000," the same did not prevail.

On motion of Mr. Crary,

The words "containing less than ——— inhabitants" were stricken out.

On motion of Mr. Crary,

The words "or disconnect the same," were added to the amendment of Mr. Morrison.

Mr. Britain moved to amend by inserting after "deeds," the words "or county clerk and judge of probate."

Which was not agreed to.

Mr. Morrison's amendment, as amended, was then adopted.

On motion of Mr. Walker,

The words "who shall be the clerk of all the courts of record to be held in the county," were stricken out of section 3.

Mr. Roberts offered the following as a substitute for the section:

"In each organized county there shall be one sheriff, a county clerk, a county treasurer, a county surveyor, and a prosecuting attorney, chosen by the qualified electors thereof, once in two years, and as often as vacancies shall happen, and whose duties and powers shall be prescribed by law: counties having more than twenty thousand inhabitants may separate the duties of register of deeds from the office of county clerk in such manner as the legislature may prescribe."

On motion of Mr. Walker,

The words "a register of deeds" were inserted after the word "treasurer."

Mr. Willard moved that the committee rise, report progress and ask leave to sit again.

But the committee refused to rise.

On motion of Mr. Crary,

All after "law," of the substitute, was stricken out.

The question then recurring upon the adoption of the substitute, and a division of the same being demanded, the committee refused to strike out section 3.

On motion of Mr. Robertson,

Section 4 was amended by striking out "prosecuting attorney," and inserting "register of deeds."

Mr. Willard moved to strike out "judge of probate;" but the committee refused to strike out.

On motion of Mr. Sutherland,

Section 6 was amended by adding at the end thereof "and as shall be prescribed by law."

On motion of Mr. Fralick,

The words "to be uniform throughout the state," were stricken out of section 6.

Mr. McClelland moved to amend section 8 by striking out to and including "mill dams," and inserting, "The board of supervisors shall have the exclusive power of organizing and dividing townships."

Which motion did not prevail.

Mr. Sutherland moved to add to section 8: "and exclusive power to pass acts creating local corporations under general laws and for such other local purposes and in such manner as the Legislature shall by law prescribe."

Pending which, on motion of Mr. Moore,

The committee rose, reported progress, and asked leave to sit again.

The committee, through their chairman, reported the same back to the convention and asked leave to sit again.

Leave was granted.

On motion of Mr. Van Valkenburg,

The Convention then adjourned.

Lansing, Wednesday, July 10, 1850.

The Convention met pursuant to adjournment and was called to order by the President.

Prayer by the Rev. Mr. Sanford.

The roll being called, there were absent on leave: Messrs. P. R. Adams and Leach, and without leave, Messrs. Daniels, Green, Hathaway, Lee, O'Brien, N. Pierce, Prevost, Raynale and Witherell.

Journal approved.

PETITIONS.

By Mr. Eaton: of David Carr and 33 others, praying for the abolition of the present grand jury system.

Referred to the committee on the bill of rights.

By Mr. McClelland: of Charles Vellet and others, of La Salle, Monroe county, about township matters.

Referred to the committee on township officers and township government.

By the President: Memorial of Geo. E. Hand and 25 others, of the bar of Wayne county, asking that the Convention will make the supreme court a separate and distinct court from the circuit, and held by separate judges.

Laid on the table.

By Mr. Cornell: of J. E. McAllister and 32 others, praying that the legislature may be prohibited from legalizing the sale of alcoholic drinks as a beverage.

Referred to the select committee upon similar subject.

By Mr. H. Bartow: of citizens of Ionia county, that an article may be incorporated in the amended constitution prohibiting the sale, manufacture or importation of intoxicating liquors, except for mechanical or medicinal purposes; also,

By Mr. Robertson: of I. B. Dickinson and sixty three others, praying for the same.

Referred to the select committee on the subject.

REPORTS.

Mr. J. Bartow, from the committee on the organization of the government of cities and villages, reported an article entitled

"Of Cities and Villages."

Which was read a first and second time by its title, referred to the committee of the whole and ordered printed.

Mr. Worden, from the committee on the punishment of crimes, to whom was referred a resolution directing said committee to inquire into the expediency of providing for the abolition of capital punishment, reported

"Article —. The punishment of death is forever prohibited in this State."

Which was read the first and second time and referred to the committee of the whole.

MOTIONS AND NOTICES.

Mr. McClelland gave notice that on to-morrow he would call up the article entitled "Legislative Department."

On motion of Mr. Cook,

The Convention resolved itself into committee of the whole, on the general order,

Mr. Eaton in the chair.

—

PROCEEDINGS IN COMMITTEE.

The committee resumed the consideration of Mr. Sutherland's amendment, which was to add at the end of section 8, "and exclusive power to pass acts creating local corporations under general laws, and for such other local purposes, and in such manner as the legislature shall by law prescribe."

The amendment did not prevail.

Mr. Walker moved to amend section 8 by inserting after "mill dams," the words "across streams not actually navigable."

Which was not agreed to.

On motion of Mr. J. Clark,

The words "or mill-dams," were stricken out of 2d line of section 8.

Mr. Fralick moved to strike out of section 8 the words, "and may grant privileges to construct bridges or mill dams, or to lay out roads in their respective counties."

Pending which, on motion of Mr. Cook,

The words "grant privileges to construct" were stricken out of section 8, and "authorizing the construction of," inserted.

The question then recurring upon Mr. Fralick's amendment, the committee refused to strike out.

On motion of Mr. McClelland,

Section 8 was amended so that the first clause would read as follows: "The board of supervisors of all organized counties shall have the exclusive power to organize new townships."

Mr. Britain offered the following as a substitute for section 8:

The board of supervisors shall have power to lay out county roads, authorize and provide for the construction of bridges, and may change the boundaries of townships in their respective counties; but no such change shall take effect until approved by a majority of the votes cast upon that subject by the electors of each of the townships effected by the change, in such manner as shall be provided by the Legislature. The Legislature shall, by general laws, provide for the organization of any United States surveyed township by the inhabitants thereof, whenever said township shall contain —— inhabitants; provided the township from which said township separates shall contain —— inhabitants; and for the organization of any legally established county by the inhabitants thereof, whenever said county shall contain —— inhabitants, provided the county from which it separates shall contain —— inhabitants.

Mr. Willard moved that the committee rise, report progress and ask leave to sit again.

But the committee refused to rise.

Mr. Fralick moved to insert after counties, in 2d line, "but the expense of laying out, constructing, and the right of way of said roads shall in all cases be paid by the township in which said roads are laid out or constructed."

Which motion did not prevail.

On motion of Mr. Storey,

The committee rose, reported progress and asked leave to sit again.

The committee, through their chairman, reported the same back to the Convention and asked leave to sit again.

Leave was granted.

On motion of Mr. McClelland,

The Convention then adjourned.

Afternoon Session.

Half-past two o'clock.

The President called the Convention to order.

A quorum of members in attendance.

On motion of Mr. Cook,

The Convention resolved itself into committee of the whole on the general order.

Mr. Eaton in the chair.

PROCEEDINGS IN COMMITTEE.

The committee resumed the consideration of "Article —, County Officers and County Government."

And the question being upon Mr. Britain's substitute for section 8, the same was modified by striking out "and provide for," and inserting after "power," in 1st line, "to authorise the."

And a division of the question being called for, the committee refused to strike out section 8.

Mr. Hanscom offered the following substitute for section 8.

"The Legislature shall, by general laws, provide for the organization and division of townships and counties; for the construction of bridges, the laying out of roads, and the erection of mill dams."

Mr. Eastman moved to add to the substitute "and the removal of county sites."

Which was not agreed to.

Mr. Cook moved to strike out "and division."

But the committee refused to strike out.

The substitute was not adopted.

Mr. Crouse moved to add to section 8 as follows: "whenever any board of Supervisors shall have organized any new township, they shall cause to be filed a certificate of the fact, together with the name and boundaries of the same, in the office of the Secretary of State."

Which did not prevail.

Mr. Van Valkenburg moved to strike out "two-thirds" and insert "majority:" and a division of the question being demanded,

The committee refused to strike out.

Mr. McLeod moved to strike out section 9.

But the committee refused to strike out.

Mr. Fralick offered the following substitute for section 10.

"Each Board of Supervisors may borrow, when necessary for the erection of public buildings of the county, or the building of bridges therein, any sum of money not exceeding 15,000 dollars in all, or may raise the same by a tax; but no Board of Supervisors shall borrow or raise by a tax for such purposes more than $2,000 in any one year unless authorized by a vote of the majority of the electors of the county, as may be prescribed by law."

Mr. Bush moved to strike out "borrow or," in 1st line of section 10.

Which motion was disagreed to.

Mr. Morrison moved to strike out "2000" and insert "1000;" and the question being divided, the committee struck out "2000."

Mr. Moore moved to fill the blank with "5000."

Which was not agreed to.

Mr. Rix Robinson moved to fill the blank with "2000."

Which was negatived.

The question then recurring upon Mr. Morrison's motion, the blank was filled with "1000."

Mr. Hascall moved to strike out "of," where it last occurs in last line of section 10, and insert "voting therefor in."

Which was disagreed to.

The question then recurring upon the substitute of Mr. Fralick, and a division of the question being called for, the committee refused to strike out section 10.

Mr. McLeod moved to strike out all after "counties," in 2d line of section 11.

Mr. J. D. Pierce moved to strike out "alteration by," in 2d line of section 11, and "or otherwise," in 3d line.

Pending which, on motion of Mr. J. Clark,

The committee rose, reported progress and asked leave to sit again.

The committee, through their chairman, reported the same back to the Convention, and asked leave to sit again.

Leave was granted.

On motion of Mr. Skinner.

The Convention adjourned.

Lansing, Thursday, July 11, 1850.

The President called the Convention to order at the usual hour.

Prayer by the Rev. Mr. Atterbury.

The roll being called, there was found absent with leave Messrs. P. R. Adams and Leach; and without leave, Messrs. Daniels, Hathaway, O'Brien, Raynale and Witherell.

Journal approved.

ABSENCE.

Mr. Comstock asked and obtained leave for Mr. Daniels until Saturday next.

PETITIONS.

By Mr. Tiffany: of the members of the bar of Lenawee county, for a separate supreme court.

Laid upon the table.

By Mr. Hascall: of Charles E. Johnson and 51 others, citizens of Kalamazoo county, praying that the traffic in ardent spirits as a beverage be prohibited.

Referred to select committee upon that subject.

By Mr. White: of Henry Wheelock and 69 others, of Lapeer county, for the equalization and collection of taxes.

Referred to the committee on finance and taxation.

By Mr. Fralick: of H. Warner and 74 others, citizens of Wayne county, praying for the adoption in the constitution of an article providing for single senatorial and representative districts.

Laid upon the table.

RESOLUTIONS.

Mr. McClelland proposed the following amendment to the 13th rule of the Convention:

Add thereto the words "which shall be the section or article under consideration, as the Convention may direct."

Upon which, after some debate, Mr. McClelland moved the previous question; and the same being seconded, the main question was ordered to be now put.

Mr. Gardiner asked the yeas and nays upon the adoption of the amendment; and the same being demanded, the amendment was made by a two-thirds vote, as follows:

YEAS.

Mr. W. Adams,
Alvord,
Arzeno,
Axford,
Backus,
Barnard,
H. Bartow,
Beardsley,
Beeson,
Alvarado Brown,
Ammon Brown,
Burns,
Butterfield,
Chandler,
Chapel,
Choate,
Church,
J. Clark,
S. Clark,
Comstock,
Cook,
Cornell,
Crary,
Crouse,

Mr. Danforth,
Desnoyers,
Dimond,
Eastman,
Fralick,
Gibson,
Graham,
Green,
Hanscom,
Hart,
Harvey,
Kinne,
Lee,
Lovell,
Marvin,
Mason,
McClelland,
Moore,
Morrison,
Mosher,
Mowry,
Newberry,
J. D. Pierce,

Mr. Prevost,
Redfield,
Roberts,
M. Robinson,
Rix Robinson,
Skinner,
Soule,
Storey,
Sturgis,
Sullivan,
Sutherland,
Tiffany,
Town,
Van Valkenburg,
Walker,
Warden,
White,
Whipple,
Whittemore,
Williams,
Willard,
Woodman,
President,

70

NAYS.

Mr. Anderson,
Bagg,

Mr. Eaton,
Edmunds,

Mr. Orr,
N. Pierce,

J. Bartow,	Gale,	Robertson,
Britain,	Gardiner,	E. S. Robinson,
Asahel Brown,	Hascall,	Wait,
Bush,	Hixon,	Webster,
Carr,	Kingsley,	Wells,
Conner,		22

Mr. Cook offered the following, which was laid upon the table:

Resolved, That the committee on schedule be instructed to fix in their report the terms of the first officers elected under the revised Constitution, so that thereafter the election of all State and county officers shall take place upon the even numbered years, excepting such as may be made elective at the spring elections.

Mr. Williams proposed the following:

Resolved, That the committee on miscellaneous provisions be instructed to inquire into the expediency of inserting a provision in the new Constitution as follows: "The navigable waters of this State shall be common highways, and forever free to the inhabitants of this State and the United States."

Mr. Morrison moved to lay the same upon the table.

Which did not prevail.

And the resolution was then adopted.

On motion of Mr. McClelland,

The Convention resolved itself into committee of the whole, on the general order,

Mr. Eaton in the chair.

PROCEEDINGS IN COMMITTEE.

The committee resumed the consideration of "Article —, County Officers and County Governments."

The question being upon Mr. J. D. Pierce's motion, to strike out "no alteration," in 2d line of section 11, and "or otherwise," in 3d line, the same prevailed.

The question then recurring upon Mr. McLeod's motion to strike out all after "counties," in 2d line,

The committee refused to strike out.

On motion of Mr. Fralick,

The words "for all services rendered for, and to be paid by, the counties," were inserted after "counties," in 2d line.

Mr. Bush offered the following substitute for section 11:

"The board of supervisors shall have the power to settle all claims for services rendered their respective counties, and from their final decision there shall be no appeal."

Mr. Walker offered the following as a substitute for the substitute:

"Sec. 11. The board of supervisors shall have the exclusive power to prescribe and fix the compensation for all services rendered for and to adjust all claims against their respective counties."

On motion of Mr. J. D. Pierce,

Mr. Walker's substitute was amended by adding "and the sum so fixed and defined shall be subject to no appeal."

The substitute of Mr. Walker, as amended, then prevailed.

The question then recurring upon striking out section 11, and the adoption of the substitute,

The same prevailed.

Mr. Robertson moved to amend as follows:

Add to end of section, "and the compensation of officers shall, in all cases, be fixed before their election, and shall not be diminished during their terms of office."

Mr. W. Adams moved to amend the amendment by striking out "diminished," and inserting "altered."

Which was disagreed to.

Mr. Robertson's amendment was negatived.

Mr. Bagg offered the following as a substitute for section 12:

"The several boards of supervisors of this state may hereafter confer upon the legislature of this state, such powers of local and general legislation and administration as they may deem proper."

And the question being divided, the committee refused to strike out section 12.

On motion of Mr. Cook,

The committee rose, reported the article back to the Convention and asked their concurrence in the amendments made thereto.

The committee, through their chairman, reported the article entitled "County Officers and County Government," with various amendments, in which the concurrence of the Convention was asked.

The committee was discharged from further consideration of the Article, and

On motion of Mr. Cook,

It was laid upon the table and ordered printed with amendments.

Mr. McClelland called from the table the article entitled "Legislative Department."

And the question being upon concurring with the amendments made in committee of the whole, and

The first amendment being under consideration,

Mr. McClelland moved further to amend by striking out the word "one," and inserting the words "not more than three."

A division of the question being called,

The yeas and nays were ordered upon the first branch of the same, when

On motion of Mr. Storey,

The Convention adjourned.

Afternoon Session.

Half-past two o'clock.

The Convention was called to order by the President.

And a quorum of members being in attendance, the consideration of the article entitled "Legislative Department" was resumed; and the question being on striking out, as proposed by Mr. McClelland, the result was as follows:

YEAS.

Mr. Alvord,	Mr. Dimond,	Mr. Roberts,
Arzeno,	Eaton,	Robertson,
Bagg,	Gibson,	M. Robinson,
J. Bartow,	Graham,	Rix Robinson,
Beeson,	Hart,	Soule,
Butterfield,	Marvin,	Storey,
Choate,	McClelland,	Sturgis,
Church,	McLeod,	Sutherland,
J. Clark,	Mosher,	Town,
Crary,	Mowry,	Whittemore,
Crouse,	J. D. Pierce,	President,
Desnoyers,	Redfield,	35.

NAYS:

Mr. W. Adams,	Mr. Cornell,	Mr. Newberry,
Anderson,	Danforth,	Orr,

Axford,
Backus,
Barnard,
H. Bartow,
Beardsley,
Britain,
Alvarado Brown,
Ammon Brown,
Asahel Brown,
Burns,
Bush,
Carr,
Chandler,
S. Clark,
Comstock,
Conner,
Cook,
Eastman,
Edmunds,
Fralick,
Gale,
Gardiner,
Green,
Hanscom,
Harvey,
Hascall,
Hixon,
Kingsley,
Kinne,
Lovell,
Mason,
Moore,
Morrison,
N. Pierce,
Prevost,
E. S. Robinson,
Skinner,
Sullivan,
Tiffany,
Van Valkenburg,
Wait,
Walker,
Webster,
Wells,
White,
Whipple,
Williams,
Willard,
Woodman, 55

So the motion to strike out did not prevail.

The first amendment made in committee was then concurred in by the following vote:

YEAS.

Mr. W. Adams,
Anderson,
Axford,
Backus,
Barnard,
H. Bartow,
Beardsley,
Britain,
Alvarado Brown,
Ammon Brown,
Asahel Brown,
Burns,
Bush,
Butterfield,
Carr,
Chandler,
S. Clark,
Comstock,
Conner,
Cook,
Cornell,
Mr. Crouse,
Danforth,
Eastman,
Edmunds.
Fralick,
Gale,
Gardiner,
Graham,
Green,
Harvey,
Hascall,
Hixon,
Kingsley,
Kinne,
Lee,
Lovell,
Mason,
Moore,
Morrison,
Mosher,
Mr. Mowry,
Newberry,
Orr,
J. D. Pierce,
N. Pierce,
Prevost,
E. S. Robinson,
Skinner,
Sullivan,
Tiffany,
Van Valkenburg,
Wait,
Walker,
Warden,
Webster,
Wells,
White,
Williams,
Willard,
Woodman, 61

NAYS.

Mr. Alvord,
Arzeno,
Bagg,
Mr. Desnoyers,
Eaton,
Gibson,
Mr. Robertson,
M. Robinson,
Rix Robinson,

J. Bartow,	Hanscom,	Soule,	
Beeson,	Hart,	Storey,	
Chapel,	Marvin,	Sturgis,	
Choate,	McClelland,	Sutherland,	
Church,	McLeod,	Town,	
J. Clark,	Redfield,	Whittemore,	
Crary,	Roberts,	President,	30

Prior to the announcement of the result,

A motion made to excuse Mr. Chapel from voting was lost, and

On motion of Mr. McLeod,

The delegate from Macomb was allowed the floor,

When, after explanation, he recorded his vote as above.

The second amendment being under consideration,

Mr. Sutherland proposed to amend the same by substituting the following:

"Provided that until the apportionment under the census of 1855, the counties of Saginaw, Tuscola, Midland, Sanilac, Newago and Montcalm shall each be entitled to at least one Representative, and all other counties now or hereafter to be organized, to at least one Representative each, whenever it shall contain 1,500 inhabitants."

Pending which,

On motion of Mr. Church,

The Convention adjourned.

Lansing, Friday, July 12, 1850.

The Convention met pursuant to adjournment and was called to order by the President.

Prayer by the Rev. Mr. Sanford.

The roll was called and there were absent on leave Messrs. P. R. Adams, and Leach.

Without leave, Messrs. Danforth, Hathaway, O'Brien, Raynale and Witherell.

Leave of absence was granted for an indefinite period to Messrs. O'Brien, Raynale, Hathaway and Witherell.

DEATH OF THE PRESIDENT OF THE UNITED STATES.

Mr. Backus rose and said—I arise, Mr. President, as well in respect for public feeling, as of the better sympathies of our common nature, to the performance of a painful duty, in the formal announcement to this Convention of the death of ZACHARY TAYLOR, President of the United States. This event took place at Washington, on the evening of the 9th instant.

Sir, the inscrutible purposes of Providence in this afflictive dispensation depriving the nation of its chief Executive Magistrate, at a juncture so big with events as the present, we can neither fathom or fully comprehend.

The ebon wing of the Angel of Death is over the nation—her head is smitten—he has bowed to the mandate of Omnipotence, "thou shalt surely die"—he is numbered with the dead. But one thing, Sir, we can do. Draw instructions from the monitions of this Providence, that again admonishes us of man's mortality—that the great leveler of human distinction, *Death*, marks indiscriminately for his victim the high and low, the great and small; that even a *nation's* confidence cannot shield its possessor from the unerring shaft of death.

It teaches too, with the same unerring certainty, that he who would be truly great must be truly good—that mortality can become immortal alone by virtues that shall leave an impress on society when the *mortal* man shall be numbered with the countless hosts of the forgotten dead.

In making this announcement, I shall, sir, be permitted to say, that not only the distinguished position, but the virtues of the man whose death it has been my duty to announce, challenge from us and the whole American people, deep sorrow for the national bereavement.

The death of the Chief Magistrate of a nation is at any time and to any people a sad disaster; to us, as a people, emphatically so. Not only from the peculiarly important matters that now engross the attention of our national councils, but also at all times from the very nature and organization of our form of government.

With us the sovereignty of the nation is invoked to select from its citizens him who is to guard and guide, as the Supreme Executive, the national destinies. None can exercise this delicate and responsible trust like him to whom the trust is directly confided. Before this fearful stroke of Providence, the rancor and commotion of partisan strife must sink back abashed, as seeing the hand of Him who doeth His pleasure in the armies of heaven, as also among the nations of the earth. The better and nobler feelings of our nature will predominate, and all concur in one common sentiment to honor, in death, him, who in life the millions of our republic have loved to honor.

This, Sir, is not the time or place for me to pronounce the eulogium of the illustrious dead; our feelings at this time are too nearly allied to despondency to permit it. I shall, however, be permitted to say of his public services, in which almost from boyhood he has been engaged, his nation's banner has been borne by him in triumph, and untarnished through all the varied scenes of a soldier's life, with honor to himself and glory to his country. His life presents an example worthy of emulation to all who may follow him, as combining the stern tenets of war happily blended with the milder sympathies of a good man and magnanimous conqueror.

As a statesman, to which position the confidence of the American people in his integrity, by their free suffrage elevated him, he brought to the councils of the nation a heart uncontaminated with the tricks of political manœuverers, and bent firmly and alone on an unwavering purpose to do his duty; this part none will deny. He has nobly and constantly aimed to perform with a single purpose to the public good. He will go down to the grave with the proudest title that man can bear—the unanimous sentiment of a great nation that he was an *honest man*.

As a man, his elements of character, as illustrated in his life, were all such as we must ever praise and admire. To those who knew him personally, his memory, as was his life, will ever be endeared by all the most pure and holy ties that can bind man to man; he was but to be seen and known to be admired and beloved; of unflinching integrity, untarnished purity. He is dead. The Angel of Death has smitten the nation; his history will become that of the nation, who elevated him to the highest station within their gift. The present will with heartfelt sorrow lament him, posterity will do him honor—he was a great, because he was a good man.

I hope, Mr. President, in testimony of our respect, and a nation's grief, under this sudden national calamity, this convention will now adjourn.

Whereupon, Mr. Roberts offered the following preamble and resolutions:

Whereas, a benignant and inscrutable Providence hath, in its wisdom, removed from the scenes of his usefulness and the great theatre of human action, a renowned warrior, a distinguished patriot, and a beloved statesman, General ZACHARY TAYLOR, the President of the United States; it is

Resolved, That this Convention, as a testimonial of their deep and profound respect for the memory of the deceased, and of their unaffected sorrow over this sudden bereavement to the Republic, will adopt the usual insignia of mourning.

Resolved, That this Convention do now adjourn over until to-morrow.

And the same were unanimously adopted.

So the Convention adjourned.

Lansing, Saturday, July 13, 1850.

The Convention met pursuant to adjournment, and was called to order by the President.

Prayer by the Rev. Mr. Sanford.

Roll called—absent with leave, Messrs. P. R. Adams, Hathaway Leach, Raynale and Witherell; without leave, Messrs. Hixon, and Whipple.

Journal approved.

PETITIONS.

By Mr. Cook: of John W. May and 81 others, citizens of Hillsdale county, asking that the new constitution may provide that the legislature shall have no power of authorizing the sale of intoxicating liquors as a beverage; also,

By Mr. Gardiner, two several petitions of 134 citizens of Washtenaw county, praying for a like provision.

Referred to select committee upon the subject.

By Mr. Williams: of E. C. White and 43 others, of Centreville, St. Joseph county, relative to the right of suffrage.

Laid upon the table.

The Convention having reached the order of

UNFINISHED BUSINESS,

Resumed the consideration of the article entitled "Legislative Department."

The question being upon Mr. Sutherland's amendment, the same was withdrawn.

Mr. Crary moved to amend the amendment made in committee by striking out the words "containing 2000 white inhabitants," and inserting in lieu thereof, the words "at the time of the adoption of this constitution."

Mr. Morrison asked a division of the question, and the yeas and nays were demanded on the motion to strike out.

Mr. Alvord moved that the Convention adjourn.

But the motion did not prevail.

The question being on striking out, as proposed by Mr. Crary, it was decided in the affirmative, as follows:

YEAS:

Mr. W. Adams,	Mr. Crary,	Mr. Mowry,
Alvord,	Crouse,	Orr,
Arzeno,	Danforth,	J. D. Pierce,
Bagg,	Desnoyers,	Prevost,
Barnard,	Dimond,	Roberts,
H. Bartow,	Eastman,	Robertson,
J. Bartow,	Edmunds,	M. Robinson,
Beardsley,	Gale,	Rix Robinson,
Britain,	Graham,	Soule,
Alvarado Brown,	Hanscom,	Sturgis,
Ammon Brown,	Hart,	Sutherland,
Asahel Brown,	Harvey,	Town,
Burns,	Hascall,	Van Valkenburg,
Bush,	Kinne,	Walker,
Chapel,	Lee,	Warden,
Choate,	Lovell,	Webster,
Church,	Marvin,	White,
J. Clark,	McClelland,	Whittemore,
Conner,	McLeod,	Willard,
Cook,	Morrison,	Woodman,
Cornell,	Mosher,	President, 63

NAYS:

Mr. Anderson,	Mr. Eaton,	Mr. E. S. Robinson,
Axford,	Fralick,	Skinner,
Backus,	Gardiner,	Storey,
Beeson,	Kingsley,	Sullivan,
Butterfield,	Mason,	Tiffany,
Carr,	Moore,	Wait,
Chandler,	Newberry,	Wells,
S. Clark,	O'Brien,	Williams,

Comstock,	N. Pierce,	Witherell,
Daniels,	Redfield,	29

On motion of Mr. Hanscom,

The Convention then adjourned.

Afternoon Session.

Half-past two o'clock.

The President called the Convention to order.

The roll being called, and a quorum of members being in attendance,

The consideration of the article entitled "Legislative Department" was resumed,

And the question being upon inserting the words "at the time of the adoption of this Constitution," proposed by Mr. Crary this morning,

And the yeas and nays being demanded, the amendment was lost, as follows:

YEAS:

Mr. Arzeno,	Mr. Danforth,	Mr. Soule,
Beardsley,	Hanscom,	Sturgis,
Bush,	Lovell,	Walker,
Chapel,	Orr,	Webster,
Church,	Rix Robinson,	14

NAYS.

Mr. W. Adams,	Mr. Crouse,	Mr. Newberry,
Alvord,	Daniels,	O'Brien,
Anderson,	Desnoyers,	J. D. Pierce,
Axford,	Dimond,	N. Pierce,
Backus,	Eastman,	Prevost,
Bagg,	Eaton,	Redfield,
Barnard,	Edmunds,	Robertson,
H. Bartow,	Fralick,	E. S. Robinson,
Beeson,	Gale,	Skinner,
Britain,	Gardiner,	Storey,
Alvarado Brown,	Graham,	Sullivan,
Ammon Brown,	Green,	Sutherland,
Asahel Brown,	Hart,	Tiffany,
Burns,	Harvey,	Town,
Butterfield,	Hascall	Van Valkenburg,
Carr,	Hathaway,	Wait,
Chandler,	Kinne,	Warden,
Choate,	Marvin,	Wells,
J. Clark,	Mason,	Whittemore,

S. Clark,
Comstock,
Conner,
Cook,
Cornell,
Crary,
McClelland,
McLeod,
Moore,
Morrison,
Mosher,
Mowry,
Williams,
Willard,
Witherell,
Woodman,
President, 74

Mr. Lovell moved to strike out the balance of the amendment made in Committee, and insert the following:

Provided, That each County having an organized County Government, and the territory attached thereto, shall be entitled to one Representative; and that each county hereafter organized, and the territory attached thereto, if any, shall be entitled to a separate representative when it shall have attained a population equal to a moiety of the ratio of representation hereafter established.

Mr. Britain moved to amend the amendment of the committee of the whole by inserting after "county" the words "with such territory as may be attached thereto."

Which was decided not in order.

A division of the question was had, on Mr. Lovell's motion,

And the motion to strike out prevailed by the following vote:

YEAS:

Mr. Anderson,
Axford,
Backus,
Bagg,
H. Bartow,
Beardsley,
Beeson,
Britain,
Alvarado Brown,
Ammon Brown,
Butterfield,
Carr,
Chandler,
Chapel,
S. Clark,
Comstock,
Conner,
Cook,
Mr. Cornell,
Daniels,
Desnoyers,
Eaton,
Fralick,
Gardiner,
Graham,
Harvey,
Hascall,
Hathaway,
Kingsley,
Marvin,
Mason,
McClelland,
Moore,
Mosher,
Newberry,
N. Pierce,
Mr. Redfield,
Robertson,
E. S. Robinson,
M. Robinson,
Skinner,
Storey,
Sullivan,
Tiffany,
Town,
Van Valkenburg,
Wait,
Warden,
Wells,
Whittemore,
Williams,
Witherell,
Woodman,
President, 54

NAYS.

Mr. W. Adams,
Alvord,
Arzeno,
Mr. Eastman,
Edmunds,
Gale,
Mr. Orr,
J. D. Pierce,
Prevost,

Barnard,	Hanscom,	Roberts,
Burns,	Hart,	Rix Robinson,
Bush,	Kinne,	Soule,
Choate,	Lee,	Sturgis,
Church,	Lovell,	Sutherland,
J. Clark,	McLeod,	Walker,
Crary,	Morrison,	Webster,
Crouse,	Mowry,	White,
Danforth,	O'Brien,	Willard,
Dimond,		37

The amendment was then adopted as follows:

YEAS:

Mr. Alvord,	Mr. Danforth,	Mr. J. D. Pierce,
Anderson,	Daniels,	N. Pierce,
Arzeno,	Desnoyers,	Prevost,
Axford,	Dimond,	Redfield,
Barnard,	Edmunds,	Roberts,
H. Bartow,	Gale,	Robertson,
Beardsley,	Gardiner,	M. Robinson,
Beeson,	Graham,	Rix Robinson,
Britain,	Green,	Skinner,
Alvarado Brown,	Hanscom,	Soule,
Ammon Brown,	Harvey,	Sturgis,
Asahel Brown,	Hascall,	Sullivan,
Burns,	Hathaway,	Sutherland,
Bush,	Kingsley,	Tiffany,
Carr,	Kinne,	Town,
Chandler,	Lee,	Van Valkenburg,
Chapel,	Lovell,	Wait.
Choate,	Marvin,	Walker,
Church,	Mason,	Warden,
J. Clark,	McClelland,	Webster,
Comstock,	McLeod,	Whittemore,
Conner,	Morrison,	Williams,
Cook,	Mosher,	Willard,
Cornell,	Mowry,	Witherell,
Crary,	Newberry,	Woodman,
Crouse,	Orr,	President, 78

NAYS:

Mr. W. Adams,	Mr. Eastman,	Mr. Moore,
Backus,	Eaton,	Storey,
Bagg,	Fralick,	Wells,
Butterfield,	Hart,	White,
S. Clark,		13

And the amendment as amended was then concurred in.

The third amendment to the article was concurred in.

The fourth amendment being under consideration,

Mr. Hanscom moved to strike out "thirty-two" and insert "twenty-two."

A division of the question was called,

And the motion to strike out was lost by the following vote:

YEAS:

Mr.	Alvord,	Mr.	J. Clark,	Mr.	N. Pierce,
	Axford,		Hanscom,		Roberts,
	Barnard,		Hart,		E. S. Robinson,
	H. Bartow,		McLeod,		Rix Robinson,
	Beeson,		Mowry,		Sturgis,
	Butterfield,		Newberry,		Warden,
	Chapel,		Orr,		Webster,
	Church,		J. D. Pierce,		President, 24

NAYS:

Mr.	W. Adams,	Mr.	Dimond,	Mr.	Morrison,
	Backus,		Eaton,		Mosher,
	Bagg,		Edmunds,		O'Brien,
	Beardsley,		Fralick,		Prevost,
	Britain,		Gale,		Redfield,
	Alvarado Brown,		Gardiner,		Skinner,
	Ammon Brown,		Graham,		Sullivan,
	Asahel Brown,		Green,		Tiffany,
	Burns,		Harvey,		Town,
	Bush,		Hascall,		VanValkenburgh,
	Carr,		Hathaway,		Wait,
	Chandler,		Kingsley,		Walker,
	S. Clark,		Kinne,		Wells,
	Comstock,		Lee,		White,
	Conner,		Lovell,		Whittemore,
	Cook,		Marvin,		Williams,
	Cornell,		Mason,		Willard,
	Crouse,		McClelland,		Witherell,
	Danforth,		Moore,		Woodman,
	Daniels,				57

Mr. Morrison moved to amend the amendment by striking out the last clause, being all after the word "inclusive" in the 2d line.

Pending which, on motion of Mr. Gardiner,

The Convention adjourned.

Lansing, Monday, July 15, 1850.

The Convention met at the usual hour and was called to order by the President.

Prayer by the Rev. Mr. Tooker.

Roll called, and Messrs. P. R. Adams, Leach and Raynale were found absent with leave.

On motion of Mr. Church,

The journal of Saturday was corrected by striking therefrom the following:

"Mr. Britain moved to amend the amendment of the committee of the whole by inserting after "county," the words "with such territory as may be attached thereto."

"Which was decided not in order."

PETITIONS.

By Mr. Backus: of H. Eisnack and 20 others, naturalized citizens, praying that the elective franchise may not be extended to foreigners until they shall have been regularly naturalized as required by existing laws.

Laid upon the table.

By Mr. White: of C. A. Shaw and 103 others, citizens of Lapeer, Oakland and Macomb counties, in relation to equalization and collection of taxes.

Referred to committee on finance and taxation.

REPORTS.

Mr. Bush, from the committee on township officers and township government, submitted "Article —, Township officers and government."

The article was read the first and second time by its title, referred to the committee of the whole and ordered printed.

RESOLUTIONS, MOTIONS, &c.

Mr. Hanscom proposed the following:

Resolved, That from and after this day the daily morning sessions of this Convention shall commence at half-past seven o'clock, A. M.

Mr. White moved to insert "six," in lieu of "half-past seven."

Mr. Bartow moved to lay the resolution upon the table.

Which was lost.

A division of the question being had on Mr. White's motion, the question upon striking out was negatived.

Mr. N. Pierce moved to strike out "half-past seven," and insert "four."

Mr. Woodman moved the previous question, which was demanded.

And the main question was ordered to be now put.

The amendment proposed by Mr. N. Pierce did not prevail.

The main question recurring upon the passage of the resolution, it was adopted.

Mr. Gale offered the following:

Resolved, That the afternoon sessions of this Convention commence hereafter at 2 o'clock.

Mr. Chapel moved to amend by inserting "one o'clock."

Mr. Alvord proposed to insert "twelve and a half."

When, on motion of Mr. Axford,

The resolution was laid upon the table.

Mr. Storey proposed to amend rule 8 of the Convention, as follows:

In line 2, strike out the words "one hour," and insert "five minutes."

On motion of Mr. W. Adams,

The proposition was laid upon the table.

Mr. Van Valkenburg presented the following, which, with the exception of the last resolution, had been presented by Mr. Axford, but withdrawn:

Whereas, This Convention did adjourn on the 29th day of June last past, until the 9th day of July instant, therefore, in the opinion of this Convention, it would be unjust to the tax payers of this state for the members or officers of this Convention to receive any pay from the public treasury of this state during said adjournment; therefore,

Resolved, That for and during said adjournment no member or officer of this Convention is justly entitled to or should receive any pay during said adjournment, and that no money shall be drawn from the public treasury of this State for that purpose.

Resolved, That the time members of this body have spent unnecessarily out of the Convention during its sessions shall be deducted in the estimate for their per diem allowance.

On motion of Mr. Axford,

The Preamble and Resolutions were indefinitely postponed.

Mr. Woodman offered the following.

Whereas, It has been formally announced to this Convention, that General ZACHARY TAYLOR, late President of the United States, departed this life on the evening of the 9th inst.;

And whereas, Not only the "distinguished position, but the virtues of the man whose death has been thus announced, challenge from us and the whole American people, deep sorrow for the National bereavement;" therefore,

Resolved, That as a "testimonial of the deep and profound respect for the memory of the deceased," and in accordance with a long established usage, that a committee of — be appointed by the President of this Convention to procure some suitable member of this body to pronounce an eulogy on the "life and public services of General Zachary Taylor, late President of the United States."

Resolved, That said committee be, and hereby are instructed to make the suitable arrangements as to time and place, and report to this Convention in due time.

The blank was filled with "nine,"

And the Preamble and Resolutions adopted.

UNFINISHED BUSINESS.

The Convention renewed the consideration of the article entitled "Legislative Department,"

And the question being upon the amendment proposed by Mr. Morrison to the 4th amendment made by the committe,

Mr. Church moved to amend the amendment by striking out all after the word "district."

But the same was lost by the following vote:

YEAS.

Mr.	Arzeno,	Mr.	Danforth,	Mr.	Rix Robinson,	
	H. Bartow,		Hart,		Sturgis,	
	Church,		Hathaway,			8

NAYS.

Mr.	W. Adams,	Mr.	Crouse,	Mr.	Mowry,
	Alvord,		Daniels,		Newberry,
	Anderson,		Desnoyers,		O'Brien,
	Axford,		Dimond,		Orr,
	Backus,		Eastman,		N. Pierce,
	Bagg,		Eaton,		Prevost,
	Barnard,		Edmunds,		Robertson,
	Beardsley,		Fralick,		E. S. Robinson,

Beeson, Britain, Alvardo Brown, Ammon Brown, Asahel Brown, Burns, Bush, Butterfield, Carr, Chandler, Chapel, Choate, S. Clark, Comstock, Conner, Cook, Cornell, Crary, Gale, Gardiner, Gibson, Graham, Green, Hanscom, Harvey, Hascall, Hixon, Kingsley, Kinne, Lee, Marvin, Mason, McClelland, Moore, Morrison, Mosher, Soule, Storey, Sullivan, Tiffany, Town, Van Valkenburg, Wait, Warden, Webster, Wells, White, Whipple, Whittemore, Williams, Willard, Witherell, President, 77

The amendment proposed by Mr. Morrison was not agreed to.

The substitute proposed by the committee for section 5 was then adopted.

The 5th amendment being under consideration,

Mr. Morrison moved to amend the same by inserting after "any county officer," the words "or the office of Supervisor of a township." Which was not agreed to.

Mr. Church moved to amend by inserting after "militia," the words "post masters."

When, after some debate, Mr. S. Clark moved the previous question, which was demanded.

The main question was ordered to be now put.

The same being first upon the amendment proposed by Mr. Church, it was rejected, as follows:

YEAS:

Mr. W. Adams, Barnard, J. Bartow, Beardsley, Asahel Brown, Bush, Butterfield, Chandler, Church, S. Clark, Mr. Desnoyers, Dimond, Edmunds, Gale, Green, Hart, Hascall, Lee, Lovell, McClelland, Mr. Redfield, E. S. Robinson, Rix Robinson, Storey, Sutherland, Tiffany, Town, Van Valkenburg, Wait, Wells,

Comstock,	Newberry,	Whipple,
Cook,	N. Pierce,	Williams,
Cornell,	Prevost,	Woodman,
Crouse,		40

NAYS:

Mr. Alvord,	Mr. Daniels,	Mr. Mowry,
Anderson,	Eastman,	O'Brien,
Arzeno,	Eaton,	J. D. Pierce,
Axford,	Fralick,	Robertson,
Backus,	Gardiner,	M. Robinson,
H. Bartow,	Gibson,	Skinner,
Beeson,	Graham,	Soule,
Britain,	Hanscom,	Sturgis,
Alvarado Brown,	Harvey,	Sullivan,
Ammon Brown,	Hathaway,	Walker,
Burns,	Hixon,	Warden,
Carr,	Kingsley,	Webster,
Chapel,	Kinne,	White,
Choate,	Marvin,	Whittemore,
Conner,	Mason,	Willard,
Crary,	Morrison,	Witherell,
Danforth,	Mosher,	President, 51

The substitute proposed by the committee of the whole was then concurred in.

The 6th and 7th amendments were severally concurred in, when Mr. Britain moved to reconsider the vote by which the 6th amendment was concurred in.

But the motion did not prevail.

The amendments to the 15th and 16th sections of the article made in committee were severally concurred in.

The amendments to section 17 being under consideration,

Mr. J. Bartow moved to strike out the last clause of the section as amended, on which

Mr. Britain asked the yeas and nays, and the Convention refused to strike out by the following vote:

YEAS.

Mr. Alvord,	Mr. Hanscom,	Mr. Sutherland,
J. Bartow,	Roberts,	VanValkenburg,
Butterfield,	Storey,	Whipple,
Carr,		10

NAYS.

Mr. W. Adams,	Mr. Daniels,	Mr. Newberry,
Anderson,	Dimond,	O'Brien,

Arzeno,	Eaton,	N. Pierce,
Bagg,	Fralick,	Redfield,
Barnard,	Gale,	Robertson,
H. Bartow,	Gardiner,	E. S. Robinson,
Beardsley,	Gibson,	M. Robinson,
Beeson,	Graham,	Rix Robinson,
Britain,	Green,	Skinner,
Alvarado Brown,	Harvey,	Soule,
Ammon Brown,	Hascall,	Sturgis,
Asahel Brown,	Hathaway,	Tiffany,
Burns,	Hixon,	Town,
Chandler,	Kingsley,	Wait,
Chapel,	Lovell,	Walker,
Church,	Marvin,	Webster,
S. Clark,	Mason,	Whittemore,
Comstock,	McClelland,	Williams,
Conner,	Moore,	Willard,
Cook,	Morrison,	Witherell,
Cornell,	Mosher,	Woodman,
Crouse,	Mowry,	President,
Danforth,		67

The amendments were then severally concurred in.

The amendment to section 19 being under consideration,

Mr. McClelland moved to strike out, and substitute the following:

"Receive the same per diem compensation and mileage as members of the Legislature, and no more."

And the same prevailed, and

The amendment as amended was concurred in.

The amendments to sections 20 and 23 were severally concurred in.

To the amendment proposed to section 25,

Mr. Gardiner moved to strike out sub-divisions 2 and 3,

And a division being had,

The Convention refused to strike out.

The amendments wese then concurred in.

The amendments to sections 26 and 27 were likewise severally concurred in.

Section 28 being under consideration,

Mr. McClelland moved to amend the amendment by striking out the words "chaplain or."

Pending which,

On motion of Mr. Danforth,

The Convention adjourned.

Afternoon Session.

½ past 2 o'clock.

The President called the Convention to order.

A quorum of members in attendance.

The consideration of the unfinished business of the morning was resumed.

The question being upon the amendment proposed by Mr. McClelland, the same was agreed to.

The amendment to the section (28th) was then concurred in by the following vote:

YEAS.

Mr. W. Adams,
Alvord,
Arzeno,
Axford,
Barnard,
Britain,
Alvarado Brown,
Ammon Brown,
Asahel Brown,
Burns,
Bush,
Carr,
Chapel,
Church,
J. Clark,
Conner,
Cook,
Cornell,
Mr. Crary,
Crouse,
Desnoyers,
Dimond,
Eastman,
Eaton,
Edmunds,
Fralick,
Gale,
Gardiner,
Graham,
Green,
Hanscom,
Hascall,
Hathaway,
Kingsley,
Kinne,
Mr. Mosher,
Newberry,
Mowry,
O'Brien,
Orr,
Redfield,
Roberts,
Rix Robinson,
Soule,
Storey,
Sturgis,
Town,
Walker,
Warden,
Wells,
Willard,
Woodman,
52

NAYS.

Mr. Anderson,
Backus,
Bagg,
H. Bartow,
Beeson,
Buttergeld,
Chandler,
Choate,
S. Clark,
Comstock,
Danforth,
Daniels,
Gibson,
Hart,
Mr. Harvey,
Hixon,
Lovell,
Marvin,
Mason,
McClelland,
Moore,
Morrison,
J. D. Pierce,
N. Pierce,
Prevost,
Robertson,
E. S. Robinson,
Mr. M. Robinson,
Skinner,
Sullivan,
Sutherland,
Tiffany,
VanValkenburg,
Wait,
Webster,
White,
Whittemore,
Williams,
Witherell,
President,
40

The amendments made in committee to sections 29, 32, 33 and 34 were severally concurred in.

The amendment to section 36 being under consideration,

On motion of Mr. Cook,

The same was amended by striking out "February," in the 2d line, and inserting in lieu thereof "January."

Mr. Church moved further to amend by inserting after "January," the words "in 1852 and."

The yeas and nays being ordered upon his motion, the same was lost by the following vote:

YEAS.

Mr. Ammon Brown,	Mr. Fralick,	Mr. Roberts,
Bush,	Hanscom,	Sullivan,
Church,	Lee,	Sutherland,
Crouse,	Prevost,	Van Valkenburg

12

NAYS.

Mr. W. Adams,	Mr. Desnoyers,	Mr. Orr,
Alvord,	Dimond,	N. Pierce,
Anderson,	Eaton,	Redfield,
Arzeno,	Edmunds,	Robertson,
Axford,	Gale,	E. S. Robinson,
Backus,	Gardiner,	M. Robinson,
Bagg,	Gibson,	Skinner,
Barnard,	Graham,	Soule,
Beardsley,	Green,	Storey,
Beeson,	Hart,	Sturgis,
Britain,	Harvey,	Tiffany,
Alvarado Brown,	Hascall,	Town,
Asahel Brown,	Hathaway,	Wait,
Butterfield,	Hixon,	Walker,
Carr,	Kingsley.	Warden,
Chandler,	Kinne,	Webster,
Chapel,	Lovell,	Wells,
Choate,	Marvin,	White,
S. Clark,	Mason,	Whittemore,
Comstock,	McClelland,	Williams,
Conner,	Moore,	Willard,
Cook,	Morrison,	Witherell,
Cornell,	Mosher,	Woodman,
Danforth,	Mowry,	President.
Daniels,	Newberry,	

74

The amendment of the committee was then concurred in.

The amendment made to section 37 was also concurred in.

Section 38 being under consideration,

Mr. Storey submitted the following substitute for the same:

Section 38. The legislature shall pass no law creating or authorizing a state paper, but shall provide for the publication of all acts of a general nature in all the newspapers of the state, under such regulations, and for such compensation as may be provided by law.

Mr. Eaton asked a division of the question.

And the yeas and nays being ordered,

The motion to strike out was lost as follows:

YEAS.

Mr. Alvord,	Mr. Hanscom,	Mr. Skinner,	
H. Bartow,	Hascall,	Soule,	
Beardsley,	Kingsley,	Storey,	
Beeson,	Lee,	Sutherland,	
Church,	Lovell,	Van Valkenburg	
Crary,	McClelland,	Warden,	
Eastman,	Roberts,	White,	
Edmunds,	Robertson,	Whipple,	
Gardiner,	Rix Robinson,	Williams,	
Gibson,			28

NAYS.

Mr. W. Adams,	Mr. Cornell,	Mr. Mosher,	
Anderson,	Crouse,	Mowry,	
Arzeno,	Danforth,	Newberry,	
Axford,	Daniels,	O'Brien,	
Backus,	Desnoyers,	Orr,	
Bagg,	Dimond,	N. Pierce,	
Barnard,	Eaton,	Prevost,	
Britain,	Fralick,	Redfield,	
Alvarado Brown,	Gale,	E. S. Robinson,	
Ammon Brown,	Graham,	M. Robinson,	
Asahel Brown,	Green,	Sturgis,	
Carr,	Hart,	Town,	
Chandler,	Harvey,	Wait,	
Chapel,	Hathaway,	Walker,	
Choate,	Hixon,	Webster,	
J. Clark,	Kinne,	Wells,	
S. Clark,	Marvin,	Whittemore,	
Comstock,	Mason,	Wiliard,	
Conner,	Moore,	Woodman,	
Cook,	Morrison,	President,	60

On motion of Mr. Walker,

The amendment was amended by adding thereto the following:

"Except for the publication of such general laws as are by the direction of the Legislature to take effect within less than ninety days after the passage thereof."

The amendment made in committee was then concurred in as amended by the following vote:

YEAS.

Mr. W. Adams,	Mr. Conner,	Mr. Morrison,
Arzeno,	Cornell,	Mosher,
Axford,	Crouse,	N. Pierce,
Backus,	Danforth,	Prevost,
Bagg,	Desnoyers,	Redfield,
Barnard,	Dimond,	E. S. Robinson,
Beardsley,	Eaton,	M. Robinson,
Beeson,	Edmunds,	Skinner,
Britain,	Fralick,	Sturgis,
Alvarado Brown,	Graham,	Tiffany,
Ammon Brown,	Green,	Town,
Burns,	Hart,	Walker,
Bush,	Hascall,	Warden,
Butterfield,	Hathaway,	Webster,
Carr,	Hixon,	Whipple,
Chandler,	Kingsley,	Williams,
Chapel,	Kinne,	Willard,
Choate,	Lee,	Witherell,
S. Clark,	Marvin,	Woodman,
Comstock,	Mason,	59

NAYS.

Mr. Alvord,	Mr. Hanscom,	Mr. Rix Robins,
H. Bartow,	Harvey,	Soule,
Asahel Brown,	Lovell,	Storey,
Church,	McClelland,	Sullivan,
Cook,	Moore,	Sutherland,
Crary,	Mowry,	Van Valkenburg,
Daniels,	Newberry,	Wells,
Eastman,	O'Brien,	White,
Gale,	J. D. Pierce,	Whittemore,
Gardiner,	Roberts,	President.
Gibson,	Robertson,	32

Mr. Mason moved to adjourn,

But the Convention refused to adjourn.

Mr. Hanscom moved that the article entitled "Legislative Department," be recommitted to the committee on that department with instructions to amend the same as follows, and report said article back to the Convention forthwith, viz:

1. Strike out section 2 and insert in lieu thereof the following.

"The number of Representatives shall not exceed eighty, nor be less than fifty, to be elected by single districts and for two years. The Senate shall consist of twenty-four members, to be elected in such manner and for such term as may be prescribed by law."

2. Amend section 3 by striking out the following.

"Provided, That each county having an organized county government, and the territory attached thereto, shall be entitled to one representative," and insert as follows. "Provided that each county whose organization on the first day of January, A. D. 1851, shall have been perfected by election of county officers, shall be entitled to at least one Representative."

3. Strike out section 5, and insert in lieu thereof the following:

"The state shall be divided into Senate districts, and in the formation of Senate districts no county shall be divided."

4. Strike out of section 15 the words "two-thirds," and insert "a majority," where the words occur in the section.

5. Strike out all of section 17, up to and including the word "thereafter," in the 3d line, and insert the following:

"Compensation of the members of the Legislature shall not exceed three dollars per day for actual attendance, unless absent by reason of sickness; and after the session of 1851 such compensation shall not extend beyond the first sixty days of the session."

6. Amend section 20 by striking out the words, at the end of the section, "and for one year thereafter."

7. Amend section 23 by striking out the words "all the members elected to," in 3d and 4th line of said section.

8. Strike out of section 25 all after the words "by law," in the 5th line, down to and including the word "oath," at the end of the 17th line.

9. Strike out section 38 and insert as follows:

All general laws shall be published in two of the newspapers having the largest circulation published in the city of Detroit, and also in the newspaper having the largest circulation published at the seat of government of the State.

Mr. Hanscom moved to adjourn; when, by consent, the President announced the following committee, under the resolution of this morning:

Messrs. Woodman, Backus, Roberts, Williams, Comstock, Whipple, Butterfield, Rix Robinson, Kingsley.

The motion to adjourn was lost.

But, after some discussion,

On motion of Mr. Roberts, the Convention adjourned.

Lansing, Tuesday, July 16, 1850.

The Convention was called to order by the President at half-past seven o'clock.

Roll called—absent with leave, Messrs. P. R. Adams, Leach and Raynale; without leave, Messrs. J. Bartow and J. Clark.

PETITIONS.

By Mr. Hascall: the argument of Joseph Miller, Jun., and others, members of the Kalamazoo bar, requesting their delegation to use their efforts in favor of an independent supreme court.

Laid upon the table.

The Convention arriving at the order of

UNFINISHED BUSINESS,

Resumed the consideration of the article entitled "Legislative Department."

The question being upon Mr. Hanscom's proposition to recommit, it was, by consent, passed over.

The amendment of the committee to the article, striking out the 39th section, being under consideration,

Mr. Van Valkenburg proposed to amend the section by striking therefrom the words "drink or beverage," and inserting the following: "except for mechanical or medicinal purposes; and all traffic in said articles is hereby forever prohibited except for the purposes aforesaid."

A division of the question was had, and the motion to strike out prevailed.

Mr. Van Valkenburg then withdrew his proposition to insert.

Mr. Britain moved to add to the section the words, "and this section shall be submitted to the people as a separate question."

And the yeas and nays being had thereon, the amendment did not prevail, as follows:

YEAS:

Mr. Alvord,
Arzeno,
Beeson,
Britain,
Alvarado Brown,
Ammon Brown,
Asahel Brown,
Burns,
Butterfield,
Mr. Carr,
Choate,
Cook,
Fralick,
Green,
Redfield,
Roberts,
Robertson,
Mr. M. Robinson,
Storey,
Town,
Walker,
Webster,
Wells,
Willard,
Witherell,

26

NAYS:

Mr. W. Adams,
Anderson,
Axford,
Backus,
Bagg,
Barnard,
H. Bartow,
Beardsley,
Bush,
Chandler,
Church,
S. Clark,
Comstock,
Conner,
Cornell,
Crary,
Crouse,
Danforth,
Desnoyers,
Dimond,
Eastman,
Eaton,
Mr. Edmunds,
Gale,
Gibson,
Graham,
Hanscom,
Hart,
Harvey,
Hascall,
Hixon,
Kingley,
Kinne,
Lee,
Lovell,
Marvin,
Mason,
McClelland,
McLeod,
Moore,
Morrison,
Mosher,
Mowry,
Mr. Newberry,
O'Brien,
Orr,
J. D. Pierce,
N. Pierce,
Prevost,
E. S. Robinson,
Rix Robinson,
Skinner,
Soule,
Sturgis,
Sutherland,
Tiffany,
VanValkenburg,
Warden,
White,
Whipple,
Whittemore,
Williams,
Woodman,
President,

64

Mr. Van Valkenburg then renewed his proposition, but the same was negatived by the following vote:

YEAS.

Mr. H. Bartow,
Butterfield,
Fralick,
Gardiner,
Lovell,
Mr. Mowry,
Roberts,
Rix Robinson,
Skinner,
Mr. Sturgis,
Van Valkenburg,
Wells,
President,

13

NAYS.

Mr. W. Adams,
Alvord,
Anderson,
Arzeno,
Axford,
Mr. Crouse,
Danforth,
Desnoyers,
Dimond,
Eastman,
Mr. Mosher,
Newberry,
O'Brien,
J. D. Pierce,
N. Pierce,

Backus,	Eaton,	Redfield,
Bagg,	Edmunds,	Robertson,
Barnard,	Gale,	E. S. Robinson,
Beardsley,	Gibson,	M. Robertson,,
Beeson,	Graham,	Soule,
Britain,	Green,	Storey,
Alvarado Brown,	Hanscom,	Sullivan,
Ammon Brown,	Hart,	Sutherland,
Asahel Brown,	Harvey,	Tiffany,
Bush,	Hascall,	Town,
Carr,	Kingsley,	Walker,
Chandler,	Kinne,	Webster,
Choate,	Lee,	White,
Church,	Marvin,	Whipple,
S. Clark,	Mason,	Whittemore,
Conner,	McClelland,	Williams,
Cook,	McLeod,	Willard,
Cornell,	Morrison,	Woodman,
Crary,		70

The question then being on concurring with the committee of the whole in striking out the section, (39th,) the yeas and nays were ordered, with the following result:

YEAS.

Mr. Alvord,	Mr. Cook,	Mr. E. S. Robinson,
Arzeno,	Danforth,	M. Robinson,
Axford,	Desnoyers,	Rix Robinson,
Beeson,	Hathaway,	Storey,
Britain,	McClelland,	Tiffany,
Ammon Brown,	Mosher,	Town,
Chapel,	Redfield,	Walker,
Choate,	Roberts,	Witherell,
Church,	Robertson,	President, 27

NAYS.

Mr. W. Adams,	Mr. Eastman,	Mr. Morrison,
Anderson,	Eaton,	Mowry,
Backus,	Edmunds.	Newberry,
Bagg,	Fralick,	O'Brien,
Barnard,	Gale,	J. D. Pierce,
H. Bartow,	Gardiner,	N. Pierce,
Beardsley,	Gibson,	Skinner,
Alvarado Brown,	Graham,	Soule,
Asahel Brown,	Green,	Sturgis,
Burns,	Hanscom,	Sullivan,
Bush,	Hart,	Sutherland,
Butterfield,	Harvey,	Van Valkenburg,
Carr,	Hascall,	Warden,
Chandler,	Hixon,	Webster,

S. Clark,	Kingsley	Wells,
Comstock,	Kinne,	White,
Conner,	Lee,	Whipple,
Cornell,	Lovell,	Whittemore,
Crary,	Marvin,	Williams,
Crouse,	Mason,	Willard,
Daniels,	McLeod,	Woodman,
Dimond,	Moore,	65

So the amendment was non-concurred in.

On motion of Mr. McClelland,

Section 2 of the article was amended by striking out in the last line the word "four," and inserting "two" in lieu thereof.

Mr. Hanscom's proposition to recommit the article with instructions being under consideration,

A division of the question was ordered, and the vote first taken upon recommitting, and the same was lost, by the following vote:

YEAS.

Mr. Alvord,	Mr. Hanscom,	Mr. Storey,
Beardsley,	Hart,	Sturgis,
Church,	McLeod,	Sutherland,
Crary,	J. D. Pierce,	White,
Crouse,	Roberts,	Whipple,
Eastman,	Rix Robinson,	President,
Gardiner,		21

NAYS.

Mr. W. Adams,	Mr. Daniels,	Mr. Mowry,
Anderson,	Desnoyers,	Newberry,
Arzeno,	Dimond,	N. Pierce,
Axford,	Eaton,	Redfield,
Backus,	Edmunds,	Robertson,
Barnard,	Fralick,	E. S. Robinson,
H. Bartow,	Gale,	M. Robinson,
Beeson,	Gibson,	Skinner,
Britain,	Graham,	Soule,
Alvarado Brown,	Green,	Sullivan,
Ammon Brown,	Harvey,	Tiffany,
Burns,	Hascall,	Town,
Bush,	Hathaway,	VanValkenburg,
Butterfield,	Hixon,	Walker,
Carr,	Kingsley,	Warden,
Chandler,	Kinne,	Webster,
Chapel,	Lovell,	Wells,
Choate,	Marvin,	Whittemore,
S. Clark,	Mason,	Williams,
Comstock,	McClelland,	Willard,

Conner,	Moore,	Witherell,
Cook,	Morrison,	Woodman,
Cornell,	Mosher,	68

Mr. Sutherland moved that the vote by which the Convention concurred in the amendment made in committee to section 3, be reconsidered.

During the discussion of the question, and while Mr. Mason had the floor,

Mr. Roberts raised a point of order, "that the gentleman from St. Clair asserts an untruth in stating that there is no organized county in the Upper Peninsula."

The President decided Mr. Mason in order, and he proceeded with his remarks.

At this stage of the proceedings, Mr. Sutherland withdrew his motion.

On motion of Mr. Lovell,

Section 3 was amended by adding thereto the following: "and that each county having said ratio, and a fraction over, equal to a moiety of said rotio, shall be entitled to two Representatives; and so on above that number, giving one additional member for each additional ratio."

Mr. Mason moved to amend the section by adding thereto as follows: "The counties of Newaygo, Tuscola and Midland shall be entitled each to one Representative.

Mr. Williams offered the following as an amendment to the amendment:

"The counties of Sanilac and Huron shall be entitled to one Representative; the county of Tuscola shall be entitled to one Representative; the counties of Saginaw, Midland, and the territory thereto attached, shall be entitled to one Representative; the counties of Montcalm, Gratiot, and the territory thereto attached, shall be entitled to one Representative; the counties of Newaygo, Oceanna, and the territory thereto attached, shall be entitled to one Representative; and the counties of Marquette, Houghton, Schoolcraft and Ontonagon shall be entitled to one Repreeentative."

When, on motion of Mr. J. D. Pierce,

The Convention adjourned.

Afternoon Session.

Half-past two o'clock.

The Convention was called to order by the President.

A quorum of members in attendance.

The consideration of the article entitled "Legislative Department," was resumed.

The question being upon the substitute proposed by Mr. Williams for the amendment of Mr. Mason, it was modified to read as follows, and then accepted by Mr. Mason:

"And provided that the county of Huron shall be attached to Sanilac, and together they shall be entitled to one Representative; the county of Tuscola shall be entitled to one Representative; the counties of Gratiot, Midland and Saranac shall be entitled to one Representative; the county of Montcalm and the counties thereto attached shall be entitled to one Representative; the counties of Newaygo, Oceana and the counties thereto attached, shall be entitled to one Representative; the counties of Houghton, Schoolcraft, Marquette and Ontonagon shall be entitled to one Representative; and the county of Delta shall be attached to Mackinac, and together they shall be entitled to one Representative."

On motion of Mr. Roberts,

The foregoing was amended by striking out so much as related to the counties of Marquette, Schoolcraft, Houghton, Ontonagon, Delta and Mackinac.

And the question being on the adoption of the amendment as amended, it was not agreed to.

Mr. McClelland proposed the following as a substitute for the section:

"3. The Legislature shall provide by law for an enumeration of the inhabitants of this State in the year eighteen hundred and fifty five, and at the end of every ten years thereafter; and at the first session after each enumeration so made, and also after each enumeration made by the authority of the United States, the Legislature shall apportion anew the Representatives and Senators among the several counties and districts, according to the number of white inhabitants; which, apportionment shall remain unaltered until the return of another enumeration. Every organized county, which with the territory that may be attached thereto for representative purposes, shall contain 2,000 inhabitants, shall be entitled to one Representative; and it shall be competent for the Legislature to authorize an enumeration of the inhabitants of such county or territory in such manner and at such time as they may deem fit."

On motion of Mr. McLeod,

The proposition was amended by inserting after the words "white inhabitants," "and civilized persons of Indian descent, not members of any tribe."

Mr. Sutherland proposed further to amend by adding:

"Provided, That Tuscola shall be entitled to one Representative; Midland, Gratiot and Saranac, one Representative; Newago and Oceana, one representative; Sanilac one representative; Montcalm one representative.

Which was disagreed to, as follows:

YEAS.

Mr. W. Adams,	Mr. Danforth,	Mr. Orr,
Alvord,	Dimond,	J. D. Pierce,
Arzeno,	Eastman,	Rix Robinson,
Bagg,	Edmunds,	Skinner,
Barnard,	Gale,	Soule,
H. Bartow,	Gardiner,	Sturgis,
Burns,	Hanscom,	Sutherland,
Bush,	Hart,	Town,
Chandler,	Hixon,	Walker,
Chapel,	Lovell,	Warden,
Church,	Mason,	White,
J. Clark,	McLeod,	Whipple,
Crary,	Mowry,	President,
Crouse,		40

NAYS.

Mr. Anderson,	Mr. Cornell,	Mr. O'Brien,
Axford,	Daniels,	N. Pierce,
Backus,	Desnoyers,	Redfield,
Beardsley,	Eaton,	Robertson,
Beeson,	Fralick,	E. S. Robinson,
Britain,	Gibson,	Storey,
Alvarado Brown,	Green,	Sullivan,
Ammon Brown,	Harvey,	VanValkenburg,
Asahel Brown,	Hascall,	Webster,
Butterfield,	Hathaway,	Wells,
Carr,	Kinne,	Whittemore,
Choate,	Marvin,	Williams,

S. Clark,	McClelland,	Willard,
Comstock,	Moore,	Witherell,
Conner,	Mosher,	Woodman,
Cook,	Newberry,	47.

Mr. Chapel moved to strike out "2,000," and insert "1,500" in lieu thereof.

But the Convention refused to strike out.

Mr. McClelland modified his proposition by inserting "1500" in lieu of "2000."

Mr. Storey moved to strike out "1500" and insert "2000."

Which was not agreed to.

The yeas and nays being demanded on the adoption of the substitute, the result was as follows:

YEAS.

Mr. W. Adams,	Mr. Crary,	Mr. J. D. Pierce,
Alvord,	Crouse,	Robertson,
Arzeno,	Danforth,	Rix Robinson,
Barnard,	Dimond,	Skinner,
H. Bartow,	Eastman,	Soule,
Britain,	Edmunds,	Storey,
Alvarado Brown,	Gale,	Sturgis,
Asahel Brown,	Gardiner,	Sutherland,
Burns,	Hanscom,	Town,
Bush,	Hart,	Walker,
Butterfield,	Kingsley,	Warden,
Chapel,	Kinne,	Webster,
Choate,	Lovell,	White,
Church,	Marvin,	Whipple,
J. Clark,	Mason,	Whittemore,
Comstock,	McClelland,	Williams,
Conner,	McLeod,	Willard,
Cook,	Mowry,	Woodman,
Cornell,	Orr,	56

NAYS.

Mr. Anderson,	Mr. Desnoyers,	Mr. Newberry,
Axford,	Eaton,	O'Brien,
Backus,	Fralick,	N. Pierce,
Bagg,	Gibson,	Redfield,
Beardsley,	Green,	E. S. Robinson,
Beeson,	Harvey,	M. Robinson,
Ammon Brown,	Hascall,	Sullivan,
Carr,	Hathaway,	Tiffany,
Chandler,	Hixon,	Van Valkenburg,
S. Clark,	Moore,	Wells,
Daniels,	Mosher,	Witherell, 33

So the substitute proposed by Mr. McClelland for section 3 was agreed too.

On motion of Mr. Danforth,

The Convention then adjourned.

Lansing, Wednesday, July 17, 1850.

The Convention met pursuant to adjournment and was called to order by the President.

Prayer by the Rev. Mr. Atterbury.

The roll being called, there were absent with leave, Messrs. P. R. Adams, Leach and Raynale; without leave Messrs. J. Bartow, McClelland and Prevost.

CORRECTION OF THE JOURNAL.

Mr. Britain moved to amend the journal of yesterday by inserting after the substitute proposed by Mr. McClelland to section 3 of the article entitled "Legislative Department," the following, viz:

"Mr. White proposed the following as an addition to the substi-
"tute, which, after some debate, was withdrawn.
"'Provided that each county whose organization on the first day
"of January, A. D. 1851, shall have been perfected by election of
"county officers, shall be entitled to at least one representative.'"

On this correction Mr. Britain asked the yeas and nays,

And the journal was ordered corrected by the following vote:

YEAS:

Mr. W. Adams,	Mr. Danforth,	Mr. Mosher,
Alvord,	Desnoyers,	Mowry,
Anderson,	Eaton,	Newberry,
Backus,	Edmunds,	O'Brien,
Bagg,	Fralick,	N. Pierce,
Barnard,	Gale,	Redfield,
H. Bartow,	Gardiner,	Robertson,
Beeson,	Gibson,	Skinner,
Britain,	Graham,	Storey,
Alvarado Brown,	Green,	Sullivan,
Asahel Brown,	Hanscom,	Town,
Burns,	Hart,	Van Valkenburg,
Bush,	Harvey,	Wait,
Carr,	Hascall,	Walker,
Chandler,	Hathaway,	Warden,
S. Clark,	Hixon,	Wells,
Comstock,	Kingley,	White,

Conner,	Kinne,	Whipple,
Cook,	Marvin,	Whittemore,
Cornell,	Moore,	Willard,
Crouse,	Morrison,	Woodman, 63

NAYS:

Mr. Arzeno,	Mr. Daniels,	Mr. Rix Robinson,
Axford,	Dimond,	Soule,
Beardsley,	Mason,	Sturgis,
Butterfield,	Orr,	Sutherland,
Choate,	J. D. Pierce,	Tiffany,
Church,	Roberts,	Williams,
Crary,	F. S. Robinson,	President, 21

On motion of Mr. J. D. Pierce,

The Journal was ordered corrected by the insertion of all amendments and substitutes yesterday proposed and withdrawn.

On motion of Mr. Britain,

The journal was corrected as follows:

"Strike out from amendment of Mr. McLeod to Mr. McClelland's
" substitute for section 3, 'not members of any tribe,' and insert as
" follows:

" Mr. Britain moved to amend the amendment, by adding thereto
" 'not members of any tribe,' which was accepted by the mover."

On motion of Mr. Britain,

The journal was further corrected by inserting after the amendment proposed by Mr. White to the substitute for section 3 offered by Mr. McClelland, the follwing, viz:

"Mr. Britain moved to amend the amendment by inserting after
"'officers,' 'and such territory as may be attached thereto for repre-
"sentative purposes,' which was accepted by the mover."

Mr. Sutherland moved to correct the journal of yesterday so that it would read as follows:

"Mr. Sutherland moved that the vote by which the Convention
" concurred in the amendment made in committee to section 3 be
" reconsidered, for the purpose of offering a substitute."

Which was withdrawn.

Mr. Van Valkenburgh moved that the journal of yesterday be corrected in which he is made to withdraw his motion to amend section 39 of legislative department.

The motion did not prevail.

LEAVE OF ABSENCE.

Mr. Lovell asked and obtained leave of absence for Mr. Prevost until Saturday; and Mr. Hixon for Mr. McClelland for an indefinite period.

PETITIONS.

By Mr. Moore: two several petitions of sundy inhabitants of St. Joseph county, praying that the legalization of the traffic in ardent spirits may be prohibited; also

By Mr. Wells: of A. U. Mack and 73 others, and of Asa B. Brown and 13 others, citizens of Kalamazoo county, praying a like prohibition.

Referred to select committee upon the subject.

By the President: of Mrs. L. J. Cardwell and 135 others, Daughters of Temperance in the village of Almont and its vicinity, praying that a clause may be inserted in the revised constitution, prohibiting the manufacture, importation, and sale of intoxicating liquors for other than medicinal and mechanical purposes.

Which, on motion of Mr. Van Valkenburgh,

Was referred to the select committee upon the subject.

The President presented a resolution adopted by the common council of the city of Detroit, requesting the incorporation of a provision into the constitution preventing banks, rail roads, and other incorporations from being exempted from municipal and county taxes.

Referred to the committee on finance and taxation.

REPORTS.

Mr. Tiffany, from a majority of the committee on exemptions and the rights of married women, submitted a report accompanied by an article entitled "Rights of Married Women."

Which was laid upon the table and ordered printed.

MOTIONS, RESOLUTIONS, &c.

Mr. Van Valkenburgh presented the following protest:

Whereas, it is made to appear, by the journals of yesterday, that I withdrew my amendment to section 39 in the article Legislative Department,

And whereas, it was my intention to withdraw only my demand for the yeas and nays, and not the original amendment offered by me, I therefore protest against the position in which I am made to appear on the said journal.

J. VAN VALKENBURGH.

And the same was ordered entered upon the journal.

On motion of Mr. Woodman,

The vote granting indefinite leave of absence to Mr. P. R. Adams was reconsidered.

Mr. Woodman moved that the Sergeant-at-arms be instructed to take Mr. P. R. Adams into immediate custody.

The motion was withdrawn.

Mr. Alvord submitted the following resolution:

Resolved, That the committee on "Exemptions and the rights of Married Women," be instructed to report to this Convention some "rule" whereby the "*thunder*" of each member may remain *inviolate.*

A motion being made to lay the resolution on the table,

Mr. Alvord withdrew it.

The Convention having reached the order of

UNFINISHED BUSINESS.

Resumed the consideration of the article entitled "Legislative Department."

Mr. Comstock moved the reconsideration of the vote by which the Convention refused to concur in the amendment made by the committee of the whole, striking out section 39.

The President called Mr. Hanscom to the chair.

Mr, Robertson moved the previous question, but by request,

He withdrew the call.

Mr. Cornell moved a call of the Convention, but withdrew the motion.

Mr. Williams renewed the motion, and the same prevailed.

The roll being called, Messrs. P. R. Adams, S. Clark, Crary, Green, M. Robinson and Sutherland, were absent without leave.

On motion of Mr. J. D. Pierce,

All further proceedings under the call were dispensed with.

The question being on Mr. Comstock's motion to reconsider,

The yeas and nays were demanded thereon, and the same was negatived by the following vote:

YEAS:

Mr. Alvord,	Mr. Crouse,	Mr. Rix Robinson,
Arzeno,	Daniels,	Skinner,

Axford, J. Bartow, Britain, Ammon Brown, Butterfield, Chapel, Church, J. Clark, Comstock, Cook, Desnoyers, Fralick, Gardiner, Harvey, Hascall, Hathaway, Roberts, Robertson, E. S. Robinson, Storey, Tiffany, Town, Walker, Webster, Wells, White, Witherell, President, — 34

NAYS:

Mr. W. Adams, Anderson, Backus, Bagg, Barnard, H. Bartow, Beardsley, Beeson, Alvarado Brown, Asahel Brown, Burns, Bush, Carr, Chandler, Choate, Conner, Cornell, Danforth, Dimond, Mr. Eastman, Eaton, Edmunds, Gale, Gibson, Graham, Hanscom, Hart, Hixon, Kingsley, Kinne, Lee, Lovell, Marvin, Mason, McLeod, Moore, Morrison, Mr. Mosher, Mowry, Newberry, O'Brien, Orr, J. D. Pierce, N. Pierce, Redfield, Souie, Sturgis, Van Valkenburg, Wait, Warden, Whipple, Whittemore, Williams, Willard, Woodman, — 55

Mr. Church moved to strike from section 25 of the article, all after the word "security" in the 4th line, to and including the word "oath" in the 17th line;

But withdrew the same, when

Mr. Goodwin offered the following:

Resolved, That section 39 be committed to the select committee on the subject to which it relates, with instructions to prepare and report a section abolishing the existing laws authorizing the licensing of the sale of spirituous liquors, and prohibiting the Legislature from hereafter passing any law authorizing the same, together with a resolution providing for submitting such section separately to the people.

Mr. White moved to adjourn.

But the Convention refused to adjourn.

The question being upon the adoption of the resolution, the yeas and nays were demanded thereon.

The Clerk having partly called the roll,

Mr. Britain addressed the chair, when a motion was made to allow him to proceed, which was lost.

The resolution was then lost by the following vote:

YEAS.

Mr. Alvord,
Beeson,
Britain,
Butterfield,
Chapel,
Church,
J. Clark,
Comstock,
Cook,
Mr. Daniels,
Desnoyers,
Fralick,
Gardiner,
Hathaway,
Roberts,
Robertson,
Rix Robinson,
Mr. Story,
Tiffany,
Walker,
Webster,
Wells,
White,
Witherell,
President, 25

NAYS.

Mr. W. Adams,
Anderson,
Axford,
Backus,
Bagg,
Barnard,
H. Bartow,
J. Bartow,
Alvarado Brown,
Ammon Brown,
Asahel Brown,
Burns,
Bush,
Carr,
Chandler,
Choate,
S. Clark,
Conner,
Cornell,
Crary,
Mr. Crouse,
Eastman,
Eaton,
Edmunds,
Gale,
Gibson,
Hanscom,
Hart,
Hascall,
Hixon,
Kingsley,
Kinne,
Lee,
Lovell,
Mason,
Moore,
Morrison,
Mosher,
Mowry,
Newberry,
Mr. O'Brien,
Orr,
J. D. Pierce,
N. Pierce,
Redfield,
M. Robinson,
Soule,
Sturgis,
Sullivan,
Sutherland,
Town,
Van Valkenburg,
Wait,
Warden,
Whipple,
Whittemore,
Williams,
Willard,
Woodman, 59

On motion of Mr. Roberts,

The Convention adjourned.

Afternoon Session.

Half past two o'clock.

The President called the Convention to order.

A quorum of members being in attendance, the Convention resumed the consideration of the unfinished business of this morning, the article entitled "Legislative Department."

Mr. Church renewed his proposition of this morning, modified so as to strike out from the word "thereof," in line four of section 25, to and inclusive of the word "oath," in line 17.

Mr. Cook raised a point of order, "that the amendment to the section having been reported by the committee of the whole and concurred in by the Convention, it is not now in order to strike out a portion of it."

The President decided the proposition of Mr. Church not in order.

Mr. J. Bartow moved to reconsider the vote by which the Convention concurred in the amendment made by the committee of the whole to section 25.

Mr. Hascall asked the yeas and nays, and the same being ordered, the motion prevailed by the following vote:

YEAS:

Mr. Alvord,
Arzeno,
Axford,
Bagg,
Barnard,
H. Bartow,
J. Bartow,
Beeson,
Ammon Brown,
Burns,
Bush,
Butterfield,
Carr,
Church,
J. Clark,
Cook,
Cornell,
Crary,
Mr. Danforth,
Eastman,
Fralick,
Gardiner,
Gibson,
Graham,
Hanscom,
Hart,
Kingsley,
Kinne,
Marvin,
Mason,
McLeod,
Mosher,
Mowry,
Newberry,
O'Brien,
Mr. Redfield,
Roberts,
Robertson,
E. S. Robinson,
Rix Robinson,
Skinner,
Soule,
Storey,
Sullivan,
Van Valkenburg,
Warden,
Webster,
White,
Whipple,
Whittemore,
Woodman,
President, 52

NAYS:

Mr. W. Adams,
Anderson,
Backus,
Beardsley,
Britain,
Asahel Brown,
Chandler,
Mr. Daniels,
Dimond,
Eaton,
Edmunds,
Gale,
Green,
Harvey,
Mr. Morrison,
Orr,
M. Robinson,
Sturgis,
Tiffany,
Town,
Wait,

Chapel,	Hascall,	Walker,
Choate,	Hathaway,	Wells,
S. Clark,	Lee,	Williams,
Comstock,	Lovell,	Willard,
Conner,	Moore,	Witherell,
Crouse,		67

Mr. Roberts offered the following, as a substitute for the entire section:

"The legislature shall provide their fuel and stationery, the printing and binding of their laws and journals, and all other printing they may wish executed, in such manner as they may deem expedient."

Mr. Witherell moved to amend the substitute by striking out the last clause, and inserting the words "by contract,"

Which he subsequently withdrew.

On motion of Mr. Church,

The amendment made in committee was amended by striking out all after the word "thereof," in the 4th line, up to and inclusive of the word "oath," in the 17th line.

The amendment as amended was then concurred in.

Mr. Britain moved to amend the section by adding thereto the words, "nor shall constructive composition or press-work in any case be paid for," upon which he asked the yeas and nays.

And the same being demanded, the amendment was disagreed to, as follows:

YEAS.

Mr. W. Adams,	Mr. Crouse,	Mr. Orr,
Anderson,	Daniels,	Redfield,
Backus,	Eaton,	Robertson,
Bagg,	Edmunds,	M. Robinson,
H. Bartow,	Gale,	Sturgis,
Beardsley,	Green,	Tiffany,
Britain,	Harvey,	Town,
Asahel Brown,	Hascall,	Wiat,
Burns,	Hathaway,	Walker,
Carr,	Hixon,	Wells,
Chandler,	Lovell,	Whipple,
Chapel,	Moore,	Williams,
S. Clark,	Morrison,	Willard,
Comstock,	Mosher,	Witherell,
Cook,	O'Brien,	44

NAYS:

Mr. Alvord,	Mr. Dimond,	Mr. Roberts,
Arzeno,	Eastman,	E. S. Robinson,
Axford,	Fralick,	Rix Robinson,
Barnard,	Gardiner,	Skinner,
J. Bartow,	Gibson,	Soule,
Beeson,	Graham,	Storey,
Alvarado Brown,	Hanscom,	Sullivan,
Ammon Brown,	Hart,	Sutherland,
Butterfield,	Kingsley,	Van Valkenburg,
Choate,	Kinne,	Warden,
Church,	Marvin,	Webster,
J. Clark,	McLeod,	White,
Conner,	Mowry,	Whittemore,
Cornell,	Newberry,	Woodman,
Crary,	J. D. Pierce,	President,
Danforth,		46

Mr. Williams moved to amend the section as follows:

Insert after "journals," in the 2d line of section 25, as follows: "all blanks, paper and printing for the executive departments; all advertisements of tax sales in counties where two or more newspapers are published."

Mr. Crary moved to amend the amendment by striking out all after the word "departments."

Mr. Williams asked the yeas and nays.

And the same being demanded, the amendment was agreed to as follows:

YEAS.

Mr. W. Adams,	Mr. Gardiner,	E. S. Robinson,
Alvord,	Graham,	Rix Robinson,
Arzeno,	Hanscom,	Skinner,
Bagg,	Hart,	Soule,
Barnard,	Hascall,	Storey,
Alvarodo Brown,	Kingsley,	Struges,
Bush,	Kinne,	Sullivan,
Chapel,	Lee,	Town,
Church,	Marvin,	Walker,
S. Clark,	McLeod,	Warden,
Cook,	Morrison,	White,
Cornell,	Newberry,	Whipple,
Crary,	J. D. Pierce,	Whittemore,
Danforth,	Redfield,	Willard,
Eaton,	Robertson,	President,
Fralick,		46

NAYS.

Mr. Axford,	Mr. Comstock,	Mr. Mowry,
Backus,	Conner,	O'Brien,
H. Bartow,	Crouse,	Orr,
J. Bartow,	Daniels,	Roberts,
Beeson,	Dimond,	M. Robinson,
Britain,	Eastman,	Sutherland,
Ammon Brown,	Edmunds,	Tiffany,
Asahel Brown,	Gibson,	Van Valkenburg,
Burns,	Green,	Wait,
Butterfield,	Harvey,	Webster,
Carr,	Hathaway,	Wells,
Chandler,	Hixon,	Williams,
Choate,	Lovell,	Witherell,
J. Clark,	Mosher,	

41

Upon Mr. Williams' amendment he asked the yeas and nays, and the same was agreed to, as follows:

YEAS.

Mr. Backus,	Mr. Danforth,	Mr. Redfield,
Bagg,	Daniels,	Robertson,
H. Bartow,	Eastman,	M. Robinson,
Beardsley,	Eaton,	Rix Robinson,
Britain,	Edmunds,	Skinner,
Alvarado Brown,	Gardiner,	Soule,
Asahel Brown,	Graham,	Sturgis,
Bush,	Green,	Sullivan,
Carr,	Harvey,	Wait,
Chandler,	Hascall,	Walker,
Chapel,	Hixon,	Warden,
Choate,	Kingsley,	Webster,
Church,	Lee,	White,
S. Clark,	Lovell,	Whipple,
Comstock,	Marvin,	Williams,
Conner,	McLeod,	Willard,
Cook,	Morrison,	Witherell,
Cornell,	Mosher,	President,
Crary,	Orr,	

56

NAYS.

Mr. Barnard,	Mr. Fralick,	Mr. Roberts,
Ammon Brown,	Gibson,	Sutherland,
Butterfield,	Hanscom,	Town,
J. Clark,	Kinne,	Whittemore,
Dimond,	Newberry,	

14

Mr. Hascall moved to amend the section by inserting after "lowest," in the 3d line, the word "responsible."

The motion was withdrawn.

The question recurring on the substitute proposed by Mr. Roberts,

Mr. Britain asked the yeas and nays.

And the same were taken with the following result:

YEAS:

Mr. McLeod,	Mr. Roberts,	Mr. Sutherland,	3

NAYS:

Mr. Alvord,	Mr. Crary,	Mr. Mowry,	
Anderson,	Crouse,	Newberry,	
Arzeno,	Danforth,	O'Brien,	
Axford,	Daniels,	Orr,	
Backus,	Dimond,	J. D. Pierce,	
Bagg,	Eastman,	Redfield,	
Barnard,	Eaton,	Robertson,	
H. Bartow,	Fralick,	Skinner,	
Beardsley,	Gardiner,	Soule,	
Beeson,	Gibson,	Sturgis,	
Britain,	Graham,	Sullivan,	
Alvarado Brown,	Green,	Tiffany,	
Ammon Brown,	Hanscom,	Town,	
Asahel Brown,	Harvey,	Van Valkenburg,	
Butterfield,	Hascall,	Wait,	
Carr,	Hathaway,	Warden,	
Chandler,	Hixon,	Webster,	
Chapel,	Kingsley,	White,	
Choate,	Kinne,	Whipple,	
Church,	Lee,	Whittemore,	
Comstock,	Lovell,	Williams,	
Conner,	Marvin,	Willard,	
Cook,	Morrison,	Woodman,	
Cornell,	Mosher,	President,	72

So the substitute was not adopted.

Mr. Willard moved to amend section 17 of the article by striking out "three," wherever it occurs, and inserting "two."

He moved a call of the house.

And the same being ordered,

The roll was called, and Messrs. P. R. Adams, J. Clark, Gale, Hart, Mason and N. Pierce were absent without leave.

On motion of Mr. Woodman,

All further proceedings under the call were dispensed with.

A division of the question was ordered upon the proposition of Mr. Willard, and the yeas and nays being demanded, the motion to strike out was lost by the following vote:

YEAS.

Mr. Backus, Ashel Brown, Bush, Carr, Chandler, S. Clark, Comstock, Cook, Danforth,

Mr. Edmunds, Green, Harvey, Hascall, Hixon, Lovell, Morrison, Newberry, Sturgis,

Mr. Town, Van Valkenburg, Wait, Webster, Wells, Williams, Willard, Witherell, 26

NAYS.

Mr. W. Adams, Alvord, Anderson, Arzeno, Axford, Bagg, Barnard, H. Bartow, J. Bartow, Beardsley, Beeson, Britain, Alvarado Brown, Ammon Brown, Burns, Butterfield, Chapel, Choate, Church, J. Clark, Conner, Cornell,

Mr. Crary, Crouse, Daniels, Desnoyers, Dimond, Eaton, Fralick, Gale, Gardiner, Gibson, Graham, Hanscom, Hart, Hathaway, Kingsley, Kinne, Lee, Marvin, McLeod, Moore, Mosher, Mowry,

Mr. O'Brien, Orr, J. D. Pierce, Redfield, Robertson, E. S. Robinson, M. Robinson, Rix Robinson, Skinner, Soule, Storey, Sullivan, Sutherland, Tiffany, Walker, Warden, White, Whipple, Whittemore, Woodman, President, 65

Prior to the announcement of the result, Mr. Roberts was excused from voting.

Mr. Bagg proposed the following amendment to the article.

Insert after "township," line 9, section 4, the words "or city," and add at the end of the section the following:

"And when any township or city shall contain a population which shall entitle it to more than one representative, then such township or city shall elect the number of Representatives to which it shall be so entitled, by general ticket.

On motion of Mr. Alvord,

The Convention adjourned.

Lansing, Thursday, July 18, 1850.

The President called the Convention to order at the usual hour.

Prayer by the Rev. Mr. Sanford.

The roll being called, Mr. P. R. Adams was absent without leave, and Messrs. Leach, McClelland and Prevost with leave.

Journal approved.

RESOLUTIONS.

Mr. Cornell submitted the following:

Resolved, That from and after to day, the morning sessions shall commence at 8 o'clock and adjourn at 11 o'clock A. M.; the afternoon sessions shall commence at 3 o'clock and adjourn at six o'clock P. M. until otherwise ordered.

Mr. Hascall moved to strike out the words "and adjourn at 11 o'clock A. M."

Which did not prevail.

Mr. Ammon Brown moved to strike out all after the words "8 o'clock."

Which was disagreed to.

Mr. Eaton moved to strike out "eight" and insert "seven."

Mr. Walker proposed the insertion of "half-past seven."

Which Mr. Eaton accepted.

Mr. Desnoyers moved to lay the resolution upon the table.

But the Convention refused to lay upon the table.

Mr. Eaton's amendment was lost.

On motion of Mr. Fralick,

So much of the resolution as related to the adjournments was stricken out.

Mr. Woodman moved to strike out "three," and insert in its stead "two."

But the motion did not prevail.

The resolution as amended was then adopted.

Mr. Britain submitted the following:

Resolved, That from and after the adoption of this resolution, no member shall speak more than eight minutes at any one time, without leave of the Convention.

Mr. Witherell moved to strike out "eight," and insert "five."

A division of the question was had, and the motion to strike out prevailed.

On motion of Mr. Woodman,

The resolution was indefinitely postponed.

UNFINISHED BUSINESS.

The Legislative article being taken up, the amendment proposed by Mr. Bagg to the 4th section was under consideration.

The yeas and nays being ordered thereon, the result was as follows:

YEAS:

Mr. W. Adams,	Mr. Danforth,	Mr. Redfield,
Alvord,	Desnoyers,	Robertson,
Arzeno,	Dimond,	M. Robinson,
Axford,	Eastman,	Rix Robinson,
Bagg,	Eaton,	Skinner,
Barnard,	Gardiner,	Soule,
J. Bartow,	Gibson,	Storey,
Beardsley,	Hanscom,	Sturgis,
Beeson,	Hart,	Sullivan,
Alvarado Brown,	Hathaway,	Town,
Ammon Brown,	Kingsley,	Van Valkenburg,
Bush,	Lee,	Walker,
Chapel,	Marvin,	Warden,
Choate,	Mason,	Whipple,
Church,	McLeod,	Whittemore,
J. Clark,	Mowry,	Witherell,
Cornell,	J. D. Pierce,	Woodman,
Crouse,	Raynale,	President, 54

NAYS.

Mr. Anderson,	Mr. Edmunds,	Mr. Mosher,
Backus,	Fralick,	Newberry,
H. Bartow,	Gale,	O'Brien,
Britain,	Graham,	Orr,
Asahel Brown,	Green,	N. Pierce,
Burns,	Harvey,	E. S. Robinson,
Butterfield,	Hascall	Tiffany,
Carr,	Hixon,	Wait,
Chandler,	Kinne,	Wells,
Comstock,	Lovell,	White,
Cook,	Moore,	Williams,
Daniels,	Morrison,	Willard, 36

So the amendment was agreed to.

Mr. Lovell moved to amend section 15 of the article by striking out in lines 4 and 6, the words "two-thirds," and inserting in their stead, "a majority."

Upon the amendment, Mr. Raynale asked the yeas and nays, and the same were taken, with the following result:

YEAS.

Mr. H. Bartow, Asahel Brown, Carr, Comstock, Mr. Edmunds, Green, Hanscom, Harvey, Mr. Lovell, Van Valkenburg, Williams, — 11

NAYS.

Mr. W. Adams, Alvord, Anderson, Arzeno, Axford, Barnard, J. Bartow, Beeson, Britain, Alvarado Brown, Ammon Brown, Bush, Butterfield, Chapel, Choate, Church, J. Clark, Conner, Cook, Cornell, Crary, Danforth, Dimond, Mr. Eastman, Eaton, Fralick, Gale, Gardiner, Gibson, Graham, Hascall, Hathaway, Hixon, Kingsley, Kinne, Marvin, Morrison, Mosher, Mowry, Newberry, O'Brien, Orr, J. D. Pierce, N. Pierce, Raynale, Mr. Redfield, Robertson, E. S. Robinson, M. Robinson, Rix Robins, Skinner, Storey, Sturgis, Sullivan, Sutherland, Town, Wait, Walker, Warden, Wells, White, Whipple, Whittemore, Willard, Witherell, Woodman, President. — 67

So the amendment did not prevail.

Mr. Kingsley moved to reconsider the vote by which the substitute of Mr. McClelland to section 3 was adopted on the 16th instant.

And the motion prevailed.

Mr. Whipple moved that the section (3) be referred to a select committee of nine; but withdrew his motion.

Mr. Kingsley moved to amend the substitute of Mr. McClelland by striking out all after the word "enumeration," and inserting the following:

Provided, That the county of Saginaw, with the territory thereto attached, shall be entitled to one Representative; the county of Tuscola and the territory thereto attached, one Representative; the county of Sanilac and the territory thereto attached, one Representative; the counties of Midland, Gratiot and Aronac, with the territory thereto attached, one Representative; the county of Montcalm with the territory attached thereto, one Representative; and the counties of Newago and Oceana with the territory attached thereto, one Representative; and each county hereafter organized, with such territory as may be attached thereto, shall be entitled to a separate Representative when it shall have attained a population equal to a moiety of the ratio of representation.

Mr. Hanscom proposed to amend the substitute offered by Mr. McClelland, by inserting after the words "representative purposes," the words, "that shall have perfected their county organization by the election of county officers by the first of January 1851."

Mr. Church moved the previous question, and the same being seconded, the question being, "shall the main question be now put?" it was decided in the affirmative.

The question first occurring on the proposition of Mr. Hanscom, it was disagreed to, by the following vote:

YEAS:

Mr. Arzeno,	Mr. Choate,	Mr. Hathaway,
H. Bartow,	Danforth,	McLeod,
Beardsley,	Hanscom,	President,
Chapel,		10

NAYS.

Mr. Alvord,	Mr. Desnoyers,	Mr. N. Pierce,
Anderson,	Dimond,	Raynale,
Axford,	Eastman,	Redfield,
Backus,	Eaton,	E. S. Robinson,
Bagg,	Fralick,	M. Robinson,
Barnard,	Gale,	Rix Robinson,
J. Bartow,	Gardiner,	Skinner,
Beeson,	Gibson,	Soule,
Britain,	Graham,	Storey,
Alvarado Brown,	Green,	Sturgis,
Ammon Brown,	Hart,	Sullivan,
Asahel Brown,	Harvey,	Sutherland,
Burns,	Hascall,	Tiffany,
Bush,	Hixon,	Town,
Carr,	Kingsley,	Van Valkenburg,

Chandler,	Kinne,	Wait,
Church,	Lee,	Walker,
J. Clark,	Lovell,	Webster,
Comstock,	Marvin,	Wells,
Conner,	Mason,	White,
Cook,	Moore,	Whipple,
Cornell,	Mosher,	Williams,
Crary,	Mowry,	Willard,
Crouse,	O'Brien,	Woodman,
Daniels,	Orr,	74

The amendment of Mr. Kingsley was then agreed to, as follows:

YEAS:

Mr. W. Adams,	Mr. Dimond,	Mr. J. D. Pierce,
Alvord,	Eastman,	N. Pierce,
Anderson,	Eaton,	Redfield,
Axford,	Edmunds,	Robertson,
Bagg,	Fralick,	E. S. Robinson,
Barnard,	Gale,	M. Robinson,
H. Bartow,	Gardiner,	Rix Robinson,
J. Bartow,	Gibson,	Skinner,
Beardsley,	Graham,	Soule,
Beeson,	Green,	Storey,
Alvarado Brown,	Hart,	Sturgis,
Ammon Brown,	Harvey,	Sullivan,
Burns,	Hascall,	Sutherland,
Bush,	Hathaway,	Tiffany,
Butterfield,	Hixon,	Town,
Chandler,	Kingsley,	Van Valkenburg,
Church,	Lee,	Warden,
J. Clark,	Lovell,	Webster,
Comstock,	Mason,	White,
Conner,	Moore,	Whipple,
Cornell,	Morrison,	Whittemore,
Crary,	Mosher,	Williams,
Crouse,	Mowry,	Woodman,
Daniels,	O'Brien,	President,
Desnoyers,	Orr,	74

NAYS:

Mr. Arzeno,	Mr. Cook,	Mr. Raynale,
Backus,	Hanscom,	Wait,
Asahel Brown,	Kinne,	Walker,
Carr,	Marvin,	Wells,
Chapel,	Newberry,	Willard,
Choate,		16

And the question being on the substitute as amended, the same was adopted.

Mr. Cornell moved a reconsideration of the vote by which the Convention concurred in the substitute of the committee of the whole for the 28th section.

Mr. Axford demanded the yeas and nays; and the same were had with the following result:

YEAS:

Mr. Anderson,
Backus,
H. Bartow,
Beardsley,
Beeson,
Butterfield,
Chandler,
Church,
Comstock,
Cook,
Cornell,
Crary,
Danforth,
Daniels,
Edmunds,
Mr. Gardiner,
Gibson,
Graham,
Hart,
Harvey,
Hixon,
Lovell,
Mason,
McLeod,
Moore,
Morrison,
J. D. Pierce,
N. Pierce,
E. S. Robinson,
Rix Robinson,
Mr. Skinner,
Soule,
Storey,
Sullivan,
Tiffany,
VanValkenburgh,
Wait,
Webster,
White,
Whipple,
Whittemore,
Williams,
Witherell,
President, 44

NAYS:

Mr. W. Adams,
Alvord,
Arzeno,
Axford,
Barnard,
Britain,
Alvarado Brown,
Ammon Brown,
Asahel Brown,
Burns,
Bush,
Carr,
Chapel,
Choate,
J. Clark,
Mr. Conner,
Crouse,
Desnoyers,
Dimond,
Eastman,
Eaton,
Fralick,
Gale,
Green,
Hanscom,
Hascall,
Hathaway,
Kinne,
Lee,
Marvin,
Mr. Mosher,
Mowry,
Newberry,
O'Brien,
Orr,
Raynale,
Redfield,
Robertson,
M. Robinson,
Sturgis,
Town,
Walker,
Wells,
Willard,
Woodman, 45

So the motion to reconsider did not prevail.

On motion of Mr. Cook,

Section 37 of the article was amended by striking out "1851," and inserting in its stead, "1852."

On motion of Mr. Barnard,

Section 18 of the article was amended as follows:

Line 1, after the words "Speaker," insert the words "during the sessions of the legislature."

Also, insert after the word "of," in line 1, the words "postage on."

Also, strike out the word "for," in line 2, and insert the word "on."

Mr. Edmunds proposed to amend section 17 by inserting after the word "message," in the 6th line, the following:

"And each session of the Legislature shall terminate on the day on which the members thereof cease to receive their pay from the State Treasury."

But the amendment was not agreed to.

Mr. Kingsley moved to reconsider the vote by which the Convention concurred in the amendment of the committee of the whole to section 7.

But the motion was lost.

Mr. McLeod moved that the vote by which the Convention concurred in the amendment made by the committee of the whole to section 38 be reconsidered.

Mr. Morrison asked the yeas and nays, and the same were demanded and the motion prevailed, as follows:

YEAS.

Mr. Alvord,	Mr. Fralick,	Mr. M. Robinson,
H. Bartow,	Gardiner,	Rix Robinson,
Beardsley,	Gibson,	Skinner,
Beeson,	Graham,	Soule,
Alvarado Brown,	Green,	Storey,
Ammon Brown,	Hanscom,	Sullivan,
Burns,	Hascall,	Tiffany,
Butterfield,	Kingsley,	VanValkenburg,
Carr,	Kinne,	Wait,
Church,	Lovell,	Wells,
J. Clark,	McLeod,	White,
Cook,	Mosher,	Whittemore,
Cornell,	J. D. Pierce,	Whipple,
Crary,	Raynale,	Williams,
Eastman,	Robertson,	President,
Edmunds,		46

NAYS.

Mr. W. Adams,	Mr. Eaton,	Mr. Orr,
Anderson,	Gale,	N. Pierce,
Arzeno,	Harvey,	Redfield,
Britain,	Hathaway,	E. S. Robinson,

Asahel Brown,	Hixon,	Sturgis,
Bush,	Marvin,	Town,
Chandler,	Mason,	Walker,
Chapel,	Moore,	Warden,
Choate,	Morrison,	Webster,
Comstock,	Mowry,	Willard,
Conner,	Newberry,	Witherell,
Crouse,	O'Brien,	Woodman,
Desnoyers,		37

On motion of Mr. Eaton,

The Convention adjourned.

Afternoon Session.

3 o'clock.

The Convention was called to order by the President.

Roll called and a quorum being present, the consideration of the Article entitled "Legislative Department" was resumed.

Mr. McLeod moved to strike out section 38, and insert:

"The Legislature shall have no power to establish a State Paper; but may provide for the publication of general laws in all the newspapers in the state, at a compensation therefor of not exceeding twenty dollars to each newspaper, which shall publish the same within forty days after their passage."

On motion of Mr. Church,

"Twenty" was stricken out and "ten" inserted.

On motion of Mr. Cook,

The word "the" was inserted before "general laws," and the words "of each session" after "laws."

Mr. Newberry moved the previous question,

But it was not seconded.

Mr. Church moved to reconsider the vote by which "twenty" was stricken out.

But the motion did not prevail.

Mr. Hascall submitted the following as a substitute for the proposition of Mr. McLeod:

"The Legislature shall have no power to establish a State Paper; but it shall provide for the publication of the general laws in one or more newspapers in each county in the State, having the largest circulation, providing the pay therefor shall not exceed twenty dollars for any one session."

Mr. Sutherland moved to postpone the further consideration of the article until Tuesday next.

Which was not agreed to.

The substitute of Mr. Hascall was rejected.

Mr. Williams offered the following as a substitute for the one proposed by Mr. McLeod:

"The Legislature shall have no power to establish a state paper, but every newspaper in the state which shall publish all the general laws of any session within forty days of their passage, shall be entitled to receive fifteen dollars therefor."

And the same was adopted.

The question now recurring on the adoption of the substitute for the section, a division being had,

The motion to strike out the section prevailed by yeas and nays, as follows:

YEAS.

Mr. Alvord,	Mr. Eaton,	Mr. Raynale,
Backus,	Edmunds,	Roberts,
H. Bartow,	Fralick,	Robertson,
Beeson,	Gardiner,	M. Robinson,
Britain,	Gibson,	Rix Robinson,
Alvarado Brown,	Green,	Skinner,
Ammon Brown,	Hanscom,	Soule,
Burns,	Hart,	Storey,
Butterfield,	Harvey,	Sturgis,
Chapel,	Hascall,	Sullivan,
Church,	Kingsley.	Town,
J. Clark,	Lovell,	Van Valkenburg
Conner,	Marvin,	Wells,
Cook,	Mason,	White,
Cornell,	McLeod,	Whittemore,
Crary,	Mosher,	Williams,
Daniels,	Mowry,	Willard,
Desnoyers,	O'Brien,	Witherell,
Eastman,	J. D. Pierce,	57

NAYS.

Mr. W. Adams,	Mr. Comstock,	Mr. Orr,
Anderson,	Crouse,	N. Pierce,
Arzeno,	Danforth,	Redfield,
Axford,	Dimond,	E. S. Robinson,
Bagg,	Gale,	Sutherland,

Barnard,	Hathaway,	Wait,
Beardsley,	Hixon,	Walker,
Asahel Brown,	Kinne,	Warden,
Bush,	Lee,	Webster,
Carr,	Moore,	Whipple,
Chandler,	Morrison,	Woodman,
Choate,	Newberry,	President. 36

Mr. White moved to amend the substitute by inserting after "re ceive," the words "a sum not exceeding."

Which was agreed to.

The substitute for the section was then agreed to by the following vote:

YEAS.

Mr. Alvord,	Mr. Eaton,	Mr. Raynale,
Backus,	Edmunds,	Roberts,
H. Bartow,	Fralick,	Robertson,
Beeson,	Gardiner,	M. Robinson,
Britain,	Gibson,	Rix Robinson,
Alvardo Brown,	Green,	Skinner,
Ammon Brown,	Hanscom,	Soule,
Burns,	Hart,	Storey,
Bush,	Hascall,	Sturgis,
Butterfield,	Kingsley,	Sullivan,
Church,	Kinne,	Sutherland,
J. Clark,	Lovell,	Town,
Conner,	Marvin,	Van Valkenburg,
Cook,	Mason,	Wells,
Cornell,	McLeod,	White,
Crary,	Mosher,	Whipple,
Crouse,	Mowry,	Whittemore,
Daniels,	O'Brien,	Williams,
Desnoyers,	Orr,	Willard,
Eastman,	J. D. Pierce,	Witherell, 60

NAYS.

Mr. W. Adams,	Mr. Choate,	Mr. Newberry,
Anderson,	Comstock,	N. Pierce,
Arzeno,	Danforth,	Redfield,
Axford,	Dimond,	E. S. Robinson,
Bagg,	Gale,	Wait,
Barnard,	Hathaway,	Walker,
Beardsley,	Hixon,	Warden,
Asahel Brown,	Lee,	Webster,
Carr,	Moore,	Woodman,
Chandler,	Morrison,	President,
Chapel,		31

And this section of the article was concurred in.

Mr. Raynale moved to amend section 7 by inserttng after "officers of the militia," the words "post masters."

The President decided the proposition not in order.

Mr. Raynale moved to insert "judges of the supreme court;" which he subsequently withdrew.

Mr. Hanscom proposed to amend section 2, by striking out the word "one."

Also, strike out section 5, and insert the following, to stand as the section:

"The number of Senators shall be thirty-two, and the Legislature shall divide the state into districts; but in the formation of such districts no county shall be divided."

Mr. Cook raised a point of order "that the amendment to the section having been reported by a committee of the whole, and concurred in by the Convention, it is not now in order to strike out a portion of it."

The chair decided the proposition not in order.

Mr. Hanscom moved to reconsider the vote by which the amendment made in committee to sec. 5 was concurred in.

The motion was lost by yeas and nays, as follows:

YEAS:

Mr. Alvord,
Arzeno,
Beeson,
Chapel,
Church,
J. Clark,
Cornell,
Crary,
Mr. Eastman,
Gibson,
Hanscom,
Hart,
Marvin,
McLeod,
Raynale,
Mr. Robertson,
Rix Robinson,
Storey,
Van Valkenburg,
Whittemore,
Woodman,
President,
22

NAYS:

Mr. W. Adams,
Anderson,
Axford,
Backus,
Bagg,
Barnard,
H. Bartow,
Beardsley,
Britain,
Alvarado Brown,
Ammon Brown,
Mr. Daniels,
Desnoyers,
Dimond,
Eaton,
Edmunds,
Fralick,
Gale,
Graham,
Green,
Harvey,
Hascall,
Mr. Mowry,
Newberry,
Orr,
N. Pierce,
Redfield,
E. S. Robinson,
M. Robinson,
Skinner,
Soule,
Sturgis,
Sullivan,

Asahel Brown,	Hathaway,	Sutherland,
Burns,	Hixon,	Tiffany,
Butterfield,	Kingsley,	Town,
Carr,	Kinne,	Wait,
Chandler,	Lee,	Walker,
Choate,	Lovell,	Webster,
Comstock,	Mason,	Wells,
Conner,	Moore,	White,
Cook,	Morrison,	Williams,
Crouse,	Mosher,	Willard,
Danforth,		64

On motion of Mr. Church,

Section 36 was amended by inserting after "meet," the words, "at the seat of government," and by striking out "period," and inserting in its stead, the words, "place or time."

Mr. Soule moved the previous question,

But withdrew the call.

Mr. Butterfield moved to re-commit the article to the committee on the Legislative Department, with instructions to amend section 28 so it will read as follows:

"The Legislature may authorize the employment of a chaplain for the State Prison, but no money shall be drawn from the Treasury for the payment of any other religious services."

Mr. Hixon moved to amend so as to read:

"The Legislature shall have no power to have any religious services performed in either House."

But the motion did not prevail.

Mr. Crary moved to amend by striking out "other," and adding to the proposition the words "in either branch of the Legislature,"

Which Mr. Butterfield accepted.

Mr. Butterfield then modified his proposition by moving that the committee on Phraseology be instructed to make the above alteration when the Legislative article should be referred to it.

And the motion as modified prevailed.

Mr. Britain moved to amend section 17 by striking out in the 8th line thereof the words "and newspapers."

Which did not prevail.

Mr. Tiffany proposed to add at the end of section 17, "nor to vacate or alter any road laid out by commissioners of highways, or any street in any incorporated city or village, or in any township plat."

Mr. Raynale moved to strike out the words "or any street in any incorporated city or village or, in any township plat."

Which motion was disagreed to.

And the amendment of Mr. Tiffany prevailed.

Mr. Bush moved to adjourn.

But the Convention refused to adjourn,

Mr. Hanscom moved to strike out of section 17, all up to and including the word "thereafter," in the 3d line, and insert:

"The compensation of members of the Legislature shall never exceed three dollars per day for actual attendance, unless absent by reason of sickness; and after the session of 1851, no compensation shall be allowed after the first sixty days of the session, and not beyond the first ninety days of the session of that year."

A division of the question being had, the motion to strike out was lost.

On motion of Mr. Whittemore,

Section 17 was amended by inserting in the 6th line, after "receive," the words "no more than."

Mr. White moved to amend section 23 by striking out "object," and inserting in its stead, "subject."

Which was not agreed to.

Mr. Hart moved to adjourn.

But the Convention refused to adjourn.

On motion of Mr. McLeod,

The article, as amended, was laid upon the table and ordered printed.

Mr. Storey moved to adjourn.

But the Convention refused to adjourn.

Mr. White moved a call of the House.

Mr. Hart moved to adjourn.

Ruled out of order.

Mr. White's move for a call was not sustained.

Mr. J. D. Pierce moved to adjourn,

But the Convention refused to adjourn by the following vote:

YEAS.

Mr. H. Bartow,	Mr. Cornell,	Mr. Kinne,
Carr,	Crary,	Lovell,
Chandler,	Daniels,	Warden,
Choate,	Desnoyers,	Wells,
J. Clark,	Green,	White,
Cook,	Hathaway,	President, 18

NAYS.

Mr. W. Adams,	Mr. Eaton,	Mr. Orr,
Anderson,	Edmunds,	N. Pierce,
Arzeno,	Fralick,	Redfield,
Axford,	Gibson,	Robertson,
Bagg,	Graham,	E. S. Robinson,
Barnard,	Hanscom,	M. Robinson,
Beeson,	Hart,	Rix Robinson,
Britain,	Harvey,	Soule,
Alvarado Brown,	Hascall,	Storey,
Ammon Brown,	Hixon,	Sturgis,
Asahel Brown,	Kingsley,	Sullivan,
Burns,	Marvin,	Town,
Bush,	Mason,	Wait,
Chapel,	McLeod,	Walker,
Church,	Morrison,	Webster,
Comstock,	Mosher,	Williams,
Crouse,	Mowry,	Wiliard,
Dimond,	Newberry,	Woodman,
Eastman,	O'Brien,	56

Mr. Hanscom moved that the Convention resolve itself into committee of the whole on the general order; but withdrew the motion.

Mr. J. D. Pierce moved a call of the House. Lost.

On motion of Mr. Cook,

The Convention adjourned.

Lansing, Friday, July 19, 1850.

The Convention met pursuant to adjournment, and was called to order by the President.

Prayer by the Rev. Mr. Tooker.

The roll being called, there were absent with leave, Messrs. Leach, McClelland and Prevost; without leave, Messrs. P. R. Adams and S. Clark.

ABSENCE.

Mr. Wells asked and obtained leave of absence for Mr. S. Clark for an indefinite period.

PETITIONS.

By Mr. Robertson: the petition of Mrs. E. A. Bentley and fifty-one other ladies of Mt. Clemens, Macomb county, praying the insertion of a provision in the constitution prohibiting the importation, sale and manufacture of intoxicating liquors from and after the 1st day of January, 1854.

Which was read and referred to the select committee on licenses.

By Mr. Hascall: the petition of N. A. Balch, Gov. Ransom and 120 others, citizens of Kalamazoo county, remonstrating against the establishment of an independent supreme court.

Which was read and laid on the table.

MOTIONS, RESOLUTIONS AND NOTICES.

On motion of Mr. Whittemore,

The article "Elections" was taken from the table.

On motion of Mr. McLeod,

The article "Mode of amending and revising the Constitution," was taken from the table.

On motion of Mr. Redfield,

The article "State Officers" was taken from the table.

On motion of Mr. Rix Robinson,

The article "County Officers and County Government" was taken from the table.

Mr. Hanscom offered the following:

Resolved, That the committee on "the Judicial and Governmental Policy of the Upper Peninsula" of the State, be requested to inquire into the expediency and practicability of a separation of said Peninsula for purposes of government, and the formation of the Upper Peninsula into a territorial government, with reference to its ultimate admission into the Union as one of the States; *Provided,* That the assent of the people of this State and of Congress can be obtained.

Resolved, That if in the judgment of said committee such separation is expedient and practicable, some plan be submitted to the Convention that in the opinion of the committee may be best adapted to secure to the inhabitants of said Upper Peninsula a separate territorial government.

Which, on motion of Mr. Witherell,

Was laid on the table.

The Convention then proceeded to the consideration of Article "Mode of amending and revising the Constitution."

Mr. J. Bartow offered the following substitute for section 1:

"Any amendment or amendments to this constitution may be proposed in the Senate or House of Representatives; and if the same shall be agreed to by two-thirds of the members elected to the two Houses, such proposed amendment or amendments shall be entered on their journals respectively, with the yeas and nays taken thereon; and shall be submitted to the people at such time and in such manner as the Legislature may provide. And if the people shall ratify and approve such amendment or amendments. by a majority of the electors qualified to vote for members of the Legislature voting thereon, such amendment or amendments shall become part of this Constitution."

Mr. White moved to insert after "people," the words "before the next ensuing legislature."

Which motion did not prevail.

Mr. Bartow's substitute was then adopted.

On motion of Mr. Cornell,

The words "decided by" were stricken out of sec. 2, line 3, and the words "submitted to" were inserted.

Mr. Bagg moved to strike out of section 2, the words "sixty-five," in line 1; "fifteenth year," in line 2; and "also," in line 2.

On motion of Mr. J. D. Pierce,

The word "five," in line 1, was stricken out, and "six" was inserted; and "fifteenth," in line 2, was stricken out, and "sixteenth" inserted.

The question then recurring upon Mr. Bagg's amendment, the same was not agreed to.

Mr. Raynale offered the following substitute for section 2:

"If at any time two-thirds of the Senate and House of Representatives shall think it necessary to revise or change this entire constitution, they shall recommend to the electors at the next election for members of the Legislature to vote for or against a Convention, and if it shall appear that a majority of the electors voting at such election have voted in favor of calling a Convention, the Legislature shall at its next session provide by law for calling a Convention to be holden within six months after the passage of such law, and such Convention shall consist of a number of members not less than that of both branches of the Legislature."

Mr. Alvord offered the following as a substitute for the substitute:

"If at any time the Legislature shall think it necessary to amend or revise this constitution, they shall provide by law for a vote of the people for or against a convention, at the next ensuing election for members of the Legislature. In case a majority of the people vote for a convention, said Legislature shall provide for an election of delegates to a convention, to be held within six months after a vote of the people in favor thereof."

Which was not adopted.

The question then recurring upon Mr. Raynale's substitute, the same was disagreed to.

The article was then ordered to a third reading.

Article —, "Elections," being under consideration,

Mr. Britain moved to amend the amendment reported by the committee of the whole, by adding thereto the following:

"And for depriving every person who shall make or become directly or indirectly interested in any bet or wager depending upon the result of any election, from the right of voting at such election."

Mr. Chapel moved to amend Mr. Britain's proposition by inserting "and also all persons intoxicated."

When Mr. Britain withdrew his proposition.

Mr. Moore renewed the same, and

Mr. Chapel also renewed his amendment.

Mr. Alvord proposed to amend Mr. Chapel's amendment by making the same include "manufacturers and venders of ardent spirits."

Mr. Chapel accepted the amendment proposed.

Mr. Whipple asked a division of the question,

But withdrew the same.

Mr. Backus renewed the call,

And the question being taken on the first clause of Mr. Chapel's amendment, the same was disagreed to, as follows:

YEAS.

Mr. Backus, H. Bartow, Butterfield, Chapel, Church, J. Clark, Eaton, Gale, Gardiner, Hanscom, Hart, Lovell, Mason, McLeod, Mowry, Newberry, Orr, N. Pierce, Robertson, E. S. Robinson, Rix Robinson, Storey, Sturgis, VanValkenburg, Webster, White, Whipple, Whittemore, Willard, 29

NAYS.

Mr. W. Adams, Anderson, Arzeno, Bagg, Barnard, J. Bartow, Beardsley, Beeson, Britain, Ammon Brown, Asahel Brown, Burns, Bush, Carr, Chandler, Choate, Comstock, Conner, Cook, Cornell, Crary, Daniels, Desnoyers, Dimond, Eastman, Edmunds, Fralick, Gibson, Graham, Green, Harvey, Hascall, Hathaway, Hixon, Kingsley, Lee, Marvin, Moore, Morrison, Mosher, O'Brien, Raynale, Redfield, M. Robinson, Skinner, Soule, Sullivan, Tiffany, Town, Wait, Walker, Warden, Wells, Williams, Witherell, Woodman, President, 57

And the remainder of the amendment was disagreed to.

Mr. Bush moved to amend Mr. Moore's amendment by inserting the following: "and any person who shall be a candidate for an office of profit at such election."

Which was withdrawn.

Mr. Church proposed to amend the amendment of Mr. Moore by adding "nor any person holding an office of profit."

Mr. Hascall moved the previous question on the section.

But the call was not sustained.

The amendment proposed by Mr. Church was disagreed to.

The proposition of Mr. Moore was then agreed to, by the following vote:

YEAS:

Mr. W. Adams, Anderson, Backus, Barnard, H. Bartow, J. Bartow, Beardsley, Beeson, Britain, Ammon Brown, Asahel Brown, Burns, Butterfield, Carr, Chandler, Comstock, Conner, Cook,

Mr. Daniels, Eastman, Edmunds, Fralick, Gale, Gardiner, Gibson, Green, Hart, Harvey, Hascall, Kingley, Lovell, McLeod, Moore, Mowry, Orr, N. Pierce,

Mr. Redfield, E. S. Robinson, M. Robinson, Skinner, Sullivan, Tiffany, Town, VanValkenburg, Warden, White, Whipple, Whittemore, Williams, Willard, Witherell, Woodman, President, 53.

NAYS:

Mr. Arzeno, Axford, Bush, Chapel, Choate, Church, J. Clark, Cornell, Crary, Danforth, Dimond,

Mr. Eaton, Graham, Hanscom, Hathaway, Hixon, Lee, Marvin, Mason, Morrison, Mosher,

Mr. Newberry, O'Brien, Raynale, Robertson, Rix Robinson, Soule, Storey, Wait, Walker, Wells, 31.

Mr. Bush moved to reconsider the last vote.

Mr. Bush moved a call of the Convention; which was not ordered.

Mr. Church moved to lay the motion to reconsider on the table.

Mr. Willard moved a call of the House.

Which did not prevail.

Mr. Bush then withdrew his motion to reconsider.

The question being on concurring with the amendment made in committee of the whole as amended, Mr. Raynale moved to strike out and substitute therefor the following:

"Laws may be passed, excluding from the right of suffrage all persons not of sound mind, or otherwise disqualified by a disordered understanding."

Mr. Britain moved to amend the section as amended, by striking out all after the words "laws may be passed," to the word "for."

Mr. Danforth moved to adjourn.

But the Convention refused to adjourn.

Mr. Crary asked the yeas and nays on the amendment of Mr. Britain, and the same were ordered and taken with the following result:

YEAS.

Mr. Arzeno,	Mr. Edmunds,	Mr. O'Brien,
Bagg,	Fralick,	Orr,
Barnard,	Graham,	J. D. Pierce,
H. Bartow,	Green,	Raynale,
Britain,	Hanscom,	Robertson,
Ammon Brown,	Hathaway,	E. S. Robinson,
Burns,	Hixon,	Rix Robinson,
Chapel,	Lovell,	Soule,
Choate,	Marvin,	Storey,
Cnurch,	Mason,	Sturgis,
J. Clark,	McLeod,	Walker,
Conner,	Morrison,	Warden,
Crary,	Mosher,	Wells,
Danforth,	Newberry,	Willard,
Eaton,		43

NAYS.

Mr. W. Adams,	Mr. Desnoyers,	Mr. Sullivan,
Backus,	Eastman,	Tiffany,
J. Bartow,	Gardiner,	Town,
Beeson,	Gibson,	Van Valkenburg,
Alvarado Brown,	Hart,	Wait,
Asahel Brown,	Harvey,	Webster,
Bush,	Hascall,	White,
Butterfield,	Kingsley,	Whipple,
Carr,	Kinne,	Whittemore,
Chandler,	Moore,	Williams,
Comstock,	N. Pierce,	Witherell,
Cook,	Redfield,	Woodman,
Cornell,	M. Robinson,	President,
Daniels,	Skinner,	41

So the amendment was agreed to.

On motion of Mr. Bagg,

The Convention adjourned.

Afternoon Session.

Three o'clock.

The Convention was called to order by the President,

The roll called, and a quorum of members being in attendance,

On motion of Mr. Hanscom,

Resolved, That the use of this House be permitted to the Rev. J. A. Baughman, on Saturday evening, half-past 7 o'clock, July 20th, for the purpose of delivering an address upon the subject of Temperance.

The Convention resumed the consideration of the article entitled "Elections."

The question being upon Mr. Raynale's substitute for section 6 as amended by committee of the whole,

A division of the question was had,

And the motion to strike out the substitute proposed by the committee prevailed.

Mr. Raynale's proposition to insert was not agreed to.

Mr. Cornell submitted the following as a substitute:

Laws may be passed to preserve the purity of elections and guard against abuses of elective franchise.

Which was adopted.

The question being upon concurring with the amendment of the committee as amended,

A division of the question was had,

And the Convention concurred in striking out the original section, by yeas and nays as follows:

YEAS:

Mr. Arzeno, H. Bartow, Beardsley, Britain, Alvarado Brown, Ammon Brown, Burns, Carr, Chapel, Church, Conner, Cook, Cornell, Danforth, Desnoyers, Dimond, Edmunds, Fralick,

Mr. Gale, Gibson, Graham, Green, Hanscom, Hathaway, Hixon, Lee, Lovell, Marvin, McLeod, Morrison, Mosher, Newberry, O'Brien, Orr, J. D. Pierce, Raynale,

Mr. Redfield, Robertson, E. S. Robinson, M. Robinson, Rix Robinson, Skinner, Soule, Storey, Sturgis, Sullivan, Town, Wait, Walker, Warden, Wells, Whipple, Willard, Woodman, 54

NAYS:

Mr. W. Adams,	Mr. Daniels,	Mr. Sutherland,
Axford,	Eastman,	Tiffany,
Backus,	Gardiner.	Van Valkenburg,
J. Bartow,	Hart,	Webster,
Beeson,	Harvey,	White,
Asahel Brown,	Hascall,	Whittemore,
Chandler,	Kingsley,	Williams,
Choate,	Mowry,	Witherell,
Comstock,	N. Pierce,	President, 27

And the substitute of Mr. Cornell was inserted.

The question being upon concurring with the committee in striking out section 8,

Mr. Van Valkenburg moved to amend the original section by adding thereto the words, "and also for preventing men from voting when they are intoxicated."

Which was not agreed to.

The amendment made in committee, as amended, was then concurred in.

Mr. Mason offered the following substitute for section 8:

"Laws shall be made for preventing the administration of oaths by boards of elections to persons intoxicated."

Mr. Raynale moved to amend by adding, "and all elections shall be opened by a temperance lecture." Which he withdrew.

Mr. Mason's proposition was then disagreed to by yeas and nays, as follows:

YEAS.

Mr. Backus,	Mr. Eaton,	Mr. N. Pierce,
Burns,	Gardiner,	Rix Robinson,
Chapel,	Green,	Sturgis,
J. Clark,	Hart,	Van Valkenburg,
Comstock,	Mason,	Williams,
Dimond,	McLeod,	Witherell,
Eastman,	Orr,	20

NAYS.

Mr. W. Adams,	Mr. Danforth,	Mr. Robertson,
Arzeno,	Daniels,	E. S. Robinson,
Axford,	Desnoyers,	M. Robinson,
Bagg,	Edmunds,	Skinner,
H. Bartow,	Fralick,	Soule,
J. Bartow,	Gibson,	Story,
Beardsley,	Graham,	Sullivan,

Beeson,	Hanscom,	Sutherland,
Britain,	Hascall,	Tiffany,
Alvarado Brown,	Hathaway,	Town,
Ammon Brown,	Kingsley,	Walker,
Asahel Brown,	Lee,	Warden,
Butterfield,	Lovell,	Webster,
Carr,	Mosher,	Wells,
Chandler,	Mowry,	White,
Choate,	Newberry,	Whipple,
Church,	O'Brien,	Whittemore,
Conner,	Raynale,	Willard,
Cook,	Redfield,	Woodman,
Cornell,	Roberts,	President, 60

The amendments to the resolution accompanying the article were concurred in.

Mr. Storey moved to amend the article by striking out the last clause of section 1.

Mr. Robertson proposed the following substitute for the entire section:

"In all elections, every white male citizen above the age of twenty-one years, every white male inhabitant of the age aforesaid who was permitted to vote under the provisions of the previous constitution of this state, every civilized male inhabitant of Indian descent of the age aforesaid, not a member of any tribe, who shall be a native of the United States, and every white male inhabitant of the age aforesaid, who shall have been a resident of this State on the first day of January A. D. 1849, shall be entitled to vote at such elections: provided, that the last mentioned persons shall first declare their intentions to become citizens of the United States, pursuant to the laws thereof; but no such citizen or inhabitant shall be entitled to vote at any such election unless he shall have resided in this State for six months next preceding such election, nor in any township or ward unless he is an actual resident thereof."

Mr. Storey's amendment did not prevail.

Mr. N. Pierce moved to strike out all after the word "every," in the first line of the section, and insert the following: "Male person above the age of twenty-one years having resided in this State for six months next and immediately preceding any election, shall be entitled to vote at such election; and every such voter shall be eligible to any office in the gift of the people of this State. But no such citizen or person shall be entitled to vote, except in the township or ward of which he is an actual resident, and in which he has resided for ten days next preceding the day of election."

Mr. Morrison moved to amend the original section by adding after "aforesaid," in the first line thereof, as follows:

"And white male persons of foreign birth, of the age aforesaid, who have resided in the United States two years, and shall have declared their intention to become citizens, (conformable to the laws of the United States on the subject of naturalization,) at least one year previous to an election, and every civilized male person of Indian blood of the age aforesaid, not a member of any tribe."

The amendment did not prevail.

Mr. N. Pierce's proposition being uuder consideration,

On motion of Mr. Woodman,

The word "male" was stricken out.

And the amendment as amended was disagreed to.

On motion of Mr. McLeod,

The original section was amended by inserting after "citizen," in line one, "and civilized persons of Indian descent, not members of any tribe."

Mr. Williams moved to add to the original section as follows:

"The legislature may at any time extend by law the right of suffrage to persons not herein enumerated, subject, however, to the approval of a majority of all the votes cast at a general election."

The yeas and nays being demanded thereon, the amendment was lost, as follows:

YEAS.

Mr. Barnard,	Mr. Green,	Mr. Sturgis,
H. Bartow,	Hart,	Wiat,
Chandler,	Hixon,	Walker,
Comstock,	Mason,	Warden,
Edmunds,	Orr,	Wells,
Gale,	N. Picree,	Williams, 18.

NAYS:

Mr. W. Adams,	Mr. Cook,	Mr. J. D. Pierce,
Anderson,	Cornell,	Raynale,
Arzeno,	Crary,	Roberts,
Axford,	Danforth,	Robertson,
Backus,	Desnoyers,	E. S. Robinson,

Bagg,	Eastman,	M. Robinson,
J. Bartow,	Eaton,	Rix Robinson,
Beardsley,	Fralick,	Skinner,
Beeson,	Gardiner,	Soule,
Britain,	Gibson,	Storey,
Alvarado Brown,	Graham,	Sullivan,
Ammon Brown,	Hanscom,	Tiffany,
Asahel Brown,	Hascall,	Town,
Burns,	Hathaway,	Van Valkenburg,
Butterfield,	Kingsley,	Webster,
Carr,	Lee,	White,
Chapel,	Marvin,	Whipple,
Choate,	Mosher,	Whittemore,
Church,	Mowry,	Willard,
J. Clark,	Newberry,	Woodman,
Conner,	O'Brien,	President, 63

Mr. Walker moved to amend the section as follows:

After the word "citizen," in first line, insert "or inhabitant;" also strike out all after the word "election," in 2d line, to and including the word "aforesaid," in fifth line.

Mr. Hanscom moved the previous question on the article without the resolution.

The call was sustained, and the main question ordered to be now put.

The same recurring first upon the amendment proposed by Mr. Walker, it was lost by the following vote:

YEAS:

Mr. Arzeno,	Mr. Gale,	Mr. Robertson,
Bagg,	Gibson,	F. S. Robinson,
Barnard,	Graham,	Soule,
Beardsley,	Hathaway,	Sturgis,
Asahel Brown,	Hixon,	Sutherland,
Carr,	Marvin,	Wait,
Chapel,	Morrison,	Walker,
Choate,	Orr,	Warden,
Crary,	J. D. Pierce,	Williams,
Eaton,	N. Pierce,	Willard,
Edmunds,	Raynale,	32

NAYS:

Mr. W. Adams,	Mr. Cornell,	Mr. Redfield,
Anderson,	Danforth,	Roberts,
Axford,	Daniels,	M. Robinson,
Backus,	Desnoyers,	Rix Robinson,
H. Bartow,	Eastman,	Skinner,

J. Bartow,
Beeson,
Britain,
Alvarado Brown,
Burns,
Butterfield,
Chandler,
Church,
J. Clark,
Comstock,
Conner,
Cook,
Fralick,
Green,
Hanscom,
Harvey,
Hascall,
Kingley,
Kinne,
Lovell,
McLeod,
Mosher,
Newberry,
O'Brien,
Storey,
Sullivan,
Tiffany,
Town,
Van Valkenburg,
Webster,
Wells,
White,
Whipple,
Whittemore,
Woodman,
President, 51

The substitute of Mr. Robertson for the section as amended, was then disagreed to by the following vote:

YEAS.

Mr. Anderson,
Arzeno,
Bagg,
Barnard,
Beardsley,
Ammon Brown,
Asahel Brown,
Chapel,
Cook,
Crary,
Desnoyers,
Eaton,
Edmunds,
Gardiner,
Mr. Gibson,
Graham,
Hanscom,
Hart,
Hathaway,
Hixon,
Kingsley,
Marvin,
McLeod,
Morrison,
Orr,
J. D. Pierce,
N. Pierce,
Raynale,
Mr. Roberts,
Robertson,
E. S. Robinson,
Skinner,
Soule,
Storey,
Sturgis,
Sutherland,
Wait,
Walker,
Warden,
Willard,
President, 41

NAYS.

Mr. W. Adams,
Axford,
Backus,
H. Bartow,
J. Bartow,
Beeson,
Britain,
Alvarado Brown,
Burns,
Butterfield,
Carr,
Chandler,
Choate,
Church,
J. Clark,
Comstock,
Mr. Conner,
Cornell,
Danforth,
Daniels,
Dimond,
Eastman,
Fralick,
Gale,
Green,
Harvey,
Hascall,
Kinne,
Lovell,
Moore,
Mosher,
Newberry,
Mr. O'Brien,
Redfield,
M. Robinson,
Rix Robinson,
Sullivan,
Tiffany,
Town,
Van Valkenburg,
Webster,
Wells,
White,
Whipple,
Whittemore,
Williams,
Woodman, 47

The question being, "shall the article entitled 'Elections' be now read a third time?"

The yeas and nays were demanded, with the following result:

YEAS.

Mr. W. Adams,	Mr. Danforth,	Mr. O'Brien,
H. Bartow,	Daniels,	N. Pierce,
J. Bartow,	Desnoyers,	Redfield,
Beeson,	Eastman,	Roberts,
Britain,	Fralick,	M. Robinson,
Asahel Brown,	Gale,	Rix Robinson,
Ammon Brown,	Graham,	Soule,
Butterfield,	Hascall,	Sullivan,
Carr,	Hathaway,	Town,
Chandler,	Kingsley,	Wait,
Church,	Kinne,	Wells,
J. Clark,	Lovell,	White,
Conner,	Mosher,	Whipple,
Cook,	Mowry,	Whittemore,
Crary,	Newberry,	Willard, 45

NAYS.

Mr. Anderson,	Mr. Gardiner,	Mr. Robertson,
Arzeno,	Gibson,	E. S. Robinson,
Backus,	Green,	Skinner,
Bagg,	Hanscom,	Storey,
Barnard,	Hart,	Sturgis,
Beardsley,	Harvey,	Sutherland,
Alvarado Brown,	Hixon,	Tiffany,
Burns,	Marvin,	VanValkenburg,
Chapel,	McLeod,	Walker,
Choate,	Moore,	Warden,
Comstock,	Morrison,	Webster,
Cornell,	Orr,	Williams,
Dimond,	J. D. Pierce,	Woodman,
Eaton,	Raynale,	President,
Edmunds,		43

So the article was ordered to a third reading.

Mr. Story moved to strike out the resolution.

On motion of Mr. Crary,

The resolution was amended as follows:

Insert in line 4, before "color," the word "every;" and strike out "citizen," in same line, and insert "inhabitant." Strike out all after "the," in 5th line, up to and including "1851," in the 6th line, and insert the rights and privileges of an elector." Also, strike out in the 17th line the words, "after the 1st day of January, 1851."

On motion of Mr. Church,

The resolution was further amended by striking out, in the 15th and 16th lines, the words "for and against the said separate amendment."

The question being upon Mr. Story's motion to strike out, the same was lost by the following vote:

YEAS.

Mr. Arzeno,	Mr. Graham,	Mr. Raynale,
Bagg,	Hanscom,	Roberts,
Beeson,	Marvin,	E. S. Robinson,
Burns,	McLeod,	M. Robinson,
Butterfield,	Mowry,	Storey,
Chapel,	Newberry,	Sullivan,
Crary,	O'Brien,	Whipple, 21

NAYS.

Mr. W. Adams,	Mr. Eaton,	Mr. Rix Robinson,
Backus,	Edmunds.	Skinner,
H. Bartow,	Fralick,	Soule,
Britain,	Gardiner,	Sutherland,
Alvarado Brown,	Green,	Tiffany,
Ammon Brown,	Hart,	Town,
Asahel Brown,	Harvey,	Van Valkenburg,
Carr,	Hascall,	Waite,
Chandler,	Hathaway,	Walker,
Choate,	Hixon,	Warden,
Church,	Kingsley,	Webster,
Comstock,	Kinne,	Wells,
Conner,	Lovell,	White,
Cook,	Morrison,	Whittemore,
Cornell,	Mosher,	Williams,
Danforth,	Orr,	Willard,
Daniels,	J. D. Pierce,	Witherell,
Desnoyers,	N. Pierce,	Woodman,
Dimond,	Redfield,	President,
Eastman,	Robertson,	59

Mr. Van Valkenburgh moved to adjourn.

But the Convention refused to adjourn.

Mr. Cook moved the previous question.

But the call was not sustained.

On motion of Mr. Desnoyers,

The Convention adjourned.

Lansing, Saturday, July 20, 1850.

The President called the Convention to order at the usual hour.

Prayer by the Rev. Mr. Baughman.

The roll being called, there were absent with leave, Messrs. S. Clark, Leach, McClelland and Prevost; without leave, Messrs. P. R. Adams, Crouse and Sutherland.

ABSENCE.

Mr. Barnard asked and obtained leave of absence for Mr. Crouse until Tuesday next.

Mr. J. Bartow for Mr. Sutherland for the day, on account of ill health.

PETITIONS.

By Mr. Story: the petition of Ichabod Cole, Henry Foster, and 292 other citizens of Jackson county, praying the insertion of a clause in the Constitution prohibiting the employment of convicts in the State Prison at those branches of mechanical labor which interfere with mechanical trades in this State.

Which was referred to the committee on miscellaneous provisions.

By the President: the petition of J. M. Cooper and 156 other citizens of Detroit, praying for an insertion of a provision in the Constitution prohibiting the legislature from passing any laws authorizing the sale of intoxicating liquors as a beverage; also the petition of Francis Raymond and 32 others; also, Wm. A. Butler and 14 others, citizens of Detroit, praying for like objects.

Also, the petitions of Eliza N. Whipple and 79 other ladies; Mrs. H. T. Backus and 203 other ladies; Mrs. W. Cole and 333 other ladies; and Mrs. D. Knight and 80 other ladies, of the city of Detroit, praying for a like prohibition.

Which were referred to the select committee on licenses.

MOTIONS, RESOLUTIONS AND NOTICES.

Mr. Witherell offered the following:

Resolved, That the President of this Convention shall be entitled to receive the sum of four dollars a day, and no more, for his services during the remainder of the session.

Which, on motion of Mr. Hanscom,

Was indefinitely postponed by the following vote:

YEAS:

Mr. W. Adams,	Mr. Daniels,	Mr. Mowry,
Alvord,	Desnoyers,	O'Brien,
Anderson,	Dimond,	Orr,
Arzeno,	Eastman,	J. D. Pierce,
Axford,	Eaton,	Raynale,
Backus,	Fralick,	Robertson,
Bagg,	Gale,	E. S. Robinson,
Barnard,	Gardiner,	M. Robinson,
H. Bartow,	Gibson,	Rix Robinson,
J. Bartow,	Graham,	Skinner,
Beardsley,	Green,	Soule,
Beeson,	Hanscom,	Storey,
Alvarado Brown,	Hart,	Tiffany,
Ammon Brown,	Harvey,	Town,
Asahel Brown,	Hascall,	Van Valkenburg,
Burns,	Hathaway,	Warden,
Carr,	Kingsley,	Webster,
Chandler,	Kinne,	Wells,
Chapel,	Lovell,	White,
Choate,	Marvin,	Whittemore,
Church,	McLeod,	Williams,
J. Clark,	Moore,	Willard,
Cook,	Morrison,	Woodman,
Cornell,	Mosher,	71

NAYS:

Mr. Butterfield,	Mr. Edmunds,	Mr. N. Pierce,
Comstock,	Hixon,	Wait,
Crary,	Mason,	Witherell,
Danforth,	Newberry,	11

Mr. Church gave notice that he would on Monday next, introduce a resolution requiring the committee on finance and taxation to report.

Mr. Crary gave notice that he would on Monday next, move to take up the Judicial Article and the resolution relating thereto.

Mr. Kingsley moved to reconsider the vote by which the article "Elections," was yesterday ordered to a third reading.

Mr. Hanscom moved to commit the article to the committee that reported it, with instructions to strike out section 1, and insert the following to stand as section 1, and report the same back to the Convention forthwith:

"In all elections, every white male citizen above the age of twenty-one years, every white male inhabitant of the age aforesaid who was permitted to vote under the provisions of the previous constitution of this State, every civilized male inhabitant of Indian descent of the age aforesaid, not a member of any tribe, who shall be a native of the United States, and every white male inhabitant of the age aforesaid who shall have been a resident of this State on the first day of January A. D. 1850, shall be entitled to vote at such elections: *Provided*, That the last mentioned persons shall have declared their intentions to become citizens of the United States, pursuant to the laws thereof, at least six months next preceding such election; but no such citizen or inhabitant shall be entitled to vote at any such election unless he shall have resided in this State for six months next preceding such election, nor in any township or ward unless he is an actual resident thereof, and shall have therein resided for ten days next preceding such election."

Mr. J. Bartow raised a question of order, that "the Article having been ordered to a third reading under a demand of the previous question, a motion to commit with instructions could not be entertained."

The President decided that as the motion to commit was a privileged motion, it was in order to entertain the same.

Mr. J. Bartow appealed from the decision; but withdrew the same previous to the question being stated.

Mr. Walker moved to amend the instructions by striking out "on the 1st day of January, A. D. 1849," and inserting "at the time of the adoption of this Constitution."

Mr. Raynale offered the following substitute for the instructions:

"In all elections, every white male citizen, and every civilized male inhabitant of Indian descent, not a member of any tribe, above the age of twenty-one years, being a native of the United States of America, having resided in this State six months next preceding an election, shall be entitled to vote at such election; and every white male inhabitant of the age aforesaid, having resided in this State two years in all, and having filed his intentions to become a citizen of the United States, according to the laws of the United States on the subject of naturalization, shall be entitled to vote at all elections: *Provided*, Such inhabitants shall have resided in this State for the six months next preceding such election; but no such citizen or inhabitant shall be entitled to vote except in the township or ward where he shall have actually resided for the ten days next preceding such election."

Mr. J. Clark moved to lay the whole subject on the table, but withdrew the same before the question was taken.

The question being on the amendment proposed by Mr. Walker, Mr. Britain moved to postpone the whole subject until Tuesday next.

Mr. Hathaway moved to amend the above motion by striking out "Tuesday" and inserting "Friday."

Which did not prevail.

The question then recurring upon Mr. Britain's motion, the same was lost, as follows:

YEAS:

Mr. Alvord,	Mr. Crary,	Mr. O'Brien,
Anderson,	Gale,	Robertson,
Beardsley,	Gardiner,	E. S. Robinson,
Britain,	Green,	Rix Robinson,
Burns,	Hanscom,	Sturgis,
J. Clark,	Hart,	Town,
Conner,	Lee,	VanValkenburgh,
Cornell,	McLeod,	White, 24

NAYS:

Mr. W. Adams,	Mr. Danforth,	Mr. Newberry,
Arzeno,	Desnoyers,	Orr,
Axford,	Dimond,	J. D. Pierce,
Backus,	Eastman,	N. Pierce,
Bagg,	Eaton,	Raynale,
Barnard,	Fralick,	Redfield,
H. Bartow,	Gibson,	M. Robinson,
J. Bartow,	Graham,	Skinner,
Beeson,	Harvey,	Soule,
Alvarado Brown,	Hascall,	Sullivan,
Ammon Brown,	Hathaway,	Tiffany,
Asahel Brown,	Hixon,	Wait,
Bush,	Kingsley,	Walker,
Butterfield,	Kinne,	Warden,
Carr,	Lovell,	Webster,
Chandler,	Marvin,	Wells,
Chapel,	Mason,	Whittemore,
Choate,	Moore,	Williams,
Church,	Morrison,	Willard,
Comstock,	Mosher,	Woodman,
Cook,	Mowry,	President, 63

Mr. Sturgis moved to amend the instructions of Mr. Hanscom by striking out "1849," and inserting "1850."

Which was accepted by Mr. Hanscom.

Mr. Walker then moved to strike out "1st day of January, 1850," and insert "at the time of the adoption of this constitution."

After some debate, Mr. Walker withdrew the motion.

The question then recurred upon the substitute offered by Mr. Raynale.

Pending which, Mr. Raynale moved a call of the Convention, and the call was ordered.

There were absent without leave, Messrs. P.R. Adams, J. Bartow, Sullivan, Story, Tiffany and Witherell.

Mr. Danforth moved to dispense with further proceedings under the call.

But the motion did not prevail.

On motion of Mr. Raynale,

The Sergeant-at-Arms was despatched after the absentees.

The Sergeant-at-Arms reported the absentees present, except Mr. P. R. Adams.

On motion of Mr. Danforth,

All further proceedings under the call were dispensed with.

The question then recurring upon the adoption of the substitute of Mr. Raynale,

Mr. Whipple moved to strike out "2 years," and insert "3 years."

Which was disagreed to, as follows:

YEAS:

Mr. Axford,	Mr. Comstock,	Mr. N. Pierce,
H. Bartow,	Cook,	M. Robinson,
J. Bartow,	Fralick,	Skinner,
Beeson,	Gardiner,	Storey,
Britain,	Mason,	Town,
Ammon Brown,	McLeod,	Webster,
Burns,	Moore,	White,
Carr,	Mowry,	Whipple,
Chandler,	Newberry,	Whittemore,
J. Clark,		29

NAYS:

Mr. W. Adams,	Mr. Eaton,	Mr. Raynale,
Alvord,	Edmunds,	Redfield,
Anderson,	Gale,	Roberts,

Arzeno,	Gibson,	Robertson,
Backus,	Green,	E. S. Robinson,
Bagg,	Hanscom,	Rix Robinson,
Barnard,	Hart,	Soule,
Beardsley,	Harvey,	Sturgis,
Alvarado Brown,	Hascall,	Sullivan,
Asahel Brown,	Hathaway,	Tiffany,
Bush,	Hixon,	Van Valkenburg,
Butterfield,	Kingsley,	Wait.
Chapel,	Lee,	Walker,
Choate,	Lovell,	Warden,
Church,	Marvin,	Wells,
Cornell,	Morrison,	Williams,
Crary,	Mosher,	Willard,
Danforth,	O'Brien,	Witherell,
Daniels,	Orr,	Woodman,
Dimond,	J. D. Pierce,	President,
Eastman,		61

Mr. Whipple moved to strike out "six months," and insert "four months."

Mr. Burns moved to amend by inserting "three months;" which was accepted by Mr. Whipple."

Mr. Backus called for a division of the question; and the words "six months" were stricken out.

The words "three months" were then inserted.

Mr. Hanscom then modified his instructions to conform to the above amendment to Mr. Raynale's substitute:

Mr. Storey moved to strike out "for the ten days next preceding such election."

Which was not agreed to.

Mr. Crary moved to strike out of the substitute "being a native of the United States."

Which was accepted by Mr. Raynale.

The yeas and nays were then ordered on the substitute and the call commenced,

When Mr. Backus moved to amend by adding at the end of the substitute the following: "and every such elector shall be eligible to all offices under this Constitution;" and was proceeding to debate the question, but was called to order by Mr. Hanscom.

The amendment was decided not in order.

Mr. Mason moved that Mr. Backus have leave to proceed.

This motion was also decided not in order, as the call of the roll had been commenced.

Mr. Raynale's substitute was then lost by a tie vote, as follows:

YEAS:

Mr. Alvord,	Mr. Desnoyers,	Mr. J. D. Pierce,
Anderson,	Eastman,	Raynale,
Arzeno,	Eaton,	E. S. Robinson,
Bagg,	Edmunds,	Rix Robinson,
Barnard,	Gibson,	Soule,
H. Bartow,	Hixon,	Sturgis,
Britain,	Kingsley,	Tiffany,
Alvarado Brown,	Lee,	Walker,
Asahel Brown,	Lovell,	Warden,
Chapel,	Marvin,	Whipple,
Choate,	Mason,	Williams,
Church,	McLeod,	Willard,
Cornell,	Morrison,	Witherell,
Crary,	O'Brien,	Woodman,
Danforth,	Orr,	President, 45

NAYS.

Mr. W. Adams,	Fralick,	Mr. N. Pierce,
Axford,	Gale,	Redfield,
Backus,	Gardiner,	Roberts,
J. Bartow,	Graham,	Robertson,
Beeson,	Green,	M. Robinson,
Ammon Brown,	Hanscom,	Skinner,
Burns,	Hart,	Storey,
Bush,	Harvey,	Sullivan,
Butterfield,	Hascall,	Town,
Carr,	Hathaway,	Van Valkenburg,
Chandler,	Kinne,	Wait,
Comstock,	Moore,	Webster,
Conner,	Mosher,	Wells,
Cook,	Mowry,	White,
Daniels,	Newberry,	Whittemore, 45

The question then recurring upon Mr. Hanscom's motion to commit with instructions,

Mr. Backus moved to amend the instructions by adding as follows: "And every such elector shall be eligible to all offices under this Constitution."

Mr. Mason moved that the Convention adjourn.

Which was disagreed to.

Mr. Backus then proceeded to debate the amendment, but gave way by request.

When, on motion of Mr. Hanscom,

The Convention adjourned.

Afternoon Session.

Three o'clock.

The Convention was called to order by the President.

A quorum of members in attendance.

The Convention resumed the consideration of the motion to commit with instructions, made by Mr. Hanscom.

The question being upon the amendment of Mr. Backus to the instructions, Mr. Backus modified his amendment so as to read as follows:

"And every such elector shall be eligible to all offices in this State, at the same age and upon the same terms of residence as is prescribed in this Constitution."

The amendment was adopted by the following vote:

YEAS.

Mr. Alvord,
Anderson,
Arzeno,
Axford,
Backus,
H. Bartow,
Alvarado Brown,
Asahel Brown,
Butterfield,
Carr,
Chandler,
Church,
J. Clark,
Comstock,
Cook,
Crary,
Danforth,
Daniels,

Mr. Eastman,
Eaton,
Edmunds,
Gale,
Gardiner,
Gibson,
Graham,
Green,
Hart,
Harvey,
Hascall,
Lee,
Lovell,
Mason,
Morrison,
Mosher,
Mowry,

Mr. Newberry,
Orr,
Raynale,
Redfield,
M. Robinson,
Rix Robinson,
Sullivan,
Van Valkenburg,
Wait,
Warden,
Webster,
Wells,
White,
Whipple,
Williams,
Willard,
Woodman,

52

NAYS.

Mr. W. Adams,
Bagg,
J. Bartow,
Beardsley,
Britain,
Ammon Brown,

Mr. Dimond,
Fralick,
Hanscom,
Hathaway,
Kingsley,
Kinne,

Mr. Roberts,
Robertson,
E. S. Robinson,
Skinner,
Soule,
Sturgis,

Choate,	Marvin,	Tiffany,
Conner,	McLeod,	Whittemore,
Cornell,	O'Brien,	President,
Desnoyers,	J. D. Pierce,	29

Mr. J. D. Pierce moved to amend the instructions by inserting after "State," in 4th line, "and also every white male inhabitant of the age aforesaid, who shall have resided in the State two and a half years, and declared his intention to become a citizen of the United States."

Mr. Robertson moved a call of the Convention, which was sustained; and upon calling the roll, Messrs. P. R. Adams, Burns, Moore, N. Pierce, Town and Witherell, were absent without leave.

Mr. Morrison moved to dispense with all further proceedings under the call.

Which was not agreed to.

Mr. Eaton moved that the Sergeant-at-Arms be despatched after the absentees.

Which motion did not prevail.

Mr. ——— moved that the Convention adjourn; but the Convention refused to adjourn.

On motion of Mr. Mason, all further proceedings under the call were dispensed with.

Mr. Backus moved to strike out of the above all after the words "aforesaid," of Mr. J. D. Pierce's amendment.

And the yeas and nays being ordered thereon, the same did not prevail, as follows:

YEAS.

Mr. Alvord,	Mr. Eastman,	Mr. Mowry,
Anderson,	Edmunds,	Newberry,
Axford,	Gale,	N. Pierce,
Backus,	Gardiner,	Rix Robinson,
Asahel Brown,	Green,	Wait,
Carr,	Harvey,	Webster,
Chandler,	Hascall,	Wells,
Church,	Lovell,	White,
Crary,	Mason,	Williams, 27

NAYS.

Mr. W. Adams,	Mr. Desnoyers,	Mr. Redfield,
Arzeno,	Dimond,	Roberts,
Bagg,	Eaton,	Robertson,

Barnard,
H. Bartow,
J. Bartow,
Beeson,
Britain,
Alvarado Brown,
Ammon Brown,
Bush,
Chapel,
Choate,
J. Clark,
Comstock,
Conner,
Cook,
Cornell,
Danforth,
Daniels,
Fralick,
Gibson,
Graham,
Hanscom,
Hart,
Hathaway,
Hixon,
Kingsley.
Kinne,
Marvin,
McLeod,
Morrison,
Mosher,
O'Brien,
Orr,
J. D. Pierce,
Raynale,
E. S. Robinson,
M. Robinson,
Skinner,
Soule,
Storey,
Sturgis,
Sullivan,
Tiffany,
Van Valkenburg
Walker,
Warden,
Whipple,
Whittemore,
Willard,
Woodman,
President. 50

The question then recurring upon the amendment of Mr. J. D. Pierce, the same was adopted by the following vote:

YEAS.

Mr. Alvord,
Anderson,
Arzeno,
Backus,
Bagg,
Barnard,
H. Bartow,
J. Bartow,
Beardsley,
Britain,
Alvardo Brown,
Bush,
Butterfield,
Chandler,
Chapel,
Choate,
Church,
Conner,
Cook,
Cornell,
Crary,
Danforth,
Mr. Desnoyers,
Eastman,
Eaton,
Edmunds,
Gale,
Gardiner,
Gibson,
Graham,
Hart,
Hascall,
Hathaway,
Hixon,
Kingsley,
Kinne,
Lee,
Lovell,
Marvin,
Mason,
McLeod,
Morrison,
Mosher,
Mowry,
Mr. Newberry,
O'Brien,
Orr,
J. D. Pierce,
N. Pierce,
Raynale,
Roberts,
Robertson,
E. S. Robinson,
Skinner,
Soule,
Sturgis,
Sullivan,
Van Valkenburg,
Walker,
Warden,
Wells,
Whipple,
Williams,
Willard,
Woodman,
President, 66

NAYS.

Mr. W. Adams,
Axford,
Beeson,
Ammon Brown,
Mr. Daniels,
Dimond,
Fralick,
Green,
Mr. Rix Robinson,
Storey,
Tiffany,
Town,

Asahel Brown,	Hanscom,	Wait,
Carr,	Harvey,	Webster,
J. Clark,	Redfield,	White,
Comstock,	M. Robinson,	Whittemore, 24

Mr. Warden moved to reconsider the vote by which the Convention adopted the amendment offered by Mr. Backus to the instructions.

Which motion was agreed to.

Mr. Walker moved to amend Mr. Backus' amendment by inserting after "State," the words "for eligibility to which, no other test is applied in this Constitution."

Which motion, after some debate, was withdrawn.

The question then recurring upon Mr. Backus' amendment, Mr. Bagg moved a call of the Convention, which being sustained, and the roll being called, Messrs. P. R. Adams, Alvarado Brown, Burns Daniels, Desnoyers, Hixon and Kinne were absent without leave.

On motion of Mr. ———,

All further proceedings under the call were dispensed with.

Mr. Backus' amendment was then disagreed to by the following vote:

YEAS:

Mr. Axford,	Mr. Gale,	Mr. N. Pierce,
Backus,	Graham,	Rix Robinson,
H. Bartow,	Green,	Sullivan,
Asahel Brown,	Harvey,	Wait,
Carr,	Hascall,	Webster,
Chandler,	Lee,	Wells,
Church,	Lovell,	White,
Comstock,	Mason,	Williams,
Cook,	Mowry,	Willard,
Crary,	Newberry,	Witherell,
Eastman,	Orr,	Woodman,
Edmunds,		34

NAYS:

Mr. W. Adams,	Mr. Danforth,	Mr. J. D. Pierce,
Alvord,	Desnoyers,	Raynale,
Anderson,	Dimond,	Redfield,
Arzeno,	Eaton,	Roberts,
Bagg,	Fralick,	Robertson,
Barnard,	Gardiner,	E. S. Robinson,
J. Bartow,	Gibson,	M. Robinson,
Beardsley,	Hanscom,	Skinner,

Beeson, Britain, Ammon Brown, Bush, Butterfield, Chapel, Choate, J. Clark, Conner, Cornell, Hart, Hathaway, Kingsley, Marvin, McLeod, Moore, Morrison, Mosher, O'Brien, Soule, Storey, Sturgis, Town, Van Valkenburg, Walker, Warden, Whipple, President, 52

The question then being upon committing with the instructions, which, as amended, were as follows:

"In all elections, every white male citizen above the age of twenty-one years, who shall have resided in this State three months next preceding any election; every white male inhabitant of the age aforesaid, who was permitted to vote under the provisions of the previous constitution of this State; and also every white male inhabitant of the age aforesaid, who shall have resided in the State two years and a half, and declared his intention to become a citizen of the United States; and every civilized male inhabitant of Indian descent, of the age aforesaid, not a member of any tribe, who shall be a native of the United States; and every white male inhabitant of the age aforesaid, who shall have been a resident of this State on the first day of January, A. D. 1850, shall be entitled to vote at such election; provided the last mentioned persons shall have declared their intention to become citizens of the United States, pursuant to the laws thereof, at least six months next preceding such election; but no such citizen or inhabitant shall be entitled to vote at any such election, unless he shall have resided in this State three months next preceding such election, nor in any township or ward, unless he is an actual resident thereof, and shall have resided therein for ten days next preceding such election."

The same prevailed by the following vote:

YEAS.

Mr. W. Adams, Alvord, Anderson, Arzeno, Bagg, Barnard, Mr. Danforth, Desnoyers, Eaton, Edmunds, Gardiner, Gibson, Mr. J. D. Pierce, Raynale, Redfield, Roberts, Robertson, E. S. Robinson,

H. Bartow,	Graham,	Rix Robinson,
Beardsley,	Hanscom,	Skinner,
Britain,	Hart,	Soule,
Alvarado Brown,	Hascall,	Storey,
Bush,	Hathaway,	Sturgis,
Butterfield,	Hixon,	Sullivan,
Chapel,	Kingsley,	Van Valkenburg,
Choate,	Kinne,	Walker,
Church,	Lee,	Warden,
J. Clark,	Marvin,	Whipple,
Conner,	McLeod,	Willard,
Cook,	Morrison,	Witherell,
Cornell,	O'Brien,	President,
Crary,	Orr,	59

NAYS.

Mr. Axford,	Mr. Fralick,	Mr. N. Pierce,
Backus,	Gale,	M. Robinson,
J. Bartow,	Green,	Town,
Beeson,	Harvey,	Wait,
Ammon Brown,	Lovell,	Webster,
Asahel Brown,	Mason,	Wells,
Carr,	Moore,	White,
Comstock,	Mosher,	Whittemore,
Daniels,	Mowry,	Williams,
Dimond,	Newberry,	Woodman,
Eastman,		31

On motion of Mr. Cornell,

The Convention adjourned.

Lansing, *Monday*, *July* 22, 1850.

The Convention met at the usual hour and was called to order by the President.

Prayer by the Rev. Mr. Sanford.

The roll being called, there were absent on leave Messrs. S. Clark, Crouse, Leach and McClelland, and without leave, Messrs. P. R. Adams, Bagg, Story, Sturgis and Whipple.

LEAVE OF ABSENCE.

Mr. Eaton asked and obtained leave of absence for Mr. Bagg for the day.

REPORTS.

Mr. Whittemore, from the committee on the "Elective Franchise," to whom was referred the article entitled "Elections," with certain instructions, reported the same back amended accordingly.

The committee appointed under the preamble and resolutions adopted in this Convention on the 15th inst., have instructed me as their chairman to make the following report:

That they have conferred with and selected the Hon. H. T. Backus, of Wayne, who has consented to deliver an eulogy on the life and public services of General Zachary Taylor, late President of the United States. And your committee would recommend Saturday, the 27th inst., at 2 o'clock, P. M., and would respectfully solicit the use of this Hall for the occasion.

E. S. WOODMAN, Ch'n.

The report was accepted.

Mr. Fralick moved to strike out "2 o'clock," and insert "7 o'clock."

Which was disagreed to.

The report was then adopted.

MOTIONS AND RESOLUTIONS.

Mr. McLeod offered the following, which was laid upon the table:

Resolved, That a select committee of seven be appointed to draft and report as early as practicable, the form of a general incorporation law, to be engrafted in the revised Constitution.

Mr. Hanscom moved to amend the 34th rule by striking out the word "ten," and inserting "twenty," so that the rule will read: "The ayes and noes may be called for by twenty members."

But two-thirds not voting therefor, it was decided in the negative, yeas 53, nays 27.

On motion of Mr. Church,

Resolved, That the committee on printing be instructed to examine into the state of the publication of the debates of this Convention, and to make arrangements, if necessary, for their earlier issue.

Mr. Hanscom moved to amend rule 8 by striking out of 2d line, "one hour," and inserting "five minutes," so that the rule shall read, "No member shall speak more than twice on the same question, nor more than five minutes at any one time, without leave of the Convention, nor more than once until every member who chooses to speak shall have spoken."

Mr. Van Valkenburg moved to strike out "five," and insert "twenty."

A division of the question being had, the motion to strike out was lost.

And the yeas and nays being asked by Mr. Crary on the amendment to the rule, the result was as follows:

YEAS:

Mr. W. Adams,	Mr. Eaton,	Mr. Mowry,
Anderson,	Edmunds,	Newberry,
Axford,	Fralick,	O'Brien,
Britain,	Gardiner,	Orr,
Alvarado Brown,	Gibson,	Redfield,
Ammon Brown,	Graham,	Robertson,
Bush,	Green,	M. Robinson,
Butterfield,	Hanscom,	Soule,
Carr,	Hart,	Storey,
Chandler,	Harvey,	Sullivan,
Choate,	Hascall,	Tiffany,
Comstock,	Hathaway,	Town,
Cook,	Hixon,	Walker,
Cornell,	Kingsley,	Warden,
Crary,	Kinne,	Whittemore,
Danforth,	Lee,	Willard,
Daniels,	Mason,	Witherell,
Desnoyers,	Morrison,	Woodman,
Dimond,	Mosher,	56

NAYS.

Mr. Alvord,	Mr. Eastman,	Mr. Rix Robinson,
Arzeno,	Gale,	Skinner,
Backus,	Lovell,	Sutherland,
Bagg,	Marvin,	Van Valkenburg,
H. Bartow,	McLeod,	Wait,
J. Bartow,	Moore,	Webster,
Beardsley,	J. D. Pierce,	White,
Asahel Brown,	N. Pierce,	Whipple,
Chapel,	Prevost,	Williams,
Church,	Raynale,	President,
J. Clark,	E. S. Robinson,	32

So, two-thirds not voting therefor, the rule was not amended as proposed.

Mr. Church moved to amend the 8th rule by striking out "one hour," and inserting "ten minutes."

Mr. N. Pierce moved to strike out "ten," and insert "fifteen."

Which did not prevail.

The amendment was then agreed to by a two-thirds vote.

THIRD READING OF ARTICLES.

The Article entitled "Mode of amending and revising the Constitution," was read a third time, passed, and referred to the committee on arrangement and phraseology.

UNFINISHED BUSINESS.

The Convention having reached the order of unfinished business, resumed the consideration of the resolution accompanying the article entitled "Elections."

On motion of Mr. Woodman,

The vote was reconsidered by which the words "for and against the said separate amendment" were stricken from the 15th and 16th lines; when Mr. Church withdrew the proposition.

Mr. Comstock moved to reconsider the vote by which all after the word "the," in the 5th line, up to and including "1851," was stricken out, and the words "the rights and privileges of an elector," inserted in lieu thereof.

Mr. Williams asked the yeas and nays thereon, and the same being demanded, the motion to reconsider was lost, as follows:

YEAS.

Mr. Arzeno,	Mr. Green,	Mr. Redfield,
H. Bartow,	Hart,	Robertson,
J. Bartow,	Harvey,	Tiffany,
Britain,	Hascall,	VanValkenburg,
Asahel Brown,	Hixon,	Wait,
Bush,	Lee,	Walker,
Chandler,	Lovell,	Webster,
Comstock,	McLeod,	Wells,
Conner,	Moore,	White,
Daniels,	Mowry,	Whittemore,
Edmunds,	Orr,	Whipple,
Gale,	N. Pierce,	Williams,
Gardiner,	Prevost,	Woodman, 39

NAYS.

Mr. W. Adams,	Mr. Cornell,	Mr. O'Brien,
Alvord,	Crary,	J. D. Pierce,
Anderson,	Danforth,	Raynale,
Axford,	Desnoyers,	Roberts,
Backus,	Eastman,	E. S. Robinson,
Barnard,	Eaton,	M. Robinson,
Beardsley,	Fralick,	Rix Robinson,
Alvarado Brown,	Gibson,	Soule,
Ammon Brown,	Graham,	Storey,

Butterfield,	Hanscom,	Sturgis,	
Carr,	Hathaway,	Sutherland,	
Chapel,	Kinne,	Town,	
Choate,	Marvin,	Warden,	
J. Clark,	Mosher,	Willard,	
Cook,	Newberry,	President,	45

The resolution was then ordered to a third reading.

Mr. Britain, by consent, presented the petition of Daniel Baker and 57 others, asking the insertion in the Constitution of an article prohibiting the manufacture and sale of intoxicating liquors as a beverage.

Referred to the select committee upon the subject.

Mr. Barnard, by consent, presented the petition of B. C. Curtis and 39 others, on the subject of convict labor in the State prison.

Referred to the committee on miscellaneous provisions.

The Article entitled "State Officers," being taken up for consideration, and the question being on concurring in the amendments made in committee of the whole,

On motion of Mr. Redfield,

The article was laid upon the table and ordered printed with amendments.

The article entitled "County Officers and County Government" being under consideration, the amendments made in committee of the whole were severally concurred in.

On motion of Mr. Britain,

Section 10 was amended by adding thereto the words, "voting upon that subject."

Mr. Eastman moved to strike out section 9.

Mr. Chapel moved to amend the section by striking out "two-thirds," and inserting in lieu thereof, "a majority;" and also, by striking out "a majority," and inserting "three-fifths."

Mr. Willard moved to amend the proposition by inserting "two-thirds," instead of "three-fifths."

Which prevailed.

The question being upon the amendment as amended,

Mr. White asked a division of the question; and the same recurring first on striking out "a majority," it was agreed to, and "two-thirds" was inserted in lieu thereof.

The question being on the second clause of the amendment,

Mr. Robertson demanded the yeas and nays; and the same being ordered,

The motion to strike out "two-thirds" prevailed, as follows:

YEAS.

Mr. W. Adams,	Mr. Crary,	Mr. J. D. Pierce,
Alvord,	Danforth,	N. Pierce,
Anderson,	Desnoyers,	Raynale,
Arzeno,	Eastman,	Redfield,
Barnard,	Eaton,	E. S. Robinson,
H. Bartow,	Fralick,	M. Robinson,
Beardsley,	Gale,	Soule,
Beeson,	Green,	Storey,
Britain,	Hanscom,	Sturgis,
Alvarado Brown,	Harvey,	Sullivan,
Ammon Brown,	Hascall,	Tiffany,
Asahel Brown,	Hathaway,	Town,
Bush,	Kinne,	Van Valkenburg,
Butterfield,	Marvin,	Walker,
Chandler,	McLeod,	Warden,
Chapel,	Moore,	Webster,
Church,	Morrison,	Whipple,
J. Clark,	Mosher,	Whittemore,
Comstock,	Mowry,	Williams,
Conner,	Newberry,	Willard,
Cook,	Orr,	Woodman,
Cornell,		64

NAYS.

Mr. J. Bartow,	Mr. Lovell,	Mr. Skinner,
Choate,	O'Brien,	Wait,
Gardiner,	Prevost,	Wells,
Hart,	Roberts,	White,
Hixon,	Robertson,	President.
Kingsley,	Rix Robinson,	17

And the words "a majority," were inserted in lieu thereof.

The motion of Mr. Eastman to strike out section 9 was then lost.

Mr. Cornell moved to amend section 8 by inserting in the first line, after "new," the words "and change the boundaries of."

And the same prevailed.

On motion of Mr. Butterfield,

The section was amended by inserting after "townships," in 2d line, the following:

"Provided, no township heretofore organized shall be divided without the sanction of a majority of the inhabitants of the territory proposed to be set off."

Mr. Arzeno offered the following substitute for the section:

"The board of supervisors of all organized counties shall have exclusive power to organize new townships and to divide townships, but no new township lines, other than those made for the purpose of organizing new townships, shall be valid unless the majority of the voters of the township, whose territory it is proposed to take, shall agree to the same in a manner to be provided by law, and no new township shall be organized of less dimensions than the United States survey thereof."

On motion of Mr. Crary,

The section was further amended by striking out "of," in 2d line of section 8, and inserting "or repair of roads or."

Mr. Backus moved to amend by striking out "United States survey thereof," and inserting in lieu thereof, the words "less than six square miles."

He afterwards modified the same by inserting "thirty-six" in lieu of "six."

Mr. Backus subsequently withdrew his amendment and substituted the following:

Add at the end of the section: "where such surveys exist."

Mr. Eastman moved to amend the amendment by adding, "and not divided by meandered streams."

Pending which,

On motion of Mr. Crary,

The Convention adjourned.

Afternoon Session.

Three o'clock.

The President called the Convention to order.

A quorum of members being in attendance, the consideration of the article entitled "County Officers and County Government" was resumed.

The question being upon Mr. Eastman's amendment, it did not prevail.

The amendment proposed by Mr. Backus was not agreed to.

On motion of Mr. Redfield,

The last clause of the section, (8,) being all after "counties," in the 3d line, was stricken out.

Mr. Arzeno then withdrew his substitute for the section.

Mr. Cornell moved to amend by adding to the same section as follows:

"The compensation of the members of the board of supervisors may be fixed by law; but shall never exceed one dollar and fifty cents each per day."

Mr. Willand moved to strike out "and fifty cents."

When Mr. Cornell withdrew his proposition.

On motion of Mr. J. Bartow,

Section 6 was amended by inserting after "powers," the words "and compensation."

Mr. Eaton proposed to amend by adding at the end of section 2 as follows: "except the county of Wayne."

But the amendment was not agreed to.

Mr. Williams moved to amend the same section by striking out "six hundred square miles," and inserting in lieu thereof "sixteen townships as surveyed by the United States."

Mr. Fralick moved to amend the amendment by inserting "four hundred," instead of "six hundred."

Which did not prevail.

The amendment proposed by Mr. Williams was then adopted.

On motion of Mr. Daniels,

Section 3 was amended by striking out of the 3d line, the words "one county surveyor."

Mr. Walker moved to amend section 3 by adding after the word "law," in the fourth line, as follows: "and any qualified elector, who shall have resided in the county six months next preceding the election, shall be eligible to the aforesaid offices."

Mr. Cook moved to amend by striking out so much as relates to the time of residence.

Mr. Walker accepted the amendment, and his proposition was then negatived.

Mr. W. Adams proposed to amend section 8 by adding thereto, as follows:

"But no township already organized embracing a territory of no more than six miles square shall be divided into two separate townships."

Which did not prevail.

Mr. Hascall moved to amend section six by adding thereto, as follows:

"But such compensation shall not exceed one dollar and twenty-five cents, for each member, per day."

Mr. Van Valkenburgh moved to strike out "twenty-five," and insert "fifty."

And the amendment prevailed by yeas and nays, as follows:

YEAS.

Mr. Arzeno,
Axford,
Backus,
Barnard,
H. Bartow,
J. Bartow,
Beardsley,
Britain,
Alvarodo Brown,
Asahel Brown,
Chandler,
Choate,
Church,
Comstock,
Conner,
Daniels,
Desnoyers,
Diamond,
Eaton,
Edmunds,
Mr. Fralick,
Gale,
Graham,
Green,
Hanscom,
Hart,
Hathaway,
Kingsley,
Kinne,
Lee,
Lovell,
Marvin,
McLeod,
Mosher,
Mowry,
Newberry,
O'Brien,
Orr,
N. Pierce,
Raynale,
Mr. Redfield,
Roberts,
Robertson,
E. S. Robinson,
M. Robinson,
Rix Robinson,
Soule,
Storey,
Struges,
Tiffany,
Van Valkenburg,
Wait,
Walker,
Warden,
Webster,
White,
Whipple,
Whittemore,
Woodman,
President, 60

NAYS.

Mr. Ammon Brown,
Cook,
Cornell,
Danforth,
Eastman,
Gardiner,
Mr. Harvey,
Hascall,
Hixon,
Morrison,
Skinner,
Mr. Sutherland
Town,
Wells,
Willard,
Witherell, 16

Mr. Hascall's proposition was then rejected.

Mr. Fralick moved to amend section 11 by inserting after "supervisors," in line 1, the words "or county auditor."

Which was not agreed to.

On motion of Mr. Tiffany,

Section 9 was amended by inserting after "electors," in the 3d line, the words "voting thereon."

Mr. Whipple moved to amend the article by striking out in section 3, "prosecuting attorney," and adding the following to stand as a new section:

"A prosecuting attorney for each judicial circuit shall be elected by the qualified electors at the same time that judicial officers are elected, as provided by this constitution, who shall hold his office for the term of four years, and whose duties and compensation shall be prescribed by law."

Which was not agreed to.

On motion of Mr. Redfield,

The vote by which Mr. Fralick's amendment to section 11 was rejected, was reconsidered.

Mr. Fralick modified his amendment by adding thereto, "for the county of Wayne."

Mr. Fralick further modified his amendment so as to read "and in the county of Wayne, the board of county auditors."

And the same was then agreed to.

On motion of Mr. Church,

The vote by which the Convention refused to strike out section 9 was reconsidered.

Mr. Eastman moved to amend the section by striking out "when once," in the first line, and inserting "now" in its stead.

But the motion was lost.

The vote being again taken upon striking out section 9, the Convention refused to strike out.

Mr. Hixon moved to amend section 10 by striking out in the 1st line "borrow or," and in the 3d line the words "borrowed or,"

Upon which he asked the yeas and nays, and the same being demanded,

The amendment was lost as follows:

YEAS:

Mr. Barnard,
Beeson,
Britain,
Alvarado Brown,
Mr. Gardiner,
Graham,
Hanscom,
Hart,
Mr. O'Brien,
Raynale,
Roberts,
Skinner,

Bush,	Hathaway,	Wait,
Carr,	Hixon,	Walker,
Choate,	Kingsley,	Warden,
Cook,	Lee,	Webster,
Eastman,	Mason,	Whipple,
Edmunds,	Newberry,	29

NAYS:

Mr. W. Adams,	Mr. Daniels,	Mr. E. S. Robinson,
Alvord,	Desnoyers,	M. Robinson,
Anderson,	Dimond,	Rix Robinson,
Arzeno,	Eaton,	Soule,
Axford,	Fralick,	Storey,
Backus,	Gale,	Sturgis,
H. Bartow,	Gibson,	Sullivan,
J. Bartow,	Green,	Sutherland,
Beardsley,	Harvey,	Town,
Ammon Brown,	Hascall,	Van Valkenburg,
Asahel Brown,	Moore,	Wells,
Chapel,	Mosher,	White,
Church,	Orr,	Whittemore,
Comstock,	J. D. Pierce,	Williams,
Conner,	N. Pierce,	Willard,
Cornell,	Redfield,	Woodman,
Danforth,	Robertson,	President, 51

Mr. Backus moved to amend section 2 by adding thereto as follows;

"But the Legislature shall have power to organize any city into a separate county when it shall have attained a population of at least twenty thousand people, without reference to geographical extent."

On motion of Mr. Desnoyers,

The foregoing was amended by adding thereto, "upon application of a majority of the legal voters of said city."

On motion of Mr. Britain,

The last vote taken was reconsidered, when Mr. Hanscom proposed the following as a substitute for the amendment, which was accepted by Mr. Desnoyers:

"When a majority of the legal voters of a county in which such city may be situated shall recommend such new organization."

And the same was agreed to.

The original proposition of Mr. Backus, as amended, was then adopted.

On motion of Mr. Storey,

Section six was amended by striking out "hereafter," and inserting after "prescribed," the words "in this Constitution."

On motion of Mr. Britain,

Section 8 was amended by striking out in the 2d line, the words, "or to lay out," and inserting in lieu thereof "the laying out and establishing of."

Mr. Edmunds moved to strike out section 8, and substitute the following:

"The Legislature shall, by general laws, confer upon the board of Supervisors of their respective counties, power to construct highways and bridges and to authorize the construction of the same, to lay out and establish roads and fix the boundaries of townships. Power shall also be conferred upon the inhabitants of any one or more surveyed townships to organize township governments therein."

Mr. Hanscom moved to amend the section by adding thereto, as follows:

"*Provided*, That any surveyed township containing 150 white inhabitants shall be entitled to a separate township organization, if a majority of the electors of such township shall so elect."

Pending which,

On motion of Mr. Cook,

The Convention adjourned.

Lansing, Tuesday, July 23, 1850.

The Convention met at the usual hour and was called to order by the President.

Prayer by the Rev. Mr. Sanford,

The roll being called, there were absent on leave Messrs. S. Clark, Crouse, Leach and McClelland; without leave, Messrs. Bagg and Lee.

PETITIONS.

By Mr. Mowry: of S. F. Hubbell and 74 others, citizens of Oakland county, praying for the insertion of a provision in the constitution, prohibiting the legislature from passing any law authorizing the sale of intoxicating liquors as a beverage; also, to make the traffic in intoxicating liquors as a beverage a penal offence.

Also, of Mrs. E. Hastings and 198 others, ladies of Milford, Oakland county, praying for a like prohibition.

By Mr. Fralick: of Mary A. Bentley, Hannah Buearly and 160 other ladies of Plymouth, praying there may be an article inserted in the revised constitution, prohibiting the manufacture, importation or sale of intoxicating drinks as a beverage.

The above were severally referred to the select committee heretofore appointed upon the subject.

RESOLUTIONS.

Mr. Woodman offered the following:

Whereas, Hon. P. R. Adams has absented himself from the sittings of this Convention during most of the session, without any apparent excuse or reason for so doing; therefore

Resolved, That the Secretary be not authorized to draw any certificate in favor of said Adams for per diem allowance, unless directed so to do by the Convention.

Mr. Danforth moved to lay the preamble and resolution upon the table.

Which did not prevail.

On motion of Mr. Hanscom,

The consideration of the same was postponed for one week.

Mr. Butterfield offered the following:

Resolved, That the afternoon sessions of this Convention will hereafter commence at two o'clock.

Mr. Alvord moved to amend by striking out "two," and inserting "one."

Which was not agreed to.

Mr. Desnoyers moved to strike out "two," and insert "half past two."

But the motion was lost.

The resolution was then adopted.

THIRD READING OF ARTICLES.

The Convention having reached the order of third reading of Articles, and the Article entitled "Elections" coming up for consideration,

On motion of Mr. J. Bartow,

It was laid upon the table until to-morrow.

UNFINISHED BUSINESS.

The Convention having under consideration the Article entitled "County Officers and County Government," and the question being upon Mr. Hanscom's amendment to section eight, Mr. Britain proposed the following substitute for the section:

"The Legislature shall provide by general laws:

"1. For the laying out and establishing State and county roads and for altering the same;

"2. For the erection of bridges;

"3. For the organization of legally established counties;

"4. For the organization of United States surveyed townships by the inhabitants thereof;

"5. For changing the boundaries of organized townships by the board of supervisors, subject to the approval of the electors of said townships."

When Mr. Hanscom withdrew his amendment.

The following substitute for the section, proposed by Mr. Edmunds yesterday, being under consideration:

"The legislature shall, by general laws, confer upon the board of supervisors of their respective counties, power to construct highways and bridges, and to authorize the construction of the same, to lay out and establish roads, and fix the boundaries of townships. Power shall also be conferred upon the inhabitants of any one or more surveyed townships to organize township governments therein."

A motion was made by Mr. Arzeno to amend the same by striking out all after the word "the," in the first line, and inserting as follows:

"Board of supervisors of all organized counties shall have exclusive power to organize and divide townships; but no new township lines, other than those made for the purpose of organizing new townships, shall be valid, unless a majority of the voters in the territory it is proposed to set off, shall agree to the same in a manner to be prescribed by law."

Mr. Eastman moved to amend the amendment by inserting after "counties," the words "by a two-thirds vote,"

But the amendment was negatived.

The amendment proposed by Mr. Arzeno to the substitute was also disagreed to.

The question then recurring on the substitute offered by Mr. Edmunds,

Mr. Britain proposed as a substitute for the same, the proposition submitted by him this morning as a substitute for the section, (8.)

After some debate, Mr. Arzeno moved the previous question on the section; and the same being sustained, the main question was ordered to be now put.

Mr. Moore moved a call of the Convention.

Which was not agreed to.

The question first recurring on the substitute of Mr. Britain for the one proposed by Mr. Edmunds, the yeas and nays were ordered, and the proposition rejected, as follows:

YEAS.

Mr. W. Adams,	Mr. Hanscom,	Mr. Raynale,
Axford,	Hart,	Redfield,
Britain,	Harvey,	Robertson,
Alvarado Brown,	Hascall,	Rix Robinson,
Chapel,	Hathaway,	Sturgis,
Choate,	Kinne,	Town,
Church,	McLeod,	Warden,
Conner,	Morrison,	White,
Cook,	Mosher,	Whipple,
Daniels,	Mowry,	Willard,
Graham,	Newberry,	Witherell,
Green,	Orr,	President, 36

NAYS.

Mr. Alvord,	Mr. Desnoyers,	Mr. J. D. Pierce,
Anderson,	Dimond,	N. Pierce,
Arzeno,	Eastman,	Prevost,
Backus,	Eaton,	E. S. Robinson,
H. Bartow,	Edmunds,	Skinner,
J. Bartow,	Fralick,	Soule,
Beardsley,	Gale,	Storey,
Ammon Brown,	Gardiner,	Sutherland,
Bush,	Gibson,	VanValkenburg,
Butterfield,	Kingsley,	Wait,
Carr,	Lee,	Walker,
Chandler,	Lovell,	Wells,
J. Clark,	Marvin,	Whittemore,
Comstock,	Moore,	Williams,
Cornell,	O'Brien,	Woodman,
Crary,		46

And the question then being upon striking out the 8th section and substituting the proposition of Mr. Edmunds in lieu thereof, Mr. Crary asked a division of the same, and asked the yeas and nays, and the same being ordered the result was as follows:

YEAS:

Mr. Anderson,	Mr. Edmuuds,	Mr. N. Pierce,
Axford,	Gale,	Prevost,
Backus,	Gardiner,	Raynale,
H. Bartow,	Green,	Robertson,
Britain,	Harvey,	Skinner,
Bush,	Hathaway,	Soule,
Carr,	Kingsley,	Storey,
Chandler,	Kinne,	Town,
Choate,	Lee,	Wait,
J. Clark,	Lovell,	Warden,
Cook,	Morrison,	White,
Crary,	Mosher,	Williams,
Daniels,	Newberry,	Witherell,
Desnoyers,	O'Brien,	Woodman,
Eaton,	J. D. Pierce,	President, 45

NAYS:

Mr. W. Adams,	Mr. Cornell,	Mr. Orr,
Alvord,	Danforth,	Redfield,
Arzeno,	Dimond,	E. S. Robinson,
Barnard,	Eastman,	Rix Robinson,
J. Bartow,	Fralick,	Sturgis,
Beardsley,	Gibson,	Sutherland,
Ammon Brown,	Graham.	VanValkenburg,
Asahel Brown,	Hanscom,	Walker,
Butterfield,	Hart,	Wells,
Chapel,	Hascall,	Whipple,
Church,	Marvin,	Whittemore,
Comstock,	Moore.	Willard,
Conner,	Mowry,	38

So the section was stricken out.

And on the question of inserting the substitute of Mr. Edmunds' the yeas and nays were ordered, and the substitute rejected by the following vote:

YEAS.

Mr. W. Adams,	Mr. Edmunds,	Mr. Prevost,
Anderson,	Gale,	Skinner,
Backus,	Gardiner,	Soule,
Asahel Brown,	Green,	Storey,
Bush,	Harvey,	Town,
Carr,	Hathaway,	Wait,

Chandler,	Kingsley,	Walker,
Church,	Lee,	White,
J. Clark,	Lovell,	Williams,
Crary,	McLeod,	Willard,
Daniels,	Mosher,	Witherell,
Desnoyers,	O'Brien,	Woodman,
Eastman,	J. D. Pierce,	President,
Eaton,	N. Pierce,	41

NAYS.

Mr. Alvord,	Mr. Conner,	Mr. Newberry,
Arzeno,	Cook,	Orr,
Axford,	Cornell,	Raynale,
Barnard,	Danforth,	Redfield,
H. Bartow,	Fralick,	Robertson,
J. Bartow,	Gibson,	E. S. Robinson,
Beardsley,	Graham,	M. Robinson,
Beeson,	Hanscom,	Rix Robinson,
Britain,	Hart,	Sturgis,
Alvarado Brown,	Hascall,	Sutherland,
Ammon Brown,	Kinne,	Van Valkenburg,
Butterfield,	Marvin,	Warden,
Chapel,	Moore,	Webster,
Choate,	Morrison,	Wells,
Comstock,	Mowry,	Whittemore, 45

Mr. Hanscom moved to amend section 2 by adding after "United States," as follows:

"Unless a majority of the qualified electors residing in the territory to be affected by such organization shall so elect."

Mr. Cook moved to amend the amendment by striking out "the territory," and inserting "each county."

And the same prevailed by the following vote:

YEAS.

Mr. W. Adams,	Mr. Eaton,	Mr. Newberry,
Anderson,	Edmunds,	Orr,
Arzeno,	Fralick,	J. D. Pierce,
Axford,	Gale,	N. Pierce,
Barnard,	Gibson,	Raynale,
H. Bartow,	Graham,	Redfield,
J. Bartow,	Green,	M. Robinson,
Beeson,	Hart,	Skinner,
Alvarado Brown,	Hascall,	Sturgis,
Ammon Brown,	Hathaway,	Sullivan,
Asahel Brown,	Kingsley,	Tiffany,
Chandler,	Kinne,	Town,
Choate,	Lee,	Wait,
Church,	Marvin,	Wells,

J. Clark,
Comstock,
Cook,
Daniels,
Dimond,
Eastman,
McLeod,
Moore,
Morrison,
Mosher,
Mowry,
Whipple,
Whittemore,
Williams,
Willard,
President, 58

NAYS:

Mr. Alvord,
Backus,
Beardsley,
Britain,
Bush,
Carr,
Chapel,
Conner,
Mr. Cornell,
Danforth,
Gardiner,
Hanscom,
Harvey,
Lovell,
O'Brien,
Prevost,
Mr. Robertson,
Rix Robinson,
Soule,
Van Valkenburg,
Walker,
Webster,
Witherell,
Woodman, 24

And the amendment of Mr. Hanscom, as amended, was then agreed to by yeas and nays as follows:

YEAS:

Mr. Alvord,
H. Bartow,
Beeson,
Britain,
Ammon Brown,
Bush,
Chapel,
Choate,
Church,
J. Clark,
Cornell,
Dimond,
Eastman,
Eaton,
Edmunds,
Mr. Fralick,
Green,
Hanscom,
Hascall,
Kinne,
Lee,
Marvin,
McLeod,
Morrison,
Mosher,
Mowry,
Newberry,
Orr,
Robertson,
M. Robinson,
Mr. Rix Robinson,
Storey,
Sturgis,
Town,
Van Valkenburg,
Walker,
Webster,
Wells,
Whipple,
Williams,
Willard,
Witherell,
Woodman,
President, 44

NAYS:

Mr. W. Adams,
Anderson,
Arzeno,
Axford,
Backus,
Barnard,
J. Bartow,
Beardsley,
Alvarado Brown,
Asahel Brown,
Butterfield,
Carr,
Chandler,
Mr. Comstock,
Conner,
Cook,
Danforth,
Daniels,
Gale,
Gardiner,
Gibson,
Hart,
Harvey,
Lovell,
O'Brien,
Mr. J. D. Pierce,
N. Pierce,
Prevost,
Raynale,
Redfield,
Skinner,
Soule,
Sullivan,
Tiffany,
Wait,
White,
Whittemore, 37

On motion of Mr. Walker,

Section 12 was amended by prefixing the following:

"The boards of supervisors of all organized counties shall have the power to provide for the laying out of highways and the construction of bridges, and for the organizing of townships, under such restrictions and limitations as shall be prescribed by law; and."

On motion of Mr. Alvord,

Section 11 was amended by striking out "and," in the first line, and inserting in its stead "or."

Mr. Britain offered the following, to stand as a new section:

"The Legislature shall authorize any United States surveyed township, having one hundred and fifty inhabitants therein, to organize for themselves a separate township government: *Provided*, the township left contains one hundred and fifty inhabitants."

Mr. Williams moved to strike from the amendment, "having one hundred and fifty inhabitants therein."

Mr. Britain then modified his proposition by striking out "one hundred and."

When Mr. J. Clark submitted the following as a substitute:

"Power shall also be conferred upon the inhabitants of any one or more surveyed townships to organize township governments therein."

Mr. Danforth moved the previous question on the Article, and the call was sustained and the main question ordered to be now put.

The substitute offered by Mr. Clark was then adopted.

The question being upon adopting the same as a new section of the article, it was decided in the negative.

And the Article was then ordered to a third reading.

The article entitled "of State Officers" was taken from the table.

The question being upon concurring with the amendments made in committee of the whole,

The 1st amendment was non-concurred in.

The 2d amendment was concurred in.

The 3d amendment being under consideration,

Mr. Witherell moved to amend the same by inserting after "each of whom," the words "except the Attorney General and Superintendent of Public Instruction."

A division of the question being had, the motion to insert "except the Attorney General," was lost.

The balance of the amendment of Mr. Witherell was also disagreed to.

The amendment of the committee of the whole to sections 2, 3, 4 and 5 were severally concurred in.

When, on motion of Mr. Cook,

The Convention adjourned.

Afternoon Session.

Two o'clock.

The Convention was called to order by the President, and a quorum of members being in attendance, resumed the consideration of the article entitled "State Officers."

The question being upon concurring with the committee of the whole in the amendments to the 6th section, they were severally concurred in.

The article being open for amendment, Mr. Redfield proposed the following as a substitute for section six:

"There shall be elected at each general election an agent of the State Prison who shall hold his office two years."

Mr. Storey moved to amend the original section by striking out all after "Constitution," in the second line, up to and inclusive of the word "hereafter," in the 6th line.

Mr. Storey withdrew the amendment.

When Mr. Redfield withdrew his proposition.

On motion of Mr. Chapel,

Section 6 was stricken from the article.

On motion of Mr. Redfield,

The second section was amended by striking out "1852," and inserting in its stead "1853."

Mr. Edmunds moved to amend the same section by striking out "day," and inserting "Monday."

Mr. J. D. Pierce proposed "Wednesday," instead of "Monday."

Mr. Edmunds accepted the amendment, and his proposition was agreed to as modified.

Mr. Moore moved to reconsider the vote by which the Convention refused to except the Attorney General and Superintendent of Public Instruction from the operation of the clause in section 1, providing for offices being kept at the seat of government, together with the vote by which the Convention concurred in that amendment to the section made by the committee of the whole.

But the motion did not prevail.

Mr. Williams moved to amend the 1st section by striking out "a," before "Superintendent," and inserting "who shall be;" but subsequently withdrew the motion.

Mr. Williams moved to amend section 1, by inserting after "Secretary of State," the words "who shall be *ex officio* State Treasurer," and by striking out "State Treasurer," at the end of line 1.

Upon which he called the yeas and nays; and the same being ordered, the result was as follows:

YEAS.

Mr. W. Adams,	Mr. Daniels,	Mr. Moore,
Anderson,	Eaton,	Mosher,
H. Bartow,	Edmunds,	Prevost,
Ammon Brown,	Fralick,	E. S. Robinson,
Asahel Brown,	Gale,	Rix Robinson,
Butterfield,	Green,	Tiffany,
Carr,	Harvey,	Town,
Chapel,	Hascall,	Wait,
Choate,	Hathaway,	Webster,
Church,	Kinne,	Whittemore,
Comstock,	Lovell,	Williams,
Cook,	Marvin,	Willard,
Crary,	Mason,	Woodman, 39

NAYS.

Mr. Alvord,	Mr. Gardiner,	Mr. Raynale,
Arzeno,	Gibson,	Redfield,
Axford,	Graham,	Robertson,
Barnard,	Hanscom,	Skinner,
Beeson,	Hart,	Soule,
Britain,	Hixon,	Storey,
Alvarado Brown,	Kingsley,	Sturgis,
Burns,	Lee,	Sullivan,
Bush,	McLeod,	Sutherland,
Conner,	Mowry,	Van Valkenburg,
Cornell,	Newberry,	Walker,
Danforth,	O'Brien,	Warden,
Desnoyers,	Orr,	White,
Dimond,	J. D. Pierce,	Whipple,
Eastman,	N. Pierce,	President, 45

So the amendment was not agreed to.

The article was then ordered engrossed for a third reading.

On motion of Mr. Robertson,

The Convention resolved itself into committee of the whole on the article entitled "Education,"

Mr. McLeod in the chair.

PROCEEDINGS IN COMMITTEE.

The question recurring upon Mr. Fralick's amendment to section 3, proposed on the 26th June last, which amendment is as follows:

Amend section 3, by striking out all after "shall," in 1st line, and inserting "provide for a system of common schools, by which a school shall be kept up and supported in each school district, at least three months in every year; and any school district neglecting to keep up and support such a school, may be deprived of its epual proportion of the interest of the public fund. And the legislature may levy a tax on the whole taxable property of the several townships or cities of this State for the support of said schools."

Mr. Van Valkenburgh moved to strike out "three months" and insert "six months."

Which motion did not prevail.

Mr. Alvord moved to strike out after "year," in 4th line of Mr Fralick's amendment, to "and," in 6th line.

The last motion being withdrawn,

On motion of Mr. Crary,

Mr. Fralick's amendment was amended by striking out all after "and," in 4th line, to "and," in 6th line, and inserting: "any school district neglecting to keep up and support a school wherein instruction in the English language is conducted, for three months in each year, shall be deprived, for the year next succeeding, of its equal proportion of the income of the public fund."

Mr. Warden moved to strike out the words "several townships or cities of this."

Pending which, on motion of Mr. Moore,

The committee rose, reported progress and asked leave to sit again.

The committee, through their chairman, reported the same back to the Convention and asked leave to sit again.

Leave was granted.

On motion of Mr Danforth,

The Convention adjourned.

Lansing, Wednesday, July 24, 1850.

The President called the Convention to order at the usual hour.

Prayer by the Rev. Mr. Tooker.

The roll being called, there were absent on leave, Messrs. S. Clark, Leach and McClelland; without leave, Messrs. P. R. Adams, Bagg, Crouse, Eaton, Lee and Warden.

LEAVE OF ABSENCE.

Mr. Soule asked leave for Mr. Eaton,

Mr. Wells for Mr. Lee,

Mr. Alvord for Mr. Bagg, and

Mr. J. Clark for Mr. Warden,

And leave was granted Messrs. Eaton, Lee, Bagg and Warden for an indefinite period.

REPORTS.

Mr. Britain, from the committee on finance and taxation, submitted an Article entitled "Finance and Taxation."

Which was read the first and second time by its title and referred to the committee of the whole and ordered printed.

MOTIONS AND RESOLUTIONS.

Mr. Storey moved to recommit the article entitled "State Officers," to the committee on that subject, with instructions to insert the following therein, to stand as section 6:

"Three Inspectors of the State Prison shall be elected at the general election, which shall be held next after the adoption of this Constitution, one of whom shall hold his office for two years, one for four years and one for six years. The board of state canvassers shall on the first Monday of January next succeeding such general election, meet at the capital and determine by lot which of said Inspectors shall hold his office for two years, which for four years, and which for six years. And there shall be one elected at each general election thereafter, who shall hold his office for six years. The Inspectors shall have the charge and superintendence of the State

Prison, and shall appoint all the officers therein. All vacancies in the office of Inspector shall be filled by the Governor till the next election."

Which, on motion of Mr. Hanscom,

Was laid upon the table.

On motion of Mr. J. Bartow,

The Convention then resolved itself into committee of the whole and resumed the consideration of the Article entitled "Education,"

Mr. McLeod in the chair.

PROCEEDINGS IN COMMITTEE.

The question being upon Mr. Warden's amendment, the same prevailed.

Mr. Fralick's amendment, as amended, was then disagreed to.

The question then recurring upon Mr. Cornell's substitute, offered on the 26th June last, which, as amended, is as follows:

"The legislature may establish free schools throughout the State, and provide for their support. After applying the primary school fund and such other funds as shall be set apart for the support of such schools, the balance shall be raised by a State tax."

Mr. Witherell moved to strike out "shall," in 4th line, and insert "may."

But the Committee refused to strike out.

Mr. Cook moved to strike out "State," in 4th line.

Which motion was negatived.

On motion of Mr. J. D. Pierce,

The word "may," in 1st line was stricken out, and "shall" inserted.

Mr. Cornell's substitute was then disagreed to.

Mr. Hanscom offered the following as a substitute for section 3:

"Sec. 3. The legislature shall, within five years from the adoption of this Constitution, provide by law for a system of primary schools, to be kept free and without charge for tuition to all children between the ages of four and twenty. Such schools to be kept at least three months in each year, in each school district of the State."

Mr. Raynale moved to strike out "within five years."

But the committee refused to strike out.

Mr. Church moved to strike out, in Mr. Hanscom's substitute, after "Constitution," and insert "establish a system of common schools, in which the instruction shall be conducted in the English language, and shall be free of charge to pupils between the ages of four and and eighteen years at least three months in each year, in each school district in the State, and shall provide by law for the support of such schools by a tax or taxes upon property."

But the committee refused to so amend.

Mr. Hanscom's substitute was then disagreed to.

Mr. Walker, from the committee on education, reported the following, as a substitute for section 3:

"Sec. 3. The legislature shall establish by law, a system of primary schools. Such schools shall be kept in each and every school district, for at least three months in each year, free and without charge for tuition, to all children between the ages of four and eighteen years. Any deficiency that may exist after the distribution of the income from the primary school fund, shall be raised by a tax upon the whole taxable property in the State. The English language shall be taught in such schools."

On motion of Mr. Woodman,

"Eighteen" was stricken out, and "twenty-one" inserted.

Mr. Crary moved to strike out all after "tax."

But the committee refused to strike out.

Mr. N. Pierce moved to strike out "and without any charge for tuition."

Pending which,

On motion of Mr. Van Valkenburg,

The committee rose, reported progress, and asked leave to sit again.

The committee, through their Chairman, reported the same back to the Convention, and asked leave to sit again.

Leave was granted.

Mr. Crary moved that the Convention resolve itself into committee of the whole on the Article entitled "Education."

But the motion did not prevail.

On motion of Mr. Woodman, the Convention adjourned.

Afternoon Session.

Two o'clock.

The Convention was called to order by the President.

The roll called, and a quorum of members being in attendance,

On motion of Mr. Sutherland,

The Convention resolved itself into committee of the whole on the article entitled "Education,"

Mr. McLeod in the chair.

PROCEEDINGS IN COMMITTEE.

The question being upon Mr. N. Pierce's amendment to Mr. Walker's substitute, the same was not agreed to.

Mr. Redfield moved to strike out "children between the ages of four and twenty-one years," and insert "persons."

But the committee refused to strike out.

The question then recurring upon Mr. Walker's substitute, the committee refused to so amend.

Mr. Morrison offered the following as a substitute for section 3:

"The legislature shall provide by law that in the year 1855, and every year thereafter, a general tax shall be levied in the State for the support of primary schools, not exceeding five mills upon each dollar of the valuation of the taxable property in the State. Such tax to be levied and collected in the same manner as the general State tax for State purposes, and apportioned for the support of primary schools throughout the State in the same manner as the primary school interest fund, and shall provide that during the time required to expend the amount thus appropriated among the several districts, a school shall be kept in each district without any charge for tuition, to all scholars residing in such district between the ages of four and twenty-one years, and the instruction in such schools shall be conducted in the English language."

Mr. Morrison moved to amend the above by striking out "for tuition."

Which motion did not prevail.

On motion of Mr. H. Bartow,

"Five mills" were stricken out and "two mills" inserted.

Mr. Moore moved to strike out "1855" and insert "1852."

But the committee refused to strike out.

On motion of Mr. W. Adams,

"Exceeding" was stricken out, and "not less" inserted.

Mr. Morrison's substitute was then disagreed to.

Mr. N. Pierce offered the following as a substitute for sec. 3:

The legislature shall establish by law a system of primary schools, by which such schools shall be kept in each and every school district for at least three months in each year, free to all children between the ages of four and eighteen years, and shall provide for the levying a tax not exceeding two mills upon the dollar, upon all the taxable property in the State, for the support of said schools; and the English language be taught in such schools.

Mr. Church moved to amend the substitute by striking out the words: "and the English language shall be taught in such schools;" and inserting the words: "and all instructions in the said schools shall be conducted in the English language."

Which was agreed to.

On motion of Mr. Robertson,

The words "and without charge for tuition," was inserted after "free."

Mr. N. Pierce's substitute, as amended, was then adopted.

Mr. Robertson moved to strike out section four.

But the committee refused to strike out.

Mr. Crary moved to strike out the 1st, 2d and 3d lines of section five.

Which did not prevail.

Mr. Bush moved to strike out section five.

But the committee refused to strike out.

Mr. Robertson moved to strike out of section six all after "University," in fifth line.

Which was disagreed to.

Mr. Mason moved to strike out section seven.

But the committee refused to strike out.

On motion of Mr. Crary,

The words "according to the terms of the grant or appropriation," were added to section eight.

On motion of Mr. Crary,

The following, to stand as section nine, was adopted:

"Institutions for the benefit of those inhabitants who are deaf, dumb, blind, or insane shall always be fostered and supported, and the proceeds from the sale of all lands that have been or shall be hereafter granted or appropriated for the support of such institutions, shall be inviolably appropriated according to the terms and conditions of such grant or appropriation."

On motion of Mr. Soule,

The following was inserted in section 9, as printed, after the word "therewith," in line 3:

"And the twenty-two sections of salt spring lands now unappropriated, or the money arising from the sale of the same, where such lands have been already sold, and any land which may hereater be granted or appropriated for such purpose, shall be set apart for the support and maintenance of such school and farm. And the proceeds of the sale of all such lands that have been, or that may be hereafter sold, shall be a perpetual fund, the interest of which, together with the rents and profits of such lands, shall be appropriated for the support of such school and farm."

Mr. Hanscom moved to strike out all after "township," in line 4, of section 9.

On motion of Mr. Raynale,

"Collected" was inserted after "assessed," in line 5.

The words proposed to be stricken out containing two propositions, Mr. Crary called for a division of the question, and the committee struck out the first, but refused to strike out the second proposition.

Mr. Woodman moved to strike out "of at least," in line 4 of section 9.

Which was disagreed to.

Mr. Crary offered the following to stand as section 11.

"Until the existing state debt is paid, all specific state taxes are set apart and appropriated to the payment annually of the interest that may become due from the state to the school and other educational funds, or so much thereof as may be necessary for such purposes, and from and after the payment of said debts, such taxes shall be inviolably appropriated annually for the support of primary schools."

After some debate, Mr. Crary withdrew his proposition.

On motion of Mr. J. D. Pierce,

The committee rose, reported the article back with the amendments, asked the concurrence of the Convention therein, and to be discharged from the further consideration of said article.

—

The committee, through their chairman, reported the same back to the Convention with amendments, in which the concurrence of the Convention was asked.

The committee was discharged from the further consideration of the same, and

On motion of Mr. Whipple,

The article was laid on the table and ordered printed.

On motion of Mr. Britain,

The Convention resolved itself into committee of the whole on the general order,

Mr. Church in the chair.

—

PROCEEDINGS IN COMMITTEE.

The committee having under consideration the article entitled "Corporations," and section 2 having been read,

Mr. Woodman moved to fill the blank with "ten."

Mr. Van Valkenburgh with "two."

Mr. Witherell with "four."

The question being taken on the largest number first,

Mr. Woodman's motion did not prevail.

Mr. Witherell's amendment prevailed, and the blank was filled with "four."

Mr. Hanscom moved to strike from the section all after "election," in the third line,

When, on motion of Mr. Cook,

The committee rose, reported progress, and asked leave to sit again.

The committee, through their chairman, reported the same back to the Convention, and asked leave to sit again.

Leave was granted.

On motion of Mr. Robertson,

The Convention adjourned.

Lansing, Thursday, July 25, 1850.

The Convention met at the usual hour and was called to order by the President.

Prayer by the Rev. Mr. Sanford.

The roll being called, there were absent on leave, Messrs. Bagg, S. Clark, Eaton, Leach, Lee and Warden, and without leave, Messrs. P. R. Adams, Beardsley, J. Clark, Crouse, Walker and Whipple.

LEAVE OF ABSENCE.

Mr. Barned asked and obtained leave of absence for Mr. J. Clark indefinitely, and

Mr. Cornell for Mr. Beardsley for the day.

PETITIONS.

By Mr. Fralick: of Seth Hughes and 55 other citizens of Wayne county, that an article may be inserted in the Constitution restraining the legislature from passing any laws granting licenses for the sale of intoxicating drinks; and if deemed expedient, to make it the duty of the legislature to pass laws making it a misdemeanor to vend intoxicating drinks as a beverage.

By Mr. Sullivan: three several petitions of citizens of the county of Cass, praying for a provision prohibiting the passage of any law authorizing the sale of intoxicating liquors as a beverage.

By the President: two petitions of ladies of the city of Detroit, for a like prohibition.

The above were severally referred to the select committee upon the subject.

By Mr. Alvarado Brown: of A. A. Amidon and 105 others, citizens of Branch county, praying the insertion of a clause in the constitution prohibiting the employment of convicts in the State Prison at those branches of mechanical labor which interfere with mechanical trades in this State.

Referred to the committee on miscellaneous provisions.

MOTIONS AND RESOLUTIONS.

On motion of Mr. Comstock,

The minority report of the committee on banking and other incorporations, except municipal, was taken from the table and referred to the committee of the whole.

Mr. Alvord submitted the following:

Resolved, That when the Convention adjourns at noon to-day, it stand adjourned until to-morrow, and that the sergeant-at-arms be instructed to remove the carpet from the floor, and thoroughly cleanse the Hall.

Mr. Crary moved to amend so as to adjourn at noon to-morrow over till Monday, but withdrew the motion.

The question was taken on the adoption of the resolution and decided in the negative.

On motion of Mr. J. Bartow,

The Convention resolved itself into a committee of the whole on the general order,

Mr. Church in the chair.

PROCEEDINGS IN COMMITTEE.

The committee resumed the consideration of "Article —, Corporations."

Mr. Hanscom withdrew his motion made yesterday to strike out all after "election," in third line of section two, and offered the following as a substitute for section two:

"No banking law or law for banking purposes, nor any act creating any association or corporation for banking purposes, shall ever be enacted by the legislature."

Mr. J. Bartow asked a division, and the question being taken on striking out, the same prevailed.

Mr. Goodwin moved to amend Mr. Hanscom's substitute by striking out all after "no," and inserting the following: "bank shall be established under any banking law or law for banking purposes, unless the question whether the same may be established, shall have been first submitted to and decided by the electors of the State, under the provisions of law."

Mr. Hanscom modified his substitute by adding after "creating," the words "or renewing."

Mr. Moore moved that the committee rise, report progress and ask leave to sit again.

But the committee refused to rise.

Mr. Goodwin's amendment was then negatived.

Mr. Woodman moved to amend the substitute by adding thereto, as follows:

"Until the same shall have been submitted to a vote of the electors of the State at some general election, and been approved by a majority of the votes cast on that subject at such election."

Mr. Moore moved that the committee rise, report progress and ask leave to sit again.

But the committee refused to rise.

Mr. Woodman's amendment was disagreed to.

On motion of Mr. Chapel,

The following was substituted for Mr. Hanscom's substitute:

"No banking law or law for banking purposes shall have any force or effect until the same shall, after its passage, have been submitted to a vote of the electors of the State, at some general election, and been approved by a majority of the votes cast on that subject at such election."

The substitute was then adopted.

On motion of Mr. Woodman,

The committee rose, reported progress, and asked leave to sit again.

The committee, through their chairman, reported progress and asked leave to sit again.

Leave was granted.

When, on motion of Mr. Cornell,

The Convention adjourned.

Afternoon Session.

Two o'clock.

The Convention was called to order by the President,

A quorum being present,

On motion of Mr. Cook,

The Convention resolved itself into a committee of the whole and resumed the consideration of the article entitled "Corporations,"

Mr. Church in the chair.

PROCEEDINGS IN COMMITTEE.

The committee resumed the consideration of "Article —, Corporations."

Section 3 was read, and

On motion of Mr. J. Bartow,

The words "as co-partners" and "of every kind," were stricken out of lines two and three.

Mr. Goodwin moved to amend section three by inserting after "association," the words "established under such laws."

Which was disagreed to.

Mr. Fralick moved to amend by inserting in line two, after "liable," the words "to the amount of their respective share or shares of stock in any such corporation or association."

The motion was withdrawn.

Mr. Sullivan moved to amend section three, by adding thereto, "which were contracted during the time of their being officers and stockholders of such corporotion or association, and for one year thereafter."

Mr. Crary moved to strike out "and for one year thereafter."

Which motion was not agreed to.

Mr. Sullivan's amendment was then adopted.

Mr. Raynale moved to strike out of section three, the words "or any kind of paper credits."

Which motion did not prevail.

On motion of Mr. Cook,

Section four was amended by striking out "ample," in second line, and inserting after "security," the following: "to the full amount of notes or paper credits so registered."

On motion of Mr. Witherell,

"On" was stricken out and "bearing" inserted, in second line.

Mr. Tiffany moved to amend section four by striking out all after "security," in second line, and inserting the following:

"For the redemption of the same in specie; such security to be in stocks, bonds or evidences of debt issued by the United States or of individual States, or both, bearing interest, which shall be deposited with the State Treasurer, and be at least, when offered, equal in value to the amount of bills or notes registered and issued for circulation."

Which was withdrawn.

Mr. Witherell moved to amend by inserting after "stocks," in 2d line, the words "of this State or of some other State, or of the United States."

Which was also withdrawn.

On motion of Mr. Cornell,

The words "which shall be deposited with the State Treasurer," were inserted after "stocks," in 2d line.

Mr. Van Valkenburgh offered the following, as a substitute for section four:

"The legislature shall provide by law for the registry of all bills or notes issued or put in circulation as money, and shall require security in the stocks of this State or of some other State of this Union, or stocks of the United States, bearing interest, for the redemption of such bills or notes in specie, to be deposited with the State Treasurer."

Which was not adopted.

On motion of Mr. Cook.

"Bill" was stricken out of first line of section 5, and "of the notes or bills" inserted after "holders."

On motion of Mr. Witherell,

The words "issuing bank notes of any description," were stricken out of section 6.

On motion of Mr. Cornell,

"Unless with" were stricken out of 3d line of section 8, and "without" inserted.

Mr. Edmunds moved to strike out of section 10, line 2, "or secured."

Which motion was withdrawn.

On motion of Mr. Witherell,

"Other than municipal" was stricken out of 1st line of sec. 10.

Mr. Whipple moved to strike out section 10.

Mr. Crary moved to amend section 10 by striking out "its own" and inserting "public."

Which motion prevailed.

Mr. Whipple then withdrew his motion to strike out.

Mr. McLeod moved to strike out the 1st line of section 11, and also the 2d line to "no."

But the committee refused to strike out.

Mr. J. D. Pierce offered the following, to stand as section 11, which was not adopted:

"Whenever damage shall be done by any corporation to private property, such corporation shall be liable to the full amount of such damage."

On motion of Mr. McClelland,

The following was inserted after "thereof," in 1st line of section 5: "issued or put in circulation as money."

On motion of Mr. Bush,

The committee rose, reported the article back with amendments, asked the concurrence of the Convention therein, and to be discharged from the further consideration of the same.

The committee, through their chairman, reported the same back with sundry amendments, in which they asked the concurrence of the Convention.

On motion of Mr. Cook,

The article was laid upon the table and ordered printed.

On motion of Mr. Storey,

The Convention then adjourned.

Lansing, Friday, July 26, 1850.

The Convention met pursuant to adjournment and was called to order by the President.

Prayer by the Rev. Mr. Sanford.

The roll being called, there were absent with leave, Messrs. Bagg, J. Clark, S. Clark, Eaton, Lee and Warden; without leave, Messrs.

Barned, Beardsley, Bush, Chapel, Crouse, Daniels, Morrison, Raynale, M. Robinson, Walker and Wells.

LEAVE OF ABSENCE

Was granted to Messrs. Kinne, Raynale, M. Robinson, Chapel Walker, Morrison and Wells for an indefinite period.

To Messrs. Beardsley and Orr till Monday.

To Mr. Barnard till Tuesday, and Mr. Daniels until Wednesday next.

PETITIONS.

By Mr. Storey: of Mrs. Electa M. Sheldon and 157 others, ladies of the village of Jackson, praying for the insertion of a provision in the constititution prohibiting the manufacture, importation and sale of intoxicating liquors to be used as a beverage.

Referred to the select committee upon that subject.

By Mr. Hascall: of Martin Wilson and 32 others, citizens of Kalamazoo county, for a like prohibition as the foregoing.

Referred to same committee.

On motion of Mr. J. Barlow,

The Convention then resolved itself into committee of the whole on the general order,

Mr. Roberts in the chair.

PROCEEDINGS IN COMMITTEE.

The committee took up for consideration "Articles —, Exemptions and the rights of Married Women," which were read, and,

On motion of Mr. J. Bartow,

Were passed over, and "Article —, Of Cities and Villages," considered.

Mr. Witherell moved to amend section one by adding the following:

"And when the boundaries of any city or village shall be enlarged, the territory annexed shall not be taxed for the payment of pre existing debts of said city."

Which motion did not prevail.

Mr. Witherell moved to amend the same section by adding thereto, as follows:

"And the boundaries of cities and villages shall not be extended over adjacent territory without the consent of a majority of the owners or occupants of such territory."

Mr. Desnoyers moved to add to the amendment, as follows:

"Unless such adjoining territory is laid out in city or village lots."

Which was accepted by Mr. Witherell.

The amendment as modified was disagreed to.

Mr. Skinner moved to insert after "villages," in 2d line, as follows: "extending or diminishing their boundaries, laying out or discontinuing streets and alleys."

But the committee refused to so amend.

Mr. Danforth moved to strike out section two.

But the committee refused to strike out.

Mr. Crary moved to strike out section three.

The motion was withdrawn.

Mr. Sullivan moved to strike out "of such city or village" from line three of section three.

Which motion did not prevail.

On motion of Mr. Witherell,

The following was adopted to stand as

"Sec. 4. Previous notice of any application for an alteration of the charter of any corporation shall be given in such manner as the legislature shall by law direct."

On motion of Mr. Crary,

The committee rose, reported the article back and asked the concurrence of the Convention to the amendment made thereto, and to be discharged from the further consideration of the article.

The committee, through their chairman, reported the article "Cities and Villages" back, with an additional section thereto, in which the concurrence of the Convention was asked.

The amendment was concurred in, and the Article being before the Convention, Mr. Skinner proposed the following as a substitute for section one:

"It shall be the duty of the legislature to provide by general laws for the organization and regulation of cities and villages."

Which was not adopted.

Mr. Fralick moved to amend section three by striking out in the second and third lines, the words "of such city or village."

And the amendment was agreed to.

The Article was then ordered engrossed for a third reading.

Mr. Moore offered the following, and moved its reference to the committee of the whole:

Resolved, That the judiciary committee be instructed to inquire into the expediency of incorporating in the Constitution, the following:

"The legislature shall, as soon as practicable, provide for the appointment of a board of commissioners, whose duty it shall be to revise, reform, simplify and abridge the rules and practice, pleadings, forms and proceedings of the courts of record of this State, and they shall provide for the abolition of the distinct forms of action at law, now in use in civil proceedings, and that justice may be administered in a uniform mode of pleadings, without reference to the distinction now existing between law and equity; and the said commissioners shall from time to time, when required, report their proceedings to the legislature, subject to the action of that body."

And the motion to refer prevailed.

On motion of Mr. Crary,

The article entitled "Judicial Department," together with the resolution of Mr. Crary, as follows:

"*Resolved,* That the article on the judicial department be recommitted to the judiciary committee with instructions that such committee so alter and modify their report as to provide that the judges of the circuit courts shall be judges of the supreme court,"

Were taken from the table.

And the question being on the adoption of the resolution,

After some debate,

On motion of Mr. Whittemore,

The Convention adjourned.

Afternoon Session.

Two o'clock.

The Convention was called to order by the President.

A quorum being present,

The Convention resumed the consideration of the resolution pending at the time of the adjournment this morning.

Mr. McClelland moved to amend the resolution by striking out all after "instructions" and inserting as follows: "to report also, as soon as practicable, a plan for a supreme court, the judges thereof to perform circuit duties."

Mr. Crary then withdrew his resolution, and on his motion,

The article entitled "Judicial Department," was referred to the committee of the whole and placed upon the general order.

Mr. Witherell moved that the Convention resolve itself into committee of the whole on the article entitled "exemptions and the rights of married women," but withdrew his motion.

On motion of Mr. J. Bartow,

The Convention resolved itself into committee of the whole on the general order, Mr. Bush in the chair.

PROCEEDINGS IN COMMITTEE.

The committee took up for consideration "Article —, Finance and Taxation."

Section one was read, when,

On motion of Mr. Britain,

The words "in defraying the current expenses of the State," were stricken out of line two of section one, and "balance of the," inserted before "State," at the end of line two.

On motion of Mr. Crary,

The words "and other educational," were inserted between "school" and "funds," in line two.

Mr. Roberts moved to insert after the word "taxes," in first line, "except on charters organizing the mining companies in the Upper Peninsula."

Which motion was disagreed to.

Mr. J. Bartow moved to strike out, at the end of line three, the words "in the order herein recited."

But the committee refused to strike out.

Mr. Witherell offered the following, to come in at the end of the third line:

"After the payment of the State debt, except the debt due to the educational fund, the said taxes shall be applied exclusively to the purposes of Education."

Mr. J. D. Pierce moved to strike out of the above "purposes of education," and insert "support of primary schools."

The motion was withdrawn, and

Mr. Witherell's amendment was then adopted.

Mr. Roberts moved to amend section 1 by inserting after "paying," in the 1st line, the words "the expense of the governmental and judicial policy of the upper peninsula."

Mr. Witherell offered the following as a substitute for the above amendment, which was accepted by Mr. Roberts and adopted by the committee:

Add at end of first subdivision of section 1, as follows: "The foregoing provisions shall not apply to specific taxes in the upper peninsula."

Mr. Van Valkenburgh moved to add at end of 5th line as follows:

"And also the necessary amount including the fund appropriated to support the free schools established by this constitution.

But the committee refused to so amend section 2.

Mr. Edmunds moved to strike out "one," at end of line 2, and insert "five."

Which was disagreed to.

Mr. Robertson moved to strike out of line three, "with compound interest at six per cent. per annum."

The motion was withdrawn.

On motion of Mr. Whipple,

"One" was stricken out of line two, and "two" inserted.

Section three was read, when,

On motion of Mr. Britain,

The blank was filled with "fifty."

Sections 4, 5, 6, 7, 8, and 9 were severally read.

Mr. Fralick moved to strike out section nine.

But the committee refused to strike out.

Mr. Cook moved to strike out section 10.

The motion was withdrawn.

Section 11 was then read.

Mr. Robertson moved to strike out of section 11, the words "and taxes shall be levied upon such property as the legislature shall prescribe."

But the committee refused to strike out.

Mr. W. Adams moved to strike out of line 1 the word "shall" and insert "may."

Which was disagreed to.

Mr. Cook moved to strike out "by a state board."

But the committee refused to strike out.

Mr. Butterfield offered the following to stand as

"Sec. 15. The Legislature shall provide by law for the final col lection of all taxes within the several townships."

Mr. White moved to add to said proposed section, the following: "at the same time and in the same manner."

On motion of Mr. Church,

The committee rose, reported progress, and asked leave to sit again.

The committee, through their chairman, reported the Article back to the Convention, and asked leave to sit again.

Leave was granted.

On motion of Mr. Van Va.kenburgh,

The Convention then adjourned.

Lansing, Saturday, July 27, 1850.

The President called the Convention to order at the usual hour.

Prayer by the Rev. Mr. Tooker.

The roll being called, there were absent on leave. Messrs. Barnard, Beardsley, Chapel, J. Clark, S. Clark, Crouse, Daniels, Eaton-Kinne, Lee, Morrison, Raynale, Walker, Warden and Wells; with, out leave, Messrs. Beeson, McLeod, N. Pierce and Soule.

LEAVE OF ABSENCE.

Mr. J. D. Pierce asked and obtained leave for Messrs. N. Pierce and Soule until Monday.

Mr. Roberts for Mr. McLeod until Monday,

And Mr. J. Bartow for Mr. Beeson till Wednesday next.

PETITIONS.

By Mr. Whittemore: four several petitions of the ladies of Pontiac, praying the incorporation of a provision in the constitution, prohibiting the manufacture and sale of alcoholic drinks as a beverage.

Referred to the select committee upon the subject.

By Mr. Church: two several petitions of the citizens of Kent county, that a clause may be inserted in the new constitution, prohibiting the employment of convicts in the State Prison in those branches of mechanical industry which interfere with those of our own citizens.

Referred to the committee on miscellaneous provisions.

RESOLUTIONS.

On motion of Mr. Rix Robinson,

Resolved, That the committee on the judiciary be instructed to inquire into the expediency of inserting a clause in the constitution prohibiting the enforcing by law the payment of any debts on contracts express or implied of a less amount than twenty-five dollars, and that they report thereon as soon as practicable.

On motion of Mr. J. Bartow,

The Convention was resolved into a committee of the whole, on the article entitled "Finance and Taxation,"

Mr. Mason in the chair.

PROCEEDINGS IN COMMITTEE.

The committee resumed the consideration of "Article —, Finance and Taxation,"

And the question being upon Mr. White's amendment to Mr. Butterfield's proposed new section,

Mr. W. Adams moved to amend the proposed substitute by inserting before "townships" the words "counties and,"

Which was not agreed to.

Mr. White's motion was also disagreed to.

Mr. Butterfield's proposed section was not adopted.

Mr. Bush moved to add a new section as follows:

"Sec. 15. Any tax deed given for land returned and sold as delinquent for taxes shall be conclusive evidence of the legality of all the proceedings prior to and including the sale, and any suit in ejectment for the recovery of said land shall be commenced within five years from the date of said deed and not thereafter, unless the original tax upon which the deed was predicated had been paid."

But the section was not adopted.

Mr. Britain offered the following as a substitute for section 1:

"Sec. 1. All specific taxes shall be applied in paying the interest upon the primary school, university and other educational funds, and of the balance of the state debt in the order herein recited, until the first of January, eighteen hundred and , at which time said specific taxes shall be added to, and forever thereafter constitute a part of, the proceeds of the primary school fund."

Mr. Britain also offered the following as an addition to the Article, viz:

"Sec. 15. Every act making an appropriation not expressly provided for by this constitution, shall contain a provision for the necessary state tax to meet such appropriation, and a statement of the year or years in which said tax is to be levied; and said act shall, before it shall take effect, be submitted to the people at a general election, or at the annual township meetings, and be approved by a majority of all the votes given for and against it at said election or annual township meetings.

"Sec. 16. All lands sold for the non-payment of taxes, even though sold by a county officer, shall be sold in the townships in which they are situated.

"Sec. 17. Every assessment roll upon which the resident taxes have been paid and which has been returned by the collector shall, with said return, be conclusive evidence of the legality of all taxes therein contained, and of everything pertaining to said taxes, except as against errors contained in said roll, and receipts for payment of taxes returned unpaid.

"Sec. 18. The Legislature may provide by law as follows:

1st. That a deed given by any legally authorized person, to a purchaser of real estate, sold for non-payment of taxes, shall be prima facia evidence of title to such real estate:

2d. That peaceable possession of real estate by any person whose title thereto shall be based upon a tax title thereof for such time as the

Legislature shall prescribe not less than six nor more than ten years, shall be conclusive evidence of title thereto:

3d. That no person whose title to real estate shall be based upon a tax deed made after the first of January, eighteen hundred and fifty shall be ejected therefrom until he be fully paid for all improvements thereon either made or purchased by him."

On motion of Mr. McClelland,

The committee rose, reported progress and asked leave to sit again.

The committee, through their chairman, reported the same back to the Convention, and asked and obtained leave to sit again.

On motion of Mr. Storey,

The Convention adjourned until Monday morning at 8 o'clock.

Lansing, Monday, July 29, 1850.

The Convention met pursuant to adjournment and was called to order by the President.

Prayer by the Rev. Mr. Merrill.

The roll being called, there were absent on leave Messrs. Barnard Beardsley, Beeson, Chapel, J. Clark, S. Clark, Crouse, Eaton, Kinne, Lee, Morrison, N. Pierce, Raynale, Soule, Walker, and Wells; without leave, Messrs. Anderson, H. Bartow, Alvarado Brown, Butterfield, Choate, Daniels, Edmunds, Green, McLeod, Orr, Roberts, M. Robinson, Whipple and Witherell.

LEAVE OF ABSENCE

Was granted to Messrs. Roberts, McLeod and Willard, until tomorrow: to Messrs. Alvarado Brown and Witherell, indefinitely; to Messrs. Butterfield and Whipple, until Wednesday, and to Mr. Anderson until Thursday.

PETITIONS:

By Mr. Warden: of Sarah McCamley and 43 other ladies of Brighton, Livingston county, praying the Convention to prohibit the sale of ardent spirits, (except for medicinal and mechanical purposes), after the 1st day of January, 1854.

Referred to select committee upon the subject.

By the President: of the officers and other members of the Detroit City Guards, that the provision in article 10, section 4, of the present constitution, in relation to money paid "by persons as an exemption from military duty" may be rescinded, and for other encouragement to volunteer companies.

Laid upon the table.

MOTIONS AND RESOLUTIONS.

Mr. McClelland submitted the following substitute for section 2, of the article entitled "Judicial Department."

"For the term of six years and thereafter until the Legislature shall otherwise provide, the Judges of the several circuit courts shall be Judges of the supreme court, three of whom shall constitute a quorum, and a concurrence of a majority of Judges present, shall be necessary to a decision. The Legislature shall have power, if they should think expedient and necessary, to provide by law for the organization of a seperate supreme court, with the jurisdiction and powers prescribed in this constitution, to consist of one Chief Justice and two associate Justices, to be elected by the qualified electors of the State. The separate court when so organized, shall not be changed or discontinued by the legislature for six years after its organization. The Judges thereof shall be so classified that but one of them shall go out of office at the same time, and their term of office shall be the same as is provided for the Judges of the circuit court."

Which, on his motion,

Was referred to the committee of the whole.

On motion of Mr. McClelland,

The article entitled "Legislative Department," was taken from the table.

On motion of Mr. J. Bartow,

The Convention resolved itself into committee of the whole and resumed the consideration of the article entitled "Finance and Taxation,"

Mr. Mason in the chair.

PROCEEDINGS IN COMMITTEE.

"Article —, Finance and Taxation," being under consideration, and the chairman of that committee being absent,

On motion of Mr. J. Bartow,

The committee rose, reported progress, and asked leave to sit again.

The same was reported back to the Convention and leave was granted the committee to sit again.

On motion of Mr. Tiffany,

The Convention was then resolved into a committee of the whole, on the article entitled "Judicial Department."

Mr. Cook in the chair.

PROCEEDINGS IN COMMITTEE.

Section 1 having been read,

Mr. Bagg moved to insert after "circuit courts," in line 1, the words "in county courts."

Which motion did not prevail.

Mr. Sullivan moved to insert after "circuit courts," the words "in county judges."

The motion was disagreed to.

On motion of Mr. Goodwin,

"Inferior local" was stricken out of 2nd line and "municipal" inserted.

Section 2 was then read, and

On motion of Mr. Mason,

"Three" was stricken out of line 1 and "four" inserted; also "two," in lines 1 and 2 were stricken out and "three" inserted.

On motion of Mr. Backus,

The following was inserted after "decision," in 2d line: "The majority of the judges shall give their opinion in every case, in writing, under their signatures."

Mr. Britain offered the following as a substitute for the section, which was not adopted.

"2d. The supreme court shall consist of four Judges, a majority of whom shall form a quorum, and a majority shall be necessary to any decision. A Judge dissenting from a decision, shall give the reasons of such dissent in writing, under his own signature."

On motion of Mr. Hanscom,

The word "final" was inserted before "decision," wherever it occurs in line 2.

Mr. McClelland offered the substitute this morning presented by him, for section 2.

On motion of Mr. Van Valkenburg,

The committee rose, reported progress, and asked leave to sit again.

The chairman reported the same back to the Convention, and asked and obtained leave to sit again.

On motion ot Mr. Desnoyers,

The Convention adjourned.

Afternoon Session.

Two o'clock.

The Convention was called to order by the President.

A quorum of members in attendance,

Mr. Moore submitted the following additional sections to the article entitled "Judicial Department," which were referred to the committee of the whole.

Sec. —. There shall be elected in each of the counties of this State one county judge, who shall hold his office for four years, who shall hold the county court and perform the duties of the office of judge of probate.

Sec. —. The county court shall have original jurisdiction in all cases, civil and criminal, in law and equity, and appellate jurisdiction in such cases as the legislature shall provide.

Sec. —. The county judge shall receive an annual salary, to be fixed by the board of supervisors, to be paid by the county.

Sec. —. The county judge of the county is authorized to hold the county courts for any other county in the State.

On motion of Mr. Backus,

The Convention resolved itself into committee of the whole and resumed the consideration of the article entitled "Judicial Department," Mr. Cook in the chair.

PROCEEDINGS IN COMMITTEE.

The committee resumed the consideration of Mr. McClelland's substitute for section 2, and after debate thereon,

On motion of Mr. J. Bartow,

The committee rose, reported progress and asked leave to sit again.

The committee, through their chairman, reported the same back and asked and obtained leave to sit again.

On motion of Mr. Mason,

The Convention adjourned.

Lansing, Tuesday, July 30, 1850.

The Convention met pursuant to adjournment, and was called to order by the President.

Prayer by the Rev. Mr. Tooker.

The roll being called, there were absent on leave Messrs. Anderson, Beeson, Alvarado Brown, Butterfield, Chapel, J. Clark, S. Clark, Daniels, Kinne, McLeod, Morrison, Raynale, Roberts, M. Robinson, Walker, Wells, Whipple, Willard and Witherell; without leave, Messrs. Edmunds, Hixon and Skinner.

ABSENCE.

Mr. McClelland asked and obtained leave of absence for Mr. McLeod; Mr. Hanscom for Mr. Roberts; Mr. Kingsley for Mr. Skinner, and Mr. Carr for Mr. Edmunds.

MOTIONS.

Mr. J. Bartow moved to go into committee of the whole on the article entitled "Judicial Department."

On motion of Mr. Hanscom,

The same was amended by inserting "Exemptions and the Rights of Married Women," in lieu of "Judicial Department," and

The Convention refused to go into committee of the whole.

On motion of Mr. J. Bartow,

The Convention then resolved itself into a committee of the whole on the general order,

Mr. Hanscom in the chair.

PROCEEDINGS IN COMMITTEE.

The committee took up for consideration "Article —, Exemptions and the Rights of Married Women."

Section 1 having been read,

Mr. Tiffany moved to strike out of line two "not less than five hundred dollars," and insert "not more than three hundred dollars."

A division of the question was called for by Mr. Woodman, when

Mr. Backus moved to strike out "less" and insert "more."

Which motion was disagreed to.

Mr. Robertson moved to strike out "not less than."

But the committee refused to strike out.

On motion of Mr. J. D. Pierce,

The following was added to section one: "issued for the collection of any debt contracted after the adoption of this constitution."

Mr. Tiffany then withdrew his amendment.

Mr. Mason moved to strike out "resident of," in line 1 and insert "person in."

Which was disagreed to.

Mr. Tiffany moved to strike out "resident," and insert "householder."

Which motion did not prevail.

Section 2 was then read.

Mr. Robertson moved to strike out "less" and "forty," in line 1, and insert "more" and "eighty."

But the committee refused to so amend.

Mr. Fralick moved to insert after "the," in line 1 the word "recorded."

Which was disagreed to.

Mr. Cook moved to amend by inserting after "plat," in 3d line as follows: "or an amount of land, equal in quantity, to one lot in such village or city on which the dwelling house is situated."

Which was not adopted.

Mr. Robertson moved to insert after "incurred," in 3d line, the words "except for the purchase money thereof."

Which was not agreed to.

Mr. Tiffany moved to insert after "plat," in 3d line, the words "to the value of one thousand dollars."

Which was disagreed to.

Mr. Beardsley moved to strike out "forty," in line 1, and insert "eighty."

But the committee refused to so amend.

Sections 3, 4 and 5 were then read, and no amendments having been offered,

Mr. Robertson moved that the committee rise, report progress and ask leave to sit again.

But the committee refused to rise.

The article in relation to capital punishment was then taken up.

Mr. Woodman moved that the committee pass over the article for the present.

Which was not agreed to.

The article having been read,

Mr. Crary moved as a substitute for the article the following: "human life shall be held inviolable."

The committee refused to adopt the substitute.

The committee then proceeded to consider "Article —, Township Officers and Government."

Mr. Robertson moved to strike out "the duties of," in 1st line, and insert, "there shall be elected in."

But the committee refused to so amend.

Mr. Woodman moved to strike out "duties of," and insert "township government of."

Which motion did not prevail.

Mr. Alvord moved to strike out "one school inspector," in 2d line.

But the committee refused to strike out.

On motion of Mr. N. Pierce,

The following was added to 2d line: "and so many overseers of highways as there are highway districts."

On motion of Mr. Hascall,

The words, "and terms of office," were added to the end of the section.

Mr. Gale moved to insert after "treasurer," the words "two highway commissioners, one poor-master."

On motion of Mr. Newberry,

"Two" was stricken out, and "one" inserted.

The amendment of Mr. Gale was then adopted as amended.

On motion of Mr. Alvord,

"And compensation," was inserted at the end of the section.

On motion of Mr. Van Valkenburgh,

The committee rose, reported progress and asked leave to sit again on the article under consideration, and to be discharged from the consideration of articles entitled "exemptions and the rights of married women," and "capital punishment."

—

The committee through their chairman reported back the article entitled "exemptions and the rights of married women," with an amendment in which the concurrence of the Convention was asked, and the article relative to capital punishment without amendment.

On motion of Mr. Cornell,

The Convention adjourned.

—

Afternoon Session.

Two o'clock.

The President called the Convention to order.

A quorum of members being in attendance,

On motion of Mr. Hanscom,

The Convention was resolved into a committee of the whole on the general order,

Mr. Hanscom in the chair.

—

PROCEEDINGS IN COMMITTEE.

The committee resumed the consideration of "Article —, Township Officers and Government."

Mr. Church offered the following as a substitute for the article:

"*Article —. Townships and Township Officers.*

"1. Each township, duly organized by law, shall be a body corporate and politic, with such rights, duties, powers, privileges and immunities, and such powers of local legislation, to be uniform throughout the State, as shall be prescribed by law. All suits and proceedings by or against any township shall be in the name thereof. And there shall be elected in each township three supervisors, who shall hold their offices for three years; two school inspectors, who shall hold their offices for two years; and annually, on the first Monday in April, a township clerk, township treasurer and such number of constables and overseers of highways as may be provided by law. The supervisors and school inspectors, at their first election, shall be divided by lot into numbers so that one supervisor and one school inspector shall be elected annually."

Mr. Crary called for a division of the question and moved that the first part of the foregoing, to and including the word "thereof," should stand as a new section of the article.

Which motion prevailed.

The remainder was then offered as a substitute for section 1.

But the committee refused to adopt the same.

On motion of Mr. Backus,

The following was substituted for section 1:

"Section 1. There shall be elected by the people annually, on the first Monday of April, in each organized township, one supervisor, one township clerk, one township treasurer, one school inspector, not exceeding four constable, and one overseer of highways for each highway district in such township, in whom, together with the justices of the peace, not to exceed four, shall be vested the township government, to be defined and limited in such manner as the Legislature shall prescribe.

Mr. Bush offered the following as a substitute for the article:

Sec. 1. All city, town and village officers whose election or appointment is not provided for by this constitution, shall be elected by the electors of such cities, towns and villages, or of some division thereof, or appointed by such authorities thereof as the legislature shall designate for that purpose. All other officers whose election or appointment is not provided for by this constitution, and all officers whose offices may hereafter be created by law, shall be elected by the people, or appointed, as the legislature may direct.

Sec. 2. When the duration of any office is not provided by this constitution, it may be declared by law; and if not so declared, such office shall be held during the pleasure of the authority making the appointment.

Sec. 3. The time of electing all officers named in the article shall be prescribed by law.

Sec. 4. The legislature may declare the cases in which any office shall be deemed vacant where no provision is made for that purpose in this constitution.

The substitute was not adopted.

On motion of Mr. Britain,

The following was adopted as a new section:

Sec. 3. The legislature shall secure to the inhabitants of every United States surveyed township having fifty inhabitants, a separate organization, provided the township left, contain fifty inhabitants.

On motion of Mr. Warden,

The committee rose, reported the Article back with the amendments, asked the concurrence of the Convention therein, and to be discharged from the further consideration thereof.

The committee through their chairman reported the same back to the Convention, with sundry amendments, in which its concurrence was asked, and the article was laid upon the table.

The article entitled "Exemptions and the rights of Married Women" coming up, and the question being upon concurring in the amendment made by the committee of the whole,

The Convention concurred therein.

The article being open for amendment,

Mr. Mason moved to strike out "resident of," in the first line of section 1, and insert the words, "person in."

Which motion was not agreed to.

Mr. Newberry moved to strike out "less," in first line of section 2, and insert in lieu thereof, "more."

Upon which he asked the yeas and nays.

And the same being had, the motion to amend was lost, as follows:

YEAS:

Mr. P. R. Adams,	Mr. Dimond,	Mr. Mowry,
Axford,	Fralick,	Newberry,
Backus,	Gibson,	Robertson,
Ammon Brown,	Graham,	E. S Robinson,
Burns,	Green,	Rix Robinson,
Carr,	Harvey,	Sturgis,
Choate,	Hathaway,	Sutherland,
Church,	Lee,	Tiffany,
Comstock,	Mason,	Wait,
Cornell,	McClelland,	White,
Crouse,	Moore,	32

NAYS.

Mr. W. Adams, Alvord, Arzeno, Bagg, H. Bartow, Beardsley, Britain, Bush, Chandler, Conner, Cook, Crary, Danforth, Eastman,
Mr. Eaton, Gale, Gardiner, Hanscom, Hart, Hascall, Kingsley, Leach, Lovell, Marvin, Mosher, O'Brien, Orr,
Mr. J. D. Pierce, Prevost, Soule, Storey, Sullivan, Town, Van Valkenburg, Warden, Webster, Whittemore, Williams, Woodman, President,

40

Mr. Fralick proposed adding at the end of the first section as follows:

"Provided, such personal property so exempt shall be designated and defined by law."

Which was lost, by yeas and nays, as follows:

YEAS:

Mr. P. R. Adams, Axford, Backus, Ammon Brown, Carr, Church, Cornell, Crouse, Dimond, Eastman,
Mr. Fralick, Gibson, Graham, Hathaway, Lee, Moore, Mowry, Newberry, Orr,
Mr. E. S. Robinson, Rix Robinson, Sturgis, Sutherland, Tiffany, Wait, White, Williams, President,

28

NAYS.

Mr. W. Adams, Alvord, Arzeno, Bagg, H. Bartow, Beardsley, Britain, Bush, Chandler, Choate, Comstock, Conner, Cook,
Mr. Crary, Danforth, Eaton, Gale, Gardiner, Hanscom, Hascall, Leach, Lovell, Marvin, Mason, McClelland, Mosher,
Mr. O'Brien, J. D. Pierce, Prevost, Robertson, Soule, Storey, Sullivan, Van Valkenburg, Warden, Webster, Whittemore, Woodman,

38

Mr. Backus moved to strike out in sec. 1, the words "exempted to the amount of not less than five hundred dollars," and to insert in lieu thereof the word "exempt."

Upon this, the yeas and nays being demanded, the vote was as follows:

YEAS:

Mr. P. R. Adams,	Mr. Dimond,	Mr. Mason,
Axford,	Fralick,	Newberry,
Backus,	Gibson,	Orr,
Burns,	Graham,	N. Pierce,
Bush,	Hart,	E. S. Robinson,
Carr,	Harvey,	Sturgis,
Church,	Leach,	Sutherland,
Cornell,	Lee,	Town,
Crouse,	Marvin,	Wait, 27

NAYS:

Mr. W. Adams,	Mr. Eaton,	Mr. Prevost,
Alvord,	Gale,	Robertson,
Arzeno,	Gardiner,	Rix Robinson,
Bagg,	Green,	Soule,
H. Bartow,	Hanscom,	Storey,
Beardsley,	Hascall,	Sullivan,
Britain,	Hathaway,	Tiffany,
Chandler,	Kingsley,	Van Valkenburg,
Choate,	Lovell,	Warden,
Comstock,	McClelland,	Webster,
Conner,	Moore,	White,
Cook,	Mosher,	Whittemore,
Crary,	Mowry,	Williams,
Danforth,	O'Brien,	Woodman,
Desnoyers,	J. D. Pierce,	President, 45

So the Convention refused to strike out.

Mr. N. Pierce moved to strike from the 2d line of section 1, the word "five" and substitute "twelve."

Mr. Alvord moved the previous question on the article, and the call being sustained,

The main question was ordered to be now put.

On the amendment proposed by Mr. N. Pierce,

A division having been called, the motion to strike out "five" was lost,

And the main question being on ordering the article to a third reading,

Mr. Alvord called the yeas and nays, and the same were ordered with the following result:

YEAS:

Mr. W. Adams, Alvord, Arzeno, Bagg, H. Bartow, Britain, Bush, Chandler, Choate, Church, Comstock, Conner, Cook, Cornell, Crary, Danforth, Eastman, Eaton, Mr. Gale, Gardiner, Gibson, Green, Hanscom, Harvey, Hascall, Hathaway, Kingsley. Leach, Lovell, Marvin, McClelland, Mosher, Mowry, O'Brien, Orr, Mr. J. D. Pierce, N. Pierce, Prevost, Robertson, Rix Robinson, Soule, Storey, Sullivan, Sutherland, Town, Van Valkenburg Warden, Webster, Whittemore, Williams, Woodman, President. 52

NAYS:

Mr. P. R. Adams, Axford, Backus, Beardsley, Ammon Brown, Carr, Crouse, Mr. Desnoyers, Dimond, Fralick, Gibson, Hart, Lee, Mason, Mr. Moore, Newberry, E. S. Robinson, Sturgis, Tiffany, Wait, White, 21

So the article was ordered to a third reading.

Mr. McClelland gave notice that he should move to-morrow to take up the Legislative Article.

On motion of Mr. Bagg,

The Convention then adjourned.

Lansing, Wednesday, July 31, 1850.

The Convention met at the usual hour and was called to order by the President.

Prayer by the Rev. Mr. Sanford.

Absent on leave, Messrs. Beeson, Alvarado Brown, Butterfield, Chapel, J. Clark, S. Clark, Daniels, Edmunds, Kinne, Morrison, Raynale, M. Robinson, Walker, Wells and Witherell; without leave Messrs. Asahel Brown, Hixon, McLeod, Roberts, Whipple and Willard.

Journal approved.

LEAVE OF ABSENCE.

Mr. McClelland asked and obtained leave of absence for Messrs. McLeod and Roberts for the day.

Mr. J. Bartow for Mr. Beeson until Monday next.

Mr. Crary for Messrs. Willard and Hixon, and

Mr. W. Adams for Asahel Brown indefinitely.

PETITIONS.

By Mr. Storey: of 19 citizens of the county of Jackson, on the subject of licences.

Laid upon the table.

Also, of 33 citizens of Leoni, Jackson county, praying the insertion of a clause in the constitution, prohibiting the employment of convicts in the State Prison in those branches of mechanical labor which interfere with mechanical trades in this State.

Referred to the committee on miscellaneous provisions.

MOTIONS.

Mr. McClelland called up the article entitled "Legislative Department,"

And the question being on ordering the same to a third reading,

Mr. Crary moved the previous question, and the same being seconded,

The question, "Shall the main question be now put?" was decided in the affirmative,

And the article was ordered to a third reading by the following vote:

YEAS.

Mr. P. R. Adams,	Mr. Eastman,	Mr. O'Brien,
W. Adams,	Eaton,	Orr,
Anderson,	Fralick,	J. D. Pierce,
Arzeno,	Gale,	N. Pierce,
Bagg,	Gardiner,	Prevost,
Barnard,	Gibson,	Robertson,
H. Bartow,	Graham,	E. S. Robinson,
Britain,	Green,	Rix Robinson,
Ammon Brown,	Harvey,	Skinner,
Burns,	Hascall,	Soule,
Chandler,	Hathaway,	Storey,
Choate,	Kingsley,	Sturgis,
Church,	Leach,	Sullivan,
Comstock,	Lee,	Sutherland,

Conner,	Lovell,	Tiffany,
Cook,	Marvin,	Warden,
Cornell,	Mason,	Webster,
Crary,	McClelland,	Whittemore,
Crouse,	Mosher,	Williams,
Danforth,	Mowry,	Woodman,
Desnoyers,	Newberry,	President,
Dimond,		64

NAYS:

Mr. Alvord,	Mr. Bush,	Mr. Town,
Axford,	Carr,	Van Valkenburg,
Backus,	Hanscom,	Wait,
J. Bartow,	Hart,	White, 12

On motion of Mr. McClelland,

The article was then read a third time by its title, and

The question being "Shall the article now pass?"

It was decided in the affirmative, and the same under the rule, referred to the committee on arrangement and phraseology.

On mo ion of Mr. J. Bartow,

The Convention resolved itself into a committee of the whole on the article entitled "Finance and Taxation,"

Mr. Mason in the chair.

PROCEEDINGS IN COMMITTEE.

The committee resumed the consideration of Mr. Britain's substitute, offered on the 27th inst., for section 1:

Mr. Britain offered the following as an amendment:

Insert in line 5, after "taxes," "except such portion of specific taxes from the upper peninsula, as the Legislature may return to the counties and townships thereof."

The motion was withdrawn.

The question being upon the adoption of the substitute,

Mr. Cook asked for a division of the question, and

Section 1 was stricken out.

Mr. Fralick offered the following as a substitute for the substitute of Mr. Britain:

"The Legislature shall provide for an, annual tax sufficient with other sources of income, to defray the estimated expenses of the State, including the interest on the debt of the State for each year;

and whenever the expenses of any year, including such interest, shall exceed the income and such tax, the Legislature shall provide for levying a tax the ensuing year, sufficient, with other sources of income, to pay the deficiency, as well as the estimated expenses of such ensuing year, including such interest."

The substitute was not adopted.

Mr. Church moved to add to Mr. Britain's substitute the following:

"The foregoing provisions shall not apply to specific taxes in the upper peninsula."

But the committee refused to so amend.

Mr. Hanscom moved to insert after "taxes," in the first line, "not otherwise appropriated by this constitution."

Which motion did not prevail.

Mr. Britain's substitute was then adopted.

Mr. Bush moved to fill the blank with "80."

Which motion was disagreed to.

Mr. Britain moved to fill the blank with "55."

This motion was also disagreed to.

Mr. Williams moved to fill with "65."

But the committee refused to so amend.

On motion of Mr. Crary,

The blank was filled with "52."

The committee then proceeded to the consideration of the new sections offered by Mr. Britain.

The question being upon the 1st, to stand as section 15,

The same was not adopted.

Mr. Britain withdrew his proposed section 16.

Mr. Britain offered the following as a substitute for the proposed section 17:

"The legislature shall provide by law for making all assessment rolls which have been returned by collectors; conclusive evidence of the legality of all assessments correctly made, contained therein, and for the correction of repeated and erroneous assessments."

The substitute was not adopted.

Mr. Britain then withdrew the remainder of his proposition made on the 27th.

On motion of Mr. Webster,

The committee rose, reported the article with amendments, asked the concurrence of the Convention, and to be discharged from the further consideration thereof.

—

The committee, through their chairman, reported the same back with amendments in which the concurrence of the Convention was asked.

On motion of Mr. Hanscom,

The article (Finance and Taxation,) as amended in committee was laid upon the table and ordered printed.

THIRD READING OF ARTICLES.

The article entitled "Elections" being before the convention,

On motion of Mr. Whittemore,

The same was passed over.

Upon the article entitled "County Officers and County Government,"

Mr. Rix Robinson moved the previous question, which was demanded, and the main question was ordered to be now put.

The article was then read a third time, and the question being "Shall the article pass?"

Mr. Mason asked the yeas and nays, and the same were taken as follows:

YEAS.

Mr. W. Adams,	Mr. Crouse,	Mr. O'Brien,
Alvord,	Danforth,	Orr,
Anderson,	Desnoyers,	J. D. Pierce,
Arzeno,	Eastman,	N. Pierce,
Axford,	Fralick,	Robertson,
Backus,	Gale,	E. S. Robinson,
H. Bartow,	Gibson,	Rix Robinson,
Britain,	Graham,	Skinner,
Ammon Brown,	Harvey,	Soule,
Burns,	Hascall,	Storey,
Carr,	Hathaway,	Sullivan,
Chandler,	Kingsley,	Tiffany,
Choate,	Marvin,	Town,
Church,	McClelland,	VanValkenburg,
Comstock,	Moore,	Wait,
Conner,	Mosher,	Webster,
Cook,	Mowry,	Williams,
Cornell,	Newberry,	Woodman, 54

NAYS.

Mr. Bagg,	Mr. Dimond,	Mr. Mason,
Barnard,	Gardiner,	Warden,
J. Bartow,	Green,	White,
Bush,	Hanscom,	Whittemore,
Crary,	Hart,	President, 15

So the article was passed and referred to the committee on arrangement and phraseology.

The article entitled "Of Cities and Villages" was read a third time, passed, and under the rule referred to the committee on arrangement and phraseology.

Mr. Mason moved to go into committee of the whole on the Judiciary article.

But the Convention refused so to do.

The article entitled "Exemptions and the rights of Married Women," was read a third time, when,

On motion of Mr. Mason,

It was laid upon the table

UNFINISHED BUSINESS.

The article relative to capital punishment, coming up as reported back yesterday by the committee of the whole,

Mr. Bagg moved to strike out the same, when,

On motion of Mr. McClelland,

It was laid upon the table.

Mr. Mason moved to go into committee of the whole on the article entitled "Judicial Department."

Which was not agreed to.

Mr. Cook called up the Article entitled "Corporations,"

And the question being upon concurring in the amendments made to the same in committee of the whole,

Mr. Hanscom moved to strike out the substitute for section 2, reported by the committee, and insert in lieu of it, as follows:

"No banking law or law for banking purposes, nor any act creating or renewing any association or corporation for banking purposes, shall ever be enacted by the legislature."

Mr. Britain moved to amend the foregoing by adding thereto, "nor shall any bank charter now in force extend beyond the first day of January, 1852."

Mr. Bagg moved to adjourn,

But the Convention refused to adjourn.

Mr. Robertson asked the yeas and nays on the amendment proposed by Mr. Britain, and the same being ordered,

The amendment prevailed as follows:

YEAS:

Mr. W. Adams, Alvord, Anderson, Axford, Barnard, Britain, Ammon Brown, Burns, Bush, Carr, Chandler, Church, Conner, Cook, Cornell,

Mr. Crary, Crouse, Danforth, Dimond, Eastman, Eaton, Gale, Gardiner, Graham, Green, Hanscom, Hart, Harvey, Hascall, Kingsley,

Mr. Lovell, Marvin, Mosher, Mowry, Newberry, O'Brien, J. D. Pierce, N. Pierce, Rix Robinson, Sturgis, Sullivan, VanValkenburg, Webster, White, Williams, 45

NAYS:

Mr. P. R. Adams, Arzeno, Backus, Bagg, H. Bartow, J. Bartow, Choate, Desnoyers, Fralick, Gibson,

Mr. Hathaway, Mason, McClelland, Moore, Orr, Robertson, E. S. Robinson, Skinner, Soule,

Mr. Storey, Sutherland, Tiffany, Town, Wait, Warden, Whittemore, Woodman, President, 28

On motion of Mr. Kingsley,

The proposition of Mr. Hanscom was further amended by adding:

"And no bank paper of any other State shall be allowed to circulate in this State as currency."

Mr. Skinner moved to adjourn.

Which was not agreed to.

Mr. McClelland moved to amend by adding after "Legislature," in the first clause of the substitute, as follows:

"Unless it shall be submitted to the people, and then been first approved by a majority of the electors of the State voting thereon in such manner as may be prescribed by the Legislature."

Mr. Van Valkenburgh moved a call of the Convention.

But the call was not sustained.

The amendment proposed by Mr. McClelland was then agreed to, as follows:

YEAS.

Mr. P. R. Adams,	Mr. Crouse,	Mr. Mowry,
W. Adams,	Danforth,	Newberry,
Alvord,	Desnoyers,	O'Brien,
Arzeno,	Eastman,	Orr,
Bagg,	Eaton,	Robertson,
H. Bartow,	Fralick,	E. S. Robinson,
J. Bartow,	Gale,	Rix Robinson,
Britain,	Gibson,	Skinner,
Ammon Brown,	Graham,	Storey,
Burns,	Harvey,	Sullivan,
Chandler,	Hathaway,	Sutherland
Choate,	Kingsley,	Town,
Church,	Marvin,	White,
Conner,	McClelland,	Williams,
Cook,	Moore,	Woodman,
Cornell,	Mosher,	President,
Crary,		49

NAYS.

Mr. Anderson,	Mr. Gardiner,	Mr. Soule,
Axford,	Green,	Sturges,
Backus,	Hanscom,	Tiffany,
Barnard,	Hart,	Van Valkenburg,
Bush,	Hascall,	Wait,
Carr,	Lovell,	Warden,
Comstock,	Mason,	Webster,
Dimond,	N. Pierce,	Whittemore, 24

Mr. Crary moved further to amend Mr. Hanscom's proposition, by inserting after the word "renewing," as follows:

"Or extended, with the privilege of making, issuing or putting in circulation any bill, check, ticket, certificate, promissory note or other paper or the paper of any bank to circulate as money."

And the amendment was agreed to.

On motion of Mr. Eaton,

The Convention adjourned.

Afternoon Session.

Two o'clock.

The President called the Convention to order.

A quorum of members being in attendance,

On motion of Mr. Mason,

Resolved, That the thanks of this Convention be tendered to the Hon. H. T. Backus for his able and eloquent eulogy upon the life and character of Zachary Taylor, late President of the United States, and that a committee of three be appointed to solicit a copy thereof for publication.

The Convention resumed the consideration of the Article entitled "Corporations."

On motion of Mr. McClelland,

The substitute proposed by the committee for section two, was amended by inserting after "purposes," in the 1st line, the words "or amendment thereof."

The question recurring on the adoption of Mr. Hanscom's proposition as amended, as a substitute for the one proposed by the committeee, Mr. Gale asked the yeas and nays, and the same being ordered, the substitute was rejected, as follows:

YEAS:

Mr. Alvord,
Anderson,
Bagg,
Beardsley,
Britain,

Mr. Comstock,
Eaton,
Hanscom,
Hathaway,

Mr. N. Pierce,
Wait,
Webs er,
White,

13

NAYS:

Mr. P. R. Adams,
W. Adams,
Arzeno,
Axford,
Backus,
Barnard,
H. Bartow,
J. Bartow,
Burns,
Carr,
Chandler,
Choate,
Church,
Conner,

Mr. Dimond,
Eastman,
Fralick,
Gale,
Gardiner,
Gibson,
Graham,
Green,
Hart,
Harvey,
Leach,
Lee,
Lovell,
Mason,

Mr. Orr,
J. D. Pierce,
Redfield,
Robertson,
E. S. Robinson,
Rix Robinson,
Skinner,
Soule,
Storey,
Sturgis,
Sullivan,
Sutherland,
Tiffany,
Town,

Cook,	McClelland,	Van Valkenburg,
Cornell,	Moore,	Warden,
Crary,	Mosher,	Whittemore,
Crouse,	Mowry,	Williams,
Danforth,	Newberry,	Woodman,
Desnoyers,	O'Brien,	President, 60

Mr. Britain moved to amend the reported substitute by adding thereto, the following:

"Nor shall any bank have any legal existence in this State after the 1st day of January, 1855, except under a general banking law," upon which the yeas anp nays were ordered.

Mr. Britain withdrew the proposition.

Mr. Crary moved the previous question on the section;

But the same was not ordered.

On motion of Mr. Britain,

The original section of the article was amended by inserting in line 1, after "purposes," the words, "or amendment thereof."

Mr. Bagg proposed the following substitute for the one proposed by the committee to section 2.

"The legislature shall have no power to pass any law creating banking privileges."

To which Mr. Britain proposed to add:

"Nor shall any bank charter now in existence, extend beyond the first day of January, 1853."

Mr. Bagg then withdrew his proposition, and offered the following as a substitute for the same:

"No banking law or law for banking purposes, nor any act creating, continuing, renewing or extending any association or corporation for banking purposes, shall ever be enacted by the Legislature."

The President deciding the proposition out of order,

Mr. Hanscom appealed from the decision of the chair.

Upon the appeal Mr. McClelland moved the previous question.

And the same being ordered,

The main question was ordered to be now put,

And the question being: "Shall the decision of the chair stand as the decision of the Convention?"

It was decided in the affirmative.

Mr. McClelland moved the previous question on the section, and the same was sustained.

And the main question ordered to be now put,

And the substitute reported by the committee of the whole for sec. 2 of the article, was concurred in by the following vote:

YEAS.

Mr. P. R. Adams,	Mr. Danforth,	Mr. Mowry,
W. Adams,	Desnoyers,	Newberry,
Alvord,	Eaton,	Orr,
Anderson,	Fralick,	J. D. Pierce,
Arzeno,	Gale,	Robertson,
Bagg,	Gibson,	E. S. Robinson,
H. Bartow,	Graham,	Rix Robinson,
Beardsley,	Green,	Skinner,
Britain,	Hart,	Soule,
Ammon Brown,	Hathaway,	Sturgis,
Burns,	Kingsley,	Sullivan,
Chandler,	Leach,	Town,
Choate,	Marvin,	Van Valkenburg,
Church,	Mason,	Whittemore,
Conner,	McClelland,	Woodman,
Cornell,	Moore,	President,
Crouse,	Mosher,	50

NAYS.

Mr. Backus,	Mr. Eastman,	Mr. Redfield,
Barnard,	Gardiner,	Storey,
J. Bartow,	Hanscom,	Sutherland,
Bush,	Harvey,	Tiffany,
Carr,	Hascall,	Warden,
Comstock,	Lee,	Webster,
Cook,	Lovell,	White,
Crary,	N. Pierce,	Williams,
Dimond,	Prevost,	26

The amendments made in committee to section 3 were concurred in.

The first amendment to section 4 being under consideration,

On motion of Mr. Cook,

The same was amended by striking out "paper credit" and inserting the word "bills."

The remainder of the amendments made in committee of the whole to the article were severally concurred in with the exception of those to section 5, in which the Convention refused to concur.

The article being open to amendment,

Mr. Van Valkenburgh moved to strike from the sixth section, up to and inclusive of the word "indirectly," in the 2nd line, and insert "the legislature shall pass no law directly or indirectly sanctioning."

Which was disagreed to.

Mr. Comstock moved to amend section 3, by inserting in line 2 after the word "liable," the words, "to the amount of their respective share or shares of stock in any such corporation or association."

But the motion was not agreed to.

On motion of Mr. Cook,

Section 6 was amended by inserting in the first line, after "law," the words "authorizing or."

Mr. J. D. Pierce moved to amend section 4, by striking therefrom, in the third line, "in State stocks;" and in the third and fourth lines, the words "bearing interest, or stock of the United States."

Pending which,

Mr. Webster moved that the article be committed to the committee on corporations, with instructions to amend the same as follows, viz: Strike out section 2, and insert as follows:

"No banking law or law for banking purposes, nor any act creating, renewing or continuing any association or corporation for banking purposes, shall ever be enacted by the Legislature."

Amend by adding a new section, to stand as section 3, as follows:

"No law now in force in this State creating or authorizing any bank or banking institution, or incorporating any company or association for banking purposes in this State, shall extend to or have any force or effect after the first day of January, 1853, and no such institution now existing in this state shall issue any note or bill to be circulated as money after the first day of January, 1851.

Mr. Cook moved the previous question on the Article, and the call being seconded by a majority of the members present, the main question was ordered to be now put.

The amendment proposed by Mr. J. D. Pierce was then rejected by the following vote:

YEAS:

Mr. P. R. Adams,	Mr. Church,	Mr. J. D. Pierce,
Backus,	Crary,	Soule,
Bagg,	Eaton,	Webster,
Barnard,	Gardiner,	White,

H. Bartow,	Hanscom,	Williams,
Beardsley,	Hascall,	Woodman,
Bush,	Lovell,	20

NAYS:

Mr. W. Adams,	Mr. Desnoyers,	Mr. Orr,
Alvord,	Dimond,	N. Pierce,
Arzeno,	Fralick,	Redfield,
Axford,	Gale,	E. S. Robinson,
J. Bartow,	Gibson,	Rix Robinson,
Britain,	Green,	Skinner,
Ammon Brown,	Hart,	Storey,
Burns,	Harvey,	Sturgis,
Chandler,	Hathaway,	Sullivan,
Choate,	Kingsley,	Tiffany,
Comstock,	Leach,	Town,
Conner,	Marvin,	Van Valkenburg,
Cook,	Mason,	Warden,
Cornell,	McClelland,	Whittemore,
Crouse,	Mosher,	President,
Danforth,	Mowry,	47

And the main question being on ordering the Article to a third reading, it was so ordered by yeas and nays, as follows:

YEAS.

Mr. P. R. Adams,	Mr. Crouse,	Mr. Mowry,
W. Adams,	Danforth,	Orr,
Arzeno,	Desnoyers,	E. S. Robinson,
Axford,	Dimond,	Rix Robinson,
H. Bartow,	Fralick,	Skinner,
Beardsley,	Gale,	Storey,
Britain,	Gibson,	Sturgis,
Ammon Brown,	Graham,	Sullivan,
Burns,	Hathaway,	Tiffany,
Chandler,	Kingsley,	Town,
Choate,	Leach,	Van Valkenburg,
Church,	McClelland,	Whittemore,
Conner,	Moore,	Woodman,
Cook,	Mosher,	President,
Cornell,		43

NAYS.

Mr. Alvord,	Mr. Green,	Mr. N. Pierce,
Backus,	Hanscom,	Redfield,
Bagg,	Hart,	Robertson,
Barnard,	Harvey,	Soule,
J. Bartow,	Hascall,	Warden,
Bush,	Lovell,	Webster,
Crary,	Marvin,	White,
Eaton,	Mason,	Williams,
Gardiner,	J. D. Pierce,	26

Mr. Bagg moved to take up the Article entitled "Elections."

Pending which,

On motion of Mr. McClelland,

The Convention adjourned.

Lansing, Thursday, August 1, 1850.

The Convention met at 8 o'clock and was called to order by the President.

Prayer by the Rev. Mr. Tooker.

The roll being called, there were absent on leave, Messrs. Beeson, Alvarado Brown, Chapel, J. Clark, S. Clark, Edmunds, Hixon. Kinne, McLeod, Raynale, Roberts, M. Robinson, Walker, Wells, Willard and Witherell; without leave, Messrs. Lee, Redfield and Wait.

LEAVE OF ABSENCE.

Mr. Hanscom obtained leave for Mr. Van Valkenburg, and

Mr. Carr for Mr. Wait until Monday next.

Mr. Gardiner for Mr. O'Brien,

Mr. Robertson for Mr. Hathaway, and

Mr. Crouse for Mr. Lee, indefinitely.

PETITIONS.

By Mr. Moore: of Jacob French and 45 others of St. Joseph county, praying an article may be incorporated in the constitution prohibiting the legislature from passing any laws authorizing the sale of ardent spirits as a beverage.

Referred to the select committee upon the subject.

Also of John Hotchin and 46 others of St. Joseph county, that the Convention will insert an article in the Constitution prohibiting the labor of convicts in the State Prison from coming into competition with other mechanical labor.

Referred to the committee on miscellaneous provisions.

REPORTS.

Mr. Gardiner, from the select committee on the traffic in ardent spirits, submitted a resolution.

Laid upon the table and ordered printed.

MOTIONS AND RESOLUTIONS.

On motion of Mr. Gardiner,

Resolved, That the Secretary be authorized to draw a certificate upon the State Treasurer in favor of Mr. Martin Mahon, for three dollars per day for his services as reporter of this Convention, commencing on the 16th day of July last.

On motion of Mr. Leach,

Resolved, That the committee on supplies be instructed to report to the Convention, as soon as practicable, the kind and quantity of stationery purchased for the use of the Convention, and the price paid for the same.

On motion of Mr. J. Bartow,

The Convention then resolved itself into committee of the whole and resumed the consideration of the Article entitled "Judicial Department,"

Mr. Cook in the chair.

PROCEEDINGS IN COMMITTEE.

The consideration of the substitute offered by Mr. McClelland for section 2 being resumed,

Mr. Warden moved to amend the same as follows:

Strike out all between the words "supreme court," in 3d line, and "shall," in the 4th line, and insert "four of whom shall constitute the supreme court, and a concurrence of three."

Mr. Church moved to amend by striking out all after the word "courts," in the second line, and inserting as follows: "shall constitute a supreme court, and four of said judges shall be a quorum able to transact business, and the concurrence of three of said quorum shall be necessary to a final decision. The Legislature shall have power, whenever they deem it expedient, to organize a separate supreme court, with the jurisdiction and powers prescribed in this constitution, to consist of one chief justice and three associate judges, to be elected by the qualified electors of this state. Said separate supreme court, when established, shall not be changed or discontinued by the Legislature for eight years after its organization. The judges thereof shall be so classified that but one of them shall go out of office at the same time, and their term of office shall be eight years."

The question being upon Mr. Warden's amendment, it was withdrawn.

The proposition of Mr. Church was adopted.

The question now recurring upon the adoption of the substitute, as amended, for section 2,

A division of the question was called, when,

On motion of Mr. Woodman,

The committee rose, reported progress and asked leave to sit again.

—

The committee, through their chairman, reported progress and asked leave to sit again.

Leave was granted.

When, on motion of Mr. Cook,

The Convention adjourned.

—

Afternoon Session.

Two o'clock.

The Convention was called to order by the President.

A quorum being present,

On motion of Mr. Storey,

The Convention resolved itself into a committee of the whole on the Judiciary article,

Mr. Cook in the chair.

—

PROCEEDINGS IN COMMITTEE.

The committee resumed the consideration of the substitute offered by Mr. McClelland, and amended by Mr. Church, and after some time spent in debate thereon,

On motion of Mr. Bush,

The committee rose, reported progress and asked leave to sit again.

—

The committee through their chairman reported the same back to the Convention and asked leave to sit again.

Leave was granted.

On motion of Mr. J. Bartow,

Rsolved, That the Secretary of this Convention be and he is hereby required to procure a sufficient quantity of parchment, upon which to enroll the new Constitution.

On motion of Mr. J. D. Pierce,

The Convention adjourned.

Lansing, Friday, August 2, 1850.

The Convention met at the usual hour and was called to order by the President.

Prayer by the Rev. Mr. Merrill.

The roll being called, there were absent on leave Messrs. Beeson, Alvarado Brown, Chapel, S. Clark, Edmunds, Hixon, Kinne, Lee, Raynale, M. Robinson, Wait, Walker, Wells, Willard and Witherell; without leave, Messrs. Crary, Danforth, Redfield and Whittemore.

ABSENCE.

Mr. Hart asked and obtained leave for Messrs. Redfield and Whittemore for the day.

The President announced Messrs. Mason, Williams and Soule a committee in conformity with the resolution adopted on Wednesday last, relative to the eulogy delivered by the Hon. H. T. Backus.

MOTIONS AND RESOLUTIONS.

Mr. Eastman moved to reconsider the vote by which the article entitled "county officers and county government" was passed.

The motion was laid upon the table.

Mr. Woodman called up his resolution relative to the absence of Mr. P. R. Adams, offered the 23d ultimo, when,

On motion of Mr. Moore,

The resolution was indefinitely postponed.

On motion of Mr. Hanscom,

The Convention proceeded to consider, in committee of the whole, the article entitled "Judicial Department,"

Mr. Cook in the chair.

PROCEEDINGS IN COMMITTEE OF THE WHOLE.

The committee resumed the consideration of the substitute for section 2,

And a division of the question being call for, section 2 was stricken out.

Mr. Hanscom offered the following as a substitute for the substitute:

"The supreme court shall consist of four judges, three of whom shall be necessary to form a quorum, and the concurrence of three shall be necessary to every final decision. The final decision of the judges shall be in writing, signed by them, and a judge dissenting from a decision shall give his reascns for such dissent in writing, under his signature. And the legislature may, if they shall deem it expedient, require each of the judges of the supreme court to hold one of the terms of the circuit court in each year in any one of the counties of the State in which more than two terms are annually held."

On motion of Mr. Hanscom,

The committee rose, reported the article back with an amendment and asked the concurrence of the Convention therein.

—

The committee through their chairman reported the same back to the Convention with an amendment in which its concurrence was asked.

The question being upon concurring in the amendment—striking out section 2 of the article—the yeas and nays were demanded, when,

On motion of Mr. McClelland,

A call of the Convention was ordered, and Messrs. Crary, Danforth, Graham and Prevost were found absent without leave.

Mr. Cook asked leave for Mr. Danforth, and

Mr. Morrison for Mr. Crary for the day, and

Leave was granted.

On motion of Mr. Cook,

The Sergeant-at-Arms was dispatched to secure the attendance of Messrs. Graham and Prevost.

Those delegates soon appearing,

On motion of Mr. McClelland,

All further proceedings under the call were dispensed with.

The amendment of the committee, striking out section 2 of the article, was then concurred in by the following vote:

YEAS.

Mr. P. R. Adams,	Mr. Choate,	Mr. McClelland,
W. Adams,	Conner,	Moore,
Anderson,	Cook,	Mosher,
Arzeno,	Cornell,	J. D. Pierce,
Barnard,	Desnoyers,	N. Pierce,
H. Bartow,	Eastman,	Prevost,
J. Bartow,	Eaton,	E. S. Robinson,
Beardsley,	Gale,	Rix Robinson,
Britain,	Gardiner,	Skinner,
Ammon Brown,	Graham,	Storey,
Asahel Brown,	Hascall,	Town,
Burns,	Kingsley,	Warden,
Bush,	Leach,	White,
Butterfield,	Marvin,	Whipple, 42

NAYS.

Mr. Alvord,	Mr. Gibson,	Mr. Roberts,
Axford,	Green,	Robertson,
Backus,	Hanscom,	Soule,
Bagg,	Hart,	Sturgis,
Carr,	Harvey,	Sullivan,
Chandler,	Lee,	Sutherland,
Church,	Lovell,	Tiffany,
J. Clark,	Mason,	Webster,
Comstock,	McLeod,	Whittemore,
Crouse,	Morrison,	Williams,
Daniels,	Mowry,	Woodman,
Dimond,	Newberry,	President,
Fralick,	Orr,	38

On motion of Mr. J. Bartow,

The article (Judiciary Department) was recommitted to the committee of the whole, and

The Convention resumed its consideration in committe, Mr. Cook in the chair.

PROCEEDINGS IN COMMITTEE.

The committee resumed the consideration of "Article —, Judicia Department."

Mr. McClelland offered the following to stand as section 2:

"For the term of six years and thereafter until the Legislature shall otherwise provide, the Judges of the several circuit courts, shall constitute a supreme court; and four of said Judges shall be a quorum able to transact business; and the concurrence of three of said quorum shall be necessary to a final decision. The Legislature shall have power, whenever they deem it expedient, to organize a separate supreme court with the jurisdiction and powers prescribed in this Constitution; to consist of one chief justice, and three associate judges, to be elected by the qualified electors of this State; said separate supreme court when established, shall not be changed or discontinued by the Legislature for eight years after its organization; the judges thereof shall be so classified that but one of them shall go out of office at the same time, and their term of office shall be eight years."

Mr. Hanscom offered the following as a substitute for the above:

"The supreme court shall consist of four judges, three of whom shall be necessary to form a quorum, and the concurrence of three shall be necessary to every final decision. The final decision of the judges shall be in writing, signed by them; and a judge dissenting from a decision, shall give his reasons for such dissent in writing, under his signature; and the Legislature may, if they shall deem it expedient, require each of the judges of the supreme court to hold one of the terms of the circuit court in each year, in any of the counties of the State in which more than two terms are annually held."

Mr. Britain moved to amend the substitute of Mr. McClelland, as follows: strike out "separate," wherever it occurs: and also strike out all after "decision," in the fifth line, to and including "State," in the 11th line, and insert, "The Legislature shall have power to provide by law for the organization of a supreme court, with the jurisdiction and powers prescribed in this Constitution; to consist of one chief justice, to be elected by the qualified electors of the State; and three associate justices, who shall be circuit judges, and taken from the respective circuits for the time being, in such manner as the Legislature may deem expedient."

But the committee refused to so amend.

Mr. Britain also offered the following amendment, which was not adopted:

Strike out "separate," wherever it occurs.

Also, strike out, after "decision," in line 5, to and including "state," in line 11, and insert, "the legislature may provide by law for the organization of a supreme court, with the jurisdiction and powers prescribed in this constitution, to consist of four judges, two of whom shall be elected by the qualified electors of the state, and two of whom shall be circuit judges, and taken from the respective judicial circuits for the time being, in such manner as they may deem expedient."

Mr. Morrison moved to strike out of Mr. McClelland's substitute "for the term of six years and thereafter."

But the committee refused to strike out.

The question then recurring upon Mr. Hanscom's substitute, the same was not adopted.

Mr. Robertson moved to strike out of Mr. McClelland's substitute the words "for the term of six years and thereafter until the legislature shall otherwise provide."

Which did not prevail.

Mr. Bagg moved to insert after "decision," the words "and they shall cast lots as to whom shall set in bank in the supreme court for each and every year."

But the committee refused to so amend.

The question being upon the adoption of Mr. McClelland's substitute,

Mr. Britain called for a division of the question, and the 1st part of the substitute was adopted.

Mr. Kingsley moved to amend the 2d branch of the substitute by inserting after "expedient," the words, "for the term of six years."

Which motion prevailed.

The substitute was then adopted.

On motion of Mr. McClelland,

The committee rose, and reported the article back to the Convention.

The committee through their chairman, reported the same back to the Convention with an amendment, in which its concurrence was asked.

On motion of Mr. McClelland,

The article with amendment was referred to the committee on the judicial department.

The article entitled "Elections," coming up on its passage,

On motion of Mr. Hanscom,

The same was laid upon the table.

THIRD READING OF ARTICLES.

The article entitled "Corporations," was read a third time; when Mr. McLeod moved to recommit it to the committee on banking and other corporations except municipal, with instructions to strike therefrom the first clause of section 11 as follows: "From and after the year 1880, the Legislature shall have the power to alter or repeal the charters of all corporations whose charters shall not have expired previous to that time."

Mr. White moved to amend the instructions by striking out the entire article, and inserting in lieu thereof as follows:

ARTICLE —.

Sec. 1. Corporations may be formed under general laws; but shall not be created by special act, except for municipal purposes. All general laws, and special acts passed pursuant to this section, may be altered from time to time, or repealed.

Sec. 2. The term "corporations," as used in this article, shall be construed to include all associations and joint stock companies having any of the powers or privileges of corporations, not possessed by individuals or partnerships. And all corporations shall have the right to sue, and shall be subject to be sued, in all courts, in like cases as natural persons.

Sec. 3. The Legislature shall have no power to pass any act granting any special charter for banking purposes; but corporations or associations may be formed for such purposes, under general laws, by a vote of two-thirds of all the members elected to both branches thereof.

Sec. 4. The Legislature shall not pass any law sanctioning in any manner, directly or indirectly, the suspension of specie payments by any person, association or corporation, issuing bank notes of any description.

Sec. 5. The Legislature shall provide by law for the registry of all bills or notes issued or put in circulation as money, and shall require ample security for the redemption of the same in specie; such security to be in stocks, (bonds or evidence of debt issued by the United States or of individual States, or both,) which shall be deposited with the State Treasurer, and be at least, when offered, equal in value to the amount of bills or notes registered and issued for circulation.

Sec. 6. The stockholders in every corporation and joint stock association for banking purposes, issuing bank notes or any kind of paper credits to circulate as money, shall be individually responsible to the amount of their respective share or shares of stock in any such corporation or association, for all its issues, debts and liabilities.

Sec. 7. All corporations and joint stock associations created by the Legislature, under and by virtue of this article, shall pay to the State Treasurer for the use of the State, at least one per centum per annum on the capital stock paid in, as a tax; and no other tax shall be assessed or collected against them.

Sec. 8. In case of the insolvency of any bank or banking association, the bill holders thereof shall be entitled to preference in payment, over all other creditors of said bank or association."

But the motion to so amend, was lost as follows:

YEAS.

Mr. Burns,	Mr. Daniels,	Mr. Harvey,
Carr,	Fralick,	Lovell,
Chandler,	Gale,	White,
Comstock,	Green,	Williams, 12

NAYS.

Mr. W. Adams,	Mr. Crouse,	Mr. Mowry,
Alvord,	Dimond,	Newberry,
Anderson,	Eastman,	Orr,
Arzeno,	Gardiner,	J. D. Pierce,
Bagg,	Gibson,	N. Pierce,
Barnard,	Hanscom,	Robertson,
H. Bartow,	Hascall,	Rix Robinson,
Beardsley,	Kingsley,	Skinner,
Britain,	Leach,	Soule,
Bush,	Mason,	Storey,
Choate,	McClelland,	Sturgis,
Church,	McLeod,	Town,
Conner,	Moore,	Warden,

Cook,	Morrison,	Webster,	
Cornell,	Mosher,	President,	45

Mr. Church moved to amend by adding further instructions, as follows:

"And to amend section 3 by striking out in lines 2 and 3, the words "all its debts," and insert "said bank notes or paper credits so circulated as money;" and to strike out in line 4, the words "for one year thereafter."

Which he subsequently withdrew.

On motion of Mr. Comstock,

The proposition of Mr. McLeod was amended by instructing the committee to report the following additional section.

"The term "corporations," as used in this article, shall be construed to include all associations and joint stock companies having any of the powers or privileges of corporations, not possessed by individuals or partnerships. And all corporations shall have the right to sue, and shall be subject to be sued, in all courts, in like cases as natural persons.

Mr. White moved further to amend by instructing the committee to add the following as an additional section:

"All the officers and stockholders of every corporation or association for banking purposes, issuing bank notes or bills, or any kind of paper credits to circulate as money, shall at all times be jointly and severally liable for all the debts and liabilities for such corporation or association."

Mr. Hanscom proposed to add "and for six years thereafter."

Which Mr. White agreed to.

And the amendment as modified was lost.

Mr. Morrison moved to amend by instructing the committee to report the following in lieu of section 2 of the article:

"Corporations for banking purposes, shall be formed, extended or renewed by special laws, but no such act of incorporation, extension or renewal, shall take effect until the same shall have been submitted to the people at the next general election, (for representatives) succeeding the passage of the same, and approved by a majority of all the votes cast at such election for and against such law. There shall not be more than one act of incorporation, extension, or renewal of any association with banking powers passed during any one session of the Legislature."

Which was not agreed to.

Mr. Moore moved to adjourn.

But the Convention refused to adjourn.

On motion of Mr. Cook,

The article was laid upon the table.

On motion of Mr. Woodman,

The article reported by the committee on the Punishment of Crimes was made the special order of the day for to-morrow.

On motion of Mr. Cornell,

The Convention adjourned.

Afternoon Session.

Two o'clock.

The Convention was called to order by the President.

A quorum of members being present,

On motion of Mr. Cook,

The article entitled "Corporations," was taken from the table.

Mr. Mason moved a call of the Convention.

And the same being ordered, after calling the roll the absentees appearing,

All further proceedings under the call were dispensed with.

At the suggestion of Mr. McClelland,

By the unanimous consent of the Convention, section 11 was amended by inserting after the word "created," in the 3d line, "except for the construction of rail roads and canals."

The proposition of Mr. McLeod, to recommit with instructions, coming up,

A division was had, and

The motion to recommit was first taken, which prevailed by yeas and nays, as follows:

YEAS.

Mr. P. R. Adams.	Mr. Eastman,	Mr. Prevost,
Arzeno,	Fralick,	Roberts,
H. Bartow,	Gale,	Robertson,
J. Bartow,	Green,	Rix Robinson,

Beardsley,	Hart,	Skinner,
Butterfield,	Harvey,	Storey,
Carr,	Kingsley,	Sturgis,
Chandler,	Lovell,	Sullivan,
Choate,	Mason,	Webster,
Church,	McClelland,	White,
Comstock,	McLeod,	Whipple,
Cornell,	Morrison,	Williams,
Daniels,	Newberry,	Woodman,
Desnoyers,	Orr,	President. 42

NAYS.

Mr. W. Adams,	Mr. Burns,	Mr. Hanscom,
Alvord,	Conner,	Mowry,
Anderson,	Cook,	J. D. Pierce,
Axford,	Crouse,	N. Pierce,
Bagg,	Dimond,	Soule,
Barnard,	Eaton,	Town,
Ammon Brown,	Gardiner,	Warden,
Asahel Brown,	Gibson,	23

The question recurring on the instructions,

Mr. Church moved to amend the same by further instructing the committee to amend section 3 by striking out in the 2d and 3d lines the words "all its debts," and inserting in lieu thereof "said bank notes and paper credits so circulated as money." Also,

To strike out in the last line of the same section the words "and for one year thereafter."

Mr. Hanscom moved to amend by further instructing the committee to strike out section 2, and insert as follows:

"No banking law or law for banking purposes, nor any act creating, renewing or continuing any association or corporation for banking purposes, shall ever be enacted by the Legislature."

Amend by adding a new section, to stand as section 3, as follows:

"No law now in force in this State, creating or authorizing any bank or banking institution, or incorporating any company or association for banking purposes in this State, shall extend to or have any force or effect after the first day of January, 1853, and no such institution now existing in this State, shall issue any note or bill to be circulated as money after the first day of January, 1851."

A division of the question was had, and on the instructions striking out section 2, and substituting as above, the yeas and nays were ordered, with the following result:

YEAS:

Mr. Anderson,	Mr. Eaton,	Mr. Robertson,
Bagg,	Gale,	Rix Robinson,
Barnard,	Gardiner,	Soule,
Beardsley,	Hanscom,	Town,
Britain,	Hart,	Warden,
Asahel Brown,	Hascall,	Webster,
Carr,	Morrison,	White,
Church,	N. Pierce,	Williams,
Dimond,	Roberts,	Woodman, 27

NAYS:

Mr. P. R. Adams,	Mr. Cook,	Mr. McClelland,
W. Adams,	Cornell,	McLeod,
Arzeno,	Crouse,	Moore,
Axford,	Eastman,	Mosher,
H. Bartow,	Fralick,	Mowry,
J. Bartow,	Gibson,	Newberry,
Ammon Brown,	Green,	Orr,
Burns,	Harvey,	Prevost,
Butterfield,	Kingsley,	Skinner,
Chandler,	Leach,	Storey,
Choate,	Lee,	Sullivan,
Comstock,	Lovell,	Whipple,
Conner,	Mason,	President, 39

So the first portion of the amendment was disagreed to; and the remainder of the proposition was also rejected by yeas and nays, as follows:

YEAS.

Mr. Alvord,	Mr. Cook,	Mr. Roberts,
Anderson,	Daniels,	Robertson,
Bagg,	Dimond,	Rix Robinson,
Beardsley,	Eaton,	Soule,
Britain,	Gardiner,	Town,
Asahel Brown,	Hanscom,	Webster,
Burns,	Hart,	White,
Carr,	Hascall,	Williams,
Church,	N. Pierce,	Woodman, 27

NAYS.

Mr. P. R. Adams,	Mr. Crouse,	Mr. Moore,
W. Adams,	Eastman,	Morrison,
Arzeno,	Fralick,	Mosher,
Axford,	Gale,	Mowry,
Barnard,	Gibson,	Newberry,
H. Bartow,	Green,	Orr,
J. Bartow,	Harvey,	J. D. Pierce,
Ammon Brown,	Kingsley,	Prevost,

Butterfield,	Leach,	Skinner,	
Chandler,	Lee,	Storey,	
Choate,	Lovell,	Sullivan,	
Comstock,	Mason,	Warden,	
Conner,	McClelland,	Whipple,	
Cornell,	McLeod,	President,	42

Upon Mr. McLeod's proposition as amended, a division of the question was had, and the instructions in regard to section 11 were agreed to by yeas and nays, as follows:

YEAS.

Mr. P. R. Adams,	Mr. Fralick,	Mr. Newberry,	
Alvord,	Gale,	Orr,	
H. Bartow,	Green,	Prevost,	
J. Bartow,	Harvey,	Roberts,	
Beardsley,	Kingsley,	Robertson,	
Butterfield,	Leach,	Rix Robinson,	
Carr,	Lee,	Skinner,	
Chandler,	Lovell,	Storey,	
Choate,	Mason,	Sullivan,	
Church,	McClelland,	White,	
Comstock,	McLeod,	Whipple,	
Cornell,	Moore,	Williams,	
Daniels,	Mosher,	Woodman,	
Eastman,	Mowry,	President,	42

NAYS.

Mr. W. Adams,	Mr. Burns,	Mr. Hart,	
Anderson,	Conner,	Hascall,	
Arzeno,	Cook,	Morrison,	
Axford,	Crouse,	J. D. Pierce,	
Bagg,	Dimond,	N. Pierce,	
Barnard,	Eaton,	Soule,	
Britain,	Gardiner,	Town,	
Ammon Brown,	Gibson,	Warden,	
Asahel Brown,	Hanscom,	Webster,	27

And the second clause of the proposition instructing the committee to report an additional section was also agreed to.

So the article was recommitted to the committee with which it originated with instructions.

Mr. Cook, from the committee on banking and other corporations except municipal, to whom was referred the article entitled "Corporations," with certain instructions, reported the same back to the Convention amended agreeably thereto.

Mr. Cook moved the previous question on the article,

And the same being sustained,

The main question was ordered to be now put.

And on the question, "Shall the article now pass ?"

The yeas and nays were ordered, with the following result:

YEAS.

Mr. P. R. Adams,	Mr. Cornell,	Mr. Orr,
W. Adams,	Crouse,	J. D Pierce,
Arzeno,	Daniels,	Rix Robinson,
Axford,	Eastman,	Skinner,
H. Bartow,	Gibson,	Soule,
Beardsley,	Harvey,	Storey,
Ammon Brown,	Kingsley,	Sullivan,
Butterfield,	Lee,	Town,
Chandler,	McClelland,	Warden,
Choate,	Mosher,	Willard,
Church,	Mowry,	Woodman,
Conner,	Newberry,	President,
Cook,		38

NAYS.

Mr. Alvord,	Mr. Fralick,	Mr. Morrison,
Bagg,	Gale,	N. Pierce,
Barnard,	Gardiner,	Prevost,
J. Bartow,	Green,	Roberts,
Britain,	Hanscom,	Robertson,
Asahel Brown,	Hart,	Webster,
Burns,	Hascall,	White,
Carr,	Lovell,	Whipple,
Comstock,	Mason,	Williams,
Eaton,	McLeod,	29

So the article (corporations) was passed, and under the rule, referred to the committee on arrangement and phraseology.

Mr. McClelland moved to adjourn.

But the Conventiou refused to adjourn.

On motion of Mr. Moore,

The article, "Exemptions and the rights of Married Women," was taken from the table,

And the question being on the passage of the same,

Mr. Axford moved that the article be committed to the committee on Exemptions and the Rights of Married Women with instructions to amend the same as follows:

Strike out sections 1 and 2, and substitute the following to stand as sections 1 and 2 of said article;

Substitute for section 1:

"Personal property to the amount of not less than two hundred and fifty dollars nor over five hundred dollars of every resident of this state shall be exempt from sale on execution or any other final process of any court of law or equity, except for the purchase money of the same, and at the first session of the legislature after the adoption of this constitution they shall provide and designate by law the kinds of property and the amount so to be exempted."

Substitute for section 2:

"A homestead of every family of this State, of forty acres and no more, not exceeding in value five hundred dollars, and which shall not be included in any city, village, or recorded town plat, or in lieu thereof any lot, in any village, city, or recorded town plat, not exceeding in value five hundred dollars, shall not be subject to any forced sale for any debt contracted after the adoption of this constitution, except for the purchase money of the same, nor shall the owner of such homested, if a married man, alienate the same by any deed of conveyance, without the consent of his wife obtained in due form of law; but no such exemption shall be valid except the owner or owners thereof shall have filed a description of the same in the office of the register of deeds in the county in which said real estate is situated."

Mr. J. D. Pierce offered the following substitute for the instructions proposed by Mr. Axford:

Amend section 1, line 1, by inserting after "state," the words, "to consist of such articles as shall be designated by law."

Also, amend section 2, line 3, after the word "plat," by inserting as follows: "or such parts of lots as shall be equal thereto, not exceeding in value $1500."

Amend section 3 by striking out of line 3 the following: "for their benefit and support during minority."

Mr. Axford moved to strike out "1500," and insert "500."

But a division being had, the Convention refused to strike out.

The substitute was then agreed to by yeas and nays, as follows:

YEAS:

Mr. P. R. Adams,	Mr. Cook,	Mr. Mosher,
W. Adams,	Cornell,	Mowry,
Alvord,	Daniels,	Orr,

Arzeno, Bagg, Barnard, H. Bartow, Britain, Ammon Brown, Asahel Brown, Burns, Chandler, Choate, Church, Comstock, Conner, Eastman, Eaton, Gale, Gardiner, Gibson, Green, Harvey, Hascall, Kingsley, Lovell, Mason, Moore, Morrison, J. D. Pierce, N. Pierce, Rix Robinson, Soule, Storey, Sturgis, Town, Warden, Webster, Whipple, Williams, Woodman, President, 48

NAYS:

Mr. Axford, Butterfield, Carr, Crouse, Mr. Fralick, Hanscom, Lee, Mr. Newberry, Robertson, Skinner, 10

Mr. Mason moved to amend the instructions by adding, amend section 1, by striking out "resident of," and inserting in lieu thereof, the words "person in."

Which did not prevail.

Mr. Moore moved to amend the same by adding, amend section 5, by inserting after "devise," the words, "otherwise than from her husband."

Which was not agreed to.

Mr. Beardsley moved to amend the instructions by adding, amend the 5th section, by adding thereto, "and she may devise the same as if she were unmarried."

Mr. Robertson moved to adjourn.

But the Convention refused to adjourn.

Mr. Beardsley's amendment was then agreed to by yeas and nays, as follows:

NAYS.

Mr. P. R. Adams, W. Adams, Alvord, Anderson, Arzeno, Bagg, Barnard, H. Bartow, Beardsley, Mr. Comstock, Crouse, Daniels, Eastman, Eaton, Gale, Gardiner, Hart, Harvey, Mr. N. Pierce, Prevost, Rix Robinson, Skinner, Soule, Storey, Sturgis, Warden, Webster,

Ammon Brown,	Hascall,	White,
Asahel Brown,	Kingsley,	Whipple,
Burns,	Moore,	Williams,
Butterfield,	Mosher,	Woodman,
Church,	Mowry,	41

YEAS.

Mr. Axford,	Mr. Desnoyers,	Mr. Newberry,
Britain,	Fralick,	Orr,
Carr,	Gibson,	J. D. Pierce,
Choate,	Hanscom,	Robertson,
Conner,	Lovell,	President,
Cook,		16

The proposition of Mr. Pierce as amended, was then agreed to, and the article recommitted with instructions.

Mr. J. D. Pierce, from the committee on Exemptions and the Rights of Married Women, reported back the article bearing that title, amended agreeably to instructions.

And the question being "shall the article now pass?"

The yeas and nays were had, as follows:

YEAS:

Mr. P. R. Adams,	Mr. Cook,	Mr. McClelland,
W. Adams,	Cornell,	Moore,
Alvord,	Daniels,	Morrison,
Anderson,	Desnoyers,	Mosher,
Arzeno,	Eastman,	Mowry,
Bagg,	Eaton,	J. D. Pierce,
Barnard,	Gale,	N. Pierce,
H. Bartow,	Gardiner.	Robertson,
Beardsley,	Gibson,	Soule,
Britain,	Green,	Storey,
Ammon Brown,	Hanscom,	Sturgis,
Asahel Brown,	Hart,	Town,
Butterfield,	Harvey,	Warden,
Chandler,	Hascall,	Webster,
Choate,	Kingsley,	White,
Church,	Lovell,	Williams,
Comstock,	Mason,	Woodman,
Conner,		52

NAYS:

Mr. Axford,	Mr. Crouse,	Mr. Orr,
Burns,	Fralick,	Rix Robinson,
Carr,	Newberry,	President, 9

So the article was passed, and under the rule referred to the committee on arrangement and phraseology.

On motion of Mr. Cook, the Convention adjourned.

Lansing, Saturday, August 3, 1850.

The Convention was called to order by the President at the usual hour.

Prayer by the Rev. Mr. Sanford.

Absent on leave, Messrs. Beeson, Alvarado Brown, Chapel, J. Clark, Edmunds, Hathaway, Hixon, Kinne, Lee, O'Brien, Raynale, M. Robinson, Van Valkenburgh, Wait, Walker, Wells, Willard and Witherell,

Without leave, Messrs. Backus, Crary, Graham, Marvin, Mason, Redfield, Sutherland, Tiffany and Whittemore.

LEAVE OF ABSENCE

Was granted to Messrs. Backus, Crary, Graham, Hixon, Mason, Redfield and Tiffany for an indefinite period, and to Mr. Whittemore for the day.

RESOLUTIONS.

On motion of Mr. Bush,

Resolved, That the committee on printing be requested to instruct the State Printer not to strike off the copies of any form of the debates set up till the Reporter who has reported the same shall have had an opportunity of examining the proof sheet.

On motion of Mr. Britain,

The vote adopting the foregoing resolution was reconsidered.

Mr. Britain moved to amend the resolution by adding thereto "and the committee on printing is discharged from further action upon the subject."

On motion of Mr. Alvord,

The resolution was indefinitely postponed.

SPECIAL ORDER.

The article reported by the committee on the punishment of crimes coming up under the resolution of yesterday, and

The question being upon ordering it to a third reading,

Mr. Fralick moved to indefinitely postpone the article.

Mr. Axford moved the previous question, but the call was not sustained.

The yeas and nays were ordered on the motion to postpone indefinitely, and the result was as follows:

YEAS.

Mr. P. R. Adams,	Mr. Conner,	Mr. Lovell,
W. Adams,	Cornell,	McClelland,
Axford,	Danforth,	Moore,
Alvord,	Fralick,	Mowry,
Anderson,	Gibson,	Roberts,
Beardsley,	Green,	Robertson,
Ammon Brown,	Hanscom,	E. S. Robinson,
Butterfield,	Hart,	Skinner,
Carr,	Harvey,	White,
Chandler,	Hascall,	Whipple,
Choate,	Kingsley,	Williams,
Church,	Leach,	President,
S. Clark,		37

NAYS.

Mr. Bagg,	Eastman,	Mr. Prevost,
H. Bartow,	Eaton,	Rix Robinson,
Britain,	Gale,	Soule,
Asahel Brown,	Lee,	Storey,
Bush,	Morrison,	Sturgis,
Comstock,	Mosher,	Town,
Cook,	Newberry,	Warden,
Crouse,	Orr,	Webster,
Daniels,	N. Pierce,	Woodman,
Mr. Dimond,		28

So the article was indefinitely postponed.

The President announced the following communication:

"Mr. J. Coates respectfully resigns his appointment as Reporter to the Convention."

And the same was laid upon the table.

On motion of Mr. Cook,

The article entitled "Finance and Taxation" was taken from the table, and

The question being upon concurring in the amendments made in committee of the whole,

On motion of Mr. Britain,

The substitute for section 1 reported by the committee was amended as follows:

Strike out in the 2d line "and of the balance of," and insert "the principal and interest of."

Also, strike out from lines 3 and 4 "until the 1st day of January 1852," and insert "until the extinguishment of the State debt, other than the amounts due to the primary school, university and other educational funds."

Mr. Church proposed the following substitute for the one reported by the committee:

"All specific taxes, save those received from the mining companies organized in the Upper Peninsula, shall be applied in paying the interest upon the state indebtedness; and to the payment of said indebtedness (save that in favor of the several educational funds) until the full extinguishment of said state indebtedness, at which time the said specific taxes shall be added to, and forever constitute a part of, the proceeds of the primary school fund."

On motion of Mr. Roberts,

A call of the Convention was ordered, and Messrs. Arzeno, Barnard, J. Bartow, Beardsley, Burns, Desnoyer, Leach, Prevost, and Sturgis were absent without leave.

Mr. Bush asked and obtained leave of absence for Mr. Barnard, and Mr. Eaton for Mr. Desnoyers.

Mr. J. D. Pierce moved that all further proceedings under the cal be dispensed with.

But the motion was lost, and

On motion of Mr. Roberts,

The Sergeant-at-Arms was despatched for the absentees.

The majority of them soon appearing,

On motion of Mr. Cook,

All further proceedings under the call were dispensed with.

Mr. J. Bartow asked and obtained leave of absence for Mr. Sutherland indefinitely.

On motion of Mr. Hanscom,

The Convention adjourned.

Afternoon Session.

Two o'clock.

The Convention was called to order by the President.

A quorum of members in attendance.

Mr. Beardsley asked and obtained leave of absence for Mr. Burns until Tuesday next.

The article, "Finance and Taxation," being under consideration,

And the question being upon the proposition Mr. Church, offered this morning,

Mr. McClelland moved to amend the substitute reported by the committee, by inserting after "taxes" in the 1st line, the words "save those received from the mining companies in the upper peninsula."

Which was agreed to, and

Mr. Church withdrew his proposition.

Mr. Fralick offered the following substitute for the one reported by the committee for section 1:

"The Legislature shall provide for an annual tax, sufficient with other sources of income to defray the estimated expenses of the State for each year, including the interest on the debt of the State, and whenever the expenses of any year, including such interest, shall exceed the income, the legislature shall provide for levying a tax the ensuing year, sufficient with other sources of income, to pay the deficiency, as well as the estimated expenses of such ensuing year, including such interest."

But the same was not agreed to.

On motion of Mr. Britain,

The amendment of the committee was so amended as to strike out but the first subdivision of section 1, and substitute as reported.

The amendments of the committee were then severally concurred in.

The Article being up for amendment,

Mr. Butterfield moved to amend section 11 by striking out the words "of taxation," in the 1st line, and inserting the following: "for the assessment and collection of all taxes."

Upon which he asked the yeas and nays, and the motion was lost, as follows:

YEAS.

Mr. W. Adams,
Anderson,
H. Bartow,
Asahel Brown,
Butterfield,
Chandler,
Gale,

Mr. Green,
Hart,
Harvey,
Leach,
Moore,
Morrison,
Orr,

Mr. N. Pierce,
Sturgis,
Webster,
White,
Williams,
Woodman, 20

NAYS.

Mr. P. R. Adams,	Mr. Daniels,	Mr. Newberry,
Axford,	Fralick,	Prevost,
Bagg,	Gardiner,	Robertson,
Beardsley,	Gibson,	E. S. Robinson,
Bush,	Hanscom,	Rix Robinson,
Choate,	Hascall,	Storey,
Church,	Kingsley	Town,
Conner,	McClelland,	Warden,
Cook,	Mosher,	Whipple,
Crouse,	Mowry,	President,
Danforth,		31

Mr. Britain moved to amend the article by adding thereto the following additional section:

"Every act making an appropriation for purposes not provided for by this constitution, shall contain a provision for the necessary state tax to meet such appropriation, and a statement of the year or years in which said tax is to be levied; and said act shall, before it shall take effect, be submitted to the people at a general election, or at the annual township meetings, and be approved by a majority of all the votes given for and against it at said election or annual township meetings."

But the motion was not agreed to.

And the article was ordered to a third reading.

On motion of Mr. J. D. Pierce,

The Convention then adjourned.

Lansing, Monday, August 5, 1850.

The Convention met pursuant to adjournment, and was called to order by the President.

Prayer by the Rev. Mr. Tooker.

Absent on leave, Messrs. Backus, Beeson, Alvarado Brown, Burns, Chapel, J. Clark, Crary, Graham, Hathaway, Hixon, Kinne, Mason, O'Brien, Raynale, Redfield, M. Robinson, Sutherland, Tiffany, Van Valkenburgh, Wait, Wells, Willard and Witherell; without leave, Messrs. J. Bartow, S. Clark, Cook, Desnoyers, Dimond, Edmunds, Marvin, Moore, Sullivan and Webster.

LEAVE OF ABSENCE

Was granted to Messrs. Moore, Sullivan, Dimond, S. Clark, J. Bartow and Cook, for an indefinite period.

RESOLUTIONS.

Mr. McClelland offered the following, which was laid upon the table.

Resolved, That this Convention will adjourn, sine die, on Monday the 19th inst.

Mr. Whittemore moved to recommit the article on elections to committee with which it originated, with instructions to strike out of section 1, the words "and also every white male inhabitant who shall have resided in the state two years and a half, and declared his intention to become a citizen of the United States," and that the article be reported back as amended forthwith.

Mr. Leach moved to amend the proposition by striking out therefrom the word "white."

Which was lost by the yeas and nays as follows:

YEAS.

Mr. H. Bartow,	Mr. Green,	Mr. Orr,
Asahel Brown,	Harvey,	N. Pierce,
Chandler,	Leach,	Prevost,
Comstock,	Lovell,	Williams,
Daniels,		

13

NAYS.

Mr. P. R. Adams,	Mr. Crouse,	Mr. Newberry,
W. Adams,	Danforth,	J. D. Pierce,
Alvord,	Eastman,	Roberts,
Anderson,	Eaton,	Robertson,
Arzeno,	Fralick,	E. S. Robinson,
Bagg,	Gardiner,	Rix Robinson,
Barnard,	Gibson,	Skinner,
Beardsley,	Hanscom,	Soule,
Britain,	Hart,	Story,
Ammon Brown,	Hascall,	Town,
Butterfield,	Kingsley,	Walker,
Carr,	McClelland,	Warden,
Choate,	McLeod,	Whittemore,
Church,	Morrison,	Woodman,
Conner,	Mosher,	President,
Cornell,		

46

Mr. Fralick moved to amend so as to instruct the committee to strike out section 1, and substitute in lieu thereof as follows:

"In all elections, every white male citizen above the age of twenty-one years, having resided in the State six months next preceding an election, shall be entitled to vote at such election; and every white male inhabitant who was permitted to vote under the provisions of the previous constitution of this State, and their male descendants of the age aforesaid, having resided in the State six months next preceding an election, shall have the right of voting as aforesaid; but no such citizen or inhabitant shall be entitled to vote except in the township or ward of which he is an actual resident, and in which he has resided for ten days next preceding the day of election."

Which was disagreed to by the following vote:

YEAS.

Mr. P. R. Adams,	Mr. McLeod,	Mr. Prevost,	
Ammon Brown,	Mowry,	Rix Robinson,	
Church,	Newberry,	Town,	
Fralick,			10

NAYS.

Mr. W. Adams,	Cornell,	Mr. Morrison,	
Alvord,	Crouse,	Mosher,	
Anderson,	Danforth,	Orr,	
Arzeno,	Daniels,	N. Pierce,	
Bagg,	Eaton,	J. D. Pierce,	
Barnard,	Gardiner,	Robertson,	
H. Bartow,	Gibson,	E. S. Robinson,	
Beardsley,	Green,	Skinner,	
Britain,	Hanscom,	Soule,	
Asahel Brown,	Hart,	Walker,	
Butterfield,	Harvey,	Warden,	
Carr,	Hascall,	Whittemore,	
Chandler,	Leach,	Williams,	
Choate,	Lee,	Woodman,	
Comstock,	McClelland,	President,	
Conner,			46

The proposition of Mr. Whittemore was then rejected by yeas and nays as follows:

YEAS.

Mr. P. R. Adams,	Mr. Gardiner,	Mr. McLeod,	
Ammon Brown,	Hanscom,	Newberry,	
Butterfield,	Hart,	Skinner,	
Danforth,	Hascall,	Storey,	
Eastman,	Kingsley,	Town,	
Fralick,	McClelland,	Whittemore,	18

NAYS.

Mr. W. Adams,	Mr. Comstock,	Mr. Mosher,

Alvord,	Conner,	Orr,
Anderson,	Cornell,	J. D. Pierce,
Arzeno,	Crouse,	N. Pierce,
Bagg,	Daniels,	Prevost,
Barnard,	Eaton,	Robertson,
H. Bartow,	Gale,	E. S. Robinson,
Beardsley,	Gibson,	Soule,
Britain,	Green,	Walker,
Asahel Brown,	Harvey,	Warden,
Carr,	Leach,	Williams,
Chandler,	Lee,	Woodman,
Choate,	Lovell,	President,
Church,	Morrison,	41

Mr. Daniels proposed the following:

Resolved, That no member shall occupy more than five minutes in speaking at any one time, either in convention or committee of the whole, from and after this date, except by leave of the convention or committee.

And the same was adopted by a two-thirds vote, as follows:

YEAS.

Mr. P. R. Adams,	Mr. Comstock,	Mr. Lovell,
W. Adams,	Conner,	McClelland,
Anderson,	Cornell,	Morrison,
Arzeno,	Crouse,	Mosher,
Bagg,	Daniels,	Mowry,
Barnard,	Eaton,	Newberry,
H. Bartow,	Fralick,	J. D. Pierce,
Beardsley,	Gale,	Prevost,
Britain,	Gibson,	Rix Robinson,
Ammon Brown,	Green,	Skinner,
Asahel Brown,	Hanscom,	Soule,
Bush,	Hart,	Town,
Butterfield,	Harvey,	Walker,
Carr,	Hascall,	Warden,
Chandler,	Kingsley,	Whittemore,
Choate,	Leach,	Williams,
Church,	Lee,	Woodman, 51

NAYS.

Mr. Alvord,	Mr. Orr,	Mr. Robertson,
McLeod,	N. Pierce,	President, 6

On motion of Mr. Green,

Resolved, That the committee on phraseology be instructed to inquire into the propriety of so altering the phraseology in the Article on Elections, as to make it unnecessary to refer to the constitution of 1835.

Mr. Hanscom asked and obtained leave to introduce an article entitled "Judicial Department," which was read the first and second time by its title, referred to the committee of the whole, and ordered printed.

Mr. Whipple, from the committee on the Executive department, to whom was referred the Article entitled "Executive Department," with instructions "to inquire into the expediency of so amending said article as to provide for the election of Speaker of the House of Representatives by the people," reported the same back, deeming such a provision inexpedient.

The report was accepted, the committee discharged, and

The report was agreed to by the following vote:

YEAS.

Mr. P. R. Adams,	Mr. Choate,	Mr. Hanscom,
Alvord,	Church,	Harvey,
Anderson,	J. Clark,	Mowry,
Arzeno,	Comstock,	N. Pierce,
Barnard,	Conner,	E. S. Robinson,
H. Bartow,	Crouse,	Rix Robinson,
Ammon Brown,	Danforth,	Skinner,
Bush,	Daniels,	Soule,
Butterfield,	Eastman,	Walker,
Carr,	Fralick,	Whipple,
Chandler,	Gibson,	President, 33

NAYS.

Mr. Bagg,	Mr. Hart,	Mr. Roberts,
Britain,	Hascall,	Robertson,
Asahel Brown,	Kingsley,	Storey,
Eaton,	Leach,	Warden,
Gale,	Lee,	Williams,
Gardiner,	Newberry,	Woodman,
Green,	Orr,	20

Mr. Eastman called up his motion to reconsider the vote by which the article entitled "County Officers and County Government" was passed.

And the motion to reconsider was lost, by yeas and nays, as follows:

YEAS.

Mr. W. Adams,	Mr. Fralick,	Mr. Mosher,
Arzeno,	Gale,	Storey,
H. Bartow,	Green,	Whipple,

Asahel Brown,	Leach,	Williams,
Bush,	Lovell,	President,
Eastman,	McLeod,	17

NAYS.

Mr. P. R. Adams,	Mr. Cornell,	Mr. Orr,
Anderson,	Crouse,	J. D. Pierce,
Axford,	Danforth,	N. Pierce,
Bagg,	Daniels,	Prevost,
Barnard,	Eaton,	Roberts,
Beardsley,	Gardiner,	Robertson,
Britain,	Gibson,	E. S. Robinson,
Ammon Brown,	Hart,	Skinner,
Butterfield,	Harvey,	Soule,
Carr,	Hascall,	Sturges,
Chandler,	Kingsley,	Town,
Choate,	McClelland,	Walker,
Church,	Morrison,	Warden,
J. Clark,	Mowry,	Whittemore,
Comstock,	Newberry,	Woodman,
Conner,		46

The article entitled "Executive Department" coming up, and the question being, shall the article now pass?

The yeas and nays were ordered, and the vote was as follows:

YEAS:

Mr. P. R. Adams,	Mr. Conner,	Mr. Mosher,
W. Adams,	Cornell,	Mowry,
Anderson,	Crouse,	Newberry,
Arzeno,	Danforth,	Orr,
Axford,	Daniels,	J. D. Pierce,
Bagg,	Eaton,	N. Pierce,
Barnard,	Fralick,	Prevost,
H. Bartow,	Gale,	Robertson,
Beardsley,	Gardiner,	E. S. Robinson,
Britain,	Gibson,	Rix Robinson,
Ammon Brown,	Green,	Skinner,
Asahel Brown,	Hart,	Soule,
Bush,	Harvey,	Sturgis,
Butterfield,	Hascall,	Town,
Carr,	Kingsley,	Walker,
Chandler,	Leach,	Warden,
Choate,	Lee,	Whittemore,
Church,	Lovell,	Williams,
J. Clark,	McClelland,	Woodman,
Comstock,	Morrison,	59

NAYS:

Mr. Alvord,	Mr. McLeod,	Mr. Whipple,
Eastman,	Roberts,	President,
Hanscom,	Storey,	8

So the article was passed, and under the rule referred to the committee on arrangement and phraseology.

The article "Of Elections" coming up on its passage with the resolution accompanying the same,

A division of the question was had,

And the article was passed by the following vote:

YEAS.

Mr. P. R. Adams,	Mr. Choate,	Mr. Morrison,
W. Adams,	Church,	Mosher,
Alvord,	Conner,	Orr,
Anderson,	Cornell,	J. D. Pierce,
Arzeno,	Crouse,	N. Pierce,
Bagg,	Danforth,	Robertson,
Barnard,	Dimond,	E. S. Robinson,
H. Bartow,	Eaton,	Soule,
Beardsley,	Gibson,	Sturgis,
Britain,	Hascall,	Walker,
Asahel Brown,	Kingsley,	Warden,
Bush,	Leach,	Williams,
Butterfield,	McClelland,	President,
Carr,		40

NAYS.

Mr. Axford,	Mr. Hart,	Mr. Roberts,
Ammon Brown,	Harvey,	Rix Robinson,
Chandler,	Leach,	Skinner,
Comstock,	Lovell,	Storey,
Fralick,	McLeod,	Town,
Gale,	Mowry,	Whipple,
Gardiner,	Newberry,	Whittemore,
Green,	Prevost,	Woodman,
Hanscom,		25

The resolution was then passed, by yeas and nays, as follows:

YEAS:

Mr. P. R. Adams,	Mr. Crouse,	Mr. Mosher,
W. Adams,	Danforth,	Mowry,
Alvord,	Daniels,	Orr,
Anderson,	Eaton,	J. D. Pierce,
Arzeno,	Fralick,	N. Pierce,
Barnard,	Gale,	Prevost,
H. Bartow,	Gardiner,	Robertson,
Beardsley,	Gibson,	Rix Robinson,
Britain,	Green,	Skinner,
Ammon Brown,	Hart,	Soule,
Asahel Brown,	Harvey,	Sturgis,
Bush,	Hascall,	Town,

Chandler,	Kingsley,	Walker,
Choate,	Leach,	Warden,
Church,	Lee,	Whittemore,
Comstock,	Lovell,	Williams,
Conner,	McClelland,	Woodman,
Cornell,	Morrison,	President, 54

NAYS.

Mr, Axford,	Mr. J. Clark,	Mr. Roberts,
Bagg,	Hanscom,	E. S. Robinson,
Butterfield,	McLeod,	Storey,
Carr,	Newberry,	Whipple, 15

And the article and resolution were, under the rule, referred to the committee on arrangement and phraseology.

The article entitled "Finance and Taxation" coming up for a third reading,

Mr. Fralick moved to pass the same over for the day.

Which was not agreed to.

The article was then read the third time, when

Mr. Bagg moved to recommit the same to the committee on finance and taxation with instructions to strike from section 11 the words, "except upon property paying specific taxes."

The President called Mr. Bush to the chair.

Mr. Goodwin moved the following addition to the instructions proposed by Mr. Bagg:

And also to add to section 1 the following:

"But the legislature may provide that when any private corporations are or shall be, in consideration of specific taxes, exempt by their charters from all other taxation, the counties, towns, cities or villages, within which such corporation may hold property which would be taxable if held by other persons, shall be entitled to an equitable proportion of such specific taxes for local purposes."

Which he subsequently withdrew.

When, after some debate,

Mr. Bagg withdrew his motion to recommit.

And the question being, "shall the article pass ?"

The yeas and nays were taken, with the following result:

YEAS.

Mr. P. R. Adams,	Mr. Daniels,	Mr. J. D. Pierce,
W. Adams,	Eaton,	N. Pierce,
Alvord,	Gardiner,	Prevost,

Anderson,
Arzeno,
Barnard,
H. Bartow,
Beardsley,
Britain,
Ammon Brown,
Asahel Brown,
Bush,
Chandler,
Church,
Conner,
Crouse,
Danforth,
Green,
Hanscom,
Hart,
Harvey,
Hascall,
Kingsley,
Lovell,
McClelland,
Morrison,
Mosher,
Mowry,
Newberry,
Orr,
Robertson,
E. S. Robinson,
Rix Robinson,
Skinner,
Soule,
Sturgis,
Town,
Walker,
Warden,
Whipple,
Whittemore,
Williams,
Woodman, 49

NAYS.

Mr. Bagg,
Butterfield,
Carr,
Choate,
Mr. Cornell,
Fralick,
Gale,
Gibson,
Mr. Lee,
McLeod,
Storey,
President, 12

So the article was passed, and under the rule, referred to the committee on arrangement and phraseology.

The President took the chair.

On motion of Mr. Robertson,

The article entitled State Officers was taken from the table.

The question being on recommitting with instructions, as proposed by Mr. Storey on the 24th ult.,

Mr. Woodman moved to amend by further instructing the committee so to amend the article that the Attorney General shall not be required to keep his office at the seat of government.

But the motion did not prevail.

A division of the question was had.

The motion to reconsider the article was lost.

Upon the question, shall the article now pass?

The vote, by yeas and nays, stood as follows:

YEAS:

Mr. P. R. Adams,
W. Adams,
Arzeno,
Bagg,
Barnard,
H. Bartow,
Beardsley,
Britain,
Mr. Crouse,
Danforth,
Daniels,
Eastman,
Eaton,
Gale,
Green,
Harvey,
Mr. Newberry,
Orr,
J. D. Pierce,
N. Pierce,
Prevost,
Robertson,
E. S. Robinson,
Rix Robinson,

Ammon Brown,	Hascall,	Town,
Asahel Brown,	Kingsley,	Walker,
Bush,	Lee,	Warden,
Carr,	Lovell,	Whipple,
Chandler,	McClelland,	Whittemore,
Choate,	Morrison,	Williams,
Church,	Mosher,	Woodman,
Comstock,	Mowry,	President,
Conner,		49

NAYS:

Mr. Fralick,	Mr. Hanscom,	Mr. Skinner,
Gardiner,	McLeod,	Storey,
Gibson,		7

So the article was passed, and under the rule, referred to the committee on arrangement and phraseology.

On motion of Mr. Storey,

The Convention resolved itself into committee of the whole on the general order,

Mr. Whipple in the chair.

—

PROCEEDINGS IN COMMITTEE.

The committee took up for consideration the resolution relative to the sale of ardent spirits.

Mr. Eaton moved to strike out the first branch of the resolution.

Pending which,

On motion of Mr. Willaims,

The committee rose and reported the resolution back to the Convention without amendment.

—

The committee through their chairman reported back the resolution to the Convention without amendment.

Mr. J. D. Pierce moved the Convention adjourn.

But the motion was lost.

Mr. Eaton moved to strike out the first branch of the resolution.

The previous question being moved,

It was demanded.

And the main question was ordered to be now put.

The amendment proposed by Mr. Eaton was then rejected, by yeas and nays, as follows:

YEAS:

Mr. Alvord,	Mr. Hanscom,	Mr. J. D. Pierce,
Anderson,	Hart,	Prevost,
Bagg,	Lee,	Soule,
Barnard,	Lovell,	Sturgis,
H. Bartow,	McClelland,	Town,
Carr,	Morrison,	Warden,
Chandler,	Mowry,	Whittemore,
Eaton,	Newberry,	Williams,
Gale,	Orr,	Woodman, 27

NAYS:

Mr. P. R. Adams,	Mr. Cornell,	Mr. Kingsley.
W. Adams,	Crouse,	Mosher,
Arzeno,	Danforth,	N. Pierce,
Beardsley,	Daniels,	Robertson,
Ammon Brown,	Eastman,	E. S. Robinson,
Asahel Brown,	Fralick,	Rix Robinson,
Butterfield,	Gardiner,	Skinner,
Choate,	Gibson,	Storey,
Church,	Green,	Walker,
Comstock,	Harvey,	Whipple,
Conner,	Hascall,	President. 33

Mr. Bagg moved a call of the Convention.

But the call was not sustained.

Mr. Britain moved to adjourn: which was lost.

Mr. Gale moved a call of the Convention.

Which was not agreed to.

Mr. Eaton moved to adjourn.

But the motion was lost.

The question being on ordering the resolution to a third reading,

The result was as follows:

YEAS:

Mr. Alvord,	Mr. Eastman,	Mr. Robertson,
Arzeno,	Fralick,	E. S. Robinson,
Ammon Brown,	Gardiner,	Rix Robinson,
Butterfield,	Gibson,	Skinner,
Choate,	Harvey,	Soule,
Church,	Hascall,	Town,
Comstock,	Mosher,	Walker,
Cornell,	J. D. Pierce,	Whipple,
Crouse,	N. Pierce,	President,
Daniels,		28

NAYS:

Mr. P. R. Adams,	Mr. Danforth,	Mr. Mowry,
W. Adams,	Eaton,	Newberry,

Anderson,	Gale,	Orr,
Bagg,	Green,	Prevost,
Barnard,	Hanscom,	Storey,
H. Bartow,	Hart,	Sturgis,
Beardsley,	Kingsley,	Warden,
Asahel Brown,	Lee,	Whittemore,
Carr,	Lovell,	Williams,
Chandler,	McClelland,	Woodman,
Conner,	Morrison,	32

So the Convention refused to order the resolution to a third reading.

On motion of Mr. J. D. Pierce,

The Convention adjourned.

Afternoon Session.

Two o'clock.

The President called the Convention to order.

A quorum of members in attendance.

Mr. Storey offered the following:

Resolved, That the resolution adopted by the Convention on the 4th day of June last, by which the Governor of the State was invited to take a seat within the bar of the Convention during its sittings, be and the same is hereby rescinded.

Mr. Hanscom moved to indefinitely postpone the resolution; when,

On motion of Mr. McClelland,

It was laid upon the table.

On motion of Mr. Whipple,

The Convention was resolved into a committee of the whole on the general order,

Mr. Hanscom in the chair.

Without action the committee rose.

Mr. Church, from the committee on the judiciary, reported back the article entitled Judicial Department, with sundry amendments thereto.

The article was laid upon the table and ordered printed.

On motion of Mr. Robertson,

Resolved, That each article of this constitution, as passed and referred to the committee on arrangement and phraseology, be printed for the use of this Convention; and

Resolved, That said committee be and they are hereby instructed to prepare a fair copy of each article, as amended by them, and procure the same to be printed before making their report.

Mr. Walker called up the article entitled "Education," and the question being upon concurring in the amendments made in committee of the whole,

The amendment to section one was concurred in.

Mr. Green moved to amend the original section by striking out all to and inclusive of "respectively," in the 6th line, and substituting as follows:

"Each of the cities and townships of this state shall, in the year , and in each and every year thereafter, raise by tax upon the real and personal estate in such cities and townships respectively, a sum equal to for each and every person residing in such cities and townships between the ages of 4 and 18 years, as shall appear by the returns of the school districts therein; which sum, together with the money apportioned to each of such cities and townships from the interest of the primary school fund, shall be apportioned pro rata among the several school districts therein according to the number of persons between the ages of 4 and 18 years residing in each, as shall appear by the last annual reports of such districts, to be used by them in payment of teachers' wages therein. The amount so to be raised may be increased or diminished by the legislature as they may deem right and proper; but such increase or dimimution shall not exceed cents per scholar, as above named, at any one session of the legislature."

But the amendment was not agreed to.

Mr. Leach moved to amend the substitute reported by the committee by striking out of lines three and four the words "not exceeding two mills upon the dollar."

Which was not agreed to.

Mr. Gale offered the following as a substitute for the one reported by the committee:

"The legislature shall establish and provide for a system of primary schools within five years from the adoption of this constitution, in which the instruction shall be conducted in the English language; and as nearly free to all scholars residing in the several districts as may be deemed practicable."

Mr. Leach moved to amend by striking out "five" and inserting "two."

Which was lost.

The proposition of Mr. Gale was disagreed to.

Mr. Hanscom offered the following substitute for the one proposed by the committee:

"The Legislature shall, within five years from the adoption of this constitution, provide for and establish a system of primary schools by which such schools shall be kept free and without charge for tuition, for at least three months in each year, in each school district within the State."

Mr. Woodman moved to strike out "3 months," and insert "4 months;" also, strike out "5 years," and insert "3 years."

A division was had, and the first branch of the amendment was lost.

The second proposition was also disagreed to by yeas and nays, as follows:

YEAS:

Mr. W. Adams,	Mr. Daniels,	Mr. J. D. Pierce,
Alvord,	Eastman,	Robertson,
Anderson,	Gale,	Skinner,
Bagg,	Green,	Soule,
Barnard,	Hart,	Sturgis,
H. Bartow,	Leach,	Walker,
Beardsley,	Lee,	Warden,
Chandler,	Lovell,	Webster,
Choate,	Mowry,	Williams,
Conner,	Orr,	Woodman,
Cornell,		31

NAYS:

Mr. P. R. Adams,	Mr. Danforth,	Mr. Morrison,
Arzeno,	Eaton,	Newberry,
Axford,	Fralick,	N. Pierce,
Britain,	Gardiner,	Prevost,
Ammon Brown,	Gibson,	Roberts,
Asahel Brown,	Hanscom,	F. S. Robinson,
Butterfield,	Harvey,	Rix Robinson,
Carr,	Hascall,	Storey,
Church,	Kingsley,	Town,
Comstock,	McClelland,	President,
Crouse,	McLeod,	32

The substitute offered by Mr. Hanscom was negatived.

Mr. Bagg offered the following as a substitute, which was rejected:

"The Legislature shall establish a uniform system of free primary schools throughout this Sta.e, by levying a State tax upon the taxable pr operty of this State."

The substitute reported by the committee of the whole (for section 3,) was then concurred in.

The amendment made to section 9 being under consideration,

Mr. Williams proposed to add thereto:

"The said school and farm shall be under the superintendence of the Regents of the University, who may locate the same on any of the University land which they may appropriate for that purpose, not exceeding 640 acres, or on any land donated for the purpose; and it shall be a branch of the University for instruction in agriculture and the natural sciences connected therewith."

But his amendment did not prevail.

Mr. Warden moved to amend the amendment made in committee by striking out "and farm," wheresoever it occurs.

But the amendment was not agreed to.

Mr. McClelland moved to amend by inserting after "and," where it first occurs, the words, "it shall be competent for the legislature to appropriate;" and also to strike out "set apart," in the 6th line of the section as amended.

And the amendment prevailed.

And the amendments of the committee were severally concurred in.

Mr. Soule proposed the following new section, to come in between sections 3 and 4:

"Any school district neglecting to keep up and support a school for three months in each year shall be deprived of its proportion of the income of the primary school fund, and of all funds arising from tax for the support of schools."

And the same was adopted.

Mr. Woodmon moved to amend sec. 11, by striking out in the 9th line, the words "at least."

But the Convention refused to strike out.

Mr. Whipple offered the following substitute for section 4 of the Article:

"There shall be appointed by the Governor, by and with the concurrence of both branches of the Legislature in joint convention assembled, in the year 1852, eight Regents of the University; two for the term of eight years, two for the term of six years, two for the term of four years, and two for the term of two years; and at each subsequent election two Regents shall be elected in the manner aforesaid, who shall hold their office for the term of eight years."

And the same was agreed to by yeas and nays, as follows:

YEAS.

Mr. P. R. Adams,	Mr. Church,	Mr. Mowry,
W. Adams,	Conner,	Newberry,
Alvord,	Cornell,	Orr,
Anderson,	Crouse,	Robertson,
Arzeno,	Gale,	Rix Robinson,
Axford,	Hanscom,	Storey,
H. Bartow,	Hart,	Webster,
Britain,	Hascall,	Whipple,
Ammon Brown,	McClelland,	Williams,
Choate,	Morrison,	Woodman, 30

NAYS.

Mr. Bagg,	Mr. Eaton,	Mr. Mosher,
Barnard,	Fralick,	N. Pierce,
Asahel Brown,	Gibson,	Prevost,
Bush,	Green,	Skinner,
Butterfield,	Harvey,	Soule,
Carr,	Kingsley,	Town,
Chandler,	Leach,	Walker,
Comstock,	Lee,	Warden,
Daniels,	Lovell,	President,
Eastman,		28

Mr. Whipple submitted the following, to stand as (a new) section 5, and the same was agreed to:

"The Regents elected pursuant to the provisions of the foregoing section, and their successors in office, shall continue to constitute the body corporate, known by the name and style of "the Regents of the University of Michigan."

Mr. Britain moved to amend section 11 by addnig after "farm," in the 8th line, the words, "until otherwise appropriated by law."

Which was agreed to.

On motion of Mr. Williams,

Section 10 was amended by inserting after "farm," in 6th line, "and it shall be competent for the legislature to make the same a branch of the University for instruction in agriculture and the natural sciences connected therewith, and place the same under the supervision of the Regents of the University."

On motion of Mr. Woodman,

The Convention adjourned.

Lansing, Tuesday, August 6, 1850.

The Convention met at the usual hour and was called to order by the President.

No clergyman in attendance.

Roll called. Absent on leave, Messrs. Backus, J. Bartow, Alvarado Brown, Burns, Chapel, S. Clark, Cook, Crary, Desnoyers, Dimond, Edmunds, Graham, Hathaway, Hixon, Kinne, Marvin, Mason, Moore, O'Brien, Raynale, Redfield, M. Robinson, Sullivan, Sutherland, Tiffany, Wells, Willard and Witherell.

Without leave, Messrs. Van Valkenburgh and White.

LEAVE OF ABSENCE.

Mr. Hart asked and obtained leave of absence for Mr. White for an indefinite period.

Mr. Whittemore for Mr. Van Valkenburgh for the day.

PETITIONS.

By Mr. Fralick: of Riley Stilwell and thirty-five other citizens of Plymouth, Wayne county, praying that a clause may be inserted in the organic law of this State whereby any convict who may be sentenced to the State Penitentiary, for any term of years not during life, may have the privilege to choose any profession or trade he may think proper; so that the learned professions may share equally in all the benefits resulting from the system of prison labor.

Referred to the committee on the judicial department.

Mr. Hanscom announced the receipt by the Secretary of a communication from the Postmaster of Lansing, by which it appeared the postage of the Convention amounted to $501 97.

Laid on the table.

MOTIONS AND RESOLUTIONS.

Mr. McClelland called up his resolution of yesterday, relative to an adjournment, and modified the same by inserting "Thursday, the 15th inst."

And the resolution as modified was adopted.

On motion of Mr. J. D. Pierce,

Resolved, That the committee on miscellaneous provisions be instructed to inquire into the expediency of incorporating a provision in the constitution to promote the early sale and settlement of the unappropriated public lands now held by the United States, exempt from taxation within this State; the Legislature shall be authorized to take all necessary and proper steps to procure the conveyance of said lands to the State whenever they can be obtained on just and advantageous terms; and whatever sum, if any, shall be realized from the sales of the lands so acquired, after repaying to the State the amount of all advances made on account of the purchase, management, sale and settlement of the same, together with interest thereon, shall constitute a permanent fund for the benefit of education, and the support of such deaf and dumb and blind and insane persons as have not the means of supporting themselves.

The Convention having reached the order of

UNFINISHED BUSINESS,

Resumed the consideration of the article entitled "Education."

Mr. Skinner moved to amend the article by adding at the end of sec. 8: "and tuition shall be free and without charge in said institution."

Which was lost.

Mr. Cornell proposed the following:

Resolved, That the article be recommitted to the committee on education, with instructions to strike out section 3, and insert as follows:

"The Legislature shall, as soon as practicable, establish a system of primary schools, the tuition of which shall be free, throughout the State, and provide for their support."

A division of the question was had.

And on the motion first to recommit, the yeas and nays were had, and the motion prevailed, as follows:

YEAS.

Mr. Arzeno,	Mr. Daniels,	Mr. Morrison,
Axford,	Eaton,	Mosher,
Bagg,	Fralick,	Newberry,
Ammon Brown,	Gale,	Orr,
Asahel Brown,	Gardiner,	J. D. Pierce,
Bush,	Gibson,	Prevost,
Carr,	Green.	E. S. Robinson,
Chandler,	Hanscom,	Rix Robinson,
Choate,	Hart,	Skinner,
Church,	Kingsley,	Storey,
J. Clark,	Leach,	Sturgis,
Conner,	Lee,	Town,
Cornell,	Lovell,	Whipple,
Crouse,	McClelland,	Whittemore,
Danforth,	McLeod,	President, 45

NAYS.

Mr. P. R. Adams,	Mr. Beeson,	Mr. Robertson,
W. Adams,	Britain,	Soule,
Alvord,	Comstock,	Warden,
Anderson,	Harvey,	Webster,
Barnard,	Mowry,	Williams,
H. Bartow,	N. Pierce,	Woodman, 18

Mr. Walker moved to amend the proposed instructions by inserting after "State" therein, the words "by which such schools shall be kept in each and every school district, for at least three months in each year."

But the amendment was lost by the following vote:

YEAS:

Mr. P. R. Adams,	Mr. Leach,	Mr. Sturgis,
W. Adams,	Morrison,	Town,
Alvord,	Mowry,	Wait,
Anderson,	J. D. Pierce,	Walker,
Arzeno,	N. Pierce,	Warden,
Barnard,	Robertson,	Webster,
Beeson,	Rix Robinson,	Williams,
J. Clark,	Skinner,	Woodman,
Eaton,		25

NAYS.

Mr. Axford,	Mr. Cornell,	Mr. Kingsley,
Bagg,	Crouse,	Lovell,
H. Bartow,	Danforth,	McClelland,
Beardsley,	Daniels,	Mosher,
Ammon Brown,	Fralick,	Newberry,
Asahel Brown,	Gale,	Orr,

Bush,	Gardiner,	Prevost,
Carr,	Gibson,	Roberts,
Chandler,	Green,	E. S. Robinson,
Choate,	Hanscom,	Soule,
Church,	Hart,	Storey,
Comstock,	Harvey,	Whittemore,
Conner,	Hascall,	President, 39

Mr. Woodman moved to amend the instructions by striking out "as soon as practicable," and inserting in lieu thereof "within three years after the adoption of this constitution."

Mr. Storey moved to amend the foregoing by striking out "three" and inserting "five."

Upon which the yeas and nays were had, and the Convention refused to strike out, as follows:

YEAS.

Mr. Arzeno,	Mr. Danforth,	Mr. Newberry,
Axford,	Fralick,	Prevost,
H. Bartow,	Gibson,	E. S. Robinson,
Ammon Brown,	Lee,	Storey,
Asahel Brown,	McLeod,	Sturgis,
Bush,	Mowry,	President,
Crouse,		19

NAYS.

Mr. W. Adams,	Mr. Daniels,	Mr. Mosher,
Alvord,	Eaton,	Orr,
Anderson,	Gale,	N. Pierce,
Bagg,	Gardiner,	Robertson,
Barnard,	Green,	Rix Robinson,
Beardsley,	Hanscom,	Skinner,
Beeson,	Hart,	Soule,
Britain,	Harvey,	Town,
Chandler,	Hascall,	Wait,
Choate,	Kingsley,	Warden,
Church,	Leach,	Webster,
J. Clark,	Lovell,	Whipple,
Comstock,	McClelland,	Whittemore,
Conner,	Morrison,	Williams,
Cornell,		43

The amendment proposed by Mr. Woodman was then rejected.

Mr. J. D. Pierce moved to amend by striking out the words "as soon as practicable."

But the Convention refused to strike out.

Upon instructing, as preposed by Mr. Cornell, the yeas and nays were ordered, and the result was as follows:

YEAS.

Mr. P. R. Adams,	Mr. Comstock,	Mr. McClelland,
Arzeno,	Conner,	McLeod,
Axford,	Cornell,	Morrison,
Bagg,	Crouse,	Mosher,
Beardsley,	Danforth,	Mowry,
Beeson,	Daniels,	Newberry,
Ammon Brown,	Fralick,	Orr,
Asahel Brown,	Gale,	Prevost,
Bush,	Gibson,	E. S. Robinson,
Butterfield,	Green,	Rix Robinson,
Carr,	Hanscom,	Storey,
Chandler,	Hart,	Town,
Choate,	Hascall,	Whipple,
Church,	Kingsley,	Whittemore,
J. Clark,	Lee,	President, 45

NAYS:

Mr. W. Adams,	Mr. Harvey,	Mr. Sturgis,
Alvord,	Leach,	Wait,
Anderson,	J. D. Pierce,	Walker,
Barnard,	N. Pierce,	Warden,
H. Bartow,	Roberts,	Webster,
Britain,	Robertson,	Williams,
Eaton,	Skinner,	Woodman,
Gardiner,	Soule,	23

So the article was recommitted with the instructions as proposed.

By unanimous consent of the Convention, the section proposed by Mr. Whipple, yesterday, and adopted, was amended by striking out "1852," and inserting "1851."

On motion of Mr. Fralick,

The Article entitled "Township Officers and Government," was taken from the table.

And the question being upon concurring in the amendments made in committee,

Mr. Woodman moved to amend the substitute reported for section 1, by striking out "four," before "constables," and inserting "two."

But the amendment was lost.

Mr. Woodman moved to amend the same by striking out before "school inspector," the word "one," and inserting "two."

But the committee refused to strike out.

Mr. Gale moved to amend by inserting after "school inspector," the words "two highway commissioners, and one overseer of the poor."

But the amendment was not agreed to.

Mr. Gale moved to amend by striking out "four," where it occurred relative to justices of the peace, and inserting "one."

Mr. Cornell moved to amend by inserting "three."

A division was had, and,

The motion to strike out was lost.

Mr. Cornell moved to strike out "not exceeding four constables."

But the amendment did not prevail.

Mr. Woodman moved to amend by inserting after "township clerk," the words "who shall be ex-officio school inspector."

And the same prevailed by yeas and nays, as follows:

YEAS.

Mr. Arzeno,	Mr. Eaton,	Mr. E. S. Robinson,	
Bagg,	Gardiner,	Rix Robinson,	
Barnard,	Hart,	Soule,	
H. Bartow,	Kingsley,	Wait,	
Beeson,	McClelland,	Webster,	
Britain,	Mosher,	Whipple,	
Carr,	Mowry,	Whittemore,	
Church,	Newberry,	Williams,	
Comstock,	N. Pierce,	Woodman,	
Cornell,	Prevost,	President,	
Daniels,	Roberts,		32

NAYS.

Mr. W. Adams,	Mr. Conner,	Hascall,	
Anderson,	Crouse,	Leach,	
Axford,	Danforth,	Robertson,	
Ammon Brown,	Fralick,	Skinner,	
Asahel Brown,	Gale,	Sturgis,	
Bush,	Gibson,	Town,	
Chandler,	Green,	Walker,	
Choate,	Hanscom,	Warden,	
J. Clark,	Harvey,		26

Mr. Fralick offered the following as a substitute for the one reported by the committee:

"All city, town and village officers, whose election or appointment is not provided for by this constitution, shall be elected by the electors of such cities, towns, and villages, and of some division thereof, or appointed by such authorities thereof as the Legislature shall designate for that purpose. All other officers whose election or appointment is not provided for by this constitution, and all officers whose offices may hereafter be created by law, shall be elected by the people, or appointed, as the Legislature may direct."

Which was not agreed to.

Mr. Newberry moved to amend the substitute reported by the committee by inserting after "school inspector,," the words "one highway commissioner."

Which was lost.

Mr. Cornell moved to amend by striking out "four," where it occurs relative to justices of the peace, and insert "two."

But the Convention refused to strike out.

Mr. Gale moved to strike out "one township treasurer."

Which was not agreed to.

The substitute proposed by the committee was then concurred in.

The second amendment made in committee, being a new section to the article, was also concurred in.

The third amendment being under consideration,

Mr. Britain moved to amend the same by inserting in the additional section proposed, after the word "left," as follows: "shall consist of one or more full United States surveyed townships, and."

And the amendment was agreed to.

Mr. Arzeno moved to add to the section proposed by the committee as follows:

"Provided, That no township in any county that shall have been organized for the term of twenty years previous to the adoption of this constitution, shall be divided without the consent of a majority of the votes thereof, expressed in a manner to be provided by law."

On motion of Mr. Cornell,

"Twenty" was stricken out and "twelve" inserted.

And the amendment as amended was agreed to.

The question being upon concurring in the section as amended, the yeas and nays were had thereon, with the following result:

YEAS.

Mr. W. Adams,	Mr. Chandler,	Mr. McClelland,
Anderson,	Choate,	Newberry,
Arzeno,	Conner,	Robertson,

Bagg,	Eaton,	Town,
Beeson,	Gardiner,	Whipple,
Britain,	Green,	Williams,
Asahel Brown,	Hascall,	Woodman,
Butterfield,		22

NAYS.

Mr. P. R. Adams,	Mr. Gale,	Mr. Prevost,
Alvord,	Gibson,	E. S. Robinson,
Barnard,	Hanscom,	Rix Robinson,
H. Bartow,	Hart,	Skinner,
Beardsley,	Harvey,	Soule,
Ammon Brown,	Lee,	Storey,
Bush,	Lovell,	Sturgis,
Carr,	Morrison,	Wait,
Church,	Mosher,	Walker,
Comstock,	Mowry,	Warden,
Crouse,	Orr,	Webster,
Daniels,	J. D Pierce,	Whittemore,
Fralick,	N. Pierce,	President, 39

So the section reported by the committee, as amended, was non-concurred in.

The article was then ordered to a third reading.

On motion of Mr. Hart,

Four members were directed to be added to the committee on the schedule.

On motion of Mr. Britain,

The communication of Mr. J. Coates, tendering his resignation, was taken from the table.

Mr. Britain moved that Mr. Coates have leave to withdraw his communication.

And leave was granted.

On motion of Mr. Crouse,

The Convention adjourned.

Afternoon Session.

Two o'clock.

The President called the Convention to order.

A quorum of members being in attendance,

Mr. Walker from the committee on education, reported back the Article entitled "Education," amended according to instructions.

Mr. Crouse moved to amend the article, by striking from the 10th section, all after "improvement," in the 2d line, to and inclusive of the word "farm," in the 8th line.

The amendment was negatived by yeas and nays, as follows:

YEAS:

Mr. Arzeno,	Mr. Choate,	Mr. Lee,
Axford,	Crouse,	Rix Robinson,
Bagg,	Eaton,	Skinner,
Barnard,	Fralick,	Sturgis,
Ammon Brown,	Gardiner,	Town,
Asahel Brown,	Gibson,	Warden, 18

NAYS:

Mr. P. R. Adams,	Mr. Green,	Mr. Prevost,
W. Adams,	Hart,	Robertson,
Alvord,	Harvey,	E. S. Robinson,
Anderson,	Hascall,	Soule,
H. Bartow,	Leach,	Storey,
Beardsley,	Lovell,	VanValkenburg,
Beeson,	McClelland,	Wait,
Britain,	McLeod,	Walker,
Butterfield,	Morrison,	Webster,
Carr,	Mosher,	Whipple,
Church,	Mowry,	Whittemore,
Comstock,	Newberry,	Williams,
Conner,	Orr,	Woodman,
Cornell,	J. D. Pierce,	President,
Danforth,	N. Pierce,	44

Mr. Eaton moved the previous question.

And the same being demanded,

The main question was ordered to be now put.

The question being upon ordering the article to a third reading,

The yeas and nays were had with the following result:

YEAS.

Mr. P. R. Adams,	Mr. Harvey,	Mr. Rix Robinson,
Butterfield,	Hascall,	Soule,
Carr,	McClelland,	Storey,
Chandler,	Morrison,	Sturgis,
Church,	Mosher,	Town,
Comstock,	Mowry,	Van Valkenburg,
Conner,	Newberry,	Whipple,
Eaton,	Orr,	Whittemore,
Fralick,	E. S. Robinson,	Williams,
Green,		28

NAYS.

Mr. W. Adams,	Mr. Asahel Brown,	Mr. McLeod,
Alvord,	Choate,	J. D. Pierce,
Anderson,	Cornell,	N. Pierce,
Arzeno,	Crouse,	Prevost,
Axford,	Gale,	Skinner,
Bagg,	Gardiner,	Wait,
Barnard,	Gibson,	Walker,
H. Bartow,	Hart,	Warden,
Beardsley,	Kingsley,	Webster,
Britain,	Leach,	Woodman,
Ammon Brown,	Lovell,	President, 33

So the article was not ordered to a third reading.

Mr. J. D. Pierce moved to reconsider the last vote, and moved to lay the motion upon the table.

Which was lost; and

The motion to reconsider then prevailed.

On motion of Mr. J. D. Pierce,

The article was laid upon the table.

The President presented a petition of I. Follensbee and fifteen others, relative to a provision making it the duty of the Legislature to endeavor to obtain from the United States a cession of certain public lands.

Referred to the committee on miscellaneous provisions.

On motion of Mr. Morrison,

The Convention resolved itself into committee of the whole on the resolution offered by Mr. Moore, relative to the appointment of a board of commissioners to revise the rules &c. of the Courts of Record in this State, &c.,

Mr. McClelland in the chair.

PROCEEDINGS IN COMMITTEE.

On motion of Mr. Robertson,

All after "resolved" was stricken out.

On motion of Mr. Walker,

The committee rose and reported the resolution back as amended.

The committee reported the resolution back, recommending that all after the resolving clause be stricken out.

On motion of Mr. Whipple,

The resolution was laid upon the table.

On motion of Mr. Leach,

Resolved, That the committee on supplies be instructed to report to the Convention to-morrow the amount and kind of stationery purchased for the use of the Convention, and the price paid for the same.

The Chair announced the following additional members to the committee on the schedule: Messrs. McClelland, Whipple, Williams and Whittemore.

Mr. Beardsley moved to reconsider the vote by which the Convention refused to order to a third reading the resolutions reported by the select committee on the license laws.

Mr. Bagg moved a call of the House.

But the call was not sustained.

The motion to reconsider was lost, by yeas and nays, as follows:

YEAS.

Mr. P. R. Adams,	Mr. Fralick,	Mr. E. S. Roberson,
Alvord,	Gardiner,	Rix Robinson,
Beardsley,	Gibson,	Skinner,
Beeson,	Green,	Sturgis,
Britain,	Hart,	Town,
Ammon Brown,	Hascall,	Wait,
Burns,	Kingsley,	Walker,
Butterfield,	J. D. Pierce,	Warden,
Church,	N. Pierce,	Webster,
Comstock,	Robertson,	Whipple,
Cornell,		

31

NAYS.

Mr. W. Adams,	Mr. Danforth,	Mr. Mosher,
Anderson,	Daniels,	Mowry,
Arzeno,	Eaton,	Newberry,
Axford,	Gale,	Orr,
Bagg,	Hanscom,	Prevost,
Barnard,	Harvey,	Soule,
H. Bartow,	Leach,	Storey,
Bush,	Lee,	Van Valkenburg,
Carr,	Lovell,	Whittemore,
Chandler,	McClelland,	Williams,
Choate,	McLeod,	Woodman,
J. Clark,	Morrison,	President.
Conner,		

37

47

Mr. Woodman offered the following:

Resolved, That the messengers of this Convention be allowed one and a half dollars per diem, for their services during the sitting of this Convention.

Mr. Fralick asked the yeas and nays.

And the same being ordered,

The resolution prevailed as follows:

YEAS.

Mr. W. Adams,	Mr. Comstock,	Mr. McLeod,
Alvord,	Conner,	Mowry,
Arzeno,	Cornell,	Orr,
Bagg,	Danforth,	J. D. Pierce,
Barnard,	Eaton,	Prevost,
H. Bartow,	Gale,	Robertson,
Beardsley,	Gardiner,	E. S. Robinson,
Beeson,	Gibson,	Rix Robinson,
Ammon Brown,	Hanscom,	Skinner,
Burns,	Hart,	Soule,
Bush,	Harvey,	Sturgis,
Butterfield,	Hascall,	Whipple,
Carr,	Leach,	Whittemore,
Choate,	Lee,	Williams,
Church,	Lovell,	Woodman,
J. Clark,	McClelland,	President, 48

NAYS.

Mr. P. R. Adams,	Mr. Fralick,	Mr. Town,
Anderson,	Green,	Van Valkenburg,
Axford,	Newberry,	Wait,
Daniels,	N. Pierce,	11

Mr. McClelland moved to adjourn.

But the Convention refused to adjourn.

On motion of Mr. Cornell,

Resolved, That the Sergeant-at-arms be required to procure a quantity of unslaked lime, or chloride of lime, to be used in and about the representative hall, and the out-buildings connected therewith.

Mr. McLeod moved to adjourn.

But the Convention refused to adjourn.

Mr. Alvord offered the following:

Resolved, That the committee on arrangement and phraseology be instructed to strike out from section five of the article on the Legislative Department, all after the word "district," in line three.

Mr. McClelland raised a point of order: "that a resolution, without going through the forms prescribed by the rules, directing a committee to substantially change any article passed by the Convention, cannot be entertained."

The Chair decided the resolution out of order.

On motion of Mr. J. D. Pierce,

The article entitled "Education" was taken from the table and recommitted to the committee on education.

Mr. Church, from the committee on miscellaneous provisions, reported back sundry resolutions, from which they asked to be and were discharged.

Also a petition referred to that committee, praying for the incorporation of a provision in the constitution prohibiting ministers of the Gospel from holding any office of honor or profit in the State; reporting adverse to the prayer of the petitioners.

The report was accepted and the committee discharged.

Mr. Church, from the same committee, reported Article —, "Miscellaneous provisions."

Which was read the first and second time, by its title, referred to the committee of the whole, and ordered printed.

Mr. J. Clark offered the following, which was laid upon the table:

Resolved, That the committee on arrangement and phraseology report to this Convention any and all changes made by them, in the articles when reported by them to the convention.

On motion of Mr. Church,

Resolved, That the committee on the government and judicial policy of the Upper Peninsula, &c., and the committee upon the mode of revising the constitution, be and the same are hereby instructed to report forthwith to this Convention, upon the subjects severally and specially committed to them.

On motion of Mr. Danforth,

The Convention adjourned.

Lansing, Wednesday, August 7, 1850.

The Convention met pursuant to adjournment and was called to order by the President.

Prayer by the Rev. Mr. Sanford.

Absent on leave, Messrs. Backus, Alvarado Brown, S. Clark, Cook, Crary, Desnoyers, Dimond, Edmunds, Graham, Hathaway, Hixon, Kinne, Marvin, Mason, Moore, O'Brien, Raynale, Redfield, M. Robinson, Sullivan, Sutherland, Tiffany, Wells, White, Willard and Witherell.

LEAVE OF ABSENCE.

Mr. Hanscom asked and obtained indefinite leave of absence for Mr. Woodman,

Mr. Cornell for Mr. E. S. Robinson, and

Mr. Church for Mr. Eastman.

PETITIONS.

By Mr. Beeson: of George Goodman, W. H. McComber and 147 others, praying the incorporation by the Convention of a clause in the constitution prohibiting the collection of all debts of a less amount than one hundred dollars, if contracted after the adoption of the constitution. Referred to the committee on the legislative department.

REPORTS.

Mr. Hanscom submitted the following:

Pursuant to the instructions of the Convention, the committee on supplies and expenditures respectfully report: That they have purchased the amount and kind of stationery specifically stated and set forth in the bills now in the hands of the Secretary of the Convention, numbered from one to five inclusive, and made a part of this report; that bills, for some small amounts purchased in this village, have not as yet been presented and filed; that one considerable item of expense incurred consisted of purchases of appropriate materials to carry out the resolution of the Convention upon the melancholy announcement of the death of General Taylor, late President of the United States. The committee respectfully refer the Convention to the proceedings of the 5th and 19th of June.

On the last named day the chairman of your committee proposed to the Convention the following resolutions, in obedience to the wishes of the committee:

"*Resolved*, That from and after this day the post master of this village be not authorized to charge to the Convention or State any postage on any mailable matter, sent or mailed by members or officers of the Convention, and that the Secretary notify the post master accordingly.

"*Resolved*, That from and after this date there be printed for the use of the Convention but 240 copies of the journal."

The passage of the resolutions had the effect to reduce the daily current and incidental expenses of the Convention to an amount varying from thirty-five to fifty dollars.

The committee also suggest, that by reason of the system of reporting, adopted by order of the Convention, an increased quantity of stationery has been necessarily required; and that for the purpose of making that branch of duties as effectually performed as practicable, and at the urgent request of the reporters, your committee purchased twelve reporter's pens, with gold points, at a cost of one dollar each. One-half have been already placed in the hands of the reporters and secretaries of the Convention. The balance, in conjunction with a large amount of the stationery purchased—ink, sand, wax, wafers, envelopes, &c. &c.—will be on hand and unused, and by the Secretary of this Convention, delivered over to the Secretary of State for the use of the State.

A comparison of the current and incidental expenses of this Convention (aside from pay of members) with former Constitutional Conventions or Legislative bodies in this State, number of members and officers and length of session considered, show, as your committee believe, a reduction of nearly two-thirds, and a consequent saving of the amount of several thousands of dollars to the tax-payers of the State.

Mr. Walker, from the committee on education, reported back the article entitled "Education" with the following amendments thereto:

1. Strike out section 3 and substitute therefor: "The legislature shall, within five years from the adoption of this constitution, provide for and establish a system of common schools. Such schools shall be kept without charge for tuition, for at least three months in each year, in every school district in the State."

2. Also insert in section 5, at the end of line 3: "with the privilege of speaking but not of voting."

3. Also strike out in section 10, line 3, the words, "with a model

farm in connection therewith;" and in lines 6 and 8 the words, "and farm."

Mr. Britain moved to lay the report on the table.

But the motion was lost.

The question being on concurring in the substitute reported by the committee for section 3,

Mr. Alvord moved to amend the same by striking out the words "within five years."

Which was lost by yeas and nays, as follows:

YEAS:

Mr. Alvord,	Mr. Cornell,	Mr. Robertson,	
Beardsley,	Fralick,	Webster,	6

NAYS:

Mr. P. R. Adams,	Mr. J. Clark,	Mr. Mosher,
W. Adams,	Comstock,	Mowry,
Anderson,	Conner,	Newberry,
Arzeno,	Crouse,	Orr,
Axford,	Daniels,	N. Pierce,
Bagg,	Eaton,	Prevost,
Barnard,	Gale,	Rix Robinson,
H. Bartow,	Gardiner,	Skinner,
J. Bartow,	Gibson,	Soule,
Beeson,	Green,	Storey,
Britain,	Hanscom,	Sturgis,
Ammon Brown,	Hart,	Town,
Asahel Brown,	Hascall,	Van Valkenburg,
Burns,	Kingsley,	Wait,
Bush,	Leach,	Walker,
Butterfield,	Leo,	Warden,
Carr,	Lovell,	Whipple,
Chandler,	McClelland,	Whittemore,
Chapel,	McLeod,	Williams,
Choate,	Morrison,	President,
Church,		61

Mr. Britain moved to add to the substitute, "and all instruction in said schools shall be conducted in the English language."

Which was accepted by the chairman on the part of the committee on education, and the addition was so made.

Mr. Fralick offered the following substitute for the one proposed by the committee, which was not agreed to:

"The Legislature shall provide for a system of primary schools, by which a school shall be kept and supported in each school district, at least three months in every year; and any school district neglecting to keep and support such school, may be deprived of its equal proportion of the interest of the public fund. And the Legislature may provide for levying a tax on the taxable property of the several townships and cities of this State, for the support of said schools."

Mr. Beardsley moved to amend the proposition of the committee, by striking out "for at least three months in each year."

But the Convention refused to strike out; and,

The substitute reported by the committee for section 3 was then concurred in.

Thd second amendment was also concurred in.

The third amendment was also concurred in, by yeas and nays as follows:

YEAS.

Mr. Arzeno,	Mr. Gale,	Mr. Prevost,
Axford,	Gardiner,	Robertson,
Bagg,	Gibson,	Rix Robinson,
Barnard,	Hanscom,	Skinner,
H. Bartow,	Hart,	Storey,
J. Bartow,	Kingsley,	Sturgis,
Ammon Brown,	Lee,	Town,
Asahel Brown,	Lovell,	Van Valkenburg,
Burns,	Morrison,	Wait,
Butterfield,	Mosher,	Walker,
Choate,	Mowry,	Warden,
J. Clark,	Newberry,	Whipple,
Crouse,	Orr,	Williams,
Eaton,	J. D. Pierce,	41

NAYS.

Mr. P. R. Adams,	Mr. Chapel,	Mr. Hascall,
W. Adams,	Church,	Leach,
Alvord,	Comstock,	McClelland,
Anderson,	Conner,	Mc Leod,
Beardsley,	Cornell,	N. Pierce,
Beeson,	Danforth,	Soule,
Britain,	Daniels,	Webster,
Bush,	Fralick,	Whittemore,
Carr,	Green,	President,
Chandler,	Harvey,	29

Mr. Bagg offered the following substitute for section 4:

"There shall be elected at the first general election for judges in this State after the ratification of this constitution, twelve regents of the University: four for the term of six years, four for the term of four years, and four for two years; and at each subsequent election for judges, there shall be four regents of the University elected, who shall hold their office for the term of six years."

Mr. McClelland moved to amend so as to make the professors of the University elective by the people.

On the suggestion of Mr. Church, Mr. Bagg modified his substitute so as to read:

"There shall be elected in each judicial circuit, at the time of the election of the judge of said circuit, a regent of the University, whose term of office shall be the same as that of said judge; and the regents then elected shall constitute the board of regents of the University of Michigan."

When Mr. McClelland withdrew his amendment.

Mr. Storey moved the previous question.

And the same being demanded,

And the main question being ordered to be now put,

The substitute proposed by Mr. Bagg, for section 4 of the article, was agreed to by yeas and nays, as follows:

YEAS.

Mr. P. R. Adams,	Mr. Church,	Mr. Lee,
Bagg,	Comstock,	Lovell,
Barnard,	Conner,	Mosher,
H. Bartow,	Cornell,	Mowry,
J. Bartow,	Crouse,	Orr,
Beardsley,	Daniels,	N. Pierce,
Beeson,	Eaton,	Prevost,
Britain,	Fralick,	Rix Robinson,
Ammon Brown,	Gale,	Soule,
Asahel Brown,	Gardiner,	Wait,
Burns,	Gibson,	Walker,
Bush,	Green,	Warden,
Carr,	Hart,	Webster,
Chandler,	Harvey,	Whittemore,
Chapel,	Leach,	44

NAYS.

Mr. W. Adams,	Mr. Hanscom,	Mr. Skinner,
Alvord,	Hascall,	Story,
Anderson,	Kingsley,	Sturgis,
Arzeno,	McClelland,	Town,
Axford,	McLeod,	Van Valkenburg,
Butterfield,	Morrison,	Whipple,
Choate,	Newberry,	Williams,
J. Clark,	J. D. Pierce,	President,
Danforth,	Robertson,	26

The article was then ordered to a third reading.

RESOLUTIONS.

Mr. Town offered the following; which,

On motion of Mr. Arzeno,

Was indefinitely postponed.

Resolved, That the members and officers of this Convention be required to pay postage on all mailable matter received by them hereafter.

On motion of Mr. Gardiner,

Resolved, That Mr. Martin Mahon be appointed a reporter of this Convention, from and after the 1st instant.

THIRD READING OF ARTICLES.

The article entitled "Township Officers and Government," was read a third time, when

Mr. Fralick moved to indefinitely postpone the same.

Which was not agreed to, by yeas and nays, as follows:

YEAS:

Mr. W. Adams,	Mr. Bush,	Mr. Lee,	
Arzeno,	Crouse,	Mosher,	
Barnard,	Daniels,	Prevost,	
Beardsley,	Fralick,	Rix Robinson,	
Britain,	Gale,	Skinner,	
Ammon Brown,	Gibson,	Town,	
Asahel Brown,	Hanscom,	President,	
Burns,	Hart,		23

NAYS:

Mr. P. R. Adams,	Mr. Cornell,	Mr. J. D. Pierce,	
Alvord,	Danforth,	N. Pierce,	
Anderson,	Eaton,	Robertson,	
Axford,	Gardiner.	Soule,	
Bagg,	Green,	Storey,	
H. Bartow,	Harvey,	Sturgis,	
J. Bartow,	Hascall,	Van Valkenburg,	
Beeson,	Kingsley,	Wait,	
Butterfield,	Leach,	Walker,	
Carr,	Lovell,	Warden,	
Chandler,	McClelland,	Webster,	
Chapel,	Morrison,	Whipple,	
Choate,	Mowry,	Whittemore,	
Church,	Newberry,	Williams,	
Conner,	Orr,		44

And on the question, shall the article now pass?

The yeas and nays were had, with the following result:

YEAS.

Mr. P. R. Adams,	Mr. Cornell,	Mr. Orr,
Anderson,	Danforth,	J. D. Pierce,
Axford,	Daniels,	N. Pierce,
Bagg,	Eaton,	Robertson,
H. Bartow,	Gardiner,	Soule,
J. Bartow,	Harvey,	Storey,
Butterfield,	Hascall,	Sturgis,
Carr,	Kingsley,	Van Valkenburg,
Chandler,	Leach,	Wait,
Chapel,	Lovell,	Walker,
Choate,	McClelland,	Warden,
Church,	Morrison,	Webster,
Comstock,	Mowry,	Whittemore,
Conner,	Newberry,	Williams, 42

NAYS.

W. Adams,	Mr. Burns,	Mr. Hart,
Alvord,	Bush,	Lee,
Arzeno,	J. Clark,	Mosher,
Barnard,	Crouse,	Prevost,
Beardsley,	Fralick,	Rix Robinson,
Beeson,	Gale,	Skinner,
Britain,	Gibson,	Town,
Ammon Brown,	Green,	Whipple,
Asahel Brown,	Hanscom,	President, 27

So the article was passed, and under the rule, referred to the committee on arrangement and phraseology.

The article entitled "Education" was read a third time by its title,

And on the question, shall the article pass?

The yeas and nays were had, as follows:

YEAS.

Mr. P. R. Adams,	Mr. Comstock,	Mr. Mowry,
W. Adams,	Conner,	Orr,
Alvord,	Cornell,	J. D. Pierce,
Arzeno,	Crouse,	N. Pierce,
Axford,	Daniels,	Prevost,
Bagg,	Eaton,	Robertson,
Barnard,	Fralick,	Rix Robinson,
H. Bartow,	Gardiner,	Soule,
Beeson,	Gibson,	Storey,
Britain,	Hanscom,	Sturgis,
Ammon Brown,	Hart,	Town,
Burns,	Harvey,	Van Valkenburg,
Butterfield,	Hascall,	Wait,
Carr,	Kingsley,	Walker,

Chandler,	Lovell,	Warden,
Chapel,	McClelland,	Whittemore,
Choate,	Morrison,	Williams,
Church,	Mosher.	53

NAYS.

Mr. Asahel Brown,	Mr. Gale,	Mr. Skinner,
Bush,	Green,	Webster,
J. Clark,	Lee,	Whipple,
Danforth,	Newberry,	President, 12

So the article was passed, and under the rule, referred to the committee on arrangement and phraseology.

On motion of Mr. McClelland,

The committee of the whole were discharged from the consideration of the articles entitled "Judicial Department;" and

The one reported by the committee on the judiciary, through Mr. Church, and numbered 28, was taken up for consideration.

Section 1 having been read,

On motion of Mr. McClelland,

The words "inferior local," were stricken therefrom, and "municipal" inserted.

Section 2 being under consideration,

Mr. Britain moved to strike therefrom, in line 5, the word "separate," and all after "constitution," in the same line.

Which was rejected by yeas and nays, as follows:

YEAS.

Mr. W. Adams,	Mr. Chapel,	Mr. Lovell,
Barnard,	J. Clark,	Morrison,
H. Bartow,	Danforth,	Mosher,
J. Bartow,	Eaton,	Rix Robinson,
Beardsley,	Gardiner,	Skinner,
Britain,	Green,	Sturgis,
Ammon Brown,	Hanscom,	Town,
Asahel Brown,	Harvey,	Wait,
Burns,	Kingsley,	Walker,
Bush,	Lee,	Whipple, 30

NAYS.

Mr. P. R. Adams,	Mr. Cornell,	Mr. Orr,
Alvord,	Crouse,	J. D. Pierce,
Arzeno,	Daniels,	N. Pierce,
Axford,	Fralick,	Robertson,
Bagg,	Gale,	Soule,
Butterfield,	Gibson,	Storey,

Carr,	Hart,	Van Valkenburg,
Chandler,	Hascall,	Warden,
Choate,	McClelland,	Whittemre,
Church,	Mowry,	Williams,
Comstock,	Newberry,	President,
Conner,		34

By consent of the Convention, the word "two," in the 6th line, was stricken out, and "three" inserted.

"Also, the word "final," was inserted before "decision," in the third line; and all after "be," in the 9th line, was stricken out, and "eight years" inserted.

On motion of Mr. Kingsley,

The section was amended by inserting after "necessary," in the 4th line, the words "after six years."

Mr. Britain moved to strike out all after "constitution," in the 5th line, to and inclusive of the word "State," in the 6th line, and insert in lieu thereof, "to be elected in such manner as the Legislature shall prescribe."

Which was not agreed to.

Mr. Robertson moved to strike out the section, (2,) and substitute the following in lieu thereof:

"The supreme court shall consist of three judges, two of whom shall form a quorum; and the concurrence of two shall be necessary to every decision. And the Legislature shall have power, after the year 1855, to provide by law for the election of an additional judge of said supreme court; and also to provide that the concurrence of three of said judges shall be necessary to every final decision. And the Legislature may also provide that each of the judges of the supreme court shall be authorized and required to hold one term of the circuit courts in each and every year in any of the counties of the State, in which more than two terms of such circuit shall be annually held. The final decisions of the judges shall be in writing, and signed by those concurring; and a judge dissenting from a decision, shall give the reasons for such dissent in writing, under his signature."

Mr. McClelland moved a call of the Convention; and the same being ordered, there were absent without leave Messrs. Barnard, J. Clark, Crouse, Lee, McLeod and Mosher.

On motion of Mr. Bagg,

The Sergeant-at-Arms was dispatched to secure the attendance of Messrs. Barnard, Crouse, Lee, McLeod and Mosher.

The absentees soon thereafter appearing,

On motion of Mr. Hanscom,

All further proceedings under the call were dispensed with.

The motion to strike out sec. 2, and substitute as proposed by Mr. Robertson, was lost, by yeas and nays, as follows:

YEAS:

Mr. Alvord,	Mr. Fralick,	Mr. Orr,
Axford,	Gibson,	Roberts,
Bagg,	Hanscom,	Robertson,
Carr,	Hart,	Rix Robinson,
Chandler,	Harvey,	Sturgis,
Chapel,	Lee,	Van Valkenburg,
Church,	Lovell,	Walker,
Comstock,	McLeod,	Webster,
Crouse,	Morrison,	Whittemore,
Daniels,	Mowry,	Williams,
Eaton,	Newberry,	President, 33

NAYS:

Mr. P. R. Adams,	Mr. Bush,	Mr. McClelland,
W. Adams,	Butterfield,	Mosher,
Anderson,	Choate,	J. D. Pierce,
Arzeno,	Conner,	N. Pierce,
Barnard,	Cornell,	Prevost,
H. Bartow,	Danforth,	Skinner,
Beardsley,	Gale,	Soule,
Beeson,	Gardiner,	Storey,
Britain,	Green,	Town,
Ammon Brown,	Hascall,	Wait,
Asahel Brown,	Kingsley,	Warden,
Burns,	Leach,	Whipple, 36

Sec. 4 having been read,

On motion of Mr. Church,

It was amended by striking out "said circuit judges," and inserting the word "law."

Sec. 5 being under consideration,

On motion of Mr. Robertson,

It was amended by striking out, in the 1st line, the words "shall have power," and inserting in lieu therof, "it shall be the duty of."

Mr, Whittemore moved further to amend the same by adding thereto as follows:

"And testimony in cases in equity shall be taken in like manner as in cases at law; and the office of master in chancery is hereby prohibited."

Pending which, on motion of Mr. Van Valkenburgh,

The Convention adjourned.

Afternoon Session.

Two o'clock.

The Convention was called to order by the President,

And a quorum being present,

Resumed the consideration of the article entitled "Judicial Department."

The question being upon the amendment of Mr. Whittemore to section 5, the same was agreed to, by yeas and nays, as follows:

YEAS.

Mr. Alvord,	Mr. Conner,	Mr. Morrison,
Arzeno,	Cornell,	Mowry,
Axford,	Fralick,	Newberry,
Barnard,	Gale,	Orr,
Beardsley,	Gardiner,	Skinner,
Britain,	Gibson,	Soule,
Burns,	Green,	Town,
Chandler,	Hanscom,	Van Valkenburg
Chapel,	Hart,	Walker,
Choate,	Harvey,	Warden,
Church,	Hascall,	Webster,
J. Clark,	Leach,	Whittemore,
Comstock,	McClelland,	38

NAYS.

Mr. P. R. Adams,	Mr. Carr,	Mr. Prevost,
W. Adams,	Crouse,	Robertson,
Anderson,	Danforth,	Rix Robinson,
Bagg,	Eaton,	Sturges,
H. Bartow,	Kingsley,	Wait,
J. Bartow,	Lee,	Whipple,
Beeson,	Lovell,	Williams,
Asahel Brown,	Mosher,	President,
Butterfield,		25

Mr. Gale moved to amend the same section by inserting after "circuit courts," "but in no case shall they deprive any citizen of the privilege of practicing in said courts."

Upon this the yeas and nays were ordered.

And the amendment was agreed to, by yeas and nays, as follows:

YEAS:

Mr. P. R. Adams,	Mr. Cornell,	Mr. Mowry,
Alvord,	Crouse,	Newberry,
Arzeno,	Eaton,	Orr,
Axford,	Gale,	N. Pierce,
Bagg,	Gardiner,	Prevost,
Barnard,	Gibson,	Robertson,
H. Bartow,	Green,	Soule,
Beardsley,	Hanscom,	Sturgis,
Britain,	Hart,	Town,
Asahel Brown,	Harvey,	Wait,
Burns,	Hascall,	Walker,
Bush,	Leach,	Warden,
Carr,	Lee,	Webster,
Chandler,	Lovell,	Whittemore,
Chapel,	Morrison,	Williams,
Comstock,	Mosher,	47

NAYS:

Mr. W. Adams,	Mr. Church,	Mr. Rix Robinson,
Anderson,	J. Clark,	Skinner,
J. Bartow,	Conner,	Storey,
Beeson,	Danforth,	Van Valkenburg,
Ammon Brown,	Fralick,	Whipple,
Butterfield,	Kingsley,	President,
Choate,	McClelland,	20

Mr. Whittemore moved further to amend by adding to the section as follows:

"And the legislature shall, as far as practicable, abolish all distinction between law and equity proceedings."

Mr. Robertson moved to strike out "as far as practicable," which was lost by yeas and nays, as follows:

YEAS.

Mr. Bagg,	Mr. Leach,	Mr. Robertson,
H. Bartow,	Lee,	Rix Robinson,
Chapel,	Morrison,	Skinner,
J. Clark,	Orr,	Soule,
Fralick,	J. D. Pierce,	Waite,
Gale,	N. Pierce,	Walker,
Hanscom,	Prevost,	Whipple, 21

NAYS.

Mr. P. R. Adams,	Mr. Chandler,	Mr. Kingsley,
W. Adams,	Choate,	Lovell,
Alvord,	Church,	McClelland,
Anderson,	Comstock,	Mosher,

Arzeno,	Conner,	Mowry,
Axford,	Cornell,	Newberry,
Barnard,	Crouse,	Storey,
Beardsley,	Danforth,	Sturgis,
Beeson,	Eaton,	Town,
Britain,	Gardiner,	Van Valkenburg,
Ammon Brown,	Gibson,	Warden,
Asahel Brown,	Green,	Webster,
Burns,	Hart,	Whittemore,
Bush,	Harvey,	Williams,
Butterfield,	Hascall,	President,
Carr,		46

Mr. Whittemore's amendment was then agreed to.

Section 6 having been read,

Mr. Church moved to amend section 6, by striking out the words "reside after the election," and insert the words "be elected by the qualified electors thereof and."

And the same prevailed.

Mr. Church moved to amend section 7 by striking out the words "of this State," in line 3 of said section, and by inserting the words "of said circuit."

And the same was agreed to.

Section 8 being under consideration,

Mr. Robertson moved to strike out, in the 2d line, the words "and not prohibited by law."

But the amendment was lost.

Mr. Robertson moved to amend section 9 by striking out of lines 2 and 3, the words "and shall hold no other office of trust or profit during the term for which they are elected," and insert, "and shall be ineligible to any other than a judicial office, during the term for which they are elected, and for one year thereafter."

Mr. Van Valkenburgh moved to amend the amendment, by striking out, "and for one year thereafter."

Which was lost by the yeas and nays as follows:

YEAS.

Mr. P. R. Adams,	Mr. Carr,	Mr. N. Pierce,
W. Adams,	Church,	Storey,
Anderson,	Cornell,	Town,
Arzeno,	Crouse,	Van Valkenburg,
Barnard,	Gale,	Warden,
H. Bartow,	Lovell,	Whipple,

Beardsley, Beeson, Bush, Butterfield, McClelland, Mowry, J. D. Pierce, Whittemore, Williams, President, 28

NAYS.

Mr. Alvord, Axford, Bagg, Britain, Asahel Brown, Burns, Chandler, Chapel, Choate, J. Clark, Comstock, Conner, Danforth, Mr. Daniels, Eaton, Fralick, Gardiner, Gibson, Green, Hanscom, Hart, Harvey, Hascall, Kingsley, Morrison, Mr. Mosher, Newberry, Orr, Prevost, Robertson, Rix Robinson, Skinner, Soule, Sturgis, Wait, Walker, Webster, 37

The amendment offered by Mr. Robertson was then agreed to.

Mr Church moved to amend section 10 by inserting after the word "decision," in 1st line, as follows: "The decisions made by the Supreme Court shall be in writing, and signed by the judges concurring therein; and any judge dissenting therefrom shall give the reasons of such dissent in writing under his signature, and said opinions shall be filed in the office of the clerk of said Supreme Court."

And the same was agreed to.

Mr. Bagg moved to amend section 11 by inserting after "purposes," in the 2d line, "and in counties containing 20,000 inhabitants, a circuit court shall be held four times in each year."

Mr. J. Clark moved to strike out "20,000," and insert in its stead "10,000."

And the amendment to the amendment prevailed by the following vote:

YEAS.

Mr. P. R. Adams, W. Adams, Alvord, Axford, Bagg, Barnard, Beardsley, Beeson, Britain, Mr. Church, J. Clark, Conner, Crouse, Danforth, Eaton, Fralick, Gale, Gardiner, Mr. Mosher, Mowry, Newberry, Robertson, Rix Robinson, Skinner, Soule, Storey, Town,

Ammon Brown,	Gibson,	Van Valkenburg,
Asahel Brown,	Hanscom,	Walker,
Burns,	Hart,	Warden,
Bush,	Kingsley,	Whittemore,
Carr,	Lee,	Williams,
Chandler,	Lovell,	President,
Chapel,	Morrison,	47

NAYS.

Mr. Anderson,	Mr. Comstock,	Mr. J. D. Pierce,
Arzeno,	Green,	N. Pierce,
H. Bartow,	Harvey,	Sturgis,
Butterfield,	Hascall,	Wait.
Choate,	McClelland,	Webster, 15

Mr. Bagg's amendment was then agreed to.

Section 16 being under consideration,

Mr. McClelland moved to strike it out and substitute the following:

"Sec. 16. The legislature may provide by law for the election of one or more persons in each organized county, who may be vested with such judicial power as the legislature may prescribe, not exceeding those of a judge of the circuit court at chambers."

A division of the question was had.

And the motion to strike out the section was first put and carried.

On motion of Mr. Bagg,

The proposition of Mr. McClelland was amended by adding thereto, "in counties having a population of less than ten thousand inhabitants, by the last preceding enumeration provided for in this constitution, these powers may be devolved upon the judge of probate."

The substitute for section 16 as amended, was then adopted.

Mr. J. D. Pierce moved to amend section 17, by striking out "four," in the 1st line, and inserting "two."

Mr. Skinner offered the following as a substitute for the section:

"There shall be two justices of the peace in each organized township. They shall be elected by the qualified electors of the township, and shall hold their offices for four years, and until their successors are elected and qualified. They shall have such criminal and civil jurisdiction, and perform such duties as may be prescribed by law. At the first election in any township, they shall be classified by law in such manner, that one justice shall be elected biennially in each township thereafter. The Legislature may increase the number of justices in cities and in townships having over in habitants."

Mr. J. D. Pierce withdrew his amendment.

On motion of Mr. Eaton,

The section was amended by inserting between "be" and "from," in the first line, the words "not exceeding."

The question recurring on the substitute offered by Mr. Skinner, it was rejected.

On motion of Mr. McClelland,

The words "and probate," were stricken out of the 1st line of section 19, and the words,

"And for the election of judges of probate courts on the first Monday of April 1853," were inserted after "1851," in the 2d line.

On motion of Mr. McClelland,

Sec. 19 was further amended by striking therefrom, in line 1, the words "judges of the supreme court."

On motion of Mr. Britain,

All after "and" in the 2d line, to and inclusive of the word "court" in the third line, was stricken out.

On motion of Mr. Walker,

The words "an election shall be held" were inserted after "thereafter," in the 3d line.

Mr. Gale moved to amend the section by striking out in line 4, the word "fourth," and inserting in its stead, "second."

But the amendment was not agreed to.

The article having been gone through with, by sections, and being open for general amendment,

Mr. J. Clark offered the following to stand as section 21:

"Any male citizen of the age of twenty-one years, of good moral character, and who possesses the requisite qualifications of learning and ability, shall be entitled to admission to practice in all the courts of this state."

Mr. Robertson moved to strike out "male citizen," and insert "person."

Which the mover accepted.

And the proposition as modified was rejected.

Mr. Williams moved the following as an additional section to the article.

"The legislature shall have power to establish courts of conciliation, with powers and duties prescribed by law."

And the same was agreed to by yeas and nays as follows:

YEAS.

Mr. W. Adams,	Mr. J. Clark,	Mr. McClelland,
Alvord,	Comstock,	Morrison,
Anderson,	Conner,	J. D. Pierce,
Arzeno,	Cornell,	N. Pierce,
Bagg,	Crouse,	Prevost,
Barnard,	Daniels,	Robertson,
H. Bartow,	Eaton,	Rix Robinson,
Beardsley,	Fralick,	Soule,
Beeson,	Gale,	Storey,
Britain,	Gardiner,	Sturgis,
Ammon Brown,	Gibson,	Town,
Asahel Brown,	Green,	Wait,
Burns,	Hanscom,	Walker,
Bush,	Hart,	Warden,
Butterfield,	Harvey,	Webster,
Chandler,	Hascall,	Whipple,
Chapel,	Kingsley,	Whittemore,
Choate,	Leach,	Williams,
Church,	Lee,	President,
Lovell,		58

NAYS.

Mr. P. R. Adams,	Mr. Mowry,	Mr. VanValkenburg,
Danforth,	Newberry,	5

Mr. Church offered the following substitute for section 20:

"Whenever a judge shall remove beyond the limits of the circuit for which he was elected, and whenever a justice of the peace shall remove from the township in which he was elected, or who, by a change in the boundaries of said township, shall be placed without he same, shall be deemed to have vacated their respective offices."

Mr. Alvord moved to adjourn.

But the Convention refused to adjourn.

The substitute proposed by Mr. Church was agreed to.

On motion of Mr. McClelland,

The vote was reconsidered, by which an amendment was made to section 19, fixing the time for the election of judges of probate in April, 1853.

The amendment was then withdrawn, and the following was inserted in its stead:

"And the election of judges of probate, on the Tuesday succeeding the first Monday of November, 1852."

On motion of Mr. Gale,

The vote adopting the amendment proposed by him to section 5, was reconsidered.

The amendment was then withdrawn, and

Mr. Gale offered the following as an additional section to the article.

"Every person of the age of 21 years, of good moral character, shall have the right to practice in any court in this State."

And the same was adopted.

On motion of Mr. Rix Robinson,

Section 5 of the article was amended as follows:

Insert in 2d line after the words "circuit courts," "and simplify the same so far as practicable."

On motion of Mr. J. Clark,

The Convention then adjourned.

Lansing, Thursday, August 8, 1850.

The Convention met at the usual hour and was called to order by the President.

Prayer by the Rev. Mr. Tooker.

The roll being called, there were absent on leave, Messrs. Backus, Alvarado Brown, S. Clark, Cook, Crary, Desnoyer, Dimond, Eastman, Edmunds, Graham, Hathaway, Hixson, Marvin, Mason, Moore, O'Brien, Raynale, Redfield, E. S. Robinson, M. Robinson, Sullivan, Sutherland, Tiffany, Wells, White, Willard, Witherell and Woodman.

Without leave, Mr. Orr.

LEAVE OF ABSENCE.

Mr. Carr asked and obtained indefinite leave of absence for Mr Orr.

On motion of Mr, Gale,

The bills alluded to in the report of the committee of supplies, in the journal of yesterday, were ordered attached thereto.

PETITIONS.

By Mr. Church: Of Geo. Coggeshall and 37 others, citizens of Kent county, praying for the insertion in the constitution of a provision directing the legislature to procure a cession from the United States of the unsold public lands within the state, &c., &c.

Laid upon the table.

Also of Edward C. Sergeant and 174 others, citizens of Kent county, praying for the establishment of an independent supreme court, &c.

Laid upon the table.

REPORTS.

Mr. Roberts from the committee on the government and judicial policy of the Upper Peninsula, submitted an article entitled "Of Upper Peninsula," accompanied by a written report.

The report was laid upon the table and ordered printed; and

The article was read the first and second time by its title, referred to the committee of the whole and ordered printed.

The convention having reached the order of

UNFINISHED BUSINESS,

Took up the article entitled "Judicial Department."

Mr. Skinner proposed to amend section 1, as follows:

Insert in the first line after the words "probate court," the following: "As many district justice courts in each organized county, as the supervisors thereof shall, in pursuance of law, establish judicial districts therein, not exceeding the number of representative districts."

Mr. Beardsley moved to amend the foregoing by adding thereto "and justice's courts are hereby abolished," which was not agreed to

The amendment of Mr. Skinner was then agreed to by yeas and nays as follows.

YEAS.

Mr. Alvord,
Axford,
Bagg,
Barnard,
Burns,

Mr. Daniels,
Eaton,
Fralick,
Gale,
Gardiner,

Mr. Mowry,
N. Pierce,
Prevost,
Rix Robinson,
Skinner,

Carr,	Green,	Sturgis,
Chandler,	Hanscom,	Town,
Chapel,	Hart,	Wait,
Choate,	Leach,	Webster,
Church,	Lovell,	Whittemore,
Cornell,	Morrison,	Williams,
Crouse,	Mosher,	35.

NAYS.

Mr. P. R. Adams,	Mr. Asahel Brown,	Mr. Newberry,
W. Adams,	Bush,	J. D. Pierce,
Anderson,	Butterfield,	Robertson,
Arzeno,	Comstock,	Soule,
H. Bartow,	Conner,	Storey,
J. Bartow,	Gibson,	Van Valkenburg,
Beardsley,	Harvey,	Walker,
Beeson,	Kingsley,	Warden,
Britain,	Lee,	President,
Ammon Brown,	McClelland,	30.

Mr. Hanscom offered the following as a substitute for the entire article.

Section 1. The judicial power is vested in one supreme court, in circuit courts, in probate courts, and in justices of the peace. Municipal courts of civil and criminal jurisdiction may be established by the legislature in cities

Sec. 2. The supreme court shall consist of three judges, two of whom shall form a quorum, and the concurrence of two shall be necessary to every decision. And the legislature shall have power, after the year 1855, to provide by law for the election of an additional judge of said supreme court; and also to provide that the concurrence of three of said judges shall be necessary to every final decision. And the legislature may also provide that each of the judges of the supreme court shall be authorized andrequired to hold one term of the circuit courts in each and every year in any of the counties of this state in which more than two terms of such circuit shall be annually held. The final decisions of the judges shall be in writing and signed by those concurring, and a judge dissenting from a decision shall give the reasons for such dissent, in writing, under his signature.

Sec. 3. The judges of the supreme court shall be elected by the qualified electors, and shall hold their offices until their successors are elected and qualified.

Sec. 4. Of the judges of the supreme court first elected, one shall hold his office for two years, one for four years and one for six years, to be determined by lot at the first session of the court after their election. Thereafter the judge elected to fill the office shall hold the same for the term of six years. The judge having the shortest time to serve shall be chief justice.

Sec. 5. The supreme court shall have a general superintending control over all inferior courts, and shall have power to issue writs of error, habeas corpus, mandamus, injunction, quo warranto, certiorari, and other original and remedial writs, and to hear and determine the same. In all other cases it shall have appellate jurisdiction only.

Sec. 6. The supreme court shall hold at least one term annually in each judicial circuit, at such time and place as may be designated by said court; and the legislature may provide for the holding of two terms in each or either of the said circuits in each and every year.

Sec. 7. The supreme court shall have power, by general rules, to establish, modify, amend and simplify the practice in said court and in the circuit courts.

Sec. 8. The state shall be divided into five judicial circuits; in each of which one circuit judge shall be elected by the qualified electors thereof, who shall hold his office for the term of six years and until his successor is elected and qualified.

Sec. 9. The Legislature may alter the limits of circuits or increase the number of the same; but no increase thereof shall be made except at the session of the legislature first held after the apportionment of senators and representatives provided for in this constitution. No alteration or increase shall have the effect to remove a judge from office. In every additional circuit established, the judge shall be elected, and his term of office shall continue as provided in this constitution for the judges of the circuit court.

Sec. 10. The circuit courts shall have original jurisdiction in all matters civil and criminal not excepted in this constitution, and not prohibited by law, and appellate jurisdiction from all inferior courts and tribunals, and a supervisory control of the same.

They shall also have power to issue writs of habeas corpus, mandamus, injunction, quo warranto, certiorari and other writs necessary to carry into effect their orders, judgments and decrees, and give them a general control over inferior courts and tribunals within their respective jurisdictions.

Sec. 11. Each of the judges of the supreme and circuit courts shall receive a salary, payable quarterly. They shall receive no fees or perquisites of office, or other compensation; and shall hold no other office of trust or profit during the term for which they are elected. All votes for either of them, for any office other than a judicial one, given either by the legislature or the people, shall be void.

Sec. 12. The judges of the supreme court may appoint a reporter of their decisions. The judges of the circuit courts within their respective jurisdiction, may fill vacancies in the office of county clerk, and of prosecuting attorney. But no judge of the supreme court or of a circuit court shall exercise any other power of appointment to public office.

Sec. 13. A circuit court shall be held at least twice in each year, in every county organized for judicial purposes. In counties having a population of 10,000 inhabitants, by the last preceding enumeration provided for in this Constitution, there shall be held not less than three terms of such court in each year, unless otherwise provided by law. Judges of the circuit court may hold courts for each other, and shall do so when required by law.

Sec. 14. The clerk of each county organized for judicial purposes shall be the clerk of the circuit court of such county, and of the supreme court when held within the same.

Sec. 15. Appeals and writs of error may be taken from the circuit court of any county, to the supreme court held in the circuit which includes such county, or with the consent of parties in the cause, to the supreme court held in any other circuit.

Sec. 16. In each of the counties organized for judicial purposes, there shall be a court of probate. The judge of such court shall be elected by the qualified electors of the county in which he resides, and shall hold his office for four years, and until his successor is elected and qualified. The jurisdiction, powers and duties of such court shall be prescribed by law. And in counties having a population of less than 10,000 inhabitants, the legislature may authorize and require the circuit courts to perform the duties of such probate courts.

Sec. 17. When a vacancy occurs in the office of judge of the supreme court, circuit court or probate court, such vacancy shall be filled by appointment of the governor, which shall continue until a successor is elected and qualified; and when elected, such successor shall hold his office the residue of the unexpired term.

Sec. 18. The supreme court, the circuit and probate courts of each county, shall be courts of record, and shall each have a common seal.

Sec. 19. The legislature may provide by law for the election of one or more persons in each organized county, who may be vested with judicial powers, not exceeding those of a judge of the circuit court at chambers. In counties having a population of less than twenty thousand inhabitants, by the last preceding enumeration provided for in this constitution, these powers may be devolved upon the judge of probate.

Sec. 20. The Legislature shall provide for the speedy publication of all statute laws of a public nature, and of such judicial decisions as it may deem expedient. All laws and judicial decisions shall be free for publication by any person.

Sec. 21. There shall be such number of justices of the peace in each organized township, not exceeding four, as may be prescribed by law. They shall be elected by the qualified electors of the township, and shall hold their offices for four years, and until their successors are elected and qualified. They shall have such criminal and civil jurisdiction, and perform such duties, as may be prescribed by law. At their first election in any township, they shall be classified by law in such manner that only 1 justice shall be elected annually in each township thereafter. The legislature may increase the number of justices in cities.

Sec. 22. Judges of the supreme court, circuit judges and justices of the peace shall be conservators of the peace within their respective jurisdictions.

Sec. 23. The first election of judges of the supreme court and judges of the circuit courts, shall be held on the first Monday in April 1851, and for the election of judges of probate courts on the first Monday of April 1853, and every two years thereafter, an election shall be held for one judge of the supreme court, and every sixth year thereafter, for judges of the circuit courts, and every fourth year thereafter, for judges of probate in such counties as by law are required to elect such judge of probate. Whenever an additional circuit is created, such provisions may be made as to hold the subsequent election of such additional judge at the regular elections herein provided.

Sec. 24. The removal of a judge beyond the limits of the jurisdiction for which he was elected, or of a justice of the peace beyond the limits of the township in which he was elected, shall vacate his office.

Sec. 25. The style of all process shall be: "In the name of the people of the State of Michigan." All indictments shall conclude: "against the peace of the people of the State of Michigan."

Mr. Williams moved the following as an additional section to the substitute:

"The Legislature shall have power to establish courts of conciliation, with powers and duties prescribed by law."

And the same was accepted by the mover.

Mr. Gale moved the following additional section to the substitute:

"Every person of the age of twenty-one years, of good moral character, shall have the right to practice in any court in this State."

Mr. McClelland moved the previous question on the article.

And the same being demanded, and the question being, shall the main question be now put?

The yeas and nays were ordered thereon, when,

On motion of Mr. Alvord,

A call of the Convention was ordered, and Messrs. McLeod and Roberts were absent without leave; when the Sergeant-at-Arms was dispatched to procure the attendance of the absentees.

Mr. Chapel moved the Convention adjourn.

But the Convention refused to adjourn by yeas and nays as follows:

YEAS:

Mr. Axford,	Mr. Hanscom,	Mr. Roberts,
Bagg,	Hart,	Robertson,
Chapel,	Lee,	Whipple,
Eaton,		10

NAYS.

Mr. P. R. Adams,	Mr. Comstock,	Mr. Mosher,
W. Adams,	Conner,	Mowry,
Alvord,	Cornell,	Newberry,
Anderson,	Crouse,	J. D. Pierce,
Arzeno,	Danforth,	N. Pierce,
Barnard,	Daniels,	Prevost,
H. Bartow,	Fralick,	Rix Robinson,
J. Bartow,	Gale,	Skinner,
Beeson,	Gardiner,	Soule,
Britain,	Gibson,	Storey,
Ammon Brown,	Green,	Sturgis,
Asahel Brown,	Harvey,	Town,
Burns,	Hascall,	VanValkenburg,
Bush,	Kingsley,	Wait,
Butterfield,	Kinne,	Warden,
Carr,	Leach,	Webster,
Chandler,	Lovell,	Whittemore,
Choate,	McClelland,	Williams,
Church,	Morrison,	President,
J. Clark,		58

The President announced the appearance of Mr. Roberts within the bar, and the confinement of Mr. McLeod to his room on account of indisposition.

On motion of Mr. Danforth,

All further proceedings under the call were dispensed with.

The question being "shall the main question be now put?" it was so ordered by yeas and nays as follows:

YEAS.

Mr. P. R. Adams,	Mr. Chandler,	Mr. Kinne,
W. Adams,	Choate,	Leach,
Anderson,	Comstock,	McClelland,
Arzeno,	Conner,	Mosher,
H. Bartow,	Cornell,	J. D. Pierce,
J. Bartow,	Danforth,	N. Pierce,
Beeson,	Daniels,	Prevost,
Britain,	Gale,	Skinner,
Ammon Brown,	Gardiner,	Soule,
Asahel Brown,	Green,	Storey,
Bush,	Harvey,	Town,
Butterfield,	Hascall,	Wait,
Carr,	Kingsley,	Whipple, 39

NAYS.

Mr. Alvord,	Mr. Eaton,	Mr. Roberts,
Axford,	Fralick,	Robertson,
Bagg,	Gibson,	Rix Robinson,
Barnard,	Hanscom,	Sturgis,
Beardsley,	Hart,	Van Valkenburgh,
Burns,	Lee,	Walker,
Chapel,	Lovell,	Warden,
Church,	Morrison,	Whittemore,
J. Clark,	Mowry,	Williams,
Crouse,	Newberry,	President, 30

The additional section proposed to the substitute by Mr. Gale was then agreed to.

The question now being on the adoption of the substitute proposed by Mr. Hanscom for the entire article,

The same was rejected by yeas and nays as follows:

YEAS:

Mr. Alvord,	Mr. Daniels,	Mr. Roberts,
Axford,	Fralick,	Robertson,
Bagg,	Gibson,	Rix Robinson,
Carr,	Hanscom,	Sturgis,
Chandler,	Hart,	VanValkenburg,
Chapel,	Harvey,	Walker,
Church,	Lee,	Whittemore,
J. Clark,	Morrison,	Williams,
Comstock,	Mowry,	President,
Crouse,	Newberry,	29

NAYS:

Mr. P. R. Adams,	Mr. Butterfield,	Mr. McClelland,
W. Adams,	Choate,	Mosher,
Anderson,	Conner,	J. D. Pierce,
Arzeno,	Cornell,	N. Pierce,
Barnard,	Danforth,	Prevost,
H. Bartow,	Eaton,	Skinner,
J. Bartow,	Gale,	Soule,
Beardsley,	Gardiner,	Storey,
Beeson,	Green,	Town,
Britain,	Hascall,	Wait,
Ammon Brown,	Kingsley,	Warden,
Asahel Brown,	Kinne,	Webster,
Burns,	Leach,	Whipple,
Bush,	Lovell,	41

Upon ordering the article to a third reading, the yeas and nays were had, and the result was as follows:

YEAS.

Mr. P. R. Adams,	Mr. Carr,	Mr. Mosher,
W. Adams,	Choate,	J. D. Pierce,
Anderson,	Conner,	N. Pierce,
Arzeno,	Cornell,	Prevost,
Barnard,	Danforth,	Robertson,
H. Bartow,	Daniels,	Skinner,
J. Bartow,	Eaton,	Soule,
Beardsley,	Gale,	Storey,
Beeson,	Gardiner,	Town,
Britain,	Green,	Van Valkenburgh,
Ammon Brown,	Hascall,	Wait,
Asahel Brown,	Kingsley,	Warden,
Burns,	Kinne,	Webster,
Bush,	Leach,	Whipple,
Butterfield,	McClelland,	44

NAYS.

Mr. Alvord,	Mr. Fralick,	Mr. Mowry,
Axford,	Gibson,	Newberry,
Bagg,	Hanscom,	Roberts,
Chandler,	Hart,	Sturgis,
Chapel,	Harvey,	Walker,
Church,	Lee,	Whittemore,
J. Clark,	Lovell,	Williams,
Comstock,	Morrison,	President,
Crouse,		25

So the article entitled "judicial department," was ordered to a third reading.

On motion of Mr. Leach,

The convention was resolved into committee of the whole on the general order,

Mr. Danforth in the chair.

PROCEEDINGS IN COMMITTEE.

The committee took up for consideration the article Miscellaneous Provisions.

Sections 1 and 2 were read.

Mr. N. Pierce moved to add to section 2, "provided, that the lands of any person shall not be flowed or used without the consent of the owner thereof."

Which amendment did not prevail.

On motion of Mr. Britain,

The following was added to section 2: "but no person shall be permitted by flowing to injure any other improved water power."

On motion of Mr. Robertson,

The words "and damages done" were added to line 2, and "damages" was inserted in 3d line, after the word "value."

On motion of Mr. Cornell,

The word "erecting" was stricken out of line 4, and "maintaining" inserted.

Mr. Cornell moved to strike out "unimproved" in line 1.

Which did not prevail.

Mr. Gale moved to insert after "paid," in line 4, the words "or tendered;" which was withdrawn.

Mr. Newberry moved to strike out section 2.

But the committee refused to strike out.

On motion of Mr. Daniels, section 4 was stricken out.

Mr. Britain offered the following as a substitute for section 5:

"No navigable stream in this state, shall be either bridged or dammed without authority from the board of supervisors of the proper county, under the provisions of existing laws. No such law shall prejudice the right of individuals to the free navigation of such streams, or preclude the state from the further improvement of the navigation of such stream."

Mr. J. D. Pierce moved to add thereto "except as shall be prescribed by law," which was subsequently withdrawn.

On motion of Mr. Hanscom the committee rose, reported progress and asked leave to sit again.

The committee through their chairman, reported the same back to the convention and asked leave to sit again.

Leave was granted, and

On motion of Mr. Alvord,

The convention adjourned.

Afternoon Session.

Two o'clock.

The Convention was called to order by the President, and a quorum of members being present, was resolved into a committee of the whole and resumed the consideration of the Article entitled "Miscellaneous Provisions,"

Mr. Danforth in the chair.

PROCEEDINGS IN COMMITTEE.

The committee resumed the consideration of Mr. Britain's substitute for section 5.

On motion of Mr. Soule,

The word "supreme" was stricken out of section 5, line 4, and "circuit" inserted.

Mr. Britain's substitue was then adopted.

On motion of Mr. Fralick,

The committee rose, reported the article back with the amendments, asked the concurrence of the Convention therein, and to be discharged from its further consideration.

—

The committee, through their chairman, reported the Article back with amendments in which the concurrence of the Convention was asked.

The first, second and third amendments made in committee were concurred in.

The 4th amendment (an addition to section two) being under consideration,

Mr. Morrison moved to amend the same by striking out the word "improved."

After some debate, the proposition was withdrawn, and Mr. Morrison offered the following as a substitute for the amendment made in committee:

"This provision shall not apply to cases where by flowing lands any other water power shall be injured."

And the same was agreed to, by yeas and nays as follows:

YEAS.

Mr.	P. R. Adams,	Mr.	Gibson,	Mr.	Prevost,
	Arzeno,		Green,		Rix Robinson,
	Axford,		Hanscom,		Skinner,
	Barnard,		Hart,		Soule,
	Beeson,		Kingsley,		Storey,
	Ammon Brown,		Lovell,		Wait,
	Bush,		McClelland,		Walker,
	Cornell,		Morrison,		Warden,
	Crouse,		Mosher,		Webster,
	Daniels,		Newberry,		Whittemore,
	Eaton,		J. D. Pierce,		President,
	Fralick,		N. Pierce,		35

NAYS:

Mr. W. Adams,
Alvord,
Anderson,
H. Bartow,
Beardsley,
Britain,
Asahel Brown,
Burns,
Butterfield,
Mr. Carr,
Chandler,
Choate,
Church,
Comstock,
Conner,
Danforth,
Harvey,
Mr. Hascall,
Leach,
Mowry,
Robertson,
Sturgis,
Town,
Van Valkenburgh,
Williams,

25.

The fourth amendment was then concurred in.

The 5th amendment, striking out section 4 of the article, being under consideratron,

Mr. N. Pierce moved to amend the same by inserting as section 4 the following:

"Sec. 4. The legislature of this state shall have the power of erecting a state prison, or removing the present prison, with the convicts therein, to the mineral country in the upper peninsula of this state near Lake Superior, for the purpose of working the mines and minerals in that district of the state."

Mr. Daniels moved the previous question.

But the call was not sustained.

The question first being upon concurrence in striking out the section (4.)

The same was non-concurred in by yeas and nays as follows:

YEAS.

Mr. Axford,
Barnard,
H. Bartow,
Beardsley,
Asahel Brown,
Bush,
Carr,
Chandler,
Daniels,
Mr. Gale,
Green,
Hart,
Harvey,
Hascall,
Kinne,
Leach,
Lovell,
Mr. Newberry,
N. Pierce,
Prevost,
Sturgis,
Town,
Wait,
Warden,
Whittemore,

25

NAYS.

Mr. P. R. Adams,
W. Adams,
Alvord,
Anderson,
Arzeno,
Beeson,
Britain,
Mr. Conner,
Cornell,
Crouse,
Danforth,
Eaton,
Fralick,
Gibson,
Mr. Mowry,
Robertson,
Rix Robinson,
Skinner,
Soule,
Storey,
Van Valkenburgh,

Ammon Brown,	Hanscom,	Walker,
Burns,	Kingsley,	Webster,
Butterfield,	McClelland,	Williams,
Choate,	Morrison,	President,
Church,	Mosher,	35

The substitute for section 5, reported by the committee, being under consideration,

On motion of Mr. McClelland,

The original section was amended by striking out "supreme" and inserting "circuit."

Upon concurring with the proposition of the committee,

A division of the question was had, and the vote upon striking out the section stood as follows:

YEAS:

Mr. P. R. Adams,	Mr. Burns,	Mr. Mowry,
W. Adams,	Chandler,	Newberry,
Alvord,	Choate,	Robertson,
Arzeno,	Conner,	Rix Robinson,
Axford,	Eaton,	Skinner,
Barnard,	Fralick,	Storey,
H. Bartow,	Gibson,	Sturgis,
Beardsley,	Green,	Town,
Beeson,	Hascall,	Walker,
Britain,	Kinne,	Warden,
Ammon Brown,	Lovell,	Webster,
Asahel Brown,	Mosher,	President, 36

NAYS.

Mr. Anderson,	Mr. Hanscom,	Mr. Prevost,
Carr,	Hart,	Soule,
Church,	Harvey,	Van Valkenburgh,
Comstock,	McClelland,	Wait,
Crouse,	Morrison,	Whittemore,
Danforth,	J. D. Pierce,	Williams,
Daniels,	N. Pierce,	20

So the Convention concurred in striking out.

The question being upon concurring in the substitute, the same was concurred in by yeas and nays as follows:

YEAS:

Mr. P. R. Adams,	Mr. Choate,	Mr. Newberry,
W. Adams,	Conner,	Robertson,
Arzeno,	Green,	Rix Robinson,
Axford,	Hart,	Soule,
H. Bartow,	Hascall,	Storey,
Beardsley,	Kinne,	Town,

Britain, Asahel Brown, Burns, Chandler, McClelland, Morrison, Mosher, Mowry, Walker, Webster, Whittemore, 29

NAYS:

Mr. Alvord, Anderson, Barnard, Ammon Brown, Carr, Church, Comstock, Crouse, Danforth, Mr. Daniels, Eaton, Fralick, Gibson, Hanscom, Harvey, Kingsley, Lovell, J. D. Pierce, Mr. N. Pierce, Prevost, Skinner, Sturgis, Van Valkenburg, Wait, Warden, Williams, President, 27

Mr. Robertson moved to adjourn.

But the Convention refused to adjourn.

The Article "Miscellaneous Provisions," being open for general amendment,

Mr. Fralick moved to strike out section two.

Mr. Hart moved to adjourn.

When, by consent, Mr. McClelland moved to reconsider the resolution adopted relative to the adjournment.

And the motion was laid upon the table.

Mr. McClelland moved to reconsider the vote by which the resolution was adopted limiting the time of speaking to five minutes.

And the motion was laid upon the table.

When the Convention adjourned.

Lansing, Friday, August 9, 1850.

The Convention was called to order by the President.

Prayer by the Rev. Mr. Sanford.

The roll being called, there were absent on leave, Messrs Backus, Alvarado Brown, S. Clark, Cook, Crary, Desnoyer, Dimond, Eastman, Edmunds, Graham, Hathaway, Hixon, Marvin, Mason, Moore, O'Brien, Orr, Raynale, Redfield, E. S. Robinson, M. Robinson, Sullivan, Sutherland, Tiffany, Wells, Willard, Witherell and Woodman.

REMONSTRANCE.

By the President: of the Mayor, Recorder and Aldermen of the city of Detroit, against the incorporation of a provision in the constitution, prohibiting the Legislature from giving to any city or village, the power of granting licenses for the sale of spirituous liquors, &c.

Referred to the committee on the legislative department.

MOTIONS AND RESOLUTIONS.

Mr. J. D. Pierce moved to recommit the article entitled "Judicial Department," (No. 28,) to a committee of one, with the following instructions:

Strike out of section 1, the following words: "As many district justices' courts in each organized county, as the supervisors thereof shall, in pursuance of law, establish judicial districts therein, not exceeding the number of representative districts."

Amend section 17, by striking out in line 3, these words: "They shall have such criminal and civil jurisdiction," and insert as follows: "They shall have civil jurisdiction to the amount of three hundred dollars; and concurrent jurisdiction to the amount of five hundred dollars, and such criminal jurisdiction."

Mr. Church moved to lay the motion and article upon the table.

Which was not agreed to, by yeas and nays, as follows:

YEAS.

Mr. Alvord,	Mr. Lee,	Mr. Town,
Axford,	McLeod,	Wait,
Carr,	Morrison,	Walker,
Church,	Newberry,	Webster,
Fralick,	Robertson,	Whittemore,
Gibson,	Rix Robinson,	Williams,
Hanscom,	Storey,	President,
Hart,		22

NAYS.

Mr. P. R. Adams,	Mr. Butterfield,	Mr. Kingsley,
W. Adams,	Chandler,	Kinne,
Anderson,	Chapel,	Leach,
Arzeno,	Choate,	Lovell,
Bagg,	Comstock,	McClelland,
Barnard,	Conner,	Mosher,
H. Bartow,	Cornell,	Mowry,
J. Bartow,	Crouse,	J. D. Pierce,
Beardsley,	Danforth,	N. Pierce,
Beeson,	Daniels,	Prevost,
Britain,	Eaton,	Skinner,
Ammon Brown,	Gardiner,	Soule,
Asahel Brown,	Green,	Van Valkenburg,
Burns,	Harvey,	Whipple,
Bush,	Hascall,	44

Upon Mr. Pierce's proposition a division of the question was had,

And the motion to recommit prevailed by yeas and nays, as follows:

YEAS:

Mr. P. R. Adams,	Mr. Butterfield,	Mr. McClelland,
W. Adams,	Chandler,	Morrison,
Anderson,	Comstock,	Mosher,
Arzeno,	Conner,	J. D. Pierce,
Bagg,	Cornell,	N. Pierce,
Barnard,	Danforth,	Prevost,
H. Bartow,	Daniels,	Soule,
J. Bartow,	Eaton,	Storey,
Beardsley,	Gardiner,	Sturgis,
Beeson,	Green,	Van Valkenburg,
Britain,	Hascall,	Walker,
Ammon Brown,	Kingsley.	Warden,
Asahel Brown,	Kinne,	White,
Burns,	Leach,	Whipple,
Bush,		43

NAYS:

Mr. Alvord,	Mr. Hart,	Mr. Rix Robinson,
Axford,	Harvey,	Skinner,
Carr,	Lee,	Town,
Choate,	Lovell,	Wait,
Church,	McLeod,	Webster,
Crouse,	Mowry,	Whittemore,
Fralick,	Newberry,	Williams,
Gibson,	Robertson,	President,
Hanscom,		25

The instructions proposed being under consideration,

Mr. Walker moved to amend the same by adding as follows:

Strike out section 4 and insert in lieu thereof, "the supreme court shall hold at least one term annually in each judicial circuit, at such time and place as may be designated by said court; and the legislature may provide for the holding of two terms in each or either of the said circuits in each and every year."

Mr. Church moved to amend the amendment as follows:

Strike out section 2 and insert therefor one which shall contain the following provisions:

"1. The supreme court shall consist of four judges, two of whom shall be elected by the qualified electors of the State and hold office six years. The other two judges of said court shall be the two circuit judges having the shortest term of service.

"2. There shall be six circuit court judges elected by the qualified electors of each circuit, to hold office for six years; such judges to be classified so that two of them will be elected biennially.

"3. At the first election, under this constitution, there shall be elected four supreme court judges, two of whom shall hold office only two years."

Mr. Chandler moved the previous question.

And the same being demanded, and the main question ordered to be now put,

The amendment offered by Mr. Church to the one proposed by Mr. Walker, was lost by yeas and nays, as follows:

YEAS.

Mr. Alvord,	Mr. Fralick,	Mr. Roberts,
Axford,	Gibson,	Robertson,
Bagg,	Hanscom,	Rix Robinson,
Burns,	Hart,	Sturgis,
Carr,	Harvey,	Van Valkenburg,
Chandler,	Lee,	Walker,
Chapel,	McLeod,	Webster,
Church,	Morrison,	Whittemore,
J. Clark,	Mowry,	Williams,
Comstock,	Newberry,	President,
Crouse,		31

NAYS.

Mr. P. R. Adams,	Mr. Choate,	Mr. McClelland,
W. Adams,	Conner,	Mosher,
Anderson,	Cornell,	J. D. Pierce,
Arzeno,	Danforth,	N. Pierce,
Barnard,	Daniels,	Prevost,
H. Bartow,	Eaton,	Skinner,
J. Bartow,	Gale,	Soule,
Beardsley,	Gardiner,	Storey,
Beeson,	Green,	Town,
Britain,	Hascall,	Wait,
Ammon Brown,	Kingsley,	Warden,
Asahel Brown,	Kinne,	White,
Bush,	Leach,	Whipple,
Butterfield,	Lovell,	41

Mr. Walker's amendment was then rejected by the following vote:

YEAS.

Mr. Alvord,	Mr. Gibson,	Mr. Roberts,
Axford,	Hanscom,	Robertson,
Britain,	Hart,	Rix Robinson,

Bush, Carr, Chapel Church, J. Clark, Crouse, Fralick, Harvey, Lee, Lovell, McLeod, Morrison, Mowry, Newberry, Sturgis, Walker, Webster, Whittemore, Williams, President, 29

NAYS:

Mr. P. R. Adams, W. Adams, Anderson, Arzeno, Bagg, Barnard, H. Bartow, J. Bartow, Beardsley, Beeson, Ammon Brown, Asahel Brown, Burns, Butterfield, Chandler, Mr. Choate, Comstock, Conner, Cornell, Danforth, Daniels, Eaton, Gale, Gardiner, Green, Hascall, Kingsley, Kinne, Leach, Mr. McClelland, Mosher, J. D. Pierce, N. Pierce, Prevost, Skinner, Soule, Storey, Town, Van Valkenburg, Wait, Warden, White, Whipple, 43

And the question recurring on the proposition of Mr. J. D. Pierce,

A division of the question was had,

And the first branch of the instructions was agreed to, by yeas and nays, as follows:

YEAS.

Mr. P. R. Adams, W. Adams, Anderson, Arzeno, Bagg, Barnard, H. Bartow, J. Bartow, Beardsley, Beeson, Britain, Ammon Brown, Asahel Brown, Burns, Bush, Butterfield, Chandler, Mr. Choate, Comstock, Conner, Cornell, Danforth, Daniels, Eaton, Gale, Gibson, Green, Hascall, Kingley, Kinne, Lee, McClelland, Morrison, Mosher, Mr. Newberry, J. D. Pierce, N. Pierce, Prevost, Robertson, Soule, Storey, Sturgis, Town, Van Valkenburg, Walker, Warden, White, Whipple, Williams, President, 50

NAYS.

Mr. Alvord, Azford, Carr, Chapel, Church, J. Clark, Crouse, Fralick,
Mr. Gardiner, Hanscom, Hart, Harvey, Leach, Lovell, McLeod,
Mr. Mowry, Roberts, Rix Robinson, Skinner, Wait, Webster, Whittemore, 22

And the remainder of the proposed instructions were also agreed to, by the following vote:

YEAS.

Mr. P. R. Adams, W. Adams, Anderson, Arzeno, Axford, Barnard, H. Bartow, Beardsley, Britain, Ammon Brown, Asahel Brown, Burns, Bush, Butterfield, Chandler,
Mr. Choate, Comstock, Conner, Cornell, Crouse, Danforth, Daniels, Eaton, Fralick, Gale, Gardiner, Green, Hascall, Kingsley, Kinne,
Mr. Leach, Lee, McClelland, Morrison, Mosher, J. D. Pierce, N. Pierce, Prevost, Soule, Story, Town, Van Valkenburg, Webster, Whipple, 44

NAYS.

Mr. Alvord, Bagg, J. Bartow, Beeson, Carr, Chapel, Church, J. Clark, Gibson,
Mr. Hanscom, Hart, Harvey, Lovell, McLeod, Mowry, Newberry, Roberts, Robertson,
Mr. Rix Robinson, Sturgis, Wait, Walker, Warden, White, Whittemore, Williams, President, 27

And the President, under the resolution, referred the article to Mr. J. D. Pierce, who forthwith reported the same back to the Convention, amended agreeably to the same.

Mr. McClelland called up his motion to reconsider the vote by which the resolution limiting the time of speaking to five minutes was adopted.

And the question being upon reconsideration,

The yeas and nays were had, and the motion prevailed, as follows:

YEAS.

Mr. P. R. Adams,	Mr. Comstock,	Mr. Morrison,
W. Adams,	Conner,	Mosher,
Arzeno,	Cornell,	N. Pierce,
Bagg,	Crouse,	Roberts,
Barnard,	Danforth,	Robertson,
J. Bartow,	Daniels,	Storey,
Asahel Brown,	Gale,	Van Valkenburg,
Burns,	Green,	Wait,
Bush,	Kingsley.	Warden,
Chapel,	Kinne,	Webster,
Choate,	Leach,	White,
J. Clark,	McClelland,	President, 36

NAYS.

Mr. Alvord,	Mr. Eaton,	Mr. Mowry,
Anderson,	Fralick,	Newberry,
Axford,	Gardiner,	Prevost,
H. Bartow,	Gibson,	Rix Robinson,
Beardsley,	Hanscom,	Skinner,
Beeson,	Hart,	Soule,
Britain,	Harvey,	Town,
Ammon Brown,	Hascall,	Walker,
Carr,	Lee,	Whittemre,
Chandler,	Lovell,	Williams,
Church,	McLeod,	32

Mr. Roberts moved to indefinitely postpone the resolution.

But the motion did not prevail.

On motion of Mr. Eaton,

The resolution was amended by striking out "by leave of the convention or committee."

Mr. Van Valkenburgh moved to strike out "five" and insert "ten,"

A division of the question was had, and

The Convention refused to strike out.

The question being upon the adoption of the resolution as amended,

The same was agreed to by a two-thirds vote, as follows:

YEAS.

Mr. P. R. Adams,	Mr. Conner,	Mr. Lee,
W. Adams,	Cornell,	McClelland,
Alvord,	Crouse,	Mosher,
Anderson,	Danforth,	Mowry,
Arzeno,	Daniels,	Newberry,
Axford,	Eaton,	J. D. Pierce,
Beardsley,	Fralick,	N. Pierce,

Britain,	Gale,	Prevost,
Ammon Brown,	Gibson,	Rix Robinson,
Asahel Brown,	Green,	Skinner,
Bush,	Hanscom,	Soule,
Carr,	Hart,	Town,
Chandler,	Harvey,	Walker,
Chapel,	Hascall,	Webster
Choate,	Kingsley,	White,
Church,	Kinne,	Whipple,
Comstock,	Leach,	Williams, 51

NAYS.

Mr. J. Bartow,	Mr. Lovell,	Mr. Storey,
Beeson,	McLeod,	Van Valkenburg,
Burns,	Morrison,	Wait,
J. Clark,	Roberts,	Whittemore,
Gardiner,	Robertson,	President, 15

The President called Mr. Britain to the chair.

THIRD READING OF ARTICLES.

The article entitled "Judicial Department" was read a third time by its title.

On motion of Mr. Bagg,

A call of the house was ordered, and

Messrs. McLeod and Roberts were found absent without leave.

On motion of Mr. Hanccom,

All further proceedings under the call were dispensed with.

And the question being,

"Shall the article entitled 'Judicial Department' now pass?"

The yeas and nays were had, and the vote was as follows:

YEAS.

Mr. P. R. Adams,	Mr. Butterfield,	Mr. McClelland,
W. Adams,	Choate,	Mosher,
Anderson,	Conner,	J. D. Pierce,
Arzeno,	Cornell,	N. Pierce,
Barnard,	Danforth,	Prevost,
H. Bartow,	Daniels,	Skinner,
J. Bartow,	Eaton,	Soule,
Beardsley,	Gale,	Storey,
Beeson,	Gardiner,	Sturgis,
Britain,	Green,	Town,
Ammon Brown,	Hascall,	Wait,
Asahel Brown,	Kingsley,	Warden,
Burns,	Kinne,	Whipple,
Bush,		40

NAYS.

Mr. Alvord,	Mr. Fralick,	Mr. Newberry,
Axford,	Gibson,	Robertson,
Bagg,	Hanscom,	Rix Robinson,
Carr,	Hart,	Van Valkenburg,
Chandler,	Harvey,	Walker,
Chapel,	Lee,	Webster,
Church,	Lovell,	White,
J. Clark,	McLeod,	Whittemore,
Comstock,	Morrison,	Williams,
Crouse,	Mowry,	President, 30

So the article was passed, and under the rule, referred to the committee on arrangement and phraseology.

The President took the chair.

UNFINISHED BUSINESS.

The Convention resumed the consideratiou of the article entitled "Miscellaneous Provisions."

And the question being upon the motion of Mr. Fralick to strike out section 2,

After some discussion,

On motion of Mr. Arzeno,

The Convention adjourned.

Afternoon Session.

Two o'clock.

The Convention was called to order by the President,

A quorum being present,

The unfinished business of the morning was resumed.

The question being on striking out section 2 of the article entitled "Miscellaneous Provisions,"

Mr. Alvord moved the previous question.

And the same being demanded,

The main question was ordered to be now put.

And the motion to strike out prevailed by yeas and nays, as follows:

YEAS:

Mr. P. R. Adams,	Mr. Conner,	Mr. Mowry,
Alvord,	Cornell,	Newberry,
Anderson,	Crouse,	N. Pierce,
Arzeno,	Daniels,	Prevost,
Axford,	Eaton,	Roberts,

Bagg,	Fralick,	Rix Robinson,
Barnard,	Gale,	Skinner,
H. Bartow,	Gibson,	Soule,
J. Bartow,	Green,	Storey,
Beardsley,	Hanscom,	Sturgis,
Beeson,	Harvey,	Town,
Ammon Brown,	Kingsley,	Van Valkenburg,
Asahel Brown,	Kinne,	Wait,
Burns,	Leach,	Walker,
Carr,	Lee,	Warden,
Chandler,	Lovell,	Webster,
Choate,	McClelland,	Whittemore,
Church,	Mosher,	President, 54

NAYS:

Mr. W. Adams,	Mr. Danforth,	Mr. Morrison,
Britain,	Gardiner.	Robertson,
Butterfield,	Hart,	White,
Chapel,	Hascall,	Williams,
Comstock,		13

Mr. Walker offered the following, to stand in lieu of the section stricken out:

Sec. 2. The Legislature shall provide by law that lands may be flowed, or water diverted for milling and manufacturing purposes, when the public good will be promoted thereby, and shall provide the manner in which the damage to individuals shall be assessed and paid."

Mr. Alvord moved the previous question.

And the same being demanded,

The main question was ordered to be now put.

And the substitute was not agreed to.

Mr. Butterfield offered the following, to stand as an additional section to the article:

Sec. 8. The Legislature shall have power, after the year 1855, to combine or abolish any of the State offices provided for in this constitution.

Mr. Robertson moved to amend the foregoing by adding "or abolish any other provisions of this Constitution," and

He moved the previous question, and

The same being demanded

And the main question ordered to be put.

The amendment proposed by Mr. Robertson was not agreed to.

The proposition of Mr. Butterfield was then rejected.

Mr. Whittemore moved to strike out section 6 of the article.

Upon which Mr. Morrison moved the previous question.

And the same was demanded, and

The main question ordered to be now put.

The motion to strike out was agreed to by yeas and nays as follows:

YEAS:

Mr. P. R. Adams,	Mr. Carr,	Mr. Lee,
W. Adams,	Chandler,	Lovell,
Arzeno,	Choate,	Morrison,
Axford,	Comstock,	Mowry,
Bagg,	Conner,	Newberry,
Barnard,	Cornell,	N. Pierce,
H. Bartow,	Daniels,	Prevost,
J. Bartow,	Fralick,	Roberts,
Beardsley,	Gale,	Town,
Beeson,	Gibson,	Van Valkenburg,
Britain,	Green,	Wait,
Ammon Brown,	Hascall,	Walker,
Asahel Brown,	Kingsley,	Warden,
Burns,	Leach,	Whittemore, 42

NAYS:

Mr. Alvord,	Mr. Gardiner,	Mr. Skinner,
Anderson,	Hanscom,	Soule,
Bush,	Hart,	Storey,
Butterfield,	Kinne,	Sturgis,
Chapel,	McClelland,	Webster,
Church,	Mosher,	White,
Crouse,	J. D. Pierce,	Williams,
Danforth,	Robertson,	President,
Eaton,	Rix Robinson,	26

Mr. Williams offered the following new section, to stand as section 5:

The waters of this State, navigable in fact, shall be common highways and for ever free to the inhabitants of this State and the United States.

Which was rejected by yeas and nays as follows:

YEAS:

Mr. P. R. Adams,	Mr. Church,	Mr. Robertson,
Arzeno,	Comstock,	Sturgis,
Bagg,	Daniels,	Town,
H. Bartow,	Gardiner,	Van Valkenburg,
J. Bartow,	Hanscom,	Walker,

	Asahel Brown,		Kinne,		Webster,
	Butterfield,		Morrison,		White,
	Carr,		Mosher,		Whittemore,
	Chandler,		Mowry,		Williams,
	Chapel,		Newberry,		29

NAYS:

Mr.	W. Adams,	Mr.	Cornell,	Mr.	Lovell,
	Alvord,		Crouse,		McClelland,
	Anderson,		Danforth,		J. D. Pierce,
	Axford,		Eaton.		N. Pierce,
	Barnard,		Fralick,		Prevost,
	Beardsley,		Gale,		Rix Robinson,
	Beeson,		Gibson,		Skinner,
	Britain,		Green,		Soule,
	Ammon Brown,		Hart,		Storey,
	Burns,		Harvey,		Wait,
	Bush,		Hascall,		Warden,
	Choate,		Kingsley,		President,
	Conner,		Lee,		37

On motion of Mr. Conner,

The following were added as additional sections to the article:

Sec. —. An accurate statement of the receipts and expenditures of the public moneys shall be attached to, and published with, the laws, at every regular session of the Legislature.

Sec. —. The Legislature shall provide for the speedy publication of all statute laws of a public nature, and of such judicial decisions as it may deem expedient. All laws and judicial decisions shall be free for publication by any person.

Mr. Daniels offered the following, to stand as a new section:

"The Legislature shall, as soon as practicable, establish a house of correction for juvenile and female offenders.

And the same was negatived by yeas and nays, as follows:

YEAS.

Mr.	P. R. Adams,	Mr.	Crouse,	Mr.	Prevost,
	Barnard,		Daniels,		Robertson,
	Beardsley,		Green,		Storey,
	Bush,		Hanscom,		Sturgis,
	Butterfield,		Harvey,		Van Valkenburg,
	Carr,		Leach,		Walker,
	Chandler,		McClelland,		White,
	Chapel,		Mowry.		Whittemore,
	Comstock,		J. D. Pierce,		Williams,
	Cornell,		N. Pierce,		29

NAYS.

Mr. W. Adams,	Mr. Burns,	Mr. Morrison,
Alvord,	Choate,	Mosher,
Anderson,	Church,	Newberry,
Arzeno,	Conner,	Rix Robinson,
Axford,	Danforth,	Skinner,
Bagg,	Eaton,	Soule,
H. Bartow,	Fralick,	Town,
J. Bartow,	Gale,	Wait,
Beeson,	Gibson,	Warden,
Britain,	Hascall,	Webster,
Ammon Brown,	Kinne,	President,
Asahel Brown,	Lovell,	35

Mr. Hascall offered the following, to stand as a separate section:

"The Legislature shall prescribe by law the manner in which the State printing shall be executed, and the accounts rendered therefor; and shall prohibit all charges for constructive labor."

Mr. Roberts moved to amend the foregoing by adding thereto, "and the legislature shall appoint their own state printer."

Which was not agreed to, by the following vote:

YEAS.

J. Bartow,	Mr. Hart,	Skinner,
Beardsley,	Hascall,	Sturgis,
Carr,	Roberts,	White,
Hanscom,		10

NAYS.

Mr. W. Adams,	Mr. Comstock,	Mr. Mosher,
Alvord,	Cornell,	Mowry,
Anderson,	Crouse,	Newberry,
Axford,	Danforth,	J. D. Pierce,
Bagg,	Daniels,	Prevost,
Barnard,	Eaton,	Rix Robinson,
H. Bartow,	Fralick,	Soule,
Beeson,	Gale,	Storey,
Britain,	Gardiner,	Town,
Ammon Brown,	Green,	Van Valkenburg,
Asahel Brown,	Harvey,	Wait,
Burns,	Kingsley,	Walker,
Butterfield,	Kinne,	Warden,
Chandler,	Leach,	Webster,
Chapel,	Lovell,	Whittemore,
Choate,	McClelland,	Williams,
Church,	Morrison,	President, 51

Mr. Leach moved the previous question, and

The same being demanded,

The main question was ordered to be now put.

And the propositon of Mr. Hascall was agreed to by the following vote:

YEAS.

Mr. P. R. Adams,	Mr. Comstock,	Mr. Mowry,
W. Adams,	Conner,	Newberry,
Anderson,	Crouse,	N. Pierce,
Bagg,	Danforth,	Prevost,
Barnard,	Daniels,	Rix Robinson,
H. Bartow,	Eaton,	Skinner,
J. Bartow,	Fralick,	Soule,
Beardsley,	Gale,	Sturges,
Beeson,	Gardiner,	Town,
Britain,	Green,	Van Valkenburg
Ammon Brown,	Hart,	Wait,
Asahel Brown,	Harvey,	Walker,
Burns,	Hascall,	Warden,
Bush,	Kinne,	Webster,
Butterfield,	Leach,	White,
Chandler,	Lovell,	Whittemore,
Chapel,	McClelland,	Williams,
Choate,	Morrison,	President,
Church,	Mosher,	56

NAYS.

Mr. Alvord,	Mr. Hanscom,	Mr. Storey,
Arzeno,	Robertson,	5

Mr. Soule offored the following, to stand as an additional section:

"The laws, public records, and the judicial and legislative written proceedings of the state shall be conducted, promulgated and preserved in the English language."

And the same was adopted.

Mr. Cornell offered the following additional section:

"The Governor, after 1856, may, in his discretion, assume the legislative and judicial departments of the governments."

Which was subsequently withdrawn.

Mr. Hart offered the following, to stand as a separate section:

"The legislature shall provide, that after the year 1854, all taxes except upon property paying specific taxes, shall be levied and collected in the townships and counties."

Mr. Arzeno moved the previous question on the article.

And the same was demanded, and the main question was ordered to be now put.

The proposition of Mr. Hart was disagreed to by the following vote:

YEAS:

Mr. W. Adams,	Mr. Gale,	Mr. Prevost,
Anderson,	Gardiner,	Skinner,
H. Bartow,	Green,	Soule,
Beardsley,	Hart,	Sturgis,
Beeson,	Harvey,	Town,
Asahel Brown,	Leach,	Wait,
Butterfield,	Lovell,	Walker,
Chandler,	Morrison,	White,
Conner,	J. D. Pierce,	Whittemore,
Eaton,	N. Pierce,	Williams, 30

NAYS:

Mr. P. R. Adams,	Mr. Church,	Mr. Kinne,
Alvord,	Comstock,	McClelland,
Arzeno,	Cornell,	Mosher,
Bagg,	Crouse,	Mowry,
Barnard,	Danforth,	Newberry,
Britain,	Daniels,	Robertson,
Ammon Brown,	Fralick,	Rix Robinson,
Burns,	Gibson,	Storey,
Bush,	Hanscom,	Warden,
Chapel,	Hascall,	President,
Choate,	Kingsley,	32

And the article was ordered to a third reading.

Mr. J. D. Pierce moved to adjourn.

Mr. Chapel moved a call of the house.

But the call was not sustained.

On motion of Mr. Hanscom,

The Convention adjourned.

Lansing, Saturday, August 10, 1850.

The Convention was called to order by the President at the usual hour.

Prayer by the Rev. Mr. Sanford.

The roll being called, there were absent on leave, Messrs. Backus, Alvarado Brown, S. Clark, Cook, Crary, Dimond, Eastman, Edmunds, Graham, Hathaway, Hixon, Marvin, Mason, Moore, O'Brien Orr, Raynale, Redfield, E. S. Robinson, M. Robinson, Sullivan, Sutherland, Tiffany, Wells, Willard, Witherell and Woodman.

Without leave, Mr. J. Clark.

LEAVE OF ABSENCE

Mr. Bagg asked and obtained leave of absence for himself, indefinitely; and

Mr. Butterfield for Mr. J. Clark, the same.

REPORTS.

Mr. Storey, from the committee on salaries, reported an article entitled "Of Salaries."

Which was read the first and second time by its title, referred to the committee of the whole, and placed on the general order.

Mr. McClelland, from the committee on the legislative department, to whom was referred the petition "of George Goodman, W. H. McComber and 147 others, praying the incorporation by the Convention of a clause in the constitution, prohibiting the collection of all debts, of a less amount than one hundred dollars, if contracted after the adoption of the constitution," reported the same back to the Convention, recommending its reference to the committee on the judicial department, and asked to be discharged from its further consideration.

The committee was so discharged, and,

On motion of Mr. Robertson,

The consideration of the petition was indefinitely postponed.

Mr. McClelland, from the same committee, to whom was referred the remonstrance of "the Mayor, Recorder and Aldermen of the city of Detroit, against the incorporation of a provision in the constitution, prohibiting the Legislature from giving to any city or village, the power of granting licenses for the sale of spirituous liquors, &c.," reported the same back, and asked to be discharged from its further consideration.

The committee was so discharged, and the remonstrance laid upon the table.

MOTIONS AND RESOLUTIONS.

Mr. Hanscom moved that the printing of the journals of the daily proceedings of the Convention, be dispensed with for the remainder of the session.

Which, after some debate, was withdrawn.

THIRD READING OF ARTICLES.

The article entitled "Miscellaneous Provisions," coming up for a third reading,

Mr. Leach moved to recommit to the committee on miscellaneous provisions, with instructions to insert the following, to stand as a separate section:

"The propertyof all persons who by law are prohibited from voting, on account of color, shall be exempt from taxation."

Mr. Church moved to amend, by adding thereto:

"Also report the following as an additional section to the article, viz:

"To promote the early sale and settlement of the unappropriated public lands now held by the United States exempt from taxation, within this State, the legislature is hereby authorized to take all necessary and proper steps to procure a cession of said lands to the State whenever they can be obtained on just and advantageous terms; and whatever sum, if any, shall be realized from the sales of the land so acquired, after repaying to the State the amount of all advances made on account of the purchase, management, sale, and settlement of the same. together with interest thereon, shall constitute a permanent fund, for the benefit of education and the support of such deaf, dumb, blind and insane persons as are unable to support themselves."

Mr. Britain moved to amend the foregoing, by inserting after the word "terms,"

"Not exceeding the average value of said lands to the United States, during the ten years next preceding the adoption of this constitution."

But the same was not agreed to.

Mr. Walker moved to amend the proposition of Mr. Cnurch, as follows:

Strike out in line 5, after the word "after," the words "repaying to the State the amount of all advances made, and insert, "deducting the amount paid."

And insert at the end thereof, the following:

"Nothing herein contained shall be construed to authorize the Legislature to pledge the payment of any sum or sums therefor, except out of the proceeds of the sale thereof."

Which was accepted by Mr. Church, and

His proposition was then disagreed to.

Mr. N. Pierce moved to amend the instructions proposed as follows:

Also to report a separate section, as follows: "The legislature shall provide that after the year 1853, all taxes, except upon property paying specific taxes, shall be levied and collected in the respective townships and counties."

Mr. Ammon Brown moved the previous question on the article.

The same being demanded,

The main question was ordered to be now put.

Mr. J. D. Pierce moved to reconsider the vote ordering the main question to be put.

And the same prevailed by yeas and nays, as follows:

YEAS.

Mr. W. Adams,	Mr. Comstock,	Mr. N. Pierce,
Anderson,	Cornell,	Prevost,
Barnard,	Gale,	Soule,
H. Bartow,	Green,	Sturgis,
J. Bartow,	Hart,	Van Valkenburg,
Beardsley,	Harvey,	Waite,
Asahel Brown,	Hascall,	Walker,
Burns,	Leach,	Webster,
Butterfield,	Lovell,	White,
Carr,	Moore,	Whittemore,
Chandler,	Morrison,	Williams,
Church,	J. D. Pierce,	President, 36

NAYS.

Mr. P. R. Adams,	Mr. Danforth,	Mr. McClelland,
Alvord,	Desnoyers,	Mosher,
Arzeno,	Eaton,	Mowry,
Axford,	Fralick,	Newberry,
Beeson,	Gardiner,	Roberts,
Britain,	Gibson,	Robertson,
Ammon Brown,	Hanscom,	Rix Robinson,
Bush,	Kingsley,	Storey,
Choate,	Kinne,	Town,
Conner,	Marvin,	Warden,
Crouse,		31

And the question being,

Shall the main question be now put,

It was decided in the negative by the following vote:

YEAS.

Mr. P. R. Adams.	Mr. Desnoyers,	Mr. McClelland,
Alvord,	Eaton,	Mosher,

Arzeno,
Axford,
Beeson,
Ammon Brown,
Bush,
Church,
Crouse,
Danforth,
Fralick,
Gardiner,
Gibson,
Hanscom,
Kingsley,
Kinne,
Marvin,
Mowry,
Newberry,
Roberts,
Rix Robinson,
Storey,
Town,
Warden, 28

NAYS.

Mr. W. Adams,
Anderson,
Barnard,
H. Bartow,
J. Bartow,
Beardsley,
Britain,
Asahel Brown,
Burns,
Butterfield,
Carr,
Chandler,
Church,
Mr. Comstock,
Conner,
Cornell,
Daniels,
Gale,
Green,
Hart,
Harvey,
Hascall,
Leach,
Lovell,
Morrison,
J. D. Pierce,
Mr. N. Pierce,
Prevost,
Robertson,
Soule,
Sturgis,
Van Valkenburg,
Wait,
Webster,
White,
Whittemore,
Williams,
President, 38

And by the rule, the consideration of the article being suspended for the day,

Mr. Hanscom moved to suspend the rule.

And the yeas and nays being had, the result was as follows:

YEAS:

Mr. P. R. Adams,
W. Adams,
Alvord,
Axford,
Barnard,
J. Bartow,
Beeson,
Ammon Brown,
Asahel Brown,
Butterfield,
Carr,
Choate,
Comstock,
Conner,
Crouse,
Danforth,
Mr. Daniels,
Desnoyers,
Fralick,
Gibson,
Green,
Hanscom,
Hart,
Harvey,
Hascall,
Leach,
Lovell,
Marvin,
McClelland,
Morrison,
Mosher,
Newberry,
Mr. J. D. Pierce,
N. Pierce,
Prevost,
Roberts,
Robertson,
Rix Robinson,
Soule,
Storey,
Wait,
Walker,
Warden,
Webster,
Whipple,
Whittemore,
Williams, 47

NAYS:

Mr. Arzeno,
H. Bartow,
Mr. Cornell,
Eaton,
Mr. Moore,
Mowry,

Britain,
Burns,
Bush,
Chandler,
Church,
Gale,
Gardiner,
Kingsley,
Kinne,
Sturgis,
Van Valkenburg,
White,
President,
19

So the rule was suspended, two-thirds having voted therefor.

Mr. McClelland moved a call of the House.

And the same was ordered, and

Messrs. Anderson, Beardsley, Chapel, Lee, McLeod and Skinner, were absent without leave.

Leave was asked and obtained for Messrs. McLeod and Skinner, and,

On motion of Mr. McClelland,

The Sergeant-at-Arms was despatched for Messrs. Anderson, Beardsley, Chapel and Lee,

Who soon thereafter appearing in their seats,

On motion of Mr. Leach,

All further proceedings under the call were dispensed with.

The question recurring upon Mr Leach's motion to recommit the article Miscellaneous Provisions with instructions,

A division of the question was had,

And the motion to recommit first put, and lost by yeas and nays as follows:

YEAS.

Mr. W. Adams,
Anderson,
H. Bartow,
J. Bartow,
Beardsley,
Asahel Brown,
Burns,
Butterfield,
Carr,
Chandler,
Mr. Comstock,
Conner,
Daniels,
Gale,
Green,
Hart,
Harvey,
Leach,
Lovell,
Moore,
Mr. Morrison,
J. D. Pierce,
N. Pierce,
Prevost,
Soule,
Town,
Van Valkenburg,
Wait,
White,
Williams, 30

NAYS.

Mr. P. R. Adams,
Alvord,
Arzeno,
Axford,
Barnard,
Beeson,
Britain,
Mr. Danforth,
Desnoyers,
Eaton,
Fralick,
Gardiner,
Gibson,
Hanscom,
Mr. Mowry,
Newberry,
Roberts,
Robertson,
Rix Robinson,
Storey,
Sturgis,

Ammon Brown,	Hascall,	Walker,
Bush,	Kingsley,	Warden,
Chapel,	Kinne,	Webster,
Choate,	Lee,	Whipple,
Church,	Marvin,	Whittemore,
Cornell,	McClelland,	President,
Crouse,	Mosher,	41

The article was then read a third time,

And on the question "shall the article now pass?"

The yeas and nays were had, and the following was the result:

YEAS:

Mr. P. R. Adams,	Mr. Conner,	Mr. Morrison,
W. Adams,	Cornell,	Mosher,
Alvord,	Crouse,	Mowry,
Arzeno,	Danforth,	Newberry,
Axford,	Desnoyers,	Robertson,
Beardsley,	Eaton,	Rix Robinson,
Beeson,	Fralick,	Soule,
Britain,	Gibson,	Storey,
Ammon Brown,	Harvey,	Town,
Burns,	Hascall,	VanValkenburg,
Bush,	Kingsley,	Walker,
Chandler,	Kinne,	Warden,
Chapel,	Lee,	Webster,
Choate,	Marvin,	Whipple,
Church,	McClelland,	Whittemore,
Comstock,		46

NAYS.

Mr. Anderson,	Mr. Gardiner,	Mr. N. Pierce,
Barnard,	Green,	Prevost,
H. Bartow,	Hanscom,	Roberts,
J. Bartow,	Hart,	Sturgis,
Asahel Brown,	Leach,	Wait,
Carr,	Lovell,	White,
Daniels,	Moore,	Williams,
Gale,	J. D. Pierce,	President, 24

So the article was passed, and under the rule, referred to the committee on arrangement and phraseology.

Mr. McClelland moved to suspend the rules limiting the time of debate, so far as it referred to proceedings in committee, during the time the article entitled Upper Peninsula was under consideration.

And the same prevailed by a two-thirds vote, as follows:

YEAS.

Mr. Anderson,	Mr. Danforth,	Mr. Newberry,
Arzeno,	Desnoyers,	N. Pierce,

Axford,	Eaton,	Roberts,
Barnard,	Gardiner,	Robertson,
H. Bartow,	Gibson,	Rix Robinson,
J. Bartow,	Hanscom,	Storey,
Beeson,	Hascall,	Sturgis,
Britain,	Kingsley,	Walker,
Ammon Brown,	Kinne,	Warden,
Burns,	Lee,	Webster,
Chapel,	Marvin,	White,
Choate,	McClelland,	Whipple,
Church,	Morrison,	Whittemore,
Cornell,	Mosher,	President,
Crouse,	Mowry,	44

NAYS.

Mr. P. R. Adams,	Mr. Green,	Mr. Prevost,
W. Adams,	Hart,	Soule,
Asahel Brown,	Harvey,	Town,
Carr,	Leach,	Wait,
Daniels,	Lovell,	Williams,
Fralick,	Moore,	17

On motion of Mr. Whipple,

The Convention resolved itself into committee of the whole on the article entitled "Of Upper Peninsula,"

Mr. Walker in the chair.

PROCEEDINGS IN COMMITTEE.

Section 1 having been read,

On motion of Mr. J. Bartow,

"One circuit," was stricken out, and the words, "a district," inserted in line 5.

On motion of Mr. J. Bartow,

"Other," was stricken out of line 6, and the words, "and hold his office for the same period," was inserted after the word "State."

On motion of Mr. Britain,

The words, "the boundaries of," were stricken out of line 2.

Mr. Williams offered the following, to be inserted in 6th line, after the word "State:"

"Provided, That for the choice of a Regent of the University, the erritory described shall be annexed to the same judicial circuit as the county of Wayne."

Which was not adopted.

On motion of Mr. Church,

The following was inserted after "district," in line 7:

"Who shall have power to issue his warrant for the arrest of offenders, in cases of felony, returnable according to provisions of law."

On motion of Mr. Kingsley,

The words "in their respective circuits," were inserted after "State," in 6th line.

On motion of Mr. Hascall,

The words "to be elected by the qualified electors of said district," were inserted in 5th line, after the word "judge."

Section 2 was read, when

Mr. Fralick moved to strike it out.

But the committee refused to strike out.

Section 3 was read, when

Mr Fralick offered the following as a substitute for said section:

"The counties of Mackinaw and Chippewa, with the territory thereto attached, shall be entitled to one representative to the State Legislature; the counties of Delta, Schoolcraft and Marquette, with the territory thereto attached, shall be entitled to one representative; and the counties of Ontonagon and Houghton, with the territory thereto attached, shall be entitled to one representative."

Pending which, on motion of Mr. Eaton,

Tthe committee rose, reported progress and asked leave to sit again.

The committee, through their chairman, reported the same back and asked and obtained leave to sit again.

On motion of Mr. Church,

The Convention adjourned.

Afternoon Session.

Two o'clock.

The Convention was called to order by the President, and a quorum being present,

On motion of Mr. Hanscom,

It was resolved into a committee of the whole on the article entitled "Of Upper Peninsula,"

Mr. Walker in the chair.

54

PROCEEDINGS IN COMMITTEE.

The committee resumed the consideration of Mr. Fralick's substitute for section 3, when it was withdrawn, and the following offered in its stead:

"The territory embraced in the first section of this article, shall be entitled to three representatives."

Mr. Cornell moved to strike out "three," and insert "four."

Which was withdrawn.

A division of the question being called for, section 3 was stricken out.

Mr. Fralick's substitute was then adopted.

Section 4 was then read; when,

Mr. N. Pierce moved that it be stricken out.

On motion of Mr. Church the word "shall" was stricken out of line 1, and "may" inserted; also the words in same line, "for the district attorney and,"

The motion to strike out did not prevail.

Section 5, 6, 7, 8 and 9 were read,

When Mr. N. Pierce moved to strike out sections 6, 7, 8 and 9.

Which motion was withdrawn,

And on motion of Mr. Leach the committee rose, reported the article back with the amendments, asked the concurrence of the convention therein, and to be discharged from the further consideration thereof.

The committee through their chairman, reported back the same with sundry amendments, in which the concurrence of the convention was asked.

Mr. Roberts moved to adjourn.

But the convention refused to adjourn.

Mr. Roberts moved that the consideration of the article, with amendments, as reported by the committee of the whole, be postponed until Monday next, and be made the special order of that day.

Upon which the yeas and nays were had.

And the motion was lost as follows:

YEAS.

Mr. Arzeno, Axford, Barnard, H. Bartow, J. Bartow, Burns, Bush, Choate, Church, Cornell, Crouse,

Mr. Danforth, Gale, Gardiner, Hanscom, Hart, Hascall, Kinne, Marvin, Moore, Morrison, Mosher,

Mr. Prevost, Roberts, Robertson, Rix Robinson, Van Valkenburg, Webster, White, Whipple, Woodman, President,

32

NAYS.

Mr. P. R. Adams, W. Adams, Alvord, Anderson, Beeson, Britain, Ammon Brown, Asahel Brown, Butterfield, Carr, Chandler, Chapel,

Mr. Comstock, Conner, Daniels, Eaton, Fralick, Gibson, Green, Harvey, Leach, Lovell, McClelland,

Mr. Mowry, Newberry, N. Pierce, Skinner, Soule, Town, Wait, Walker, Warden, Whittemore, Williams,

34

On motion of Mr. McClelland,

The article was laid upon the table.

On motion of Mr. McClelland,

The committee of the whole was discharged from the consideration of the article entitled "Of Salaries," and

The same was taken up for consideration.

Mr. Fralick moved to amend the article by striking out "one thousand," when it occurs relative to the State Treasurer, and inserting "eight hundred."

Mr Roberts moved to amend the same by inserting "$250."

Which was not agreed to.

Upon the proposition submitted by Mr. Fralick, the yeas and nays were had,

And the same was not agreed to as follows:

YEAS.

Mr. P. R. Adams, Barnard, H. Bartow, Ammon Brown,

Mr. Fralick, Gale, Gardiner, Hart,

Mr. Mosher, Newberry, N. Pierce, Prevost,

Asahel Brown,	Harvey,	Skinner,
Butterfield,	Hascall,	Town,
Carr,	Kinne,	Wait,
Chandler,	Leach,	Warden,
Crouse,	Lee,	Webster,
Daniels,	Lovell,	Woodman,
Eaton,	Moore,	32

NAYS.

Mr. W. Adams,	Mr. Choate,	Mr. Roberts,
Alvord,	Church,	Robertson,
Anderson,	Conner,	Rix Robinson,
Arzeno,	Cornell,	Soule,
Axford,	Danforth,	VanValkenburg,
J. Bartow,	Desnoyers,	Walker,
Beeson,	Hanscom,	White,
Britain,	Marvin,	Whipple,
Burns,	McClelland,	Whitemore,
Bush,	Morrison,	Williams,
Chapel,	Mowry,	President, 33

Mr. Hascall moved to amend so much of the article as relates to judges of the supreme court, by striking out "fifteen hundred" and inserting "twelve hundred."

Mr. Roberts moved to insert "sixteen hundred."

A division of the question was had on striking out the amount contained in the article,

And the motion to strike out was lost by yeas and nays as follows:

YEAS.

Mr. Britain,	Mr. Gardiner,	Mr. N. Pierce,
Bush,	Green,	Prevost,
Carr,	Harvey,	Skinner,
Chandler,	Hascall,	Wait,
Fralick,	Lovell,	Webster,
Gale,	Newberry,	17

NAYS.

Mr. P. R. Adams,	Mr. Church,	Mr. Morrison,
W. Adams,	Conner,	Mosher,
Alvord,	Cornell,	Mowry,
Anderson,	Crouse,	Roberts,
Arzeno,	Danforth,	Robertson,
Axford,	Daniels,	Rix Robinson,
Barnard,	Desnoyers,	Soule,
H. Bartow,	Eaton,	Town,
J. Bartow,	Gibson,	VanValkenburgh,
Beeson,	Hanscom,	Walker,
Ammon Brown,	Hart,	Warden,

Asahel Brown,	Kinne,	White,
Burns,	Lee,	Whittemore,
Butterfield,	Marvin,	Williams,
Chapel,	McClelland,	Woodman,
Choate,	Moore,	President, 48

Mr. Church moved to amend by adding to the article, "and no fees whatever for the performance of any duties connected with their office."

Mr. Williams moved to insert after "fees," the words "or perquisites," which prevailed.

And the amendment as amended was agreed to.

Mr. Eaton moved to adjourn,

But the Convention refused to adjourn.

Mr. McClelland moved to strike out the entire article.

Mr. Danforth moved to adjourn.

But the convention refused to adjourn.

Mr. Britain offered the following substitute for the article:

"Executive, judicial and state officers shall receive such compensation as shall be prescribed by law, but such compensation shall neither be increased nor diminished during their continuance in office."

Mr. Alvord moved the previous question on the article,

And a quorum not voting thereon,

Mr. Moore moved a call of the Convention.

Mr. J. Bartow moved to adjourn.

But the Convention refused to adjourn.

Upon the question for a call of the Convention, the yeas and nays were had,

And the same was lost, as follows:

YEAS.

Mr. Anderson,	Mr. Danforth,	Mr. Rix Robinson,
Arzeno,	Gardiner,	Van Valkenburg,
J. Bartow,	Hart,	Wait.
Britain,	Marvin,	Webster,
Chandler,	Mosher,	White,
Crouse,	Robertson,	17

NAYS.

Mr. P. R. Adams,	Mr. Conner,	Mr. Moore,
W. Adams,	Cornell,	Mowry,
Alvord,	Daniels,	Morrison,
Barnard,	Desnoyers,	Newberry,

H. Bartow,	Eaton,	N. Pierce,
Beeson,	Fralick,	Soule,
Ammon Brown,	Gibson,	Town,
Asahel Brown,	Green,	Walker,
Burns,	Hanscom,	Warden,
Butterfield,	Harvey,	Whipple,
Carr,	Hascall,	Whittemore,
Chapel,	Kinne,	Williams,
Choate,	Lee,	Woodman,
Church,	Lovell,	President,
Comstock,	McClelland,	44

Mr. Robertson moved to adjourn.

But the Convention refused to adjourn.

The question being on seconding the previous question,

The same was demanded.

And the main question was ordered to be now put, by yeas and nays, as follows:

YEAS:

Mr. P. R. Adams,	Mr. Choate,	Mr. Hascall,
W. Adams,	Church,	Kinne,
Alvord,	Comstock,	McClelland,
Anderson,	Conner,	Moore,
Arzeno,	Cornell,	Mosher,
Barnard,	Crouse,	Mowry,
J. Bartow,	Daniels,	Newberry,
Beeson,	Desnoyers,	Rix Robinson,
Ammon Brown,	Eaton,	Soule,
Asahel Brown,	Fralick,	Walker,
Burns,	Gibson,	Whipple,
Carr,	Hanscom,	Whittemore,
Chandler,	Harvey,	Williams, 39

NAYS:

Mr. Britain,	Mr. Hart,	Mr. Van Valkenburg,
Bush,	Lovell,	Wait,
Butterfield,	Morrison,	Warden,
Chapel	N. Pierce,	Webster,
Gardiner,	Robertson,	White,
Green,	Town,	President, 18

And the question being upon striking out the entire article entitled "Of Salaries,"

The yeas and nays were ordered, and the result was as follows:

YEAS.

Mr. P. R. Adams,	Mr. Choate,	Mr. Robertson,
Arzeno,	Hart,	Rix Robinson,
J. Bartow,	Lovell,	White,
Britain,	McClelland,	President, 14
Burns,	Roberts,	

NAYS.

Mr. W. Adams, Anderson, Alvord, Barnard, Beeson, Ammon Brown, Asahel Brown, Bush, Butterfield, Carr, Chandler, Chapel, Church, Comstock, Conner, Cornell, Mr. Crouse, Danforth, Daniels, Desnoyers, Eaton, Fralick, Gardiner, Gibson, Green, Hanscom, Harvey, Hascall, Kinne, Lee, Marvin, Moore, Mr. Morrison, Mosher, Mowry, Newberry, N. Pierce, Soule, Town, Van Valkenburg, Wait, Warden, Webster, Whipple, Whittemore, Williams, Woodman, 47

So the article was not stricken out.

Mr. Barnard moved to adjourn.

But the Convention refused to adjourn.

The article was ordered to a third reading.

Mr. Britain moved to reconsider the vote by which the article entitled "Miscellaneous Provisions" was passed, which motion he moved to lay upon the table.

The convention refused to lay the motion on the table, when.

Mr. Britain withdrew it.

Mr. Walker moved to reconsider the vote by which the article entitled "Salaries" was ordered to a third reading.

Mr. Williams moved the previous question.

Mr. Robertson moved to adjourn.

And the convention adjourned.

Lansing, Monday, August 12, 1850.

The President called the Convention to order at the usual hour.

Prayer by the Rev. Mr. Tooker.

The roll being called, there were absent on leave, Messrs Backus, Bagg, Alvarado Brown, S. Clark, J. Clark, Cook, Crary, Dimond, Eastman, Graham, Hathaway, Hixon, Mason, Moore, Raynale, Redfield, E. S. Robinson, M. Robinson, Sullivan, Sutherland, Tiffany, Wells, Willard and Witherell.

LEAVE OF ABSENCE.

Mr. Britain asked and obtained leave of absence for Mr. McClelland for the day, and

Mr. Butterfield for Mr. Story, for an indefinite period.

PETITIONS.

By Mr. Leach: of Norman Little and 71 others of Saginaw Co., praying for the insertion of an article in the Constitution, making it the duty of the Legislature to obtain if possible a cession of all unsold lands in this State, &c., &c.

Laid upon the table.

REPORTS.

Mr. Hart, from the Committee on schedule, submitted an article entitled "Schedule," which was read 1st and 2d time by its title, laid upon the table, and ordered printed.

MOTIONS AND RESOLUTIONS.

Mr. Gale offered the following:

Resolved, That the committee on printing be requested to cause the report of the committee on supplies and expenditures to be printed and laid upon the table of the members of the Convention on Thursday morning next.

Mr. Robertson moved to amend, by adding, "and that one thousand copies be ordered printed for the use of the delegate from Genesee, Mr. Gale, which he subsequently withdrew.

Mr. Alvord move to indefinitely postpone the resolution, which motion was withdrawn.

Mr. Britain moved to amend the resolution, by adding, "and such printing shall appear in the Journal of the last day's proceedings of the Convention."

But the amendment did not prevail.

Mr. Gale modified his resolution, so that the matter required to be printed should appear in the printed journal of to-day's proceedings; and as modified, the resolution was adopted.

M. Hanscom submitted the following report on the 7th inst.:

"Pursuant to the instructions of the Convention, the committee on supplies and expenditures respectfully report: That they have purchased the amount and kind of stationery specifically stated and set forth in the bills now in the hands of the Secretary of the Convention, numbered from one to five inclusive, and made a part of this report; that bills, for some small amounts purchased in this village, have not as yet been presented and filed; that one considerable item of expense incurred consisted of purchases of appropriate materials to carry out the resolution of the Convention upon the melancholy announcement of the death of General Taylor, late President of the United States. The committee respectfully refer the Convention to the proceedings of the 5th and 19th of June.

On the last named day the chairman of your committee proposed to the Convention the following resolutions, in obedience to the wishes of the committee:

"*Resolved*, That from and after this day the post master of this village be not authorized to charge to the Convention or State any postage on any mailable matter, sent or mailed by members or officers of the Convention, and that the Secretary notify the post master accordingly.

"*Resolved*, That from and after this date there be printed for the use of the Convention but 240 copies of the journal."

The passage of the resolutions had the effect to reduce the daily current and incidental expenses of the Convention to an amount varying from thirty-five to fifty dollars.

The committee also suggest, that by reason of the system of reporting, adopted by order of the Convention, an increased quantity of stationery has been necessarily required; and that for the purpose of making that branch of duties as effectually performed as practicable, and at the urgent request of the reporters, your committee purchased twelve reporter's pens, with gold points, at a cost of one dollar each. One-half have been already placed in the hands of the reporters and Secretaries of the Convention. The balance, in conjunction with a large amount of the stationery purchased—ink, sand, wax, wafers, envelopes, &c., &c.—will be on hand and unused, and by the Secretary of the Convention, delivered over to the Secretary of State for the use of the State.

A comparison of the current and incidental expenses of this Convention (aside from pay of members) with former Constitutional Conventions or Legislative bodies in this State, number of members and officers and length of session considered, show, as your committee believe, a reduction of nearly two-thirds, and a consequent saving of the amount of several thousands of dollars to the tax-payers of the State."

The Constitutional Convention,

	To Turner & Seymour,	Dr.
To 6 Ink-stands,		$1 50
2 reams Letter Paper,		5 00
5¾ " Cap "		22 75
		$29 25

Rec'd payment, July 20, 1850,

TURNER & SEYMOUR.

State of Michigan,

	To Mrs. Allen,	Dr.
To repairing flag,		$0 50

State of Michigan,

	To F. M. Cowles & Co.,	Dr.
To bill of Inkstands, per E. B. Danforth,		$2 00

A. H. Hanscom,

	To O. P. Burt,	Dr.
To 6 quire of fine Envelope Paper, for use of the Convention,		$2 25

Lansing, August 5, 1850.

The Constitutional Convention,

		To Jas. A. Bascom,	Dr.
1850.—June 6.	To	1 Broom, 1s. 3d.,	16
" 14,		1 " 1s. 3d.,	16
" 15,		1 Pail, 2s. 6d.,	31
" 28,		1 Broom, 1s. 3d.,	16
July 10,		5½ Crape, 4s.,	2 75
" "		1 paper Pins, 10c.,	10
" "		6¾ Bombazines, 8s.,	6 75
" 12,		⅜ Crape, 4s.,	19
" "		1 pair Shears, 4s.,	50
" 18,		1 " 4s.,	50
" 23,		1 Broom, 1s. 3d.,	16
			$11 74

Lansing, August 2, 1850.

Detroit, June 7, 1850.

State of Michigan,

Bought of F. P. Markham & Bro.:

12 doz. Inkstands, 8s.,	$12 00
1 gross Penholders, 20s.,	2 50
4 gross Gillott's Steel Pens, 163, $1,87½,	7 50
25 lbs. Sealing Wax, 12s.,	37 50
3000 Quills, No. 60, $2,87½,	86 25
20 doz. Lead Pencils, 4s.,	10 00
5 reams Letter Paper, P. & S., 20s.,	12 50
10 Gum Arabic, 8s.,	10 00
20 doz Red Tape, 4s.,	10 00
10 M Envelopes, 12s.,	15 00
11½ lbs. Wafers, 8s.,	11 50
10 reams P. O. Envelope Paper, $5,00,	50 00
1 do Blotting Paper,	5 00
5 do Engrossing Paper, $6,50,	32 50
8 doz. Inks, (pints,) $3,50,	28 00
4 doz. " (quarts,) $4,50,	18 00
10 reams cap Paper, $3,00.	30 00
2 gross Paper Sand, $6,00,	12 00
12 doz. Sand Boxes, $2,00	24 00
12 doz. Wafer Boxes, $2,00,	24 00
10 doz. Letter Folders, (ivory,) $3,00,	30 00
	$468 25
Freight by express train,	5 50
	$473 75

Detroit, July 6, 1850.

State of Michigan,

To F. P. Markham & Bro., Dr.

(Per order of A. H. Hanscom, Com. on Supplies,)

June 7—	For bill of Stationery rendered,	$473 75
" 18,	1000 Envelopes,	2 00
" 18,	paid freight on box to Jackson,	50
July 1,	1 doz. Gold Pens,	12 00
" 1,	1 gross Steel Pens, 163 Gillott's,	2 00.

July 1,	1 gross Pen Holders,	2 25
" 1,	1 gross Lead Pencils,	6 00
" 5,	5 reams Letter Paper, $3,50,	17 50
" 6,	5 do do in 4to. packages, $4,	20 00
" 6,	paid freight on box to Jackson, and cart'ge,	1 00
		$537 00
	Deduct 5 reams letter paper not received,	20 00
		$517 00

Received, Lansing, July 20, 1850, of A. H. Hanscom, Chairman of the committee on supplies and expenditures, a certificate of the principal Secretary of the Convention, countersigned by the President of the Convention, for the amount of $517, (five hundred and seventeen dollars,) in full for stationery furnished the Convention to this date. (Signed,)

F. P. MARKHAM & BRO.,
By F. Lyon.

On motion of Mr. Green,

Resolved, That the Secretary be instructed to report to the Convention, the amount of stationary on hand, specifying the different items and the cost of each as per bill.

UNFINISHED BUSINESS.

The article entitled "Salaries" being under consideration, and the question being on ordering the previous question on the article,

The same was demanded, and

The main question ordered to be now put.

And that being, "shall the article now pass?"

The same was decided in the affirmative, by yeas and nays, as follows:

YEAS:

Mr. Alvord,	Mr. Comstock,	Mr. Mowry,
Anderson,	Danforth,	Newberry,
Arzeno,	Desnoyes,	Orr,
Axford,	Eaton,	J. D. Pierce,
Barnard,	Fralick,	Prevost,
Beardsley,	Gardiner,	Robertson,
Beeson,	Gibson,	Soule,
Ammon Brown,	Hanscom,	Town,
Asahel Brown,	Hascall,	Van Valkenburg,
Butterfield,	Kinne,	Walker,

Carr,	Moore,	Whittemore,
Chandler,	Morrison,	Williams,
Choate,	Mosher,	Woodman,
Church,		40

NAYS:

Mr. P. R. Adams,	Mr. Crouse,	Mr. Marvin,
W. Adams,	Daniels,	McLeod,
H. Bartow,	Edmunds,	N. Pierce,
J. Bartow,	Gale,	Roberts,
Britain,	Green,	Rix Robinson,
Burns,	Hart,	Skinner,
Bush,	Harvey,	Wait,
Chapel,	Leach,	Warden,
Conner,	Lee,	Webster,
Cornell,	Lovell,	White, 30

And the article was referred to the committee on arrangement and phraseology.

Mr. Barnard moved a reconsideration of the last vote,

And the same prevailed by yeas and nays, as follows:

YEAS.

Mr. P. R. Adams,	Mr. Conner,	Mr. Marvin,
W. Adams,	Cornell,	McLeod,
Barnard,	Crouse,	Mosher,
H. Bartow,	Daniels,	O'Brien,
J. Bartow,	Desnoyers,	Orr,
Beardsley,	Eaton,	N. Pierce,
Beeson,	Edmunds,	Prevost,
Britain,	Gale,	Rix Robinson,
Asahel Brown,	Gardiner,	Skinner,
Burns,	Green,	Soule,
Bush,	Hanscom,	Town,
Carr,	Hart,	Van Valkenburg,
Chandler,	Harvey,	Wait,
Chapel,	Hascall,	Walker,
Choate,	Kingsley,	Warden,
Church,	Leach,	Webster,
Comstock,	Lovell,	Whittemore, 51

NAYS.

Mr. Alvord,	Mr. Danforth,	Mr. Morrison,
Anderson,	Fralick,	Newberry,
Arzeno,	Gibson,	Williams,
Axford,	Moore,	11

And the question being on the passage of the article, the result was as follows:

YEAS.

Mr. Alvord,	Mr. Conner,	Mr. Morrison,
Anderson,	Danforth,	Mosher,
Arzeno,	Desnoyers,	Mowry,
Axford,	Eaton,	Newberry,
Beardsley,	Fralick,	J. D. Pierce,
Beeson,	Gibson,	Soule,
Ammon Brown,	Hanscom,	Town,
Butterfield,	Hascall,	Van Valkenburg,
Chandler,	Kinne,	Whittemore,
Choate,	Marvin,	Williams,
Church,	Moore,	Woodman, 33

NAYS.

Mr. P. R. Adams,	Mr. Daniels,	Mr. Orr,
W. Adams,	Edmunds,	N. Pierce,
Barnard,	Gale,	Prevost,
H. Bartow,	Gardiner,	Roberts,
J. Bartow,	Green,	Robertson,
Britain,	Hart,	Rix Robinson,
Asahel Brown,	Harvey,	Skinner,
Burns,	Kingsley,	Wait,
Bush,	Leach,	Walker,
Carr,	Lee,	Warden,
Chapel,	Lovell,	Webster,
Cornell,	McLeod,	White,
Crouse,	O'Brien,	President, 39

So the Convention refused to pass the article.

Mr. Walker moved that the same be recommitted to the committee on "Salaries."

Mr. Pierce moved to add "with instructions to fix the salaries as follows:

"Governor, $1,000, Judges, $1,200, Treasurer, $1,000, Auditor General, $0,800, Commissioner of State Land Office, $1,000, Secretary of State, $0,800, Attorney General, $0,500, Superintendent of Public Instruction, $0,800. They shall receive no more than is provided for in this constitution."

Mr. Walker offered the following substitute for the instructions proposed:

"The Governor shall receive a salary of one thousand dollars per annum. The Auditor General, State Treasurer, Secretary of State, Commissioner of the Land Office, and Superintendant of Public Instruction, each such salary as shall be prescribed by law, not exceedceeding one thousand dollars each per annum. The Attorney General shall receive a salary to be prescribed by law, not exceeding eight hundred dollars per annum. The circuit judges shall each receive an annual salary of not less than fifteen hundred dollars each, per annum to be prescribed by law. The judge of the district court for the upper peninsula shall receive such annual salary, not exceeding one thousand dollars, as shall be prescribed by law. And no fees or perquisites of office shall be received by any such officer in addition to the salaries above named."

Mr. Chapel moved to strike out in the substitute the words "not less," where it occurs, and insert "not more."

At this stage of the proceedings the motion to recommit was withdrawn, and,

On motion of Mr. Bush,

The vote by which the Convention refused to pass the article was reconsidered,

And the question again recurring on its passage,

Mr. N. Pierce moved to recommit the article with instructions, as heretofore proposed by him.

Mr. Danforth proposed to substitute the following for the instructions:

To add to the article, "and it shall not be competent for the Legislature to increase the salaries herein provided."

And the substitute prevailed.

The article was recommitted with the instructions proposed.

Mr. Van Valkenburgh, from the committee on salaries, reported back the article amended agreeably to instructions; and, as amended,

The article was passed, and referred to the committee on arrangement and phraseology.

On motion of Mr. Woodman,

The resolution offered by Mr. Story, on the 5th inst., was taken from the table and indefinitely postponed.

On motion of Mr. Fralick,

The article entitled "Of Upper Peninsula of Michigan," was taken from the table.

The question being upon concurring in amendments made in committee of the whole,

Those to section 1 were severally concurred in.

The substitute for section 3, proposed by the committee, being under consideration,

Mr. Cornell offered the following substitute for it, which was not adopted:

"The counties of Mackinac and Chippewa, and the territory thereto attached, shall be entitled to one representative; the county of Marquette and Schoolcraft, and the territory thereto attached, one representative; the county of Houghton and territory thereto attached, one representative; the county of Ontonagon and territory thereto attached, one representative."

Mr. Morrison offered the following substitute for the same:

"The county of Mackinac wtth the territory which may be thereto attached, shall be entitled to one representative to the state legislature; the county of Chippewa, and the territory which may be thereto attached, one representative; the counties of Houghton and Ontonagon, and the territory which may be thereto attached, one representative; the counties of Delta, Schoolcraft and Marquette, and the territory which may be thereto attached, one representative."

Which was not agreed to by yeas and nays, as follows:

YEAS:

Mr. Alvord,	Mr. Cornell,	Mr. O'Brien,
Arzeno,	Danforth,	Roberts,
Axford,	Gardiner,	Robertson,
H. Bartow,	Hanscom,	Rix Robinson,
J. Bartow,	Hart,	Town,
Beeson,	Kingsley.	Van Valkenburg,
Burns,	Lee,	Walker,
Bush,	Lovell,	White,
Chapel,	McLeod,	Whittemore,
Church,	Morrison,	Woodman,
Conner,	Mosher,	President, 33

NAYS:

Mr. P. R. Adams,	Mr. Crouse,	Mr. Marvin,
W. Adams,	Daniels,	Moore,
Anderson,	Desnoyers,	Mowry,
Barnard,	Eaton,	Newberry,
Beardsley,	Edmunds,	N. Pierce,
Britain,	Fralick,	Prevost,
Ammon Brown,	Gale,	Skinner,
Asahel Brown,	Gibson,	Soule,
Butterfield,	Green,	Wait,

Carr,	Harvey,	Warden,
Chandler,	Hascall,	Webster,
Choate,	Kinne,	Williams,
Comstock,	Leach,	38

Mr. Hanscom offered the following substitute for the one proposed by the committee:

"Until after the census of 1855 there shall be elected in the territory defined in the first section of this article, four members of the House of Representatives; and the legislature shall, at its next session, divide said territory into four representative districts."

And the yeas and nays were had, and the proposition was rejected as follows:

YEAS:

Mr. Alvord,	Mr. Edmunds,	Mr. Robertson,
Arzeno,	Gardiner,	Rix Robinson,
Axford,	Hanscom,	Skinner,
H. Bartow,	Hart,	Town,
J. Bartow,	Kingsley,	Van Valkenburg,
Beeson,	Lee,	Walker,
Burns,	Lovell,	White,
Chapel,	McLeod,	Whittemore,
Church,	Morrison,	Woodman,
Cornell,	Mosher,	President,
Danforth,	Roberts,	32

NAYS:

Mr. P. R. Adams,	Mr. Comstock,	Mr. Kinne,
W. Adams,	Conner,	Leach,
Anderson,	Crouse,	Marvin,
Barnard,	Daniels,	Moore,
Beardsley,	Desnoyers,	Mowry,
Britain,	Eaton,	Newberry,
Ammon Brown,	Fralick,	N. Pierce,
Asahel Brown,	Gale,	Prevost,
Butterfield,	Gibson,	Soule,
Carr,	Green,	Wait,
Chandler,	Harvey,	Warden,
Choate,	Hascall,	Williams, 36

Mr. Robertson moved to amend by inserting before the word "three" the word "at least."

Which was not agreed to.

And the substitute proposed by the committee was then concurred in.

The amendment to section 4 was non-concurred in.

The article being up for general amendment,

Mr. McLeod moved to amend section 4 by inserting after "district attorney," the words, "by tax on said district,"

And the same was agreed to.

Mr. Robertson moved to amend section 4 as amended, by striking out all after "district," in the foregoing amendment, and insert in lieu thereof, "the senators and representatives provided for in this notice, shall receive the sum of — dollars each and no more, as compensation for detention and delays in the performance of their duties, in addition to the mileage and per diem allowance provided for in this constitution, to members of the senate and house of representatives."

Mr. Roberts moved that the article entitled "Of Upper Peninsula of Michigan," be recommitted to the committee on the "Governmental and Judicial policy of the Upper Peninsula," with instructions to so amend the same that the salaries of the district judge and district attorney, together with the expenses of a senator and their representatives, shall be paid out of the treasuries of the several counties: that the counties may be subject to taxation for county and township purposes the same as counties of the lower peninsula, and that all monies paid into the state treasury by mining companies, or as a tax for county and township purposes, shall be refunded to the treasuries of the several counties from which it may be received, deducting expenses of collection if there be any.

Mr. N. Pierce moved to strike from the proposed instructions, so much as relates "to per centage of mining companies," which was lost.

And the motion to re-commit did not prevail.

The amendment offered to section 4 by Mr. Robertson was lost.

Mr. Williams offered the following substitute for the section (4):

"The Legislature may provide for the payment of said district judge, not exceeding $1000 per annum, and of said district attorney, not exceeding $500 per annum. In cases of delay and detention, it shall be competent for the Legislature to make extra compensation to the members of the Legislature, from said discribed territory not exceeding two dollars per day during the session of the Legislature."

On motion of Mr. Moore, "five hundred" was stricken out, and "seven hundred" inserted.

And the substitute as amended, was agreed to.

Mr. Britain offered the following substitute for section 6.

"One half of all money received into the treasury from corporations in the upper peninsula paying a State tax of one per cent per annum, shall be paid to the treasurers of the counties from which it is received, to be applied for township and county purposes as provided by law."

Mr. Fralick moved to strike out section 6.

Mr. Roberts moved a call of the covention, and the same being ordered,

Messrs. Axford, Barnard, Bush, Kinne, Leach, J. D. Pierce, Warden and Whipple were absent without leave.

Mr. Britain asked and obtained leave for Mr. Whipple, when

On motion of Mr. Roberts,

The Convention adjourned.

—

Afternoon Session.

Two o'clock.

The Convention was called to order by the President,

And a quorum being present,

Resumed the consideration of the unfinished business of the morning, being the article entitled, "of Upper Peninsula of Michigan."

The question being on Mr. Britain's substitute for section 6,

Mr. Hanscom moved to amend the same by adding thereto, "but the Legislature shall have power after the year 1855 to reduce the per centum to be refunded."

And the amendment was agreed to.

A division of the question being had on the adoption of the substitute,

The question was first taken on striking out the section (6) and the same prevailed.

And in inserting the proposition of Mr. Britain, the yeas and nays were had, and the same prevailed as follows:

YEAS:

Mr. W. Adams,	Mr. Cornell,	Mr. Marvin,
Alvord,	Crouse,	Mowry,
Anderson,	Danforth,	O'Brien,
Arzeno,	Desnoyers,	Roberts,
Axford,	Edmunds,	Robertson,
H. Bartow,	Gale,	Rix Robinson,
J. Bartow,	Gardiner.	Skinner,
Beardsley,	Green,	Soule,
Beeson,	Hanscom,	Town,
Britain,	Hart,	Van Valkenburg,
Asahel Brown,	Hascall,	Walker,
Burns,	Kingsley,	White,
Bush,	Kinne,	Whittemore,
Butterfield,	Lee,	Woodman,
Conner,	Lovell,	President, 45

NAYS:

Mr. P. R. Adams,	Mr. Daniels,	Mr. Newberry,
Ammon Brown,	Eaton,	Orr,
Carr,	Fralick,	N. Pierce,
Choate,	Gibson,	Wait,
Church,	Harvey,	Warden,
Comstock,	Moore,	Williams, 18

On motion of Mr. Hanscom,

Sections 7 and 8 were striken from the article.

Mr. White moved to amend section 1 by striking out all after "elected" in the 8th line and inserting, "for the term of two years."

And the same prevailed.

On motion of Mr. Church,

The following was adopted in lieu of section 2.

"The territory described in the above section shall, at all times, be entitled to at least one Senator in the Senate of the State."

Mr. Moore moved to strike out section 9, and asked the yeas and nays thereon.

And the motion was lost, as follows:

YEAS.

Mr. P. R. Adams,	Mr. Eaton,	Mr. Moore,
W. Adams,	Edmunds,	Newberry,
Anderson,	Fralick,	N. Pierce,
Barnard,	Gale,	Skinner,
Britain,	Gibson,	Wait,
Ammon Brown,	Harvey,	Warden,
Comstock,	Hascall,	Williams,
Daniels,	Lovell,	23

NAYS.

Mr. Alvord,	Mr. Church,	Mr. Mosher,
Arzeno,	Conner,	Mowry,
Axford,	Cornell,	O'Brien,
H. Bartow,	Crouse,	Orr,
J. Bartow,	Danforth,	J. D. Pierce,
Beardsley,	Desnoyers,	Roberts,
Beeson,	Gardiner,	Rix Robinson,
Asahel Brown,	Green,	Soule,
Burns,	Hanscom,	Town,
Bush,	Hart,	Van Valkenburg,
Butterfield,	Kingley,	Walker,
Carr,	Kinne,	White,
Chandler,	Lee,	Whittemore,
Chapel,	Marvin,	President,
Choa'e,	Morrison,	44

Mr. Chapel offered the following as a new section to the article, and the same was adopted:

"Sec. —. The legislature may change the location of the State Prison from Jackson to the Upper Peninsula of Michigan."

Mr. Britain moved to amend section 9 by adding thereto, "but no such corporation shall be permitted to purchase any real estate except such as shall be necessary for the exercise of the corporate franchises of such company."

And the same was agreed to.

And the question being on ordering the article to a third reading,

It was so ordered by yeas and nays as follows:

YEAS.

Mr. Alvord,	Mr. Cornell,	Mr. Mowry,
Arzeno,	Crouse,	Orr,
Axford,	Danforth,	J. D. Pierce,
H. Bartow,	Desnoyers,	N. Pierce,
J. Bartow,	Eaton,	Roberts,
Beardsley,	Edmunds,	Robertson,
Beeson,	Gardiner,	Rix Robinson,
Britain,	Green,	Skinner,
Burns,	Hanscom,	Soule,
Bush,	Hascall,	Town,
Butterfield,	Kingsley	Van Valkenburg,
Carr,	Kinne,	Wait,
Chandler,	Lee,	Walker,
Chapel,	Marvin,	Whittemre,
Church,	Morrison,	Woodman,
Conner,	Mosher,	President, 48

NAYS.

Mr. P. R. Adams,	Mr. Comstock,	Mr. Harvey,
W. Adams,	Daniels,	Lovell,
Anderson,	Fralick,	Moore,
Barnard,	Gale,	Warden,
Ammon Brown,	Gibson,	White,
Asahel Brown,	Hart,	Williams,
Choate,		19

The article was then read a third time by its title, passed and referred to the committee on arrangement and phraseology.

On motion of Mr. Bush,

The Convention adjourned.

Lansing, Tuesday, August 13, 1850.

The Convention met at the usual hour and was called to order by the President.

Prayer by the Rev. Mr. Merrill,

The roll being called, there were absent on leave, Messrs. Backus, Bagg, Alvarado Brown, S. Clark, J. Clark, Cook, Dimond, Eastman, Hathaway, Graham, Hixson, Mason, Raynale, E.S. Robinson, M. Robinson, Sullivan, Sutherland, Tiffany, Wells, Willard, and Witherell.

PETITIONS.

By the President: of Ross Wilkins, D. V. Bell, A. H. Redfield, and fifty others, praying for the insertion of an article in the constitution, making it the duty of the legislature to obtain, if possible, a cession to the State, of all unsold and unappropriated public lands lying within its limits, &c.

Laid upon the table.

By Mr. Redfield: of sundry inhabitants of the county of Cass praying a constitutional bar to all the negro race.

Laid on the table.

REPORTS.

Mr. McClelland from the committee on arrangement and phraseology, reported that the duty assigned that committee had been performed, and that in conformity with a rosolution of the Convention, the several articles had been placed in the hands of the printer.

RESOLUTIONS.

On motion of Mr. Gardiner,

Resolved, That the printing of the daily journals of the Convention be suspended until after the final adjournment.

On motion of Mr. Beeson,

Resolved, That a committee of three be appointed to superintend the enrollment of the constitution, preparatory to its being signed.

On motion of Mr. Woodman,

Resolved, That the chairman of the committee on supplies be authorized and required to furnish the Post Master of Lansing with a copy of the manual of this convention.

Mr. Alvord offered the following:

Resolved, That the Secretaries, Reporters, Messengers, Sergeant-at-Arms, and Door-keeper, who were appointed at the commencement of the Convention, be entitled to mileage; and that the Secretary be instructed to draw a warrant for the same.

On motion of Mr. Church,

The resolution was laid upon the table.

On motion of Mr. Church,

Resolved, That the committee on supplies be and are hereby requested to make some arrangement with the Post Master of this place, for the payment of the postage upon mailable matter received by the Convention since the first day of August, present, and report the same.

On motion of Mr. Britain,

The article entitled "Schedule," was taken from the table, and

It was read the first and second time by its title, and taken up for consideration in Convention.

Section 4 being under consideration.

On motion of Mr. Robertson,

The words, "to the people of the State of Michigan," were inserted after "laws," in the 4th line.

On motion of Mr. Cornell,

The word "other," was stricken out of the 3d line.

On motion of Mr. Robertson,

The word "any," before "public," in the same line was stricken out.

Mr. Alvord moved to strike out the word "any," in the 4th line.

But the motion was lost.

Section 6 having been read,

On motion of Mr. Robertson,

The words "election and" were stricken from the 3d line, and the words "election, qualification and duties of," were inserted in lieu thereof.

On motion of Mr. Gale,

The word "day" was stricken out in the 2d line, and "Monday," inserted.

Section 7 being under consideration,

On motion of Mr. Robertson,

The words "judges of the" were inserted before "county courts," in the second line."

On motion of Mr. Hanscom,

Section 8 was amended by adding thereto, "and of the district court of the Upper Peninsula."

Section 12 being under consideration.

Mr. Church moved to amend the same by preceding it with the following:

"The Governor, after the adoption of this constitution by the people, shall appoint ——— persons; whose duty it shall be to adapt the present body of statute law of this State to the provisions of this constitution, (but who shall have no power to make any alteration or modification of the laws now in force otherwise than is clearly designated in or required by this constitution;) and who shall present to the Legislature for their action at its next session their proposed alterations and modifications of said statute law; and."

Mr. Walker moved to amend by adding to the foregoing, "who shall receive such compensation, not exceeding seventy-five dollars each, as shall be allowed by the Legislature, and."

The amendment was accepted by Mr. Church.

Mr. Hanscom offered the following substitute for the proposition of Mr. Church:

"The Attorney General of the State is required to prepare and report to the next Legislature, at the commencement of the session, such changes and modifications in existing laws as may be deemed necessary to adapt the same to this constitution, and may be best calculated to carry out its provisious, and who shall receive no additional compensation."

Mr. Church withdrew his amendment.

The amendment of Mr. Hanscom was agreed to.

On motion of Mr. Morrison,

Section 13 was amended by striking out "county" and inserting "territory."

On motion of Mr. Church,

The same section was amended by striking out at the end thereof the words "in the legislature."

Mr. Woodman moved to amend section 14 by striking out all after "election" in the 6th line.

Mr. Williams moved to amend the clause proposed to be stricken out by striking out "six" and inserting "three," and striking out "fifty" and inserting "fifteen."

Mr. Hanscom moved to pass over the section, but the motion was lost.

Mr. J. Bartow moved to amend Mr. Williams' amendment by inserting "four" and "twenty" in lieu of "three" and "fifteen."

Which was accepted by the mover, and the amendment was not agreed to.

Mr. Morrison moved to amend the clause by striking out in the 7th line, the words "for six successive weeks previous to said election," and inserting after the word "publishing," the words "in the month of September next."

Mr. Leach moved the previous question.

But the same was not sustained.

Mr. Morrison modified his amendment by adding, also strike out "fifty," and insert "fifteen."

Mr. Walker moved to amend the clause by striking out the words "for" and "successive."

Which was lost.

A division was had on Mr. Morrison's proposition, and the first clause of the same was agreed to.

Mr. J. Bartow moved to amend the second branch of the proposition by inserting "twenty-five" instead of "fifteen."

A division of the question was had, and the question was first taken on striking out "fifty" in the section, and the same prevailed by yeas and nays as follows:

YEAS.

Mr. W. Adams,	Mr. Cornell,	Mr. Mowry,
Arzeno,	Daniels,	Newberry,
Axford,	Eaton,	Orr,
H. Bartow,	Edmunds,	J. D. Pierce,
Beeson,	Fralick,	N. Pierce,
Britain,	Gibson,	Prevost,
Ammon Brown,	Green,	Rix Robinson,
Asahel Brown,	Harvey,	Skinner,
Carr,	Hascall,	Soule,
Chandler,	Kinne,	Wait,
Chapel,	Lee,	Walker,
Choate,	Lovell,	Warden,
Comstock,	Marvin,	Webster,
Conner,	Moore,	Williams,
Cornell,	Morrison,	Woodman,
Crouse,	Mosher,	President, 48

NAYS.

Mr. Alvord,	Mr. Hart,	Mr. Van Valkenburgh,
J. Bartow,	O'Brien,	White,
Church,	Roberts,	Whipple,
Gardiner,	Robertson,	Whittemore,
Hanscom,	Town,	14

And the question being on filling the blank,

Mr. Eaton proposed inserting "twenty."

Mr. Britain with "thirty," and

Mr. White with "forty."

Mr. Rix Robinson moved the previous question on the section, and the same was demanded and the main question ordered to be now put.

The question being on filling the blank, and the vote being taken on the highest number first, the motion to fill the same with "forty" was lost by yeas and nays, as follows:

YEAS.

Mr. Alvord,	Mr. Hanscom,	Mr. White,
J. Bartow,	Hart,	Whipple,
Church,	Roberts,	Whittemore,
Gardiner,	Robertson,	11

NAYS.

Mr. W. Adams,	Mr. Daniels,	Mr. Newberry,
Anderson,	Desnoyers,	O'Brien,
Arzeno,	Eaton,	Orr,
Axford,	Edmunds,	J. D. Pierce,
Barnard,	Fralick,	N. Pierce,

Beeson,	Gale,	Prevost,
Ammon Brown,	Gibson,	Rix Robinson,
Asahel Brown,	Green,	Skinner,
Burns,	Harvey,	Soule,
Carr,	Hascall,	Wait,
Chandler,	Lee,	Walker,
Chapel,	Lovell,	Warden,
Choate,	Marvin,	Webster,
Comstock,	Moore,	Williams,
Conner,	Morrison,	Woodman,
Cornell,	Mosher,	President,
Crouse.		49

The motion to fill the blank with "thirty" was also disagreed to.

Upon filling the same with "twenty-five," the yeas and nays were had, with the following result:

YEAS.

Mr. Alvord,	Mr. Cornell,	Mr. J. D. Pierce,
Arzeno,	Desnoyers,	Prevost,
Axford,	Gardiner,	Roberts,
H. Bartow,	Gibson,	Robertson,
J. Bartow,	Hanscom,	Rix Robinson,
Beeson,	Hart,	Town,
Britain,	Hascall,	Van Valkenburg
Ammon Brown,	Lovell,	Walker,
Burns,	Marvin,	White,
Butterfield,	McClelland,	Whipple,
Choate,	Mosher,	Whittemore,
Church,	O'Brien,	President,
Conner,		37

NAYS.

Mr. W. Adams,	Mr. Eaton,	Mr. Orr,
Anderson,	Edmunds,	N. Pierce,
Barnard,	Fralick,	Redfield,
Asahel Brown,	Gale,	Soule,
Carr,	Green,	Wait,
Chandler,	Harvey,	Warden,
Chapel,	Lee,	Webster,
Comstock,	Moore,	Williams,
Crouse,	Morrison,	Woodman,
Daniels,	Newberry,	29

So the blank was filled with "twenty-five."

The question recurring upon striking out the last clause of the section,

The same was not agreed to.

On motion of Mr. Robertson,

Section 17 was amended by inserting after the words "near as may be," as follows: "and the returns thereof shall be directed to the Secretary of State."

Mr. J. Bartow moved to fill the first blank in the section with "16th day of December next."

And the same prevailed.

On motion of Mr. Robertson,

The blank in the 8th line was filled so as to read "1st day of January, 1851."

The article having been gone through with by sections, and being open for general amendment,

Mr. Walker offered the following to stand as a separate section:

"*Resolved*, That at the next general election, and at the same time when the votes of the electors shall be taken for the adoption or rejection of the revised constitution, the additional amendment in the words following, to wit:

"'The Legislature shall have no power to pass any act to grant any license for the sale of ardent spirits or other intoxicating liquor,'

"Shall be separately submitted to the electors of this State for their adoption or rejection, in form following, to wit: A separate ballot may be given by every person having the right to vote for the revised constitution, to be deposited in a separate box. Upon the ballots given for the adoption of the said separate amendment shall be written or printed, or partly written and partly printed, the words 'No license of the sale of spiritous liquors;' and upon all ballots given against the adoption of the said separate amendment, in like manner, the words 'License of the sale of spiritous liquors.' And on such ballots shall be written or printed, or partly written and partly printed, the words 'Constitution:. Spiritous liquors,' in such manner that such words shall appear on the outer side of such ballot when folded. If, at said election, a majority of all the votes given for and against the said separate amendment shall contain the words 'No license of the sale of spiritous liquors,' then the said separate amendment, after the day of one thousand eight hundred and , shall be a separate section of artice four of the constitution, in full force and effect, anything in the constitution to the contrary notwithstanding."

Mr. Williams moved the previous question on the section,

And the same being demanded,

The main question was ordered to be now put,

And the proposition of Mr. Walker was rejected by yeas and nays as follows:

YEAS:

Mr. Alvord,	Mr. Danforth,	Mr. Robertson,
Arzeno,	Desnoyers,	Rix Robinson,
J. Bartow,	Fralick,	Town,
Beeson,	Gardiner,	Van Valkenburgh,
Britain,	Gibson,	Wait,
Ammon Brown,	Hart,	Walker,
Butterfield,	Kinne,	White,
Chapel,	McClelland,	Whipple,
Church,	Mosher,	Whittemore,
Cornell,	O'Brien,	President, 30

NAYS.

Mr. W. Adams,	Mr. Crouse,	Mr. Morrison,
Anderson,	Daniels,	Mowry,
Axford,	Eaton,	Newberry,
Barnard,	Edmunds,	Orr,
H. Bartow,	Gale,	N. Pierce,
Asahel Brown,	Green,	Prevost,
Burns,	Harvey,	Redfield,
Carr,	Kingsley,	Soule,
Chandler,	Lovell,	Warden,
Choate,	Marvin,	Williams,
Comstock,	Moore,	Woodman,
Conner,		34

Mr. Lovell moved to strike out sec. 11 of the article.

Mr. Hart moved to adjourn,

But the Convention refused to adjourn.

Mr. Lovell's motion prevailed.

Mr. Britain offered the following to stand as sec. 11.

"Reprints of the laws shall only be made after the same shall have been compiled by a person appointed by the legislature in joint convention, and certified by three persons appointed by the governor, to be a true and accurate compilation, and of all the general laws of Michigan actually in force. No alteration of the legal import of any law shall be permitted in such compilation. No revision of the laws shall ever be made and submitted to the legislature."

When, on motion of Mr. Bush,

The Convention adjourned.

Afternoon Session.

Two o'clock.

The Convention was called to order by the President,

The roll being called a quorum of members answered to their names.

The President announced as the committee under the resolution of this morning, Messrs. Beeson, Fralick and Whittemore.

The consideration of the article entitled "Schedule," was resumed; and

The question being on Mr. Britain's proposition to stand as section 11,

Mr. Britain withdrew the same, and proposed the following in lieu thereof:

"No general revision of the laws shall hereafter be made.

"When a reprint thereof becomes necessary, the Legislature in joint convention, shall appoint a suitable person to collect together such acts and parts of acts as are in force, and without alteration arrange them under appropriate head and titles.

"The laws so arranged shall be submitted to — commissioners appointed by the Governor, for examination; and if certified by them to be a correct compilation of all general laws in force, shall be printed in such manner as shall be provided by law."

Mr. Morrison moved to strike out "Commissioners" and insert "Attorney General,"

Which was not agreed to.

On motion of Mr. Britain,

The blank before "commissioners" was filled with "two."

On the adoption of the section the yeas and nays were had as follows:

YEAS.

Mr. W. Adams,	Mr. Daniels,	Mr. Robertson,
Axford,	Edmunds,	Rix Robinson,
H. Bartow,	Gardiner,	Soule,
J. Bartow,	Green,	Sturgis,
Beeson,	Hanscom,	Town,
Britain,	Kingsley,	Walker,
Asahel Brown,	Kinne,	Webster,
Burns,	Leach,	White,
Chandler,	Lovell,	Whipple,

Church,	McClelland,	Williams,	
Conner,	Redfield,	Woodman,	33

NAYS.

Mr. Alvord,	Mr. Danforth,	Mr. Mosher,	
Arzeno,	Eaton,	Mowry,	
Ammon Brown,	Fralick,	Newberry,	
Bush,	Gale,	Orr,	
Butterfield,	Gibson,	N. Pierce,	
Carr,	Hart,	Van Valkenburg,	
Choate,	Harvey,	Wait,	
Comstock,	Marvin,	Warden,	
Cornell,	Moore,	Whittemore,	
Crouse,	Morrison,	President,	30

So the same was agreed to.

On motion of Mr. McClelland,

Section 17 was amended by inserting in the 8th line, after "1851" the words "except as herein otherwise provided."

On motion of Mr. Whipple,

The following was added as a separate section of the article:

"The causes pending and indisposed of in the late court of chancery, at the time of the adoption of this constitution, shall continue to be heard and determined by the judges of the supreme court. But the legislature shall, at its session in 1851, provide by law for the transfer of said causes that may remain undisposed of on the first Monday of   next, to the supreme or circuit court, established by this constitution, or require that the same may be heard and determined by the circuit judges."

On motion of Mr. Williams,

The following to stand as sec. 5, was adopted.

"Sec. 5. A Governor and Lieutenant Governor shall be chosen under the existing constitution and laws, to serve after the expiration of the present gubernatorial term, until superseded by this constitution."

Mr. Williams offered the following to stand as sec. 6.

"The senators and representatives chosen at the general election in November 1850, shall hold their offices till superseded by a legislature chosen under this constitution."

Mr. Robertson offered the following substitute for the foregoing.

Sec. 6. The members of the Senate and House of Representatives of the Legislature of 1851, shall continue in office under the provisions of law, until superseded by their successors elected and qualified under this constitution.

And the same was accepted by Mr. Williams,

And adopted by the Convention.

On motion of Mr. Robertson,

The following was added to section 17:

"And in case of the adoption of this Constitution, said officers shall immediately, or as soon thereafter as practicable, proceed to open the statement of votes returned from the several counties for judges of the supreme court and state officers under the act entitled, "an act to amend the Revised Statutes and to provide for the election of certain officers by the people, in pursuance to an amendment of the Constitution," approved Feb. 16, 1850, and shall ascertain, determine and certify the results of the election for said officers, under said act, in the same manner, as near as may be, as is now provided by law in regard to the election of Representatives in Congress.

"And the several judges and officers so ascertained to have been elected, may be qualified and enter upon the duties of their respective offices on the first Monday of January next, or as soon thereafter as practicable."

Mr. Moore moved the following additional section to the article:

"From and after the year 1855 the Legislature shall provide by law a uniform system for the collection of all taxes throughout the State."

Mr. Britain proposed the following substitute for the foregoing:

"The Legislature shall, on or before 1855, provide that all taxes shall be collected in the respective counties, and that the state tax shall have precedence over every other tax; such law shall protect the interest of the state in all lands liable to the state in consequence of non-payment of taxes."

Mr. McClelland moved the previous question, and the same being demanded, the main question was ordered to be now put.

The substitute of Mr. Britain was not agreed to.

The proposition of Mr. Moore was rejected by yeas and nays, as follows:

YEAS:

Mr. Anderson,	Mr. Carr,	Mr. Gale,	
Asahel Brown,	Edmunds,	Moore,	6.

NAYS.

Mr. W. Adams,	Mr. Cornell,	Mr. Mosher,
Alvord,	Crouse,	Newberry,

Arzeno,	Danforth,	O'Brien,
Axford,	Daniels,	Orr,
Barnard,	Desnoyers,	N. Pierce,
H. Bartow,	Eaton,	Prevost,
J. Bartow,	Fralick,	Redfield,
Beardsley,	Gardiner,	Robertson,
Beeson,	Gibson,	Rix Robinson,
Britain,	Green,	Soule,
Ammon Brown,	Hanscom,	Sturgis,
Burns,	Hart,	Town,
Bush,	Hascall,	Van Valkenburg,
Butterfield,	Kingsley,	Walker,
Chandler,	Kinne,	Warden,
Chapel,	Leach,	White,
Choate,	Lovell,	Whipple,
Church,	Marvin,	Whittemore,
Comstock,	McClelland,	Woodman,
Conner,	Morrison,	President, 60

Mr. Britain offered the following as an additional section.

"The legislature shall on or before 1855, provide that all taxes, except specific taxes, shall be collected in the respective counties, and that the state tax shall have precedence over every other tax. Such law shall protect the interest of the State in all lands liable to the State in consequence of the non-payment of taxes."

Mr. Danforth moved to strike out, "except specific taxes."

Mr. McClelland moved the previous question.

And the same being demanded, the main question was ordered to be now put.

Mr. Danforth's amendment was lost, as follows:

YEAS.

Mr. Arzeno,	Mr. Choate,	Mr. Fralick,
Axford,	Cornell,	Gibson,
Burns,	Crouse,	Hanscom,
Bush,	Danforth,	Robertson, 12

NAYS.

Mr. W. Adams,	Mr. Eaton,	Mr. Orr,
Alvord,	Edmunds,	N. Pierce,
Barnard,	Gale,	Prevost,
H. Bartow,	Gardiner,	Redfield,
J. Bartow,	Green,	Rix Robinson,
Beeson,	Hart,	Soule,
Britain,	Harvey,	Town,
Ammon Brown,	Kingsley,	Van Valkenburgh,
Asahel Brown,	Leach,	Walker,

58

Butterfield,	Lovell,	Warden,
Carr,	McClelland,	Webster
Chandler,	Morrison,	White,
Chapel,	Mosher.	Whipple,
Church,	Mowry,	Whittemore,
Conner,	Newberry,	Woodman,
Daniels,	O'Brien,	President,
Desnoyers,		49

Mr. Britain's proposition was rejected by yeas and nays, as follows:

YEAS.

Mr. W. Adams,	Mr. Edmunds,	Mr. O'Brien,
Barnard,	Gale,	Orr,
Beeson,	Green,	N. Pierce,
Britain,	Hart,	J. D. Pierce,
Asahel Brown,	Harvey,	Prevost,
Butterfield,	Leach,	Soule,
Carr,	Lee,	Warden,
Chandler,	Lovell,	White,
Conner,	Moore,	Whittemore,
Daniels,	Morrison,	Woodman, 30

NAYS:

Mr. Alvord,	Mr. Cornell,	Mr. Mosher,
Arzeno,	Crouse,	Mowry,
Axford,	Danforth,	Newberry,
J. Bartow,	Desnoyers,	Redfield,
H. Bartow,	Eaton,	Robertson,
Beardsley,	Fralick,	Rix Robinson,
Ammon Brown,	Gardiner,	Town,
Burns,	Gibson,	Van Valkenburgh,
Bush,	Hanscom,	Walker,
Chapel,	Kingsley,	Webster,
Choate,	Kinne,	Whipple,
Church,	Marvin,	President,
Comstock,	McClelland,	38

On motion of Mr. McClelland,

The following was added as a new section to the article:

"Sec. —. The term of office of governor and lieutenant governor shall commence on the first Monday of January next after the election thereof."

On motion of Mr. Whipple,

The article was referred to the committee on Arrangement and Phraseology, and

Mr. Robertson was added as an additional member to that committee.

Mr. McClelland from the Committee on Arrangement and Phraseology, reported

ARTICLE I.

BOUNDARIES.

"The State of Michigan consists of and has jurisdiction over the territory embraced within the following boundaries, to wit: Commencing at a point on the eastern boundary line of the State of Indiana, where a direct line drawn from the southern extremity of Lake Michigan to the most northerly cape of the Maumee Bay shall intersect the same—said point being the north-west corner of the State of Ohio, as established by act of Congress, entitled "an act to establish the northern boundary line of the State of Ohio and to provide for the admission of the State of Michigan into the Union upon the conditions therein expressed," approved June fifteenth, one thousand eight hundred and thirty-six; thence with the said boundary line of the State of Ohio till it intersects the boundary line between the United States and Canada in Lake Erie; thence with said boundary line between the United States and Canada, through the Detroit river, Lake Huron and Lake Superior to a point where the said line last touches Lake Superior; thence in a direct line through Lake Superior to the mouth of the Montreal river; thence through the middle of the main channel of the said river Montreal to the head waters thereof; thence in a direct line to the centre of the channel between Middle and South Islands in the Lake of the Desert; thence in a direct line to the southern shore of Lake Brule; thence along said southern shore and down the river Brule to the main channel of the Menominie river; thence down the centre of the main channel of the same to the centre of the most usual ship channel of the Green Bay of Lake Michigan; thence through the centre of the most usual ship channel of the said Bay, to the middle of Lake Michigan; thence through the middle of Lake Michigan to the northern boundary of the State of Indiana, as that line was established by the act of Congress of the nineteenth of April, eighteen hundred and sixteen; thence due east with the north boundary line of the said State of Indiana to the north-east corner thereof; and thence south with the eastern boundary line of Indiana to the place of beginning."

And the same was agreed to as one of the articles of the Constitution.

Mr. McClelland from the same committee, reported the following as a caption for the Constitution:

"The People of the State of Michigan do ordain this Constitution."

And the same was agreed to.

Mr. McClelland from the same committee, reported

ARTICLE II.

SEAT OF GOVERNMENT.

"The Seat of Government shall be at Lansing, where it is now located."

Mr. McClelland, from the same committee, reported

ARTICLE III.

DIVISION OF THE POWERS OF GOVERNMENT.

Section 1. The Powers of Government are divided into three departments: The Legislative, Executive and Judicial.

Sec. 2. No person belonging to one of these departments shall exercise the powers properly belonging to another, except in the cases expressly provided for in this constitution.

The amendments were concurred in.

On motion of Mr. McClelland,

Article 3 was amended by striking out "for" in the 3rd line.

On motion of Mr. McClelland,

It was ordered that the articles, as reported by the committee on arrangement and phraseology, with amendments as concurred in, be referred to the committee on Enrollment.

Mr. Hanscom offered the following:

Resolved, That Thomas Palmer and ——— Holden be and they are hereby appointed Messengers of this Convention, from this day to the end of the session.

Which was not agreed to.

On motion of Mr. Bush,

The Convention adjourned.

Lansing, Wednesday, August 14, 1850.

The Convention met at the usual hour and was called to order by the President.

Prayer by the Rev. Mr. Sanford.

The roll being called, there were absent with leave, Messrs. Backus, Bagg, Alvarado Brown, S. Clark, J. Clark, Cook, Dimond, Eastman, Graham, Hathaway, Hixon, Mason, Raynale, Redfield, M. Robinson, Sullivan, Sutherland, Tiffany, Wells, Willard and Witherell.

RESOLUTIONS.

Mr. Hart offered the following:

Resolved, That a committee of eight be appointed, whose duty it shall be to recommend a plan for dividing the State, exclusive of the Upper Peninsula, into eight judicial circuits, with instructions to report as soon as practicable.

Mr. W. Adams moved to strike out "as soon as practicable," and insert "this afternoon."

Which amendment was accepted by the mover.

Mr. Crouse moved to indefinitely postpone the resolution,

But the motion was lost.

Mr. Walker moved to strike out "a committee of eight," and insert "the committee on Schedule."

Which was lost.

Mr. Woodman moved to strike out "eight," and insert "eleven."

Which was lost.

The resolution was then adopted by yeas and nays, as follows:

YEAS:

Mr. W. Adams,	Mr. Church,	Mr. O'Brien,
Anderson,	Comstock,	Orr,
H. Bartow,	Conner,	Robertson,
J. Bartow,	Cornell,	E. S. Robinson,
Beardsley,	Desnoyers,	Rix Robinson,
Beeson,	Eaton,	Skinner,
Britain,	Edmunds,	Sturgis,
Ammon Brown,	Gale,	VanValkenburg,
Asahel Brown,	Gardiner,	Walker,
Burns,	Hart,	Webster,
Bush,	Kinne,	Whipple,
Butterfield,	Leach,	Williams,
Chapel,		

NAYS.

Mr. Alvord,	Mr. Hanscom,	Mr. Newberry,
Arzeno,	Harvey,	J. D. Pierce,
Axford,	Hascall,	N. Pierce,
Barnard,	Lee,	Prevost,
Carr,	Lovell,	Redfield,
Chandler,	Marvin,	Soule,
Choate,	McClelland,	Warden,
Crouse,	Moore,	Whittemore,
Daniels,	Mosher,	Woodman,
Fralick,	Mowry,	President,
Gibson,		31

Mr. Gardiner offered the following:

Resolved, That C. J. Fox, one of the Reporters of this Convention, be and he hereby is authorized and required to superintend the proof reading and publication of the debates of the Convention, and to complete the index of the same.

On motion of Mr. Fralick,

The resolution was laid upon the table.

On motion of Mr. McClelland,

Resolved, That the committee on printing be instructed to inquire into the propriety of publishing the old and new constitutions in the Dutch, German and French languages.

On motion of Mr. McClelland,

The following resolutions were adopted:

Resolved, That there be allowed to John Swegles, Jr., Secretary of this Convention, the sum of two hundred and fifty dollars, for compiling and preparing for publication, making index and superintending the printing of the journals and documents of the Convention, to be paid on the certificate of the Secretary of State that the work is correctly done.

Resolved, That there be allowed to Horace S. Roberts, one of the Secretaries of this Convention, the sum of eight cents per folio for making a fair copy of the journals of the Convention, to be paid on the certificate of the Secretary of State (who shall certify the number of folios) that the work has been correctly done and deposited in his office.

Mr. Britain moved to reconsider the last vote, which was lost by yeas and nays, as follows:

YEAS.

Mr. W. Adams,	Mr. Gale,	Mr. Redfield,
Britain,	Gardiner,	Skinner,
Asahel Brown,	Gibson,	Soule,
Carr,	Hascall,	Sturgis,
Comstock,	Leach,	Town,
Conner,	Lovell,	Van Valkenburg,
Cornell,	Moore,	Wait,
Crary,	Newberry,	Warden,
Crouse,	O'Brien,	Williams,
Edmunds,	J. D. Pierce,	Woodman,
Fralick,	N. Pierce,	32

NAYS.

Mr. Alvord,	Mr. Chapel,	Mr. Morrison,
Anderson,	Choate,	Mosher,
Arzeno,	Church,	Mowry,
Axford,	Danforth,	Orr,
Barnard,	Daniels,	Roberts,
H. Bartow,	Hanscom,	Robertson,
J. Bartow,	Hart,	Rix Robinson,
Beeson,	Harvey,	Walker,
Burns,	Kinne,	Webster,
Bush,	Lee,	White,
Butterfield,	Marvin,	Whittemore,
Chandler,	McClelland,	President, 36

On motion of Mr. Gardiner,

Resolved, That there be allowed to A. T. Welch, George W. Osborn, Henry Starkey, A. J. Vandenbergh, Stephen P. Mead, J. H. Titus, Jr., O. S. Case, F. M. Creps, J. Whitman, and Wm. Gumbrecht, the sum of four dollars each; and to J. Reeves, Charles Holbrook, Mary Teeter, and Maria Balch, the sum of two dollars each, for extra services in the printing office and bindery, and that a certificate be issued therefor to the chairman of the printing committee.

Mr. Crary, from the committee on arrangement and phraseology, reported back

ARTICLE IV.

LEGISLATIVE DEPARTMENT.

Section 1. The Legislative power is vested in a Senate and House of Representatives.

Sec. 2. The Senate shall consist of thirty-two members. Senators shall be elected for two years, and by single districts. Such districts shall be numbered from one to thirty-two inclusive; each of which shall choose one senator. No county shall be divided in the formation of senate districts, except such county shall be equitably entitled to two or more senators.

Sec. 3. The House of Representatives shall consist of not less than sixty-four, nor more than one hundred members. Representatives shall be chosen for two years, and by single districts. Each representative district shall contain, as nearly as may be, an equal number of white inhabitants, and civilized persons of Indian descent not members of any tribe, and shall consist of convenient and contiguous territory. But no township or city shall be divided in the formation of a representative district. When any township or city shall contain a population which entitles it to more than one representative, then such township or city shall elect by general ticket the number of representatives to which it is entitled. Each county hereafter organized, with such territory as may be attached thereto, shall be entitled to a separate representative when it has attained a population equal to a moiety of the the ratio of representation. In every county entitled to more than one representative, the board of supervisors shall assemble at such time and place as the Legislature shall prescribe, and divide the same into representave districts, equal to the number of Representatives to which such county is entitled by law, and shall cause to be filed in the offices of the Secretary of State and clerk of such county, a description of such representative districts, specifying the number of each district, and the population thereof, according to the last preceding enumeration.

Sec. 4. The Legislature shall provide by law for an enumeration of the inhabitants in the year eighteen hundred and fifty-five, and every ten years thereafter; and at the first session after each enumeration so made, and also at the first session after each enumeration by the authority of the United States, the Legislature shall apportion anew the senators and representatives among the counties and districts, according to the number of white inhabitants and civilized persons of Indian descent, not members of any tribe. Each apportionment, and the division into representative districts by any board of supervisors, shall remain unaltered until the return of another enumeration.

Sec. 5. Senators and Representatives shall be citizens of the United States, and qualified electors in the respective counties and districts which they represent. A removal from their respective counties or districts shall be deemed a vacation of their seats.

Sec. 6. No person holding any office under the United States or this State, or any county office, except notaries public, officers of the militia, and officers elected by townships, shall be eligible to or have a seat in either house of the Legislature; and all votes given for any such person shall be void.

Sec. 7. Senators and Representatives shall, in all cases except treason, felony or breach of the peace, be privileged from arrest. They shall not be subject to any civil process during the session of the Legislature, or for fifteen days next before the commencement and after the termination of each session; they shall not be questioned in any other place for any speech in either house.

Sec. 8. A majority of each house shall constitute a quorum to do business; but a smaller number may adjourn from day to day, and compel the attendance of absent members, in such manner and under such penalties as each house may prescribe.

Sec. 9. Each house shall choose its own officers, determine the rules of its proceedings, and judge of the qualifications, elections and returns of its members; and may, with the concurrence of two-thirds of all the members elected, expel a member. No member shall be expelled a second time for the same cause; nor for any cause known to his constituents antecedent to his election; the reason for such expulsion shall be entered upon the journal, with the names of the members voting on the question.

Sec. 10. Each house shall keep a journal of its proceedings, and publish the same, except such parts as may require secrecy. The yeas and nays of the members of either house, on any question, shall be entered on the journal at the request of one-fifth of the members elected. Any member of either house may dissent from and protest against any act, proceeding or resolution which he may deem injurious to any person or the public, and have the reason of his dissent entered on the journal.

Sec. 11. In all elections by either house, or in joint convention, the votes shall be given viva voce. All votes on nominations to the Senate, shall be taken by yeas and nays, and published with the journal of its proceedings.

Sec. 12. The doors of each house shall be open, unless the public welfare requires secrecy. Neither house shall, without the consent of the other, adjourn for more than three days, nor to any other place than where the Legislature may then be in session.

Sec. 13. Bills may originate in either house of the Legislature.

Sec. 14. Every bill and concurrent resolution except of adjournment, passed by the Legislature, shall be presented to the Governor before it becomes a law. If he approves, he shall sign it; but if not, he shall return it with his objections to the house in which it originated, which shall enter the objections at large upon their journal, and reconsider it. On such reconsideration, if two-thirds of the members elected agree to pass the bill, it shall be sent with the objections, to the other house, by which it shall be reconsidered. If approved by two-thirds of the members elected to that house, it shall become a law. In such case, the vote of both houses shall be determined by yeas and nays, and the names of the members voting for and against the bill shall be entered on the journals of each house respectively. If any bill be not returned by the Governor within ten days, Sundays excepted, after it has been presented to him, the same shall become a law, in like manner as if he had signed it, unless the Legislature, by their adjournment, prevent its return; in which case it shall not become a law. The Governor may approve, sign, and file in the office of the Secretary of State, within five days after the adjournment of the Legislature any act passed during the last five days of the session; and the same shall become a law.

Sec. 15. The compensation of the members of the Legislature shall be three dollars a day for actual attendance and when absent on account of sickness, for the first sixty days of the session of 1851, and for the first forty days of every subsequent session, and nothing thereafter. When convened in extra session their compensation shall be three dollars a day for the first twenty days, and nothing thereafter; and they shall legislate on no other subjects than those expressly stated in the Governor's proclamation, or submitted to them by special message. They shall be entitled to ten cents, and no more, for every mile actually traveled, in going to and returning from the place of meeting, on the usually traveled route; and for stationery and newspapers not exceeding five dollars for each member during any session. Each member shall be entitled to one copy of the laws, journals and documents of the Legislature of which he was a member; but shall not receive, at the expense of the State, books, newspapers or other perquisites of office, not expressly authorized by this constitution.

Sec. 16. The Legislature may provide by law for the payment of postage on all mailable matter received by its members and officers during the session of the Legislature, but not on any sent or mailed by them.

Sec. 17. The President of the Senate and the Speaker of the House of Representatives shall be entitled to the same per diem compensation and mileage as members of the Legislature, and no more.

Sec. 18. No person elected a member of the Legislature shall receive any civil appointment within this State, or to the Senate of the United States, from the Governor, the Governor and Senate, from the Legislature, or any other State authority, during the term for which he is elected. All such appointments and all votes given for any person so elected for any such office or appointment, shall be void. No member of the Legislature shall be interested, directly or indirectly, in any contract with the State, or any county thereof, authorized by any law passed during the time for which he is elected, and for one year thereafter.

Sec. 19. Every bill and joint resolution shall be read three times in each house before the final passage thereof. No bill or joint resolution shall become a law without the concurrence of a majority of all the members elected to each house. On the final passage of all bills the vote shall be by ayes and nays, and entered on the journal.

Sec. 20. No law shall embrace more than one object, which shall be expressed in its title. No public act shall take effect or be in force until the expiration of ninety days from the end of the session at which the same is passed, unless the Legislature shall otherwise direct, by a two-thirds vote of the members elected to each house.

Sec. 21. The Legislature shall not grant nor authorize extra compensation, to any public officer, agent or contractor, after the service has been rendered or the contract entered into.

Sec. 22. The Legislature shall provide by law that the fuel and stationery furnished for the use of the State, the printing and binding the laws and journals, all blanks, paper and printing for the executive departments, and all other printing ordered by the Legislature, shall be let by contract to the lowest bidder or bidders, who shall give adequate and satisfactory security for the performance thereof. The Legislature shall prescribe by law the manner in which the State printing shall be executed, and the accounts rendered therefor; and shall prohibit all charges for constructive labor. The Legislature shall not rescind nor alter such contract, nor release the person or persons taking the same, or his or their sureties, from the performance of any of the conditions of the contract. No member of the Legislature nor officer of the State shall be interested directly or indirectly in any such contract.

Sec. 23. The Legislature shall not authorize, by private or special law, the sale or conveyance of any real estate belonging to any person; nor vacate nor alter any road laid out by commissisnors of highways, or any street in any city or village, or in any recorded town plat.

Sec. 24. The Legislature may authorize the employment of a chaplain for the State Prison; but no money shall be appropriated for payment of any religious services in either house of the Legislature.

Sec. 25. No law shall be revised, altered or amended by reference to its title only; but the act revised, and the section or sectious of the act altered or amended shall be re-enacted and published at length.

Sec. 26. Divorces shall not be granted by the Legislature.

Sec. 27. The Legislature shall not authorize any lottery, nor permit the sale of lottery tickets.

Sec. 28. No new bill shall be introduced into either house during the last three days of the session, without the unanimous consent of the house in which it originates. In case of a contested election, the person only shall receive from the State per diem compensation and mileage who is declared to be entitled to a seat by the house in which the contest takes place.

Sec. 29. No collector, holder nor disburser of public moneys, shall have a seat in the Legislature, or be eligible to any office of trust or profit under this State, until he shall have accounted for and paid over, as provided by law, all sums for which he may be liable.

Sec. 30. The Legislature shall not audit nor allow any private claim or account.

Sec. 31. The Legislature, on the day of final adjournment, shall adjourn at twelve o'clock at noon.

Sec. 32. The Legislature shall meet at the seat of government on the first Wednesday in February next, and on the first Wednesday in January of every second year thereafter, and at no other place or time, unless provided in this constitution.

Sec. 33. The election of Senators and Representatives, pursuant to the provisions of this constitution, shall be held on the Tuesday succeeding the first Monday of November, in the year 1852, and on the Tuesday succeeding the first Monday of November of every second year thereafter.

Sec. 34. The Legislature shall not establish a State Paper. Every newspaper in the State which shall publish all the general laws of any session within forty days of their passage, shall be entitled to receive a sum not exceeding fifteen dollars therefor.

Sec. 35. The Legislature shall provide for the speedy publication of all statute laws of a public nature, and of such judicial decisions as it may deem expedient. All laws and judicial decisions shall be free for publication by any person.

Sec. 36. The Legislature may declare the cases in which any office shall be deemed vacant, and also the manner of filling the vacancy, where no provision is made for that purpose in this constitution.

Sec. 37. The Legislature may confer upon organized townships, incorporated cities and villages, and upon the board of supervisors of the several counties, such powers of a local, legislative and administrative character as they may deem proper.

Sec. 38. The Legislature shall pass no law to prevent any person from worshipping Almighty God according to the dictates of his own conscience; or to compel any person to attend, erect, or support any place of religious worship, or to pay tithes, taxes or other rates for the support of any minister of the gospel.

Sec. 39. No money shall be appropriated or drawn from the treasury for the benefit of any religious sect or society, theological or religious seminary, nor shall property belonging to the State be appropriated for any such purposes.

Sec. 40. The Legislature shall not diminish or enlarge the civil or political rights, privileges and capacities of any person, on account of his opinion or belief concerning matters of religion.

Sec. 41. No law shall ever be passed to restrain or abridge the liberty of speech or of the press; but every person may freely speak, write and publish his sentiments on all subjects, being responsible for the abuse of such right.

Sec. 42. The Legislature shall pass no bill of attainder, ex post facto law, or law impairing the obligation of contracts.

Sec. 43. The privilege of the writ of habeas corpus remains and shall not be suspended by the Legislature, except in case of rebellion or invasion the public safety require it.

Sec. 4. The assent of two-thirds of the members elected to each house of the Legislature shall be requisite to every bill appropriating the public money or property for local or private purposes.

Sec. 45. The Legislature may authorize a trial by a jury of a less number than twelve men.

Sec. 46. The Legislature shall not pass any act authorizing the grant of license for the sale of ardent spirits or other intoxicating liquors.

Sec. 47. The style of the laws shall be "The People of the State of Michigan enact."

On motion of Mr. Crary,

Section 4 was amended by inserting between "shall" and "apportion," in the 5th line, the words "re-arrange the senate districts and;" and also by striking out the words "Senators and," in line 6.

On motion of Mr. McClelland,

The rule being suspended, section 4 was amended by striking out at the beginning of the section, "1855," and inserting in lieu thereof, "1854."

On motion of Mr. Britain,

Section 28 was ordered divided so as to make two sections.

On motion of Mr. Williams,

Section 18 was amended by striking out in line 9, the word "and" and inserting "nor."

On motion of Mr. Barnard,

Section 22 was amended by inserting before "fuel," in 1st line, the words "furnishing of," and also by striking out "furnished," after "stationery."

On motion of Mr. Crary,

Section 22 was amended by striking out in the 9th line, the words "the Legislature" and inserting "they."

With the foregoing amendments, made by unanimous consent of the Convention,

The article was referred to the committee on Enrollment.

Mr. Crary from the committee on Arrangement and Phraseology, reported

ARTICLE V.

EXECUTIVE DEPARTMENT.

Sec. 1. The executive power is vested in a Governor, who shall hold his office for two years. A Lieutenant Governor shall be chosen for the same term.

Sec. 2. No person shall be eligible to the office of Governor or Lieutenant Governor, who has not been five years a citizen of the United States, and a resident of this State two years next preceding his election; nor shall any person be eligible to either office who has not attained the age of thirty years.

Sec. 3. The Governor and Lieutenant Governor shall be elected at the times and places of choosing members of the Legislature. The person having the highest number of votes for Governor or Lieutenant Governor shall be elected. In case two or more persons shall have an equal and the highest number of votes for Governor or Lieutenant Governor, the Legislature shall, by joint vote, choose one of such persons.

Sec. 4. The Governor shall be commander-in-chief of the military and naval forces, and may call out such forces to execute the laws, to suppress insurrections and to repel invasions.

Sec. 5. He shall transact all necessary business with officers of government, and may require information, in writing, from the officers of the executive department upon any subject relating to the duties of their respective offices.

Sec. 6. He shall take care that the laws be faithfully executed.

Sec. 7. He may convene the Legislature on extraordinary occasions.

Sec. 8. He shall give to the Legislature, and at the close of his official term to the next Legislature, information by message of the condition of the State, and recommend such measures to them as he shall deem expedient.

Sec. 9. He may convene the Legislature at some other place when the seat of government becomes dangerous from disease or a common enemy.

Sec. 10. He shall issue writs of election to fill such vacancies as occur in the Senate and House of Representatives.

Sec. 11. He may grant reprieves, commutations and pardons, after conviction, for all offences except treason and cases of impeachment, upon such conditions, and with such restrictions and limitations, as he may think proper, subject to such regulations as are provided by law, relative to the manner of applying for pardons. Upon conviction for treason, he may suspend the execution of the sentence until the case shall be reported to the Legislature at its next session, when the Legislature shall either pardon, or commute the sentence, direct the execution of the sentence, or grant a further reprieve. He shall communicate to the Legislature at each session, information of each case of reprieve, commutation or pardon granted, and the reasons therefor.

Sec. 12. In case of the impeachment of the Governor, his removal from office, death, inability, resignation, or absence from the State, the powers and duties of the office shall devolve upon the Lieutenant Governor, for the residue of the term, or until the disability ceases. When the Governor shall be out of the State in time of war, at the head of a military force thereof, he shall continue commander-in-chief of all the military force of the State.

Sec. 13. During a vacancy in the office of Governor, if the Lieutenant Governor die, resign, be impeached, displaced, be incapable of performing the duties of his office, or absent from the State, the President *pro tempore* of the Senate shall act as Governor, until the vacancy be filled, or the disability cease.

Sec. 14. The Lieutenant Governor shall, by virtue of his office, be President of the Senate. In committee of the whole he may debate all questions; and when there is an equal division, he shall give the casting vote.

Sec. 15. No member of Congress, nor any person holding office under the United States, or this State, shall execute the office of Governor.

Sec. 16. No person elected Governor or Lieutenant Governor, shall be eligible to any office or appointment from the Legislature or either house thereof during the time for which he was elected. All votes for either of them, for any such office, shall be void.

Sec. 17. Whenever a vacancy occurs in the office of Governor or Lieutenant Governor, the person executing the duties of the office of Governor shall give notice thereof by proclamation; and the electors shall, on the Tuesday succeeding the first Monday of November thereafter, choose a person to fill such vacancy.

Sec. 18. The Lieutenant Governor and President of the Senate, *pro tempore,* when performing the duties of Governor, shall receive the same compensation as the Governor.

Sec. 19. All official acts of the Governor, the approval of the laws excepted, shall be authenticated by the great seal of the State which shall be kept by the Secretary of State.

Sec. 20. All commissions issued to persons holding office under the provisions of this constitution, shall be in the name and by the authority of the people of the State of Michigan, sealed with the great seal of the State, signed by the Governor, and countersigned by the Secretary of State.

On motion of Mr. Britain,

Section 11 was amended by striking out in line 4, the word "such," and also the words "as are."

On motion of Mr. J. D. Pierce,

The rule was suspended in order to entertain a motion to strike out section 17.

And the question being on striking out the section,

Mr. Robertson moved to amend the same by substituting the word "and" in lieu of the word "or," between "Governor and Lieutenant Governor."

And the motion prevailed.

The section was then stricken out.

60

And the article, with the foregoing amendments, was referred to the committee on Enrollment.

Mr. McClelland from the committee on Arrangement and Phraseology, reported

ARTICLE VI.

JUDICIAL DEPARTMENT.

Sec. 1. The judicial power is vested in one supreme court, in circuit courts, in probate courts, and in justices of the peace. Municipal courts of civil and criminal jurisdiction may be established by the Legislature in cities.

Sec. 2. For the term of six years, and thereafter, until the Legislature otherwise provide, the judges of the several circuit courts shall be judges of the supreme court, four of whom shall constitute a quorum. A concurrence of three shall be necessary to a final decision. After six years the Legislature may provide by law for the organization of a separate supreme court, with the jurisdiction and powers prescribed in this constitution, to consist of one chief justice and three associate justices, to be chosen by the electors of the State. Such supreme court, when so organized, shall not be changed or discontinued by the legislature for eight years thereafter. The judges thereof shall be so classified that but one of them shall go out of office at the same time. Their term of office shall be eight years.

Sec. 3. The supreme court shall have a general superintending control over all inferior courts, and shall have power to issue writs of error, habeas corpus, mandamus, injunction, quo warranto, procedendo, and other original and remedial writs, and to hear and determine the same. In all other cases it shall have appellate jurisdiction only.

Sec. 4. Four terms of the supreme court shall be held annually at such times and places as may be designated by law.

Sec. 5. The supreme court shall, by general rules, establish, modify and amend the practice in such court and in the circuit courts, and simplify the same. The Legislature shall, as far as practicable, abolish distinctions between law and equity proceedings. The office of master in chancery is prohibited.

Sec. 6. The state shall be divided into eight judicial circuits; in each of which the electors thereof shall elect one circuit judge, who shall hold his office for the term of six years and until his successor is elected and qualified.

Sec. 7. The Legislature may alter the limits of circuits or increase the number of the same. No alteration or increase shall have the effect to remove a judge from office. In every additional circuit established, the judge shall be elected by the electors of such circuit, and his term of office shall continue as provided in this constitution for judges of the circuit court.

Sec. 8. The circuit courts shall have original jurisdiction in all matters, civil and criminal, not excepted in this constitution, and not prohibited by law; and appellate jurisdiction from all inferior courts and tribunals, and a supervisory control of the same. They shall also have power to issue writs of habeas corpus, mandamus, injunction, quo warranto, certiorari and other writs necessary to carry into effect their orders, judgements and decrees, and give them a general control over inferior courts and tribunals within their respective jurisdictions.

Sec. 9. Each of the judges of the circuit courts shall receive a salary, payable quarterly. They shall receive no fees or perquisites of office, or other compensation; and shall be ineligible to any other than a judicial office during the term for which they are elected, and for one year thereafter. All votes for any person elected a judge, for any office other than the one held by them, given either by the Legislature or the people, shall be void.

Sec. 10. The supreme court may appoint a reporter of its decisions. The decisions of the supreme court shall be in writing, and signed by the judges concurring therein. Any judge dissenting therefrom shall give the reasons of such dissent in writing, under his signature. All such opinions shall be filed in the office of the clerk of the supreme court. The judges of the circuit court within their respective jurisdictions, may fill vacancies in the office of county clerk and of prosecuting attorney; but no judge of the supreme court, or circuit court, shall exercise any other power of appointment to public office.

Sec. 11. A circuit court shall be held at least twice in each year in every county organized for judicial purposes, and four times in each year in counties containing ten thousand inhabitants. Judges of the circuit court may hold courts for each other, and shall do so when required by law.

Sec. 12. The clerk of each county organized for judicial purposes shall be the clerk of the circuit court of such county, and of the supreme court when held within the same.

Sec. 13. In each of the counties organized for judicial purposes, there shall be a court of probate. The judge of such court shall be elected by the electors of the county in which he resides, and shall hold his office for four years, and until his successor is elected and qualified. The jurisdiction, powers and duties of such court shall be prescribed by law.

Sec. 14. When a vacancy occurs in the office of judge of the supreme, circuit or probate court, it shall be filled by appointment of the Governor, which shall continue until a successor is elected and qualified. When elected, such successor shall hold his office the residue of the unexpired term.

Sec. 15. The supreme court, the circuit and probate courts of each county, shall be courts of record, and shall each have a common seal.

Sec. 16. The Legislature may provide by law for the election of one or more persons in each organized county, who may be vested with judicial powers not exceeding those of a judge of the circuit court at chambers.

Sec. 17. There shall be not exceeding four justices of the peace in eaah organized township. They shall be elected by the electors of the township, and shall hold their offices for four years, and until their successors are elected and qualified. At the first election in any township they shall be classified as shall be prescribed by law. A justice elected to fill a vacancy shall hold for the residue of the unexpired term. The Legislature may increase the number of justices in cities.

Sec. 18. In civil cases justices of the peace shall have exclusive jurisdiction to the amount of one hundred dollars, and concurrent jurisdiction to the amount of three hundred dollars, which may be increased to five hundred dollars, with such exceptions and restrictions as may be provided by law. They shall also have such criminal jurisdiction and perform such duties as shall be prescribed by the Legislature.

Sec. 19. Judges of the supreme court, circuit judges, and justices of the peace, shall be conservators of the peace within their respective jurisdictions.

Sec. 20. The first election of judges of the circuit courts shall be held on the first Monday in April, 1851, and every sixth year thereafter. Whenever an additional circuit is created, such provision may be made as to hold the subsequent election of such additional judge at the regular elections herein provided.

Sec. 21. The first election of judges of the probate courts shall be held on the Tuesday succeeding the first Monday of November, 1852, and every fourth year thereafter.

Sec. 22. Whenever a judge shall remove beyond the limits of the jurisdiction for which he was elected, and a justice of the peace from the township in which he was elected, or who, by a change in the boundaries of such township, shall be placed without the same, shall be deemed to have vacated their respective offices.

Sec. 23. The Legislature may establish courts of conciliation, with such powers and duties as shall be prescribed by law.

Sec. 24. Any suitor in any court of this State shall have the right to prosecute or defend his suit, either by his own proper person, or by an attorney or agent of his choice.

Sec. 25. In all prosecutions for libels, the truth may be given in evidence to the jury; and if it shall appear to the jury that the matter charged as libellous is true, and was published with good motives and for justifiable ends, the party shall be acquitted. The jury shall have the right to determine the law and the fact.

Sec. 26. The person, houses, papers and possessions of every person shall be secure from unreasonable searches and seizures. No warrant to search any place or to seize any person or things, shall issue without describing them, nor without probable cause, supported by oath or affirmation.

Sec. 27. The right of trial by jury shall remain, but shall be deemed to be waived in all civil cases unless demanded by one of the parties in such manner as shall be prescribed by law.

Sec. 28. In every criminal prosecution the accused shall have the right to a speedy and public trial by an impartial jury, which may consist of less than twelve men in all courts not of record; to be informed of the nature of the accusation; to be confronted with the witnesses against him; to have compulsory process for obtaining witnesses in his favor; and have the assistance of counsel for his defence.

Sec. 29. No person, after acquittal upon the merits, shall be tried for the same offence. All persons shall, before conviction, be bailable by sufficient sureties, except for murder and treason when the proof is evident or the presumption great.

Sec. 30. Treason against the State shall consist only in levying war against it, or in adhering to its enemies, giving them aid and comfort. No person shall be convicted of treason unless upon the testimony of two witnesses to the same overt act, or on confession in open court.

Sec. 31. Excessive bail shall not be required; excessive fines shall not be imposed; and cruel or unusual punishment shall not be inflicted, nor shall witnesses be unreasonably detained.

Sec. 32. No person shall be compelled, in any criminal case, to be a witness against himself, nor be deprived of life, liberty or property, without due process of law.

Sec. 33. No person shall be imprisoned for debt, arising out of or founded on a contract, express or implied, except in cases of fraud or breach of trust, or of moneys collected by public officers or in any professional employment. No person shall be imprisoned for a militia fine in time of peace.

Sec. 34. No person shall be rendered incompetent to be a witness on account of his opinions on matters of religious belief.

Sec. 35. The style of all process shall be: "In the name of the people of the State of Michigan."

On motion of Mr. Hanscom,

The word "separate" was stricken out of the 6th line of sec. 2.

On motion of Mr. Whipple,

Sec. 3 was amended by striking out in line 3 the word "injunction."

On motion of Mr. Morrison,

Sec. 9 was amended by striking out in the 6th line, the words "the one held by them," and inserting in lieu thereof the word "judicial."

On motion of Mr. McClelland,

The same section was amended by substituting for the letter "a," before "judge," the word "such."

Mr. Crouse moved to suspend the rule, for the purpose of striking out "for one year thereafter," in section 9.

But the Convention refused to suspend the rule.

On motion of Mr. Williams,

Section 9 was amended by striking out the words "shall receive no fees or perquisites of office or other compensation; and."

A discussion arising as to the alterations made by the committee to sections 17 and 18 of the article,

The report regarding section 17, was concurred in.

On motion of Mr. Crary,

The section was amended by inserting after "hold," the words "his office."

And the question being upon concurring in section 18, as reported by the committee on arrangement and phraseology, the same was concurred in, as follows:

YEAS:

Mr. W. Adams, Anderson, Arzeno, Barnard, H. Bartow, J. Bartow, Beeson, Britain, Ammon Brown, Burns, Bush, Butterfield, Chandler, Chapel Choate, Church, Conner, Cornell,

Mr. Crary, Danforth, Daniels, Edmunds, Fralick, Gardiner, Gibson, Hanscom, Harvey, Hascall, Kinne, Marvin, McClelland, Morrison, Mosher, Mowry, Orr,

Mr. J. D. Pierce, Redfield, Roberts, Robertson, E. S. Robinson, Rix Robinson, Skinner, Soule, Sturgis, Town, Van Valkenburg, Walker, Warden, White, Whipple, Whittemore, Williams,

52

NAYS:

Mr. Alvord, Axford,

Mr. Desnoyers, Eaton,

Mr. Newberry, O'Brien,

Beardsley,	Gale,	N. Pierce,
Asahel Brown,	Hart,	Prevost,
Carr,	Lee,	Wait,
Comstock,	Lovell,	Woodman,
Crouse,	Moore,	President, 31

On motion of Mr. Eaton,

The Convention adjourned.

Afternoon Session.

Two o'clock.

The President called the Convention to order.

A quorum of members in attendance.

The President announced the following committee under resolution of this morning: Messrs. Hart, Alvord, Hanscom, Cornell, Comstock, Britain, Hascall and Rix Robinson.

The consideration of the article "Judicial Department," as reported by the committee on arrangement and phraseology, was resumed.

On motion of Mr. Lovell,

Section 20 was amended by striking out the words "such" and "may," and inserting in lieu of the latter, the word "shall."

On motion of Mr. Church,

Section 22 was amended by striking out "who," in 3d line, and inserting in the 4th line, between "same" and "shall," the word "they."

On motion of Mr. Leach,

The word "and," before "cruel," in section 31, was stricken out.

The article was then referred, with the foregoing amendments, to the committee on enrollment.

Mr. McClelland, from the committee on arrangement and phraseology, reported

ARTICLE VII.

ELECTIONS.

Sec. 1. In all elections every white male citizen, every white male inhabitant residing in the State on the 24th day of June, 1835: every white male inhabitant residing in this State on the first day of January, 1850, or who has resided in this State two years and six months' and declared his intention to become a citizen of the United States, pursuant to the laws thereof, six months preceding an election, and every civilized male inhabitant of Indian descent, a native of the United States and not a member of any tribe, shall be an elector and entitled to vote; but no such citizen or inhabitant shall be an elector or entitled to vote at any election, unless he shall be above the age of twenty-one years, and has resided in this State three months, and in the township or ward in which he offers to vote, ten days next preceding such election.

Sec. 2. All votes shall be given by ballot, except for such township officers as may be authorized by law to be otherwise chosen.

Sec. 3. Every elector, in all cases, except treason, felony, or breach of the peace, shall be privileged from arrest during his attendance at election, and in going to and returning from the same.

Sec. 4. No elector shall be obliged to do militia duty on the day of election, except in time of war or public danger, or attend court as a suitor or witness.

Sec. 5. No elector shall be deemed to have gained or lost a residence, by reason of his being employed in the service of the United States, or of this State; nor while engaged in the navigation of the waters of this State or of the United States, or of the high seas; nor while a student of any seminary of learning; nor while kept at any alms-house or other asylum at public expense; nor while confined in any public prison.

Sec. 6. Laws may be passed to preserve the purity of elections, and guard against abuses of the elective franchise.

Sec. 7. No soldier, seaman, nor marine in the army or navy of the United States, shall be deemed a resident of this State, in consequence of being stationed in any military or naval place within the same.

Sec. 8. Any inhabitant who may hereafter be engaged in a duel, either as principal or accessory before the fact, shall be disqualified from holding any office under the constitution and laws of this State and shall not be permitted to vote at any election.

Section 4 of the foregoing article having been altered by the committee, by adding thereto the words "or attend court as a suitor or witness," the same was concurred in.

Mr. Butterfield moved to suspend the rule, in order that a motion might be entertained to strike out of the 1st section, the words "residing in this State on the first day of January, 1850, or."

The yeas and nays were ordered thereon with the following result:

YEAS.

Mr. J. Bartow,	Mr. Fralick,	Mr. Town,
Burns,	Mowry,	White,
Butterfield,	Newberry,	Whipple,
Chandler,	Roberts,	Whittemore,
Comstock,	Robertson,	Woodman,
Crouse,	Skinner,	17

NAYS.

Mr. W. Adams,	Mr. Connor,	Mr. Mosher,
Anderson,	Danforth,	O'Brien,
Arzeno,	Daniels,	Orr,
Axford,	Desnoyers,	N. Pierce,
Barnard,	Eaton,	Prevost,
H. Bartow,	Edmunds,	Redfield,
Beardsley,	Gale,	E. S. Robinson,
Beeson,	Gibson,	Soule,
Ammon Brown,	Harvey,	Sturgis,
Asahel Brown,	Kinne,	Waite,
Bush,	Leach,	Walker,
Carr,	Lee,	Warden,
Chapel,	Marvin,	Williams,
Choate,	McClelland,	President,
Church,	Morrison,	44

So two-thirds not voting therefor the rule was not suspended.

Mr. Walker moved to amend section 1 as follows: Insert after "1850," 4th line, "who has declared his intention to become a citizen of the United States, pursuant to the laws thereof, six months preceding an election." Also strike out all after the word "intention," in line 5, and all of line 6, and insert the words "as aforesaid."

And the same was agreed to.

The article was then referred to the committee on enrollment.

Mr. Marvin moved that the vote by which the Convention refused to pass the resolution offered by Mr. Walker yesterday, in relation to the license question, be reconsidered.

The President decided the same not in order.

On motion of Mr. Redfield,

Resolved, That when the Convention adjourn, it adjourn to meet at 7 o'clock this evening.

Mr. Williams, from the committee on arrangement and phraseology, reported

ARTICLE VIII.

OF STATE OFFICERS.

Sec. 1. There shall be elected at each general biennial election, a Secretary of State, a Superintendent of Public Instruction, a State Treasurer, a Commissioner of the Land Office, an Auditor General, and an Attorney General, for the term of two years. They shall keep their offices at the seat of government, and shall perform such duties as may be prescribed by law.

Sec. 2. Their term of office shall commence on the first day of January, 1853, and of every second year thereafter.

Sec. 3. Whenever a vacancy shall occur in any of the state offices, the Governor shall fill the same by appointment, to continue until the office can be supplied by an election, at such time, and in such manner as may be provided for by law.

Sec. 4. The Secretary of State, State Treasurer, and Commissioner of the State Land Office shall constitute a board of state auditors, to examine and adjust all claims against the State not otherwise provided for by general law. They shall constitute a board of state canvassers to determine the result of all elections for Governor, Lieutenant Governor, and State Officers, and of such other officers, as shall by law be referred to them.

Sec. 5. In case two or more persons have an equal and the highest number of votes for any office, as canvassed by the board of state canvassers, the legislature, in joint convention, shall choose one of said persons to fill such office. When the determination of the board of state canvassers is contested, the legislature in joint convention shall decide which person is elected.

On motion of Mr. Williams,

Section 3 was amended by striking out all after the word "appointment," and inserting "by and with the advise and consent of the Senate, if in session."

The article was then referred to the committee on enrollment.

Mr. Williams also reported

ARTICLE IX.

SALARIES.

Sec. 1. The governor shall receive an annual salary of one

thousand dollars; the judges of the circuit court shall each receive an annual salary of fifteen hundred dollars; the state treasurer shall receive an annual salary of one thousand dollars; the auditor general shall receive an annual salary of one thousand dollars; the superintendent of public instruction shall receive an annual salary of one thousand dollars; the secretary of state shall receive an annual salary of eight hundred dollars; the commissioner of the land office shall receive an annual salary of eight hundred dollars; the attorney general shall receive an annual salary of eight hundred dollars. They shall receive no fees or perquisites, whatever, for the performance of any duties connected with their offices. It shall not be competent for the legislature to increase the salaries herein provided.

And there being no alterations to the same, it was referred to the committee on enrollment.

Mr. Gardiner reported

ARTICLE X.

COUNTY OFFICERS AND GOVERNMENT.

Sec. 1. Each organized county shall be a body corporate, with such powers and immunities as shall be established by law. All suits and proceedings by or against a county shall be in the name thereof.

Sec. 2. No organized county shall ever be reduced by the organization of new counties to less than sixteen townships, as surveyed by the United States, unless, in pursuance of law, a majority of the electors residing in each county to be affected thereby shall so decide. The legislature may organize any city into a separate county, when it has attained a population of twenty thousand inhabitants, without reference to geographical extent, when a majority of the electors of a county in which such city may be situated, voting thereon, shall be in favor of a separate organization.

Sec. 3. In each organized county there shall be a sheriff, a county clerk, a county treasurer, a register of deeds and a prosecuting attorney, chosen by the electors thereof, once in two years, and as often as vacancies shall happen, whose duties and powers shall be prescribed by law. The board of supervisors in any county may unite the offices of county clerk and register of deeds in one office, or disconnect the same.

Sec. 4. The county clerk, county treasurer, judge of probate and register of deeds, shall hold their offices at the county seat.

Sec. 5. The sheriff shall hold no other office, and shall be incapable of holding the office of sheriff longer than four in any period of six years. He may be required by law to renew his security from time to time; and in default of giving such security, his office shall be deemed vacant. The county shall never be responsible for his acts.

Sec. 6. A board of supervisors, consisting of one from each organized township, shall be established in each county, with such powers as shall be prescribed by law.

Sec. 7. Cities shall have such representation in the board of supervisors of the counties in which they are situated, as the legislature may direct.

Sec. 8. No county seat once established shall be removed until the place to which it is proposed to be removed shall be designated by two-thirds of the board of supervisors of the county, and a majority of the electors voting thereon shall have voted in favor of the proposed location, in such manner as shall be prescribed by law.

Sec. 9. The board of supervisors of any county may borrow or raise by tax one thousand dollars, for constructing or repairing public buildings, highways or bridges; but no greater sum shall be borrowed or raised by tax for such purpose in any one year, unless authorized by a majority of the electors of such county voting thereon.

Sec. 10. The board of supervisors. or in the county of Wayne, the board of county auditors, shall have the exclusive power to prescribe and fix the compensation for all services rendered for, and to adjust all claims against their respective counties, and the sum so fixed or defined shall be subject to no appeal.

Sec. 11. The board of supervisors of each organized county may provide for laying out highways, for construction of bridges, and for organizing of townships, under such restrictions and limitations as shall be prescribed by law.

On motion of Mr. Williams,

The title was changed to "counties."

On motion of Mr. McClelland,

Section 11 was amended by striking out the word "for" before "organizing," and "of" after the same word.

On motion of Mr. Robertson,

Section 4 was amended by inserting "Sheriff," before "County Clerk."

The article was then referred to the committee on enrollment.

Mr. Williams, from the committee on arrangement and phraseology, reported

ARTICLE XI.

TOWNSHIPS.

Sec. 1. There shall be elected annually, on the first Monday of April, in each organized township, one supervisor, one township clerk, who shall be ex officio school inspector, one township treasurer, one school inspector, not exceeding four constables, and one overseer of highways for each highway district, in whom, together with the justices of the peace, shall be vested the township government, to be defined and limited by the legislature.

Sec. 2. Each organized township shall be a body corporate, with such powers and immunities as shall be prescribed by law. All suits and proceedings by or against a township, shall be in the name thereof.

Mr. J. Bartow moved to suspend the rule in order that a motion might be entertained to amend section 1, by inserting in line 2, the words "one commissioner of highways."

The yeas and nays were had on the motion to suspend the rule, and the result was as follows:

YEAS.

Mr. W. Adams,	Mr. Crouse,	Mr. Newberry,
Anderson,	Desnoyers,	O'Brien,
Arzeno,	Eaton,	Prevost,
Axford,	Edmunds,	Robertson,
Barnard,	Gale,	E. S. Robinson,
H. Bartow,	Gardiner,	Skinner,
J. Bartow,	Green,	Sturgis,
Beardsley,	Kinne,	Van Valkenburg,
Asahel Brown,	Lovell,	Wait,

Burns,	Marvin,	Webster,
Carr,	McClelland,	White,
Chandler,	Moore,	Whipple,
Choate,	Mosher,	Woodman,
Church,	Mowry,	41

NAYS.

Mr. Beeson,	Mr. Fralick,	Mr. N. Pierce,
Ammon Brown,	Harvey,	Town,
Butterfield,	Leach,	Warden,
Conner,	Morrison,	Whittemore,
Danforth,	Orr,	Williams,
Daniels,	J. D. Pierce,	17

So two-thirds voting therefor, the rule was suspended.

The question being upon inserting as proposed by Mr. J. Bartow,

Mr. N. Pierce moved to amend the same by inserting, "the justice of the peace whose term of office will first expire in each town shall be commissioner of highways;" which was lost, and

Mr. Bartow's amendment was then agreed to.

Mr. Green moved to suspend the rule, in order that the following might be added to the article:

"The word "town," instead of "township," may be used in all cases where it refers to a corporate body, or to territory within the jurisdiction of such corporate body."

But the Convention refused to suspend the rule.

The article was then referred to the committee on enrollment.

Mr. McClelland, from the committee on arrangement and phraseology, reported

ARTICLE XII.

IMPEACHMENTS AND REMOVALS FROM OFFICE.

Sec. 1. The House of Representatives shall have the sole power of impeaching civil officers for corrupt conduct in office, or for crimes and misdemeanors; but a majority of the members elected shall be necessary to direct an impeachment.

Sec. 2. Every impeachment shall be tried by the Senate. When the Governor or Lieutenant Governor is tried, the chief justice of the supreme court shall preside. When an impeachment is directed the Senate shall take an oath or affirmation truly and impartially to try and determine the same according to the evidence. No person shall be convicted without the concurrence of two-thirds of the members elected. Judgment in case of impeachment shall not extend further than removal from office, but the party convicted shall be liable to punishment according to law.

Sec. 3. When an impeachment is directed the House of Representatives shall elect from their own body three members, whose duty it shall be to prosecute such impeachment. No impeachment shall be tried until the final adjournment of the Legislature, when the Senate shall proceed to try such impeachment.

Sec. 4. No judicial officer shall exercise his office after an impeachment is directed until he is acquitted.

Sec. 5. The Governor may make a provisional appointment to fill a vacancy occasioned by the suspension of an officer until he shall be acquitted, or until after the election and qualification of a successor.

Sec. 6. For reasonable cause, which shall not be sufficient ground for the impeachment of a judge, the Governor shall remove him on a concurrent resolution of two-thirds of the members elected to each house of the Legislature; but the cause for which such removal is required, shall be stated at length in such resolution.

Sec. 7. The Legislature shall provide by law for the removal of any officer elected by a county, township or school district, in such manner and for such cause as to them shall seem just and proper.

On motion of Mr. J. Bartow,

Section 3 was amended by striking out at the end of the same, the words "such impeachment," and inserting "the same;" and the article was referred to the committee on enrollment.

Mr. Crary reported

ARTICLE XIII.

EDUCATION.

Sec. 1. The Superintendent of Public Instruction shall have the general supervision of public instruction, and his duties shall be prescribed by law.

Sec. 2. The proceeds from the sales of all lands that have been, or hereafter may be granted by the United States to the State for educational purposes, and the proceeds of all lands or other property given by individuals, or appropriated by the State for like purposes, shall be and remain a perpetual fund, the interest and income of which, together with the rents of all such lands as may remain unsold, shall be inviolably appropriated and annually applied to the specific objects of the original gift, grant or appropriation.

Sec. 3. All lands, the titles to which shall fail from a defect of heirs, shall escheat to the State; and the interest on the clear proceeds from the sales thereof, shall be appropriated exclusively to the support of primary schools.

Sec. 4. The Legislature shall, within five years from the adoption of this constitutioe, provide for and establish a system of common schools, whereby a school shall be kept without charge for tuition, at least three months in each year, in every school district in the State; and all instruction in said schools shall be conducted in the English language.

Sec. 5. A school shall be kept up and supported in each school district, at least three months in each year. Any school district neglecting to keep up and support such school, shall be deprived for the ensuing year, of its proportion of the income of the primary school fund, and of all funds arising from taxes, for the support of schools.

Sec. 6. There shall be elected in each judicial circuit, at the time of the election of the judge of such circuit, a regent of the University, whose term of office shall be the same as that of such judge; and the regents thus elected, shall constitute the board of regents of the University of Michigan.

Sec. 7. The regents of the University and their successors in office, shall continue to constitute the body corporate, known by the name and title of "the regents of the University of Michigan."

Sec. 8. The regents of the University shall, at their first annual meeting, or as soon thereafter as may be, elect a president of the University, who shall be ex-officio a member of their board, with the privilege of speaking, but not of voting. He shall preside at the meetings of the regents, and be the principal executive officer of the University. The board of regents shall have the general supervision of the University, and the direction and control of all expenditures from the university interest fund.

Sec. 9. There shall be elected at the general election in the year one thousand eight hundred fifty-two, three members of a State board of education; one for two years, one for four years, and one for six years; and at each succeeding biennial election, there shall be elected one member of such board, who shall hold his office for six years. The Superintendent of Public Instruction shall be ex officio a member and secretary of such board. The board shall have the general supervision of the State normal school, and their duties shall be prescribed by law.

Sec. 10. Institutions for the benefit of those inhabitants who are deaf, dumb, blind or insane, shall always be fostered and supported.

Sec. 11. The Legislature shall encourage the promotion of intellectual, scientific and agricultural improvement; and shall, as soon as practicable, provide for the establishment of an agricultural school. And the Legislature may appropriate the twenty-two sections of salt spring lands now unappropriated, or the money arising from the sale of the same, where such lands have been already sold, and any land which may hereafter be granted or appropriated for such purpose, for the support and maintenance of such school, and may make the same a branch of the University, for instruction in agriculture and the natural sciences connected therewith, and place the same under the supervision of the regents of the University.

Sec. 12. The Legislature shall also provide for the establishment of at least one library in each township; and all fines assessed and collected in the several counties and townships for any breach of the penal laws, shall be exclusively applied to the support of such libraries.

On motion of Mr. J. D. Pierce,

The article was amended by striking out "common," wheresoever it occurs, and inserting "primary."

On motion of Mr. Williams,

Section 5 was amended by striking out "kept up and supported," in the 1st line, and also "keep up and support," in the 3d line, and the words "maintained and" were inserted in lieu thereof.

The amendments were concurred in, and the article was referred to the committee on enrollment.

Mr. Williams reported

ARTICLE XIV.

FINANCE AND TAXATION.

Sec. 1. All specific state taxes, except those received from the mining companies of the upper peuinsula, shall be applied in paying the interest upon the primary school, university and other educational funds, and the interest and principal of the State debt, in the order herein recited, until the extinguishment of the state debt, other than the amounts due to educational funds; when such specific taxes shall be added to, and constitute a part of the proceeds of the primary school fund. The legislature shall provide for an annual tax, sufficient, with other resources, to pay the estimated expenses of the State government, the interest of the State debt, and such deficiency as may occur in the resources.

Sec. 2. The legislature shall provide by law, a sinking fund of at least twenty thousand dollars a year, to commence in eighteen hundred and fifty-two, with compound interest at six per cent. per annum, and an annual increase of at least five per cent., to be applied solely to the payment and extinguishment of the principal of the State debt, other than the amounts due to educational funds, and shall be continued until the extinguishment thereof. The unfunded debt shall not be funded or redeemed at a value exceeding that established by law in eighteen hundred and forty-eight.

Sec. 3. The state may contract debts to meet deficits in revenues. Such debts shall not in the aggregate at any one time exceed fifty thousand dollars. The moneys so raised shall be applied to the purposes for which they were obtained, or to the payment of the debts so contracted.

Sec. 4. The state may contract debts to repel invasion, suppress insurrection, or defend the state in time of war. The money arising from the contracting of such debts shall be applied to the purpose for which it was raised, or to repay such debts.

Sec. 5. No money shall be paid out of the treasury except in pursuance of appropriations made by law.

Sec. 6. The credit of the state shall not be granted to or in aid of any person, association or corporation.

Sec. 7. No scrip, certificate, or other evidence of state indebtedness shall be issued, except for the redemption of stock previously issued, or for such debts as are expressly authorized in this constitution.

Sec. 8. The state shall not subscribe to or be interested in the stock of any company, association or corporation.

Sec. 9. The state shall not be a party to or interested in any work of internal improvement, nor engaged in carrying on any such work, except in the expenditure of grants to the state, of land or other property.

Sec. 10. The state may continue to collect all specific taxes accruing to the treasury under existing laws. The legislature may provide for the collection of specific taxes, from banking, rail road, plank road and other corporations hereafter created.

Sec. 11. The legislature shall provide an uniform rule of taxation, except on property paying specific taxes; and taxes shall be levied on such property as shall be prescribed by law.

Sec. 12. All assessments hereafter authorized shall be on property at its cash value.

Sec. 13. The legislature shall provide for an equalization by a state board in 1851, and every fifth year thereafter, of assessments on all taxable property except that paying specific taxes.

Sec. 14. Every law which imposes, continues or revives a tax, shall distinctly state the tax, and the object to which it is to be applied; and it shall not be sufficient to refer to any other law to fix such tax or object.

On motion of Mr. Robertson,

Section 2 was amended by inserting between the words "at" and "six," the words "the rate of."

On motion of Mr. Crary,

The word "interest" was inserted between the words "school" and "fund," in line 8 of section 1, and the words "proceeds of" were stricken out of the same line, and

The article was referred to the committee on enrollment.

Mr. Williams, from the committe on arrangement and phraseology, reported

ARTICLE XV.

CORPORATIONS.

Sec. 1. Corporations may be formed under general laws; but shall not be created by special act, except for municipal purposes.

All laws passed pursuant to this section may be altered, amended or repealed.

Sec. 2. No banking law or law for banking purposes, or amendments thereof, shall have effect until the same shall, after its passage, be submitted to a vote of the electors of the State, at a general election, and be approved by a majority of the votes cast thereon at such election.

Sec. 3. The officers and stockholders of every corporation or association for banking purposes, issuing bank notes or paper credits to circulate as money, shall be individually liable for all debts contracted during the time of their being officers or stockholders of such corporation or association.

Sec. 4. The legislature shall provide by law for the registry of all bills or notes issued or put in circulation as money, and shall require security to the full amount of notes and bills so registered in State or United States stocks bearing interest, which shall be deposited with the State Treasurer for the redemption of such bills or notes in specie.

Sec. 5. In case of the insolvency of any bank or banking association, the bill holders thereof shall be entitled to preference in payment, over all other creditors of such bank or association.

Sec. 6. The legislature shall pass no law authorizing or sanctioning the suspension of specie payments by any person, association or corporation.

Sec. 7. The stockholders of all corporations and joint stock associations shall be individually liable for all labor performed for such corporation or association.

Sec. 8. The legislature shall pass no law altering or amending any act of incorporation heretofore granted, without the assent of two-thirds of the members elected to each house; nor shall any such act be renewed or extended. This restriction shall not apply to municipal corporations.

Sec. 9. The property of no person shall be taken by any corporation for public use, without compensation being first made or secured, in such manner as may be prescribed by law.

Sec. 10. No corporation except for municipal purposes or for the construction of rail roads and canals, shall be created for a longer time than thirty years.

Sec. 11. The term "corporations," as used in the preceding sections of this article, shall be construed to include all associations and joint stock companies having any of the powers or privileges of corporations, not possessed by individuals or partnerships. And all corporations shall have the right to sue and be subject to be sued, in all courts, in like cases as natural persons.

Sec. 12. No corporation shall hold any real estate hereafter acquired foı a longer period than ten years, except such real estate as shall be actually occupied by such corporation in the exercise of its franchises.

Sec. 13. The legislature shall provide for the incorporation and organization of cities and villages and shall restrict their powers of taxation, borrowing money, contracting debts, and loaning their credit.

Sec. 14. Officers of cities and villages shall be elected at such time and in such manner as the legislature may direct.

Sec. 15. Private property shall not be taken for improvements in cities and villages without the consent of the owner, unless the compensation therefor shall first be determined by a jury of freeholders and actually paid or secured in the manner provided by law.

Sec. 16. Previous notice of any application for an alteration of the charter of any corporation shall be given in such manner as may be prescribed by law.

Mr. Morrison moved to insert in section 3, after the word "during," the words "and for one year thereafter."

Which was not agreed to.

On motion of Mr. McClelland,

Section 14 was amended by inserting the word "judicial" at the commencement of the section, and the words "and all other officers shall be elected or appointed," after "elected," in the 1st line of the section.

On motion of Mr. Whipple,

Section 15 was amended by inserting before "improvements" the word "public."

On motion of Mr. Skinner,

The rule was suspended and section 10 was amended by inserting after "rail roads," the words "plank roads."

And the article was referred to the committee on enrollment.

By unanimous consent, on motion of Mr. Crary,

The article entitled "townships" was amended by striking out all after "highway district," and inserting "whose powers and duties shall be prescribed by law."

Mr. McClelland, from the committee on arrangement and phraseology, reported

ARTICLE XVI.

EXEMPTIONS.

Sec. 1. The personal property of every resident of this State, is to consist of such articles only as shall be designated by law, shall be exempted to the amount of not less than five hundred dollars, from sale on execution or other final process of any court, issued for the collection of any debt contracted after the adoption of this Constitution.

Sec. 2. A homested of not more than forty acres of land, used for agricultural purposes, and the dwelling house thereon, and the appurtenances to be selected by the owner thereof, and not included in any town plat, city or village; or instead thereof, at the option of the owner, any lot in any city, village or recorded town plat, or such parts of lots as shall be equal thereto, and the dwelling house thereon, and its appurtenances, owned and occupied by any resident of the State, not exceeding in value fifteen hundred dollars, shall be exempt from forced sale on execution, or any other final process from a court, for any debt contracted after the adoption of this Constitution. Such exemption shall not extend to any mortgage thereon lawfully obtained; but such mortgage or other alienation of such land by the owner thereof, if a married man, shall not be valid without the signature of the wife to the same.

Sec. 3. The homested of a family, after the death of the owner thereof, shall be exempt from the payment of his debts, contracted after the adoption of this constitution, in all cases where any minor children shall survive the death of such owner, for their benefit and support during minority.

Sec. 4. If the owner of a homested die, leaving a widow, but no children, the same shall be exempt, and the rents and profits thereof shall accrue to her benefit during the time of her widowhood, unless she be the owner of a homested in her own right.

Sec. 5. The real and personal estate of every female, acquired before marriage, and all property to which she may afterwards become entitled, by gift, grant, inheritance or devise, shall be and remain the estate and property of such female, and shall not be liable for the debts, obligations or engagements of her husband, and may be devised by her as if she were unmarried.

On motion of Mr. Church,

The Convention adjourned.

Evening Session.

7 o'clock.

The President called the Convention to order.

A quorum of members being in attendance,

Mr. Hart, from a majority of the committee appointed to divide the State into judicial districts, submitted the following report:

1st District.—Monroe, Lenawee and Hillsdale.

2d.—Branch, St. Joseph, Cass and Berrien.

3d.—Wayne.

4th.—Washtenaw, Jackson and Ingham.

5th.—Calhoun, Kalamazoo, Allegan, Barry and Van Buren.

6th.—St. Clair, Macomb and Oakland.

7th—Lapeer, Genesee, Saginaw, Shiawassee and Livingston.

8th.—Eaton, Kent, Ottawa, Ionia, Clinton and Montcalm.

Mr. Hanscom, from the same committee, submitted a minority report, as follows:

The minority of the committee appointed under the resolution to prepare and report upon the subject of a division of the State into judicial circuits, report and recommend that the districts be composed as follows:

1st District.—Wayne and Washtenaw.

2d.—Monroe, Lenawee and Hillsdale.

3d.—Branch, St. Joseph, Cass and Berrien.

4th.—Jackson, Calhoun, Kalamazoo and Van Buren.

5th.—Oakland, Macomb and St. Clair.

6th.—Livingston, Ingham, Eaton, Barry and Allegan.

7th.—Lapeer, Genesee, Shiawassee, Saginaw, Tuscola and Sanilac.

8th.—Ionia, Kent, Ottawa, Newaygo, Clinton and Montcalm.

The following is the number of terms that would be required to be held in the different circuits under the above arrangement of circuits, as is now believed from the best estimate of the population of the respective counties: 1st circuit, 8 terms; 2nd, 12; 3d, 14; 4th, 14; 5th, 12; 6th, 14; 7th, 16; 8th, 16.

The undersigned respectfully suggests to the Convention, that among the reasons that induced the placing of Wayne and Washtenaw together and constituting them a circuit, instead of making the county of Wayne a circuit of itself, the following had much weight, and they ask for them the consideration of the Convention.

By the provisions already incorporated into the Constitution which we have framed, Wayne county (or the city of Detroit, in which a large majority of the judicial business of that county originates,) can be relieved by the legislature by the organization of municipal courts. Just as much of the duties imposed upon the circuits can be imposed upon such courts as the exigencies of business may require. This exception, though general in the Constitution, as applied to cities, has really no practicable operation except in the county of Wayne.

Another reason is the contiguity of the places of holding the courts in the respective counties. One or two hour's ride, at a nominal cost, takes the judge from Detroit to Ann Arbor, and *vice versa*. Not so as applied to the judges who hold the northern or western circuits. They have to travel hundreds of miles of bad roads at all seasons of the year, at great labor and expense, as well as serious loss of time.

Another fact is submitted that should have its influence upon this question. Under the proposed division of the majority of the committee, only four terms are to be held by the judge of that circuit, while in some of the others terms to the number of sixteen will be required; and that, too, by judges residing in districts where all the expenses, trouble, and labor of traversing the circuit is far greatest.

But one other reason is respectfully urged. It is unjust to the other portions of the State to withdraw from the judicial force of the

State the sole labors of one of the judges, where neither population nor the business that will be imposed upon this circuit court, warrants it.

There is in fact now in existence, in the county of Wayne, a local tribunal, that relieves the circuit and county courts of a large mass of business.

Such are some of the reasons that influence the undersigned to dissent from the report of the majority, and induce the submission of the proposition just read. A. H. HANSCOM.

On motion of Mr. McClelland,

The two reports were laid upon the table, and so much of the same as contained the apportionment, ordered printed.

The Convention resumed the consideration of the article "Exemptions."

Mr. Fralick moved to suspend the rule in order to move the indefinite postponement of the article.

The yeas and nays were had, and the Convention refused to suspend the rule, as follows:

YEAS.

Mr. Axford,	Mr. Comstock,	Mr. E. S. Robinson,
Ammon Brown,	Crouse,	Rix Robinson,
Burns,	Desnoyers,	Skinner,
Butterfield,	Edmunds,	Wait.
Carr,	Fralick,	White,
Chapel,	Gibson,	President,
Church,	Newberry,	20

NAYS.

Mr. W. Adams,	Mr. Daniels,	Mr. Orr,
Alvord,	Eaton,	J. D. Pierce,
Anderson,	Gale,	N. Pierce,
Arzeno,	Gardiner,	Prevost,
Barnard,	Green,	Redfield,
H. Bartow,	Hart,	Roberts,
J. Bartow,	Harvey,	Robertson,
Beardsley,	Hascall,	Soule,
Beeson,	Kinne,	Sturgis,
Britain,	Leach,	Town,
Asahel Brown,	Lovell,	Van Valkenburg,
Bush,	McClelland,	Walker,
Chandler,	Morrison,	Warden,
Choate,	Mosher,	Whittemore,
Conner,	Mowry,	Williams,
Danforth,	O'Brien,	Woodman, 48

On motion of Mr. McClelland,

Section 1 was amended by striking out "articles," and inserting "property."

Mr. Skinner moved to suspend the rule in order to move to strike out "resident," in section 1, and insert "house-holder."

But the Convention refused to suspend the rule by yeas and nays as follows:

YEAS.

Mr. Axford,	Mr. Edmunds,	Mr. Newberry,
Burns,	Fralick,	Robertson,
Butterfield,	Gibson,	Skinner,
Carr,	Lee,	Wait,
Chapel,	McClelland,	White,
Church,	Moore,	Whipple,
Crouse,	Mowry,	President,
Desnoyers,		22

NAYS.

Mr. W. Adams,	Mr. Cornell,	Mr. O'Brien,
Alvord,	Danforth,	Orr,
Anderson,	Daniels,	J. D. Pierce,
Arzeno,	Eaton,	N. Pierce,
Barnard,	Gale,	Prevost,
H. Bartow,	Gardiner,	Redfield,
J. Bartow,	Green,	Rix Robinson,
Beardsley,	Hanscom,	Soule,
Beeson,	Hart,	Sturgis,
Britain,	Harvey,	Town,
Ammon Brown,	Hascall,	Van Valkenburg,
Asahel Brown,	Kinne,	Warden,
Bush,	Leach,	Webster,
Chandler,	Lovell,	Whittemore,
Choate,	Morrison,	Williams,
Comstock,	Mosher,	Woodman,
Conner,		49

Section. 1 as amended was then concurred in.

Mr. McClelland moved to amend section 2 by striking out "a homested of not more than," and inserting "every homsted not exceeding."

And the same was agreed to.

The committee having amended section 2 by inserting in the 1st line the words "and for agricultural purposes,"

Mr. Redfield moved to insert after "used" the words "or designed."

And the same was agreed to.

The Convention then refused to concur in the amendment made by the committee, by yeas and nays, as follows;

YEAS.

Mr. W. Adams, Anderson, Arzeno, Beeson, Britain, Ammon Brown, Bush, Butterfield, Choate, Cornell, Danforth, Mr. Daniels, Desnoyers, Eaton, Fralick, Gardiner, Gibson, Green, Harvey, McClelland, Moore, Mosher, Mr. Mowry, O'Brien, J. D. Pierce, Redfield, Robertson, E. S. Robinson, Town, Van Valkenburg, Whipple, Williams, Woodman, 33

NAYS.

Mr. Alvord, Axford, Barnard, H. Bartow, J. Bartow, Beardsley, Burns, Carr, Chandler, Chapel, Church, Comstock, Mr. Crouse, Edmunds, Gale, Hart, Hascall, Kinne, Leach, Lovell, Morrison, Newberry, Orr, N. Pierce, Mr. Prevost, Rix Robinson, Skinner, Soule, Sturgis, Wait, Walker, Warden, Webster, White, Whittemore, President, 36

So the words "used for agricnltural purposes," were not incorporated in the 2d section of the article.

Mr. Walker moved to suspend the rule, in order to move the insertion in section 2, after "villages," where it first occurs, the words "not exceeding in value fifteen hundred dollars."

But the Convention refused to suspend the rule.

Mr. Beardsley moved to suspend the rule, that he might be enabled to move to insert in section 2, after the word "State" in line 5, the words "said village lot or lots."

But the Convention refused to suspend the rule.

Mr. Williams moved to strike from section 3 all after "survive," in last line.

And the same was done by unanimous consent.

On motion of Mr. Church,

Section 3 was amended by striking out "where any children shall survive," and inserting "during the minority of his children."

Mr. Beardsley moved to suspend the rule, in order to amend section 5 by inserting in the last line, after "devised," the words "or bequeathed."

And the same was agreed to, and the amendment made.

The article was then referred to the committee on enrollment.

Mr. McClelland reported

ARTICLE XVII.

MILITIA.

Sec. 1. The militia shall be composed of all able bodied white male citizens between the ages of eighteen and forty-five years, except such as are exempted by the laws of the United States or of this State; but all such citizens of any religious denomination whatever, who, from scruples of conscience, may be averse to bearing arms, shall be excused therefrom, upon such conditions as shall be prescribed by law.

Sec. 2. The Legislature shall provide by law for organizing, equipping and disciplining the militia, in such manner as they shall deem expedient, not incompatible with the laws of the United States.

Sec. 3. Officers of the militia shall be elected or appointed, and be commissioned in such manner as may be provided by law.

The same was concurred in, and referred to the committee on enrollment.

Mr. Williams, from the committee on arrangement and phraseology, reported

ARTICLE XVIII.

MISCELLANEOUS PROVISIONS.

Sec. 1. Members of the legislature, and all officers, executive and judicial, except such inferior officers as may by law be exempted, shall, before they enter on the duties of their respective offices, take and subscribe the following oath or affirmation: "I do solemnly swear (or affirm) that I will support the constitution of the United States and the constitution of this State, and that I will faithfully discharge the duties of the office of according to the best of my ability." And no other oath, declaration or test shall be required as a qualification for any office or public trust.

Sec. 2. When private property is taken for the use or benefit of the public, the necessity for using such property, and the just compensation to be made therefor, except when to be made by the state, shall be ascertained by a jury of twelve freeholders, residing in the vicinity of such property, or by not less than three commissioners, appointed by a court of record, as shall be prescribed by law.

Sec. 3. No mechanical trade shall hereafter be taught to covicts in the state prison of this state. except the manufacture of those articles, of which the chief supply for home consumption is imported from other states or countries.

See. 4. No navigable stream in this state shall be either bridged or damed without authority from the board of supervisors of the proper county, under the provisions of law. No such law shall prejudice the right of individuals to the free navigation of such streams, or preclude the state from the further improvement of the navigation of such streams.

Sec. 5. An accurate statement of the receipts and expenditures of the public moneys shall be attached to, and published with, the laws, at every regular session of the legislature.

Sec. 6. The laws, publie records, and the written judicial and legislative proceedings of the state shall be conducted, promulgated and preserved in the English language.

Sec. 7. Every person has a right to bear arms for the defence of himself and the state.

Sec. 8. The military shall, in all cases, and at all times, be in strict subordination to the civil power.

Sec. 9. No soldier shall, in time of peace, be quartered in any house without the consent of the owner or occupant, nor in time of war, except in a manner prescribed by law.

Sec. 10. The people have the right peaceably to assemble together, to consult for the common good, to instruct their representatives, and to petition the Legislature for redress of grievances.

Sec. 11. Neither slavery, nor involuntary servitude, unless for the punishment of crime, shall ever be tolerated in this State.

Sec. 12. No lease or grant hereafter of agricultural land for a longer period than twelve years, reserving any rent or service of any kind, shall be valid.

Sec. 13. Aliens who are, or who may hereafter become *bona fide* residents of this State, shall enjoy the same rights in respect to the possession, enjoyment and inheritance of property, as native born citizens.

Sec. 14. The property of no person shall be taken for public use without just compensation therefor. Private roads may be opened in the manner to be prescribed by law; but in every case the necesities of the road and the amount of all damage to be sustained by the opening thereof, shall be first determined by a jury of freeholders; and such amount, together with the expenses of proceedings, shall be paid by the person or persons to be benefitted.

On motion of Mr. Edmunds,

The word "inferior" was stricken from the 2d line of section 1.

Mr. J. Bartow moved to suspend the rule, in order to strike out section 12.

But the Convention refused to suspend rule.

The article was referred to the committee on enrollment.

Mr. Williams reported

ARTICLE XIX.

UPPER PENINSULA.

Section 1. The counties of Mackinac, Chippewa, Delta, Marquette, Schoolcraft, Houghton and Ontonagon, and the islands thereunto attached, the islands of Lake Superior, Huron and Michigan and in Green Bay, and the straits of Mackinac and the River Ste Marie, shall constitute a separate judicial district, and be entitled to a district judge and district attorney.

Sec. 2. The district judge shall be elected by the electors of such district, and shall perform the same duties and possess the same powers as a circuit judge in his circuit, and shall hold his office for the same period.

Sec. 3. The district attorney shall be elected every two years by the electors of the district, shall perform the duties of prosecuting attorney throughout the entire district, and may issue warrants for the arrest of offenders in cases of felony, to be proceeded with as shall be prescribed by law.

Sec. 4. Such judicial district shall be entitled at all times to at least one Senator, and until entitled to more by its population, it shall have three members of the House of Representatives, to be apportioned among the several counties by the Legislature.

Sec. 5. The Legislature may provide for the payment of the district judge a salary not exceeding one thousand dollars a year, and the district attorney not exceeding seven hundred dollars a year; and may allow extra compensation to the members of the Legislature from such territory, not exceeding two dollars a day during any session.

Sec. 6. The elections for all district or county officers, State Senator or Representatives, within the boundaries defined in this article, shall take place on the last Tuesday of September in the respective years in which they may be required. The county canvass shall be held on the first Tuesday in October thereafter, and the district canvass on the last Tuesday of said October.

Sec. 7. One moiety of the taxes received into the treasury from mining corporations in the upper peninsula paying an annual State tax of one per cent., shall be paid to the treasurers of the counties from which it is received; to be applied for township and county purposes, as provided by law. The Legislature shall have power, after the year 1855, to reduce the amount to be refunded.

Sec. 8. The Legislature may change the location of the State prison from Jackson to the Upper Peninsula.

Sec. 9. The charters of the several mining corporations may be modified by the Legislature, in regard to the term limited for subscribing to stock, and in relation to the quantity of land which a corporation shall hold; but the capital shall not be increased, nor the time for the existence of charters extended. No such corporation shall be permitted to purchase or hold any real estate, except such as shall be necessary for the exercise of its corporate franchises.

On motion of Mr. Moore,

Section 1 was amended by inserting after "islands," the words "and territory."

Mr. Robertson moved to amend section 7 by striking out the word "moiety" and inserting "half."

And the same was agreed to.

Mr. Butterfield moved to suspend the rule, in order to strike out section 8.

But the Convention refused to suspend.

And the article was referred to the committee on enrollment.

Mr. McClelland, from the committee on arrangement and phraseology, reported

ARTICLE XX.

AMENDMENT AND REVISION OF THE CONSTITUTION.

Section 1. Any amendment or amendments to this constitution may be proposed in the senate or house of representatives. If the same shall be agreed to by two-thirds of the members elected to each house, such amendment or amendments shall be entered on their journals respectively, with the yeas and nays taken thereon, and the same shall be submitted to the electors at the next general election thereafter, and if a majority of the electors qualified to vote for members of the legislature voting thereon, shall ratify and approve such amendment or amendments, the same shall become part of the constitution.

Sec. 2. At the general election to be held in the year eighteen hundred and sixty-six, and in each sixteenth year thereafter; and also at such other times as the legislature may by law provide, the question of a general revision of the constitution shall be submitted to the electors qualified to vote for members of the legislature; and in case a majority of the electors so qualified, voting at such election, shall decide in favor of a convention for such purpose, the legislature, at the next session, shall provide by law for the election of delegates to such convention. All the amendments shall take effect at the commencement of the political year after their adoption.

The amendments made by the committee were concurred in, and the article was referred to the committee on enrollment.

Mr. McClelland, from the committee on arrangement and phraseology, to whom was referred the "Bill of Rights," for the distribution of its sections, reported back the following, and recommended their indefinite postponement.

Sec. 1. All political power is inherent in the people.

Sec. 2. Government is instituted for the protection, security and benefit of the people; and they have the right at all times to alter or reform the same, and to abolish one form of government and establish another, whenever the public good requires it.

Sec. 3. No man or set of men are entitled to exclusive or separate privileges.

Sec. 30. All acts of the Legislature, contrary to this or any other article of this Constitution, shall be void."

And the same were indefinitely postponed.

Mr. McClelland, from the same committee, reported back the resolution relative to the question of "colored suffrage."

And the same was referred to the committee on the schedule.

On motion of Mr. Beeson,

Resolved, That the sum of twenty dollars be paid to James Marsden, Oliver C. Wiswell, Gideon Paul and Edward P. Rankin, for enrolling the Constitution, and that the officers of the Convention be authorized to issue their warrant for the same.

Mr. Moore offered the following:

Resolved, That when this Convention adjourn, it shall meet again at 7 o'clock in the morning.

And the same was agreed to.

Mr. Whipple, from the committee on arrangement and phraseology, reported

ARTICLE XXI.

SCHEDULE.

That no inconvenience may arise from the changes in the constitution of this State, and in order to carry the same into complete operation, it is hereby declared, that

Sec. 1. The common law and the statute laws now in force, not repugnant to this constitution, shall remain in force until they expire by their own limitations, or are altered or repealed by the Legislature.

Sec. 2. All writs, actions, causes of action, prosecutions and rights of individuals and of bodies incorporate, and of the State, and all charters of corporation, shall continue; and all indictments which shall have been found, or which may hereafter be found, for any crime or offence committed before the adoption of this constitution, may be proceeded upon as if no change had taken place. The several courts, except as herein otherwise provided, shall continue with the like powers and jurisdiction, both at law and in equity, as if this constitution had not been adopted, and until the organization of the judicial department under this constitution.

Sec. 3. That all fines, penalties, forfeitures and escheats accruing to the State of Michigan under the present constitution and laws, shall accrue to the use of the State under this constitution.

Sec. 4. That all recognizances, bonds, obligations, and all other instruments entered into or executed before the adoption of this constitution, to the people of the State of Michigan, to any State, county or township, or any public officer or public body, or which may be entered into or excuted under existing laws, "to the people of the State of Michigan," to any such officer or public body, before the complete organization of the departments of government under this constitution, shall remain binding and valid; and rights and liabilities upon the same shall continue, and may be prosecuted as provided by law. And all crimes and misdemeanors and penal actions, shall be tried, punished and prosecuted, as though no change had taken place, until otherwise provided by law.

Sec. 5. A Governor and Lieutenant Governor shall be chosen under the existing constitution and laws, to serve after the expiration of the term of the present incumbent.

Sec. 6. All officers, civil and military, now holding any office or appointment, shall continue to hold their respective offices, unless removed by competent authority, until superseded under the laws now in force, or under this constitution.

Sec. 7. The members of the Senate and House of Representatives of the Legislature of one thousand eight hundred and fifty-one, shall continue in office under the provisions of law, until superseded by their successors elected and qualified under this constitution.

Sec. 8. All county officers, unless removed by competent authority, shall continue to hold their respective offices until the first day of January, in the year one thousand eight hundred and fifty-three. The laws now in force as to the election, qualification and duties of township officers, shall continue in force until the Legislature shall, in conformity to the provisions of this constitution, provide for the holding of elections to fill such offices, and prescribe the duties of such officers respectfully.

Sec. 9. On the first day of January, in the year one thousand eight hundred and fifty-two, the terms of office of the judges of the supreme court, under existing laws, and of the judges of the county courts, and of the clerks of the supreme court, shall expire on the said day.

Sec. 10. On the first day of January, in the year one thousand eight hundred and fifty-two, the jurisdiction of all suits and proceedings then pending in the present supreme courts, shall become vested in the supreme court established by this constitution, and shall be finally adjudicated by the court where the same may be pending. The jurisdiction of all suits and proceedings at law and equity, then pending in the circuit courts and county courts for the several counties, shall become vested in the circuit courts of the said counties, and district court for the Upper Peninsula.

Sec. 11. The probate courts, the courts of justices of the peace and the police court authorized by an act entitled "an act to establish a police court in the city of Detroit," approved April second, one thousand eight hundred and fifty, shall continue to exercise the jurisdiction and powers now conferred upon them respectively, until otherwise provided by law.

Sec. 12. The office of State Printer shall be vested in the present incumbent until the expiration of the term for whtch he was elected under the law then in force; and all the provisions of the said law relating to his duties, rights, privileges and compensation, shall remain unimpaired and inviolate until the expiration of his said term of office.

Sec. 13. It shall be the duty of the Legislature, at their first session, to adapt the present laws to the provisions of this constitution, as far as may be.

Sec. 14. The Attorney General of the State is required to prepare and report to the Legislature, at the commencement of the next session, such changes and modifications in existing laws as may be deemed necessary to adapt the same to this constitution, and as may be best calculated to carry into effect its provisions; and he shall receive no additional compensation therefor.

Sec. 15. Any territory attached to any county for judicial purposes, if not otherwise represented, shall be considered as forming part of such county, so far as regards elections for the purpose of representation.

Sec. 16. This constitution shall be submitted to the people for their adoption or rejection, at the general election to be held on the first Tuesday of November, one thousand eight hundred and fifty; and there shall also be submitted for adoption or rejection, at the same time the separate resolution in relation to the elective franchise; and it shall be the duty of the Secretary of State, and all other officers required to give or publish any notice in regard to the said general election, to give notice, as provided by law in case of an election of Governor, that this constitution has been duly submitted to the electors at said election. Every newspaper within this State pnblishing in the month of September next, this constitution as submitted, shall receive, as compensation therefor, the sum of twenty-five dollars, to be paid as the Legislature shall direct.

Sec. 17, Any person entitled to vote for members of the Legislature, by the constitution and laws now in force, shall, at the said election, be entitled to vote for the adoption or rejection of this constitution, and for or against the resolution separately submitted, at the places and in the manner provided by law for the election of members of the Legislature.

Sec. 18. At the said general election, a ballot box shall be kept by the several boards of inspectors thereof, for receiving the votes cast for or against the adoption of this Constitution; and on the ballots shall be written or printed, or partly written and partly printed, the words "Adoption of the constitution—yes," or "Adoption of the constitution—no."

Sec. 19. The canvass of the votes cast for the adoption or rejection of this Constitution and the provision in relation to the elective franchise separately submitted, and the returns thereof shall be made by the proper canvassing officers, in the same manner as now provided by law for the canvass and return of the votes cast at an election for Governor, as near as may be, and the return thereof shall be directed to the Secretary of State. On the sixteenth day of December next, or within five days thereafter, the Auditor General, State Treasurer and Secretary of State shall meet at the capitol and proceed in presence of the Governor, to examine and canvass the returns of the said votes, and proclamation shall forthwith be made by the Governor of the result thereof. If it shall appear that a majority of the votes cast upon the question have thereon "Adoption of the Constitution—yes," this constitution shall be the supreme law of the State from and after the first day of January, one thousand eight hundred and fifty-one, except as is herein otherwise provided; but if a majority of the votes cast upon the question have thereon "Adoption of the Constitution—no," the same shall be null and void. And in case of the adoption of this constitution, said officers shall immediately, or as soon thereafter as practicable, proceed to open the statements of votes returned from the several counties for judges of the supreme court and State officers under the act entitled "An act to amend the revised statutes and to provide for the election of certain officers by the people in pursuance to an amendment of the Constitution, approved February sixteenth, one thousand eight hundred and fifty," and shall ascertain, determine and certify the results of the election for said officers under said acts, in the same manner, as near as may be, as is now provided by law in regard to the election of Representatives in Congress. And the several judges and officers so ascertained to have been elected may be qualified and enter upon the duties of their respective offices, on the first Monday of January next, or as soon thereafter as practicable.

Sec. 20. The salaries or compensation of all persons holding office under the present canstitution shall continue te be the same as now provided by law, until superseded by their successors elected or appointed under this constitution; and it shall not be lawful hereafter for the Legislature to increase or diminish the compensation of any officer during the term for which he is elected or appointed.

Sec. 21. The Legislature, at their first session, shall provide for the payment of all expenditures of the Convention to revise the constitution and of the publication of the same as is provided in this article.

Sec. 22. Every county except Mackinaw and Chippewa, entitled to a representative in the Legislature, at the time of the adoption of this constitution, shall continue to be so entitled under this constitution; and the county of Saginaw, with the territory that may be attached, shall be entitled to one representative; the county of Tuscola, and the territory that may be attached, one representative; the county of Sanilac, and the territory that may be attached, one representative; the counties of Midland and Aronac, with the territory that may be attached, one representative; the county of Montcalm, with the territory that may be attached thereto, one representative; and the counties of Newaygo and Oceana, with the territory that may be attached thereto, one representative. Each county having a ratio of representation and a fraction over, equal to a moiety of said ratio, shall be entitled to two representatives, and so on above that number, giving one additional member for each additional ratio.

Sec. 23. The cases pending and undisposed of in the late court of chancery at the time of the adoption of this constitution, shall coninue to be heard and determined by the judges of the supreme court. But the Legislature shall, at its session in one thousand eight hundred and fifty one, provide by law for the transfer of said causes that may remain undisposed of on the first day of January, one thousand eight hundred and fifty-two, to the supreme or circuit court established by this constitution, or require that the same may be heard and determined by the circuit judges.

Sec. 24. The term of office of the Governor and Lieutenant Governor shall commence on the first day of January next after their election.

Sec. 25. The territory described in the article entitled "Upper Peninsula," shall be attached to and constitute a part of the third circuit for the election of a Regent of the University.

Sec. 26. The Legislature shall have authority, after the expiration of the term of office of the district judge first elected for the "Upper Peninsula," to abolish said office of district judge and district attorney, or either of them.

Sec. 27. The Legislature shall, at its session of one thousand eight hundred and fifty-one, apportion the Representatives among the several counties and districts, and divide the State into Senate districts, pursuant to the provisions of this constitution.

Sec. 28. The terms of office of all State and county officers, of the circuit judges, members of the board of education, and members of the Legislature, shall begin on the first day of January next succeeding their election.

RESOLUTION.

Sec. 29. At the next general election, and at the same time when the votes of the electors shall be taken for the adoption or rejection of this constitution, an additional amendment to section one of article seven, in the words following:

"Every colored male inhabitant possessing the qualifications required by the first section of the second article of the Constitution, shall have the rights and privileges of an elector,"

Shall be separately submitted to the electors of this State for their adoption or rejection, in form following, to wit: A separate ballot may be given by every person having a right to vote for the revised Constitution, to be deposited in a separate box. Upon the ballots given for the adoption of the said separate amendment shall be written or printed, or partly written and partly printed, the words "Equal suffrage to colored persons? Yes;" and upon all ballots given against the adoption of the said separate amendment, in like manner, the words "Equal suffrage to colored persons? No." And on such ballots shall be written or printed, or partly written and partly printed, the words "Constitution: Suffrage," in such manner that such words shall appear on the outer side of such ballot when folded. If, at said election, a majority of all the votes given for and against the said separate amendment shall contain the words, "Equal suffrage to colored persons? Yes," then there shall be inserted in the first section of the article, between the words "tribe" and "shall," these words, "and every colored male inhabitant," anything in the Constitution to the contrary notwithstanding.

And the amendments were severally concurred in.

The article was ordered to a third reading, and so read, when,

Mr. Chapel moved to lay the same on the table and order it printed.

But the motion was lost.

And the article was then passed.

On motion of Mr. Gardiner,

The Convention adjourned.

Lansing, Thursday, August 15, 1850.

The Convention met pursuant to adjournment, and was called to order by the President.

Prayer by the Rev. Mr. Tooker.

The roll being called, there were absent on leave, Messrs. Backus, Bagg, Alvarado Brown, J. Clark, S. Clark, Cook, Dimond, Eastman, Graham, Hathaway, Hixon, Mason, Raynale, M. Robinson, Story, Sullivan, Sutherland, Tiffany, Wells, Willard and Witherell; and without leave, Messrs. P. R. Adams and McLeod.

RESOLUTIONS.

On motion of Mr. Hart,

Resolved, That the Secretary of the Convention draw a certificate in favor of Ezra Willis, for the sum of three dollars, for services as door keeper the first day of the session, and for cleaning and putting the Hall in order after the adjournment of the Convention.

On motion of Mr. Hascall,

Resolved, That the State Printer deposit with the Secretary of State the journals, reports and documents to which each member and officer of the Convention is entitled, put up in separate parcels, and marked with the name of the member and officer entitled to each, subject to his order.

The President called Mr. Williams to the chair.

Mr. Gardiner offered the following:

Resolved, That 2400 copies of the Constitution, as adopted by this Convention, be printed in a pamphlet form, to be distributed one to each of the newspapers of the State, and the remainder equally amongst the members of this Convention.

And the yeas and nays being ordered thereon, the resolution was adopted, as follows:

YEAS:

Mr. Alvord,	Mr. Daniels,	Mr. Mosher,
Anderson,	Desnoyers,	O'Brien,
Arzeno,	Gardiner,	Orr,
Britain,	Gibson,	Robertson,
Ammon Brown,	Hart,	E. S. Robinson,
Chandler,	Harvey,	Rix Robinson,
Choate,	Kingsley,	Town,
Church,	Marvin,	Van Valkenburgh,

Comstock,	McClelland,	Warden,
Conner,	Moore,	Williams, 30

NAYS.

Mr. W. Adams,	Mr. Cornell,	Mr. Prevost,
Axford,	Crary,	Redfield,
Barnard,	Danforth,	Roberts,
H. Bartow,	Green,	Skinner,
J. Bartow,	Hascall,	Sturgis,
Beardsley,	Leach,	Wait,
Bush,	Lee,	Walker,
Butterfield,	Lovell,	White,
Carr,	Newberry,	Woodman,
Chapel,	N. Pierce,	29

Mr. Alvord offered the following:

Resolved, That the secretary of this Convention, and the reporters appointed under resolution of June 3d, and the door-keeper, be and they are hereby allowed the same mileage as is allowed to the members of this Convention.

Mr. Woodman moved to insert, "and messengers;" which was lost.

On motion of Mr. Woodman,

The resolution was indefinitely postponed.

Mr. Church offered the following:

Resolved, That the sum of twenty-five dollars be and is hereby allowed to Edwin R. Merrifield, for extra services as door-keeper and sergeant-at-arms *pro tempore* to this Convention, and that a certificate be drawn for the same, in the usual manner.

Mr. Fralick moved to indefinitely postpone the same, and the yeas and nays being had thereon, the motion to indefinitely postpone was lost as follows:

YEAS.

Mr. W. Adams,	Mr. Danforth,	Mr. Marvin,
Axford,	Daniels,	Morrison,
Barnard,	Desnoyers,	Newberry,
H. Bartow,	Fralick,	N. Pierce,
Britain,	Gibson,	Skinner,
Ammon Brown,	Green,	Sturgis,
Asahel Brown,	Harvey,	Town,
Burns,	Hascall,	Wait,
Carr,	Kingsley,	Williams,
Comstock,	Leach,	Woodman,
Cornell,		31

NAYS.

Mr. Alvord,	Mr. Gale,	Mr. Prevost,
Anderson,	Gardiner,	Redfield,
Arzeno,	Hart,	Roberts,
J. Bartow,	Lee,	Robertson,
Beardsley,	McClelland,	E. S. Robinson,
Chapel,	Moore,	Rix Robinson,
Choate,	Mosher,	Van Valkenburg
Church,	O'Brien,	Walker,
Conner,	Orr,	Warden,
Crary,	J. D. Pierce,	White,
Edmunds,		31

And on the adoption of the resolution the yeas and nays were had and the result was as follows:

YEAS.

Mr. Alvord,	Mr. Crary,	Mr. O'Brien,
Anderson,	Edmunds,	Prevost,
Arzeno,	Gardiner,	Roberts,
Barnard,	Hanscom,	Robertson,
H. Bartow,	Hart,	E. S. Robinson,
J. Bartow,	Lee,	Van Valkenburgh,
Beardsley,	Lovell,	Walker,
Beeson,	McClelland,	Warden,
Bush,	McLeod,	Webster
Chapel,	Morrison,	White,
Church,	Mosher,	Whipple, 33

NAYS.

Mr. W. Adams,	Mr. Danforth,	Mr. Newberry,
Axford,	Daniels,	Orr,
Britain,	Desnoyers,	N. Pierce,
Ammon Brown,	Fralick,	Redfield,
Asahel Brown,	Gibson,	Rix Robinson,
Burns,	Green,	Skinner,
Carr,	Harvey,	Sturgis,
Chandler,	Hascall,	Town,
Choate,	Kingsley,	Wait,
Comstock,	Leach,	Whittemore,
Conner,	Marvin,	Williams,
Cornell,	Moore,	35

So the resolution was not adopted.

On motion of Mr. Edmunds,

Resolved, That the thanks of this Convention be unanimously tendered to the Hon. Daniel Goodwin, President of the Convention, for the able and impartial manner in which he has discharged the duties of presiding officer of this body.

Mr. Lovell offered the following:

Resolved, That the thanks of this Convention be presented to John Swegles Jun., H. S. Roberts, and Charles Hascall, for the faithfulness and ability with which they have discharged their duties as secretaries.

And the resolution was unanimously adopted.

On motion of Mr. Hart,

The majority report of the select committee upon dividing the State into judicial districts was taken from the table.

Mr. J. Bartow offered the following, based upon the report, to stand as a seperate section of the "Schedule."

"The State, exclusive of the Upper Peninsula, shall be divided into eight judicial circuits, and the counties of Monroe, Lenewee and Hillsdale shall constitute the first circuit.

The counties of Branch, St. Joseph, Cass and Berren shall constitute the second circuit.

The county of Wayne shall constitute the third circuit.

The counties of Washtenaw, Jackson and Ingham shall constitute the fourth circuit.

The counties of Calhoun, Kalamazoo, Allegan, Barry and Van Buren shall constitute the fifth circuit.

The counties of St. Clair, Macomb and Oakland shall constitute the sixth circuit.

The counties of Lapeer, Genesee, Saginaw, Shiawassee, Livingston, Tuscola and Midland shall constitute the seventh circuit.

And the counties of Eaton, Kent, Ottawa, Iona, Clinton and Montcalm shall constitute the eighth circuit."

Mr. Bush moved to substitute for the foregoing, the minority report of the committee.

Mr. Morrison moved the indefinite postponement of the whole subject.

Which was lost.

Mr. Walker submitted the following substitute for the one proposed by Mr. Bush:

"The State is hereby divided into eight judicial circuits, to wit:

The first circuit shall consist of the counties of Monroe, Lenawee and Hillsdale.

The second circuit shall consist of the counties of Branch, St. Joseph, Cass and Berrien.

The third circuit shall consist of the counties of Wayne and Washtenaw.

The fourth circuit shall consist of the counties of Jackson, Calhoun, Kalamazoo, Van Buren and Allegan.

The fifth circuit shall consist of the counties of Kent, Ottawa, Iona, Barry and Montcalm.

The sixth circuit shall consist of the counties of Eaton, Clinton, Shiwassee, Ingham and Livingston.

The seventh circuit shall consist of the counties of Oakland, Genesee and Saginaw.

The eighth circuit shall consist of the counties of Macomb, St. Clair, Lapeer and Sanilac."

And the yeas and nays being had on the adoption of Mr. Walker's proposition,

The same was rejected, as follows:

YEAS.

Mr. Axford,	Mr. Crouse,	Mr. Rix Robinson,
Barnard,	Danforth,	Van Valkenburgh,
Burns,	Hanscom,	Walker,
Bush,	Lee,	Warden,
Chapel,	Mowry,	Whittemore,
Choate,	Newberry,	Williams,
Church,	Robertson,	Woodman, 21

NAYS:

Mr. W. Adams,	Mr. Desnoyers,	Mr. Marvin,
Alvord,	Eaton,	Morrison,
Anderson,	Edmunds,	Mosher,
Arzeno,	Fralick,	O'Brien,
J. Bartow,	Gale,	J. D. Pierce,
H. Bartow,	Gardiner,	N. Pierce,
Britain,	Gibson,	Prevost,
Ammon Brown,	Green,	E. S. Robinson,
Asahel Brown,	Hart,	Skinner,
Butterfield,	Harvey,	Soule,
Carr,	Hascall,	Town,
Chandler,	Kingsley,	Wait,
Comstock,	Kinne,	Webster,
Cornell,	Leach,	White,
Crary,	Lovell,	President,
Daniels,		46

Mr. J. Bartow modified his proposition by adding the county of Sanilac to the 6th district.

Mr. Butterfield moved to amend the proposition of Mr. Bush by striking from the apportionment for the 4th district, the county of Van Buren, and attaching the same to the 3d district.

But the amendment did not prevail.

And on the adoption of the minority report proposed by Mr. Bush, as a substitute for Mr. Bartow's proposition,

The yeas and nays were ordered, and the result was as follows:

YEAS.

Mr. Anderson,
Barnard,
Burns,
Bush,
Butterfield,
Chapel,
Conner,
Cornell,
Crary,
Crouse,
Mr. Danforth,
Hanscom,
Kinne,
Lee,
Morrison,
Mowry,
Newberry,
N. Pierce,
Robertson,
Mr. E. S. Robinson,
Soule,
Sturgis,
Walker,
Warden,
Webster,
Whittemore,
Williams,
Woodman, 28

NAYS.

Mr. W. Adams,
Alvord,
H. Bartow,
J. Bartow,
Beeson,
Britain,
Ammon Brown,
Asahel Brown,
Carr,
Chandler,
Choate,
Church,
Comstock,
Daniels,
Mr. Desnoyers,
Eaton,
Edmunds,
Fralick,
Gale,
Gardiner,
Gibson,
Green,
Hart,
Harvey,
Hascall,
Kingsley,
Leach,
Lovell,
Mr. Marvin,
Mosher,
O'Brien,
Orr,
Prevost,
Redfield,
Rix Robinson,
Skinner,
Town,
Van Valkenburg,
Wait,
White,
President, 41

So the substitute was not adopted.

The question recurring on the adoption of Mr. J. Bartow's proposition,

Mr. Church moved to amend the same by transferring in the apportionment for the fifth and eighth districts the counties of Barry and Eaton, so that the county of Barry should be placed in the eighth district, and the county of Eaton in the fifth.

And the amendment was accepted by Mr. Bartow.

Mr. Robertson moved the following as an addition to the proposition under consideration:

"Sec.—. Any citizen of this State shall be eligible to the office of circuit judge in any judicial circuit, without reference to his residence at the time of his election."

Mr. Eaton moved the previous question, and the same being seconded, the main question was ordered to be now put.

Mr. Robertson's amendment was then disagreed to.

And the question being on the adoption of Mr. J. Bartow's proposition,

The same was agreed to as an additional section to the schedule.

On motion of Mr. Van Valkenburgh,

Resolved, That the thanks of the Convention be tendered to Edwin R. Merrifield, for the efficient and courteous manner in which he has discharged his duties as door-keeper during the session.

The President took the chair.

Mr. Gardiner called up his resolution of yesterday, relative to the supervision and printing of the reports.

Mr. Walker moved to strike out "C. J. Fox," and insert "Joseph Coates."

Mr. Robertson moved the previous question, and the same being seconded, the main question was ordered to be now put.

The amendment of Mr. Walker was disagreed to by yeas and nays, as follows:

YEAS:

Mr. W. Adams,	Mr. Eaton,	Mr. E. S. Robinson,
Anderson,	Edmunds,	Skinner,
Axford,	Fralick,	Sturgis,
Barnard,	Lee,	Van Valkenburg,
H. Bartow,	Moore,	Walker,
Asahel Brown,	Mowry,	Warden,
Chapel,	Newberry,	Webster,
Crouse,	N. Pierce,	Williams,
Danforth,	Prevost,	Woodman, 27

NAYS:

Mr. Alvord,	Mr. Gardiner,	Mr. Mosher,
Arzeno,	Green,	O'Brien,
J. Bartow,	Hanscom,	Orr,
Beeson,	Hart,	J. D. Pierce,

Britain,	Harvey,	Redfield,
Burns,	Hascall,	Robertson,
Chandler,	Kingsley,	Rix Robinson,
Choate,	Kinne,	Town,
Church,	Lovell,	Wait,
Comstock,	Marvin,	White,
Conner,	McClelland,	Whipple,
Daniels,		43

And the question being on the adoption of the resolution proposed by Mr. Gardiner,

The same was agreed to by yeas and nays, as follows:

YEAS.

Mr. Alvord,	Mr. Daniels,	Mr. Morrison,
Arzeno,	Gale,	Mosher,
J. Bartow,	Gardiner,	Mowry,
Beeson,	Green,	O'Brien,
Britain,	Hanscom,	J. D. Pierce,
Burns,	Hart,	N. Pierce,
Bush,	Harvey,	Redfield,
Butterfield,	Hascall,	Roberts,
Carr,	Kingsley,	Robertson,
Chandler,	Kinne,	Rix Robinson,
Choate,	Leach,	Town,
Church,	Lovell,	White,
Comstock,	Marvin,	Whipple,
Conner,	McClelland,	President,
Cornell,	Moore,	44

NAYS.

Mr. W. Adams,	Mr. Chapel,	Mr. Soule,
Anderson,	Danforth,	Sturgis,
Axford,	Desnoyers,	Wait,
Barnard,	Edmunds,	Walker,
H. Bartow,	Gibson,	Warden,
Ammon Brown,	Newberry,	Whittemore,
Asahel Brown,	Prevost,	Woodman, 21

Mr. Gardiner, from the committee on printing, to whom was referred the resolution of yesterday, directing them to inquire into the expediency of ordering the old and new constitutions printed in the Dutch, German and French languages, reported the same back, and that in their opinion it would be inexpedient.

And the report was accepted and adopted.

Mr. Woodman offered the following:

Resolved, That the committee soliciting subscriptions to pay the clergy for services performed in this Convention, are hereby required to report as soon as convenient, the amount of funds received, and the manner in which the same have been disposed of.

On motion of Mr. Church,

The resolution was indefinitely postponed.

On motion of Mr. Cornell,

The committee alluded to in the foregoing resolution were allowed liberty to report.

Mr. J. D. Pierce reported, verbally, that the sum of $132 had been raised and disbursed to the officiating clergymen.

On motion of Mr. Church,

Resolved, That the members of this convention now absent, be requested and are hereby authorized to affix their signatures to the constitution adopted by this convention and enrolled by its order, whenever it may be convenient for them so to do.

Mr. McClelland moved that when this constitution shall be enrolled it shall be signed by the members by counties as the same shall be called.

And the same was agreed to.

On motion of Mr. Woodman,

Resolved, That the thanks of this convention are hereby tendered to the messengers for the faithful discharge of their duties.

On motion of Mr. Beeson,

Resolved, That the Governor be and he is hereby requested to draw his warrant upon the contingent fund for $550 and 62 one-hundredths in favor of the post master of Lansing, in full for the postage of this convention.

On motion of Mr. Gardiner,

Resolved, That Wm. Coates, Joseph Coates and Martin Mahon, be allowed their per diem allowance as reporters of the Convention, for eight days after the adjournment of the same, to complete their reports and prepare them for the press.

On motion of Mr. Hanscom,

Resolved, That the thanks of the Convention be tendered to the various reporters, for the efficient, accurate and prompt manner in which they have performed their duties.

On motion of Mr. Britain,

Resolved, That the Secretary of this Convention be instructed to draw his certificate in favor of Joseph Coates, William Coates and Martin Mahon, for the amounts due them respectively for eight day's services, authorized in the resolution this morning adopted.

The President submitted the following report of the Secretary of the Convention:

CONSTITUTIONAL CONVENTION,
Lansing, August 15, 1850.

To the Honorable the Constitutional Convention of the State of Michigan:

The undersigned, in compliance with a resolution adopted on the 12th inst., would respectfully report, that there is now on hand, ready to be delivernd over to the Secretary of State, the following articles of stationery, which, as per bill now in possession of the undersigned, amount to the sum of $184,09, as follows:

½ doz. Ink Stands, 8s per doz.,	$,50
80 Pen Holders, 20s per gross,	1,30
7 large and 150 small sticks sealing wax, at 12s per lb., (having no scales and weights to weigh the same,) say,	20,00
675 quills at $2,87½ per C.,	19,40
3½ doz. Lead Pencils, 4s per doz.,	1,75
Gum Arabic, at 8s per lb., say,	5,00
3000 Envelopes,	4,50
1⅔ ream Engrossing paper,	10,83
4 do do do (allowed, but not received, and now charged to F. P. Markham & Brother,)	19,50
1 doz. Sand Boxes, 16s per doz.,	2,00
1 " Wafer Boxes, 16s per doz.,	2,00
225 Envelopes,	,44
5¾ doz. Inks, (pints,) $3,50 per doz.,	19,62
1¾ " " " broken in transportation,	6,63
1¾ " " (quarts,) $4,50 per doz.,	12,37
½ " " " broken in transportation,	2,25
1 " small bottles of Ink,	,50
8¾ Reams Envelope paper, $5,00 per ream,	43,75
1⅓ gross paper sand, $6,00 per gross,	6,75
⅓ doz. Gold Pens, $12,00 per doz.,	4,00
The undersigned proposes to return his pen after the adjournment, (it is as good as new,)	1,00
	$184,09

In addition to the foregoing, the following articles may, with propriety, be reported, viz:

2 brushes, 2 cups, 1 gal. measure, 1 blank book for accounts with members,	$1,36
4 brooms, 1s 3d. each, for sweeping hall,	,64
1 pail, 2 pr. shears for Secretaries,	1,31
5½ yds. crape, ⅜ do. 4s,	2,94
4½ " Bombazine, 10s,	5,63
6¾ " " 8s,	6,75
7¼ " black crape, 6s, (torn up for badges,)	5,44
1 paper pins, lacking 3 rows,	,10
	$24,17

A portion of the above articles are nearly worthless. A portion however, are nearly as good as new, and will be disposed of as the Convention may see fit to direct.

The undersigned begs leave to say, that in consequence of the rejection by the Convention, of a resolution reported by the committee on supplies and expenditures, on the 6th day of June last, he deems himself entirely relieved from any responsibility as to the manner of the distribution of said stationery, yet at the request of the committee on supplies and expenditures, he has, in a measure, taken charge of the same, and by minutes which he has kept, finds the stationery delivered to each member, to amount to sums varying from three to five dollars.

All of which is respectfully submitted.

JOHN SWEGLES, Jr.,
Secretary Convention.

On motion of Mr. Hanscom,

Resolved, That this Convention recommend to the next Legislature, that proper compensation be paid by the State, to the proprietors of the various Newspaper Press, who have regularly furnished the members of this Convention with their papers.

On motion of Mr. Britain,

Resolved, That the State Printer be requested to complete the publication of the daily journals, and forward the same to the members respectively by mail, with as little delay as practicable.

Mr. Beeson, from the select committee upon enrollment, reported the Constitution and Schedule as correctly enrolled, and submitted the same to the Convention, reading as follows:

CONSTITUTION OF THE STATE OF MICHIGAN.

The People of the State of Michigan do ordain this Constitution:

ARTICLE I.

BOUNDARIES.

The State of Michigan consists of and has jurisdiction over the territory embraced within the following boundaries, to wit: Commencing at a point on the eastern boundary line of the State of Indiana, where a direct line drawn from the southern extremity of Lake Michigan to the most northerly cape of the Maumee Bay shall intersect the same—said point being the north-west corner of the State of Ohio, as established by act of Congress, entitled "an act to establish the northern boundary line of the State of Ohio, and to provide for the admission of the State of Michigan into the Union upon the conditions therein expressed," approved June fifteenth, one thousand eight hundred and thirty-six; thence with the said boundary line of the State of Ohio till it intersects the boundary line between the United States and Canada in Lake Erie; thence with said boundary line between the United States and Canada through the Detroit river, Lake Huron and Lake Superior to a point where the said line last touches Lake Superior; thence in a direct line through Lake Superior to the mouth of the Montreal river; thence through the middle of the main channel of the said river Montreal to the head waters thereof; thence in a direct line to the centre of the channel between Middle and South islands in the Lake of the Desert; thence in a direct line to the southern shore of Lake Brule; thence along said outhern shore and down the river Brule to the main channel of the Menominie river; thence down the centre of the main channel of the same to the centre of the most usual ship channel of the Green Bay of Lake Michigan; thence through the centre of the most usual ship channel of the said bay to the middle of Lake Michigan; thence through the middle of Lake Michigan to the northern boundary of the State of Indiana, as that line was established by the act of Congress of the nineteenth of April, eighteen hundred and sixteen; thence due east with the north boundary line of the said State of Indiana to the north-east corner thereof; and thence south with the eastern boundary line of Indiana to the place of beginning.

ARTICLE II.

SEAT OF GOVERNMENT.

§ 1. The Seat of Government shall be at Lansing, where it is now established.

ARTICLE III.

DIVISION OF THE POWERS OF GOVERNMENT.

§ 1. The powers of government are divided into three departments: the Legislative, Executive and Judicial.

§ 2. No person belonging to one department shall exercise the powers properly belonging to another, except in the cases expressly provided in this constitution.

ARTICLE IV.

LEGISLATIVE DEPARTMENT.

§ 1. The legislative power is vested in a Senate and House of Representatives.

§ 2. The Senate shall consist of thirty-two members. Senators shall be elected for two years, and by single districts. Such districts shall be numbered from one to thirty-two inclusive; each of which shall choose one Senator. No county shall be divided in the formation of Senate districts, except such county shall be equitably entitled to two or more Senators.

§ 3. The House of Representatives shall consist of not less than sixty-four, nor more than one hundred members. Representatives shall be chosen for two years, and by single districts. Each Representative district shall contain, as nearly as may be, an equal number of white inhabitants, and civilized persons of Indian descent, not members of any tribe, and shall consist of convenient and contiguous territory. But no township or city shall be divided in the formation of a Representative district. When any township or city shall contain a population which entitles it to more than one Representative, then such township or city shall elect by general ticket the number of Representatives to which it is entitled. Each county hereafter organized, with such territory as may be attached thereto, shall be entitled to a separate Representative when it has attained a population equal to a moiety of the ratio of representation. In every county entitled to more than one Representative, the board of supervisors shall assemble at such time and place as the Legislature shall prescribe, and divide the same into Representative districts, equal to the number of Representatives to which such county is entitled by law, and shall cause to be filed in the offices of the Secretary of State and clerk of such county a description of such Representative districts, specifying the number of each district, and the population thereof, according to the last preceding enumeraticn.

§ 4. The Legislature shall provide by law for an enumeration of the inhabitants in the year eighteen hundred and fifty-four, and every ten years thereafter; and at the first session after each enumeration so made, and also at the first session after each enumeration by the authority of the United States, the Legislature shall re-arrange the Senate districts and apportion anew the Representatives among the counties and districts, according to the number of white inhabitants and civilized persons of Indian descent, not members of any tribe. Each apportionment and the division into Representative districts, by any board of supervisors, shall remain unaltered until the return of another enumeration.

§ 5. Senators and Representatives shall be citizens of the United States, and qualified electors in the respective counties and districts which they represent. A removal from their respective counties or districts shall be deemed a vacation of their office.

§ 6. No person holding any office under the United States [or this State,] or any county office, except notaries public, officers of the militia and officers elected by townships, shall be eligible to or have a seat in either house of the Legislature, and all votes given for any such person shall be void.

§ 7. Senators and Representatives shall, in all cases, except treason, felony or breach of the peace, be privileged from arrest. They shall not be subject to any civil process during the session of the Legislature, or for fifteen days next before the commencement and after the termination of each session. They shall not be questioned in any other place for any speech in either house.

§ 8. A majority of each house shall constitute a quorum to do business; but a smaller number may adjourn from day to day, and compel the attendance of absent members, in such mannner and under such penalties as each house may prescribe.

§ 9. Each house shall choose its own officers, determine the rules of its procedings, and judge of the qualifications, elections and returns of its members; and may, with the concurrence of two-thirds of all the members elected, expel a member. No member shall be expelled a second time for the same cause, nor for any cause known to his constituents antecedent to his election. The reason for such expulsion shall be entered upon the journal, with the names of the members voting on the question.

§ 10. Each house shall keep a journal of its proceedings, and publish the same, except such parts as may require secrecy. The yeas and nays of the members of either house, on any question, shall be entered on the journal at the request of one-fifth of the members elected. Any member of either house may dissent from and protest against any act, proceeding or resolution which he may deem injurious to any person or the public, and have the reason of his dissent entered on the journal.

§ 11. In all elections by either house or in joint convention the votes shall be given *viva voce*. All votes on nominations to the Senate shall be taken by yeas and nays, and published with the journal of its proceedings.

§ 12. The doors of each house shall be open, unless the public welfare require secrecy. Neither house shall, without the consent of the other, adjourn for more than three days, nor to any other place than where the Legislature may then be in session.

§ 13. Bills may originate in either house of the Legislature.

§ 14. Every bill and concurrent resolution, except of adjournment, passed by the Legislature shall be presented to the Governor before it becomes a law. If he approve, he shall sign it; but if not, he shall return it with his objections to the house in which it originated, which shall enter the objections at large upon their journal, and reconsider it. On such reconsideration, if two-thirds of the members elected agree to pass the bill, it shall be sent, with the objections, to the other house, by which it shall be reconsidered. If approved by two-thirds of the members elected to that house, it shall become a law. In such case, the vote of both houses shall be determined by yeas and nays, and the names of the members voting for and against the bill shall be entered on the journals of each house respectively. If any bill be not returned by the Governor within ten days, Sundays excepted, after it has been presented to him, the same shall become a law, in like manner as if he had signed it, unless the Legislature, by their adjournment, prevent its return; in which case it shall not become a law. The Governor may approve, sign and file in the office of the Secretary of State, within five days after the adjournment of the Legislature, any act passed during the last five days of the session; and the same shall become a law.

§ 15. The compensation of the members of the Legislature shall be three dollars a day for actual attendance and when absent on account of sickness, for the first sixty days of the session of the year one thousand eight hundred and fifty-one, and for the first forty days of every subsequent session, and nothing thereafter. When convened in extra session their compensation shall be three dollars a day for the first twenty days, and nothing thereafter; and they shall legislate on no other subjects than those expressly stated in the Governor's proclamation, or submitted to them by special message. They shall be entitled to ten cents and no more for every mile actually traveled, going to and returning from the place of meeting, on the usually traveled route; and for stationery and newspapers not exceeding five dollars for each member during any session. Each member shall be entitled to one copy of the laws, journals and documents of the Legislature of which he was a member; but shall not receive at the expense of the State, books, newspapers, or other perquisites of office, not expressly authorized by this constitution.

§ 16. The Legislature may provide by law for the payment of postage on all mailable matter received by its members and officers during the sessions of the Legislature, but not on any sent or mailed by them.

§ 17. The President of the Senate and the Speaker of the House of Representatives shall be entiled to the same per diem compensation and mileage as members of the Legislature, and no more.

§ 18. No person elected a member of the Legislature shall receive any civil appointment within this State, or to the Senate of the United States, from the Governor, the Governor and Senate, from the Legislature, or any other State authority, during the term for which he is elected. All such appointments and all votes given for any person so elected for any such office or appointment, shall be void. No member of the Legislature shall be interested, directly or indirectly, in any contract with the State, or any county thereof, authorized by any law passed, during the time for which he is elected, nor for one year thereafter.

§ 19. Every bill and joint resolution shall be read three times in each house, before the final passage thereof. No bill or joint resolution shall become a law without the concurrence of a majority of all the members elected to each house. On the final passage of all bills the vote shall be by ayes and nays, and entered on the journal.

§ 20. No law shall embrace more than one object, which shall be expressed in its title. No public act shall take effect or be in force until the expiration of ninety days from the end of the session at which the same is passed, unless the Legislature shall otherwise direct, by a two-thirds vote of the members elected to each house.

§ 21. The Legislature shall not grant nor authorize extra compensation to any public officer, agent or contractor, after the service has been rendered or the contract entered into.

§ 22. The Legislature shall provide by law that the furnishing of fuel and stationery for the use of the State, the printing and binding the laws and journals, all blanks, paper and printing for the executive departments, and all other printing ordered by the Legislature, shall be let by contract to the lowest bidder or bidders, who shall give adequate and satisfactory security for the performance thereof. The Legislature shall prescribe by law the manner in which the State printing shall be executed, and the accounts rendered therefor; and shall prohibit all charges for constructive labor. They shall not rescind nor alter such contract, nor release the person nor persons taking the same, or his or their sureties, from the performance of any of the conditions of the contract. No member of the Legislature nor officer of the State, shall be interested directly or indirectly in any such contract.

§ 23. The Legislature shall not authorize, by private or special law, the sale or conveyance of any real estate belonging to any person; nor vacate nor alter any road laid out by commissioners of highways, or any street in any city or village, or in any recorded town plat.

§ 24. The Legislature may authorize the employment of a chaplain for the State prison; but no money shall be appropriated for the payment of any religious services in either house of the Legislature.

§ 25. No law shall be revised, altered or amended by reference to its title only; but the act revised, and the section or sections of the act altered or amended, shall be re-enacted and published at length.

§ 26. Divorces shall not be granted by the Legislature.

§ 27. The Legislature shall not authorize any lottery, nor permit the sale of lottery tickets.

§ 28. No new bill shall be introduced into either house during the last three days of the session, without the unanimous consent of the house in which it originates.

§ 29. In case of a contested election, the person only shall receive from the State per diem compensation and mileage, who is declared to be entitled to a seat by the house in which the contest takes place.

§ 30. No collector, holder, nor disburser of public moneys, shall have a seat in the Legislature, or be eligible to any office of trust or profit under this State, until he shall have accounted for and paid over, as provided by law, all sums for which he may be liable.

§ 31. The Legislature shall not audit nor allow any private claim or account.

§ 32. The Legislature, on the day of final adjournment, shall adjourn at twelve o'clock at noon.

§ 33. The Legislature shall meet at the seat of government on the first Wednesday in February next, and on the first Wednesday in January of every second year thereafter, and at no other place or time, unless as provided in this constitution.

§ 34. The election of Senators and Representatives, pursuant to the provisions of this Constitution, shall be held on the Tuesday succeeding the first Monday of November in the year one thousand eight hundred and fifty-two, and on the Tuesday succeeding the first Monday of November of every second year thereafter.

§ 35. The Legislature shall not establish a State paper. Every newspaper in the State which shall publish all the general laws of any session within forty days of their passage, shall be entitled to receive a sum not exceeding fifteen dollars therefor.

§ 36. The Legislature shall provide for the speedy publication of all statute laws of a public nature, and of such judicial decisions as it may deem expedient. All laws and judicial decisions shall be free for publication by any person.

§ 37. The Legislature may declare the cases in which any office shall be deemed vacant, and also the manner of filling the vacancy, where no provision is made for that purpose in this constitution.

§ 38. The Legislature may confer upon organized townships, incorporated cities and villages, and upon the board of supervisors of the several counties, such powers of a local, legislative and administrative character as they may deem proper.

§ 39. The Legislature shall pass no law to prevent any person from worshiping Almighty God according to the dictates of his own conscience, or to compel any person to attend, erect or support any place of religious worship, or to pay tithes, taxes or other rates for the support of any minister of the gospel or teacher of religion.

§ 40. No money shall be appropriated or drawn from the treasury for the benefit of any religious sect or society, theological or religious seminary, nor shall property belonging to the State be appropriated for any such purposes.

§ 41. The Legislature shall not diminish or enlarge the civil or political rights, privileges and capacities of any person on account of his opinion or belief concerning matters of religion.

§ 42. No law shall ever be passed to restrain or abridge the liberty of speech or of the press; but every person may freely speak, write and publish his sentiments, on all subjects, being responsible for the abuse of such right.

§ 43. The Legislature shall pass no bill of attainder, ex-post facto law, or law impairing the obligation of contracts.

§ 44. The privilege of the writ of habaes corpus remains and shall not be suspended by the Legislature, except in case of rebellion or invasion the public safety require it.

§ 45. The assent of two-thirds of the members elected to each house of the Legislature shall be requisite to every bill appropriating the public money or property for local or private purposes.

§ 46. The Legislature may authorize a trial by a jury of a less number than twelve men.

§ 47. The Legislature shall not pass any act authorizing the grant of license for the sale of ardent spirits or other intoxicating liquors.

§ 48. The style of the laws shall be "The People of the State of Michigan enact."

ARTICLE V.

EXECUTIVE DEPARTMENT.

§ 1. The Executive power is vested in a Governor, who shall hold his office for two years. A Lieutenant Governor shall be chosen for the same term.

§ 2. No person shall be eligible to the office of Governor or Lieutenant Governor, who has not been five years a citizen of the United States, and a resident of this State two years next preceding his election; nor shall any person be eligible to either office who has not attained the age of thirty years.

§ 3. The Governor and Lieutenant Governor shall be elected at the times and places of choosing the members of the Legislature. The person having the highest number of votes for Governor or Lieutenant Governor shall be elected. In case two or more persons shall have an equal and the highest number of votes for Governor or Lieutenant Governor, the Legislature shall, by joint vote, choose one of such persons.

§ 4. The Governor shall be Commander-in-Chief of the military and naval forces, and may call out such forces to execute the laws, to suppress insurrections and to repel invasions.

§ 5. He shall transact all necessary business with officers of government, and may require information, in writing, from the officers of the Executive department, upon any subject relating to the duties of their respective offices.

§ 6. He shall take care that the laws be faithfully executed.

§ 7. He may convene the Legislature on extraordinary occasions.

§ 8. He shall give to the Legislature, and at the close of his official term to the next Legislature, information by message of the condition of the State, and recommend such measures to them as he shall deem expedient.

§ 9. He may convene the Legislature at some other place when the seat of government becomes dangerous from disease or a common enemy.

§ 10. He shall issue writs of election to fill such vacancies as occur in the Senate or House of Representatives.

§ 11. He may grant reprieves, commutations and pardons after convictions, for all offences except treason and cases of impeachment, upon such conditions, and with such restrictions and limitations, as he may think proper, subject to regulations provided by law, relative to the manner of applying for pardons. Upon conviction for treason, he may suspend the execution of the sentence until the case shall be reported to the Legislature at its next session, when the Legislature shall either pardon, or commute the sentence, direct the execution of the sentence, or grant a further reprieve. He shall communicate to the Legislature at each session information of each case of reprieve, commutation or pardon granted, and the reasons therefor.

§ 12. In case of the impeachment of the Governor, his removal from office, death, inability, resignation, or absence from the State, the powers and duties of the office shall devolve upon the Lieutenant Governor for the residue of the term, or until the disability ceases. When the Governor shall be out of the State in time of war, at the head of a military force thereof, he shall continue Commander-in-Chief of all the military force of the State.

§ 13. During a vacancy in the office of Governor, if the Lieutenant Governor die, resign, be impeached, displaced, be incapable of performing the duties of his office, or absent from the State, the President *pro tempore* of the Senate shall act as Governor, until the vacancy be filled, or the disability cease.

§ 14. The Lieutenant Governor shall, by virtue of his office, be President of the Senate. In committee of the whole he may debate all questions; and when there is an equal division, he shall give the casting vote.

§ 15. No member of Congress, nor any person holding office under the United States, or this State, shall execute the office of Governor.

§ 16. No person elected Governor or Lieutenant Governor, shall be eligible to any office or appointment from the Legislature, or either house thereof during the time for which he was elected. All votes for either of them, for any such office, shall be void.

§ 17. The Lieutenant [Governor] and President of the Senate *pro tempore*, when performing the duties of Governor, shall receive the same compensation as the Governor.

§ 18. All official acts of the Governor, his approval of the laws excepted, shall be authenticated by the Great Seal of the State, which shall be kept by the Secretary of State.

§ 19. All commissions issued to persons holding office under the provisions of this constitution, shall be in the name and by the authority of the people of the State of Michigan, sealed with the Great Seal of the State, signed by the Governor, and countersigned by the Secretary of State.

ARTICLE VI.

JUDICIAL DEPARTMENT.

§ 1. The judicial power is vested in one supreme court, in circuit courts, in probate courts, and in justices of the peace. Municipal courts of civil and criminal jurisdiction may be established by the Legislature in cities.

§ 2. For the term of six years, and thereafter, until the Legislature otherwise provide, the judges of the several circuit courts shall be judges of the supreme court, four of whom shall constitute a quorum. A concurrence of three shall be necessary to a final decision. After six years the Legislature may provide by law for the organization of a supreme court, with the jurisdiction and powers prescribed in this constitution, to consist of one chief justice and three associate justices, to be chosen by the electors of the State. Such supreme court, when so organized shall not be changed or discontinued by the Legislature for eight years thereafter. The judges thereof shall be so classified that but one of them shall go out of office at the same time. Their term of office shall be eight years.

§ 3. The supreme court shall have a general superintending control over all inferior courts, and shall have power to issue writs of error, habeas corpus, mandamus, quo warranto, procedendo, and other original and remedial writs, and to hear and determine the same. In all other cases it shall have appellate jurisdiction only.

§ 4. Four terms of the supreme court shall be he held annually, at such times and places as may be designated by law.

§ 5. The supreme court shall, by general rules, establish, modify and amend the practice in such court and in the circuit courts, and simplify the same. The Legislature shall, as far as practicable, abolish distinctions between law and equity proceedings. The office of master in chancery is prohibited.

§ 6. The State shall be divided into eight judicial circuits; in each of which the electors thereof shall elect one circuit judge, who shall hold his office for the term of six years, and until his successor is elected and qualified.

§ 7. The Legislature may alter the limits of circuits or increase the number of the same. No alteration or increase shall have the effect to remove a judge from office. In every additional circuit established the judge shall be elected by the electors of such circuit, and his term of office shall continue as provided in this constitution for judges of the circuit court.

§ 8. The circuit courts shall have original jurisdiction in all matters civil and criminal, not excepted in this constitution, and not prohibited by law; and appellate jurisdiction from all inferior courts and tribunals, and a supervisory control of the same. They shall also have power to issue writs of habeas corpus, mandamus, injunction, quo warranto, certiorari and other writs necessary to carry into effect their orders, judgments and decrees, and give them a general control over inferior courts and tribunals within their respective jurisdictions.

§ 9. Each of the judges of the circuit courts shall receive a salary payable quarterly. They shall be ineligible to any other than a judicial office during the term for which they are elected, and for one year thereafter. All votes for any person elected such judge for any office other than judicial, given either by the Legislature or the people, shall be void.

§ 10. The supreme court may appoint a reporter of its decisions. The decisions of the supreme court shall be in writing, and signed by the judges concurring therein. Any judge dissenting therefrom, shall give the reasons of such dissent in writing, under his signature. All such opinions shall be filed in the office of the clerk of the supreme court. The judges of the circuit court within their respective jurisdictions, may fill vacancies in the office of county clerk and of prosecuting attorney; but no judge of the supreme court, or circuit court, shall exercise any other power of appointment to public office.

§ 11. A circuit court shall be held at least twice in each year in every county organized for judicial purposes, and four times in each year in counties containing ten thousand inhabitants. Judges of the circuit court may hold courts for each other, and shall do so when required by law.

§ 12. The clerk of each county organized for judicial purposes shall be the clerk of the circuit court of such county, and of the supreme court when held within the same.

§ 13. In each of the counties organized for judicial purposes, there shall be a court of probate. The judge of such court shall be elected by the electors of the county in which he resides, and shall hold his office for four years, and until his successor is elected and qualified. The jurisdiction, powers and duties of such court shall be prescribed by law.

§ 14. When a vacancy occurs in the office of judge of the supreme, circuit or probate court, it shall be filled by appointment of the Governor, which shall continue until a successor is elected and qualified. When elected, such successor shall hold his office the residue of the unexpired term.

§ 15. The supreme court, the circuit and probate courts of each county, shall be courts of record, and shall each have a common seal.

§ 16. The Legislature may provide by law for the election of one or more persons in each organized county, who may be vested with judicial powers, not exceeding those of a judge of the circuit court at chambers.

§ 17. There shall be not exceeding four justices of the peace in each organized township. They shall be elected by the electors of the townships, and shall hold their offices for four years, and until their successors are elected and qualified. At the first election in any township, they shall be classified as shall be prescribed by law. A justice elected to fill a vacancy shall hold his office for the residue of the unexpired term. The Legislature may increase the number of justices in cities.

§ 18. In civil cases justices of the peace shall have exclusive jurisdiction to the amount of one hundred dollars, and concurrent jurisdiction to the amount of three hundred dollars, which may be increased to five hundred dollars, with such exceptions and restrictions as may be provided by law. They shall also have such criminal jurisdiction and perform such duties as shall be prescribed by the Legislature.

§ 19. Judges of the supreme court, circuit judges, and justices of the peace, shall be conservators of the peace within their respectives jurisdictions.

§ 20. The first election of judges of the circuit courts, shall be held on the first Monday in April, one thousand eight hundred and fifty-one, and every sixth year thereafter. Whenever an additional circuit is created, provision shall be made to hold the subsequent election of such additional judges at the regular elections herein provided.

§ 21. The first election of judges of the probate courts shall be held on the Tuesday succeeding the first Monday of November, one thousand eight hundred and fifty-two, and every fourth year thereafter.

§ 22. Whenever a judge shall remove beyond the limits of the jurisdiction for which he was elected, or a justice of the peace from the township in which he was elected, or by a change in the boundaries of such township shall be placed without the same, they shall be deemed to have vacated their respective offices.

§ 23. The Legislature may establish courts of conciliation with such powers and duties as shall be prescribed by law.

§ 24. Any suitor in any court of this State shall have the right to prosecute or defend his suit, either in his own proper person, or by an attorney or agent of his choice.

§ 25. In all prosecutions for libels, the truth may be given in evidence to the jury; and if it shall appear to the jury, that the matter charged as libellous, is true, and was published with good motives and for justifiable ends, the party shall be acquitted. The jury shall have the right to determine the law and the fact.

§ 26. The person, houses, papers and possessions of every person shall be secure from unreasonable searches and seizures. No warrant to search any place or to seize any person or things, shall issue without describing them, nor without probable cause, supported by oath or affirmation.

§ 27. The right of trial by jury shall remain, but shall be deemed to be waived in all civil cases unless demanded by one of the parties in such manner as shall be prescribed by law.

§ 28. In every criminal prosecution, the accused shall have the right to a speedy and public trial by an impartial jury, which may consist of less than twelve men in all courts not of record; to be informed of the nature of the accusation; to be confronted with the witnesses against him; to have compulsory process for obtaining witnesses in his favor, and have the assistance of counsel for his defence.

§ 29. No person, after acquittal upon the merits, shall be tried for he same offence; all persons shall, before conviction, be bailable by sufficient sureties, except for murder and treason, when the proof is evident or the presumption great.

§ 30. Treason against the State shall consist only in levying war against, or in adhering to its enemies, giving them aid and comfort. No person shall be convicted of treason unless upon the testimony of two witnesses to the same overt act, or on confession in open court.

§ 31. Excessive bail shall not be required; excessive fines shall no be imposed; cruel or unusual punishment shall not be inflicted, nor shall witnesses be unreasonably detained.

§ 32. No person shall be compelled, in any criminal case, to be a witness against himself, nor be deprived of life, liberty or property, without due process of law.

§ 33. No person shall be imprisoned for debt arising out of, or founded on a contract, express or implied, except in cases of fraud or breach of trust, or of moneys collected by public officers or in any professional employment. No person shall be imprisoned for a militia fine in time of peace.

§ 34. No person shall be rendered incompetent to be a witness ont account of his opinions on matters of religious belief.

§ 35. The style of all process shall be: "In the name of the people of the State of Michigan."

ARTICLE VII.

ELECTIONS.

§ 1. In all elections. every white male citizen every white male inhabitant residing in the State on the twenty-fourth day of June, one thousand eight hundred and thirty-five; every white male inhabitant residing in this State on the first day of January, one thousand eight hundred and fifty, who has declared his intention to become a citizen of the United States, pursuant to the laws thereof, six months preceding an election, or who has resided in this State two years and six months, and declared his intention as aforesaid, and every civilized male inhabitant of Indian descent, a native of the United States and not a member of any tribe, shall be an elector and entitled to vote; but no citizen or inhabitant shall be an elector or entiled to vote at any election, unless he shall be above the age of twenty-one years, and has resided in this State three months, and in the township or ward in which he offers to vote, ten days next preceding such election.

§ 2. All votes shall be given by ballot, except for such township officers as may be authorized by law to be otherwise chosen.

§ 3. Every elector, in all cases, except treason, felony, or breach of the peace, shall be privileged from arrest during his attendance at election, and in going to and returning from the same.

§ 4. No elector shall be obliged to do militia duty on the day of election, except in time of war or public danger, or attend court as a suitor or witness.

§ 5. No elector shall be deemed to have gained or lost a residence, by reason of his being employed in the service of the United States, or of this State; nor while engaged in the navigation of the waters of this State or of the United States, or of the high seas; nor while a student of any seminary of learning; nor while kept at any alms-house or other asylum at public enpense; nor while confined in any public prison.

§ 6. Laws may be passed to preserve the purity of elections, and guard against abuses of the elective franchise.

§ 7. No soldier, seaman, nor marine, in the army or navy of the United States, shall be deemed a resident of this State,in consequence of being stationed in any military or naval place within the same.

§ 8. Any inhabitant who may hereafter be engaged in a duel, either as principal or accessory before the fact, shall be disqualified from holding any office under the constitution and laws of this State and shall not be permitted to vote at any election.

ARTICLE VIII.

STATE OFFICERS.

§ 1. There shall be elected at each general biennial election a Secretary of State, a Superintendent of Public Instruction, a State Treasurer, a Commissoner of the Land Office, an Auditor General, and an Attorney General, for the term of two years. They shall keep their offices at the seat of government, and shall perform such duties as may be prescribed by law.

§ 2. Their term of office shall commence on the first day of January, one thousand eight hundred and fifty-three, and of every second year thereafter.

§ 3. Whenever a vacancy shall occur in any of the State offices, the Governor shall fill the same by appointment, by and with the advice and consent of the Senate, if in session.

§ 4. The Secretary of State, State Treasurer, and Commissioner of the State Land Office shall constitute a Board of State Auditors to examine and adjust all claims against the State, not otherwise provided for by general law. They shall constitute a Board of State Canvassers to determine the result of all elections for Governor, Lieutenant Governor and State Officers, and of such other officers as shall by law be referred to them.

§ 5. In case two or more persons have an equal and the highest number of votes for any office, as canvassed by the Board of State Canvassers, the Legislature, in joint Convention, shall choose one of of said persons to fill such office. When the determination of the Board of State Canvassers is contested, the Legislature, in Joint Convention, shall decide which person is elected.

ARTICLE IX.

SALARIES.

§ 1. The Governor shall receive an annual salary of one thousand dollars; the Judges of the Circuit Court shall each receive an annual salary of one thousand five hundred dollars; the State Treasurer shall receive an annual salary of one thousand dollars; the Auditor General shall receive an annual salary of one thousand dollars; the Superintendent of Public Instruction shall receive an annual salary of one thousand dollars; the Secretary of State shall receive an annual salary of eight hundred dollars; the Commissioner of the Land Office shall receive an annual salary of eight hundred dollars; the Attorney General shall receive an annual salary of eight hundred dollars. They shall receive no fees or perquisites, whatever, for the performance of any duties connected with their offices. It shall not be competent for the Legislature to increase the salaries herein provided.

ARTICLE X.

COUNTIES.

§ 1. Each organized county, shall be a body corporate with such powers and immunities as shall be established by law. All suits and proceedings, by or against a county, shall be in the name thereof.

§ 2. No organized county, shall ever be reduced by the organization of new counties to less than sixteen townships, as surveyed by the United States, unless in pursuance of law, a majority of electors residing in each county to be affected thereby, shall so decide. The Legislature may organize any city into a separate councy, when it has attained a population of twenty thousand inhabitants, without reference to geographical extent, when a majority of the electors of a county in which such city may be situated, voting thereon, shall be in favor of a separate organization.

§ 3. In each organized county there shall be a sheriff, a county clerk, a county treasurer, a register of deeds and a prosecuting attorney, chosen by the electors thereof, once in two years, and as often as vacancies shall happen, whose duties and powers shall be prescribed by law. The board of supervisors in any county may unite the offices of county clerk and register of deeds in one office, or disconnect the same.

§ 4. The sheriff, county clerk, county treasurer, judge of probate and register of deeds, shall hold their offices at the county seat.

§ 5. The sheriff shall hold no other office, and shall be incapable of holding the office of sheriff longer than four in any period of six years. He may be required by law to renew his security from time to time, and in default of giving such security, his office shall be deemed vacant. The county shall never be responsible for his acts.

§ 6. A board of supervisors, consisting of one from each organized township, shall be established in each county, with such powers as shall be prescribed by law.

§ 7. Cities shall have such representation in the board of supervisors of the counties in which they are situated, as the Legislature may direct.

§ 8. No county seat, once established, shall be removed, until the place to which it is proposed to be removed shall be designated by two-thirds of the board of supervisors of the county, and a majority of the electors voting thereon shall have voted in favor of the proposed location, in such manner as shall be prescribed by law.

§ 9. The board of supervisors of any county may borrow or raise by tax one thousand dollars, for constructing or repairing public buildings, highways or bridges; but no greater sum shall be borrowed or raised by tax for such purpose in any one year, unless authorized by a majority of the electors of such county voting thereon.

§ 10. The board of supervisors, or in the county of Wayne, the board of county auditors, shall have the exclusive power to prescribe and fix the compensation for all services rendered for, and to adjust all claims against their respective counties, and the sum so fixed or defined shall be subject to no appeal.

§ 11. The board of supervisors of each organized county may provide for laying out highways, constructing bridges, and organizing townships, under such restrictions and limitations as shall be prescribed by law.

ARTICLE XI.

TOWNSHIPS.

§ 1. There shall be elected annually, on the first Monday of April, in each organized township, one supervisor, one township clerk, who shall be ex-officio school inspector, one commissioner of highways, one township treasurer, one school inspector, not exceeding four constables, and one overseer of highways for each highway district, whose powers and duties shall be prescribed by law.

§ 2. Each organized township shall be a body corporate, with such powers and immunities as shall be prescribed by law. All suits and proceedings by or against a township, shall be in the name thereof.

ARTICLE XII.

IMPEACHMENTS AND REMOVALS FROM OFFICE.

§ 1. The House of Representatives shall have the sole power of impeaching civil officers for corrupt conduct in office, or for crimes or misdemeanors; but a majority of the members elected shall be necessary to direct an impeachment.

§ 2. Every impeachment shall be tried by the Senate. When the Governor or Lieutenant Governor is tried, the Chief Justice of the Supreme Court shall preside. When an impeachment is directed the Senate shall take an oath or affirmation truly and impartially to try and determine the same according to the evidence. No person shall be convicted without the concurrence of two-thirds of the members elected. Judgment, in case of impeachment, shall not extend further than removal from office; but the party convicted shall be liable to punishment according to law.

§ 3. When an impeachment is directed the House of Representatives shall elect from their own body three members, whose duty it shall be to prosecute such impeachment. No impeachment shall be tried until the final adjournment of the Legislature, when the Senate shall proceed to try the same.

§ 4. No judicial officer shall exercise his office, after an impeachment is directed, until he is acquitted.

§ 5. The Governor may make a provisional appointment to fill a vacancy occasioned by the suspension of an officer until he shall be acquitted, or until after the election and qualification of a successsor.

§ 6. For reasonable cause, which shall not be sufficient ground for the impeachment of a judge, the Governor shall remove him on a concurrent resolution of two-thirds of the members elected to each house of the Legislature; but the cause for which such removal is required shall be stated at length in such resolution.

§ 7. The Legislature shall provide by law for the removal of any officer elected by a county, township or school district, in such manner and for such cause as to them shall seem just and proper.

ARTICLE XIII.

EDUCATION.

§ 1. The Superintendent of Public Instruction shall have the general supervision of public instruction, and his duties shall be prescribed by law.

§ 2. The proceeds from the sales of all lands that have been or hereafter may be granted by the United States to the State, for educational purposes, and the proceeds of all lands or other property given by individuals or appropriated by the State for like purposes, shall be and remain a perpetual fund, the interest and income of which, together with the rents of all such lands as may remain unsold, shall be inviolably appropriated and annually applied to the specific objects of the original gift, grant or appropriation.

§ 3. All lands, the titles to which shall fail from a defect of heirs, shall escheat to the State; and the interest on the clear proceeds from the sales thereof, shall be appropriated exclusively to the support of primary schools.

§ 4. The Legislature shall, within five years from the adoption of this constitution, provide for and establish a system of primary schools, whereby a school shall be kept without charge for tuition, at least three months in each year, in every school district in the State, and all instruction in said schools shall be conducted in the English language.

§ 5. A school shall be maintained in each school district at least three months in each year. Any school district neglecting to maintain such school, shall be deprived for the ensuing year, of its proportion of the income of the primary school fund, and of all funds arising from taxes for the support of schools.

§ 6. There shall be elected in each judicial circuit, at the time of the election of the judge of such circuit, a regent of the University, whose term of office shall be the same as that of such judge. The regents thus elected shall constitute the Board of Regents of the University of Michigan.

§ 7. The regents of the University and their successors in office, shall continue to constitute the body corporate, known by the name and title of "the regents of the University of Michigan."

§ 8. The regents of the University shall, at their first annual meeting, or as soon thereafter as may be, elect a President of the University, who shall be *ex officio* a member of their board, with the privilege of speaking but not of voting. He shall preside at the meetings of the regents, and be the principal executive officer of the University. The board of regents shall have the general supervision of the University, and the direction and control of all expenditures from the University interest fund.

§ 9. There shall be elected at the general election in the year one thousand eight hundred and fifty-two, three members of a State Board of Education, one for two years, one for four years, and one for six years; and at each succeeding biennial election, there shall be elected one member of such board, who shall hold his office for six years. The Superintendent of Public Instruction shall be *ex officio* a member and secretary of such board. The board shall have the general supervision of the State Normal School, and their duties shall be prescribed by law.

§ 10. Institutions for the benefit of those inhabitants who are deaf, dumb, blind or insane, shall always be fostered and supported.

§ 11. The Legislature shall encourage the promotion of intellectual, scientific and agricultural improvement; and shall, as soon as practicable, provide for the establishment of an agricultural school. The Legislature may appropriate the twenty-two sections of salt spring lands now unappropriated, or the money arising from the sale of the same, where such lands have been already sold, and any land which may hereafter be granted or appropriated for such purpose, for the support and maintenance of such school, and may make the same a branch of the University for instruction in agriculture and the natural sciences connected therewith, and place the same under the supervision of the Regents of the University.

§ 12. The Legislature shall also provide for the establishment of at least one library in each township; and all fines assessed and collected in the several counties and townships for any breach of the penal laws, shall be exclusively applied to the support of such libraries.

ARTICLE XIV.

FINANCE AND TAXATION.

§ 1. All specific State taxes, except those received from the mining companies of the Upper Peninsula, shall be applied in paying the interest upon the primary school, university and other educational funds, and the interest and principal of the State debt, in the order herein recited, until the extinguishment of the State debt, other than the amounts due to educational funds, when such specific taxes shall be added to, and constitute a part of the primary school interest fund. The Legislature shall provide for an annual tax, sufficient, with other resources, to pay the estimated expenses of the State Government, the interest of the State debt, and such deficiency as may occur in the resources.

§ 2. The Legislature shall provide by law, a sinking fund of at least twenty thousand dollars a year, to commence in eighteen hundred and fifty-two, with compound interest at the rate of six per cent per annum, and an annual increase of at least five per cent., to be applied solely to the payment and extinguishment of the principal of the State debt, other than the amounts due to educational funds, and shall be continued until the extinguishment thereof. The unfunded debt shall not be funded or redeemed at a value exceeding that established by law in one thousand eight hundred and forty-eight.

§ 3. The State may contract debts to meet deficits in revenue. Such debts shall not in the aggregate at any one time exceed fifty thousand dollars. The moneys so raised shall be applied to the purposes for which they were obtained, or to the payment of the debts so contracted.

§ 4. The State may contract debts to repel invasion, suppress insurrection, or defend the State in time of war. The money arising from the contracting of such debts shall be applied to the purposes for which it was raised, or to repay such debts.

§ 5. No money shall be paid out of the treasury except in pursuance of appropriations made by law.

§ 6. The credit of the State shall not be granted to, or in aid of any person, association or corporation.

§ 7. No scrip, certificate or other evidence of State indebtedness shall be issued, except for the redemption of stock previously issued, or for such debts as are expressly authorized in this constitution.

§ 8. The state shall not subscribe to, or be interested in, the stock of any company, association or corporation.

§ 9. The State shall not be a party to, or interested in, any work of internal improvement, nor engaged in carrying on any such work, except in the expenditure of grants to the State of land or other property.

§ 10. The State may continue to collect all specific taxes accruing to the treasury under existing laws. The Legislature may provide for the collection of specific taxes, from banking, rail road, plank road, and other corporations hereafter created.

§ 11. The Legislature shall provide an uniform rule of taxation, except on property paying specific taxes and taxes shall be levied on such property as shall be prescribed by law.

§ 12. All assessments hereafter authorized shall be on property at its cash value.

§ 13. The Legislature shall provide for an equalization by a State Board, in the year one thousand eight hundred and fifty-one, and every fifth year thereafter, of assessments on all taxable property, except that paying specific taxes.

§ 14. Every law which imposes, continues or revives a tax, shall distinctly state the tax, and the object to which it is to be applied; and it shall not be sufficient to refer to any other law to fix such tax or object.

ARTICLE XV.

CORPORATIONS.

§ 1. Corporations may be formed under general laws; but shall not be created by special act, except for municipal purposes. All laws passed pursuant to this section may be altered, amended or repealed.

§ 2. No banking law or law for banking purposes, or amendments thereof, shall have effect until the same shall, after its passage, be submitted to a vote of the electors of the State, at a general election, and be approved by a majority of the votes cast thereon at such election.

§ 3. The officers and stockholders of every corporation or association for banking purposes, issuing bank notes or paper credits to circulate as money, shall be individually liable for all debts contracted during the time of their being officers or stockholders of such corporation or association.

§ 4. The Legislature shall provide by law for the registry of all bills or notes issued or put in circulation as money, and shall require security to the full amount of notes and bills so registered in State or United States stocks, bearing interest, which shall be deposited with the State Treasurer, for the redemption of such bills or notes in specie.

§ 5. In case of the insolvency of any bank or banking association, the bill holders thereof shall be entitled to preference in payment, over all other creditors of such bank or association.

§ 6. The Legislature shall pass no law authorizing or sanctioning the suspension of specie payments by any person, association or corporation.

§ 7. The stockholders of all corporations and joint stock associations shall be individually liable for all labor performed for such corporation or association.

§ 8. The Legislature shall pass no law altering or amending any act of incorporation heretofore granted, without the assent of two-thirds of the members elected to each house; nor shall any such act be renewed or extended. This restriction shall not apply to municipal corporations.

§ 9. The property of no person shall be taken by any corporation for public use without compensation being first made or secured, in such manner as may be prescribed by law.

§ 10. No corporation, except for municipal purposes, or for the construction of rail roads, plank roads and canals, shall be created for a longer time than thirty years.

§ 11. The term "corporations," as used in the preceding sections of this article, shall be construed to include all associations and joint stock companies having any of the powers or privileges of corporations, not possessed by individuals or partnerships. All corporations shall have the right to sue, and be subject to be sued, in all courts, in like cases as natural persons.

§ 12. No corporation shall hold any real estate hereafter acquired, for a longer period than ten years, except such real estate as shall be actually occupied by such corporation in the exercise of its franchises.

§ 13. The Legislature shall provide for the incorporation and organization of cities and villages, and shall restrict their powers of taxation, borrowing money, contracting debts and loaning their credit.

§ 14. Judicial officers of cities and villages shall be elected, and all other officers shall be elected or appointed at such time and in such manner as the Legislature may direct.

§ 15. Private property shall not be taken for public improvements in cities and villages without the consent of the owner, unless the compensation therefor shall first be determined by a jury of freeholders, and actually paid or secured in the manner provided by law.

§ 16. Previous notice of any application for an alteration of the charter of any corporation shall be given in such manner as may be prescribed by law.

ARTICLE XVI.

EXEMPTIONS.

§ 1. The personal property of every resident of this State, to consist of such property only as shall be designated by law, shall be exempted to the amount of not less than five hundred dollars from sale on execution or other final process of any court issued for the collection of any debt contracted after the adoption of this constitution.

§ 2. Every homested of not exceeding forty acres of land, and the dwelling-house thereon, and the appurtenances to be selected by the owner thereof, and not included in any town plat, city or village; or instead thereof, at the option of the owner, any lot in any city, village, or recorded town plat, or such parts of lots as shall be equal thereto, and the dwelling-house thereon and its appurtenances, owned and occupied by any resident of the State, not exceeding in value fifteen hundred dollars, shall be exempt from forced sale on execution or any other final process from a court, for any debt contracted after the adoption of this constitution. Such exemption shall not extend to any mortgage thereon lawfully obtained; but such mortgage or other alienation of such land, by the owner thereof, if a married man, shall not be valid without the signature of the wife to the same.

§ 3. The homested of a family, after the death of the owner thereof, shall be exempt from the payment of his debts, contracted after the adoption of this constitution, in all cases, during the minority of his children.

§ 4. If the owner of a homested die, leaving a widow, but no children, the same shall be exempt, and the rents and profits thereot shall accrue to her benefit during the time of her widowhood, unless she be the owner of a homested in her own right.

§ 5. The real and personal estate of every female, acquired before marriage, and all property to which she may afterwards become entitled, by gift, grant, inheritance or devise, shall be and remain the estate and property of such female, and shall not be liable for the debts, obligations or engagements of her husband; and may be devised or bequeathed by her as if she were unmarried.

ARTICLE XVII.

MILITIA.

§ 1. The militia shall be composed of all able bodied white male citizens between the ages of eighteen and forty-five years, except such as are exempted by the laws of the United States or of this State; but all such citizens of any religious denomination whatever, who, from scruples of conscience, may be averse to bearing arms, shall be excused therefrom, upon such conditions as shall be prescribed by law.

§ 2. The Legislature shall provide by law for organizing, equipping and disciplining the militia, in such manner as they shall deem expedient, not incompatible with the laws of the United States.

§ 3. Officers of the militia shall be elected or appointed and be commissioned in such manner as may be provided by law.

ARTICLE XVIII.

MISCELLANEOUS PROVISIONS.

§ 1. Members of the Legislature, and all officers, executive and judicial, except such officers as may by law be exempted, shall, before they enter on the duties of their respective offices, take and subscribe the following oath or affirmation: "I do solemnly swear (or affirm,) that I will support the constitution of the United States and the constitution of this State, and that I will faithfully discharge the duties of the office of   according to the best of my ability." And no other oath, declaration or test shall be required as a qualification for any office or public trust.

§ 2. When private property is taken for the use or benefit of the public, the necessity for using such property, and the just compensation to be made therefor, except when to be made by the State, shall be ascertained by a jury of twelve freeholders, residing in the vicinity of such property, or by not less than three commissioners, appointed by a court of record, as shall be prescribed by law.

§ 3. No mechanical trade shall hereafter be taught to convicts in the state prison of this State, except the manufacture of those articles, of which the chief supply for home consumption is imported from other states or countries.

§ 4. No navigable stream in this State, shall be either bridged or damed without authority from the board of supervisors of the proper county, under the provisions of law. No such law shall prejudice the right of individuals to the free navigation of such streams, or preclude the State from the further improvement of the navigation of such stream.

§ 5. An accurate statement of the receipts and expenditures of the public moneys shall be attached to, and published with the laws, at every regular session of the Legislature.

§ 6 The laws, public records, and the written judicial and Legislative proceedings of the State, shall be conducted, promulgated and preserved in the English language.

§ 7. Every person has a right to bear arms for the defence of himself and the State.

§ 8. The military shall, in all cases, and at all times, be in strict subordination to the civil power.

§ 9. No soldier shall, in time of peace, be quartered in any house without the consent of the owner or occupant, nor in time of war, except in a manner prescribed by law.

§ 10. The people have the right peaceably to assemble together, to consult for the common good, to instruct their Representatives, and to petition the Legislature for redress of grievances.

§ 11. Neither slavery, nor involuntary servitude, unless for the punishment of crime, shall ever be tolerated in this State.

§ 12. No lease or grant hereafter of agricultural land for a longer period than twelve years, reserving any rent or service of any kind, shall be valid.

§ 13. Aliens who are, or who may hereafter become *bona fide* residents of this State, shall enjoy the same rights in respect to the possession, enjoyment and inheritance of property, as native born citizens.

§ 14. The property of no person shall be taken for public use without just compensation therefor. Private roads may be opened in the manner to be prescribed by law; but in every case the necessity of the road and the amount of all damages to be sustained by the opening thereof, shall be first determined by a jury of freeholders; and such amount, together with the expenses of proceedings, shall be paid by the person or persons to be benefitted.

§ 15. No general revision of the laws shall hereafter be made. When a re-print thereof becomes necessary, the Legislature in joint convention, shall appoint a suitable person to collect together such acts and parts of acts as are in force, and without alteration, arrange them under appropriate heads and titles. The laws so arranged shall be submitted to two commissioners appointed by the Governor for examination, and if certified by them to be a correct compilation of all general laws in force, shall be printed in such manner as shall be prescribed by law.

ARTICLE XIX.

UPPER PENINSULA.

§ 1. The counties of Mackinac, Chippewa, Delta, Marquette, Schoolcraft, Houghton and Ontonagon, and the islands and territory thereunto attached, the islands of Lake Superior, Huron and Michigan, and in Green Bay, and the straits of Mackinac and the River Ste Marie, shall constitute a separate judicial district, and be entitled to a district judge and district attorney.

§ 2. The district judge shall be elected by the electors of such district, and shall perform the same duties and possess the same powers as a circuit judge in his circuit, and shall hold his office for the same period.

§ 3. The district attorney shall be elected every two years by the electors of the district, shall perform the duties of prosecuting attorney throughout the entire district, and may issue warrants for the arrest of offenders in cases of felony, to be proceeded with as shall be prescribed by law.

§ 4. Such judicial district shall be entitled at all times to at least one Senator, and until entitled to more by its population, it shall have three members of the House of Representatives, to be apportioned among the several counties by the Legislature.

§ Sec. 5. The Legislature may provide for the payment of the district judge a salary not exceeding one thousand dollars a year, and of the district attorney not exceeding seven hundred dollars a year; and may allow extra compensation to the members of the Legislature from such territory, not exceeding two dollars a day during any session.

§ 6. The elections for all district or county officers, State Senator or Representatives, within the boundaries defined in this article, shall take place on the last Tuesday of September in the respective years in which they may be required. The county canvass shall be held on the first Tuesday in October thereafter, and the district canvass on the last Tuesday of said October.

§ 7. One-half of the taxes received into the treasury from mining corporations in the Upper Peninsula paying an annual State tax of one per cent., shall be paid to the treasurers of the counties from which it is received, to be applied for township and county purposes, as provided by law. The Legislature shall have power, after the year one thousand eight hundred and fifty-five, to reduce the amount to be refunded.

§ 8. The Legislature may change the location of the State Prison from Jackson to the Upper Peninsula.

§ 9. The charters of the several mining corporations may be modified by the Legislature, in regard to the term limited for subscribing to stock, and in relation to the quantity of land which a corporation shall hold; but the capital shall not be increased, nor the time for the existence of charters extended. No such corporation shall be permitted to purchase or hold any real estate, except such as shall be necessary for the exercise of its corporate franchises.

ARTICLE XX.

AMENDMENT AND REVISION OF THE CONSTITUTION.

§ 1. Any amendment or amendments to this constitution may be proposed in the Senate or House of Representatives. If the same shall be agreed to by two-thirds of the members elected to each house, such amendment or amendments shall be entered on their journals respectively, with the yeas and nays taken thereon; and the same shall be submitted to the electors at the next general election thereafter, and if a majority of the electors qualified to vote for members of the Legislature voting thereon, shall ratify and approve such amendment or amendments, the same shall become part of the constiution.

§ 2. At the general election to be held in the year one thousand eight hundred and sixty-six, and in each sixteenth year thereafter, and also at such other times as the Legislature may by law provide, the question of a general revision of the constitution shall be submitted to the electors qualified to vote for members of the Legislature; and in case a majority of the electors so qualified, voting at such election, shall decide in favor of a convention for such purpose, the Legislature, at the next session, shall provide by law for the election of delegates to such convention. All the amendments shall take effect at the commencement of the political year after their adoption.

SCHEDULE.

That no inconvenience may arise from the changes in the constitution of this State, and in order to carry the same into complete operation, it is hereby declared, that

§ 1. The common law and the statute laws now in force, not repugnant to this constitution, shall remain in force until they expire by their own limitations, or are altered or repealed by the Legislature.

§ 2. All writs, actions, causes of action, prosecutions and rights of individuals and of bodies corporate, and of the State, and all charters of incorporation, shall continue; and all indictments which shall have been found, or which may hereafter be found, for any crime or offence committed before the adoption of this constitution, may be proceeded upon as if no change had taken place. The several courts, except as herein otherwise provided, shall continue with the like powers and jurisdiction, both at law and in equity, as if this constitution had not been adopted, and until the organization of the judicial department under this constitution.

§ 3. That all fines, penalties, forfeitures and escheats accruing to the State of Michigan under the present constitution and laws, shall accrue to the use of the State under this constitution.

§ 4. That all recognizances, bonds, obligations, and all other instruments entered into or executed before the adoption of this constitution, to the people of the State of Michigan, to any State, county or township, or any public officer or public body, or which may be entered into or executed, under existing laws, "to the people of the State of Michigan," to any such officer or public body, before the complete organization of the departments of government under this constitution, shall remain binding and valid; and rights and liabilities upon the same shall continue, and may be prosecuted as provided by law. And all crimes and misdemeanors and penal actions, shall be tried, punished and prosecuted, as though no change had taken place, until otherwise provided by law.

§ 5. A Governor and Lieutenant Governor shall be chosen under the existing constitution and laws, to serve after the expiration of the term of the present incumbent.

§ 6. All officers, civil and military, now holding any office or appointment, shall continue to hold their respective offices, unless removed by competent authority, until superseded under the laws now in force, or under this constitution.

§ 7. The members of the Senate and House of Representatives of the Legislature of one thousand eight hundred and fifty-one, shall continue in office under the provisions of law, until superseded by their successors elected and qualified under this constitution.

§ 8. All county officers, unless removed by competent authority, shall continue to hold their respective offices until the first day of January, in the year one thousand eight hundred and fifty-three. The laws now in force as to the election, qualification and duties of township officers, shall continue in force until the Legislature shall, in conformity to the provisions of this constitution, provide for the holding of elections to fill such offices, and prescribe the duties of such officers respectively.

§ 9. On the first day of January, in the year one thousand eight hundred and fifty-two, the terms of office of the judges of the supreme court, under existing laws, and of the judges of the county courts, and of the clerks of the supreme court, shall expire on the said day.

§ 10. On the first day of January, in the year one thousand eight hundred and fifty-two, the jurisdiction of all suits and proceedings then pending in the present supreme courts, shall become vested in the supreme court established by this constitution, and shall be finally adjudicated by the court where the same may be pending. The jurisdiction of all suits and proceedings at law and equity, then pending in the circuit courts and county courts for the several counties, shall become vested in the circuit courts of the said counties, and district court for the Upper Peninsula.

§ 11. The probate courts, the courts of justices of the peace and the police court authorized by an act entitled "An act to establish a police court in the city of Detroit," approved April second, one thousand eight hundred and fifty, shall continue to exercise the jurisdiction and powers now conferred upon them respectively, until otherwise provided by law.

§ 12. The office of State Printer shall be vested in the present incumbent until the expiration of the term for which he was elected under the law then in force; and all the provisions of the said law relating to his duties, rights, privileges and compensation, shall remain unimpaired and inviolate until the expiration of his said term of office.

§ 13. It shall be the duty of the Legislature, at their first session, to adapt the present laws to the provisions of this constitution, as far as may be.

§ 14. The Attorney General of the State is required to prepare and report to the Legislature, at the commencement of the next session, such changes and modifications in existing laws as may be deemed necessary to adapt the same to this constitution, and as may be best calculated to carry into effect its provisions; and he shall receive no additional compensation therefor.

§ 15. Any territory attached to any county for judicial purposes, if not otherwise represented, shall be considered as forming part of such county, so far as regards elections for the purpose of representation.

§ 16. This constitution shall be submitted to the people for their adoption or rejection, at the general election to be held on the first Tuesday of November, one thousand eight hundred and fifty; and there shall also be submitted for adoption or rejection, at the same time the separate resolution in relation to the elective franchise; and it shall be the duty of the Secretary of State, and all other officers required to give or publish any notice in regard to the said general election, to give notice, as provided by law in case of an election of Governor, that this constitution has been duly submitted to the electors at said election. Every newspaper within this State publishing in the month of September next, this constitution as submitted, shall receive, as compensation therefor, the sum of twenty-five dollars, to be paid as the Legislature shall direct.

§ 17. Any person entitled to vote for members of the Legislature, by the constitution and laws now in force, shall, at the said election, be entitled to vote for the adoption or rejection of this constitution, and for or against the resolution separately submitted, at the places and in the manner provided by law for the election of members of the Legislature.

§ 18. At the said general election, a ballot box shall be kept by the several boards of inspectors thereof, for receiving the votes cast for or against the adoption of this Constitution; and on the ballots shall be written or printed, or partly written and partly printed, the words "Adoption of the constitution—yes." or "Adoption of the constitution—no."

§ 19. The canvass of the votes cast for the adoption or rejection of this Constitution and the provision in relation to the elective franchise separately submitted, and the returns thereof shall be made by the proper canvassing officers, in the same manner as now provided by law for the canvass and return of the votes cast at an election for Governor, as near as may be, and the return thereof shall be directed to the Secretary of State. On the sixteenth day of December next, or within five days thereafter, the Auditor General, State Treasurer and Secretary of State shall meet at the capitol and proceed in presence of the Governor, to examine and canvass the returns of the said votes, and proclamation shall forthwith be made by the Governor of the result thereof. If it shall appear that a majority of the votes cast upon the question have thereon "Adoption of the Constitution—yes," this constitution shall be the supreme law of the State from and after the first day of January, one thousand eight hundred and fifty-one, except as is herein otherwise provided; but if a majority of the votes cast upon the question have thereon "Adoption of the Constitution—no," the same shall be null and void. And in case of the adoption of this constitution, said officers shall immediately, or as soon thereafter as practicable, proceed to open the statements of votes returned from the several counties for judges of the supreme court and State officers under the act entitled "An act to amend the revised statutes and to provide for the election of certain officers by the people in pursuance to an amendment of the Constitution, approved February sixteenth, one thousand eight hundred and fifty," and shall ascertain, determine and certify the results of the election for said officers under said acts, in the same manner, as near as may be, as is now provided by law in regard to the election of Representatives in Congress. And the several judges and officers so ascertained to have been elected may be qualified and enter upon the duties of their respective offices, on the first Monday of January next, or as soon thereafter as practicable.

§ 20. The salaries or compensation of all persons holding office under the present constitution shall continue to be the same as now provided by law, until superseded by their successors elected or appointed under this constitution; and it shall not be lawful hereafter for the Legislature to increase or diminish the compensation of any officer during the term for which he is elected or appointed.

§ 21. The Legislature, at their first session, shall provide for the payment of all expenditures of the convention to revise the constitution and of the publication of the same as is provided in this article.

§ 22. Every county except Mackinaw and Chippewa, entitled to a representative in the Legislature, at the time of the adoption of this constitution, shall continue to be so entitled under this constitution; and the county of Saginaw, with the territory that may be attached, shall be entitled to one representative; the county of Tuscola, and the territory that may be attached, one representative; the county of Sanilac, and the territory that may be attached, one representative; the counties of Midland and Aronac, with the territory that may be attached, one representative; the county of Montcalm, with the territory that may be attached thereto, one representative; and the counties of Newaygo and Oceana, with the territory that may be attached thereto, one representative. Each county having a ratio of representation and a fraction over, equal to a moiety of said ratio, shall be entitled to two representatives, and so on above that number, giving one additional member for each additional ratio.

§ 23. The cases pending and undisposed of in the late court of chancery at the time of the adoption of this constitution, shall continue to be heard and determined by the judges of the supreme court. But the Legislature shall, at its session in one thousand eight hundred and fifty-one, provide by law, for the transfer of said causes that may remain undisposed of on the first day of January, one thousand eight hundred and fifty-two, to the supreme or circuit court established by this constitution, or require that the same may be heard and determined by the circuit judges.

§ 24. The term of office of the Governor and Lieutenant Governor shall commence on the first day of January next after their election.

§ 25. The territory described in the article entitled "Upper Peninsula." shall be attached to and constitute a part of the third circuit for the election of a Regent of the University.

§ 26. The Legislature shall have authority after the expiration of the term of office of the district judge first elected for the "Upper Peninsula," to abolish said office of district judge and district attorney, or either of them.

§ 27. The Legislature shall, at its session of one thousand eight hundred and fifty-one, apportion the Representatives among the several counties and districts, and divide the State into Senate districts, pursuant to the provisions of this constitution.

§ 28. The terms of office of all State and county officers, of the circuit judges, members of the board of education, and members of the Legislature, shall begin on the first day of January next succeeding their election.

§ 29. The State, exclusive of the Upper Peninsula, shall be divided into eight judicial circuits, and the counties of Monroe, Lenawee and Hillsdale shall constitute the first circuit; the counties of Branch, St. Joseph, Cass and Berrien shall constitute the second circuit; the county of Wayne shall constitute the third circuit; the counties of Washtenaw, Jackson and Ingham shall constitute the fourth circuit; the counties of Calhoun, Kalamazoo, Allegan, Eaton and Van Buren shall constitute the fifth circuit; [the] counties of St. Clair, Macomb, Oakland and Sanilac shall constitute the sixth circuit; the counties of Lapeer, Genesee, Saginaw, Shiawassee, Livingston, Tuscola and Midland shall constitute the seventh circuit; and the counties of Barry, Kent, Ottawa, Ionia, Clinton and Montcalm shall constitute the eighth circuit.

RESOLUTION.

§ 30. At the next general election, and at the same time when the votes of the electors shall be taken for the adoption or rejection of this constitution, an additional amendment to section one of Article seven, in the words following:

"Every colored male inhabitant possessing the qualifications required by the first section of the second article of the Constitution, shall have the rights and privileges of an elector,"

Shall be separately submitted to the electors of this State for their adoption or rejection, in form following, to wit: A separate ballot may be given by every person having the right to vote for the revised Constitution, to be deposited in a separate box. Upon the ballots given for the adoption of the said separate amendment shall be written or printed, or partly written and partly printed, the words "Equal suffrage to colored persons? Yes;" and upon all ballots given against the adoption of the said separate amendment, in like manner, the words "Equal suffrage to colored persons? No." And on such ballots shall be written or printed, or partly written and partly printed, the words "Constitution: Suffrage," in such manner that such words shall appear on the outer side of such ballot when folded. If, at said election, a majority of all the votes given for and against the said separate amendment shall contain the words, "Equal suffrage to colored persons? Yes," then there shall be inserted in the first section of the article, between the words "tribe and shall," these words, "and every colored male inhabitant," anything in the Constitution to the contrary notwithstanding.

Done in Convention, at the Capitol of the State, this fifteenth day of August, in the year of our Lord one thousand eight hundred and fifty, and of the Independence of the United States the seventy-fifth.

On motion of Mr. Woodman,

A call of the Convention was had, and

Messrs. J. Bartow, Butterfield, Bush, Carr, Kingsley, Lovell, Newberry, Orr, N. Pierce and Rix Robinson were found absent without leave.

On motion of Mr. Whittemore,

The Sergeant-at-Arms was despatched for the absentees, who soon thereafter appearing,

On motion of Mr. Leach,

All further proceedings under the call were dispensed with.

Mr. McClelland then moved the adoption of the Constitution,

And the yeas and nays being had thereon, the motion prevailed as follows:

YEAS:

Mr. W. Adams,	Mr. Crary,	Mr. Mosher,
Alvord,	Crouse,	Mowry,
Anderson,	Danforth,	O'Brien,
Arzeno,	Daniels,	Orr,
Axford,	Desnoyers,	J. D. Pierce,
Bagg,	Eaton,	N. Pierce,
Barnard,	Edmunds,	Prevost,
H. Bartow,	Fralick,	Redfield,
J. Bartow,	Gale,	Robertson,
Beardsley,	Gardiner,	E. S. Robinson,
Beeson,	Gibson,	Rix Robinson,
Britain,	Green,	Skinner,
Ammon Brown,	Harvey,	Soule,
Asahel Brown,	Hascall,	Sturgis,
Burns,	Kingsley,	Town,
Butterfield,	Kinne,	Van Valkenburg,
Chandler,	Leach,	Wait,
Chapel,	Lee,	Walker,
Choate,	Lovell,	Warden,
Church,	Marvin,	Webster,
Comstock,	McClelland,	Whipple,
Conner,	Moore,	Williams,
Cornell,	Morrison,	Woodman, 69

NAYS:

Mr. Bush,	Mr. McLeod,	Mr. White,
Carr,	Newberry,	Whittemore,
Hanscom,	Roberts,	President,
Hart,	Storey,	11

Mr. Bush presented the following:

The undersigned, members of this Convention, solemnly protest against the adoption of the proposed Constitution, for that

1st. Having full confidence in the integrity of the people, and in their ability to successfully maintain a representative government, they believe that all abuses can and will be corrected by an enlightened public opinion through the ballot box.

2d. That our State being new, and consequently but partially developed, they believe that the detail of the Constitution which has been carried out in its every article, even to the one on township government, is not adapted to its changing condition and rapid growth and improvement.

3d. That distrust in the intelligence of the people, stamped upon every article of the Constitution, is, in their opinion, a stigma upon their character, not justified by the history of the State.

C. P. BUSH,
WM. NORMAN McLEOD,
E. J. ROBERTS.

In accordance with the resolution adopted this morning,

The constitution was signed in the following order, to wit:

By the President—D. Goodwin.

From the County of *Allegan*—Oka Town.

Barry—Joseph W. T. Orr.

Berrien—Jacob Beeson, Calvin Britain and Charles W. Whipple.

Branch—Wales Adams and Asahel Brown.

Calhoun—Isaac E. Crary, W. V. Morrison, John D. Pierce, Nathan Pierce and Milo Soule.

Cass—George Redfield.

Clinton—David Sturgis.

Eaton—Charles E. Beardsley and J. D. Burns.

Genesee—John Bartow, Elbridge G. Gale and DeWitt C. Leach.

Hillsdale—D. Kinne and John Mosher.

Ingham—Charles P. Bush and Ephraim B. Danforth.

Ionia—Henry Bartow and Cyrus Lovell.

Jackson—Robert H. Anderson, John L. Butterfield, Jerry G. Cornell, Elisha S. Robinson and Wilbur F. Storey.

Kalamazoo—Volney Hascall.

Kent & Ottawa—Thomas B. Church and Rix Robinson.

Lapeer—N. H. Hart and Joseph R. White.

Lenawee—Charles Chandler, Addison J. Comstock, Ebenezer Daniels, Nelson Green and George C. Harvey.

Livingston—Eli Barnard, Robert Crouse, D. S. Lee and Robert Warden, Jun.

Mackinac—Wm. Norman McLeod.

Macomb—C. W. Chapel, A. S. Robertson and D. C. Walker.

Monroe—Robert McClelland, H. B. Marvin, Emerson Choate and A. M. Arzeno.

Oakland—Wm. Axford, A. H. Hanscom, Z. M. Mowry, Seneca Newberry, James Webster, Gideon O. Whittemore, Elias S. Woodman and Jacob Van Valkenburgh.

Shiawassee—Francis J. Prevost.

St. Joseph—E. S. Moore, William Conner and J. R. Williams.

Washtenaw—W. S. Carr, J. M. Edmunds, E. P. Gardiner, James Kingsley, Morgan O'Brien, E. M. Skinner and B. W. Wait.

Wayne—Henry J. Alvord, Joseph H. Bagg, Ammon Brown, Peter Desnoyer, Ebenezer E. Eaton, Henry Fralick and John Gibson.

John Swegles, Jr., Horace S. Roberts, Charles Hascall, Secretaries.

The Constitution, as enrolled and signed, was then transmitted to the Secretary of State.

The delegate from Chippewa, Elijah J. Roberts, declined signing.

There were absent at the time of the adoption of the Constitution, Messrs. P. R. Adams, Backus, Alvarado Brown, J. Clark, S. Clark, Cook, Dimond, Eastman, Graham, Hathaway, Hixon, Mason, Raynale, M. Robinson, Sullivan, Sutherland, Tiffany, Welles, Willard, and Witherell.

There being no further business before the Convention,

At the suggestion of Mr. J. D. Pierce,

The Rev. Mr. Tooker closed the deliberations of the body with prayer.

Mr. Desnoyers moved that the Convention adjourn *sine die.*

The motion prevailed.

Whereupon, the President addressed the Convention as follows:

Gentlemen of the Convention:

The expression of your approbation of the manner in which I have discharged my duties as your presiding officer, contained in the resolution adopted this morning, has awakened in my bosom emotions of high gratification. I thank you for it, and shall ever recur to it with pleasure. The task of framing the institutions by which the rights, interests and liberties of a people are to be guarded and secured, is at any time important; especially is it so at a period like the present, when the spirit of free inquiry is bringing to the test of observation, of experience and of close scrutiny, the principles which lie at the foundation of civil government, and State after State is revising and reconstructing its fundamental law. At such a period it was to be expected that diversities of opinion would exist, and that the variety and moment of topics arising for consideration, would lead to extended discussion and earnest debate. It cannot be otherwise than a source of gratification, that in the midst of these, and the labors to which you have devoted yourselves with so much zeal and fidelity, there have so uniformly prevailed that dignity and urbanity which would ever be expected from a body of intelligent citizens convened for such high purposes.

I feel under great obligations to you, gentlemen, for the kindness and courtesy so generally extended to me throughout your arduous session. For them I tender to you my sincere thanks; and as we are about to part, allow me in conclusion, to express to you each and all, my earnest wishes for your welfare and prosperity.

I now pronounce this Convention adjourned without day.

INDEX.

A.

Absence, leave granted to,
Adams, P. R., 74, 112, 147.
Alvord, H. J., 147.
Anderson, R. H., 295.
Backus, H. T., 74, 339.
Bagg, J. H., 252, 274, 418.
Barnard, E., 147, 287, 341.
Bartow, H., 125.
Bartow, J., 344.
Beadsley, J. E., 281, 287.
Beeson, J., 74, 147, 292, 308.
Brown, Alvarado, 147, 295.
Brown, Asahel, 308.
Burns, J. D., 79, 341.
Butterfield, J. L., 111, 295.
Chandler, C., 112, 147.
Chapel, C. W., 287.
Clark, J., 281, 418.
Clark, S., 225, 344.
Cook, J. P., 101, 140, 344.
Crary, I. E., 324, 339.
Crouse, C., 111.
Danforth, E. B., 324.
Daniels, E., 166, 287.
Desnoyers, P., 341.
Dimond R. B., 147, 344.
Eastman, T., 372.
Eaton, E. C., 112, 274.
Edmunds, J. M., 113, 299.
Gale, E. G., 97.

Absence, leave granted to,
Graham, J. B., 339.
Green, N., 140.
Hanscom, A. H., 30.
Hart, N. H., 140.
Harvey, G. C., 147.
Hascall, V., 79, 153.
Hathaway, H. 172, 320.
Hixon, D., 147, 308, 339.
Kinne, D., 287.
Leach, D. W. C., 154.
Lee, D. S., 79, 274, 320.
Marvin. H. B., 79.
Mason, L. M., 90, 339.
McClelland, R., 60, 140, 202, 432.
McLeod, W. N., 79, 140, 292, 295, 299, 308, 422.
Moore, E. S., 344.
Morrison, W. V., 287.
Mowry, Z. M., 145.
O'Brien, M., 172, 320.
Orr, J. W. T., 71, 287, 389.
Pierce, J. D., 147.
Pierce, N., 292.
Prevost, F. J., 90, 201.
Raynale E., 172, 287.
Redfield' G., 323, 339.
Roberts, E. J., 79, 295, 299, 308.
Robinson, E. S., 372.
Robinson, M., 74, 287.
Skinner, E. M., 299, 422.
Soule, M., 292.
Storey, W. F., 432.
Sullivan, J., 147, 344.
Sutherland, J. G., 341.
Tiffany, A. R., 74, 339.
Van Valkenburgh, J., 320, 359.
Waite, B. W., 147, 320.
Walker, D. C., 287.
Warden, R. Jr., 121, 274.
Webster, J., 147.
Wells, H. G., 287.
White, J. R., 140, 359.
Whipple, C. W., 60, 295, 443.
Whittemore, G. O., 147, 323.
Willard, J. W., 113, 295, 308.
Witherell, B. F. H., 74, 172, 295.
Woodman, E. S., 113, 372.

Appeals from decisions, by
Bartow, J., 242.
Hanscom, A. H., 316.
Mason, L. M., 156.
Address of the President (D. Goodwin,) on taking the chair, 3.
adjournment *sine die*, 563.
Articles, action on,
1. Boundaries, 459, 524.
2. Seat of Government, 64, 71, 142, 144, 460, 525.
3. Division of the Powers of Government, 50, 81, 82, 109, 460, 525.
4. Legislative Department, 59, 83, 86, 88, 91, 94, 100, 106, 108, 170, 175, 183, 192, 203, 213, 308, 463, 525.
5. Executive Department, 79, 125, 128, 141, 154, 347, 348, 471, 532.
6. Judicial Department, 98, 289, 296, 297, 321, 322, 323, 347, 354, 379, 390, 404, 410, 474, 534.
7. Elections, 112, 142, 145, 228, 241, 252, 255, 264, 328, 344, 349, 480, 538.
8. State Officers, 64, 120, 149, 151, 256, 270, 274, 351, 483, 540.
9. Salaries, 418, 427, 436, 483, 540.
10. Counties, 148, 157, 159, 162, 164, 168, 256, 265, 311, 347, 484, 541.
11. Townships, 181, 301, 302, 363, 377, 486, 542.
12. Impeachments and Removals from Office, 60, 81, 82, 109, 487, 542.
13. Education, 90, 131, 136, 138, 273, 275, 277, 355, 360, 366, 373, 378, 488, 543.
14. Finance and Taxation, 274, 290, 293, 296, 309, 340, 350, 490, 545.
15. Corporations, 97, 116, 280, 282, 284, 312, 328, 492, 547.
16. Exemptions, 121, 202, 287, 300, 304, 312, 335, 495, 549.
17. Militia, 75, 123, 140, 501, 550.
18. Miscellaneous Provisions, 371, 398, 411, 418, 501, 550.
19. Upper Peninsula, 390, 424, 439, 503, 552.
20. Amendment and Revision of the Constitution, 36, 81, 82, 227, 255, 505, 553.
Schedule, 432, 447, 506, 554.
Bill of Rights, 36, 58, 63, 65, 69, 72, 76, 82, 109, 112, 116.
Cities and Villages, 162, 287, 312.
Capital Punishment, 162, 301, 312, 339.

B.

Bushnell, D. P., appointed Secretary *pro tem.*, 2.
resolution of thanks to, 9.
Bloss, Daniel, appointed messenger, 14.

C.

Convention called to order by Secretary of State, 1.
adjourned *sine die*, 563.

Constitution, adopted, 524.
signed, 562.
transmitted to Secretary of State, 563.
Crary, I. E., appointed President *pro tem.*, 2.
Communication from the Secretary of State, 10.
from the common council of Detroit, 49.
from O. B. Dibble, 49.
from Auditor General, 113.
from Commissioner of the Land Office, 138.
from J. Coates, 340, 366.
from Postmaster at Lansing, 359.
Coates, J. and W., appointed reporters, 16.
Committee to wait on President elect to the chair, 3.
on rules, 5, 17.
on newspapers and postage, 6, 18.
on reporters, 7, 16, 19.
on mode of proceeding, 8, 15, 18.
on clergymen, 8.
on national flag, 9.
on supplies and expenditures, 19.
on printing, 21.
standing, appointed, 30, 57, 58.
select, on licenses, 78, 369.
on public lands, 132.
on eulogy on President Taylor, 192.
on enrollment, 454.
on judicial circuits, 480.
of the whole, chairman of,
Mr. J. Bartow, 142, 145.
Britain, 58, 63, 65, 68, 72, 76.
Bush, 290.
Church, 280, 282, 284.
J. Clark, 123.
S. Clark, 132, 137, 138.
Cook, 297, 299, 321, 322, 323, 325.
Danforth, 398, 399.
Eaton, 157, 159, 162, 164, 168.
Hanscom, 17, 300, 302, 354.
McClelland, 80, 368.
McLeod, 273, 275, 277.
Mason, 293, 296, 309.
Morrison, 151.
J. D. Pierce, 120.
Roberts, 287.
Walker, 125, 424, 426.
Wells, 83, 86, 89, 91, 95, 100, 101, 106, 108.
Whipple, 352.
Williams, 149.

Call of the Convention, moved by
Mr. Alvord, 395.
Bagg, 250, 353, 369, 410.
Bush, 280.
Cornell, 203.
Chapel, 417.
Gale, 353.
McLeod, 153.
Moore, 266, 429.
McClelland, 324, 380, 422.
Mason, 331.
Roberts, 133, 341, 443.
Raynale, 244.
Robertson, 248.
Storey, 154.
Van Valkenburgh, 314.
Willard, 210, 230.
White, 224.
Woodman, 560.

D.

Doorkeeper, appointed, 5.
Daniels, Ebenezer, appeared and took his seat, 15.
Death of the President, announced, 172.

E.

Edmunds, James M., appeared and took his seat, 19.

F.

Fox, C. J., appointed Reporter, 16.

G.

Goodwin, Daniel, elected President, 3.
Graham, Jonatban B., appeared and took his seat, 36.
Goodridge, Moses H., appointed Messenger, 14.

H.

Hubbard, Diodate, appointed Sergeant-at-Arms *pro tem*, 2.
Hascall, Charles, appointed Assistant Secretary, 4.
Hubbard, David, Jr., appointed Sergeant-at-Arms, 4.
Hathaway, Hiram, appeared and took his seat, 36.

J.

Journals, 1000 copies ordered, 5.
corrected, 181, 200, 201.

M.

Members, names of, 1, 2.
Merrifield, E. R., appointed Doorkeeper, 14.
Messengers appointed, 14.
Mahon, Martin, appointed Reporter, 377.

P.

President *pro tem*, Isaac E. Crary, 2.
Daniel Goodwin elected, 3.

Prevost, F. J., appeared and took his seat, 3.

Protest, of Jacob Van Valkenburgh, 202.
Messrs. Bush, McLeod and Roberts, 561.

Petitions presented by
Mr. P. R. Adams, of John Crawford and others relative to the State Prison, 68.
Alvord, of George Duffield and others relative to the elective franchise, 74.
David Thomas and 185 others of Genesee County relative to the elective franchise, 103.
J. H. Sanford and 200 others of Lapeer county relative to the elective franchise, 103.
Also, of W. Bancroft and 74 others of Macomb county on the same subject, 103.
Arzeno, of H. V. Mann and 40 others of Monroe county on the same subject, 133.
Backus, of H. Eisnack and 20 others of Wayne county relative to foreigners voting, 181.
Barnard, of B. C. Curtis and 39 others relative to the State Prison, 256.
H. Bartow, of citizens of Ionia county relative to the sale of ardent spirits, 161.
Beeson, of C. Jewitt and 106 others of Berrien county against the emigration of slaves, 121.
Also, of G. Woodman and W. H. McComber and 147 others relative to the collection of debts, 372.
Britain, of D. Baker and 57 others relative to the sale of ardent spirits, 256,
Alvarado Brown, of A. A. Amidon and 105 others of Branch county relative to State Prison, 231.
Bush, of citizens of Lansing relative to the elective franchise, 90.
Church, of A. D. Rathbone against ministers holding office, 75.
of citizens of Kent county relative to State Prison, 293.
and of Geo. Coggeshall and 37 others of Kent county relative to the purchase of Public lands, 390.
of E. C. Sargeant relative to Supreme Courts, 390.
Comstock, of Israel Pennington and others relative to the elective franchise, 85.
Cook, of H. Waldron, E. H. C. Wilson and others of Hillsdale county relative to the elective franchise, 36.

Petitions presented by
Mr. Cook, of John W. May and 81 others of Hillsdale county relative to the sale of ardent spirits, 175.
Crary, of L. Wilmonth and others relative to the Grand Jury, 36.
Cornell, of J. E. McAllister and 22 others relative to the sale of ardent spirits, 161.
Eaton, of David Carr and 33 others relative to Grand Juries, 161.
Fralick, of E. J. Penniman and others in favor of Biennial Sessions and single districts, 49.
of H. Warner and 74 others of Wayne county in favor of single districts, 167.
of Mary A. Bentley, Hannah Buerly and 160 others of Plymouth, Wayne county, relative to the sale of ardent spirits, 264.
and of S. Hughs and 55 others of Wayne county on the same subject, 281.
also, of Riley Stilwell and 35 othors of Wayne county relative to the State Prison, 359.
Gardiner, of citizens of Pittsfield, Washtenaw county, relative to the sale of ardent spirits, 74.
of citizens of Washtenaw county on the same subject, 175.
Goodwin, of Wm. P. Patrick and others relative to Adjutant and Quarter Master General and State Armory, 85.
of Geo. E. Hand and 25 others of Wayne county relative to the Supreme Court, 161.
of L. J. Caldwell and 135 others, Daughters of Temperance, of Almont and vicinity relative to the sale of ardent spirits, 202.
of common council of Detroit, in relation to taxes on banks and other incorporations, 202.
of J. M. Cooper and 156 others of Detroit, in relation to sale of ardent spirits, 240.
of Eliza N. Whipple and 79 other ladies; of Mrs. H. T. Backus and 203 other ladies; of Mrs. W. Cole and 333 other ladies, and of Mrs. D. Knight and 80 other ladies of Detroit, relative to sale of ardent spirits, 240.
of ladies of Detroit, relative to same subject, 281.
of officers and members of City Guards, in relation to exemption from military duty, 296.
of J. Follensbee and 15 others, relative to purchase of public lands, 368.

Petitions presented by
Mr. Goodwin, of mayor, recorder and aldermen of Detroit, remonstrating against prohibiting the granting of licenses, 503.
of Ross Wilkins, D. V. Bell, A. H. Redfield, and 50 others, relative to purchase of public lands, 446.
Hanscom, of R. Manning and others, relative to the judiciary, 85.
of Moses S. Collins, relative to elective franchise, 90.
Hascall, of C. E. Johnson and 51 others of Kalamazoo county, relative to sale of ardent spirits, 166.
the argument of Joseph Miller, Jr., and others of Kalamazoo county, relative to supreme court, 192.
of N. A. Balch, Gov. Ransom and 120 others of Kalamazoo county, relative to same, 226.
of M. Wilson and 32 others of Kalamazoo county, relative to the sale of ardent spirits, 287.
Kingsley, of citizens of Washtenaw county, relative to elective franchise, 79, 85.
Leach, of Norman Little and 71 others of Saginaw county, relative to the purchase of the public lands, 432.
Lovell, of D. C. Case and 13 others, relative to sale of ardent spirits, 121.
McLeod, of Robert Banks and 134 other citizens of Detroit, on various subjects, 74.
of Wm. M. Johnson, in behalf of various civilized Indians, in regard to citizenship, 74.
Morrison, of James Russell and 71 others of Calhoun county, relative to the sale of ardent spirits, 97.
McClelland, of C. Vellett and others of Monroe county, in relation to township matters, 161.
Moore, of citizens of St. Joseph county, in relation to sale of ardent spirits, 202.
of J. French and 45 others of St. Joseph county, in relation to same, 320.
of John Hotchin and 46 others, relative to the State prison, 320.
Mowry, of S. F. Hubbell and 74 others of Oakland county, in relation to sale of ardent spirits, 263.
of Mrs. E. Hastings and 198 other ladies of Oakland county, on the same subject, 264.
Robertson, of J. B. Dickinson and 63 others, relative to sale of ardent spirits, 162.

Petitions presented by
Mr. Robertson, of Mrs. E. A. Bentley and 51 other ladies, relative to the sale of ardent spirits, 226.
Redfield, of sundry inhabitants of Cass County, relative to constitutional bar to all the the negro race, 446.
Storey, of G. F. Gardiner and 150 others of Jackson county, in relation tn the elective franchise, 115.
of S. Higbee, L. Chapman and 38 others, of Jackson county, relative to the Supreme Court, 133.
of J. Cole, H. Foster and 292 others of Jackson county, realtive to the State prison, 240.
of Mrs. Electa M. Sheldon and 157 other ladies of Jackson, relative to sale of ardent spirits, 287.
of 19 citizens of Jackson, on the same subject, 308.
of 33 citizens of Leoini, relative to the State prison, 308.
Sullivan, of citizens of Cass county, relative to the sale of ardent spirits, 281.
Town, of John Mabbs and others, relative to the elective franchise, 68.
Tiffany, of members of the bar of Lenawee county, relative to the Supreme Court, 166.
Van Valkenburgh, of H. Barrett and others, on various subjects, 49.
Walker, proceedings of a public meeting at Romeo, 74.
White, of H. Wheelock and 69 others of Lapeer county, relative to collection and sale for taxes, 166.
of C. A. Shaw and 103 others, on same subject, 181.
Williams, of C. E. White and 43 others of St. Joseph county, relative to elective franchise, 175.
Wells, of A. N. Mack and 73 others, and A. B. Brown and 13 others, of Kalamazoo county, relato the sale of ardent spirits, 202.
Whittemore, of Ladies of Pontiac, relative to sale of ardent spirits, 293.
Warden, of Sarah McCamly and 43 other ladies of Livingston county, relative to the same, 275.
Previous question, moved by
Mr. Alvord, 133, 306, 411, 412, 429.
Arzeno, 266, 416.
Axford, 105, 339.
Ammon Brown, 420.
Clark, S., 184.

Previous question, moved by
Mr. Church, 215.
Cook, 239, 318, 334.
Crary, 308, 314.
Chandler, 406.
Danforth, 270.
Danieis, 401.
Eaton, 367, 519.
Hanscom, 122, 134, 236.
Hascall, 229.
Leach, 415, 449.
McClelland, 135, 167, 314, 315, 395, 456, 457.
Morrison, 413.
Robertson, 203, 412, 519.
Rix Robinson, 311, 450.
Story, 133, 376.
Soule, 223.
Woodman, 182.
Williams, 431, 152.

Q.

Questions of order, raised by
Mr. J. Bartow, 242.
Cook, 206, 222.
Hanscom, 245.
McClelland, 371.
J. D. Pierce, 118.
Roberts, 196.

R.

Rules of Convention, 4, 11, 17, 26, 49, 102, 212, 253, 254, 423.
Report from committee on mode of procedure, 15, 18.
Reporters, 16.
Newspapers and postage, 18.
Supplies and Expenditures, 20, 21, 372, 432.
Clergymen, 20, 68.
Mode of amending and revising Constitution, 36.
Bill of Rights, 36.
Printing, 36, 50, 520.
Rules, 10, 17, 49.
Division of the powers of Government, 50.
Impeachments and removals from office, 59.
Legislative Department, 59, 418.
State officers, 64.
Seat of government, 64.
Militia, 75.
Executive Department, 79, 347.
Judicial Department, 408, 79, 354, 98.
Education, 90, 366, 273.
Banks and incorporations, 97, 333, 116.
Elections, 112, 252.
Exemptions, 121, 202, 338.

Report from committee on Counties, 148.
Cities and villages. 162.
Capital punishment, 162.
Townships, 181.
Eulogy, 253.
Finance and taxation, 274.
Traffiic in ardent spirits, 320.
Miscellaneous provisions, 371.
Upper Peninsula, 390.
Salaries, 418.
Schedule, 432.
Arrangement and phraseology, 446, 459, 460, 463, 471, 474, 480, 483, 484, 486, 487, 488, 490, 492, 495, 501, 503, 505, 506.
Judicial districts, 496.
Secretary of Convention, 522.
Committee on enrollment, 524.
Roberts, Horace S., appointed Assistant Secretary, 4.
Roberts, E. J., declined signing constitution, 563.
Resolutions, presented by
Mr. Alvord, of instructions to com. on legislative dep't, 44.
do do judiciary, 54.
do do exemptions, 203.
do do education, 38.
do do arangement and phraseology, 370.
relative to adjournment, 133.
cleaning the Hall, 282.
mileage of officers, 514, 447.
Arzeno, do stationery, 21.
Axford, do per diem of members, 109, 112.
Backus, of instruction to com. on legislative department, 35, 53, 54.
of instructions to com. on miscellaneous provisions. 54.
of instructions to com. on counties, 61, 62.
do do finance and taxation, 123.
of instructions to com. on public lands, 128.
Bagg, do do legislative dep'nt, 41.
do do judicial do 52.
do do seat of gov'nt, 62.
relative to adjournment, 148.
of instructions to com, on banks and incorporations, 38.
Britain, relative to furnishing newspapers with journals, 6.
relative to postage, 23.
printing, 50.

Resolutions, presented by
Mr. Britain, relative to rules, 80.
adjournment, 149.
of instructions to com. on State officers, 42.
do do printing, 46.
do do State printer, 523,55.
do do executive dep't, 154.
do do rules, 212.
do to Secretary, 521.
Butterfield, relative to newspapers for delegates, 6.
stationery, 22.
debates, 99.
afternoon sessions, 96, 264.
of instructions to com. on judicial dep'nt, 37.
do do finance & taxa'n, 44.
Beardsley, do do elections, 43.
do do exemptions, 53, 47.
do do judiciary, 64, 53, 47.
Bush, do do legislative dep'nt, 43.
relative to State printer and debates, 339.
H. Bartow, of instructions to com. on education, 43.
J. Bartow, do to Sec'y of Convention, 322.
Beeson, do to com. on exemptions, 44.
relative to com. on enrollment, 447.
do pay for clerks for enrolling constitution, 506.
relative to postage, 521.
Ammon Brown, of instructions to com. on legislative department, 51.
Burns, of instructions to com. on counties, 62.
Cook, relative to Secretaries, 4.
do daily journals, 5.
do daily sessions, 75, 5.
do pay of officers, 86.
of instructions to com. on schedule, 168.
Crary, relative to door-keeper and messengers, 5.
from com. on judicial department, 79
of instructions to above committee, 289, 98.
Crouse, do to com. on rules, 7.
do do printing, 41.
S. Clark, do do education, 54.
J. Clark, do do arrange't and phraseology, 371.
Chapel, relative to per diem of members, 56.
adjournment, 59, 156.
of instructions to com. on legislative dep't, 57.
Comstock, do do militia, 60.
Church, do do bill of rights, 119.
do do Upper Peninsula, 371.

Resolutions, presented by
Mr. Church, relative to daily sessions, 62.
do debates, 253, 99.
do commissioner of land office, 122.
do postage of members, 447.
do extra pay to door-keeper, 514.
do absentees signing the constitution, 521
Cornell, of instructions to committee on townships, 65,57.
relative to daily sessions, 212.
requiring sergeant-at-arms to scatter lime, 370.
Daniels, of instructions to committee on crimes, 55.
limiting time of speaking, 346.
Eaton, of instructions to com. on elections, 39.
do do education, 39.
do do finance & taxat'n, 60.
relative to adjournment, 62.
Edmunds, of thanks to President, 515.
Fralick, of instructions to com. on townships, 44.
do do legislative department, 41, 51.
do do militia, 61.
Gardiner, relative to com. on printing, 21.
pay of reporter, 321.
appointing M. Mahon reporter, 377.
suspending printing journals, 447.
C. J. Fox, superinten'dg do debates, 462.
relative to extra pay to printers, 46?.
printing constitution in pamphlet form, 513.
paying reporters for extra services, 521.
Gibson, of instructions to com. on elections, 54.
Green, do do education, 79.
do do arrangement and phraseology, 346.
do to Secretary, 436.
Graham, relative to adjournment, 103.
Gale, afternoon sessions, 182.
printing bills of stationery, 432.
Goodwin, sale of spirituous liquors, 204.
Hanscom, rules, 4.
newspapers and postage, 6.
com. on supplies and exp'rs., 19.
postage and printing, 93.
adjournment, 106, 112.
pay of President, Secretary and Serg't-at-Arms, *pro tem.*, 155.
morning sessions, 181.
Upper Peninsula, 226.

Resolutions presented by
Mr. Hanscom, relative to granting use of Hall, 232.
messengers, 460.
of thanks to reporters, 521.
relative to pay for newspapers, 523.
Hascall, drawing for seats, 5.
of instructions to com. on State officers, 44.
do do exemptions, 48.
relative to per diem of members, 136, 141.
of instructions to State printer, 513.
Hart, do com. on judiciary, 56, 45.
relative to com. on judicial circuits, 461.
pay to E. Willis, as door-keeper, 513.
Hixon, of instructions to com. on judicial depm't, 57.
Kingsley, relative to com. on rules, 5.
constitutions of States, 31.
Leach, biennial sessions, 45.
debates, 86.
report of com. on supplies, 369, 321.
Lovell, of thanks to Secretaries, 516.
McClelland, relative to com. on mode of proceeding, 5.
printing debates in Dutch, German and French, 9.
revising constitution, 32.
of instructions to com. on judicial dep't, 42.
do do banks and inc'ns, 42,
do do counties, 42.
do do mode of amending and revising constitution, 133,
relative to adjournment *sine die*, 344, 360, 403.
appointing John Swegles, Jr., to superintend printing journals, 462.
appointing Horace S. Roberts, to record do, 462.
relative to printing constitution in Dutch, German and French, 462.
McLeod, clergymen, 32.
seat of government, 61.
granting hall to Mr. Bibb, 76.
general incorporation law, 253.
Moore, of instructions to com. on legislative dep't, 47.
relative to adjournment, 506, 103.
of instructions to com. on judicial dep't, 289.
Morrison, do do corporations, 51.
do do exemptions, 52.
relative to compensation for property for public uses, 51.
relative to elective franchise, 65.
Mason, of thanks to H. T. Backus, for eulogy, 315.
Orr, of instructions to com. on judiciary, 61, 42.
do do banks and inc's., 47.

Resolutions presented by
Mr. O'Brien, instructions to com. on exemptions, 54.
N. Pierce, do do supplies, 31.
relative to revising constitution, 32.
adjournment, 145.
J. D. Pierce, of instructions to com. on judiciary, 39.
do do banks and incorporations, 40.
relative to granting use of hall, 108.
purchase of public lands, 360.
Roberts, Sergeant-at-Arms, 4.
of thanks to D. P. Bushnell, 9.
relative to national flag, 9.
com. on Upper Peninsula, 21.
clergymen, 32.
printing, 39.
com. on printing and debates, 91, 96, 99.
supplies, 94.
newspapers, 94, 98.
death of President Taylor, 175.
Raynale, clergyman, 32.
of instructions to com. on miscellaneous provisions, 57.
Robertson, do do legislative dep't, 45.
do do education, 55.
do do arrange't & phraseology, 355.
Redfield, relative to adjournment, 482, 148.
Rix Robinson, of instructions to com. on judiciary, 293.
Storey, relative to reporters, 32, 6.
constitutions of States, 10.
printing and binding of journals and documents, 21.
of instructions to com. on legislative dep't, 41.
do do miscellaneous provisions, 52.
do do legislative dep't and State officers, 55.
relative to postage and printing, 93.
adjournment, 156.
rescinding invitation to Gov'nor, 354.
Sutherland, of instructions to com. on finance and taxation, 43.
do do on impeachments & removals, 60.
relative to daily sessions, 100.
Soule, of instructions to com. on judiciary, 43.
Sturgis, do do legislative dep't, 44.
Skinner, do do judiciary, 55.

Resolutions presented by
Mr. Town, of instructions to com. on counties, 54.
relative to members paying their own postage, 377.
Van Valkenburgh, relative to clergymen, 8.
stationery, 22.
of instructions to com. on townships, 42.
do do legislative dep't, 52.
relative to manual, 47.
per diem of members, 182.
of thanks to door-keeper, 519.
White, relative to stationery, 7, 8.
Auditor General, 60.
adjournment, 121.
Whittemore, stationery, 7.
Witherell, Governor, 9.
of instructions to com. on judiciary, 45, 38.
relative to electing Presidents of Conventions, 51.
of instructions to com. on legislative dep't 53.
do do schedule, 57.
relative to per diem of President, 240.
Wells, of instructions to com. on judiciary, 39.
do do education, 65.
Warden, do do elections, 39.
do do capital punishm't, 42.
Walker, do do legislative dep't, 43.
Willard, relative to adjournment, 45.
Williams, of instructions to com. on judiciary, 56.
do do finance and taxation, 56.
do do miscellaneous provisions, 168, 56.
do do exemptions, 56.
relative to granting use of hall, 116.
per diem of members, 135.
Woodman, of instructions to com. on crimes, 62.
relative to the death of the President, 183.
per diem of messengers, 370.
furnishing Post Master with manual, 447.
com. on clergy, 520.
of thanks to messengers, 521.
Chairman of committee on reporters, 16.
do do supplies, 20.
do do printing, 37.

S.

Swegles, John Jr., appointed Secretary, 4
Secretary *pro tem.*, chosen, 2.

Sergeant-at-Arms *pro tem.*, chosen, 2.
Secretaries, Assistant appointed, 4.
Stockton, William C., appointed Messenger, 14.
Special orders, 109, 123, 331, 339.

T.

Tellers appointed, (Messrs. Story and Hanscom,) 3.
Toan, Charles E., appointed messenger, 14.

U.

Unfinished business, 112, 116, 141, 175, 183, 192, 203, 213, 255, 265, 312, 360, 390, 411, 436.

V.

Van Valkenburgh, J., protest of, 202.

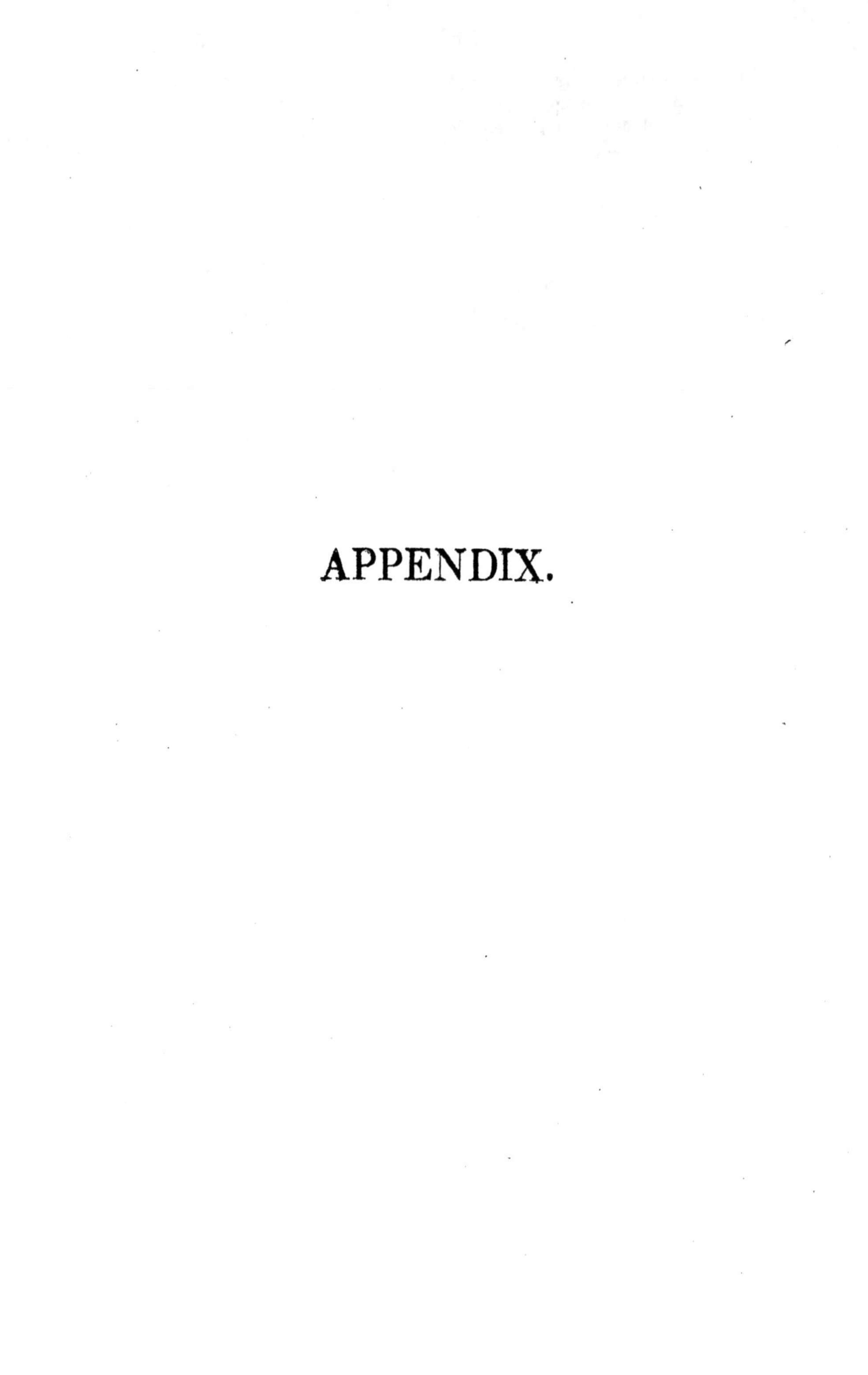

APPENDIX.

STATE OF MICHIGAN.

[Doc. No. 1.]

In Convention to Revise the Constitution, 1850.

COMMUNICATION from the Secretary of State.

Office of the Secretary of State,
Lansing, June 4, 1850.

Hon. Daniel Goodwin, *President of the Convention:*

In compliance with the requirements of Joint Resolution No. 19 of the session laws of 1850, I have the honor to transmit herewith an abstract of the reports of the County Clerks of the several counties, relative to the expenses of the circuit and county courts of this State, so far as the same have been received at this office.

The Joint Resolution above referred to also required of me a further report "of the whole expenses of courts and officers in the year 1846." I have made thorough search and have been unable to find any reports or documents in this office giving the information desired.

Very respectfully, yours,

C. H. TAYLOR,

Secretary of State.

ABSTRACT of Reports of County Clerks relative to Court Expenses, for the year 1849.

CIRCUIT COURT—1849.

COUNTIES	No. of days Circuit Court was in session.	No. of Petit Jurors in criminal cases.	No. of days Petit Jurors attended in criminal cases.	Amount paid Petit Jurors in criminal cases.	No. of days' attendance of Sheriffs and Deputies.	Fees of Sheriffs and Deputies for attendance.	No. of days' attendance of Constables.	Constables' fees for attendance.	No. of Witnesses on the part of the people.	Amount allowed Witnesses for attendance.
Allegan,	6			$	6	$ 9 00	6	$6 00		$
Barry,	2				2	3 00	2	4 50		
Berrien,	9			B. 13 50	A 9					
Branch,	3	21		73 92	3	4 50			2	3 03
Calhoun,	19	2		226 32	39	58 50	24	21 00	51	197 36
Cass,	6				6	9 00				
Chippewa,	2				2	3 00				
Clinton,	5				8	12 00				
Eaton,	2				2	3 00				
Genesee,	3				3	3 00				
Hillsdale,	3				6	9 00				
Ingham,	3				3	4 50				
Ionia,	1				1	1 00				
Jackson,	20				A 4[illegible]½	AC 267 75				
Kalamazoo,	3				3	4 50			C. 30	
Kent,	15				17	25 50				
Lapeer,	4				4	6 00	2	2 00		
Lenawee,	10				16	A. 24 00				
Livingston,	4				A 18	A. 25 00				
Mackinac,	No report.									
Macomb,	6				A 18					
Monroe,	15				19	28 50				

COUNTY COURT—1849.

COUNTIES	No. of days Supreme Court was in session	No. of days County Court was in session.	No. of days Grand Jury was in session	Amount paid Grand Jurors.	No. of Grand Jurors.	No. of Petit Jurors in criminal cases	No. of days Petit Jurors attended in criminal cases.	Amount paid Petit Jurors in criminal cases.	No. of Witnesses on the part of the people.	Witnesses' fees for attendance	No. of days' attendance of Sheriffs and Deputies.	Sheriffs' and Deputies' fees for attendance.	No. of days' attendance of Constables	Constables' fees for attendance.	Salary of County Judge.	Amount allowed County Judge upon appeal.
Allegan,		26	3	$ 76 80	18			$		$	26	$ 35 00		$	$ 150 00	$ 300 00
Barry,		12													300 00	
Berrien,		29	4			C. 94		[illegible] 255 02	49		[illegible] 3[illegible]				401 66	
Branch,		39	5	138 76		17		41 96	8		31	46 50			350 00	
Calhoun,		83	14	334 32		1		83 76	17	59 40	72	198 00	25½	25 50	H. 500 00	
Cass,		26	2	63 60							2[illegible]	39 00			H. 200 00	
Chippewa,		17									17	15 00			100 00	
Clinton,		4	4	111 04	22	32		138 51	18	60 75	44	63 00	2	2 50	H 216 63	
Eaton,		22	5	121 20	20	12	1	12 90	8	10 19	21	31 50	5	5 0	H. 150 00	
Genesee,		34									34	34 00			450 00	
Hillsdale,		57	9	170 92		12	2	26 18	11	27 44	86	120 00			300 00	
Ingham,		51	5	D. 395 76		36			150	700 00	51	77 00				
Ionia,		20									26	20 00	19	10 00	150 00	
Jackson,	4	123	1[illegible]	233 80		58		274 2[illegible]	49	93 17	A 130				H. 700 00	
Kalamazoo,	1	59	3	101 96	39			C. 143 52			57	85 50	13	15 00	500 00	
Kent,		73	9	193 22	37	44		255 22	G. 2	11 3[illegible]	84	123 0	17	17 00	500 00	
Lapeer,		32	2	53 41			1	12 72			5	7 50			300 00	
Lenawee,		61	7	190 07		57		148 85	43	129 4[illegible]	44	A 66 00			800 00	
Livingston,		60	2	D. 99 18		12			2	19 66	A. 65	A. 90 00			500 00	
Mackinac,																
Macomb,		35	4	D. 387 5[illegible]		63			66	117 57	A. 59	A. 80 50			500 00	
Monroe,		18	2	55 80	18		6	9 33			14	21 00			250 00	

Oakland,	59				50	75 00					5	127	9	252 02		139		416 78	74	217 74	127	190 50	208	203 00	H. 600 00	
Ottawa,	2				2							9	2								4	6 00			2[illegible]0 00	
Saginaw,	4				4	6 00	2	2 00				27			13						27	4[illegible] 50	25	25 0	300 0[illegible]	
Shiawassee,	7											31	3	97 20			2	17 0[illegible]	8	24 50	c.38	c.57 00	[illegible].3	c.3 [illegible]0	F. 250 00	
St. Clair,	No report.																									
St. Joseph,	6			88 72	8	12 00	13	13 00		30 54		40	4	88 21	18	65		114 66	25	16 78	50	75 00	10½	10 50	350 00	
Van Buren,	2												3	74 83		24		38 80			16	24 00			82 0[illegible]	
Washtenaw,	21				21	31 50						63	8	212 48	41	27		215 84	29	66 45	150	225 00			600 00	
Wayne,	5[illegible]		72	90 90	183	224 50			7	55 68		1[illegible]9	24	433 [illegible]	5		109	421 00	27	93 54	5[illegible]1	8[illegible]6 50	71	71 00	1,400 00	
	291	46	72	$493 36	501½	$850 75	49	$51 50	90	$[illegible]85 64	10	1348	141	$3,871 3[illegible]	281	[illegible]11	121	$2,881 43	58[illegible]	$1,707 41	1880	$2,514 00	390	$39[illegible] 00	$11103 32	$300 00

A. Constables included.
B. Sheriffs, Constables and Witnesses included.
C. Circuit and County.
D. Petit Jurors included.
E. Sheriffs, Constables, Witnesses and Grand Jurors included.
F. First and Second Judge.
G. To whom pay was allowed.
H. Appeal taken, but not yet decided.

STATE OF MICHIGAN.

[Doc. No. 2.]

In Convention to Revise the Constitution, 1850.

REPORT of the Committee on Education.

The committee on education, to whom was referred so much of the organic law as relates to the subject of education, have instructed me to report the accompanying Article, No. —.

The most important change that your committee have deemed it expedient to engraft upon the existing fundamental law of the State, is the introduction of a provision for the establishment of a system of primary schools, by which the children and youth of our State, (if it be adopted,) will have placed within their reach the opportunity of acquiring a good education free of any charge for instruction. In recommending this important change in the organic law, your committee are entirely unanimous; and we cannot but believe that in so doing, we have correctly interpreted and inscribed the views, the wishes, and the sense of sacred duty, of the great mass of the people of Michigan. If there is any one subject, of paramount importance to all others, that will come before this convention for adjustment, in the consequences that must result from its decision to the interests, the happiness, the future greatness and proud destiny of the millions to whom after us will be assigned the occupation of our now infant cities and villages, our rich agricultural districts, and as yet unbroken forests—it is the one now presented for your consideration. It is unnecessary for us to remind this convention how indispensible is the universal education of the youth of our country to the purity and permanency of our democractic institutions and system of government. It is a proposition so obvious, so universally assented to, that no one can be found in this enlightened age, who will for one moment call it in question. And yet, at this peculiar epoch, at which every day we are astonished anew by some previously unparalelled discovery in the arts and sciences—when new avenues are daily being opened to the rapid acquisition of wealth, and fortunes are acquired in a day—when the whole body politic is exhilerated to a degree amounting to phrenzy—when greater changes are effected in a year than were formerly in an age—when the teeming millions of agitated Europe, despairing of the re-establishment of civil liberty in their own country, and attracted by the bright beacon of our prosperity, rendered more visible by the darkness which surrounds them, are spreading the annual waves of emigration farther and farther into the forests of the—to us, now—far west. In this, in such an age, may we not well inquire whether, in this general scramble for wealth and power—at this period of rapid progression and transition—there may not be great danger, that unless more vigor is imparted into our system of education, and an efficiency infused into it commensurate with the exigency of the age, the foundations of our government may be undermined and the beautiful superstructure itself prostrated. The great facility and cheapness with which a freehold can be acquired in our State, has hitherto served as a perfect exemption from that extreme of poverty among any part of our population, which is beginning to exhibit itself in many of the older States of the Union, and in some of those, too, in which was first inculcated the principle that universal education was indispensible to the preservation of civil and religious liberty and the perpetuity of democratic governments—an extreme which, whenever and wherever it may exist, or from whatever cause it may be produced, must necessarily, in process of time, oppose an insurmountable barrier to that universal education and consequent intelligence of the masses which is on all hands conceded to be so indispensible, unless a timely and adequate preventative be administered. Your committee are of the opinion that no time should be lost in providing such a preventative in this State; and that the only sensible, just and adequate one within our reach is the insertion within our constitution of a mandatory clause, enjoining it upon the legislative department to provide a system of schools by which all the children and youth within our borders shall be educated at the charge of the common wealth. There was a great truth developed in the principle asserted by the Spartan law-giver, that all the children within the State were the property of the State, and should be fed at the public tables, and be trained at the public expense—a principle as essential to the preservation of the peaceful institutions of our own government as it was, at that time, to the perpetuity of the warlike system of the Lacedemonians.

Your committee have been unable to obtain any reliable data on which to base an estimate of the proportion which it would become necessary to raise by taxation, as compared with the amount distributed per scholar from the primary school interest fund, for sustaining free schools for three, six, nine or twelve months. The only data we have upon this point are those derived from the operation of the free school system in the city of Detroit. The total expense of keeping up the schools of that city for the year 1849, was about $4,950. The number of children between the ages of 4 and 18 years, was 5,846. Amount received from the primary school interest fund, $1,929, or a trifle less than the amount required for the support of their schools for one-third of the year. It is apparent, however, that the expense of maintaining such schools in the agricultural districts of the State, and especially where the population is sparse and schools small, must necessarily be much greater in proportion to the number of children between said ages than in the city of Detroit.

If there should be any who are disposed to hesitate in view of the expense of the proposed system, your committee would inquire of them whether it would not be better to be taxed for the diffusion of intelligence and virtue among the associates of their offspring, than for the support of poor houses and prisons, which would necessarily be filled up by poverty, vice and crime, the legitimate offspring of that prolific mother—ignorance.

The proposed system of free schools is by no means an untried experiment. It has been enjoined by constitutional enactment in five of the States of the Union, viz: in Indiana in 1816, in Missouri, in 1821, in Texas and Louisiana in 1845, and in Wisconsin in 1848.

It was also submitted to the people of the State of New-York by legal enactment for their approval or rejection in 1849, and was established by an overwhelming majority, and has since been carried into successful oporation. In most of the New England States, although they have no constitutional provision establishing schools entirely free, yet their schools approximate very nearly to this system.

We have already alluded to the fact that the free school system had been adopted in the city of Detroit. It was introduced there by an act of the Legislature in 1842, and has been for several years in successful operation; and although at first it encountered a violent opposition, it has since become one of its most cherished institutions, and the proudest monument of the City of the Straits.

There is another modification, intimately connected with the foregoing, which your committee have introduced into the Article herewith submitted, and which they consider too important to pass over without notice, viz: the provision requiring the English language, and no other, to be taught in all our primary schools. This provison your committee believe to be of great importance, not only to our native citizens, but more especially to the great mass of the emigrants from countries speaking a different language from our own, who have already settled among us, and to immense numbers of others of the same character, whom we have good reason to hope and believe will be induced to occupy the vast tracts of rich and beautiful lands within our State, that as yet have remained untouched by the axe or the plow of the white man, and where the iron heel of oppression never trod, and we trust never will. It is obvious that it is alike essential to them and to us, that all who are to exercise in common the high privilege of the elective franchise—to sit together in the same legislative halls—to make, to unmake and to obey the same laws, should be taught to speak and write the same language. Without such a common medium for the easy interchange of views and sentiments, distinct classes will be preserved, and animosities and prejudices engendered, disastrous alike to all, while through the medium of a common tongue, the different divisions of the European race will readily re-unite and commingle, producing a new variety of the same race, distinct from either of its ingredients, and both physically and mentally superior to each.

Your committee have so modified the provisions in relation to the Superintendent of Public Instruction and Regents of the University, as to make them elective, and dispensing with all ex-officios. We have also provided for the continuance and government of the Normal School, and for the establishment by the legislature of an agricultural school at the earliest practical period. The utility and importance of these modifications, it is believed by your committee, are too apparent to require any comment from us.

D. C. WALKER, Ch'n.

STATE OF MICHIGAN.

[Doc. No. 3.]

In Convention to Revise the Constitution, 1850.

REPORT of Committtee on Incorporations.

The undersigned, minority of the committee to whom was referred the subject of corporations, other than municipal, having had the same under consideration, beg leave to report, that on so much of the subject referred as related to banks, the committee could not agree.

In order to secure to the people of this State, under existing circumstances, a sufficiently safe, ready and ample circulating medium to meet the wants of the commercial and business portion of community, a system of banking, founded on a specie paying basis, with ample security for the redemption in specie of all bills put in circulation as money, appears to the undersigned to be absolutely necessary.

And when we take a view of the peninsular State, surrounded as it nearly is by navigable waters, which are continuous to other States, with a coast of more than eighteen hundred miles in extent, lined with fisheries inexhaustible, a fertility of soil unsurpassed in the variety and extent of its productions; bearing on its surface extensive forests of valuable timber, and enriched beneath by natural resources of unlimited mineral wealth, with its mines of iron and copper, its beds of coal and plaster, and salt springs, the conclusion is irresistible that a vast trade must grow up, which will demand an increased corresponding circulating medium.

It is, therefore, the part of wisdom and sound policy, that a system of banking be established that shall induce the aggregation and employment of foreign capital in our State, and shut out from circulation bills of less reliable institutions from other States.

It is the opinion of the committee, that by providing for such a system of banking as we have recommended, that it will be, not only a salutary aid in carrying on the already large and increasing commerce and trade within the State, but that it will prove highly advantageous to every branch of industry, and satisfactory to the people at large.

The committee therefore beg leave to report the following Article, No. —.

A. J. COMSTOCK,
J. R. WHITE,
Minority of Committee.

Corporations, other than Municipal.

ARTICLE —.

Sec. 1. Corporations may be formed under general laws; but shall not be created by special act, except for municipal purposes. All general laws, and special acts passed pursuant to this section, may be altered from time to time, or repealed.

Sec. 2. The term "corporations," as used in this article, shall be construed to include all associations and joint stock companies having any of the powers or privileges of corporations, not possessed by individuals or partnerships. And all corporations shall have the right to sue, and shall be subject to be sued, in all courts, in like cases as natural persons.

Sec. 3. The Legislature shall have no power to pass any act granting any special charter for banking purposes; but corporations or associations may be formed for such purposes, under general laws, by a vote of two-thirds of all the members elected to both branches thereof.

Sec. 4. The Legislature shall not pass any law sanctioning in any manner, directly or indirectly, the suspension of specie payments by any person, association or corporation, issuing bank notes of any description.

Sec. 5. The Legislature shall provide by law for the registry of all bills or notes issued or put in circulation as money, and shall require ample security for the redemption of the same in specie; such security to be in stocks, (bonds or evidence of debt issued by the United States or of individual States, or both,) which shall be deposited with the State Treasurer, and be at least, when offered, equal in value to the amount of bills or notes registered and issued for circulation.

Sec. 6. The stockholders in every corporation and joint stock association for banking purposes, issuing bank notes or any kind of paper credits to circulate as money, shall be individually responsible to the amount of their respective share or shares of stock in any such corporation or association, for all its issues, debts and liabilities.

Sec. 7. All corporations and joint stock associations created by the Legislature, under and by virtue of this article, shall pay to the State Treasurer for the use of the State, at least one per centum per annum on the capital stock paid in, as a tax; and no other tax shall be assessed or collected against them.

Sec. 8. In case of the insolvency of any bank or banking association, the bill holders thereof shall be entitled to preference in payment, over all other creditors of said bank or association.

Respectfully submitted.

A. J. COMSTOCK,
J. R. WHITE,
of Committee, &c.

STATE OF MICHIGAN.

[Doc. No. 4.]

In Convention to Revise the Constitution, 1850.

COMMUNICATION from the Commissioner of the State Land Office.

STATE LAND OFFICE,
Lansing, June 26, 1850.

Hon. D. GOODWIN, *President of the Convention:*

In compliance with the resolution adopted by the Convention on the 26th instant, I have the honor to present the annexed schedule, (marked A.,) which exhibits brief answers to interrogatories 1, 2, 3, 4, 5, 6, 7 and 8.

The schedule, (marked B.,) also annexed, exhibits answers to interrogatories 9 and 10.

All which is respectfully submitted.

PORTER KIBBEE,
Commissioner Land Office.

[SCHEDULE A.]

Abstract of the quantity of unsold Primary School, University, Salt Spring, State Building, Asylum, Normal School, Internal Improvement and Asset Lands:

Variety of Land.	Acres.	Price p'r acre	Amount.
Primary School,	871,859	$4 00	$3,487,436 00
University,	23,508	12 00	282,096 00
Salt Spring,	1,642	4 00	6,568 00
State Building,	800	8 00	6,400 00
Asylum,	16,000	4 00	64,000 00
Normal School,	16,000	4 00	64,000 00
Internal Improvement,	102,107		
Asset lands, including village lots at appraised value,			20,356 79
Lots in Lansing,			63,699 00
	1,031,916		$3,994,555 79

The internal improvement lands are not included in the aggregate valuation, as they are all appropriated.

[SCHEDULE B.]

Abstract of the number of Sales on which individual accounts have been opened from 1837, to June, 1850, inclusive:

Year.	Primary School.	University.	Salt Spring.	State Building.	M. Asylums.	Total.
1837,	508	198				706
1838,	124	9				133
1839,	114	8				122
1840,	22	27				49
1841,	263	110				373
1842,	309	35				344
1843,	152	58		9		219
1844,	145	69		6		220
1845,	159	38		11		208
1846,	151	23		3		177
1847,	673	22	20			715
1848,	423	37	16			476
1849,	240	1	12			253
1850,	151	4		1	8	164
	3434	639	48	30	8	4159

Total number of forfeitures on Primary School and University lands during the current year, ending May 1st, 1850, 561. These forfeitures are not absolute until the improvements are appraised and the lands offered for sale at public auction.

Total amount of penalties on said forfeitures, $1,822 12.

STATE OF MICHIGAN.

[Doc. No. 5.]

In Convention to Revise the Constitution, 1850.

REPORT from the Committee on Exemptions and the Rights of Married Women.

To the Honorable the Convention to revise the Constitution of the State of Michigan:

The undersigned, a majority of the committee on Exemptions and the Rights of Married Women, to whom were referred the various resolutions on those subjects, have had the same under consideration and would respectfully report:

That after mature deliberation of the various matters embraced in the several resolutions referred to them, they are of an opinion, and so recommend to the Convention, that on the subject of exemptions no provision is required, nor is it expedient that any should be incorporated in the constitution.

The whole subject, without any such provision, being within the competency of Legislative action, except so far as the same is limited and restrained by the provisions of the constitution of the United States, any constitutional provision on this subject, unless in restraint, would manifestly be unnecessary and unwise, and clearly better left to legislatlve discretion, so to mould the exercise of the power as to meet, without restraint, the changing circumstances of society, and enable them to grant such measure of relief as the exigencies of the time really seem to require.

In the opinion of the undersigned, on principle, except to a very limited extent, the whole system of exemptions is essentially wrong. It is followed by consequences, when adopted, to a greater or less extent, subversive of that personal economy and commercial integrity so essential to the prosperity of any people.

The changing exigencies of society really, sometimes, require, in this respect, legislative intervention. In most of the cases when exercised, it is injurious rather than beneficial, not only to the creditor, but also the debtor portion of community. The organic law cannot, therefore, with any safety, prescribe any fixed rule.

The undersigned therefore hope, and relying on the innate integrity of our people, have reason to believe, as the capacities and business energies of our state are developed and matured, the necessity and desire of any system of exemptions will and ought to decrease, and believe the time is not very remote when exemptions should not extend beyond the mere indispensable necessities of a household. It should be, and your committee hope it will be the highest ambition of our citizens, to be just and absolutely punctual in all their engagements. Property is the legitimate source for the payment of debts, and should, for that purpose, be faithfully applied as between debtor and creditor. All exemptions, in the opinion of your committee, upon principle, operate most injuriously as a withdrawal of so much available capital from the active business of society, and can alone be justified to any extent by the most imperious necessity of family existence.

In relation to the rights of married women, the undersigned respectfully report the annexed article.

SENECA NEWBERRY,
HENRY FRALICK,
DANIEL S. LEE,
A. R. TIFFANY.

July 16, 1850.

STATE OF MICHIGAN.

[Doc. No. 6.]

In Convention to Revise the Constitution, 1850.

Articles of the Constitution, as referred to the Committee on Arrangement and Phraseology.

ARTICLE —.

Bill of Rights.

§ 1. All political power is inherent in the people.

§ 2. Government is instituted for the protection, security and benefit of the people; and they have the right at all times to alter or reform the same, and to abolish one form of government and establish another, whenever the public good requires it.

§ 3. No man or set of men are entitled to exclusive or separate privileges.

§ 4. Every person has a right to worship Almighty God according to the dictates of his own conscience; and no person can of right be compelled to attend, erect, or support, against his will, any place of religious worship, or pay any tithes, taxes, or other rates, for the support of any minister of the gospel, or teacher of religion.

§ 5. No money shall be drawn from the treasury for the benefit of religious societies, or theological or religious seminaries, nor property belonging to the State be appropriated for any such purposes.

1A

§ 6. The civil and political rights, privileges and capacities of no individual shall be diminished or enlarged on account of his opinions or belief concerning matters of religion.

§ 7. Every person may freely speak, write and publish his sentiments on all subjects, being responsible for the abuse of that right; and no law shall be passed to restrain or abridge the liberty of speech or of the press. In all prosecutions for libels, the truth may be given in evidence to the jury; and if it shall appear to the jury that the matter charged as libellous is true, and was published with good motives and for justifiable ends, the party shall be acquitted; and the jury shall have the right to determine the law and the fact.

§ 8. The person, houses, papers and possessions of every individual shall be secure from unreasonable searches and seizures; and no warrant to search any place or to seize any person or things, shall issue without describing them, nor without probable cause, supported by oath or affirmation.

§ 9. The right of trial by jury shall remain inviolate, but shall be deemed to be waived in all civil cases, unless demanded by one of the parties, in such manner as shall be directed by law; and the Legislature may authorize a trial by a jury of a less number than twelve men.

§ 10. In all criminal prosecutions, the accused shall have the right to a speedy and public trial by an impartial jury, which may consist of less than twelve men in all courts not of record; to be informed of the nature of the accusation; to be confronted with the witnesses against him; to have compulsory process for obtaining witnesses in his favor; to have the assistance of counsel for his defence.

§ 11. No person, after acquittal upon the merits, shall be tried for the same offence; all persons shall, before conviction, be bailable by sufficient sureties, except for murder and treason, when the proof is evident or the presumption great; and the privilege of the writ of *habeas corpus* shall not be suspended, unless when, in case of rebellion or invasion, the public safety may require it.

§ 12. Every person has a right to bear arms for the defence of himself and the State.

§ 13. The military shall in all cases and at all times be in strict subordination to the civil power.

§ 14. No soldier shall, in time of peace, be quartered in any house without the consent of the owner or occupant; nor in time of war, but in a manner prescribed by law.

§ 15. Treason against the State shall consist only in levying war against it, or in adhering to its enemies, giving them aid and comfort; no person shall be convicted of treason, unless on the testimony of two witnesses to the same overt act, or on confession in open court.

§ 16. No bill of attainder, ex-post facto law, or law impairing the obligation of contracts, shall be passed.

§ 17. Excessive bail shall not be required; excessive fines shall not be imposed; and cruel or unusual punishments shall not be inflicted, nor shall witnesses be unreasonably detained.

§ 18. The property of no person shall be taken for public use without just compensation therefor. Private roads may be opened in the manner to be prescribed by law; but in every case the necessities of the road and the amount of all damage to be sustained by the opening thereof, shall be first determined by a jury of freeholders; and such amount, together with the expenses of proceedings, shall be paid by the person or persons to be benefitted.

§ 19. The people have the right peaceably to assemble together, to consult for the common good, to instruct their representatives, and to petition the Legislature for a redress of grievances.

§ 20. No person shall be compelled in any criminal case to be a witness against himself, nor be deprived of life, liberty or property, without due process of law.

§ 21. Aliens who are, or who may hereafter become, *bona fide* residents of this State, shall enjoy the same rights in respect to the possession, enjoyment and inheritance of property, as native born citizens.

§ 22. Neither slavery nor involuntary servitude, unless for the punishment of crime, shall ever be tolerated in this State.

§ 23. No person shall be imprisoned for debt, arising out of, or founded on a contract, express or implied; except in cases of fraud or breach of trust, or of moneys collected by public officers, or in any professional employment; and no person shall be imprisoned for a militia fine in time of peace.

§ 24. No person shall be rendered incompetent to be a witness on account of his opinions on matters of religious belief.

§ 25. Any citizen of this State who may hereafter be engaged, either directly or indirectly, in a duel, either as principal or accessory before the fact, shall forever be disqualified from holding any office under the constitution and laws of this State, nor be permitted to vote at any election.

§ 26. The assent of two-thirds of the members elected to each branch of the Legislature, shall be requisite to every bill appropriating the public moneys or property for local or private purposes.

§ 27. No lease or grant of agricultural land for a longer period than twelve years, hereafter made, in which shall be reserved any rent or service of any kind, shall be valid.

§ 28. No corporation shall hold any real estate hereafter acquired for a longer period than ten years, except such real estate as shall be actually occupied by such corporation in the exercise of its franchises.

§ 29. All lands, the title to which shall fail from a defect of heirs, shall escheat to the State, and shall be appropriated exclusively to the support of primary schools.

§ 30. All acts of the Legislature, contrary to this or any other article of this Constitution, shall be void.

ARTICLE —.

Elections.

§ 1. In all elections, every white male citizen above the age of twenty-one years, who shall have resided in this State three months next preceding any election; every white male inhabitant of the age aforesaid, who was permitted to vote under the provisions of the previous constitution of this State; and also every white male inhabitant of the age aforesaid, who shall have resided in the State two years and a half, and declared his intention to become a citizen of the United States; and every civilized male inhabitant of Indian descent, of the age aforesaid, not a member of any tribe, who shall be a native of the United States; and every white male inhabitant of the age aforesaid, who shall have been a resident of this State on the first day of January, A. D. 1850, shall be entitled to vote at such election; provided the last mentioned persons shall have declared their intention to become citizens of the United States, pursuant to the laws thereof, at least six months next preceding such election; but no such citizen or inhabitant shall be entitled to vote at any such election, unless he shall have resided in this State three months next preceding such election, nor in any township or ward, unless he is an actual resident thereof, and shall have resided therein for ten days next preceding such election.

§ 2. All votes shall be given by ballot, except for such township officers as may by law be directed to be otherwise chosen.

§ 3. Electors shall, in all cases except treason, felony, or breach of of the peace, be privileged from arrest during their attendance at election, and in going to and returning from the same.

§ 4. No elector shall be obliged to do militia duty on the day of election, except in time of war or public danger.

§ 5. For the purpose of voting, no person shall be deemed to have gained or lost a residence, by reason of his presence or absence while employed in the service of the United States or of this State; nor while engaged in the navigation of the waters of this State, or of the United States, or of the high seas; nor while a student of any seminary of learning; nor while kept at any alms-house or other asylum at public expense; nor while confined in any public prison.

§ 6. Laws may be passed to preserve the purity of elections, and guard against abuses of the elective franchise.

§ 7. No soldier, seaman, or marine, in the army or navy of the United States, shall be deemed a resident of this State, in consequence of being stationed in any military or naval place within the same.

RESOLUTION.

Resolved, That at the next general election, and at the same time when the votes of the electors shall be taken for the adoption or rejection of the revised Constitution, the additional amendment in the words following:

"Every colored male inhabitant, possessing the qualifications required by the first section of the second article of the Constitution, shall have the rights and privileges of an elector,"

Shall be separately submitted to the electors of this State for their adoption or rejection, in form following, to wit: A separate ballot may be given by every person having the right to vote for the revised Constitution, to be deposited in a separate box. Upon the ballot given for the adoption of the said separate amendment, shall be written or printed, or partly written and partly printed, the words "Equal suffrage to colored persons? Yes;" and upon all ballots given against the adoption of the said separate amendment, in like manner, the words, "Equal suffrage to colored persons? No." And on such ballots shall be written or printed, or partly written and partly printed, the words, "Constitution: Suffrage;" in such manner that such words shall appear on the outer side of such ballot when folded. If, at said election, a majority of all the votes given for and against the said separate amendment, shall contain the words "Equal suffrage to colored persons? Yes," then the said separate amendment shall be a separate section of article second of the Constitution, in full force and effect, any thing in the constitution to the contrary notwithstanding.

ARTICLE —.

Legislative Department.

§ 1. The legislative power shall be vested in a Senate and House of Representatives.

§ 2. The number of Representatives shall never be less than sixty-four, nor more than one hundred, and shall be chosen for two years, and by single districts; the Senate shall consist of thirty-two members, and the Senators, one from each district, shall be elected for two years.

§ 3. The Legislature shall provide by law for an enumeration of the inhabitants of this State in the year eighteen hundred and fifty-five, and at the end of every ten years thereafter; and at the first session after each enumeration so made, and also after each enumeration made by the authority of the United States, the Legislature shall apportion anew the Representatives and Senators among the several counties and districts, according to the number of white inhabitants and civilized persons of Indian descent, not members of any tribe; which apportionment shall remain unaltered until the return of another enumeration: *Provided*, That the county of Saginaw, with the territory thereto attached, shall be entitled to one Representative; the county of Tuscola, and the territory thereto attached, one Representative; the county of Sanilac, and the territory thereto attached, one Representative; the counties of Midland, Gratiot and Aronac, with the territory thereto attached, one Representative; the county of Montcalm, with the territory attached thereto, one Representative; and the counties of Newaygo and Oceana, with the territory attached thereto, one Representative; and each county hereafter organized, with such territory as may be attached thereto, shall be entitled to a separate Representative, when it shall have attained a population equal to a moiety of the ratio of representation.

§ 4. The boards of supervisors in such counties as may be entitled to more than one member of the House of Representatives, shall assemble at such time and place as the Legislature shall prescribe, and divide their respective counties into representative districts, equal to the number of Representatives to which such counties may severally be entitled by law, and shall cause to be filed in the offices of the Secretary of State and the clerks of their respective counties, a description of such representative districts, specifying the number of each district, and the population thereof, according to the last preceding enumeration, as near as can be ascertained. Each representative district shall contain, as nearly as may be, an equal number of white inhabitants, and shall consist of convenient and contiguous territory; but no township or city shall be divided in the formation of representative districts. And when any township or city shall contain a population which shall entitle it to more than one Representative, then such township or city shall elect the number of Representatives to which it shall be so entitled by general ticket.

§ 5. The State shall be divided into thirty-two districts, to be called Senate districts, each of which shall choose one Senator. The districts shall be numbered from one to thirty-two, inclusive. No county shall be divided in the formation of Senate districts, except such county shall be equitably entitled to two or more Senators.

§ 6. Senators and Representatives shall be citizens of the United States, and be qualified electors in the respective counties and districts which they represent; and a removal from their respective counties or districts shall be deemed a vacation of their seats.

§ 7. No persons holding any office under the United States or this State, or any county office, (notaries public, officers of the militia and officers elected by townships excepted,) shall be eligible to or have a seat in either house of the Legislature, and all votes given for any such person shall be void.

§ 8. Senators and Representatives shall, in all cases, except treason, felony or breach of the peace, be privilged from arrest; nor shall they be subject to any civil process during the session of the Legislature, nor for fifteen days next before the commencement and after the termination of each session; and for any speech in either house, they shall not be questioned in any other place.

§ 9. A majority of each house shall constitute a quorum to do business; but a smaller number may adjourn from day to day, and may compel the attendance of absent members, in such mannner and under such penalties as each house may provide.

§ 10. Each house shall choose its own officers, and shall determine the rules of its procedings, and judge of the qualifications, elections and returns of its own members; and may, with the concurrence of two-thirds of all the members elected, expel a member; but no member shall be expelled a second time for the same cause, nor for any cause known to his constituents antecedent to his election; and the reason for such expulsion shall be entered upon the journal, with the names of the members voting on the question.

§ 11. Each house shall keep a journal of its proceedings, and publish the same, except such parts as may require secrecy; and the yeas and nays of the members of either house, on any question, shall, at the request of one-fifth of the members elected, be entered on the journal. Any member of either house shall have liberty to dissent from and protest against any act, proceeding or resolution which he may think injurious to the public or an individual, and have the reason of his dissent entered on the journal.

§ 12. In all elections by either or both houses, the votes shall be given *viva voce;* and all votes on nominations made to the Senate, shall be taken by yeas and nays, and published with the journals of its proceedings.

§ 13. The doors of each house shall be open, except when the public welfare shall require secrecy. Neither house shall, without the consent of the other, adjourn for more than three days, nor to any other place than where the Legislature may then be in session.

§ 14. Any bill may originate in either house of the Legislature.

§ 15. Every bill passed by the Legislature shall, before it becomes a law, be presented to the Governor; if he approves it, he shall sign it; but if not, he shall return it with his objections to that house in which it originated, who shall enter the objections at large upon their journal, and proceed to reconsider it. If, after such reconsideration, two-thirds of all the members elected agree to pass the bill, it shall be sent, with the objections, to the other house, by whom it shall likewise be reconsidered; and if approved also by two-thirds of all the members elected to that house, it shall become a law; but in such case, the vote of both houses shall be determined by yeas and nays, and the names of the members voting for or against the bill shall be entered on the journals of each house respectively; and if any bill be not returned by the Governor within ten days, Sundays excepted, after it has been presented to him, the same shall become a law, in like manner as if he had signed it, unless the Legislature, by their adjournment, prevent its return; in which ease it shall not become a law. But the Governor may approve and sign and file in the office of the Secretary of State, within five days after the adjournment of the two houses, any act passed during the last five days of the session; in which ease it shall become a law.

§ 16. Every resolution, to which the concurrence of the Senate and House of Represenntatives may be necessary, except in case of adjournment, shall be presented to the Governor; and before the same shall take effect, shall be proceeded upon in the same manner as in the case of a bill.

§ 17. The members of the Legislature shall receive for their services only three dollars a day for actual attendance and when absent from sickness, for the first sixty days of the session of 1851, and for the first forty days of every subsequent session, and nothing thereafter. When convened in extra session by the Governor, they shall receive three dollars a day for the first twenty days, and nothing thereafter; and shall legislate on no other subjects than those expressly stated in the Governor's proclamation, or submitted to them by his special message. They shall also receive no more than ten cents for every mile they shall actually travel, in going to and returning from their place of meeting, on the usually traveled route; and for stationery and newspapers, not exceeding five dollars for each member during any session. Each member of the Legislature shall be entitled to one copy of the laws, journals and documents of the Legislature of which he was a member; but the Legislature shall not, at the expense of the State, provide for its members books, newspapers or other perquisites of office, not expressly authorized by this constitution.

§ 18. The Legislature may provide by law for the payment of postage on all mailable matter received by the members, Lieutenant Governor and Speaker, during the sessions of the Legislature, but not on any sent or mailed by them.

§ 19. The President of the Senate and the Speaker of the House of Representatives shall receive the same per diem compensation and mileage as members of the Legislature, and no more.

§ 20. No member of the Legislature shall receive any civil appointment within this State, or to the Senate of the United States, by the Governor, the Governor and Senate, from the Legislature, or any other State authority, during the term for which he shall have been elected; and all such appointments, and all votes given for any such member for any such office or appointment, shall be void; nor shall any member of the Legislature be interested, either directly or indirectly, in any contract with the State, or any county thereof, authorized by any law passed during the time for which he shall have been elected, and for one year thereafter.

§ 21. The Governor shall issue writs of election to fill such vacancancies as may occur in the Senate and House of Representatives.

§ 22. All bills and joint resolutions shall be read three times in each house before the final passage thereof; and no bill or joint resolution shall become a law without the concurrence of a majority of all the members elect in each house; and on the final passage of all bills, the vote shall be by yeas and nays, and shall be entered on the journal.

§ 23. No law shall embrace more than one object, which shall be expressed in its title; and no public act shall take effect or be in force until the expiration of ninety days from the end of the session at which the same may be passed, unless the Legislature, by a two-thirds vote of all the members elected to each house, shall otherwise direct.

§ 24. The Legislature shall never grant or authorize extra compensation to any public officer, agent, servant or contractor, after the service shall have been rendered or the contract entered into.

§ 25. The Legislature shall provide by law that the fuel and stationery furnished for the use of the State, the printing and binding the laws and journals, all blanks, paper and printing for the executive departments, and all other printing ordered by the Legislature, shall be let by contract to the lowest bidder or bidders, who shall give adequate and satisfactory security for the performance thereof. And it shall not be competent for the Legislature to rescind or alter such contract, or to release the person or persons taking the same, or his or their sureties, from the performance of any of the conditions of the contract; and no member of the Legislature, or other officer of the State, shall be interested, either directly or indirectly, in any such contract.

§ 26. The Legislature shall have no power to authorize, by private or special law, the sale or conveyance of any lands or other real estate belonging in whole or in part to any person or persons; nor to vacate or alter any road laid out by commissioners of highways, or any street in any incorporated city or village, or in any township plat.

§ 27. The Legislature may authorize the employment of a chaplain for the state prison, but no money shall be drawn from the treasury for the payment of any religious services in either branch of the Legislature.

§ 28. No law shall be revised or amended by reference to its title only; but the act revised, and the section or sections of the act amended, shall be re-enacted and published at length.

§ 29. Divorces shall not be granted by the Legislature; and no lottery shall be authorized, nor shall the sale of lottery tickets be permitted.

§ 30. No new bill shall be introduced into either house during the last three days of the session, unless by the unanimous consent of the house in which it originates.

§ 31. In case of contested elections, the person only shall receive from the State per diem compensation or mileage who is declared by the house in which the contest takes place, to be entitled to a seat.

§ 32. No person who may hereafter be a collector, or holder of public moneys, shall have a seat in either house of the Legislature, or be eligible to any office of trust or profit under this State, until he shall have accounted for and paid over, as provided by law, all sums for which he may be liable.

§ 33. The Legisiature shall not audit or allow any private claim or account.

§ 34. Whenever the Legislature fixes upon the day of adjournment, they shall adjourn at twelve o'clock at noon of that day.

§ 35. The Legislature shall meet at the seat of government on the first Wednesday in February next, and on the first Wednesday of January of every second year thereafter, and at no other place or time, unless as provided by this Constitution.

§ 36. The election of Senators and Representatives, pursuant to the provisions of this Constitution, shall be held on the Tuesday succeeding the first Monday of November in the year 1852, and on the Tuesday succeeding the first Monday of November of every second year thereafter.

§ 37. The Legislature shall have no power to establish a State paper; but every newspaper in the State which shall publish all the general laws of any session within forty days of their passage, shall be entitled to receive a sum not exceeding fifteen dollars therefor.

§ 38. The style of the laws of this State shall be "The People of the State of Michigan enact."

§ 39. The Legislature shall have no power to pass any act to grant any license for the sale of ardent spirits or other intoxicating liquors.

ARTICLE —.

Executive Department.

§ 1. The Executive power shall be vested in a Governor, who shall hold his office for two years. A Lieutenant Governor shall be chosen at the same time and for the same term.

§ 2. No person shall be eligible to the office of Governor or Lieutenant Governor, who shall not have been five years a citizen of the United States, and a resident of this State two years next preceding his election; nor shall any person be eligible to the office of Governor who shall not have attained the age of thirty years.

§ 3. The Governor and Lieutenant Governor shall be elected at the times and places of choosing members of the Legislature; the persons respectively having the highest number of votes for Governor and Lieutenant Governor shall be elected; but in case two or more shall have an equal and the highest number of votes for Governor and Lieutenant Governor, the Legislature shall, by joint vote, choose one of the said persons so having an equal and the highest number of votes.

§ 4. The Governor shall be Commander-in-Chief of the military and naval forces of this State; and he shall have power to call forth the militia, to execute the laws of the State, to suppress insurrections, and to repel invasions.

§ 5. He shall transact all necessary business with the officers of government, civil and military; and may require information, in writing, from the officers of the Executive department, upon any subject relating to the duties of their respective offices.

§ 6. He shall take care that the laws be faithfully executed.

§ 7. He shall have power to convene the Legislature on extraordinary occasions. He shall communicate by message, at such times as he may deem necessary and proper, to the existing Legislature, and at the close of his official term of service, to the next Legislature, the condition of the State, and recommend such matters to them as he shall deem expedient.

§ 8. He may direct the Legislature to meet at some other place than the seat of government, if that shall become dangerous from a common enemy or disease.

§ 9. The Governor shall have the power to grant reprieves, commutations and pardons, after conviction, for all offences except treason and cases of impeachment, upon such conditions, and with such restrictions and limitations as he may think proper, subject to such regulations as may be provided by law, relative to the manner of applying for pardons. Upon conviction for treason, he shall have power to suspend the execution of the sentence until the case shall be reported to the Legislature at its next meeting, when the Legislature shall either pardon, or commute the sentence, direct the execution of the sentence, or grant a further reprieve. He shall communicate to the Legislature at each session, each case of reprieve, commutation or pardon granted; stating the name of the convict, the crime of which he was convicted, the sentence and its date, and the date of the reprieve, commutation or pardon.

§ 10. In case of the impeachment of the Governor, his removal from office, death, inability to discharge the powers and duties of the said office, resignation, or absence from the State, the powers and duties of the office shall devolve upon the Lieutenant Governor for the residue of the term, or until the disability shall cease. But when the Governor shall, with the consent of the Legislature, be out of the State in time of war, at the head of a military force thereof, he shall continue Commander-in-Chief of all the military force of the State.

§ 11. If, during a vacancy of the office of Governor, the Lieutenant Governor shall be impeached, displaced, resign, die, or be incapable of performing the duties of his office, or be absent from the State, the President of the Senate shall act as Governor until the vacancy be filled, or the disability shall cease.

§ 12. The Lieutenant Governor shall, by virtue of his office, be President of the Senate. In committee of the whole he may debate all questions; and when there is an equal division, he shall give the casting vote.

§ 13. No member of Congress, nor any other person holding office under the United States, or this State, shall execute the office of Governor; nor shall the Governor or Lieutenant Governor be eligible to any office or appointment from the Legislature, or either branch thereof, for the time for which they may have been elected; and all votes given for either of them for any such office shall be void.

§ 14. Whenever the office of Governor or Lieutenant Governor becomes vacated, the person executing the duties of Governor for the time being shall give notice thereof; and the electors shall, on the Tuesday succeeding the first Monday of November next, choose a person to fill such vacancy.

§ 15. The Lieutenant Governor and President of the Senate *pro tempore*, when performing the duties of Governor, shall receive the same compensation as is allowed to the Governor.

§ 16. The great seal of the State shall continue to be kept by the Secretary of State; and all official acts of the Governor, his approval of the laws excepted, shall thereby be authenticated.

ARTICLE —.

Of State Officers.

§ 1. There shall be a Secretary of State, a Superintendent of Public Instruction, a State Treasurer, a Commissioner of the Land Office, an Auditor General, elected at each biennial general election, who shall hold their respective offices for the term of two years, and each of whom shall keep an office at the seat of government, and shall perform such duties as may be prescribed by law.

§ 2. The terms of office of the incumbents to be elected under the foregoing provisions, shall commence on the first Wednesday of January, 1853, and of every second year thereafter.

§ 3. Whenever a vacancy shall occur in any of the above mentioned State offices, the Governor (by and with the advice and consent of the Senate, if in session,) shall fill the same by appointment, to continue until the office can be supplied by an election, at such time and in such manner as shall be provided for by law.

§ 4. The Secretary of State, State Treasurer and Commissioner of the State Land Office, shall constitute a Board of State Auditors, for the examination and adjustment of all claims against the State, not otherwise provided for by law, or specially referred by the Legislature to some other tribunal. And shall also constitute a Board of

State Canvassers, for determining the result of all elections for Governor, Lieutenant Governor, Judges and State officers, and of such other elections as shall by law be referred to said board.

§ 5. In all cases of two or more persons having an equal and the highest number of votes for any office, as canvassed by the Board of State Canvassers, the two houses of the Legislature, in joint convention, shall choose one of said persons to fill such office; and in all cases where the determination of the Board of State Canvassers shall be contested, the two houses, in joint convention, shall direct which person shall be deemed to have been duly elected.

ARTICLE —.

Impeachments and Removals from Office.

§ 1. The House of Representatives shall have the sole power of impeaching civil officers of the State, for corrupt conduct in office, or for crimes and misdemeanors; but a majority of all the members elected shall be necessary to direct an impeachment.

§ 2. All impeachments shall be tried by the Senate. When the Governor or Lieutenant Governor shall be tried, the Chief Justice of the Supreme Court shall preside. Before the trial of an impeachment, the members of the court shall take an oath or affirmation truly and impartially to try and determine the charge in question, according to the evidence; and no person shall be convicted without the concurrence of two-thirds of the members elect. Judgment, in case of impeachment, shall not extend further than removal from office; but the party convicted shall be liable to indictment and punishment according to law.

§ 3. The House of Representatives shall, when an impeachment is directed, elect from their own body three members, whose duty it shall be to prosecute impeachments. No impeachment shall be tried till the Legislature shall have adjourned *sine die;* when the Senate shall proceed to try such impeachment.

§ 4. No judicial officer shall exercise his office, after he shall have been impeached, until he shall be acquitted.

§ 5. The Governor may make a provisional appointment to fill the vacancy occasioned by the suspension of an officer until he shall have been acquitted, or until after the election and qualification of a successor.

§ 6. For any reasonable cause, which shall not be sufficient ground for the impeachment of the judges of any of the courts, the Governor shall remove any of them on a concurrent resolution of two-thirds of the members elected to each branch of the Legislature; but the cause or causes for which such removal may be required, shall be stated at length in the address.

§ 7. The Legislature shall provide by law for the removal of justices of the peace and other county, township and school district officers, in such manner and for such causes as to them shall seem just and proper.

ARTICLE —.

Finance and Taxation.

§ 1. 1st. All specific taxes, save those received from the mining companies of the Upper Peninsula, shall be applied in paying the interest upon the primary school, university and other educational funds, the principal and interest of the State debt, in the order herein recited, until the extinguishment of the State debt, other than the amounts due to the primary school, university and other educational funds, at which time said specific taxes shall be added to, and forever thereafter constitute a part of the proceeds of the primary school fund. The Legislature shall provide for an annual tax, sufficient, with other resources of the State, to pay the estimated expenses of the State, and the interest of the State debt. The Legislature shall also, by taxes, supply any deficiency which may occur in the resources of the State.

§ 2. 1st. The Legislature, in addition to the above named taxes, shall provide by law for a sinking fund of at least twenty thousand dollars a year, to commence in eighteen hundred and fifty-two, with compound interest at six per cent per annum, and an annual increase of at least five per cent. 2d. Said sinking fund shall be applied solely to the payment and extinguishment of the principal of the State debt, other than the amounts due to the University and the primary school funds;

and said tax shall be continued so long as shall be necessary to secure the extinguishment of the existing funded and fundable debt. 3d. Said fundable debt may only be funded or redeemed at a value not exceeding that established by law in eighteen hundred and forty-eight.

§ 3. The State may, to meet casual deficits or failures in revenues or expenses not provided for, contract debts; but such debts, direct and contingent, shall not in the aggregate, at any one time, exceed fifty thousand dollars; and the moneys arising from the loans creating such debts, shall be applied to the purposes for which they were obtained, or the payment of the debts so contracted, and for no other purpose whatever.

§ 4. The State may contract debts to repel invasion, suppress insurrection, and defend the State in time of war; but the money arising from the contracting of such debts shall be applied to the purpose for which it was raised, or to repay such debts, and to no other purpose whatever.

§ 5. No money shall be paid out of the treasury of this State, or any of its funds, or any of the funds under its management, except in pursuance of appropriations made by law.

§ 6. The credit of the State shall not in any manner be given or loaned to, or in aid of any individual, association or corporation.

§ 7. No scrip, certificate or other evidence of State indebtedness whatsoever, shall be issued, except for the redemption of stock previously issued, or for such debts as are expressly authorized in this article.

§ 8. The state shall never subscribe for, or become the owner of, or interested in the stock of any company, association or corporation.

§ 9. The State shall never be a party to, or interested in, any work of internal improvement, nor engaged in carrying out any such work, except in the expenditure of grants or donations of land or other property made to the State.

§ 10. The State may continue to collect all specific taxes now accruing to the treasury under existing laws. And the legislature may provide for the collection of specific taxes, from such banking, railroad, plank road, and other corporations, hereafter formed or created, as they may deem expedient.

§ 11. The Legislature shall provide a uniform rule of taxation, except upon property paying specific taxes; and taxes shall be levied upon such property as the Legislature shall prescribe.

§ 12. All assessments hereafter authorized shall be made upon property at its cash value.

§ 13. The Legislature shall provide by law for an equalization of assessments upon all taxable property, except that paying specific taxes, by a State Board, in eighteen hundred and fifty-one, and on every fifth year thereafter.

§ 14. Every law which imposes, continues or revives a tax, shall distinctly state the tax, and the object to which it is to be applied; and it shall not be sufficient to refer to any other law to fix such tax or object.

ARTICLE —.

Corporations.

§ 1. Corporations may be formed under general laws; but shall not be created by special act, except for municipal purposes. All laws passed pursuant to this section may be altered from time to time, or repealed.

§ 2. No banking law or law for banking purposes, or amendments thereof, shall have any force or effect until the same shall, after its passage, have been submitted to a vote of the electors of the State, at some general election, and been approved by a majority of the votes cast on that subject at such election.

§ 3. The officers and stockholders of every corporation or association for banking purposes, issuing bank notes or any kind of paper credits to circulate as money, shall be individually liable for all its debts which were contracted during the time of their being officers and stockholders of such corporation or association, and for one year thereafter.

§ 4. The Legislature shall provide by law for the registry of all bills or notes issued or put in circulation as money, and shall require security to the full amount of notes or bills so registered, in State stocks, which shall be deposited with the State Treasurer, bearing interest, or stocks of the United Stated States, for the redemption of such bills or notes in specie.

§ 5. In case of the insolvency of any bank or banking association, the holders of the notes or bills thereof issued or put in circulation as money, shall be entitled to preference in payment, over all other creditors of such bank or association.

§ 6. The Legislature shall have no power to pass any law authorizing or sanctioning in any manner, directly or indirectly, the suspension of specie payments by any person, association or corporation.

§ 7. The stockholders of all corporations and joint stock associations shall be individually responsible for all debts contracted for labor performed for such corporation or association.

§ 8. The Legislature shall pass no bill altering or amending any act of incorporation heretofore granted, without the assent of two-thirds of the members elect to each house; nor shall any act of incorporation, heretofore granted, be renewed or extended. The provisions of this section shall not apply to municipal corporations.

§ 9. The State shall not become subscriber to the stock of any corporation or joint stock association.

§ 10. The property of no individual shall be taken by any corporation for public use, without compensation being first made or secured, in such manner as may be prescribed by law.

§ 11. No corporation hereafter to be created, except for the construction of rail roads and canals, shall ever endure for a longer term than thirty years, except those which are municipal.

§ 12. The term "corporations," as used in this article, shall be construed to include all associations and joint stock companies having any of the powers or privileges of corporations, not possessed by individuals or partnerships. And all corporations shall have the right to sue, and shall be subject to be sued, in all courts, in like cases as natural persons.

ARTICLE —.

County Officers and County Government.

§ 1. Each county, duly organized by law, shall be a body corporate and politic, with such rights, duties, powers, privileges and immunities as shall be established by law. All suits and proceedings, by or against any county, shall be in the name thereof.

§ 2. No county, now organized by law, shall ever be reduced by the organization of new counties to less than sixteen townships, as surveyed by the United States, unless a majority of the qualified electors residing in each county to be affected by such organization shall so elect. But the Legislature shall have power to organize any city into a separate county, when it shall have attained a population of at least twenty thousand people, without reference to geographical extent, when a majority of the legal voters of a county in which such city may be situated shall recommend such new organization.

§ 3. In each organized county there shall be one sheriff, a county clerk, a county treasurer, a register of deeds, one county surveyor, a prosecuting attorney, chosen by the qualified electors thereof, once in two years, and as often as vacancies shall happen, and whose duties and powers shall be prescribed by law. It shall be competent for the board of supervisors in the several counties to combine the offices of county clerk and register of deeds in one office, or discontinue the same.

§ 3. The county clerk, county treasurer, judge of probate and register of deeds, shall hold their offices at the county seat.

§ 5. The sheriff shall hold no other office, and shall be incapable of holding the office of sheriff longer than four in any term of six years. He may be required by law to renew his security from time to time, and in default of giving such security, his office shall be deemed vacant; but the county shall never be made responsible for his acts.

§ 6. A board of supervisors, consisting of one to be chosen from each organized township, shall be established in each county, with such powers and compensation as are prescribed in this constitution, and as shall be prescribed by law.

§ 7. All incorporated cities shall have such representation in the board of supervisors of the counties in which they are situated, as the Legislature may direct.

§ 8. No county seat, when once established, shall be removed, until the place to which it is proposed to be removed shall be designated by two-thirds of the board of supervisors of said county, and a majority of the qualified electors voting thereon shall have voted in favor of the proposed location, in such manner as shall be prescribed by law.

§ 9. The board of supervisors of any county may borrow or raise by tax one thousand dollars, for constructing or repairing public buildings, highways or bridges; but no greater sum shall be borrowed or raised by tax for such purpose in any one year, unless authorized by the votes of a majority of the electors of said county voting on that subject.

§ 10. The board of supervisors, or in the county of Wayne the board of county auditors, shall have the exclusive power to prescribe and fix the compensation for all services rendered for, and to adjust all claims against their respective counties, and the sum so fixed or defined shall be subject to no appeal.

§ 11. The boards of supervisors of all organized counties shall have the power to provide for the laying out of highways and the construction of bridges, and for the organizing of townships, under such restrictions and limitations as shall be prescribed by law; and the Legislature may hereafter confer upon the board of supervisors of the several counties of this State, such further powers of local legislation and administration as they may deem proper.

ARTICLE —.

Mode of Amending and Revising the Constitution.

§ 1. Any amendment or amendments to this constitution may be proposed in the Senate or House of Representatives; and if the same shall be agreed to by two-thirds of the members elected to the two houses, such proposed amendment or amendments shall be entered on their journals respectively, with the yeas and nays taken thereon; and shall be submitted to the people at such time and in such manner as the Legislature may provide. And if the people shall ratify and approve such amendment or amendments by a majority of the electors qualified to vote for members of the Legislature voting thereon, such amendment or amendments shall become part of this constitution.

§ 2. At the general election to be held in the year eighteen hundred and sixty-six, and in each sixteenth year thereafter, and also at such times as the Legislature may by law provide, the question of a general revision of the constitution shall be submitted to the electors qualified to vote for members of the Legislature; and in case a majority of the electors so qualified, voting at such election, shall decide in favor of a convention for such purpose, the legislature, at its next session, shall provide by law for the election of delegates to such convention.

ARTICLE —.

Division of the Powers of Government.

§ 1. The powers of this government shall be divided into three distinct departments—the Legislative, Executive and Judicial.

§ 2. No person or persons belonging to any of these departments, nor either of the departments, shall exercise any of the powers properly belonging to either of the others, except in the cases expressly provided for in this constitution.

ARTICLE —.

Militia.

§ 1. The militia of this State shall be composed of all able bodied white male citizens between the ages of eighteen and forty-five years, except such as are, or may hereafter be exempt by laws of the United States or of this State. But all such inhabitants of this State, of any religious denomination whatever, as, from scruples of conscience, may be averse to bearing arms, shall be excused therefrom, upon such conditions as shall be prescribed by law.

§ 2. The Legislature shall provide by law for organizing, equipping and disciplining the militia, in such manner as they shall deem expedient, not incompatible with the laws of the United States.

§ 3. Officers of the militia shall be elected or appointed in such manner as the Legislature shall from time to time direct, and shall be commissioned in such manner as may be provided by law.

ARTICLE —.

Exemptions and the Rights of Married Women.

§ 1. The personal property of every resident of this State, to consist of such articles as shall be designated by law, shall be exempted to the amount of not less than five hundred dollars from sale on execution or other final process of any court of law or equity, issued for the collection of any debt contracted after the adoption of this constitution.

§ 2. The homested of every family, of not less than forty acres, which shall not be included in any city, village or recorded town plat; or in lieu thereof, any lot in any city, village, or recorded town plat, or such parts of lots as shall be equal thereto, not exceeding in value fifteen hundred dollars, shall not be subject to forced sale for any debt hereafter incurred; nor shall the owner of such homestead, if a married man, alienate the same by any deed of conveyance, without the consent of his wife, obtained in due form of law.

§ 3. The homested of any family, after the death of the owner thereof, shall likewise be exempt from the payment of his debts, contracted after the adoption of this constitution, in all cases where any minor children shall survive the death of such owner.

§ 4. Whenever the owner of any homested shall decease, leaving a widow, but no children, the same shall also be exempt, and the rents and profits thereof shall accrue to her benefit during the time she shall remain a widow; provided she be not the owner of a homested in her own right.

§ 5. The real and personal estate of every female, acquired before marriage, and all property to which she may afterwards become entitled, by any gift, grant, inheritence or devise, shall be and remain the estate and property of such female, and shall not be liable for the debts, obligations or engagements of her husband; and she may devise the same as if she were unmarried.

ARTICLE —.

Of Cities and Villages.

§ 1. It shall be the duty of the Legislature to provide for the organization of cities and incorporated villages, and to restrict their powers of taxation, assessment, borrowing money, contracting debts, and loaning their credit, so as to prevent abuses in assessments and in contracting debts by such corporations.

§ 2. All judicial officers of cities and villages shall be elected at such time and in such manner as the Legislature may direct; all other officers of such cities and villages shall be elected by the electors thereof, or appointed by such authorities thereof as the Legislature shall designate for that purpose.

§ 3. Private property shall not be taken for improvements in cities and villages without the consent of the owner, unless the compensation therefor shall first be determined by a jury of freeholders, and actually paid or tendered in the manner to be provided by law.

§ 4. Previous notice of any application for an alteration of the charter of any corporation, shall be given in such manner as the Legislature shall by law direct.

ARTICLE —.

Seat of Government.

§ 1. The seat of government of the State shall be in the township of Lansing in the county of Ingham, where it is now located.

ARTICLE —.

Township Officers and Government.

§ 1. There shall be elected by the people annually, on the first Monday of April, in each organized township, one supervisor, one township clerk, who shall be *ex-officio* school inspector, one township treasurer, one school inspector, not exceeding four constables, and one overseer of highways for each highway district in such township, in whom, together with the justices of the peace, not to exceed four, shall be vested the township government, to be defined and limited in such manner as the Legislature shall prescribe.

§ 2. Each township, duly organized by law, shall be a body corporate and politic, with such rights, duties, powers, privileges and immunities, and such powers of local legislation, to be uniform throughout the State, as shall be prescribed by law. All suits and proceedings by or against any township, shall be in the name thereof.

ARTICLE —.

Education.

§ 1. The Superintendent of Public Instruction shall have the general supervision of public instruction, and his duties shall be prescribed by law.

§ 2. The proceeds from the sale of all lands that have been or hereafter may be granted by the United States to this State, for the support of schools, shall be and remain a perpetual fund, the interest of which, together with the rents of all such lands as remain unsold, shall be inviolably appropriated to the support of primary schools throughout the State, and shall be annually distributed for such purpose, upon such fair and equitable basis as shall be provided by law.

§ 3. The Legislature shall, within five years from the adoption of this constitution, provide for and establish a system of common schools. Such schools shall be kept without charge for tuition, for at least three months in each year, in every school district in the State, and all instruction in said schools shall be conducted in the English language.

§ 4. Any school district neglecting to keep up and support a school for three months in each year, shall be deprived of its proportion of the income of the primary school fund, and of all fnnds arising from tax for the support of schools.

§ 5. There shall be elected in each judicial circuit, at the time of the election of the judge of said circuit, a regent of the University, whose term of office shall be the same as that of said judges; and the regents thus elected shall constitute the Board of Regents of the University of Michigan.

§ 6. The regents elected pursuant to the provisions of the foregoing section, and their successors in office, shall continue to constitute the body corporate, known by the name and style of "the Regents of the University of Michigan."

§ 7. The regents of the University shall, at their first annual meeting, or as soon thereafter as may be, elect a President of the University of Michigan, who shall be *ex officio* a member of their board, and shall preside at the meetings of said regents, and who shall be the principal executive officer, with the privilege of speaking but not of voting, of the University. Said board of regents shall have the general supervision of the University, and the direction and control of all expenditures from the University interest fund.

§ 8. The proceeds from the sale of all lands that have been or may hereafter be granted by the United States to this State, for the support of a University, and all funds accruing from any other source, for the purpose aforesaid, shall be and remain a perpetual fund, the interest of which, together with the rents of all such lands as may remain unsold, shall be inviolably appropriated to the support of the University, with such branches as the public good may require, for the promotion of literature and the arts and sciences.

§ 9. There shall be elected at the first general election in this State, after the ratification of this constitution, three members of the State Board of Education, one for the term of two years, one for the term of four years, and one for the term of six years; and at each succeeding biennial election, there shall be one member of said board elected, who shall hold his office for the term of six years. The Superintendent of Public Instruction shall be *ex officio* a member and secretary of said board. Said board shall have the general supervision of the State Normal School, and their duties shall be prescribed by law.

§ 10. The proceeds from the sale of all lands that have been or shall be hereafter granted or appropriated for the use of the State Normal School, shall be and remain a perpetual fund, the interest of which, together with the rents and profits of such of said lands as shall remain unsold, shall be inviolably appropriated for the support of said Normal School, according to the terms of the grant or appropriation.

§ 11. Institutions for the benefit of those inhabitants who are deaf, dumb, blind or insane, shall always be fostered and supported, and the proceeds from the sale of all lands that have been or shall be hereafter granted or appropriated for the support of such institutions, shall be inviolably appropriated according to the terms and conditions of such grant or appropriation.

§ 12. The Legislature shall encourage, by all suitable means, the promotion of intellectual, scientific and agricultural improvement; and shall, as soon as practicable, provide for the establishment of an agricultural school. And it shall be competent for the legislature to appropriate the twenty-two sections of salt spring lands now unappropriated, or the money arising from the sale of the same, where such lands have been already sold, and any land which may hereafter be granted or appropriated for such purpose, for the support and maintenance of such school, and it shall be competent for the legislature to make the same a branch of the University for instruction in agriculture and the natural sciences connected therewith, and place the same under the supervision of the Regents of the University. And the proceeds of the sale of all such lands that have been, or that may be hereafter sold, shall be a perpetual fund, the interest of which, together with the rents and profits of such lands, shall be appropriated for the support of such school until otherwise appropriated by law. The Legislature shall also provide for the establishment of at least one library in each township; and all fines assessesed and collected in the several counties for any breach of the penal laws, shall be exclusively applied to the support of said libraries.

ARTICLE —.

Judicial Department.

§ 1. The judicial power is vested in one supreme court, in circuit courts, in probate courts, and in justices of the peace. Municipal courts of civil and criminal jurisdiction may be established by the Legislature in cities.

§ 2. For the term of six years, and thereafter, until the Legislature shall otherwise provide, the judges of the several circuit courts shall be judges of the supreme court, four of whom shall constitute a quorum, and a concurrence of three shall be necessary to a final decision. The Legislature shall have power, if they should think expedient and necessary, after six years, to provide by law for the organization of a separate supreme court, with the jurisdiction and powers prescribed in this constitution, to consist of one chief justice and three associate justices, to be elected by the qualified electors of the State. The separate court, when so organized, shall not be changed or discontinued by the Legislature for eight years after its organization. The judges thereof shall be so classified that but one of them shall go out of office at the same time, and their term of office shall be eight years.

§ 3. The supreme court shall have a general superintending control over all inferior courts, and shall have power to issue writs of error, habeas corpus, mandamus, injunction, quo warranto, certiorari, and other original and remedial writs, and to hear and determine the same. In all other cases it shall have appellate jurisdiction only.

§ 4. Four terms of the supreme court shall be he held annually, at such times and places as may be designated by law.

§ 5. It shall be the duty of the supreme court, by general rules, to establish, modify and amend the practice in said court and in the circuit courts, and simplify the same so far as practicable; and testimony in cases in equity shall be taken in like manner as in cases at law, and the office of master in chancery is hereby prohibited. And the Legislature shall, as far as practicable, abolish all distinction between law and equity proceedings.

§ 6. The State shall be divided into eight judicial circuits; in each of which one circuit judge shall be elected by the qualified electors thereof, and who shall hold his office for the term of six years, and until his successor is elected and qualified.

§ 7. The Legislature may alter the limits of circuits or increase the number of the same. No alteration or increase shall have the effect to remove a judge from office. In every additional circuit established the judge shall be elected by the qualified electors of said circuit, and his term of office shall continue as provided in this constitution for judges of the circuit court.

§ 8. The circuit courts shall have original jurisdiction in all matters civil and criminal, not excepted in this constitution, and not prohibited by law; and appellate jurisdiction from all inferior courts and tribunals, and a supervisory control of the same. They shall also have power to issue writs of habeas corpus, mandamus, injunction, quo warranto, certiorari and other writs necessary to carry into effect their orders, judgments and decrees, and give them a general control over inferior courts and tribunals within their respective jurisdictions.

§ 9. Each of the judges of the circuit courts shall receive a salary payable quarterly. They shall receive no fees or perquisites of office, or other compensation; and shall be ineligible to any other than a judicial office during the term for which they are elected, and for one year thereafter. All votes for either of them, for any office other than the one held by them, given either by the Legislature or the people, shall be void.

§ 10. The supreme court may appoint a reporter of its decisions. The decisions made by the supreme court shall be in writing, and signed by the judges concurring therein; and any judge dissenting therefrom, shall give the reasons of such dissent in writing, under his signature; and all said opinions shall be filed in the office of the clerk of said supreme court. The judges of the circuit courts within their respective jurisdictions, may fill vacancies in the office of county clerk and of prosecuting attorney; but no judge of the supreme court, or of a circuit court, shall exercise any other power of appointment to public office.

§ 11. A circuit court shall be held at least twice in each year in every county organized for judicial purposes, and in counties containing ten thousand inhabitants, a circuit court shall be held four times a year. Judges of the circuit court may hold courts for each other, and shall do so when required by law.

§ 12. The clerk of each county organized for judicial purposes shall be the clerk of the circuit court of such county, and of the supreme court when held within the same.

§ 13. In each of the counties organized for judicial purposes, there shall be a court of probate. The judge of such court shall be elected by the qualified electors of the county in which he resides, and shall hold his office for four years, and until his successor is elected and qualified. The jurisdiction, powers and duties of such court shall be prescribed by law.

§ 14. When a vacancy occurs in the office of judge of the supreme court, circuit court or probate court, such vacancy shall be filled by appointment of the governor, which shall continue until a successor is elected and qualified; and when elected, such successor shall hold his office the residue of the unexpired term.

§ 15. The supreme court, the circuit and probate courts of each county, shall be courts of record, and shall each have a common seal.

§ 16. The Legislature may provide by law for the election of one or more persons in each organized county, who may be vested with judicial powers, not exceeding those of a judge of the circuit court at chambers. In counties having a population of less than ten thousand inhabitants, by the last preceding enumeration provided for in this constitution, these powers may be devolved upon the judge of probate.

§ 17. There shall be not exceeding four justices of the peace in each organized township. They shall be elected by the qualified electors of the township, and shall hold their offices for four years, and until their successors are elcted and qualified. They shall have civil jurisdiction to the amount of three hundred dollars, and concurrent jurisdiction to the amount of five hundred dollars, and such criminal jurisdiction and perform such duties as may be prescribed by law. At the first election in any township, they shall be classified by law in such manner that one justice shall be elected annually in each township thereafter. The Legislature may increase the number of justices in cities.

§ 18. Judges of the supreme court, circuit judges, and justices of the peace, shall be conservators of the peace within their respectives jurisdictions.

§ 19. The first election of judges of the circuit courts, shall be held on the first Monday in April, 1851; and for the election of judges of the probate courts on the Tuesday succeeding the 1st Monday of November 1852, and every sixth year thereafter an election shall be held for judges of the circuit court, and every fourth year thereafter for judges of probate. Whenever an additional circuit is created, such provision may be made as to hold the subsequent election of such additional judge at the regular elections herein provided.

§ 20. Whenever a judge shall remove beyond the limits of the circuit for which he was elected, and whenever a justice of the peace shall remove from the township in which he was elected, or who, by a change in the boundaries of said township, shall be placed without the same, shall be deemed to have vacated their respective offices.

§ 21. The Legislature shall have power to establish courts of conciliation, with powers and duties prescribed by law.

§ 22. The style of all process shall be: "In the name of the people of the State of Michigan." All indictments shall conclude: "against the peace of the people of the State of Michigan."

§ 23. Every person of the age of 21 years, of good moral character, shall have the right to practice in any court in this State.

ARTICLE —.

Miscellaneous Provisions.

§ 1. Members of the Legislature, and all officers, executive and judicial, except such inferior officers as may by law be exempted, shall, before they enter on the duties of their respective offices, take and subscribe the following oath or affirmation: "I do solemnly swear (or affirm, as the case may be,) that I will support the Constitution of the United States and the Constitution of this State, and that I will faithfully discharge the duties of the office of according to the best of my ability." And no other oath, declaration or test shall be required as a pualification for any office or public trust.

§ 2. When private property is taken for the use or benefit of the public, the necessity for using such property, and the just compensarion to be made therefor, (except when to be made by the State,) shall be ascertained by a jury of twelve freeholders, residing in the vicinity of such property, or by not less than three commissioners, appointed by a court of record, as shall be prescribed by law.

§ 3. No mechanical trade shall hereafter be taught to convicts in the State prison of this State, except the manufacture of those articles of which the chief supply for home consumption is imported from other states or countries.

§ 4. No navigable stream in this State, shall be either bridged or dammed without authority from the board of supervisors of the proper county, under the provisions of existing laws. No such law shall prejudice the right of individuals to the free navigation of such streams, or preclude the State from the further improvement of the navigation of such stream.

§ 5. An accurate statement of the receipts and expenditures of the public moneys shall be attached to, and published with the laws, at every regular session of the Legislature.

§ 6. The Legislature shall provide for the speedy publication of all statute laws of a public nature, and of such judicial decisions as it may deem expedient. All laws and judicial decisions shall be free for publication by any person.

§ 7. The Legislature shall prescribe by law the manner in which the State printing shall be executed, and the accounts rendered therefor; and shall prohibit all charges for constructive labor.

§ 8. The laws, public records, and the judicial and legislative written proceedings of the State shall be conducted, promulgated and preserved in the English language.

§ 9. The Legislature may declare the cases in which any office shall be deemed vacant, and also the manner of filling the vacancy, where no provision is made for that purpose in this Constitution.

§ 10. All commissions, issued to persons holding office under the provisions of this Constitution, shall be in the name and by the authority of the people of the State of Michigan, sealed with the great seal of the State, signed by the Governor and countersigned by the Secretary of State.

ARTICLE —.

Of Upper Peninsula of Michigan.

§ 1. That all that portion of the public domain within the territorial limits of the State of Michigan, including the islands of Lakes Superior, Huron and Michigan, and in Green Bay, the Straits of Mackinac and the River Ste Marie, known as the counties of Mackinac, Chippewa, Delta, Marquette, Schoolcraft, Houghton and Ontonagon, and the islands thereunto attached, shall constitute a separate judicial district, and be entitled to a district judge, to be elected by the qualified electors of said district, who shall perform the same duties and possess the same powers of circuit judges of the State in their respective circuits, and hold his office for the same period; and to one district attorney, who shall have power to issue his warrant for the arrest of offenders in cases of felony, returnable according to the provisions of law, and who shall be elected for the term of two years.

§ 2. The territory described in the preceding section shall be entitled at all times to at least one Senator in the Senate of the State.

§ 3. The territory embraced in the first section of this article shall be entitled to three Representatives.

§ 4. The Legislature may provide for the payment of said district judge, not exceeding one thousand dollars per annum; and for said district attorney, not exceeding seven hundred dollars per annum.

In cases of delay and detention it shall be competent for the Legislature to make extra compensation to the members of the Legislature from the above described territory, not exceeding two dollars per day during the session of the Legislature.

§ 5. The elections for all district or county officers, State Senator or Representatives, within the boundaries defined in this article, shall take place on the last Tuesday of September in the respective years in which they may be required. The county canvass shall be had on the first Tuesday in October thereafter, and the district canvass on the last Tuesday of said October.

§ 6. One-half of all moneys received into the treasury from corporations in the Upper Peninsula paying a State tax of one per cent. per annum, shall be paid to the treasurers of the counties from which it is reccived, to be applied for township and county purposes, as provided by law; and the Legislature shall have power after the year 1855 to reduce the per centum to be refunded.

§ 7. The Legislature may change the location of the State Prison from Jackson to the Upper Peninsula of Michigan.

§ 8. The charters of the several mining companies may be modified by the Legislature, in regard to the term limited for subscribing to stock, and in relation to the quantity of land which a company shall hold, but the capital shall not be increased nor the time for the existence of charters extended; but no such corporation shall be permitted to purchase any real estate except such as shall be necessary for the exercise of the corporate franchises of such company.

ARTICLE —.

Salaries.

§ 1. The Governor shall receive an annual salary of one thousand dollars; the Judges of the Circuit Courts shall each receive an annual salary of fifteen hundred dollars; the State Treasurer shall receive an annual salary of one thousand dollars; the Auditor General shall receive an annual salary of one thousand dollars; the Superintendent of Public Instruction shall receive an annual salary of one thousand dollars; the Secretary of State shall receive an annual salary of eight hundred dollars; the Commissioner of the Land

Office shall receive an annual salary of eight hundred dollars; the Attorney General shall receive an annual salary of eight hundred dollars, and no fees or perquisites whatever for the performance of any duties connected with their offices; and it shall not be competent for the legislature to increase the salaries therein provided.

ARTICLE —.

Schedule.

That no inconvenience may arise from the changes in the constitution of this State, and in order to carry the same into complete operation, it is hereby declared, that

§ 1. The common law and the statute laws now in force, not repugnant to this constitution, shall remain in force until they expire by their own limitations, or are altered or repealed by the Legislature.

§ 2. All writs, actions, causes of action, prosecutions and rights of individuals and of bodies corporate, and of the State, and all charters of incorporation, shall continue; and all indictments which shall have been found, or which may hereafter be found, for any crime or offence committed before the adoption of this constitution, may be proceeded upon as if no change had taken place. The several courts, except as herein otherwise provided, shall continue with the like powers and jurisdiction, both at law and in equity, as if this constitution had not been adopted, and until the organization of the judicial department under this constitution.

§ 3. That all fines, penalties, forfeitures and escheats accruing to the State of Michigan under the present constitution and laws, shall accrue to the use of the State under this constitution.

§ 4. That all recognizances, bonds, obligations, and all other instruments entered into or executed before the adoption of this constitution, to the people of the State of Michigan, to any State, county or township, or any public officer or public body, or which may be entered into or executed, under existing laws, "to the people of the State of Michigan," to any such officer or public body, before the complete organization of the departments of government under this constitution, shall remain binding and valid; and rights and liabilities upon the same shall continue, and may be prosecuted as provided by law. And all crimes and misdemeanors and penal actions, shall be tried, punished and prosecuted, as though no change had taken place, until otherwise provided by law.

§ 5. A Governor and Lieutenant Governor shall be chosen under the existing constitution and laws, to serve after the expiration of the term of the present incumbent.

§ 6. All officers, civil and military, now holding any office or appointment, shall continue to hold their respective offices, unless removed by competent authority, until superseded under the laws now in force, or under this constitution.

§ 7. The members of the Senate and House of Representatives of the Legislature of one thousand eight hundred and fifty-one, shall continue in office under the provisions of law, until superseded by their successors elected and qualified under this constitution.

§ 8. All county officers, unless removed by competent authority, shall continue to hold their respective offices until the first day of January, in the year one thousand eight hundred and fifty-three. The laws now in force as to the election, qualification and duties of township officers, shall continue in force until the Legislature shall, in conformity to the provisions of this constitution, provide for the holding of elections to fill such offices, and prescribe the duties of such officers respectively.

§ 9. On the first day of January, in the year one thousand eight hundred and fifty-two, the terms of office of the judges of the supreme court, under existing laws, and of the judges of the county courts, and of the clerks of the supreme court, shall expire on the said day.

§ 10. On the first day of January, in the year one thousand eight hundred and fifty-two, the jurisdiction of all suits and proceedings then pending in the present supreme courts, shall become vested in the supreme court established by this constitution, and shall be finally adjudicated by the court where the same may be pending. The jurisdiction of all suits and proceedings at law and equity, then pending in the circuit courts and county courts for the several counties, shall become vested in the circuit courts of the said counties, and district court for the Upper Peninsula.

§ 11. The probate courts, the courts of justices of the peace and the police court authorized by an act entitled "An act to establish a police court in the city of Detroit," approved April second, one thousand eight hundred and fifty, shall continue to exercise the jurisdiction and powers now conferred upon them respectively, until otherwise provided by law.

§ 12. The office of State Printer shall be vested in the present incumbent until the expiration of the term for which he was elected under the law then in force; and all the provisions of the said law relating to his duties, rights, privileges and compensation, shall remain unimpaired and inviolate until the expiration of his said term of office.

§ 13. It shall be the duty of the Legislature, at their first session, to adapt the present laws to the provisions of this constitution, as far as may be.

§ 14. The Attorney General of the State is required to prepare and report to the Legislature, at the commencement of the next session, such changes and modifications in existing laws as may be deemed necessary to adapt the same to this constitution, and as may be best calculated to carry into effect its provisions; and he shall receive no additional compensation therefor.

§ 15. Any territory attached to any county for judicial purposes, if not otherwise represented, shall be considered as forming part of such county, so far as regards elections for the purpose of representation

§ 16. This constitution shall be submitted to the people for their adoption or rejection, at the general election to be held on the first Tuesday of November, one thousand eight hundred and fifty; and there shall also be submitted for adoption or rejection, at the same time the separate resolution in relation to the elective franchise; and it shall be the duty of the Secretary of State, and all other officers required to give or publish any notice in regard to the said general election, to give notice, as provided by law in case of an election of Governor, that this constitution has been duly submitted to the electors at said election. Every newspaper within this State publishing in the month of September next, this constitution as submitted, shall receive, as compensation therefor, the sum of twenty-five dollars, to be paid as the Legislature shall direct.

§ 17. Any person entitled to vote for members of the Legislature, by the constitution and laws now in force, shall, at the said election, be entitled to vote for the adoption or rejection of this constitution, and for or against the resolution separately submitted, at the places and in the manner provided by law for the election of members of the Legislature.

§ 18. At the said general election, a ballot box shall be kept by the several boards of inspectors thereof, for receiving the votes cast for or against the adoption of this Constitution; and on the ballots shall be written or printed, or partly written and partly printed, the words "Adoption of the constitution—yes." or "Adoption of the constitution—no."

§ 19. The canvass of the votes cast for the adoption or rejection of this Constitution and the provision in relation to the elective franchise separately submitted, and the returns thereof shall be made by the proper canvassing officers, in the same manner as now provided by law for the canvass and return of the votes cast at an election for Governor, as near as may be, and the return thereof shall be directed to the Secretary of State. On the sixteenth day of December next, or within five days thereafter, the Auditor General, State Treasurer and Secretary of State shall meet at the capitol and proceed in presence of the Governor, to examine and canvass the returns of the said votes, and proclamation shall forthwith be made by the Governor of the result thereof. If it shall appear that a majority of the votes cast upon the question have thereon "Adoption of the Constitution—yes," this constitution shall be the supreme law of the State from and after the first day of January, one thousand eight hundred and fifty-one, except as is herein otherwise provided; but if a majority of the votes cast upon the question have thereon "Adoption of the Constitution—no," the same shall be null and void. And in case of the adoption of this constitution, said officers shall immediately, or as soon thereafter as practicable, proceed to open the statements of votes returned from the several counties for judges of the supreme court and State officers under the act entitled "An act to amend the revised statutes and to provide for the election of certain officers by the people in pursuance to an amendment of the Constitution, approved February sixteenth, one thousand eight hundred and fifty," and shall ascertain, determine and certify the results of the election for said officers under said acts, in the same manner, as near as may be, as is now provided by law in regard to the election of Representatives in Congress. And the several judges and officers so ascertained to have been elected may be qualified and enter upon the duties of their respective offices, on the first Monday of January next, or as soon thereafter as practicable.

§ 20. The salaries or compensation of all persons holding office under the present constitution shall continue to be the same as now provided by law, until superseded by their successors elected or appointed under this constitution; and it shall not be lawful hereafter for the Legislature to increase or diminish the compensation of any officer during the term for which he is elected or appointed.

§ 21. The Legislature, at their first session, shall provide for the payment of all expenditures of the convention to revise the constitution and of the publication of the same as is provided in this article.

§ 22. Every county except Mackinaw and Chippewa, entitled to a representative in the Legislature, at the time of the adoption of this constitution, shall continue to be so entitled under this constitution; and the county of Saginaw, with the territory that may be attached, shall be entitled to one representative; the county of Tuscola, and the territory that may be attached, one representative; the county of Sanilac, and the territory that may be attached, one representative; the counties of Midland and Aronac, with the territory that may be attached, one representative; the county of Montcalm, with the territory that may be attached thereto, one representative; and the counties of Newaygo and Oceana, with the territory that may be attached thereto, one representative. Each county having a ratio of representation and a fraction over, equal to a moiety of said ratio, shall be entitled to two representatives, and so on above that number, giving one additional member for each additional ratio.

§ 23. The cases pending and undisposed of in the late court of chancery at the time of the adoption of this constitution, shall continue to be heard and determined by the judges of the supreme court. But the Legislature shall, at its session in one thousand eight hundred and fifty-one, provide by law, for the transfer of said causes that may remain undisposed of on the first day of January, one thousand eight hundred and fifty-two, to the supreme or circuit court established by this constitution, or require that the same may be heard and determined by the circuit judges.

§ 24. The term of office of the Governor and Lieutenant Governor shall commence on the first day of January next after their election.

§ 25. The territory described in the article entitled "Upper Peninsula." shall be attached to and constitute a part of the third circuit for the election of a Regent of the University.

§ 26. The Legislature shall have authority after the expiration of the term of office of the district judge first elected for the "Upper Peninsula," to abolish said office of district judge and district attorney, or either of them.

§ 27. The Legislature shall, at its session of one thousand eight hundred and fifty-one, apportion the Representatives among the several counties and districts, and divide the State into Senate districts, pursuant to the provisions of this constitution.

§ 28. The terms of office of all State and county officers, of the circuit judges, members of the board of education, and members of the Legislature, shall begin on the first day of January next succeeding their election.

RESOLUTION.

§ 29. At the next general election, and at the same time when the votes of the electors shall be taken for the adoption or rejection of this constitution, an additional amendment to section one of Article seven, in the words following:

"Every colored male inhabitant possessing the qualifications required by the first section of the second article of the Constitution, shall have the rights and privileges of an elector,"

Shall be separately submitted to the electors of this State for their adoption or rejection, in form following, to wit: A separate ballot may be given by every person having the right to vote for the revised Constitution, to be deposited in a separate box. Upon the ballots given for the adoption of the said separate amendment shall be written or printed, or partly written and partly printed, the words "Equal suffrage to colored persons? Yes;" and upon all ballots given against the adoption of the said separate amendment, in like manner, the words "Equal suffrage to colored persons? No." And on such ballots shall be written or printed, or partly written and partly printed, the words "Constitution: Suffrage," in such manner that such words shall appear on the outer side of such ballot when folded. If, at said election, a majority of all the votes given for and against the said separate amendment shall contain the words, "Equal suffrage to colored persons? Yes," then there shall be inserted in the first section of the article, between the words "tribe and shall," these words, "and every colored male inhabitant," anything in the Constitution to the contrary notwithstanding.

STATE OF MICHIGAN.

[Doc. No. 7.]

In Convention to Revise the Constitution, 1850.

Mr. ROBERTS made the following REPORT:

[To accompany Article—, Of Upper Peninsula.]

The Committee on the Governmental and Judicial Policy of the Upper Peninsula of the State of Michigan, respectfully report:

That the progress and settlement which have marked, within a few years, that portion of the State of Michigan denominated the Upper Peninsula, has at length began to attract a deep and lively attention to its interests. Embracing more than 20,000 square miles, it includes within its boundaries all that part of the public domain lying within the territorial limits of the sovreignty of Michigan, designated as the counties of Mackinac, Chippewa, Delta, Marquette, Schoolcraft, Houghton and Ontonagon, together with the islands of Lake Superior, Huron and Michigan, and in Green Bay, the Straits of Mackinac and the river Ste Marie within the jurisdiction of the United States. Isolated in geographical position almost from the rest of the world, the God of nature has bestowed upon its face the most bountiful gifts of his handiwork and imbeded in its bosom the richest treasures of his hand. No region of country within the broad limits of our national domain, affords a subject of more interesting contemplation. With fisheries, acknowledged by the most scientific and literary men in the country, to exceed in richness and their boundless resource even those of New-Foundland—with Copper Mines, the wealth of which astounds the world, and with iron mountains yielding a richer ore than has hitherto come to the knowledge of mankind, she would seem to require nothing but the fostering care of the General Government and of our own State to successfully develope greater wealth than any other section of our country, and in so doing become tributary to the greatness of both.

But the isolated position of the Upper Peninsula demands separate considerations from those which control and direct the interests of the Lower Peninsula, and their judiciary, their elections, their taxation, indeed their entire policy, should be arranged under a separate article to be incorporated in the constitution; and with this view, after giving some of the reasons which influence your committee, they will introduce such provisions as seem to them to be demanded by locality and reference to the disabilities under which her people are laboring.

Mackinac and her Straits, with the islands in Lake Huron and the river Ste Marie, have long been celebrated for their furs, plaster, and inexhaustable supplies of Lake Trout and White Fish. Chippewa, with her like advantages, extends into Lake Superior, forms the great portage for transhipment to the mining country, and throughout that immense range of Lake and River to the newly organized Territory of Minnesota. Delta constitutes the great lumbering country, on the Green Bay division, with Michigan and Wisconsin. And these counties are all so separated from the Lake Superior counties, and by their own magnitude and extent they severally require representation of their own. Schoolcraft is situated one hundred and fifty miles above the Saut Ste Marie, and with her harbors and bays and general resorts for fishing purposes, equals if she does not excel in richness in this branch of business. West of Schoolcraft, and bordering upon her, lies the immense iron country of Marquette, now becoming as densely populated with her miners, as Delta with her lumbermen; but such is the position of the two counties that it is presumed justice may be rendered by associating them together as a Representative District. Houghton county, one hundred and twenty-five miles from either the principal towns of Marquette or Schoolcraft, farther up the Lake, and only to be approached by water communication for business purposes, is made up of the

Keewenaw Bay and Point, L'Ance, Portage Lake, Bete de Greise, Isle Royal, &c., and is one of the two great copper Mining counties. Ontonagon, the capital of which is seventy-five miles still farther up Lake Superior from Houghton, is the other celebrated copper district; and by reference to maps and to facts being daily realized, it would seem impossible for one representative to be enabled to do justice to the interests of both of these counties.

It should be borne in mind by the Convention that, from the organization of the State, Mackinac and Chippewa have alone been entitled to Representatives in the Legislature—that Mackinac, the islands in the Straits, and an immense contiguous country, of which Delta has formed a part, have been obliged to be represented by one person, and that elections could not be held in Delta and on the islands, or if they were, that their returns could never be made in season, owing to distances and inclement seasons. So with Chippewa, which has had attached to her for judicial and representative purposes, Schoolcraft, Marquette, Houghton and Ontonagon, few of the townships of which could even have succeeded in sending their returns in time to the county seat of Houghton, any more than the latter could render hers in time at the county seat of Chippewa.

And whilst referring to this subject of distances and the difficulties of legislation for that section of country, your Committee will make an extract from the report of the Auditor General for 1849. That Report says :

"No returns of election, either for electors or Representative in Congress, have been received by messenger or mail from Houghton county, or any other county in the Upper Peninsula beyond Chippewa; and in regard to the time of holding elections and making returns thereof, as well as in regard to the time of assessing and collecting taxes, the inhabitants of that portion of the state would seem to require separate and different legislative and constitutional provisions from that of the rest of the state. It would also seem doubtful whether a legislature composed almost entirely of representatives from the counties in the Lower Peninsula, having of course very inadequate means of judging of the wants and interests of that remote region, and sitting in the winter time, when the mail and travel has to pass through portions of three other states to get to or from the capitol of the state, can ever properly legislate for that country; and perhaps still more doubtful, whether our tax and other laws can ever be properly enforced or observed there. Whether the interests of that country would be best subserved by the organization of a separate territory there by Congress, or by attaching the largest portion or all of the Upper Peninsula to Wisconsin, it is not the province of this department to judge. It has only become my duty to state to the legislature the want of election and tax returus from that portion of the state; the first, because it was found physically impossible to get them here within the time required by law, and the latter, for some cause here unknown."

The cause of the latter appears to be explained in a history of the mining companies, which next occupies our attention. Wrongs and injuries to the mining country, owing to imperfect legislation, appear to call for a more than ordinary share of attention. In 1844,it seems the Secretary of War granted to individuals permits to locate tracts of land in the mineral region on the Southern shore of Lake Superior, of three miles square, for a period of three years, subject to renewals; the lessees or permittees to pay to the Government six per cent on all mineral raised during the first term, and ten per centum after removal of leases. The demand for permits becoming numerous, it was thought proper in a short time to stop the issue for three miles square and substitute one mile square. Under this arrangement more permits were granted than there were lands to be covered, and contentions arising, Congress interfered and passed the Act of March 1, 1847, entitled "An act to establish a land office in the "northern part of Michigan, and to provide for the sale of mineral "lands in the State of Michigan."

By this Act the charge of these lands was transferred to the Treasury Department, a geological survey ordered, and full directions given to bring the mineral lands into market, the lessees or permittees to be protected by giving them the privilege to purchase at $2,50 per acre if they should take the whole they had located, or $5 the acre for not less than a quarter section; and $5 to be paid by all entering after the lands had been duly placed in market. Accordingly, in 1848, a portion of these lands were placed in market by the customary proclamation, but under the adverse circumstances of a doubtful survey, and at a time when those who were in occupancy questioned the propriety of taking them up at those prices, even if they possessed the means to do so, the Government having failed to fulfill the promise of its agents in building a ship canal around Saut Ste Marie, and in every other respect. Some three or four did, however, accede to the terms, whilst others whose leases had not yet expired held over, and many abandoned their locations. These latter were succeeded in many instances by more wealthy capitalists; and new explorations, developing richer veins of mineral, many substantial companies were established, additional capital called in to the aid of the old ones, and the labor of mining was renewed with a vigor which has continued without abatement until the present time; although they have had to, and are still contending against the most discouraging and oppressive embarrassments, arising from the neglect of the general government, and partially from a want of proper legislation and action on the part of our State Government.

At the session of our Legislature, 1848, twenty-one charters were granted to these companies, viz: to the Copper Falls, North Western, Pittsburgh and Boston, Lake Superior Fishing and Mining, Lac la Belle, Bohemian, Albion, Douglass Houghton, Eagle Harbor, Medora, Ontonagon, North American, Quincy, New York and Michigan, New England, Algonquin, Michigan, National, Lake Superior, Jackson, Mackinac, and Lake Superior Mining Companies. These charters were considered liberal, except in respect to the payment of one per centum into the State Treasury on the entire amount of their real estate, the capital stock paid in, and upon all sums of money borrowed by them, as well as any portion of the nett profits invested in the business of the company, which tax was "*to be in lieu of all* " *other taxes upon the personal property of the companies, and in lieu* "*of all other state taxes on their real estate.*" The charters were liberal inasmuch as they did not restrict them in the quantity of land they might hold, and thus enforce them by limiting their localities to pay the United States the double rate, and because they did not compel them to pay in a grater amount perhaps, than their works would require, by a given period. Illiberal, in putting them upon a par with banks and railroads, in their exactions, for that because it was desirable to possess chartered privileges, to invite capital from abroad in aid of digging copper and iron out of the mineral bearing rocks of Lake Superior, when compelled to pay ten per centum of whatever they raised to the United States, or double or quadruple per acre for their bleak and apparently barren possessions, more than their fellow citizens of the Lower Peninsula for the fertile soil from which they dig their potatoes and gather their rich harvests; and for that it would deprive them of healthy county and township government in as much as they left little or nothing to enforce a tax upon for such purposes, and in so doing visited an act of injustice upon the few for the benefit of the many. But, these charters of 1848 possessed the virtue of uniformity. No one company could complain of being deprived of advantages that its neighbor possessed.

At the session of the Legislature, 1849, nine more of these companies were chartered, viz: the Ohio Trap Rock, Minnesota, North West, Siskowiet, Isle Royal, Native Copper, Phoenix, Union, and Pittsburgh and Isle Royal Mining Companies. Six of these are, in all things material, in uniformity with those chartered in 1848; but in the charter of the Ohio Trap Rock, when we come to the regulation of the one per centum to be paid into the State Treasury, we find it to read, "*which tax shall be in lieu of* ALL *taxes on the* PERSONAL *and* REAL *estate of said company.*" Next, on examining the charter of the Minnesota, we read, " *and said tax shall be in lieu of all other* STATE *taxes on the* PERSONAL *property of said company, and in lieu of all other* STATE *taxes on the* REAL *estate of said company.*" The first of these two companies was approved on the 5th March, and the latter on the 7th March. Your committee would here have thought it but reasonable to infer that the discrepancy was caused by clerical error, but from the fact that on reaching the remaining company unaccounted for, the Native Copper Company, approved March 31, they find it to read, "*which tax shall be in lieu of the* STATE *tax upon* "*the* PERSONAL *and* REAL *estate of said company.*" Thus it would seem that the Ohio Trap Rock is to be relieved from *all other taxes whatever,* whilst the Minnesota and the Native Copper, although paying the same per centage, are only to be relieved from further *State* taxes.

Your Committee now come to the consideration of the charters granted at the session of our Legislature, 1850. This year there were eighteen companies chartered—the Forest, Piscataqua, Swamscot, Copper Harbor, Cleveland Iron, Eureka, Detroit and Lake Superior, Hungarian, Adventure, Iron City, Carp River Iron, Merchants, Chesapeake, Cape, Aztec, Ripley, Ridge, and Peninsular Mining Companies. The three first are measurably on the plan of the twenty-one of 1848, and the six of the nine of 1849, except that in lieu of the one per centum to be paid into the State Treasury, *one half per centum is substituted*, saying, "*said tax to be in lieu of all "other State tax upon the real estate and personal property of said "company:* Provided, *That nothing contained in this section shall be "so construed as to release real estate and personal property from "taxation for County and Township purposes.*" In the remaining fifteen are several important changes. The section regulating the corporate succession, the capital stock, and allowing the companies to hold such real and personal estate as their business may require, to an amount not exceeding the capital stock, has added to it, "*but "said company shall not hold more than six hundred and forty acres "of land in legal subdivisions in the Upper Peninsula, except a ware-"house, lot and office, and such as may be necessary for smelting pur-"poses.*" The amount fixed upon to be paid into the State Treasury is *one per centum*, and "*said tax shall be in lieu of all State taxes upon the real and personal estate of said company.*"

From "An act authorizing the State Treasurer to refund certain moneys to the treasurers of the counties of Houghton, Schoolcraft, Marquette and Ontonagon," approved April 2, 1850, the same time of the approval of the mining bills, in which it is enacted "that the State Treasurer be, and he is hereby authorized to refund and pay over unto the treasurer of the county of Houghton, one-half of all moneys collected in the counties of Houghton, Schoolcraft, Marquette and Ontonagon, in pursuance and by virtue of any act of incorporation creating any mining company in any and each of said counties," it may be inferred that the Legislature, in the passage of the first three named acts of 1850, intended to equalize the taxation by dividing between the state and the counties equally, the per centage heretofore and hereafter to be received from companies exempt from taxation on their personal property; and that by some misunderstanding between the two Houses, or changed policy, the fifteen acts appear in the shape they do, when, from facts before your committee, the original intention of both was, to exact in the new charters but one-half per centum for the state, leaving them open to county and township taxes; and thus refunding the one-half paid in by the companies at one per cent, placing the companies upon an equality.

The state of affairs in relation to the charters of these mining companies, as they now present themselves to your committee, is far from a just and equitable dispensation of legislative power; and calls for a summary and permanent remedy of the evils which have been entailed upon a most valuable class of our fellow citizens, and upon a section of our state which demands, if not our fostering care, at least the prompt and effectual justice which is within our power to mete out to the injured.

It appears in the session laws of 1848, that by the provisions of "An act to organize four counties in the Upper Peninsula and define the boundaries of the same," the counties of Marquette, Houghton, Schoolcraft and Ontonagon, were united and set off into a judicial district, the powers in which were to be held and exercised by a district judge with the jurisdiction of a circuit court in the several organized counties in this State, as well in criminal proceedings as in civil cases and in equity. By the records in the office of the secretary of state, an election took place under this act, on the first Tuesday of July, 1848, at which a district judge and other officers were chosen, and the organization of this judicial district perfected. A prosecuting attorney and notaries public were appointed by the Governor. Courts have been held as designated by the act; grand juries summoned, petit juries impannelled, and several convictions had in criminal cases. Yet the facts are before your committee that no provision has been made to pay this district judge, the prosecuting attorney, sheriff, clerk and other officers of the court, nor the grand and petit jurors—that the district is as yet destitute of a court house, and furnished only with a temporary jail. That although each township has its supervisors, assessors, and other township officers, and the board of supervisors hold their meetings, the difficulties which present themselves in the history of the mining charters, are an almost insurmountable obstacle to the levying of an equitable tax. So both township and county expenses must be made up by commutation amongst individuals, or be accumulating as a debt.

The mining companies constitute the great bulk of the inhabitants, and are the owners of the property which should have been taxable for county, township and highway purposes. But comparatively few of them have as yet the title to their location from the general government, and of course have no real estate to be taxed. They pay their one per centum on their capital into the State treasury, and their personal property is excused from further taxation by their charters. The majority of the stockholders who ma live in the Eastern States, far removed from the scene of action, subscribe for their stock or invest their money with the understanding that the amount of their tax is fixed and unalterable. Each mining company is a community —a village—separate and independent of its neighbors. The few farmers, and the mechanics, merchants, hotel keepers and others, who live at the landings, and are separated from these companies, are but few in numbers. It would be manifestly unjust to make these pay for all the crime and poverty and misfortune inseparable from great communities, or to expect them to build the roads and bridges necessary for the accommodation of the masses. Instance, there are probably at the Boston and Pittsburgh mines, at least four hundred souls; and at the North American, more than two hundred. These companies, with the Albion, worked and inhabited by less numbers, are all within the township of Houghton, of which the mouth of the Eagle river is the landing, or the point at which they ship their copper and receive their supplies. Should the entire expense for township purposes fall upon the taxable inhabitants at the landing, place? Certainly not. Upon the companies? They pay their one per centum and cut their own roads. It is enough. The Pittsburgh and Boston company alone, as appears by the books of the State Treasurer, pays in annually upwards of $1,250. If taxed, as their charter permits, for county and township purposes, on their real estate, it would be but upon a mere trifle of the $125,000 on which they are paying this one per centum. Upon the same principle, it may be asked whether the inhabitants of the few landing places, a few farmers, and the agricultural township of L'Ance, should pay the taxes of the mining townships of Copper Harbor, Eagle Harbor, Houghton, Portage, Algonquin and Isle Royal, composing the county of Houghton; or that the township of Ontonagon, which contains no mines, should pay the expenses of the townships of Minesota and Pe-wa-be, in the county of Ontonagon, where there are more than a dozen companies in active operation, and probably not an inhabitant disconnected with them!

"The principles which have authorized and sanctioned numerous grants to the States, for turnpikes, canals and rail roads, through, or leading to, the public domain, designed to promote the sales of government lands, to facilitate the settlement of a new country, to develope new resources of public wealth, and to open new fields for enterprising labor," never appear to have been applied to this section of our country. The General Government, though repeatedly appealed to for appropriations to build a ship canal around the Falls of the Saut Ste Marie, and for Harbors and other public works on Lake Superior, appears to have paid little attention to their wants and requirements more than to obtain exhorbitant prices for their mineral lands. And although the United States have realized many millions of dollars in the sales of lands in this State, over and above all expenses, and have upwards of twenty-four millions of acres still unsold and unappropriated, they have never put it in our power to render a service to the Upper Peninsula through their benificence. The little the State has at any time received from the General Government, had been appropriated before their wants were sufficiently explained, and as yet they have not been so positioned to require any portion from the University or Primary School Funds.

To reach and to remedy their many evils, and to adjust the differences apparent in the mining charters, so far as may be in our power, your committee herewith submit provisions in an article for the consideration of the Convention, proposing—

1. That the entire Upper Peninsula shall constitute a judicial district, with the privilege of electing a circuit judge and a district attorney.

2. That the same district of country shall constitute a Senatorial district.

3. That in addition to Mackinac and Chippewa, Delta, Houghton and Ontonagon, shall be entitled to one representative each, and the counties of Marquette and Schoolcraft, to one Representative.

4. That the elections in said counties, wherein they will not interfere with the choice of members of Congress or Presidential electors, shall be held in September.

5, 6 and 7. That provision be made for the refunding to the treasuries of those counties, a certain portion of the moneys paid into the State treasury by the mining companies, to be used by them in defraying county and township expenses.

8. That the Legislature be empowered to modify certain mining charters.

All of which is respectfully submitted.

E. J. ROBERTS, Chairman.

STATE OF MICHIGAN.

[Doc. No. 8.]

In Convention to Revise the Constitution, 1850.

MAJORITY REPORT of the Committee appointed to recommend a division of the State into Judicial Districts.

1st District.—Monroe, Lenawee and Hillsdale.

2d.—Branch, St. Joseph, Cass and Berrien.

3d.—Wayne.

4th.—Washtenaw, Jackson and Ingham.

5th.—Calhoun, Kalamazoo, Allegan, Barry and Van Buren.

6th.—St. Clair, Macomb and Oakland.

7th.—Lapeer, Genesee, Saginaw, Shiawassee and Livingston.

8th.—Eaton, Kent, Ottawa, Ionia, Clinton and Montcalm.

MINORITY REPORT of the Committee appointed to recommend a division of the State into Judicial Districts.

1st District.—Wayne and Washtenaw.

2d.—Monroe, Lenawee and Hillsdale.

3d.—Branch, St. Joseph, Cass and Berrien.

4th.—Jackson, Calhoun, Kalamazoo and Van Buren.

5th.—Oakland, Macomb and St. Clair.

6th.—Livingston, Ingham, Eaton, Barry and Allegan.

7th.—Lapeer, Genesee, Shiawassee, Saginaw, Tuscola and Sanilac.

8th.—Ionia, Kent, Ottawa, Newaygo, Clinton and Montcalm.

www.ingramcontent.com/pod-product-compliance
Lightning Source LLC
LaVergne TN
LVHW021054110826
845150LV00001B/71